"I REALIZE TH[...] WILL PROVIDE GRIST FOR MANY SENSATIONAL STORIES IN THE PRESS ... THEY WILL EMBARRASS ME AND THOSE WITH WHOM I HAVE TALKED ... THEY WILL BECOME THE SUBJECT OF SPECULATION AND EVEN RIDICULE ... CERTAIN PARTS OF THEM WILL BE SEIZED UPON BY POLITICAL AND JOURNALISTIC OPPONENTS."

RICHARD M. NIXON
in his nationwide TV address

MAX MASON

Why, then, did Richard Nixon make these extraordinary transcripts of private conversations public?

Because he claims they will completely exonerate him of all guilt in the Watergate affair.

But do they?

There is only one way for every American to decide for himself or herself.

Read them. They are all here. And they are very important.

THE PRESIDENTIAL TRANSCRIPTS

IN CONJUNCTION WITH THE STAFF OF

The Washington Post

A DELL BOOK

Published by
Dell Publishing Co., Inc.
1 Dag Hammarskjold Plaza
New York, New York 10017

Dell ® TM681510, Dell Publishing Co., Inc.
Printed in the United States of America
First printing—May 1974

Contents

Background Of The Dispute
By Thomas W. Lippman

On July 16, 1973, Alexander P. Butterfield, a former presidential aide, disclosed publicly for the first time that, since early 1971, virtually all conversations in the President's White House office (Oval Room) had been preserved on tape recordings. Here is a chronology of the struggle for access to the tapes.

July 17-23: The Senate select Watergate committee and Archibald Cox, then the Watergate special prosecutor, asked for tapes concerning the Watergate affair, were turned down by the President and then they separately issued subpoenas demanding the tapes.

Aug. 9: The committee filed suit in U.S. District Court in an attempt to secure the tapes.

Aug. 29: Chief Judge John J. Sirica ordered the President to give him the tapes so the judge could decide if they should be turned over to the Watergate grand jury. The President refused and decided to appeal Sirica's order.

Oct. 12: The U.S. Court of Appeals upheld Judge Sirica.

Oct. 19—The President announced he would not appeal the tapes decision to the U.S. Supreme Court, but also said he would not comply with the order to give the tapes to Sirica. He ordered Cox to abandon his request for the tapes. In an effort at heading off what many viewed as a constitutional crisis, he offered to submit a summary of the tapes, authenticated by Sen. John C. Stennis (D-Miss.) to the committee and the grand jury. The leaders of the committee accepted this proposal but Cox rejected it.

Oct. 20—The President ordered Attorney General Elliot L. Richardson to fire Cox. Richardson refused and resigned. The same thing then happened to Deputy Attorney General William Ruckelshaus. The President named Solicitor General Robert Bork as acting Attorney General, and Bork fired Cox.

Oct. 23—In a startling turnabout, lawyers for the President announced in Sirica's courtroom that the President would give the tapes to the court.

Oct. 31—Fred J. Buzhardt, White House counsel, said that two of the tape recordings—of a conversation between Mr. Nixon and former Attorney General John N. Mitchell on June 20, 1972, and between Mr. Nixon and John Dean on April 15, 1973, never existed.

Nov. 21—White House lawyers told Sirica that an 18½-minute segment was effaced from the tape of a June 20, 1972, conversation between Mr. Nixon and his former chief of staff, H. R. Haldeman.

Jan. 15, 1974—A panel of technical experts reported to the court that the tape gap was the result of at least five separate manual erasures.

March 25—On orders from Sirica, upheld by the Court of Appeals, the Watergate grand jury's report on the President, including material from the tapes, was turned over to the House Judiciary Committee, which had begun an investigation to determine whether Mr. Nixon should be impeached.

April 11—The House Committee subpoenaed tapes and other materials related to 42 presidential conversations relating to the alleged Watergate coverup. The materials given to the Committee yesterday and simultaneously made public were the White House's response to this subpoena.

April 18—The office of Special Prosecutor Leon Jaworski, who succeeded Cox, issued a new subpoena, for tapes, memos and other materials relating to 64 conversations of Mr. Nixon, and others between June 20, 1972, and June 4, 1973. The White House was given until Thursday May 2 to respond.

April 30—An edited transcript of some of the requested tapes was released.

Introduction To Commentaries

These commentaries, written by various staff reporters of *The Washington Post* were published by that newspaper on the first and second days following the release of the Presidential transcripts.

Nixon Hoped To Keep Cap On Bottle
By Bob Woodward and Carl Bernstein

President Nixon, during a lengthy meeting in the Oval Office on March 21, 1973, told White House counsel John W. Dean III that "you have no choice but to come up with the $120,000" demanded as blackmail payment by one of the Watergate burglars, according to an edited transcript of the meeting.

The transcript reveals that Mr. Nixon, on his own initiative, discussed accommodating blackmail demands on at least a half-dozen occasions during the meeting without once suggesting that paying the men for their silence would be wrong.

Instead, the transcript reveals, Mr. Nixon repeatedly discussed different methods by which as much as $1 million could be paid to the burglars without the payments being traced to the White House. The purpose of such payments, in the President's own words, would be "to keep the cap on the bottle," to "buy time," to "tough it through."

"How much money do you need?" the President asked Dean early in the March 21 conversation, according to the transcript.

"I would say these people are going to cost a million dollars over the next two years," Dean replied.

"We could get that," the President continued. "You could get a million dollars. You could get it in cash. I know where it could be gotten. It is not easy, but it could be done. But the question is who the hell would handle it? Any ideas on that?"

In the ensuing discussion, the President went on to suggest that his personal attorney, Herbert W. Kalmbach, could be relied on to raise the money, that payments to the burglars could be made under the cover of a Cuban defense committee and that the facts could be concealed from a grand jury.

Mr. Nixon repeatedly has said that he first learned of the Watergate cover-up and hush money payments at the March 21, 1973, meeting and that he believed payment of hush money would be wrong.

Throughout the conversation as recorded, however, the President returned repeatedly to the joint theme of avoiding "criminal liability" to members of the White House staff at all costs: the desirability of meeting the blackmail demands immediately, and the necessity of expediting another meeting at which his top aides—Dean, John Mitchell, John Ehrlichman and H. R. Haldeman—could "get a decision on it."

Within 12 hours of the Oval Office discussion, Watergate conspirator E. Howard Hunt Jr. received $75,000 cash—a key element in the conspiracy to obstruct justice indictment returned against seven of the President's men on March 1, 1974.

What transpired at the morning March 21, 1973, meeting of Dean, the President and Haldeman is considered crucial by both Mr. Nixon and his critics to answering whether Mr. Nixon himself was a participant in the alleged conspiracy.

The White House released transcript of the March 21 meeting reveals that the President considered the following basic options for dealing with a deteriorating situation described by Dean as a growing cancer on the Presidency:

1 Granting executive clemency to Howard Hunt—"You don't do it politically until after the '74 elections, that's for sure," Mr. Nixon told Dean. When Dean suggested that "it may further involve you in a way you should not be involved in this," the President replied: "No—it is wrong, that's for sure."

2 Granting parole to Hunt, an alternative first suggested by the President. "The only thing we could do with him would be to parole him like the (unintelligible) situation. But you couldn't buy clemency," the President told Dean and Haldeman. Mr. Nixon added: "Parole is something I think in Hunt's case you could do but you couldn't do with the others (the other burglars). You understand."

3 Convening a new grand jury, which could be controlled by the White House, an alternative first suggested by Dean. During several discussions of the idea, Mr. Nixon noted that such a procedure would offer the protection of the Fifth Amendment for White House witnesses and that "you can say 'I don't remember.' You can say 'I can't recall. I can't give any answer to that that I can recall.' "

4 Co-opting Assistant Attorney General Henry E. Petersen, by having him appointed as a special Watergate prosecutor or, alternatively, as Mr. Nixon said: "Why

couldn't the President call him in as special counsel to the White House for the purpose of conducting an investigation . . . having him the special counsel to represent us before the Grand Jury?"

5 Using a national security argument to prevent any testimony before a grand jury regarding the White House-sponsored break-in at the office of Daniel Ellsberg's psychiatrist. The object, as described in the meeting with Dean, would be to prevent a grand jury from learning that White House aide Egil (Bud) Krogh had perjured himself earlier when he falsely testified that he had not known the Cuban-Americans who broke into the Watergate (and the psychiatrist's office).

At no point in the 103-minute meeting in the Oval Office did Mr. Nixon suggest that his aides simply testify fully before the then-existing Federal Watergate grand jury, tell the whole truth and accept the consequences.

Instead, he returned to the theme of avoiding "criminal liability" and—far more often than any other alternative to achieving that objective—meeting the Watergate burglars' blackmail demands.

"Now let me tell you," the President told Dean and Haldeman at one such juncture. "We could get the money. There is no problem in that. We can't provide the clemency. Money could be provided. Mitchell could provide the way to deliver it. That could be done. See what I mean?"

At another point in the discussion the President asked Dean:

"What do you think? You don't need a million right away, but you need a million? Is that right?"

Dean: "That is right."

The President: "You need it in cash don't you? I am just thinking out loud here for a moment. Would you put that through the Cuban Committee (through which payments to the Watergate conspirators had been funneled for months).

Dean: "No."

The President: "It is going to be checks, cash money, etc. How if that ever comes out, are you going to handle it? Is the Cuban Committee an obstruction of justice, if they want to help?"

Dean: "Well they have priests in it."

The President: "Would that give a little bit of cover?"

The edited transcript shows the following interchange near the end of the meeting:

XIII

President: "That's why for your immediate thing you have no choice but to come up with the $120,000, or whatever it is. Right?"

Dean: "That's right."

President: "Would you agree that that's the prime thing that you damn well better get done?"

Dean: "Obviously he (Hunt) ought to be given some signal anyway."

President: "(expletive deleted), get it . . ."

Then the conversation shifted to a discussion about who should talk to Hunt. The President suggested his former special counsel, Charles W. Colson. The transcript makes clear that Colson earlier had discussed clemency for Hunt with Hunt's attorney, William O. Bittman.

In the discussion of how to raise the cover-up payment, the President asked how the money would be delivered.

"You have to wash the money," Dean responded. "You can get a $100,000 out of a bank, and it all comes in serialized bills."

"I understand," the President said.

Dean continued: "And that means you have to go to [Las] Vegas with it or a bookmaker in New York City.

There is next deleted expletive of Haldeman's. The President then said that Kalmbach must have some money which could be used, but he was told by Dean that "Kalmbach doesn't have a cent."

A special $350,000 cash White House fund then was discussed and Haldeman observed that, "We are so (adjective deleted) square that we get caught at everything." This is an apparent reference to the discovery by the press of secret cash funds controlled by Haldeman and others.

The President then started to make a suggestion and Haldeman said, "Be careful . . ."

According to testimony later given at the Senate Watergate committee, the President and Haldeman were aware that the Oval Office meeting was being recorded. Dean, however, was not aware of the taping system.

The edited transcript of the meeting helps explain Dean's sworn testimony before the Senate Watergate committee about the President's suggestion that the Cabinet be briefed about Watergate. During his Senate testimony Dean expressed surprise at the President's proposal.

The transcript of the March 21 meeting indicates that the President did not want Dean to tell the Cabinet the truth.

"Still consider my scheme of having you brief the Cabinet," the President said, "just in very general terms and the (congressional) leaders in very general terms and maybe some very general statement with regard to my investigation. Answer questions, basically on the basis of what they (the witnesses) told you, not what you know."

During the last portion of the meeting, the President voiced concern about former Attorney General John N. Mitchell and proposed that Mitchell be praised for containing the Watergate probe.

The President specifically proposed telling Mitchell the following: "No doubt about the right plan before the election. You handled it just right. You contained it. And now after the election we have to have another plan. Because we can't for four years have this thing eating away."

While discussing the proposed meeting with Mitchell on the matter of the cover-up, the President said that "Mitchell has to be there because he is seriously involved and we are trying to keep him with us."

Haldeman then noted that the Watergate case may touch the President. "The erosion here now is going to you, and that is the thing that we have to turn off at whatever cost. We have to turn it off at the lowest cost we can, but at whatever cost it takes."

"That's what we have to do," Dean responded.

The President then said: "Well, the erosion is inevitably going to come here, apart from anything and all the people saying well the Watergate isn't a major issue. It isn't. But it will be. It's bound to. (Unintelligible) has to go out. Delaying is the great danger to the White House area. We don't, I say that the White House can't do it. Right?"

"Yes, sir," Dean responded and the meeting apparently ended at that point.

The unintelligible part of the conversation may be crucial. If, for example, the President said that the truth "has to go out," then it would be highly favorable to his defense. On the other hand, if he said that the money or the $120,000 "has to go out," it would be extremely damaging.

At one point in the conversation, the President asked Dean, "What would you go to jail for?"

"The obstruction of justice," Dean answered.

The President seemed puzzled: "The obstruction of justice?"

Even after learning that the Watergate defendants had

been paid for their silence and that Hunt was black-mailing the White House, the President said that the obstruction of justice "could be cut off at the pass."

In the discussion of granting clemency to Hunt, the following interchange took place:

Dean: "I am not sure that you will ever be able to deliver on the clemency. It may be just too hot."

President: "You can't do it politically until after the '74 elections, that's for sure. Your point is that even then you couldn't do it."

Dean: "That's right. It may further involve you in a way you should not be involved in this."

President: "No—it is wrong that's for sure."

The President has used that statement in his defense, though the edited transcript indicates that the statement was made in the context of the political ramifications of the 1974 elections, rather than the moral or legal "wrong."

The President then suggested that White House aide Richard A. Moore and Colson not sit in on any such meeting. Mr. Nixon gave no reason to exclude Moore, but said that Colson "talks too much" and is "a name-dropper."

The President also said that he did not worry about the unfavorable publicity that might follow disclosure of the cover-up.

"The point is," the President said, "that I don't want any criminal liabilities. That is the thing that I am concerned about for members of the White House staff, and I would trust for members of the (re-election) committee."

To avoid those "criminal liabilities," the President said that it "means keeping it off" Dean, Kalmbach, Haldeman, Mitchell, and former White House aides Dwight Chapin and Gordon Strachan.

The President then proposed looking at the course of action "to try to cut our losses . . . First it is going to require approximately a million dollars to take care of the jackasses who are in jail. That can be arranged. But you realize that after we are gone (presumably in 1977, when Mr. Nixon's term expires) and assuming we can expend this money then they are going to crack and it would be an unseemly story . . . People won't care, but people are going to be talking about it, there is no question."

The President also proposed that the White House put out the story that the initial payments to the Watergate defendants before the election came from some Cuban defense committee.

"Well, yeah," Dean answered. "We can put it together. That isn't of course quite the way it happened, but—"

"I know," the President said, "but that's the way it is going to have to happen."

Initial Reaction On Hill Divided Along Party Lines
By Haynes Johnson

The Nixon Watergate papers, the most extraordinary documents ever to come out of the White House, have been made public to the Congress and the American people.

They are massive in content (more than 200,000 words), riveting in language and characterization of public figures, and explosive in their revelations about the President's role in Watergate.

Release of the 1,254 pages of the secretly recorded conversations of crucial Watergate-related meetings from September, 1972, through April, 1973, came in two distinct installments yesterday.

The first segment, made public in the morning after the President's nationally televised address, was in the form of a White House summary of the conversations—in effect, an official "white paper" on the Watergate affair.

Its tone was that of a lawyer's brief, strongly arguing that the public disclosure will establish, once and for all, the President's innocence.

"In all of the thousands of words spoken," the White House summary said, "even though they often are unclear and ambiguous, not once does it appear that the President of the United States was engaged in a criminal plot to obstruct justice."

Throughout the morning and early afternoon an intensive White House public relations effort was under way across the country to reinforce that view. White House aides were calling editors and reporters in an attempt to demonstrate that the "truth" of Watergate, as now made public, completely absolves the President.

The immediate reaction on Capitol Hill divided along political lines. John Rhodes of Arizona, the House Republican leader, said the transcripts showed the President "in substantial compliance" with a House Judiciary Committee subpoena.

Democratic response tended to follow the lead of House Speaker Carl Albert. "Why substitute other evidence when the direct evidence [the actual tapes] is available?" he said.

Then, shortly after 3 p.m., the second wave struck in the release of the edited documents. They, clearly, were open to other interpretations than those given by the White House brief.

The conversations show the President discussing at length raising blackmail money; discussing the merits of offering clemency or parole; suggesting how to handle possible perjury or obstruction of justice charges; urging the adoption of a "national security" defense for potential White House defendants.

They are candid beyond any papers ever made public by a President. Even though the transcripts were edited to remove expletives, they still contain occasional profanities and harsh judgments on individuals. They also contain disclosures of a kind that are certain to inspire even stronger future controversy about Mr. Nixon's role.

The controversy over Mr. Nixon's compliance with the congressional subpoena also continues. Today the House Judiciary Committee will meet to give its formal response on whether its members find the President in compliance with their legal request for the production of 42 tapes and related materials—or whether they will initiate contempt proceedings in Congress.

Such a finding could become a key charge in the impeachment proceedings now under way.

The transcripts, even in their expurgated form, are certain to be talked about and read long after Mr. Nixon leaves the White House.

The conversations are laced with references to "laundering" money and cash payments, to "coded" phone conversations and burglaries and break-ins and even, in one instance, to a Mafia-type operation. In that conversation, Dean had complained that the people at the White House were not "pros" at "this sort of thing. This is the sort of thing Mafia people can do. . . ."

"That's right," the President responded.

The conversation continued:

Dean: It is a tough thing to know how to do.

Mr. Nixon: Maybe it takes a gang to do that.

His release of his private conversations comes exactly a

year to the day after he first reported in full to the public on the Watergate affair.

Now he is even more deeply engaged in fighting the most difficult political battle of his life.

President Initiated Talk About Clemency
By Lawrence Meyer

President Nixon raised the question of executive clemency for the original seven Watergate defendants during a conversation with White House counsel John W. Dean III on Feb. 28, 1973, according to edited transcripts of presidential conversations released yesterday by the White House.

"Do they expect clemency in a reasonable time?" Mr. Nixon asked Dean. "What would you advise on that?"

Dean replied that clemency "is one of those things we will have to watch closely."

Mr. Nixon responded, "You couldn't do it, say, in six months."

"No, you couldn't," Dean replied. "This thing may become so political as a result of these hearings (the Watergate trial) that it is a vendetta."

Mr. Nixon has said publicly that he ruled out clemency for the Watergate defendants and instructed his aides not to discuss the matter. He has never said whether he himself discussed the possibility of granting clemency.

The discussion of clemency by Mr. Nixon and Dean came in one of a series of meetings that the two men held in late 1972 and early 1973 as they attempted to come to grips with the problem of dealing publicly with the Watergate affair.

The transcripts lift the curtain on meetings from September, 1972, through April, 1973, at which the two men—the President of the United States and his official White House lawyer—talked informally, with mutual familiarity and apparently using salty language about the problems posed for the White House by the sentencing of the seven Watergate burglary defendants and the rapidly approaching Senate Watergate committee hearings.

Dean has testified under oath that throughout this period he was attempting to get the President to "get out in front" and take the lead in making public the Watergate affair. Dean has testified that Mr. Nixon was aware of the Watergate cover-up as early as Sept. 15, 1972 when he had his first conversation with Mr. Nixon about Watergate.

Mr. Nixon has claimed that he wanted the full story of Watergate told, that he struggled to have it made public and that he knew nothing of the cover-up until Dean told him about it in detail on March 21, 1973.

The transcripts, edited by the White House before they were released yesterday, present a third version, however, one that simultaneously substantiates and refutes significant portions of both the Dean and Nixon accounting of what the two men said to each other.

A White House summary accompanying the transcripts and preceding it states that Dean had threatened on April 27—three days before President Nixon fired Dean—through his lawyers that unless Dean received immunity from prosecution, " 'We will bring the President in—not in this case but in other things.' "

The summary quotes Mr. Nixon telling Assistant Attorney General Henry E. Petersen, who conveyed the message of Dean's alleged threat, "All right. We have got the immunity problem resolved. Do it, Dean, if you need to, but boy, I am telling you—there ain't going to be any blackmail."

In addition to showing that Mr. Nixon raised the issue of clemency Feb. 28, 1973, the transcripts also show that the President was told by Dean on March 13, 1973, that Gordon Strachan, an aide to White House chief of staff H. R. (Bob) Haldeman, knew about the Watergate affair prior to June 17, 1972, when the Watergate break-in occurred.

"Well, then," President Nixon commented when Dean told him about Strachan, "he probably told Bob (Haldeman). He may not have."

Dean assured Mr. Nixon that Strachan "is as tough as nails. He can go in and stonewall, and say, 'I don't know anything about what you are talking about.' He has already done it twice you know, in interviews."

"I guess he should, shouldn't he?" President Nixon replied. "I suppose we can't call that justice, can we?"

Strachan is presently under indictment, along with Haldeman and five other former White House and Nixon campaign officials on charges of conspiracy to obstruct justice and making false statements to a federal grand jury, charges stemming from the Watergate cover-up.

Dean also told Mr. Nixon that deputy Nixon campaign manager Jeb Stuart Magruder also knew about the Watergate break-in. "Oh, I see," Mr. Nixon said, "The other weak link for Bob (Haldeman) is Magruder."

Mr. Nixon also was told by Dean on March 13, 1973, that former Attorney General John N. Mitchell and special presidential counsel Charles W. Colson also could be involved in the Watergate affair.

The edited transcripts do not substantiate Dean's testimony before the Senate select Watergate committee, however, that he told Mr. Nixon on Sept. 15, 1972—the day the original Watergate indictments were returned—"that all that I had been able to do was to contain the case and assist in keeping it out of the White House. I also told him that there was a long way to go before this matter would end and that I certainly could make no assurances that the day would not come when this matter would start to unravel."

In fact, the transcript shows Dean telling Mr. Nixon:

"Three months ago I would have had trouble predicting there would be a day when this would be forgotten, but I think I can say that 54 days from now nothing is going to come crashing down to our surprise."

"That what?" President Nixon asked.

"Nothing is going to come crashing down to our surprise," Dean replied.

"Oh, well," President Nixon responded, "This is a can of worms. As you know a lot of this stuff went on. And the people who worked this way are awfully embarrassed. But the way you have handled all this seems to me has been very skillful, putting your fingers in the leaks that have sprung here and sprung there."

The summary prepared by the White House to accompany the transcripts explains that this last remark by Mr. Nixon, "was said in the context not of a criminal plot to obstruct justice as Dean alleges, but rather in the context of the politics of the matter, such as civil suits, countersuits, Democratic efforts to exploit Watergate as a political issue and the like . . . This is an example of the possible ambiguities that the President says exists in these tapes that someone with a motive to discredit the President could take out of context and distort to suit his own purposes."

In other detail, the transcript bears out Dean's version of this meeting, including an extensive discussion on how hearings being proposed by House Banking and Currency

Committee Chairman Wright Patman (D-Texas) could be clocked and President Nixon's suggestion that "comprehensive notes on all those who tried to do us in" should be kept. "They were doing this quite deliberately," Mr. Nixon said, "and they are asking for it and they are going to get it.

"We have not used the power in this four years as you know. We have never used it. We have not used the Bureau (FBI) and we have not used the Justice Department, but things are going to change now. And they are either going to do it right or go," Mr. Nixon said.

"What an exciting prospect," Dean replied.

Although President Nixon has said publicly that he wanted the full story of the Watergate affair told publicly after the 1972 election, a conversation with Dean on March 13 indicates that he was at least ambivalent on the point.

"Now the other thing that we have talked about in the past, and I still have the same problem, is to have a 'here it all is' approach," Dean told Mr. Nixon. "If we do that . . ."

"And let it all hang out," Mr. Nixon interrupted.

"And let it all hang out," Dean repeated.

"We have passed that point," Mr. Nixon said.

"Plus the fact, they are not going to believe the truth. That is the incredible thing," Dean said.

"They won't believe the truth," Mr. Nixon said, "and they have committed seven people."

"That's right. They will continually try to say there is (unintelligible)," Dean answered.

One of the ironies of the Watergate affair is illustrated by President Nixon's next remark, speaking as he was in confidence to the man who later became his principal accuser.

"They hope," Mr. Nixon told Dean, "one will say one day, 'Haldeman did it,' and one day one will say I did it."

Beyond what the actual language of the conversations shows about the two men, about their motivations and intentions, the full context of their conversations shows that Dean was not so earnest in trying to convince Mr. Nixon that continuing the cover-up was not only impractical but wrong. At the same time, the conversations show that Mr. Nixon, although expressing surprise at some of Dean's revelations, did not appear bent on revealing the truth whatever the cost.

President Nixon has explained in his discussions about

the March 21 meeting that he was exploring options with Dean.

Dean mentioned to Mr. Nixon that Colson had discussed commutation of E. Howard Hunt's prison sentence indirectly with Hunt. "All of these things are bad. They are promises, they are commitments," Dean said. "They are the very sort of thing that the Senate is going to be looking most for. I don't think they can find them, frankly."

"Pretty hard," Mr. Nixon responded.

"Pretty hard. Damn hard. It's all cash," Dean said, referring to money that had been paid to the seven original Watergate defendants.

Dean mentioned to Mr. Nixon that $1 million would be needed over the next two years to pay the Watergate defendants.

"We could get that," Mr. Nixon responded. "But the question is who the hell would handle it? Any ideas on that?"

Dean responded, "Well, I think that is something that Mitchell ought to be charged with."

"I would think so too," Mr. Nixon said.

Periodically in the March 21 meeting, Dean returned to his opening theme of a "cancer" threatening Mr. Nixon's presidency. At one point, Dean told Mr. Nixon that presidential aide Egil (Bud) Krogh had committed perjury in testimony before the federal grand jury.

"He might be able to—" Mr. Nixon responded. "I am just trying to think. Perjury is an awful hard rap to prove. If he could just say that I—well, go ahead."

At another point, in discussing the money demands of Hunt and the other defendants, Mr. Nixon said, "Let me put it frankly: I wonder if that doesn't have to be continued? Let me put it this way: Let us suppose that you get the million bucks, and you get the proper way to handle it. You could hold that side?"

"Uh huh," Dean replied.

"It would seem to me that would be worthwhile," Mr. Nixon said.

Later, Mr. Nixon expresses concern that "we are going to be bled to death. And in the end, it is going to come out anyway. Then you get the worst of both worlds. We are going to lose, and the people are going to—"

"And look like dopes," interjected Haldeman, who had joined the meeting.

Moments later, despite Mr. Nixon's public statements

that he rejected paying money to Hunt, he told Dean:

"That's why for your immediate things you have no choice but to come up with $120,000, or whatever it is. Right?"

"That's right," Dean agreed.

"Would you agree," Mr. Nixon said, "that that's the prime thing that you damn well better get that done?"

Tapes Indicate Nixon Knew Of Cover-up Early
By Bob Woodward and Carl Bernstein

The edited transcripts of President Nixon's conversations indicate that Mr. Nixon was aware of the possible criminal involvement of his top aides well before March 21, 1973, the date he has maintained he first learned of the Watergate cover-up.

The tapes show that on Sept. 15, 1972, and Feb. 28, March 13 and March 20, 1973, Mr. Nixon, a lawyer, made statements, asked questions and received information that indicated he knew there was far more to the Watergate story than government investigators said they had been told by that time.

For example, on March 13, 1973, White House Counsel John W. Dean III specifically told Mr. Nixon that White House aide Gordon Strachan was aware of the illegal Watergate bugging operation during the period in 1972 when telephones at Democratic National Committee headquarters were tapped.

"I will be damned!" the President responded.

A key issue in the House impeachment inquiry could be whether President Nixon failed in this and other instances documented in the transcripts, to inform Watergate prosecutors about his knowledge of possibly criminal acts.

At that time, the seven original Watergate defendants, the only ones against whom the prosecutors then had evidence, were awaiting sentencing following their January, 1973, convictions.

The President and the White House have characterized Mr. Nixon's actions, before March 21, 1973, as being designed to quiet a political problem and not to obstruct justice. Unless there is uncontradicted evidence that the President did obstruct justice or otherwise broke the law, Mr.

Nixon and his advisers have contended, he cannot be impeached.

The President's response to Dean's information about Strachan on March 13 is consistent with other instances recorded in the transcripts in which Mr. Nixon received or discussed the possible criminal involvement of his aides.

At no time in the conversations before March 21—and rarely in those after that critical date—did the President or his advisers even discuss telling the whole truth to either the public or law enforcement authorities.

Instead, the tapes reveal discussions of alternatives ranging from public relations offensives to total silence to the possibility of extending executive clemency to the Watergate burglars.

The conversation about Strachan's involvement—like many others in the pre-March 21 transcripts—took place against the backdrop White House planning for the then-upcoming Senate Watergate committee hearings.

Early in the same March 13 discussion Dean told Mr. Nixon: "These questions are just not going to go away."

It was two weeks earlier, on Feb. 28, that the transcripts show that Mr. Nixon raised the question of offering executive clemency to some of the Watergate burglars.

Told by Dean, "Well, there is every indication that they (the burglars) are hanging in tough right now"—an apparent reference to their silence about the Watergate raid—Mr. Nixon responded:

"What the hell do they expect, though? Do they expect clemency in a reasonable time? What would you advise on that?"

Dean: "I think it is one of those things we will have to watch very closely . . ."

During the same meeting, which occurred several weeks before the sentencing of the seven original Watergate defendants, the President asked Dean if federal Judge John J. Sirica "is trying to work on them to see who will break them down."

"Well, there is some of that," Dean replied in an apparent reference to publicly unrevealed facts known to the burglars.

"How the hell does Liddy stand up so well?" the President asked Dean on March 13.

"He's a strange man, Mr. President," Dean told him, ". . . Strange and strong. His loyalty is—I think it is just beyond the pale. . . ."

The President then asked Dean, "Is it too late to go the hang-out road?"—apparently meaning to take a candid approach—and was told by his counsel:

". . . There is a certain domino situation here. If some things start going, a lot of other things are going to start going, and there can be a lot of problems if everybody starts falling. So there are dangers, Mr. President. I would be less than candid if I didn't tell you there are. There is a reason for not everyone going up and testifying" (before the Senate committee).

According to the same page of the transcript, Dean also told Mr. Nixon on March 13, "I think there are some people (in the White House) who saw the fruits of "the Watergate wiretap—though Dean added that they did not know of "the criminal conspiracy to go in there" (the Democrats' Watergate headquarters).

Mr. Nixon did not ask Dean for details.

Earlier, on Feb. 28, Dean and the President engaged in the following colloquy during their discussion of the upcoming Senate hearings:

Dean: Well I was—we have come a long road on this thing now. I had thought it was an impossible task to hold together until after the election until things started falling out, but we have made it this far and I am convinced we are going to make it the whole road and put this thing in the funny pages of the history books rather than anything serious because actually—

Mr. Nixon: It will be somewhat serious but the main thing, of course, is also the isolation of the President.

Dean: Absolutely! Totally true!

Mr. Nixon: Because that, fortunately, is totally true.

Dean: I know that sir!

Mr. Nixon: (expletive deleted) Of course, I am not dumb and I will never forget when I heard about this (adjective deleted) forced entry and bugging. I thought, what in the hell is this? What is the matter with these people? Are they crazy. I thought they were nuts! A prank!

But it wasn't! It wasn't very funny. I think that our Democratic friends know that, too. They know what the hell it was. They don't think we'd be involved in such.

Dean: I think they do too.

Mr. Nixon: Maybe they don't. They don't think I would be involved in such stuff. They think I have people capable of it. And they are correct, in that Colson (special presidential counsel Charles W. Colson) would do anything . . . Colson's got (characterization deleted), but

I really, really—this stuff here, let's forget this. But let's remember this was not done by the White House. This was done by the Committee to Re-elect, and Mitchell was the chairman, correct?

Dean: That's correct!

The President then observed that if the Senate hearings "get out of hand," the result "is going to potentially ruin John Mitchell."

At the time of the discussion, investigators still had failed to establish the existence of a cover-up in Watergate or the involvement of high-level officials at either the White House or the Committee for the Re-election of the President.

In a later conversation, Dean briefed the President on preparations for sidetracking Watergate hearings then being planned by the House Banking and Currency Committee.

"You really can't sit and worry about it all the time," the President advised Dean. "The worst may happen but it may not. So you just try to button it up as well as you can and hope for the best, and remember basically the damn business is unfortunately trying to cut our losses."

Nixon's 'Probe Order' Not Supported By Transcripts
By Lawrence Meyer

President Nixon's assertion that he began "intensive new inquiries" into the Watergate affair on March 21, 1973, personally ordering "those conducting the investigations to get all the facts and to report them directly to me" is not supported by the edited transcripts of recorded White House conversations released Tuesday.

What the transcripts show instead is that the President and senior White House officials tried to gather information primarily for internal strategy purposes, rather than to turn over new information to the prosecutors, and to put together the semblance of a record, for later use, if necessary, to show that they had attempted to learn what happened.

In his televised speech of April 30, 1973, Mr. Nixon said, "On March 21, I personally assumed the responsibility for coordinating intensive new inquiries into the matter, and I personally ordered those conducting the investigations to get all the facts and to report them directly—to me, right here in this office."

The law enforcement officials in charge of the Watergate investigation, Attorney General Richard G. Kleindienst, Assistant Attorney General Henry E. Petersen and acting FBI Director L. Patrick Gray III, later testified under oath that they had received no such instructions from Mr. Nixon.

When pressed by reporters to detail what he had done to investigate and whom he had ordered to report to him, Mr. Nixon said that he had ordered White House counsel John W. Dean III to write a report concerning what he knew about the Watergate affair. Mr. Nixon said he had asked his top domestic adviser, John D. Ehrlichman, to conduct an investigation. And Mr. Nixon said that he had asked Ehrlichman to direct Kleindienst to report directly to Mr. Nixon any information he should have about the Watergate affair.

The transcripts show that the contact with Kleindienst was an attempt to use him as a conduit for information so that Mr. Nixon and his senior staff assistants, Ehrlichman and White House chief of staff H. R. (Bob) Haldeman, could keep abreast of developments inside the federal grand jury, which had resumed its investigation of the Watergate affair.

Increasingly, the transcripts show, Mr. Nixon, Haldeman and Ehrlichman became concerned that former Attorney General John N. Mitchell would be named as being involved in the planning and execution of the Watergate break-in.

The following transcript excerpt, from a March 27, 1973, meeting in President Nixon's Executive Office Building office shows how Kleindienst was to be approached.

Mr. Nixon: This is a bad rap here. We are not going to allow it. Our real problem is Mitchell. Now what about this? What are you going to do about it? . . . Of course, we ought to know—can't the Attorney General call Silbert (Principal Assistant U.S. Attorney Earl J. Silbert, then in charge of the Watergate investigation), or is that too dangerous for him?

Ehrlichman: Well he doesn't have to do that. Henry Petersen follows that thing on a daily basis.

Mr. Nixon: Henry Petersen?

Ehrlichman: Henry can let Dick (Kleindienst) know, and that's all there is to it.

Mr. Nixon: All right. You just tell Dick. You see the problem is, there, that Dick thinks I am—if he says he has furnished the grand jury things to the White House that there is a problem.

Ehrlichman: It's a tender problem. I think what he has to do—

Mr. Nixon: No, you could say this. Our need—our interest here—you could say it whether there are any White House people involved here and we will move on them.

Ehrlichman: That's right. And the President wants to know.

Mr. Nixon: That is the purpose. Not to protect anybody, but to find out what the hell they are saying.

Ehrlichman: Absolutely. That is the only basis on which to go.

President Nixon has left the inference, through his public statements, that his directions to Kleindienst covered the entire Watergate affair, the June 17 break-in, the decisions leading up to it and the cover-up that followed it. In an Aug. 22, 1973, press conference, Mr. Nixon was Ehrlichman directed Kleindienst "to report to me anything he found in this particular area."

A telephone conversation between Ehrlichman and Kleindienst on March 28, 1973, however, shows that Ehrlichman's instructions to the Attorney General were much narrower.

"OK, now," Ehrlichman told Kleindienst, according to the transcript of that conversation. "The President said for me to say this to you. That the best information he had and has is that neither Dean nor Haldeman nor (special President counsel Charles W.) Colson nor I nor anybody in the White House had any prior knowledge of this burglary. He said that he's counting on you to provide him with any information to the contrary if it ever turns up and you just contact him direct. Now as far as the Committee to Re-elect is concerned he said that serious questions are being raised with regard to Mitchell and he would likewise want you to communicate to him any evidence or inferences from evidence on that subject."

Dean, President Nixon told the Aug. 22, 1973, press conference, had earlier been "given the responsibility to write his own report . . ."

The transcript of a March 22, 1973, meeting in Mr. Nixon's Executive Office Building office shows that Mr. Nixon told Dean, "It (the report) is a negative in setting forth general information involving questions. Your consideration—your analysis, et cetera. You have found this, that. Rather than going into every news story and every charge, et cetera, et cetera. This, this, this—put it down. I don't know but—"

A moment later, Ehrlichman, speaking about the report Dean was assigned to write, said, "That would be my scenario. He presents it to you at your request. You then publish—(inaudible).

"And I am looking to the future," Ehrlichman continued later, speaking to Mr. Nison, "assuming that some corner of this thing comes unstuck, you are then in a position to say, 'Look, that document I published is the document I relied on, that is, the report I relied on.'"

"This is all we knew," Mr. Nixon said.

"This is all the stuff we could find out—" Haldeman added.

Dean, however, did not write the report. He testified before the Senate select Watergate committee last summer that he believed such a report would be used to further the cover-up, a move he said he opposed and which he would not assist.

Finally, Mr. Nixon said on Aug. 22, "I gave a responsibility for Mr. Ehrlichman on the 29th of March to continue the investigation that Mr. Dean was unable to conclude."

Ehrlichman, however, testified before the senate select Watergate committee that he could not characterize the interviews he conducted as comprising an "investigation." Ehrlichman said, rather, that he had conducted an "inquiry."

Ehrlichman's report to Mr. Nixon on April 14 on the results of his inquiries show a concern for public relations at a time when new facts about the Watergate affair, and the possible involvement of White House officials, were becoming known to the Watergate prosecutors and the public.

Mr. Nixon: We have to prick the boil and take the heat. Now that's what we are doing here. We're going to prick this boil and take the heat. I—am I overstating?

Ehrlichman: No, I think that's right. The idea is, this will prick the boil. It may not. The history of this thing has to be, though, that you did not tuck this under the rug yesterday or today, and hope it would go away.

Mr. Nixon: Now. In the scenario. I sort of go out and tell people that I have done this.

Ehrlichman: I don't know. It depends on how it all

turns out. If he does not go to the U.S. attorney, if Magruder decides to stay clammed up—

Haldeman: What would you do?

Mr. Nixon: Well, that, well, let's suppose they still indict. You don't want them to indict and then have to say that on Saturday, the 14th of April, you, John Ehrlichman—

Ehrlichman: The problem is that you if you were to go out on this kind of hearsay and say we know who did it, then you've prejudiced their rights.

Mr. Nixon: Then your thought is just to make a record of the decision?

Ehrlichman: When somebody comes to (unintelligible) what the hell was the White House doing all this time? Then you're in a position to say, well, we began to investigate personally the external circumstances and we came to some conclusions—we acted on those conclusions.

Mr. Nixon then went on to say that it might be officially announced that John Ehrlichman conducted an investigation.

Watergate Seemed To Be A Simple
Public Relations Crisis
By Haynes Johnson

At one point, Richard M. Nixon turns to his men and asks, "How do you handle that PR wise?" A not unusual question for an executive—including the President—to ask in this age of images, mass communications and public relations campaigns, to be sure.

Watergate, too, it now seems clear from reading the 1,254 pages of Nixon transcripts, was regarded by the President and his most trusted advisers as essentially a PR problem. Traumatic and troubling, yes, but basically a problem to be handled by seizing the initiative, by minimizing the public impact, by cutting losses, by bold and vigorous counterattacks.

The Nixon men had a phrase for it: getting out in front. If successful, they would put the President "on top" and out of reach.

Listen, for instance, to the conversation between the President, H. R. (Bob) Haldeman, John D. Ehrlichman, John W. Dean III and John N. Mitchell on March 22 a year ago. It is the day after Dean has reported on criminal involvement and they are discussing using Dean's report on his Watergate "investigation" so the White House can cite its striving for the full truth—and that Dean can use if he is called to testify.

The President: Well, on the Dean thing—you simply say, well, that [testifying] is out. Dean has made this report and here is everything Dean knows.

Ehrlichman: I think, John, on Monday you could say to Ervin if the question comes up, "I know the President's mind on this and he has always indicated that the fruits of my investigation should be available to you." And just leave it at that for the time being.

Dean: One issue that may come up as the hearings go along is the fact that the focus on this book is that Dean knows. I was all over this thing like a wet blanket. I was everywhere—everywhere they look they are going to find Dean.

President: Sure.

Haldeman: Well, I don't think that is bad.

Ehrlichman: I don't either. You were supposed to be.

President. You were our investigator. You were directed by the President to get me all the facts. Second, as White House counsel you were on it to assist people in the executive branch who were being questioned. Say you were there for the purpose of getting information. That was your job.

Dean: That's right.

President: But the main point certainly is that Dean had absolutely no operational activity. The wonderful thing about your position is that as far as they are concerned—your position has never been as operative.

Moments later, the President continues: ". . . . We've got to keep our eye on the Dean thing—just give them some of it—not all of it. I don't suppose they say John—no—we won't take it. Just take the heat. . . ."

The conversation turns to the possibilities of White House subpoenas being issued.

"They can subpoena any of us," Dean says. "There is no doubt about that. If they don't serve it here it's because they can't get in. They can serve you at home somewhere. They can always find you."

Haldeman speaks up. "We move to Camp David and hide! They can't get in there."

Thus, as the drama slowly unfolds inside the White House, the Nixon men continually debate their PR and political strategies. They weigh the consequences of each possible move, rehearse their public statements, act out their various and constantly changing "scenarios," draft imaginary news accounts to determine the public reaction, check and counter-check.

March 27, the President, Haldeman, Ehrlichman and press secretary Ronald L. Ziegler are meeting to handle publicly a deteriorating situation. Finally, the President tells Ziegler:

". . . Just get out there and act like your usual cocky, confident self."

Ziegler: Then if I am asked a question about whether or not Dean would appear before the grand jury, if I am asked that question—

President: Yeah.

Ziegler: How should I handle that?

President: That's tough.

Ziegler: I could—Two options: one would be to say that (unintelligible) the other would be to say the (unintelligible).

After a brief exchange, the President suggests: "Why don't you say, 'We have indicated cooperation and when we see the form of the request, or whatever it is—' "

Ziegler, interrupting and continuing the dialogue to be delivered to the press: "These matters must proceed in an orderly manner and I am not going up here and comment on the possibility of—"

President: Of future action (unintelligible).

Ehrlichman: The other thing you might do is—this would put our friend John Dean III in a tough spot—say, "While there have been some accusations against him, he's really in the poorest position to defend himself of anybody in the government."

In the peculiar shorthand language they employed so familiarly in the privacy of their deliberations, the Nixon men spoke of "confining the situation," of "stonewalling," of "stroking" less resolute members of their team, of taking the "let-it-all-hang-out" or "the limited let-it-all-hang-out" of getting to the "bottom line."

What is singularly missing from these glimpses of life inside the White House is a sense of moral outrage, a ringing declaration from anyone, at any time, that wrongs had been committed that must be corrected.

Instead, by their own admittedly incomplete testimony, they reacted to the growing knowledge of possible Watergate-related crimes—obstruction of justice, break-ins, burglaries, bugging, plans to commission prostitutes and mugging teams—by devising PR and political tactics to deal with them.

They spoke of trying to use, it would seem, everyone and everything at their command. The list is long and inclusive.

The FBI. The Attorney General, Senators Baker, Gurney and Goldwater. Prosecutor Henry Petersen. The grand jury. Secretary of State Rogers. The Library of Congress. The IRS. The Chief Justice. Judge Ritchie. Private records of past administrations to demonstrate that the Democrats—and Democratic Presidents—did it too. "Friendly" news organizations and newsmen favored with selective leaks. The "Dean Report."

National security, executive privilege and the constitutional doctrine of separation of powers also became vehicles in their public campaign of counterattack.

The final question of the guilt or innocence of these participants is still to be determined, but the record that has now been made public goes a long way to help understand the official climate and attitudes during the long months of the Watergate crisis.

What emerges is a picture of no master plot hatched by master conspirators, but of a desperate struggle to put the best face on a steadily worsening situation.

The President and his men are trapped by events, and those events begin to have an inexorable life of their own that sweep the main actors along from scene to scene. They improvise. They deliberate. They see the tide turning in on them. They recognize, finally, that some—and maybe most—face criminal indictments and possible imprisonment.

As the transcripts make clear, they are all fighting to limit the scope of the investigations and the final consequences. They are trying to keep the inquiries focused on the event—the break-in and burglary at the Watergate office building. But Watergate will not stay within its channels; it spills out into other areas—the Ellsberg burglary case, the Huston surveillance plan, the Vesco affair.

The transcripts strongly indicate that few of them had a clear picture of any one aspect. Some know only a fragment, some have a larger understanding. The President appears, in these accounts, to have been the one person most in the dark.

Whatever his own knowledge—and these transcripts are open to questions since he, at least, knew that every word he uttered was being secretly recorded—his reaction to the disclosures is consistent from beginning to end. He, too, frequently views them as a PR-political problem to be confronted.

When Dean tells him on March 21 how Watergate really began—"It started with an instruction to me from Bob Haldeman to see if we couldn't set up a perfectly legitimate campaign intelligence operation over at the re-election committee"—he listens quietly.

When Dean informs him of the Ellsberg break-in, he says, "Oh, yeah." When Dean explains, "I worked on a theory of containment—to try to hold it right where it was," he replies, "Sure," and "Right."

One of the most fascinating portraits of Mr. Nixon as President is in his relationship to his two key aides, Haldeman and Ehrlichman. They speak as equals. There is none of the "Sirs" that Dean always employs, none of the "Mr. President" that John Mitchell uses to address the Chief Executive.

Together, they argue out strategy and tactics—whether to go public, and in what form; whether to permit aides to testify; whether to appoint a special prosecutor; whether to yield on executive privilege and "national security."

In the end, the case unravels, but the PR struggle continues to this day.

Now those once-secret conversations have become a critical factor in the President's campaign to win public support. And even they come before the public with a touch of the PR man's hand about them.

They begin with a White House position paper affirming the President's innocence and an explanation that certain things were said not in the context of a criminal plot, "but rather in the politics of the matter" and the "handling of the political and public relations aspect of the matter."

They end with a presidential speech of a year ago concluding with the words, "God bless America and God bless each and every one of you."

Names That Figure In The Transcripts

Code for initials used in the transcripts to identify major personalities involved in the Oval Room, and EOB office talks and the telephone conversations as well as the full names and biographical sketches of other people often referred to in the tapes.

P.—President Nixon.
D.—John W. Dean, III, Mr. Nixon's counsel.
E.—John D. Ehrlichman, former Assistant to the President for Domestic Affairs.
K.—Richard G. Kleindienst, former U.S. Attorney General.
H.—H. R. Haldeman, former White House chief of staff.
L.H.—Lawrence M. Higby, deputy assistant to the President.
M.—John N. Mitchell, former U.S. Attorney General.
H.P.—Henry E. Petersen, Assistant U.S. Attorney General.
R.—William P. Rogers, former Secretary of State.
S.—Frank H. Strickler, attorney for Nixon aide, Ehrlichman.
W.—John J. Wilson, lawyer for former White House aides Haldeman and Ehrlichman.
Z.—Ronald L. Ziegler, press secretary to President Nixon.

Sen. Howard H. Baker, Jr. (R-Tenn.)—Baker, 48, is Vice-Chairman and ranking minority member of the Senate Watergate Committee. Shortly after the committee was formed in February, 1973, Baker met secretly with President Nixon.
Dwight L. Chapin—Chapin, 33, was appointed secretary to the President in the first Nixon administration. He was convicted in April, 1974, of perjury in connection with his relationship to political saboteur, Donald H. Segretti.
Charles W. Colson—Colson, 42, a special counsel to Mr. Nixon until March, 1973, was known as the President's troubleshooter. He has been indicted for conspir-

acy and obstruction of justice in the Watergate cover-up, and with conspiracy in the 1971 break-in at the office of Daniel Ellsberg's psychiatrist.

John W. Dean, III—Dean, 35, a rising young man as counsel to Mr. Nixon, was the first ranking member of the Nixon camp to confess criminal acts in the Watergate cover-up. Dean claims to have had Mr. Nixon's best interests in mind, but he has been pictured as the President's chief accuser.

John D. Ehrlichman—Ehrlichman, 48, was the President's Assistant for Domestic Affairs and was closer to Mr. Nixon than almost anyone other than Ehrlichman's own close friend, H. R. Haldeman. In the Watergate cover-up, he has been charged with conspiracy, obstruction of justice and making false statements to a grand jury or a court and to the FBI. Ehrlichman also has been charged in the Ellsberg psychiatrist's break-in with conspiracy to violate the civil rights of the psychiatrist and with four counts of lying to a federal grand jury and to FBI agents.

Sen. Sam J. Ervin, Jr. (D.-N.C.)—Ervin, 76, is chairman of the seven-member select committee on the Senate that investigated the Watergate affair.

L. Patrick Gray, III—Gray, 57, was acting head of the FBI during the first Watergate investigation and resigned April 27, 1973, when it was revealed that he had destroyed material given him by John W. Dean, III and John D. Ehrlichman. Before then, Senate hearings on Gray's nomination to be permanent FBI Director became the first serious inquiry into the Watergate scandal.

H. R. Bob Haldeman—Haldeman, 47, President Nixon's former chief of staff, has worked for Richard Nixon since 1956 and was reputedly the only aide who entered the Oval Office without knocking. He has been indicted for conspiracy, obstruction of justice and perjury in the Watergate cover-up.

E. Howard Hunt, Jr.—Hunt, 55, one of those convicted in the first Watergate trial in 1973, was a 21-year veteran of the CIA who retired in 1970. He was brought to the White House by his friend Charles W. Colson the following year, and engaged in political spying including the Ellsberg psychiatrist's break-in and gathering information on Sen. Edward M. Kennedy.

Herbert W. Kalmbach—Kalmbach, 52, President Nixon's personal attorney, raised secret funds to help support the Watergate defendants and pay their legal fees. He has pleaded guilty to peddling an ambassadorship and for illegal fund raising in 1970.

Richard G. Kleindienst—Kleindienst, 50, became a friend and close associate of several Watergate conspirators. He became Attorney General in 1972 and was forced to resign on April 30, 1973, along with John D. Ehrlichman and H. R. Haldeman.

Egil Krogh, Jr.—Krogh, 34, was head of the White House "Plumbers" and was sentenced to six months after pleading guilty to involvement in the Ellsberg psychiatrist's break-in.

Frederick C. La Rue—La Rue, 44, a wealthy Mississippian, was an aide and close friend of John N. Mitchell when Mitchell directed the 1972 Nixon campaign. La Rue has pleaded guilty to charges of conspiracy to obstruct justice in the Watergate cover-up.

G. Gordon Liddy—Liddy, 43, a former FBI agent, prosecutor and unsuccessful candidate for Congress, worked with the White House "Plumbers" on the Ellsberg psychiatrist's break-in; as an aide at the Nixon re-election committee, he directed the ill-fated Watergate break-in of June 17. Aside from a criminal sentence, he has been found in contempt of Congress and contempt of court as he has refused, apparently alone among all the Watergate underlings, to cooperate in any investigation.

Jeb S. Magruder—Magruder, 39, was a White House aide under H. R. Haldeman and then no. 2 man to John N. Mitchell in the Nixon re-election committee at the time of the Watergate arrests. He has admitted planning the break-in and pleaded guilty to obstruction of justice and defrauding the United States in the cover-up.

Robert C. Mardian—Mardian, 50, is a former assistant Attorney General under John N. Mitchell and left that position to work for Mitchell in the 1972 Nixon re-election campaign. He has been charged with conspiracy in the Watergate cover-up.

James W. McCord, Jr.—McCord, 50, a retired CIA official, joined the Nixon re-election committee in 1972 as security coordinator and was among the five men caught in Democratic headquarters. A letter he sent to Judge John J. Sirica in March 1973 is credited with having been a major factor in the collapse of the Watergate cover-up.

John N. Mitchell—Mitchell, 60, Attorney General in the first Nixon administration, is accused by aides of having approved the Watergate bugging—a charge he denies.

Acquitted in a New York trial in April 1974, on charges of perjury and conspiracy in another case related to the 1972 Presidential campaign, Mitchell still faces formal charges of conspiracy, obstruction of justice, making false statements to a grand jury or a court, perjury and making false statements to the FBI in the Watergate cover-up.

Richard M. Nixon—Mr. Nixon, 61, was in the Bahamas with his friend Robert Abplanalp June 17, 1972, when he first heard of the arrests at the Watergate. Victor in a re-election landslide 5½ months later. Mr. Nixon has seen his second administration turned into a shambles, has been forced to call for the resignations of his closest associates, has sunk precipitously in public opinion polls and, at the time of publication, was fighting to avoid impeachment.

Henry E. Petersen—Petersen, 53, a career Justice Department official and a Democrat who rose to the position of Assistant Attorney General in charge of the Criminal Division, played a controversial role in the first Watergate investigation.

Donald H. Segretti—Segretti, 32, was a classmate of Dwight Chapin and was recruited by Chapin and another White House aide, Gordon Strachan, to conduct political sabotage in the 1972 campaign. He pleaded guilty and was sentenced to six months for so-called "dirty tricks" performed in Florida during the election campaign.

Earl J. Silbert—Silbert, 37, was chief prosecutor in the original Watergate trial. While some have questioned his integrity, others have staunchly defended it. He was nominated in early 1974 as U. S. Attorney for the District of Columbia.

John J. Sirica—Sirica, 70, a little known federal district court judge until the Watergate affair, was named man-of-the-year by TIME magazine at the end of 1973 for his role in helping unravel the conspiracy.

Maurice H. Stans—Stans, 66, was chief of the Nixon finance committee in the 1972 re-election campaign that raised more than $60 million dollars for President Nixon—$22 million of it in secret contributions. He, along with John N. Mitchell, was acquitted in the New York trial on charges of perjury and conspiracy in the case of a $200,000 campaign contribution and alleged influence peddling before the Securities and Exchange Commission.

Gordon C. Strachan—Strachan, 30, an attorney who worked for H. R. Haldeman in the White House, was liaison for Haldeman with the re-election committee in the

1972 campaign. He has been indicted on charges of conspiracy, obstruction of justice, and making false statements to a grand jury or a court in the Watergate cover-up.

Sen. Lowell P. Weicker, Jr.—Weicker, 42, Connecticut Republican member of the Senate Watergate Committee, was among the first politicians to attack high White House aides as culpable in the Watergate affair. Early, Weicker demanded the resignation of H. R. Haldeman, and as the Senate committee's investigations were played out, Weicker often was the most outspokenly critical Senator.

John J. Wilson—Wilson, 73, became attorney for H. R. Haldeman and John D. Ehrlichman on the recommendation of former Secretary of State, William Rogers. In April, 1973, he met twice with President Nixon to discuss their defense, and one of those talks is among the tapes made public.

Ronald L. Ziegler—Ziegler, 35, was brought to the White House as press secretary for Mr. Nixon after having worked in advertising for H. R. Haldeman. As member after member of the original Nixon team left the White House under a Watergate cloud, Ziegler remained and reportedly became one of Mr. Nixon's closest associates and advisers.

The White House Summary

Following is the text of a 50-page statement sent by President Nixon to the House Judiciary Committee Tuesday, April 30, 1974. In it, Mr. Nixon explains his objections to what he calls a "Broad scale subpoena" by the Committee and offers a summary of the edited transcripts of tapes of 31 White House conversations that he also sent to the Committee yesterday.

The following text makes several references to testimony before the Senate Watergate Committee last summer. That testimony is now in book form, and the references are indicated in this manner: "(Bk.-, P.-)."

Phrases that appear in italicized type are those in which the emphasis was supplied by the White House.

On April 11, 1974, the Committee on the Judiciary of the House of Representatives of the Congress caused a subpoena to be issued to the President of the United States, returnable on April 25, 1974. The subpoena called for the production of tapes and other materials relating to forty-two Presidential conversations. With respect to all but three of these conversations, the subpoena called for the production of the tapes and related materials without regard to the subject matter, or matters, dealt with in these conversations. In the President's view, such a broad scale subpoena is unwarranted. As the U.S. Court of Appeals in *Nixon* vs. *Sirica* has stated, "wholesale public access to Executive deliberations and documents would cripple the Executive as a co-equal branch," and as the President has repeatedly stated, he will not participate in the destruction of the office of the Presidency of the United States by permitting unlimited access to Presidential conversations and documents.

The President, on the other hand, does recognize that the House Committee on the Judiciary has constitutional responsibilities to examine fully into his conduct and therefore the President has provided the annexed transcripts of all or portions of the subpoenaed conversations that were recorded and of a number of additional nonsubpoenaed conversations that clearly show what knowledge

1

the President had of an alleged cover-up of the Watergate break-in and what actions he took when he was informed of the cover-up. The President believes that these are the matters that primarily concern the Congress and the American people.

In order that the Committee may be satisfied that he has in fact disclosed this pertinent material to the Committee, the President has invited the Chairman and ranking minority member to review the subpoenaed tapes to satisfy themselves that a full and complete disclosure of the pertinent contents of these tapes has, indeed, been made. If, after such review they have any questions regarding his conduct, the President has stated that he stands ready to respond under oath to written interrogatories and to meet with the Chairman and ranking minority member of the Committee at the White House to discuss these matters if they so desire.

The President is making this response, which exceeds the material called for in the subpoena, in order that the Committee will be able to carry out its responsibilities and bring this matter to an expeditious conclusion.

The attached transcripts represent the best efforts accurately to transcribe the material contained on the recording tapes. Expletives have been omitted in the interest of good taste, except where necessary to depict accurately the context of the conversation. Characterization of third persons, in fairness to them, and other material not relating to the President's conduct has been omitted, except where inclusion is relevant and material as bearing on the President's conduct.

In order that the material submitted in this response to the Committee's subpoena can be viewed in the context of the events surrounding the Watergate incident and thereafter, the following summary is provided.

The Break-in at the Watergate - June 17, 1972

When the break-in at Watergate occurred and the participants were arrested, the President was in Florida. As he has stated many times, he had no prior knowledge of this activity and had nothing whatsoever to do with it. No one has stated otherwise, not even Mr. Dean, former Counsel to the President, who is the only one who has made any charges against the President. During the course of Dean's conversation with the President on February 28, 1973, the President stated to Dean:

2

P.   Of course I am not dumb and I will never forget when I heard about this - forced entry and bugging. I thought "what is this? What is the matter with these people, are they crazy?" I thought they were nuts.

During the conversation between the President and Dean on the morning of March 21, 1973, the tape of which has also previously been provided the Committee, Dean strongly disclaimed to the President that anyone at the White House knew of the break-in in advance.

D.   I honestly believe that no one over here knew that. I know that as God is my maker I had no knowledge that they were going to do this.

In the conversation of the President with Mr. Haldeman and Mr. Ehrlichman on the 27th of March 1973, the following exchange, which conclusively demonstrates the President's lack of foreknowledge, took place:

H.   O'Brien raised the question whether Dean actually had no knowledge of what was going on in the intelligence area between the time of the meetings in Mitchell's office, when he said don't do anything, and the time of the Watergate discovery. And I put that very question to Dean, and he said, "Absolutely nothing."

P.   I would—the reason I would totally agree—that I would believe Dean there (unintelligible) he would be lying to us about that. But I would believe for another reason—that he thought it was a stupid damn idea.

E.   There just isn't a scintilla of hint that Dean knew about this. Dean was pretty good all through that period of time in sharing things, and he was tracking with a number of us on—

P.   Well, you know the thing the reason that (unintelligible) thought—and this incidentally covers Colson—and I don't know whether—. I know that most everybody except Bob, and perhaps you, think Colson knew all about it. But I was talking to Colson, remember exclusively about—and maybe that was the point—exclusively about issues . . .

* * *

P. Right. That was what it is. But in all those talks he had plenty of opportunity. He was always coming to me with ideas, but Colson in that entire period, John, didn't mention it. I think he would have said, "Look we've gotten some information," but he never said they were. Haldeman, in this whole period, Haldeman I am sure—Bob and you, he talked to both of you about the campaign. Never a word. I mean maybe all of you knew but didn't tell me, but I can't believe that Caslon—well—

Allegations of a Cover-up Prior to March 21, 1973

Of all the witnesses who have testified publicly with respect to allegations of an illegal cover-up of the Watergate break-in prior to March 21, 1973, only Mr. Dean has accused the President of participation in such a cover-up. In his testimony before the Senate Select Committee Dean stated (Bk. 4, p. 1435)[1] that he was "certain after the September 15 meeting that the President was fully aware of the cover-up." However, in answering questions of Senator Baker, he modified this by stating it "is an inference of mine." (Bk. 4, p. 1475) Later he admitted he had no personal knowledge that the President knew on September 15th about a cover-up of Watergate. (Bk. 4, p. 1482)

The tape of the conversation between the President and Dean on September 15, 1972, does not in any way support Dean's testimony that the President was "fully aware of the cover-up." The tape of September 15, 1972, does indeed contain a passage in which the President does congratulate Dean for doing a good job:

P. Oh well, this is a can of worms as you know a lot of this stuff that went on. And the people who worked this way are awfully embarrassed. But the way you have handled all this seems to me has been very skillful putting your fingers in the leaks that have sprung here and sprung there.

[1] References to testimony before the Senate Select Committee are indicated "(Bk.———, p.———)."

This was said in the context not of a criminal plot to obstruct justice as Dean alleges, but rather in the context of the politics of the matter, such as civil suits, counter-suits, Democratic efforts to exploit Watergate as a political issue and the like. The reference to "putting your finger in the leaks" was clearly related to the handling of the political and public relations aspect of the matter. At no point was the word "contained" used as Dean insisted had been the case in his testimony. (Bk. 4, pp. 1476, 1477)

This is an example of the possible ambiguities that the President says exists in these tapes that someone with a motive to discredit the President could take out of context and distort to suit his own purposes.

If Dean did in fact believe that the President was aware of efforts illegally to conceal the break-in prior to March 21, 1973, it is strange that Dean on that date felt compelled to disclose to the President for the first time what he later testified the President already knew.

Further questions of Dean's credibility concerning the President's conduct are raised by his testimony before the Senate Select Committee that it was on March 13, 1973, that he told the President about money demands and threats of blackmail (Bk. 3, pp. 995, 996). He said he was "very clear" about this date. (Bk. 4, p. 1567) It now develops that the conversation with the President, on the date of which Dean was so clear, did not in fact take place until the morning of March 21, 1973, as the President has always contended. At no point in the tape of the March 13, 1973, conference between the President and Dean is there any reference to threats of blackmail or raising a million dollars. These references are contained in the tape of the March 21, 1973, A.M. meeting between the President and Dean.

This discrepancy in Dean's testimony from the tapes of these two meetings is surprising in the light of Dean's self-professed excellent memory (Bk. 4, p. 1433) and the certainty with which he fixed the date of the blackmail disclosure as March 13, 1973, rather than March 21, 1973. Curiously, on April 16, 1973, as evidenced by the recording of his meeting on that morning with the President, Dean recalled very specifically that his revelation to the President was on the Wednesday preceding the Friday (March 23) that the Watergate defendants were sentenced.

Dean's testimony to the Senate may have been simply an error of course, or it may have been an effort to have his disclosures to the President predate what was then at least thought to be the date of the last payment to Hunt's attorney for his fees, namely March 20, 1973, (Bk. 9, p. 3799). As far as the President is concerned, however, it makes no difference when this payment was made; he not only opposed the payment, but never even knew that it had been made until mid-April when the facts were finally disclosed to him.

In this connection it is interesting to note that Dean testified that on March 30, 1973, he told his attorneys "everything that I could remember." (Bk. 3, p. 1009) Yet Dean's list of April 14 of persons whom he believed were indictable did not include the President. (Ex. 34-37) Attorney General Kleindienst testified that Mr. Silbert, who had been interviewing Mr. Dean and conferring at length with his counsel, reported on the night of April 14, 1973, that "Nothing was said to me that night that would implicate the President of the United States." (Bk. 9, p. 3586) This same thing was confirmed by Mr. Petersen who testified that as of April 27 they had no information implicating the President. (Bk. 9, pp. 3635, 3636) In fact it was not until after April 30, 1973, when Dean was discharged that he for the first time charged the President with knowledge of a cover-up as early as September 15, 1972.

The Meeting of March 21, 1973, A.M. Between the President and Dean and later Haldeman

On or about February 27, 1973, Dean had been instructed to report directly to the President regarding the Executive Privilege issues raised in the context of the Gray nomination hearings and the prospective Ervin Committee hearings, rather than to Ehrlichman as it was taking up too much of Mr. Ehrlichman's time from his regular duties. (Bk. 7, p. 2739) Previous to this Dean had been keeping himself informed as to the progress of the FBI and Department of Justice investigation on Watergate so that he could keep Ehrlichman and Haldeman informed. Both Attorney General Kleindienst and Mr. Petersen confirmed that Dean had represented to them that he was "responsible to keep the President informed." (Bk. 9, p. 3618); that he "had been delegated by the President to be posted and kept informed throughout the course of the investigation." (Bk. 9, pp. 3575, 3576, 3652) It is equally clear from the recorded conversations between Dean and the President that he did not keep the President fully informed until March 21, 1973.[2] Indeed, on April 16, 1973, Dean so acknowledged that fact to the President, when he said:

> D. I have tried all along to make sure that anything I passed to you didn't cause you any personal problem.

An analysis of the March 21, 1973, A.M. conversation thus becomes important in assessing the conduct of the President. On the previous evening the President and Dean talked by telephone and Dean requested a meeting with the President. They met the next morning, alone, at first, and later Mr. Haldeman joined them about half way through the meeting, rather than for only the last few minutes, as Dean testified. (Bk. 4, p. 1383) After some preliminary remarks concerning the Gray confirmation hearings, Dean stated the real purpose for the meeting:

> D. The reason that I thought we ought to talk this morning is because in our conversations *I have the impression that you don't know everything I know* and it makes it very difficult for you to make judgments that only you can make on some of these things and I thought that—(Emphasis supplied)

He then proceeded to detail for the President what he be-

[2] Apparently Dean even on March 21, 1973, concealed other matters from the President as well. In *U.S.* v. *Stans, et al*, he testified that despite the fact that he had made calls to the SEC, he told the President "no one at the White House has done anything for Vesco." Of course the statement to the President was not true if Dean did make such calls for he certainly was at the White House.

Among the other significant matters which Dean did not report to the President, even on March 21, 1973, were (1) that Dean had assisted Magruder in preparing his perjured Grand Jury testimony; (2) that Dean had authorized promises of executive clemency to be made to Watergate defendants; (3) that he had personally handled money which went to the Watergate defendants; (4) that he had delivered documents from Hunt's safe to F.B.I. Director Gray; (5) that Dean had personally destroyed documents from Hunt's safe; or (6) that Dean had ordered Hunt out of the country, and then retracted the order.

7

lieved the President should be made aware of, first in the "overall."

Dean stated, "We have a cancer within, close to the Presidency, that is growing." and that "people are going to start perjuring themselves . . ." He described the genesis of the DNC break-in; the employment of Liddy; the formulation of a series of plans by Liddy which Dean disavowed, as did Mr. Haldeman; the belief that the CREP had a lawful intelligence gathering operation and the receipt of information from this source; and the arrest at the DNC on June 17, 1972. He then informed the President of a call to Liddy shortly thereafter inquiring ". . . whether anybody in the White House was involved in this" and the response "No, they weren't."

Dean then advised the President of the allegation that Magruder and Porter had committed perjury before the grand jury in denying knowledge that the DNC was to be bugged. He did not tell the President he had helped "prepare" Magruder's testimony as he later admitted before the Senate Committee. (Bk. 3, p. 1206) Dean said he did not know what Mitchell had testified to before the grand jury.

Dean next laid out for the President what happened after June 17. He informed the President "I was under pretty clear instructions not to investigate this . . . I worked on a theory of containment - to try to hold it right where it was," and he admitted that he was "totally aware" of what the FBI and grand jury was doing. Throughout these disclosures the President asked Dean a number of questions such as:

P. Tell me this: did Mitchell go along?

P. Did Colson know what they (Liddy and Hunt) were talking about?

P. Did he (Colson) talk with Haldeman?

P. Did he (Haldeman) know where it (the information) was coming from?

All together, the President asked Dean more than 150 questions in the course of this meeting.

Dean then described to the President the commencement of what he alleges was a cover-up involving himself and others. Implicit in these revelations, of course, is that

8

the President was not involved but rather he was learning of these allegations for the first time. In fact, later in the conversation, Dean said:

> D. I know, sir, I can just tell from our conversation that these are things *you have no knowledge of.* (Emphasis supplied)

Dean next recited receiving a demand "from Hunt to me" through an intermediary for "$120,000 for personal expenses and attorney's fees."

> D. ". . . he wanted it as of the close of business yesterday" (March 20).

Dean told how he rejected the demand

> D. "If you want money, you came to the wrong man, fellow. I am not involved in the money. I don't know a thing about it. I can't help you. You better scramble about elsewhere."

Dean also claimed that Hunt had threatened Ehrlichman if he wasn't paid the money he demanded. Dean analyzed the situation as he saw it, pointing out that a number of people know about these events, including Mrs. Hunt who had died in a plane crash. At the mention of Mrs. Hunt, the President interjected that this was a "great sadness" and that he "recalled a conversation with someone about Hunt's problem on account of his wife and the President said that "of course commutation could be considered on the basis of his wife's death, and that was the only conversation I ever had in that light." During their conversations, the President repeatedly and categorically rejected the idea of clemency.

Following this lengthy description of what had transpired, the conversation dealt with what should be done about the situation presented by Hunt's demands. A number of alternatives were considered. Dean pointed out that the blackmail would continue, that it would cost a million dollars and it would be difficult to handle.

> D. What really bothers me is this growing situation. As I say, it is growing because of the continued need to provide support for the Watergate people who are going to hold us up for everything we've got,

and the need for some people to perjure themselves as they go down the road here. If this thing ever blows, then we are in a cover-up situation. I think it would be extremely damaging to you and the—

    P.   Sure. The whole concept of administration (of) justice which we cannot have.

Dean then made a recommendation: Dean was unsure of the best course to follow, but stated the approach he preferred.

    D.   That's right. I am coming down to what I really think, is that Bob and John and John Mitchell and I can sit down and spend a day, or however long, to figure out, one, how this can be carved away from you, so that it does not damage you or the Presidency. It just can't. You are not involved in it an it is something you shouldn't . . .

    P.   That is true!

The President then began to press Dean for his advice as to what should be done.

    P.   So what you really come to is what we do. . . . Complete disclosure isn't that the best way to do it?

    D.   - Well, one way to do it is -

    P.   - That would be my view

Dean then suggested that another grand jury be convened but Dean points out that "some people are going to have to go to jail. That is the long and the short of it also."

Among the alternatives considered were the payment of the money generally and the payment of the amount demanded by Hunt, specifically. The mechanics of these alternatives, such as how the money could be raised and delivered, were explored.

The President expressed the belief that the money could be raised, and perhaps, even, a way could be found to deliver it. However, he recognized and pointed out that blackmail would continue endlessly, and in the final analysis would not be successful unless the Watergate defendants were given executive clemency, which he said adamantly, could not be done. The President stated:

> P.   No, it is wrong that's for sure.

After the alternatives were explored, the President's conclusion regarding the demands for money were clearly stated:

> P.   . . . But in the end, we are going to be bled to death. And in the end, it is all going to come out anyway. Then you get the worst of both worlds. We are going to lose and the people are going to—
>
> H.   And look like dopes.
>
> P.   And in effect look like a cover-up. So that we can't do . . .

Restating it, the President said:

> P.   But my point is, do you ever have any choice on Hunt? That is the point. No matter what we do here now, John, whatever he wants if he doesn't get it—immunity, etc., he is going to blow the whistle.

Finally the discussion as to what should be done was concluded by the President, at least tentatively decided to have another grand jury investigation at which members of the White House staff would appear and testify:

> P.   I hate to leave with differences in view of all this stripped land. I could understand this, but I think I want another grand jury proceeding and we will have the White House appear before them Is that right, John?
>
> D.   Uh huh.

Further discussion ensued concerning the benefits of calling for a grand jury investigation - political as well as substantive - and the meeting ended with an agreement to have Dean, Mitchell, Haldeman and Ehrlichman meet the next day to consider what they would recommend. The conclusion of the meeting, however, was not ambiguous:

11

H. We should change that a little bit. John's point is exactly right. The erosion here now is going to you, and that is the thing that we have to turn off at whatever cost. We have to turn it off at the lowest cost we can, but at whatever cost it takes.

D. That's what we have to do.

P. Well, the erosion is inevitably going to come here, apart from anything and all the people saying well the Watergate isn't a major issue. It isn't. But it will be. It's bound to. (Unintelligible) has to go out. Delaying is the great danger to the White House area. We don't, I say that the White House can't do it. Right?

D. Yes, Sir.

As the President has stated, the transcript of the meeting on the morning of March 21, 1973, contains ambiguities and statements which taken out of context could be construed to have a variety of meanings. The conversation was wide ranging, consideration was given to a number of different possibilities, but several things clearly stand out:

1. The President had not previously been aware of any payments made allegedly to purchase silence on the part of the Watergate defendants.

2. The President rejected the payment of $120,-000 or any other sum to Hunt or other Watergate defendants.

3. The President determined that the best way to proceed was to have White House people appear before a grand jury even though it meant that some people might have to go to jail.

Tapes of recorded conversations following the meeting in the morning of March 21, 1973, further establish that the President not only did not approve of any payment to Hunt, but he did not even know a payment had been made to Hunt's lawyer in the amount of $75,000.

In the afternoon of the same day, March 21, 1973, the President met again with Dean, Haldeman and now Ehrlichman. This conversation makes it even more clear that

12

the President did not suggest that blackmail should be paid to Hunt. Ehrlichman pointed out:

> E. The problem of the Hunt thing or some of these other people, there is just no sign off on them. That problem goes on and on.

The President again reiterated his view:

> P. Maybe we face the situation. We can't do a thing about the participants. If it is going to be that way eventually why not now? That is what you are sort of resigned to, isn't it?

And later near the end of the meeting:

> P. You see, if we go your route of cutting the cancer out - if we cut it out now. Take a Hunt, well wouldn't that knock the hell out from under him?

> D. That's right.

Shortly after this the President terminated the meeting, apparently rather abruptly, inquiring as to the time for the meeting the next day among Mitchell, Dean, Haldeman and Ehrlichman.

Again the recorded conversation clearly discloses that not only did the President not approve or even know of a payment made or to be made to Hunt. It is in fact quite clear that, subject to some other solution being suggested at a meeting scheduled for the next day at which Mr. Mitchell would attend, he favored "cutting the cancer out . . . now."

The President next met with his principal aides and now Mitchell on the afternoon of March 22, 1973. This was the first meeting of the President with John Mitchell following the disclosures of March 21, 1973. Mitchell and the others had met that morning as the President had requested. If the allegations of the grand jury as stated in pending indictments are correct as to when the arrangements for the payment of Hunt's legal fees were made, they would have had to have been made prior to this meeting on the afternoon of March 22nd. The tape recording of this meeting establishes that no one at the meeting disclosed to the President that such an arrangement had been made. In fact, the President was not informed

13

about these arrangements until mid-April when Ehrlichman was reporting the results of his investigation to the President. In attempting to pin down what had happened, the President was given two versions, one by Ehrlichman and Haldeman on April 14 and another by John Dean on April 16.

Ehrlichman and Haldeman explained to the President what had transpired:

P. What happened?

E. And he just said, "It's taken care of."

H. Mitchell raised the problem to Dean and said, "What have you done about that other problem?" Dean said, he kind of looked at us, and then said, "Well, you know, I don't know." And Mitchell said, "Oh, I guess that's been taken care of." Apparently through LaRue.

P. Apparently who?

H. LaRue. Dean told us, LaRue.

On April 16 Dean described how it happened that Hunt's legal fees were paid. After repeating Hunt's threat against Ehrlichman he said:

D. . . . Alright I took that to John Ehrlichman. Ehrlichman said "Have you talked to Mitchell about it?" I said "No I have not." He said "Well, will you talk to Mitchell?" I said "Yes I will." I talked to Mitchell. I just passed it along to him. And then we were meeting down here a few days later in Bob's office with Bob, and Ehrlichman and Mitchell and myself, and Ehrlichman said at that time, "Well is that problem with Hunt straightened out?" He said it to me and I said "Well, ask the man who may know; Mitchell." Mitchell said "I think that problem is solved."

P. That's all?

D. That's all he said.

If Dean's disclosure to the President on April 16, 1973,

about the payment of Hunt's legal fees is to be believed, then it is clear that this fact was concealed from the President when he met with Mitchell and the others on the afternoon of March 22nd. The explanation for this concealment perhaps is contained in a significant statement made by Dean to the President at their meeting on the morning of April 16, 1973:

> D. I have tried all along to make sure that anything I passed to you myself didn't cause you any personal problems.

This explanation for not making a full disclosure to the President may have been well intentioned at the time but in the last analysis only served to prolong the investigation.

The Conduct of the President Following the Disclosures Made on March 21, 1973

Dean disclosed for the first time on March 21, 1973, that he had been engaged in conduct that might have amounted to obstruction of justice and allegations that other high officials and former officials were also involved. These matters were thoroughly probed by the President in his talk with Dean, with the President often taking the role of devil's advocate; sometimes merely thinking out loud.

Having received this information of possible obstruction of justice having taken place following the break-in at the DNC the President promptly undertook an investigation into the facts. The record discloses that the President started his investigation the night of his meeting with Dean on March 21st, as confirmed by Dean in his conversation with the President on April 16, 1973.

> P. Then it was that night that I started my investigation.

> D. That's right . . .

> P. . . . That is when I frankly became interested in the case and I said, "Now I want to find out the score" and set in motion Ehrlichman, Mitchell and— not Mitchell but a few others.

At the meeting with Mitchell and the others on the afternoon of March 22nd, the President instructed Dean to prepare a written report of his earlier oral disclosures:

> H. I think you (Dean) ought to hole up for the weekend and do that and get it done.

> P. Sure.

> H. Give it your full attention and get it done.

> P. I think you need - why don't you do this? Why don't you go up to Camp David.

> D. I might do it, I might do it.

> P. Completely away from the phone. Just go up there and (inaudible). *I want a written report*. (Emphasis supplied)

Later during this same conversation the President said:

> P. I feel that at a very minimum we've got to have this statement. Let's look at it. I don't know what it - where is it - If it opens up doors, it opens up doors - you know.

The recording of this conversation in which the President instructed Dean to go to Camp David to write a report should be compared with Dean's testimony in which he stated:

> "He (the President) *never at any time* asked me to write a report, and it wasn't until after I had arrived at Camp David that I received a call from Haldeman asking me to write the report up." (Bk. 4, p. 1385) (Emphasis supplied)

Dean in fact did go to Camp David and apparently did some work on such a report but he never completed the task. The President then assigned Ehrlichman to investigate these allegations.

By as early as March 27, the President met with Ehrlichman and Haldeman to discuss the evidence thus far developed and how it would be best to proceed.

Again the President stated his resolve that White House officials should appear before the grand jury:

P. . . . Actually if called, we are not going to refuse for anybody called before the grand jury to go, are we, John?

The President then reviewed with Haldeman and Ehrlichman the evidence developed to that time. They stated that they had not yet talked to Mitchell and indicated this would have to be done. They reviewed what they had been advised was Magruder's current position as to what had happened and compared that with what Dean had told them. They reported that Hunt was before the grand jury that same day. It is interesting to note that neither the President, Haldeman nor Ehrlichman say anything that indicate surprise in Hunt's testifying before the grand jury. If in fact he had been paid to keep quiet, it might have been expected that someone would have expressed at least disappointment that he was testifying before the grand jury less than a week later.

They confirmed to the President, as Dean had, that no one at the White House had prior knowledge of the Watergate break-in. Ehrlichman said, "There just isn't a scintilla of a hint that Dean knew about this." The President asked about the possibility of Colson having prior knowledge and Ehrlichman said, "His response was one of total surprise . . . He was totally non-plussed, as the rest of us." Ehrlichman then revived with the President the earlier concern that they had for national security leaks and the steps taken to find out about how they occurred.

It was decided to ask Mitchell to come to Washington to receive a report of the facts developed so far and a call was placed to him for that purpose. It was also decided that Ehrlichman should also call the Attorney General and review the information on hand with him. It was during this meeting that the possibility of having a commission or a special prosecutor appointed in order to avoid the appearance of the Administration investigating itself and a call was placed to former Attorney General Rogers to ask him to meet with the President to discuss the situation.

The next day Ehrlichman, pursuant to the President's direction given the previous day, called Attorney General Kleindienst and among other things advised him that he was to report directly to the President if any evidence turns up of any wrongdoing on the part of anyone in the White House or about Mitchell. Kleindienst raised the

17

question of a possibility of a conflict of interest and suggests that thought be given to appointing a special prosecutor.

On March 30, 1973, consideration was given to the content of a press briefing with respect to White House officials appearing before the grand jury. As a result thereof, Mr. Ziegler stated at the Press briefing that day:

> "With regard to the grand jury, the President reiterates his instructions that any member of the White House staff who is called by the grand jury will appear before the grand jury to answer questions regarding that individual's alleged knowledge or possible involvement in the Watergate matter."[3]

Even prior to the completion of Ehrlichman's investigation, the President was taking steps to get the additional facts before the grand jury. On April 8, 1973, on the airplane returning to Washington from California, the President met with Haldeman and Ehrlichman and directed they meet with Dean that day and urge him to go to the grand jury - "I am not going to wait, he is going to go." (Bk. 7, p. 2757) Haldeman and Ehrlichman met with Dean that afternoon from 5 to 7. At 7:33 Ehrlichman reported the results of that meeting to the President by telephone:

> P. Oh, John, Hi

> E. I just wanted to post you on the Dean meeting. It went fine. He is going to wait until after he'd had a chance to talk with Mitchell and to pass the word to Magruder through his lawyers that he is going to appear at the grand jury. His feeling is that Liddy has pulled the plug on Magruder and that (unintelligible) he thinks he knows it now. And he says there's no love lost there, and that that was Liddy's motive in communicating informally.

Indeed, Dean did, in fact, communicate his intentions to Mitchell and Magruder not to support Magruder's previous testimony to the grand jury. (Bk. 6, p. 1006) This no doubt was the push, initially stimulated by the President, which got Magruder to go to the U.S. Attorneys on

[3] Copy submitted with transcript of conversations.

the following Saturday, April 14, and change his testimony.

On the morning of April 14, 1973, the President met again with Haldeman and Ehrlichman to discuss the Watergate matter. This was an in-depth discussion lasting more than two and one-half hours. The obvious purpose was to review the results of three week's investigation on the part of Ehrlichman and Haldeman and determine what course of action they would recommend.

Several conclusions were reached at that meeting by the President. From Ehrlichman's report on what Ehrlichman called "hearsay" facts, the President concluded, with regard to Mitchell:

> P. I'm not convinced he's guilty but I am convinced that he ought to go before a grand jury.

There was a discussion as to who would be the appropriate person to talk to Mitchell and tell him that continued silence did not well serve the President. Ultimately, it was decided that Haldeman should call Mitchell to come to Washington and that Ehrlichman should talk to him.

With respect to Magruder, the President said:

> P. We've come full circle on the Mitchell thing. The Mitchell thing must come first. That is something today. We've got to make this move today. If it fails, just to get back our position I think you ought to talk to Magruder.

> H. I agree.

> P. And you tell Magruder, now Jeb, this evidence is coming in, you ought to go to the grand jury. Purge yourself if you're perjured and tell this whole story.

> H. I think we have to.

> P. Then, well Bob, you don't agree with that?

> H. No, I do.

The President instructed Ehrlichman to see Magruder, also, and tell him that he did not serve the President by remaining silent.

The President's decision to urge Mitchell and Magruder to go to the grand jury was based on his recognition of his duty to act on the body of information Ehrlichman had reported to him:

> E.   Here's the situation. Look again at the big picture. You now are possessed of a body of fact.

> P.   That's right.

> E.   And you've got to - you can't just sit there.

> P.   That's right.

> E.   You've got to act on it. You've got to make some decisions and the Dean thing is one of the decisions you have to make . . .

At another point in the discussion, the same point was reiterated:

> E.   Well, you see, that isn't that kind of knowledge that we had was not action knowledge like the kind of knowledge that I put together last night. I hadn't known really what had been bothering me this week.

> P.   Yeah.

> E.   But what's been bothering me is -

> P.   That with knowledge we're still not doing anything.

> E.   Right.

> P.   That's exactly right. The law and order - That's the way I am. You know it's a pain for me to do it - the Mitchell thing is damn painful.

A decision was reached to speak to both Mitchell and Magruder before turning such information as they had developed over to the Department of Justice in order to afford them "an opportunity to come forward." The President told Ehrlichman that when he met with Mitchell to advise him that "the President has said let the chips fall where they may. He will not furnish cover for anybody."

The President summed up the situation by stating:

> P. No, seriously, as I have told both of you, the boil had to be pricked. In a very different sense - that's what December 18th was about. We have to prick the boil and take the heat. Now that's what we're doing here. We're going to prick this boil and take the heat. I - am I overstating?

> E. No, I think that's right. The idea is this will prick the boil. It may not. The history of this thing has to be though that you did not tuck this under the rug yesterday or today, and hope it would go away.

The decision was also made by the President that Ehrlichman should provide the information which he had collected to the Attorney General. Ehrlichman called the Attorney General, but did not reach him.

Mitchell came to Washington that afternoon and met with Ehrlichman. Immediately following that meeting, Ehrlichman reported to the President, stating Mitchell protested his innocence, stating:

> "You know, these characters pulled this thing off without my knowledge . . . I never saw Liddy for months at a time . . . I didn't know what they were up to and nobody was more surprised than I was . . . I can't let people get away with this kind of thing . . . I am just going to have to defend myself every way I can."

Ehrlichman said he explained to Mitchell that the President did not want anyone to stand mute on his account; that everyone had a right to stand mute for his own reasons but that the "interests of the President . . . were not served by a person standing mute for that reason alone."

Ehrlichman said that he advised Mitchell that the information that had been collected would be turned over to the Attorney General and that Mitchell agreed this would be appropriate.

Even later on April 14, Ehrlichman finally was able to reach Magruder and met with Magruder and his lawyers for the purpose of informing him that he should not remain silent out of any misplaced loyalty to the President. Ehrlichman found, however, that Magruder had just come from a meeting with the U.S. Attorneys where he had told the full story as he knew it. He, Magruder, told Ehrlichman what he had told the U.S. Attorney, which Ehrlichman duly reported to the President.

During this meeting with the President, Ehrlichman's earlier call to the Attorney General was completed, and Ehrlichman spoke to the Attorney General from the President's office. Ehrlichman told the Attorney General that he had been conducting an investigation for about the past three weeks for the President as a substitute for Dean on White House and broader involvement. He also told him that he had reported his findings to the President the day before and that he had advised people not to be reticent on the President's behalf about coming forward. He informed the Attorney General that he had talked to Mitchell and had tried to reach Magruder, but that he had not been able to meet with Magruder until after Magruder had conferred with the U.S. Attorneys. He offered to make all of his information available if it would be in any way useful.

Following the telephone call Ehrlichman said that the Attorney General wanted him to meet with Henry Petersen the next day regarding the information he had obtained. During the course of the conversation relating to Magruder changing his testimony the President stated:

> P. It's the right thing. We all have to do the right thing. Damn it! We just cannot have this kind of business, John. Just cannot be.

Late on the evening of April 14th, after the Correspondents' dinner, the President spoke by telephone first with Haldeman and then with Ehrlichman. The President told each that he now thought all persons involved should testify in public before the Ervin Committee.

On the morning of Sunday, April 15th, the President talked with Ehrlichman and told him that he had received a call from the Attorney General who had advised him that he had been up most of the night with the U.S. Attorney, and with Assistant Attorney General Peterson. The Attorney General had requested to see the President, personally, the President told Ehrlichman, and the President had agreed to see him after Church. The President and Ehrlichman again reviewed the available evidence developed during Ehrlichman's investigation and the status of relations with the media.

In the early afternoon of April 15, the President met with Attorney General Kleindienst. Kleindienst confirmed to the President that the U.S. Attorneys had broken the case and knew largely the whole story as a result of Magruder's discussions with them and from disclosures made by Dean's attorneys, who were also talking to the U.S. Attorney. The Attorney General anticipated indictments of Mitchell, Dean and Magruder and others, possibly including Haldeman and Ehrlichman. Kleindienst indicated that he felt that he could not have anything to do with these cases especially because of his association with Mitchell, Mardian and LaRue. The President expressed reservations about having a special prosecutor:

> P. First it's a reflection - it's sort of an admitting mea culpa for our whole system of justice. I don't want to do that . . .

The President then suggested that Kleindienst step aside and that the Deputy Attorney General, Dean Sneed, be placed in charge of the matter. The President expressed confidence in Silbert doing a thorough job.

Kleindienst pointed out that even if he were to withdraw, his deputy is still the President's appointee and that he would be "in a tough situation . . ." Kleindienst recommended that a Special Prosecutor be appointed and a number of names were suggested. The President's reaction to the idea of a Special Prosecutor was negative.

> P. ". . . I want to get some other judgments because I - I'm open on this. I lean against it and I think it's too much of a reflection on our system of justice and everything else."

Following a further review of the evidence, Kleindienst raised the question about what the President should do in the event charges are made against White House officials. The President resisted the suggestion that they be asked to step aside on the basis of charges alone.

> P. . . . the question really is basically whether an individual, you know, can be totally, totally - I mean, the point is if a guy isn't guilty, you shouldn't let him go.

> K. That's right, you shouldn't.

P. It's like me - wait now - let's stand up for people if there - even though they are under attack.

Further discussion on this subject included the suggestion
that Assistant Attorney General Henry Petersen might be
placed in charge rather than the Deputy Attorney General. Kleindienst pointed out, "He's the first career Assistant Attorney General I think in the history of the Department."

Shortley after this the tape at the President's office in
the Executive Office Building ran out. It is clear, however,
from a recorded telephone conversation between the President and Kleindienst that he and Henry Petersen met
later in the afternoon with the President. This was verified
by Mr. Petersen's testimony before the Senate Committee.
It was during this meeting that the President assigned the
responsibility for the on-going investigation to Mr. Petersen.

At his meeting with the President, Assistant Attorney
General Petersen presented to the President a summary of
the allegations which related to Haldeman, Ehrlichman
and Strachan, and that the summary indicated no case of
criminal conduct by Haldeman and Ehrlichman at that
time. (Bk.9, p.3875)

The President, on the afternoon of April 15, 1973, had
every reason to believe that the judicial process was moving rapidly to complete the case. He continued to attempt
to assist. He had four telephone conversations with Petersen after their meeting. In the afternoon, having been told
that Liddy would not talk unless authorized by "higher
authority," who all assumed was Mitchell, the President
directed Petersen to pass the word to Liddy through his
counsel that the President wanted him to cooperate. Subsequently, the President told Petersen that Dean doubted
Liddy would accept the word of Petersen, so Petersen was
directed to tell Liddy's counsel that the President personally would confirm his urging of Lijdy to cooperate. The
President stated:

P I just want him (Liddy) to be sure to understand that as far as the President is concerned, everybody in this case is to talk and to tell the truth. You
are to tell everybody, and you don't even have to call
me on that with anybody. You just say those are
your orders.

24

The President continued to seek additional facts and details about the whole matter. Petersen could not reveal the details of the further disclosures by Dean's attorneys, so the President sought Petersen's advice about getting further information from Dean.

P. Right. Let me ask you this - why don't I get him in now if I can find him and have a talk with him?

HP. I don't see any objection to that, Mr. President.

P. Is that all right with you?

HP. Yes, sir.

P. All right - I am going to get him over because I am not going to screw around with this thing. As I told you.

HP. All right.

P. But I want to be sure you understand, that you know we are going to get to the bottom of this thing.

HP. I think the thing that -

P. What do you want me to say to him? Ask him to tell me the whole truth?

After talking with Dean and reviewing Dean's further information, the President raised the question about when Dean and perhaps Haldeman and Ehrlichman should resign and Petersen responded, "We would like to wait, Mr. President."

On the morning of April 16, the President began a long series of meetings on the entire subject. Being uncertain of when the case would become public, the President decided he wanted resignations or requests for leave in hand from those against whom there were allegations. He had Erlichman draft such letters, and discussed them with Haldeman and Ehrlichman.

The President then met with Dean and discussed with

him the manner in which his possible resignation would be handled. Dean resisted the idea of his resigning without Haldeman and Ehrlichman resigning as well. The President reviewed with Dean the disclosures Dean made to the President on March 21st and on the evening of April 15th.

The President had some more advice for John Dean on this occasion:

> P. Thank God. Don't ever do it, John. Tell the truth. That is the thing I have told everybody around here - tell the truth! All they do, John, is compound it. That Hiss would be free today if he hadn't lied. If he had said, "Yes, I knew Chambers and as a young man I was involved with some Communist activities but I broke it off a number of years ago." And Chambers would have dropped it. If you are going to lie, you go to jail for the lie rather than the crime. So believe me, don't ever lie."

As to the President's actions, he told Dean:

> P. No, I don't want, understand when I say don't lie. Don't lie about me either.

> D. No, I won't sir - you -

The President met with Haldeman at noon on April 16th to discuss at length how and when Haldeman should make a public disclosure of his actions in the Segretti and Watergate matters. Haldeman reported that Mr. Garment recommended that he and Ehrlichman resign. Garment had been assigned by the President on April 9 to work on the matter. The President stated that he would discuss that problem with William Rogers that afternoon and asked Haldeman to get with Ehrlichman and fill in Rogers on the facts.

The President met in the early afternoon alone with Henry Petersen for nearly two hours in the Executive Office Building. They discussed the effect the Senate Committee hearings would have on the trials in the event indictments are returned.

The President then asked Petersen what he should do about Dean's resignation.

> HP. Yes. As Prosecutor I would do something

different but from your point of view I don't think
you can sit on it. I think we have the information under control but that's a dangerous thing to say in this
City.

P.   Ah

HP.   And if this information comes out I think
you should have his resignation and it should be effective . . .

Petersen, however, urged the President not to announce
the resignation if the information did not get out, as that
would be "counter-productive" in their negotiations with
Dean's counsel. Petersen reviewed the status of the evidence at length with the President with a view toward
making a press release before an indictment or information was filed in open Court.

During the course of the conversation Petersen informed the President that they were considering giving
Dean immunity. As for Haldeman and Ehrlichman, Petersen recommended that they resign. The status of the situation was reviewed as follows:

P.   Okay. All right come to the Haldeman/Ehr-
lichman thing. You see you said yesterday they
should resign. Let me tell you they should resign in
my view if they get splashed with this. Now the
point is, is the timing. I think that it's, I want to get
your advice on it, I think it would be really hanging
the guy before something comes in if I say look, you
guys resign because I understand that Mr. Dean in
the one instance, and Magruder in another instance,
made some charges against you. And I got their oral
resignations last night and they volunteered it. They
said, look, we want to go any time. So I just want
your advice on it. I don't know what to do, frankly.
(Inaudible) so I guess there's nothing in a hurry
about that is there? I mean I—Dean's resignation. I
have talked, to him about it this morning and told
him to write it out.

HP.   (Inaudible).

P.   It's under way—I asked for it. How about
Haldeman and Ehrlichman? I just wonder if you

27

have them walk the plank before Magruder splashes and what have you or what not. I mean I have information, true, as to what Magruder's going to do. (Inaudible) nothing like this (inaudible).

HP. Or for that matter, Mr. President.

P. Yeah.

HP. Its confidence in the Office of the Presidency.

P. Right. You wouldn't want—do you think they ought to resign right now?

HP. Mr. President, I am sorry to say it. I think that mindful of the need for confidence in your office—yes.

P. (Inaudible) basis?

HP. That has nothing to do—that has nothing to do with guilt or innocence.

At the end of the meeting with Petersen, the President had every reason to believe that a public disclosure of the entire case in court would be made within forty-eight hours and perhaps sooner. The remaining questions for Presidential decision were: (1) What action he should take on the resignation, suspension or leave of Haldeman, Ehrlichman and Dean and whether it should be before or after they were formally charged; (2) what position he should take on immunity for Dean; and (3) what statement he should issue prior to the public disclosure in court.

On the afternoon of April 17, the President discussed the problem of granting immunity to White House officials with Henry Petersen. Petersen pointed out that he was opposed to immunity but he pointed out that they might need Dean's testimony in order to get Haldeman and Ehrlichman. The President agreed that under those circumstances he might have to move on Haldeman and Ehrlichman, provided Dean's testimony was corroborated. The President told Petersen:

P. That's the point. Well, I feel it strongly - I

28

mean - just understand - I am not trying to protect anybody - I just want the damn facts if you can get the facts from Dean and I don't care whether -

HP.   Mr. President, if I thought you were trying to protect somebody, I would have walked out.

As for Dean, the President told Petersen:

P.   ". . . No I am not going to condemn Dean until he has a chance to present himself. No he is in exactly the same position they are in."

The President remained convinced, however, that a grant of immunity to a senior aide would appear as a cover-up.

P.   What you say - Look we are having you here as a witness and we want you to talk.

HP.   That is described as immunity by estoppel.

P.   I see, I see - that's fair enough.

HP.   That is really the prosecutor's bargain.

P.   That is much better basically than immunity - let me say I am not, I guess my point on Dean is a matter of principle - it is a question of the fact that I am not trying to do Dean in - I would like to see him save himself but I think find a way to do it without - if you go the immunity route I think we are going to catch holy hell for it.

HP.   Scares hell out of me.

The President went over the draft of his proposed statement with Petersen. Petersen further counseled the President that no discussion of the facts of the case could be made without prejudicing the case and the rights of the defendants.

Later on the afternoon of April 17, the President issued his statement, revealing that he had new facts and had begun his own investigation on March 21; that White House staff members who were indicted would be suspended, and if they were convicted, they would be discharged. He announced that all members of the White House staff would appear and testify before the Senate Committee. The President further stated that:

> I have expressed to the appropriate authorities my view that no individual holding, in the past or present, a position of major importance in the Adminstration should be given immunity from prosecution.

In addition he stated that all White House staff employees were expected fully to cooperate in this matter.

After making his public statement, the President met with Secretary of State Rogers, and they were joined later by Haldeman and Ehrlichman. Secretary Rogers reiterated his advice that the President could not permit any senior official to be given immunity. He also reiterated his advice that for the President to discharge his senior aides before they were formally charged with a crime would highly prejudice their legal rights and convict them without a trial.

The President had concluded that he should treat Dean, Haldeman and Ehrlichman in the same manner. Petersen had advised the President that action on Dean would prejudice the negotiations of the U.S. Attorneys with Dean's lawyers, and that Dean's testimony might be needed for the case.

On the evening of April 19, the President met with Messrs. Wilson and Strickler, counsel retained by Haldeman and Ehrlichman upon recommendation of Secretary Rogers. Wilson and Strickler made strong arguments that Haldeman and Ehrlichman had no criminal liability and should not be discharged.

The President continued to struggle with the question of administrative action against his aides.

On April 27, Petersen reported to the President that Dean's lawyer was threatening that unless Dean got immunity. "We will bring the President in - not in this case but in other things."

On the question of immunity in the face of these threats, the President told Petersen:

> P.   All right. We have got the immunity problem resolved. Do it, Dean if you need to, but boy I am telling you - there ain't going to be any blackmail.

On April 27, the President was also advised by Petersen

that the negotiations with Dean's attorneys had bogged down, and action by the President against Dean, Haldeman and Ehrlichman would now be helpful to the U.S. Attorney.

Three days later, on April 30, the President gave a nationwide address. He announced that he accepted the resignations of Haldeman, Ehrlichman, Attorney General Kleindienst and Dean. The President then announced the nomination of Elliot Richardson as the new Attorney General.

Conclusion

Throughout the period of the Watergate affair the raw material of these recorded confidential conversations establishes that the President had no prior knowledge of the break-in and that he had no knowledge of any cover-up prior to March 21, 1973. In all of the thousands of words spoken, even though they often are unclear and ambiguous, not once does it appear that the President of the United States was engaged in a criminal plot to obstruct justice.

On March 21, 1973, when the President learned for the first time of allegations of such a plot and an alleged attempt to blackmail the White House, he sought to find out the facts first from John Dean then others. When it appeared as a result of these investigations that there was reason to believe that there may have been some wrongdoing he conferred with the Attorney General and with the Assistant in charge of the criminal division of the Department of Justice and cooperated fully to bring the matter expeditiously before the grand jury.

Ultimately Dean has plead guilty to a felony and seven former White House officials stand indicted. Their innocence or guilt will be determined in a court of law.

This is as it should be.

The recent acquittals of former Secretary Stans and former Attorney General Mitchell in the Vesco case demonstrate the wisdom of the President's actions insisting that the orderly process of the judicial system be utilized to determine the guilt or innocence of individuals charged with crime, rather than participating in trials in the public media.

Meeting: The President, Haldeman and Dean,
Oval Office, September 15, 1972.
(5:27 - 6:17 pm)

The following are edited transcripts of conversations between President Nixon and his advisors.

The conversations, recorded by hidden microphones in the President's Oval Office occurred at a time of increasing pressure on the White House by both the U.S. prosecutor and the Senate Watergate committee to cooperate more fully with their investigations.

These transcripts have been edited by White House officials to remove matters of obscenities and personal characterizations, the White House announced.

This opens just as Dean comes in the door.

P   Hi, how are you? You had quite a day today didn't you. You got Watergate on the way didn't you?
D   We tried.
H   How did it all end up?
D   Ah, I think we can say well at this point. The press is playing it just as we expect.
H   Whitewash?
D   No, not yet—the story right now—
P   It is a big story
H   Five indicted plus the WH former guy and all that.
D   Plus two White House fellows
H   That is good that takes the edge off whitewash really that was the thing Mitchell kept saying that to people in the country Liddy and Hunt were big men. Maybe that is good.
P   How did MacGregor handle himself?
D   I think very well he had a good statement which said that the Grand Jury had met and that it was now time to realize that some apologies may be due.
H   Fat chance.
D   Get the damn (inaudible)
H   We can't do that.
P   Just remember, all the trouble we're taking, we'll have a chance to get back one day. How are you doing on your other investigations?
H   What has happened on the bug?

32

P What bug?

D The second bug there was a bug found in the tele-phone of one of the men at the DNC.

P You don't think it was left over from the other time?

D Absolutely not, the Bureau has checked and re-checked the whole place after that night. The man had specifically checked and re-checked the telephone and it was not there.

P What the hell do you think was involved?

D I think DNC was planted.

P You think they did it?

D Uh huh

P (Expletive deleted)—do they really want to believe that we planted that?

H Did they get anything on the finger prints?

D No, nothing at all—either on the telephone or on the bug. The FBI has unleashed a full investigation over at the DNC starting with O'Brien right now.

H Laughter. Using the same crew—

D The same crew—the Washington Field Office.

P What kind of questions are they asking him?

D Anything they can think of because O'Brien is charging them with failing to find all the bugs.

H Good, that will make them mad.

D So Gray is pissed and his people are pissed off. So maybe they will move in because their reputation is on the line. I think that is a good development.

P I think that is a good development because it makes it look so (adjective deleted) funny. Am I wrong?

D No, no sir. It looks silly. If we can find that the DNC planted that, the whole story will reverse.

P But how could they possibly find it, though?

D Well, they are trying to ascertain who made the bug. It is a custom made product. If they can get back to the man who manufactured it and who he sold it to and how it came down through the chain.

P Boy, you never know when those guys get after it—they can really find it.

D The resources that have been put against this whole investigation to date are really incredible. It is truly a larger investigation than was conducted against the after inquiry of the JFK assassination.

P Oh.

D Good statistics supporting the finding.

H Isn't that ridiculous—this silly thing.

P   Yes (Expletive deleted). Goldwater put it in context when he said "(expletive deleted) everybody bugs everybody else. You know that."

D   That was priceless.

P   It happens to be totally true. We were bugged in '68 on the plane and in '62 even running for Governor—(expletive deleted) thing you ever saw.

D   It is a shame that evidence to the fact that that happened in '68 was never around. I understand that only the former Director had that information.

H   No, that is not true.

D   There was evidence of it?

H   There are others who have information.

P   How do you know? Does DeLoache know?

D   DeLoache?

H   I have some stuff too—on the bombing incident and too in the bombing halt stay.

P   The difficulty with using it, of course, is it reflects on Johnson. If it weren't for that, I would use it. Is there any way we could use it without using his name—saying that the DNC did it? No—the FBI did the bugging.

D   That is the problem—would it reflect on Johnson or Humphrey?

H   Johnson. Humphrey didn't do it.

P   Oh, hell no.

H   He was bugging Humphrey, too.

P   (Expletive deleted)

P   Well, on the other hand. I want you to ask Connally. What crazy things we do. That this might help with the bombing. I don't think he will talk to Johnson—and also it would reflect on the Bureau. They hate to admit that.

H   It is a rough one on them with all this stuff that they don't do Congressmen, etc.

P   It isn't worth it—the hell with it. What is the situation on the little red box? Have they found the box yet?

D   Gray has never had access to the box. He is now going to pursue the box. I spoke to him just about thirty minutes ago. Pat said "I don't know about the box. Don't know where it is now. We never had an opportunity before when it was first released in the press that there was a box to go in but we have decided now we have grounds to go in and find it."

H   The latest public story was that she handed it over to Edward Bennett Williams.

D   That is right.

34

H The Bureau ought to go into Edward Bennett Williams and start questioning him and have him tied up for a couple of days.

P Yeah, I hope they do. The Bureau better get over pretty quick and get that little red box. We want it cleared up. We want to get to the bottom of it. If any body is guilty over here we want to know.

H It will probably be in the news!

D You might be interested in some of the allocations we got. The Stans' libel action was assigned to Judge Ritchie.

P (Expletive deleted)

D Well now that is good and bad. Judge Ritchie is not known to be one of the (inaudible) on the bench, that is considered by me. He is fairly candid in dealing with people about the question. He has made several entrees off the bench—one to Kleindienst and one to Roemer McPhee to keep Roemer abreast of what his thinking is. He told Roemer he thought Maury ought to file a libel action.

P Did he?

H Can he deal with this concurrently with the court case?

D Yeah. The fact that the civil case drew to a halt— that the depositions were halted he is freed.

H It was just put off for a few days, wasn't it?

D It did more than that—he had been talking to Silbert, one of the Assistant U.S. Attorneys down here. Silbert said, "We are going to have a hell of a time drawing these indictments because these civil depositions will be coming out and the Grand Jury has one out on this civil case but it is nothing typical."

Someone asked the President if he wanted Mitchell's call—he said, "Yeah."

D Based on that when Silbert had told Ritchie this and with a casual encounter—in fact it was just in the hall, so Ritchie stopped the civil case so Silbert can get the indictment down.

Telephone call from John Mitchell:

Hello

P—comments only from here on until end of call:

Well are you still alive.

I was just sitting here with John Dean and he tells me you were going to be sued or something.

Good, Good.

Yeah.

Good.

Sure.

Well I tell you just don't let this keep you or your colleagues from concentrating on the big game. This thing is just one of those side issues and a month later everybody looks back and wonders what all the shooting was about. OK, John, Good night. Get a good night's sleep. And don't bug anybody without asking me? OK?

Yeah.

Thank you."

D   Three months ago I would have had trouble predicting there would be a day when this would be forgotten, but I think I can say that 54 days from now nothing is going to come crashing down to our surprise.

P   That what?

D   Nothing is going to come crashing down to our surprise.

P   Oh well, this is a can of worms as you know a lot of this stuff that went on. And the people who worked this way are awfully embarrassed. But the way you have handled all this seems to me has been very skillful putting your fingers in the leaks that have sprung here and sprung there. The Grand Jury is dismissed now?

D   That is correct. They have completed and they have let them go so there will be no continued investigation prompted by the Grand Jury's inquiry. The GAO report referred over to Justice is on a shelf right now because they have hundreds of violations—they have violations of McGovern, of Humphrey, violations of Jackson, and several hundred Congressional violations. They don't want to start prosecuting one any more than they prosecute the other.

P   They definitely will not prosecute us unless they prosecute the others.

D   Well, we are talking about technical violations referred over also.

P   What about watching the McGovern contributors and all that sort of thing?

D   We have (inaudible) eye out on that. His I understand is not in full compliance.

P   He asked?

D   No.

P   Well, not yet. His 300 committees—have they all reported yet?

D   We have a couple delinquent state committees.

P   It said in the paper that McGovern had 300 committees reported.

D   No, they have not. There are a lot of things he has
never done—as he has never disclosed the fact that he has
some 300 committees. The Wall Street Journal piece that
picked it up and carried that story brought out his committees.

P   Can we say anything publicly about it?

D   Purpose there hasn't been a tax sham—it is hard to
comprehend why he set up that many committees. He
doesn't have that many large contributors, but they may
have to disburse through a great number of smaller committees.

H   Unless someone is stealing $900,000.

D   That's right.

P   It could be. That could be possible.

H   He may be getting $900,000 from somebody. He
may have two or three angles.

P   I don't think he is getting a hell of a lot of small
money. I don't believe (expletive deleted) Have you had
the P.O. checked yet?

H   That is John's area. I don't know.

P   Well, let's have it checked.

D   Well as I see it, the only problems we may have
are the human problems and I will keep a close watch on
that.

P   Union?

D   Human.

H   Human frailities.

D   People get annoyed—some finger pointing—false
accusations—any internal dissension of any nature.

P   You mean on this case?

D   On this case. There is some bitterness between the
Finance Committee and the Political Committee—they
feel they are taking all the heat and all the people upstairs
are bad people—not being recognized.

P   We are all in it together. This is a war. We take a
few shots and it will be over. We will give them a few
shots and it will be over. Don't worry. I wouldn't want to
be on the other side right now. Would you?

D   Along that line, one of the things I've tried to do, I
have begun to keep notes on a lot of people who are
emerging as less than our friends because this will be over
some day and we shouldn't forget the way some of them
have treated us.

P   I want the most comprehensive notes on all those who tried to do us in. They didn't have to do it. If we had had a very close election and they were playing the other side I would understand this. No—they were doing this quite deliberately and they are asking for it and they are going to get it. We have not used the power in this first four years as you know. We have never used it. We have not used the Bureau and we have not used the Justice Department but things are going to change now. And they are either going to do it right or go.

D   What an exciting prospect.

P   Thanks. It has to be done. We have been (adjective deleted) fools for us to come into this election campaign and not do anything with regard to the Democratic Senators who are running, et cetera. And who the hell are they after? They are after us. It is absolutely ridiculous. It is not going to be that way any more.

H   Really, it is ironic that we have gone to extremes. You and your damn regulations. Everybody worries about not picking up a hotel bill.

D   I think you can be proud of the White House staff. It really has had no problems of that sort. And I love this GAO audit that is going on now. I think they have some suspicion that even a cursory investigation is going to discover something here. I don't think they can find a thing. I learned today, incidentally, and have not confirmed it, that the GAO auditor who is down here is here at the Speaker of the House's request.

P   That surprises me.

H   Well, (expletive deleted) the Speaker of the House. Maybe we better put a little heat on him.

P   I think so too.

H   Because he has a lot worse problems than he is going to find down here.

D   That's right.

H   That is the kind of thing that, you know, we really ought to do is call the Speaker and say, "I regret to say your calling the GAO down here because of what it is going to cause us to do to you."

P   Why don't you see if Harlow will tell him that.

H   Because he wouldn't do it—he would just be pleasant and call him Mr. Speaker.

D   I suppose the other area we are going to see some publicity on in the coming weeks because I think now that the indictments are down there will be a cresting on

38

that—the white wash—the civil rights cases in advance. But <u>Wright Patman's hearings—his banking and currency</u> committee—whether we will be successful in turning that off or not I don't know. We have a plan where Rothblatt and Bittman who were counsel for the seven who were indicted today are going to go up and visit the five top members and say that if you commence hearings you are going to jeopardize the civil rights of these individuals in the worst way and they will never get a fair trial.

P Why not ask that they request to be heard by the committee?

D They could say, "If you do commence with these hearings we intend to come up and say what you are doing to the rights of individuals." Something to that effect.

P They could even get a motion in court to get the thing dismissed.

H Going the other way—

P Getting the criminal charges dismissed on the grounds of civil rights.

D We have someone approaching the ACLU for these guys—having them exert some pressure because we don't just want Stans up there in front of the cameras with Patman asking all these questions. It is going to be the whole thing over and over again. I understand too, or I have been told, that <u>John Connally</u> is close to Patman and if anyone could talk turkey to Patman, Connally could. <u>Jerry Ford</u> is not really taking an active interest in this matter that is developing so Stans is going to see Jerry Ford and try to brief him and explain to him the problems he has. The other things we are going to do—we are looking at all the campaign reports of every member of that committee because we are convinced that none of them complied exactly with the law either. If they want to play rough— some day we better say, "Gentlemen, we want to call your attention that you have not complied with A,B,C, and F and we are not going to hold that a secret if you start talking campaign violations here."

P What about Ford? Do you think so? Connally can't because of the way he is set up. If anybody can do it, Connally could, but if Ford can get the minority members. They have some weak men and women on that committee, unfortunately. Heckler is alright.

D Heckler was great.

P Widnall, et cetera. Jerry should talk to Widnall. After all, if we ever win the House, Jerry will be the Speaker and he could tell him if he did not get off—he will not be Chairman ever.

D   That would be very helpful to get all of these people at least pulling together. If Jerry could get a little action on this.

H   Damn it Jerry should. That is exactly the thing he was talking about, that the reason they are staying is so that they can run investigations.

P   The point is that they ought to raise hell about these hearings. I don't know that the counsel calls the members of the committee often. I think if they have to have this blunderbuss in the public arena then this is all it is.

D   That is the last forum where we have the least problem right now. Kennedy has already said he may call hearings of the Administrative Practices sub-committee. As these committees spin out oracles we used to get busy on each one. I stopped doing that about two months ago. We just take one thing at a time.

P   You really can't sit and worry about it all the time. The worst may happen but it may not. So you just try to button it up as well as you can and hope for the best, and remember basically the damn business is unfortunately trying to cut our losses.

D   Certainly that is right and certainly it has had no effect on you. That's the good thing.

H   No, it has been kept away from the White House and of course completely from the President. The only tie to the White House is the Colson effort they keep trying to pull in.

D   And, of course, the two White House people of lower level—indicted—one consultant and one member of the Domestic Staff. That is not very much of a tie.

H   That's right.

P   Or Manson. (expletive deleted). If they had been killers. Isn't that true?

H   It is certainly true.

P   These (characterization deleted) they have had no way. They ought to move the trial away from—

D   There has been extensive clipping on the part of the counsel in this case. They may never get a fair trial. They may never get a jury that will convict them. The Post, you know, that they have a real large team assigned to cover this case. Believe me, the Maury Stans story about his libel suit that had so much coverage in the

40

Evening News they put way back on page 8 of the Post and did not even cover it in total.

H   Yes, I will talk to Bill.

D   I think Dick Cook has been working on it.

P   Maybe Mitchell should do.

H   Could Mitchell do it?

P   No.

D   I don't think it would be good to draw him into it. I think Maury could talk to Ford if that would do any good. I think Maury ought to brief Ford on exactly what his whole side of the story is. Maury understands the law.

H   I will talk to Cook.

P   Maybe Ehrlichman should talk to him. Ehrlichman understands the law.

H   Is that a good idea? Maybe it is.

P   I think maybe that is the thing. This is a big play. He has to know that it comes from the top. While I can't talk for myself he has to get at this and—the thing up.

D   Well, if we got that slide up there—it is a tragedy to let them have a field day up there.

P   What is the first move? When does he call his witnesses?

D   Well, he has not even gotten the vote of his committee—he hasn't even convened his committee as to whether he can call hearings. That is why he won't come Monday morning. His attorney is going to arrive on the doorstep of the chairman and to tell him what to do and he proceeds. One of the members of the committee, Jerry Brown, wrote Kliendienst a letter saying, "If the chairman holds committee hearings on this, isn't this going to jeopardize your criminal case?"

P   That is smart politics for Michigan and some tie into Ford. He is a very smart fellow.

D   Good lawyer and being helpful. He is anxious to help.

P   Tell Ehrlichman to get Brown and Ford in together and they can work out something. They ought to get off their—and push it. No use to let Patman have a free ride here.

D   Well we can keep them well briefed on moves if they will move when we provide them with the strategy. And we will have a raft of depositions going the other way soon. We will be hauling the O'Briens in and the like on our due process soon.

P   What did they ask—any questions?

D   No. I saw Rothblatt laughing at the start of the

41

symposium. He is quite a character. He has been getting into the sex life of some of the members of the DNC.

P   Why? What is the justification?

D   Well, he is working on the entrapment theory that they were hiding something and they had secret information of theirs to hide and if they could someway conspire to bring this thing about themselves. It is a way-out theory that no one had caught.

H   (Laughter)

D   He had scheduled Patricia Harris and she did not show up. She went to the beauty parlor instead so he went down to the Court House and she had been directed to show up and then the next day the Judge cut all the depositions off. But he had a host of wild questions about where O'Brien got his compensation when he was Chairman. Not that he would know anything about that, but it was just an interesting question he might want to ask the Chairman under oath.

H   That's what Gibbons said—the same hunting license that gave them.

D   No—that is right.

H   So we can play the same game they are playing. We ought to be able to do better at it.

P   Well.

H   Are those depositions sealed?

D   That's right.

H   They are?

D   But that argues that they will want them unsealed less than we will, and we may be arguing at some point to get them unsealed.

P   Yeah.

D   I think what is going to happen on the civil case is that the Judge is going to dismiss the complaint that is down there right now. They will then file a new complaint which will come back to Ritchie again. That will probably happen the 20th, 21st, 22nd. Then 20 days will run before any answers have to filed and the depositions will be commenced so we are eating up an awful lot of time.

P   Why will the Judge dismiss the complaint?

D   Probably on the middle ground—both on the substantive ground that they haven't stated a good course of action—that there is improper class actions filed. O'Brien doesn't indeed represent any class. And he will just dismiss it on the merits. It is not a good complaint. He has already shaved it down to almost nothing on his original order. They will then have to re-design it in a much narrower action but the Judge himself can't suggest something to counsel. He has to do a cute argument here. If he dismisses on the merits, that they can't file another suit. They are out of the court totally.

H But our two suits go hang?

D We have two suits—we have the abuse of process and the libel suit.

H We can take depositions on both of those?

D Absolutely.

P Hell yes.

(Inaudible)

H (Laughter)

D We can blunder down the road anyway.

NOTE

(Further conversation following unrelated to Watergate.)

Meeting: The President and Dean, Oval Office, February 28, 1973. (9:12 - 10:23 am)

D Good morning, Sir.

P Oh, hi.

D How are you?

P I wanted to talk with you about what kind of a line to take. I now want Kleindienst on the—it isn't a matter of trust. You have it clearly understood that you will call him and give him directions and he will call you, et cetera, and so on. I just don't want Dick to go off—you see, for example, on executive privilege—I don't want him to go off and get the damn thing—get us—

D Make any deals on it—

P Make a deal—that is the point. Baker, as I said, is going to keep at arm's length and you've got to be very firm with these guys or you may not end up with many things. Now as I said the only back-up position I can possibly see is one of a (inaudible) if Kleindienst wants to back (inaudible) for (inaudible)—didn't want to but suggested we ought to back them heavily, send them up there in executive session. Well, now you all know that under executive session we still have the problem, and it ain't good. Well, I am thinking particularly of Baker because it will go to him without any question and that is going to be far more significant. This bothers us at the moment, but that's (inaudible) to me. And they will haul him up there and bull-rag him around the damn place and it will raise holy hell with Rogers and all our—the other people.

D   Yeah.

P   I sent some notes out—a couple of yellow pages—something on the teachers' thing that I am not doing today. Just send it back to me, please.

Secretary   Alright, Sir.

P   So you see, I think you better have a good, hard face to face talk with him and say, look, we have thought this thing over. And you raise the point with him that this cannot be in executive session because he is likely to float it out there and they will grab it.

D   That's right, and as I mentioned yesterday, he is meeting with Sam Ervin and Baker in this joint session and that is probably one of the first things they will discuss.

P   The main thing Ervin is going to be talking about is executive privilege. Has that meeting been set yet, though?

D   No, it has not. There is ample time to have Dick go up there—

P   You have a talk with him and say we had a talk about this—now your position now I know (inaudible) which they probably never accept but it will make his position be reasonable in the public mind. That is what we have in mind.

D   Right. Correct.

P   Another possibility is the one that Ehrlichman has suggested. If you could have an agreement that the Chairman and the ranking member could question basically the same under very restricted—a little bit early (inaudible)

D   Them coming down here, say?

P   Basically, that is the suggestion.

D   I think that is sort of "if" we couldn't get the written interrogatories. That is still a serious precedent to deal with if they come down here and start questioning people I think the issues would have to be so narrowed for even that situation. And that sort of thing would evolve with the narrowing of the issues where what information a Haldeman or Ehrlichman might have. The Committee needs to be complete in its report of its investigation.

P   Yeah. We will say that you can have written interrogatories under oath, then answer questions.

D   Publicly you are not withholding any information

and you are not using the shield of the Presidency.

P When you talk to Kleindienst—because I have raised this (inaudible) thing with him on the Hiss Case—he has forgotten, I suppose. Go back and read the first chapter of SIX CRISES. But I know, as I said, that was espionage against the nation, not against the party. FBI, Hoover, himself, who's a friend of mine said "I am sorry I have been ordered not to cooperate with you" and they didn't give us one (adjective omitted) thing. I conducted that investigation with two (characterization omitted) committee investigators—that stupid—they were tenacious. We got it done. Then we worked that thing. We then got the evidence, we got the typewriter, we got the Pumpkin Papers. We got all of that ourselves. The FBI did not cooperate. The Justice Department did not cooperate. The Administration would not answer questions except, of course, for Cabinet officers, I mean like Burling came down and some of the others.

D Funny, when the shoe is on the other foot how they look at things, isn't it?

P Well, as I said, the New York Times, the Washington Post and all the rest. They put it in terms of executive privilege because they were against the investigation. So the real question now is say that I having been through that—we have talked it over and that I have always felt very miffed about that because I thought that was very wrong and now this is another matter. But I think we ought to cooperate in finding an area of cooperation. Here it is. You see, the Baker theory is that he wants to have a big slambang thing for a whole week and then he thinks interest in the whole thing will fall off. And he is right about that. But his interest in having a big slambang for a week is that we bring all the big shots up right away. The big shots you could bring up. They could bring up Stans. They have to put him on, and they've got to put Mitchell on. They would like, of course, to get Haldeman, Ehrlichman and Colson.

D I understand that you and Bob have talked about running Stans out as sort of a stalking horse on it, on another post.

P It is not my idea. I guess Moore or somebody mentioned it.

D I think it was my idea. I think it could be one defusing factor in the hearings. Stans would like to get his story out. He is not in any serious problem ultimately. It could be rough and tumble, but Maury is ready to take it and it would be a mini-hearing there is no doubt about it. But this further detracts from the other committee.

P   It would be a mini-hearing, it is true. Except knowing the Press and knowing—like they have taken—they sold several of these stories about Colson and Haldeman about four times.

D   Well, I know that.

P   Well, I just wonder if that doesn't do that?

D   At present I hesitate to send Stans. They would give him a hot seat.

P   Somebody is after him about Vesco. I first read the story briefly in the Post. I read, naturally, the first page and turned to the Times to read it. The Times had in the second paragraph that the money had been returned, but the Post didn't have it.

D   That is correct. •

P   The Post didn't have it until after you continued to the back section. It is the (adjective omitted) thing I ever saw.

D   Typical.

P   My guess is the Star pointed out (inaudible) that they—(inaudible). Actually they got the money after the 10th, but I don't think they pointed out that Sears got it before.

D   For all purposes, the donor - Vesco—

P   Stans would never do a thing like that! Never. Never. Never.

D   I think we have a good strong case that the donor had relinquished control of the money, and constructive possession of the money was in the hands of the finance committee, Sears and the like. So that there is not—ah—

P   How did they get my brother in it? Eddie?

D   That was sheer sandbagging of your brother. Here is what they did. They called him down here in Washington . . .

P   Who did?

D   It was Vesco and Sears and said that, "we want to talk to you about the nature of this transaction because we have had earlier conversations with Stans." He really wasn't privy to it, and didn't know much about it, but what the long and short of it was that they were after him to find out from Stans whether they wanted cash or checks. Stans just responded to your brother and said, "I don't really care—whatever they want to do," and that is what he relayed back. He didn't even understand why he

46

was there. He is just as clean as a whistle. There is just nothing there at all.

P I know that. I know that myself. So you sort of lean to having Stans starting out there?

D I think it would take a lot of the teeth out of the—you know—the stardom of the people are trying to build up to. If Stans has already gone to a hearing in another committee, obviously they will use everything they have at that time and it won't be a hell of a lot. It confuses the public. The public is bored with this thing already.

P Yeah.

D One of the things I think we did succeed in before the election—

P Stans is very clean. Unless I make a mistake on this thing, the way I analyze it, and I have stayed deliberately away from it, but I think I can sense what it is. The way I analyze the thing, Stans would have been horrified at any such thing. And, what happened was he honestly is outraged. He thinks—what happened was he thinks he eventually found a line on somebody's hard earned cash and got into this silly business with it.

D He does and he is a victim of circumstances, of innuendo, of false charges. He has a darn good chance of winning that libel suit he has against Larry O'Brien.

P Has he?

D That's right.

P Good. That's why Larry filed a counter suit.

D That's right.

P I see. Ziegler was disturbed at the news that they supoenaed newsmen. Did that disturb you?

D No, it didn't disturb me at all. No Sir. I talked with Ron at some length about it the other night. I said, "Ron, first of all you can rest assured that the White House was not involved in that decision." Exceptional case.

P It should involve prosecution.

D No, it is a civil deposition and it is not because we haven't reached the newsman's privilege issue yet, and that is way down the road yet, if for some reason they refuse to testify on some given evidence. What they are trying to establish is the fact that Edward Bennett Williams' law firm passed out an amended complaint that libeled Stans before it was into the Court process, so it was not privileged. And the newsmen are the people who can answer that question. Also they are trying to find out how Larry

O'Brien and Edward Bennett Williams made statements to the effect that this law suit—the first law suit they had filed against the Committee—was not really to establish any invasion of privacy threat, rather they were harrassing the Committee.

P The Committee to Re-Elect?

D They made this off the record to several newsmen and we know they did this. That this was a drummed up law suit.

P So therefore that proves also malice, doesn't it?

D It makes the abuse of process case that we have against them on a counter suit. And the lawyers made a very conscious and good decision to proceed with the suit and if they did, they were going to have to have this information and it doesn't bother me if they supoenaed nine or ten—

P Well, one hell of a lot of people don't give one damn about this issue of the suppression of the press, etc. We know that we aren't trying to do it. They all squeal about it. It is amusing to me when they say—I watched the networks and I thought they were restrained. What (expletive omitted) do they want them to do—go through the 1968 syndrome when they were 8 to 1 against us. They are only three to one this time. It is really sickening though to see these guys. These guys have always figured we have the press on our side. You know we receive a modest amount of support—no more. Colson sure making them move it around, saying we don't like this or that and (inaudible)

D Well, you know Colson's threat of a law suit which was printed in Evans and Novak had a very sobering effect on several of the national magazines. They are now checking before printing a lot of this Watergate junk they print. They check the press office trying to get a confirmation or denial, or call the individuals involved. And they have said they are doing it because they are afraid a libel suit on them. So it did have a sobering effect. We will keep them honest if we can remind them that they can't print anything and get away with it.

P Well, as you of course know, at the time of the Hills case (inaudible)

D Yes, I have noticed. We have to establish, one, malice for reckless disregard (inaudible)

P Yeah. Malice is impossible for (inaudible) It has to get, it's got to get up in through me. (inaudible) Reckless disregard maybe.

D   Tough. That is a bad decision, Mr. President. It really is a bad decision.

P   What is the name of the case—horrible.

D   (inaudible) & Sullivan and it came out of the South on a civil rights . . .

P   It was about some guy who was a police chief or something. Anyway, I remember reading it at the time when I thought we were suing LIFE for Hills. When LIFE was guilty as hell.

D   Did you win it?

P   Supreme Court—four to three. There were a couple missing or it would have probably been five to three and one-half.

P   Well, let's go back so it is clearly understood. We must go forward on that. I think you had better go over and get in touch with Dick. And say Dick you keep it at your level.

P   My guess is that he is going to be in the end, and I would say, "this is the position, Dick, you should take on this." Tell him I took that position with Baker. Baker is a smoothy - impressive - The President didn't say this or that - they recommended it and the President has approved it. Right? Is that what you would say?

D   Yes sir, I think that is absolutely on all fours. And how about our dealings with Baker? Under normal Congressional relations, viz-a-viz Timmons and Baker, should we have Timmons dealing?

P   Well, he objected to (inaudible) something that is a curious thing on that (inaudible) made a very big gaff calling him and urging and trying to influence who would be on his staff. (expletive omitted) I don't know why he did that, if he did. But if he did, I don't know why Baker would resent it. But, nevertheless, I don't know how to deal with him, frankly.

H   Why don't you ask (inaudible) to see him.

P   I gathered the impression that Baker didn't want to talk with anyone but Kleindienst.

D   Well, OK, I think that is one we will just have to monitor and that is one we will have to know an awful lot about along the road.

P   Well let Timmons tell Baker that if he wants to talk with anybody at the White House, if he says he doesn't want to talk to Haldeman, doesn't want to talk to Ehrlichman, that you, Dean, are available. But nobody else. How does that sound to you?

D   I think that sounds good.

P You tell Timmons that he sees him privately, and tells him that's it. We are not pressing him. We don't care, because Baker . . .

D I would suspect if we are going to get any insight to what that Committee is going to do, it is going to be through Gurney. I don't know about Weicker, where he is going to fall out on this thing.

P Weicker, I think the line to Weicker is through Gray. Gray has to shape up here and handle himself well too. Do you think he will?

D I do. I think Pat has had it tough. He goes up this morning as you know. He is ready. He is very comfortable in all of the decisions he has made, and I think he will be good.

P But he is close to Weicker - that is what I meant.

D Yes, he is.

P And so, Gray . . .

D Has a lead in there—yes.

P One amusing thing about the Gray thing, and I knew this would come. They say Gray is a political crony and a personal crony of the President's. Did you know that I have never seen him socially?

D Is that correct? No, I didn't.

P I think he has been to a couple White House events, but I have never seen him separately.

D The Press has got him meeting you at a social function. And, back in 1947, (inaudible) is something I have read.

P Maybe at a Radford party or something like that. That's all. I don't know. But Gray is somebody that I know only—He was Radford's Assistant, used to attend NSC meetings. He has never been a social friend. Edgar Hoover, on the other hand, I have seen socially at least a hundred times. He and I were very close friends.

D This is curious the way the press—

P (expletive deleted)—Hoover was my crony. He was closer to me than Johnson, actually although Johnson used him more. But as for Pat Gray, (expletive deleted) I never saw him.

D While it might have been a lot of blue chips to the late Director, I think we would have been a lot better off during this whole Watergate thing if he had been alive. Because he knew how to handle that Bureau—knew how to keep them in bounds.

P Well, Hoover performed. He would have fought. That was the point. He would have defied a few people.

He would have scared them to death. He has a file on everybody.

P But now at the present time, the Bureau is leaking like a sieve to Baker, (inaudible). It isn't coming from Henry Petersen is it?

D No. I would just not believe that.

P Is isn't coming from that (unintelligible).

D No. Well, they are getting the raw data. They are getting what they call the 302 forms. Actually, the summaries of the interviews.

P If you could handle it that way, I think that is the best thing to do. Do you ever wonder really if Colson (characterization deleted) should bring a suit. For example, I notice that Colson has a lot of vulnerabilities. You know, in terms of people that he knew, et cetera, et cetera. But I mean on a narrow issue—

D Well, Chuck and I talked about this. He could possibly win a suit, but lose the war, for this reason: A counter-discovery in a libel action has no bounds.

P I get it. OK.

D That's the problem there.

P That the District Court (inaudible).

D Federal Court. They could just come in and depose him on everything he has done at this point in time.

P Keep him out of it. Keep him out of it.

D That's right.

P What—Why doesn't Stans be the sue-er?

D He's got a good one, and he may well prevail. It may well be the decisive settlement of all these other suits we've got out there. You know, we have 14 million dollar suits against us, and we have 7 or 10 against them. (expletive deleted) They ought to all get together and drop them.

D That is what we are trying to get accomplished.

P Hell, yes!

D It is just causing everybody problems.

P That is right—they've got problems, and we've got problems.

P You see this Vesco thing coming up burns my tail. I raised hell with Haldeman on this and he didn't do anything about. I guess he couldn't. What (expletive omitted) became of our investigation of their financial activities? (Expletive omitted) They cancelled debts, they borrowed money. What the hell is that?

D It is still going on, Mr. President. McGovern's stuff is in such bad shape. That is another unfortunate thing.

The GAO comes into audit us. They find all the documents, so they are able to make—

P   Just like two year old state tax.

D   They have now, but it gets about that much coverage in the paper. They can't even figure out what McGovern's done, the books are such a mess, but you haven't seen them say anything yet. And that is one of the things that hopefully we will bring out in hearings, as to what a mess this was, et cetera.

P   How are you going to bring it out? You can't bring it out in these hearings.

D   Well I think I would rather do it independently, so that the media types will bring it out. Chuck is going to be of aid when he is out there not connected with the White House, coming through with bits of tidbits. Chuck will still have his channels to flip things out.

P   Sure! Sure! In my view—of course it is hard to believe since he loves the action and the rest—but apart from the financial—for the country's aid, etc.—I don't care what you think: Colson can be more valuable out than in, because, basically in, he has reached the point that he was too visible.

D   A lightning rod.

P   And outside he can start this and say that I am a private citizen and I can say what I (expletive omitted) please.

D   Right. I think Chuck can be of great aid in this thing, and I think he will do it.

P   Now, as to the other thing. Just to recap. You will talk to Timmons about Baker, and get that tied down if you can. I doubt if much can be done there. Then when you talk to Kleindienst, he should know that it has been decided, and that's it. Well, he will say they won't take me. Then say "why not?" We shall see. Going on to the interrogatory thing—we shall see—your view would not to give any further ground on that?

D   I would say hope not. You initially hold the line as far as you can go. If it becomes necessary for informational purposes, the President is not going to hide any information. He has just given a sworn statement through an interrogatory—send your questions down they will be answered. We won't hide the information—we won't diminish the ability of the President to operate internally and the like because we have a political circus going.

P   OK. I understand that Mollenhoff still thinks everybody should go up and testify.

D   Yeah.

P   At least you had a talk with him. I do want you to look at the case, though.

D   Yes Sir.

P   If the guy's got a bad rap, this man, (expletive omitted) we will get him out of it!

D   I am doing that. I talked with Clark yesterday. I talked with him last night again. He is on this as hot and heavy as can be and—

P   Does he think he's got a bad rap?

D   He does—he thinks he's got a bad rap. I know Rule hasn't a bad rap. When a bureaucrat takes it upon himself to go out, and go way beyond the pale in terms of attacking an Administration that can't be tolerated. Suppose a Congressman or a Senator or one of his Administrative Assistants went out and attacked one of his contributors. What would he do? Fire him! That's right.

P   I noticed where several of our Congressmen and Republican Senators called upon us to reinstate Rule. Congress is, of course, on its (inaudible). And yet they are so enormously frustrated that they are exhausted. Isn't that the point?

D   I think there is a lot of that.

P   It is too bad. We can take very little comfort from it because we have to work with them. But they become irrelevant because they are so damned irresponsible, as much as we would like to say otherwise.

D   Yes, sir. I spent some years on the Hill myself and one of the things I always noticed was the inability of the Congress to deal effectively with the Executive Branch because they have never provided themselves with adequate staffs, had adequate information available—

P   Well now they have huge staffs compared to what we had.

D   Well they have huge staffs, true, as opposed to what they had years ago. But they are still inadequate to deal effectively—

P   (Expletive deleted) Don't try to help them out!

D   I am not suggesting any reserve money for them. I ought to keep my observations to myself. I think this is going to be very different. It will be hot, I think they are going to be tough. I think they are going to be gory in some regards, but I am also absolutely convinced that if everyone pulls their own oar in this thing, in all those we've got with various concerns, we can make it through these things and minimal people will be hurt. And they may even paint themselves as being such partisans and off base, that they are really damaging to the institutions of the government themselves.

P   I frankly say that I would rather they would be partisan—rather than for them to have a facade of fairness and all the rest. Ervin always talks about his being a great Constitutional lawyer. (expletive deleted) He's got Baker totally toppled over to him. Ervin works harder than most of our Southern gentlemen. They are great politicians. They are just more clever than the minority. Just more clever!

D   I am convinced that he has shown that he is merely a puppet for Kennedy in this whole thing. The fine hand of the Kennedys' is behind this whole hearing. There is no doubt about it. When they considered the resolution on the Floor of the Senate I got the record out to read it. Who asked special permission to have their Staff man on the floor? Kennedy brings this man Flug out on the floor when they are debating a resolution. He is the only one who did this. It has been Kennedy's push quietly, his constant investigation. His committee did the (unintelligible) subpoenas to get at Kalmbach and all these people.

P   Uh, huh.

D   He has kept this quiet and constant pressure on this thing. I think this fellow Sam Dash, who has been selected Counsel, is a Kennedy choice. I think this is also something we will be able to quietly and slowly document. Leak this to the press, and the parts and cast become much more apparent.

P   Yes, I guess the Kennedy crowd is just laying in the bushes waiting to make their move. I had forgotten, by the way, we talk about Johnson using the FBI. Did your friends tell you what Bobby did?

D   I haven't heard but I wouldn't be—

P   Johnson believed that Bobby bugged him.

D   That wouldn't surprise me.

P   Bobby was a ruthless (characterization omitted.) But the FBI does blatantly tell you that—or Sullivan told you about the New Jersey thing. He did use a bug up there for intelligence work. (inaudible)

D   (inaudible) Intelligence workers had agents all over the property.

P   The doctors say that the poor old gent had a tumor. The FBI said he had one.

D   He had Abe Fortas and Deke DeLoache backed up by some other people in the Bureau and try to talk this

54

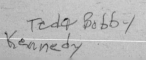
Tedq Bobby
Kennedy

doctor into examining this guy to say the man had a brain tumor. He was very (unintelligible) ill, slightly eratic, but eager. This doctor wouldn't buy it.

P   The doctor had never examined him before or anything.

D   No.

P   They were trying to set it up though, huh? What other kind of activities?

D   Well, as I say, I haven't probed Sullivan to the depths on this thing because I want to treat him at arm's length until he is safe, because he has a world of information that may be available.

P   But he says that what happened on the bugging thing. Who told what to whom again?

D   On the '68 thing—I was trying to track down the leaks. He said that the only place he could figure it coming from would be one of a couple of sources he was aware of that had been somewhat discovered publicly. He said that Hoover had told Patrick Coyne about the fact that this was done. Coyne had told Rockefeller—now Rockefeller had told Kissinger. I have never run it any step beyond what Mr. Sullivan said there. The other thing is that when the records were unavailable for Mr. Hoover all these logs, etc. Hoover tried to reconstruct them by going to the Washington Field Office and he made a pretty good stir about what he was doing when he was trying to get the record and reconstruct it. He said that at that time we probably hit the grapevine in the Bureau that this had occurred. But there is no evidence of it. The records show at the Department of Justice and the FBI that no such surveillance was ever conducted.

P   Shocking to me!

D   What the White House had from reporters in LIFE. The other person who knows and is aware of it is Mark Felt, and we have talked about Mark Felt before.

P   Let's face it. Suppose Felt comes out now and unwraps. What does it do to him?

D   He can't do it.

P   How about (unintelligible)? Who is going to hire him? Let's face it—the guy who goes out—he couldn't do it unless he had a guarantee from somebody like TIME Magazine who would say look we will give you a job for life. Then what do they do? He would go to a job at LIFE, and everyone would treat him like a pariah. He is in a very dangerous situation. These guys you know—the informers. Look what it did to Chambers. Chambers informed because he didn't give (expletive deleted). But then one of the most brilliant writers according to Jim Shepley we have ever seen in this country—and I am not referring to the Communist issue—greatest writer of his time, - about 30 years ago, probably TIME's best writer of the century—they finished him. Either way, the informer is not one in our society. Either way, that is the one thing people can't survive. They say no civilized (characterization deleted) informs. Hoover to Coyne to Nelson Rockefeller to Kissinger. Right?

D That's right.

P Why did Coyne tell it to Nelson Rockefeller? I have known Coyne for years. I haven't known him well, but he was a great friend of one of my Administrative Assistants, Bob King, who used to be a Bureau head.

D Now this is Sullivan's story. I have no reason to know whether it is true, but I don't have any reason to doubt that it is true.

P Hoover told me, and he also told Mitchell personally that this had happened.

D I was talking the '68 incident that occurred. I wasn't referring to that now. When this Coyne, etc., this was the fact that newsmen—excuse me I thought you were making reference to the fact that three years ago the White House had allegedly—

P Oh, sure, sure. That is not the same one.

D On the '68 incident all I have been able to find out is what you told me that Hoover had told you, what he had told Mitchell.

P Yeah. Mitchell corroborates that, doesn't he?

D Kevin Phillips called Pat Buchanan the other day with a tidbit that Dick Whelan on the NSC staff has seen memoranda between the NSC and the FBI that the FBI had been instructed to put surveillance on Anna Chennault, the South Vietnamese Embassy and the Agnew plane. This note also said that Deke DeLoach was the operative FBI officer on this.

P The Agnew plane? I think DeLoach's memory now is very very hazy. He doesn't remember anything.

D I talked to Mitchell about this and he has talked to DeLoach. DeLoach has in his possession, and he has let Mitchell review them, some of the files on this.

P But not—

D But they don't go very far; this is DeLoach protecting his own hide.

P It is just as well because we can't do anything with

56

it. So Hoover told Coyne, who told Rockefeller, that newsmen were being bugged.

P   That tickles you. That is right.

P   Why do you suppose they did that?

D   I haven't the foggiest idea. It is a Sullivan story as to where the leak might have come from about the current Time Magazine story, which we are stonewalling totally here.

P   Oh, absolutely.

(Material not related to Presidential action deleted)

P   Well, is this the year you are going to try to get out the '68 story?

D   Well, I think the threat of the '68 story when Scott and others were arguing that the Committee up on the Hill broadened its mandate to include other elections. They were hinting around at something in 1968 and 1964 that should be looked at.

P   Yeah, Goldwater claims he was bugged.

D   That's right. Now I think that threats—

P   Didn't you say that Johnson did bug Goldwater?

D   Well, I don't know if he bugged him.

P   He did intelligence work?

D   He did intelligence up one side and down the other—

P   From the FBI?

D   Just up one side and down the other on Goldwater. I haven't had a chance to talk to the Senator, and I have known the Senator for twenty years. He is the first man in public life I ever met. Barry Jr. and I were roommates in school together, so I can talk to the man. So I am really going to sit down with him one day and see what really happened.

P   Does he have any hard evidence?

D   Then we can go from there and . . .

P   Right.

D   Get some stuff written, etc. I do think you have to remember, as I am sure you realize, this is mainly a public relations thing anyway.

P   What is the situation anyway with regard to the situation of the sentencing of the seven? When in the hell is that going to occur?

D   That is likely to occur, I would say, as early as late this week, but more likely sometime next week.

P   Why has it been delayed so long?

D   Well, they have been in the process of preparing a pre-sentence report. The Judge sends out probation officers to find out everybody who knew these people, and then he will . . .

P   He is trying to work on them to see who will break them down?

D   Well, there is some of that. They are using the probation officer for more than the normal probation report. They are trying to do a mini-investigation by the judge himself which is his only investigative tool here so they are virtually completed now. The U.S. Attorneys handles these, the Assistant U.S. Attorneys.

P   You know when they talk about a 35 year sentence, here is something to think about. There were no weapons! Right? There were no injuries! Right? There was no success! Why does that sort of thing happen? It is just ridiculous!

(Characterization deleted)

Are they in jail?

D   Well, all but one. Hunt made the bond—everybody else is in jail. They have a $100,000 surety bond which means that they have to put actual collateral, and none of these people have $100,000. The Court of Appeals has been sitting for two weeks or better now on a review of the bond issue and letting people out for charity cases.

(Material unrelated to Presidential action deleted)

P   You still think Sullivan is basically reliable?

D   I have nothing to judge that on except that I have watched him for a number of years. I watched him when he was working with Tom Huston on domestic intelligence, and his desire to do the right thing. I tried to stay in touch with Bill, and find out what his moods are. Bill was forced on the outside for a long time. He didn't become bitter. He sat back and waited until he could come back in. He didn't try to force or blackmail his way around with knowledge he had. So I have no signs of anything but a reliable man who thinks a great deal of this Administration and of you.

(Material unrelated to Presidential action deleted.)

D   I have got to say one thing. There has never been a leak out of my office. There never will be a leak out of my office. I wouldn't begin to know how to leak and I don't want to learn how you leak.

P   Well, it was a shocking thing. I was reading a book last night. A fascinating book, although fun book, by Malcolm Smith Jr. on Kennedy's Thirteen Mistakes, the great mistakes. And one of them was on the Bay of Pigs. And what had happened, there was Chester Bowles had learned about it, and he deliberately leaked it. Deliberately, because he wanted the operation to fail! And he admitted it! Admitted it!

D   Interesting. Interesting

P   This happens all the time. Well, you can follow these characters to their Gethsemane. I feel for those poor guys in jail, particularly for Hunt with his wife dead.

D   Well there is every indication they are hanging in tough right now.

P   What the hell do they expect though? Do they expect clemency in a reasonable time? What would you advise on that?

D   I think it is one of those things we will have to watch very closely. For example,—

P   You couldn't do it, say, in six months.

D   No, you couldn't. This thing may become so political as a result of these hearings that it is a vendetta. This judge may go off the deep end in sentencing, and make it so absurd that its clearly injustice that they have been heavily—

P   Is there any kind of appeal left?

D   Right. Liddy and McCord, who sat through the trial, will both be on appeal and there is no telling how long that will last. It is one of these things we will just have to watch.

P   My view though is to say nothing about them on the ground that the matter is still in the courts and on appeal. Second, my view is to say nothing about the hearings at this point, except that I trust they will be conducted the proper way and I will not comment on the hearings while they are in process. Of course if they break through—if they get muckraking—It is best not to cultivate that thing here at the White House. If it is done at the White House again they are going to drop the (adjective deleted) thing. Now there, of course, you say but you leave it all to them. We'll see as time goes on. Maybe we will have to change our policy. But the President should not become involved in any part of this case. Do you agree with that?

D   I agree totally, sir. Absolutely. That doesn't mean that quietly we are not going to be working around the office. You can rest assured that we are not going to be sitting quietly.

P   I don't know what we can do. The people who are most disturbed about this (unintelligible) are the (adjective deleted) Republicans. A lot of these Congressmen, financial contributors, et cetera, are highly moral. The Democrats are just sort of saying, "(expletive deleted) fun and games!"

D   Well, hopefully we can give them Segretti.

P   (Expletive deleted) He was such a dumb figure, I don't see how our boys could have gone for him. But nevertheless, they did. It was really juvenile! But, nevertheless, what the hell did he do? What in the (characterization deleted) did he do? Shouldn't we be trying to get intelligence? Weren't they trying to get intelligence from us?

D   Absolutely!

P   Don't you try to disrupt their meetings? Didn't they try to disrupt ours? (expletive deleted) They threw rocks, ran demonstrations, shouted, cut the sound system, and let the tear gas in at night. What the hell is that all about? Did we do that?

D   McGovern had Dick Tuck on his payroll, and Dick Tuck was down in Texas when you were down at the Connally ranch and set up to do a prank down there. But it never came off.

P   What did Segretti do that came off?

D   He did some humorous things. For example, there would be a fund-raising dinner, and he hired Wayne the Wizard to fly in from the Virgin Islands to perform a magic show. He sent invitations to all the black diplomats and sent limousines out to have them picked up, and they all showed up and they hadn't been invited. He had 400 pizzas sent to another—

P   Sure! What the hell! Pranks! Tuck did all those things in 1960, and all the rest.

D   I think we can keep the Segretti stuff in perspective because it is not that bad. Chapin's involvement is not that deep. He was the catalyst, and that is about the extent of it.

P   Sure, he knew him and recommended him.

D   That's right.

P   But he didn't run him. He was too busy with us.

D   The one I think they are going to go after with a vengeance—and I plan to spend a great deal of time with next week, as a matter of fact a couple of days getting this all in order—is Herb Kalmbach.

P Yes.

D Herb—they have subpoenaed his records, and he has records that run all over hell's acres on things. You know Herb has been a man who has been moving things around for Maury and keeping things in tow and taking care of—

P What is holding up his records?

D They already have gotten to the banks that had them, and what I think we will do is that there will be a logical, natural explanation for every single transaction. It is just a lot of minutia we've got to go through but he is coming in next week and I told him we would sit down and he is preparing everything—all that is available, and we are going to sit down with Frank DeMarco and see if we can't get this whole thing—

P They can't get his records with regard to his private transactions?

D No, none of the private transactions. Absolutely, that is privileged material. Anything to do with San Clemente and the like—that is just so far out of bounds that—

P Did they ask for them?

D No. No indication.

P Kalmbach is a decent fellow. He will make a good witness.

D I think he will.

P He is smart.

D He has been tough thus far. He can take it. His skin is thick now. Sure it bothered him when all this press was being played up. LA Times were running stories on him all the time and the like. Local stations have been making him more of a personality and his partners have been nipping at him, but Herb is tough now. He is ready and he is going to go through. He is hunkered down and he is ready to handle it, so I am not worried about Herb at all.

P Oh well, it will be hard for him. I suppose the big thing is the financing transaction that they will go after him for. How does the money get to the Bank of Mexico, etc.

D Oh, well, all that can be explained.

P It can?

D Yes, indeed! Yes, sir! They are going to be disappointed with a lot of the answers they get. When they actually get the facts—because the Times and the Post had such innuendo—when they get the facts, they are going to be disappointed.

P The one point that you ought to get to Baker. I tried to get it through his thick skull. His skull is not thick but tell Kleindienst in talking to Baker—and Herb should emphasize that the way to have a successful hearing and a fair one is to run it like a court: no hearsay, no innuendo! Now you know—

D That's a hell of a good point.

P (expletive deleted) well, they are not going to but tell them that is the way Nixon ran the Hiss Case. As a matter of fact some innuendo came out, but there was (adjective deleted) little hearsay. We really just got the facts, and tore them to pieces. Say "no hearsay" and "no innuendo." Ervin should sit like a court there: that is hearsay, and the counsel for our people should get up and say, "I object to that, Mr. Chairman," on the basis that it is hearsay.

D That is a heck of an idea, Mr. President. Some of these early articles said—will Sam Ervin, Constitutional man, be a judge? Will he admit hearsay? We can try to get some think pieces out to try to get a little pressure on him to perform that way, to make it look like partisan when he doesn't.

P The point that Kleindienst gets out: no hearsay, no innuendo! There will be no hearsay, no innuendo. This will be a model of a Congressional hearing. That will disappoint the (adjective deleted) press. No hearsay! No innuendo! No leaks!

D Well, there are a lot of precedents. I have been involved in two Congressional investigations. One was the Adam Clayton Powell investigation when I was working over there as the Minority Counsel of the House Judiciary. We didn't take hearsay. We stuck to the facts on that. We did an investigation of the Oklahoma judges. Again, the same sort of thing. We went into executive session when necessary. I bet if we look around, respectable investigations that have been held up there that could be held up, and some of it should be coming forth to set the stage for these hearings. I am planning a number of brain sessions with some of the media people to—

P I know. It is very important, but it seems like a terrible waste of your time. But it is important in the sense that all this business is a battle and they are going to wage the battle. A lot of them have enormous frustrations about those elections, state of their party, etc. And their party has its problems. We think we have had problems, look at some of theirs. Strauss has had people and all the actors, and they haven't done that well you know.

D   Well I was—we have come a long road on this thing now. I had thought it was an impossible task to hold together until after the election until things started falling out, but we have made it this far and I am convinced we are going to make it the whole road and put this thing in the funny pages of the history books rather than anything serious because actually—

P   It will be somewhat serious but the main thing, of course, is also the isolation of the President.

D   Absolutely! Totally true!

P   Because that, fortunately, is totally true.

D   I know that sir!

P   (expletive deleted) Of course, I am not dumb and I will never forget when I heard about this (adjective deleted) forced entry and bugging. I thought, what in the hell is this? What is the matter with these people? Are they crazy? I thought they were nuts! A prank! But it wasn't! It wasn't very funny. I think that our Democratic friends know that, too. They know what the hell it was. They don't think we'd be involved in such.

D   I think they do too.

P   Maybe they don't. They don't think I would be involved in such stuff. They think I have people capable of it. And they are correct, in that Colson would do anything. Well, ok.—Have a little fun. And now I will not talk to you again until you have something to report to me.

D   Alright, sir.

P   But I think it is very important that you have these talks with our good friend Kleindienst.

D   That will be done.

P   Tell him we have to get these things worked out. We have to work together on this thing. I would build him up. He is the man who can make the difference. Also point out to him what we have. (expletive deleted) Colson's got (characterization deleted), but I really, really,—this stuff here—let's forget this. But let's remember this was not done by the White House. This was done by the Committee to Re-Elect, and Mitchell was the Chairman, correct?

D   That's correct!

P   And Kleindienst owes Mitchell everything. Mitchell wanted him for Attorney General. Wanted him for Deputy, and here he is. Now, (expletive deleted). Baker's got to realize this, and that if he allows this thing to get out of hand he is going to potentially ruin John Mitchell. He won't. Mitchell won't allow himself to be ruined. He will put on his big stone face. But I hope he does and he will. There is no question what they are after. What the Committee is after is somebody at the White House. They would like to get Haldeman or Colson, Ehrlichman.

D   Or possible Dean.—You know, I am a small fish.

P   Anybody at the White House they would—but in your case I think they realize you are the lawyer and they know you didn't have a (adjective deleted) thing to do with the campaign.

D   That's right.

P   That's what I think. Well, we'll see you.

D   Alright, sir.—Good bye.

Meeting: The President and Dean, Oval Office, March 13, 1973. (12:42 - 2:00 pm)

H   Say, did you raise the question with the President on Colson as a consultant?

D   No, I didn't.

H   Was that somebody else?

D   The thought was as a consultant, without doing any consulting, he wants it for continued protection on—

H   Solely for the purpose of executive privilege protection, I take it.

D   It is one of those things that is kept down in the personnel office, and nothing is done on it.

P   What happens to Chapin?

D   Well, Chapin doesn't have quite the same problem in appearing as Colson will.

H   Yeah—you have the same problems of Chapin appearing as Colson.

P   Well, can't—that would such an obvious fraud to have both of them as consultants, that that won't work. I think he is right. You would have to leave Chapin.

H   Well, you can't make Chapin a consultant, because we have already said he is not.

D   Yeah.

H   Because we wanted the separation. The question is, are you then, as of now, the way they have interpreted executive privilege, is that you are not going to let Chapin testify.

P Anybody.

H Because it applies to executive privilege by the former people in relation to matters while they were here.

D And the problem area is . . .

H And that same thing would apply to Colson.

D Well, yes, if Chuck were truly going to be doing nothing from this day on.

H That's alright. He is concerned with what he is doing. Colson is concerned with what he is doing from now on, and he would apply the consulting tactic if he were called with regard to actions taken now . . .

D That's right.

H that relate to the Watergate action.

D The problem is, I think, he will be out stirring up counter-news attacks and things of this nature.

P (expletive deleted) Is he supposed to do that and be consulting with the President on it?

D No, no. But he is consulting. It is a wide open consultantship. It doesn't mean he would be consulting with you.

H Yeah. Your idea was just to put this in the drawer, in case.

D Put it in the drawer, and then decide it.

H It would be a consultant without pay.

D I wouldn't even tell Chuck this. Just tell Chuck there is something in the drawer.

H There is no reason to tell Chuck is there? Why . . .

P I would tell Chuck. Tell him he is not to say anything, frankly.

H The point would be to date it back on Saturday, so it is that day.

D Continuous.

P His consultant fee stopped for the present time, but he is still available for purposes of consulting on various problems and the like.

D Right.

P Unpaid consultants?

D Yes.

H We have some of those.

D Good ones.

P Well, what are the latest developments Bob should get something on?

D Yeah.

P Before we get into that I was wondering about that

jackassery about some kid who (unintelligible)—which of course is perfectly proper couse of action if it works. I would expect we were heavily infiltrated that way too.

D   The only problem there Mr. President is that . . .

P   Did he get paid?

D   He was paid.

P   By check?

D   He was paid by personal check of another person over there who, in turn, was taking it out of expense money. The ultimate source of the money—and this is ticklish—is that it is pre-April 7th money, and there could be some potential embarrassment for Ken Reitz along the way.

P   Oh!

D   So he is. But I think it is a confined situation. Obviously it is something that will come up in the Ervin Committee, but it is not another new Liddy-Hunt operation.

P   It is just a (adjective deleted) thing.

D   Oh, it is.

P   What happened to the kid? Did he just decide to be a hero?

D   That's right. He probably chatted about it around school, and the word got out, and he got confronted with it and he knew he had chatted about it, so there he was. Its absurd, it really is. He didn't do anything illegal.

P   Illegal? Of course not! Apparently you haven't been able to do anything on my project of getting on the offensive?

D   But I have sir, to the contrary!

P   Based on Sullivan, have you kicked a few butts around?

D   I have all of the information that we have collected. There is some there, and I have turned it over to Baroody. Baroody is having a speech drafted for Barry Goldwater. And there is enough material there to make a rather sensational speech just by: Why in the hell isn't somebody looking into what happened to President Nixon during his campaign? Look at these events! How do you explain these? Where are the answers to these questions? But, there is nothing but threads. I pulled all the information. . . .

P   Also, the Senator should then present it to the Ervin Committee and demand that that be included. He is a Senator, a Senator . . .

D   What I am working on there for Barry is a letter to Senator Ervin that this has come to my attention, and why shouldn't this be a part of the inquiry? And he can spring out 1964 and quickly to '72. We've got a pretty good speech there, if we can get out our materials.

P   Good!

D   So it's in the mill.

H   We have finally started something.

P   (expletive deleted) Why haven't we had anyone involved in it before? Just didn't have enough stuff? For example, investigations were supposed to have been taken for the 34 (unintelligible) contributed to McGovern. And they say (expletive deleted) it is all hanky-panky, and their records are just too bad to find out. Is that the problem?

H   Won't that be an issue?

D   That will be an issue. There is a crew working that, also.

P   Do you need any IRS stuff?

D   There is no need at this hour for anything from IRS, and we have a couple of sources over there that I can go to. I don't have to go around with Johnnie Walters or anybody, but we can get right in and get what we need. I have been preparing the answers for the briefing book and I just raised this with Ron; in my estimation, for what it is worth, that probably this week will draw more Watergate questions than any other week we are likely to see, given the Gray hearings, the new revelations—they are not new, but they are now substantiated—about Kalmbach and Chapin that have been in the press.

P   To the effect of what phase?

D   That Chapin directed Kalmbach to pay Segretti, the alleged saboteur, somewhere between $35 and $40,000. There is an awful lot of that hot in the press now. There is also the question of Dean appearing, not appearing—Dean's role. There are more stories in the Post this morning that are absolutely inaccurate about my turning information over to the Re-Election Committee for some woman over there. Mrs. Hoback signed an affidavit and gave it to Birch Bayh, and said that "I was brought into Bob Mardian's office within 48 hours after a private interview I had with the jury and confronted with it." How did they know that? It came from internal sources over there. That's how they knew it!

P   From what?

D   Internal sources—this girl had told others that she was doing this, and they just told. They just quickly sent it to the top that she was out on her own.

P   Did she quit?

D   She did. There have been two or three of those.

H   Why did she do that? Was she mad?

D   She is a registered Democrat.

H   Why did we take her in?

D   To this day, I do not know what she was doing.

P   Who was she working for?

. D   She worked in Stans' operation.

P   Why did he have her working for him?

D   It wasn't a good move. In fact that was one of our problems—the little pocket of women who worked for Maury Stans. There is no doubt that things would have sailed a lot smoother without that pack. Not that they have or had anything that was devastating.

P   Well, now, with regard to the question, etc., it would be my opinion not to dodge it just because there are going to be questions.

D   Well you are probably going to get more questions this week. And the tough questions. And some of them don't have easy answers. For example, did Haldeman know that there was a Don Segretti out there? That question is likely.

P   Did he? I don't know.

D   Yes, he had knowledge that there was somebody in the field doing prankster-type activities.

P   Well, I don't know anything about that. What about my taking, basically, just trying to fight this thing one at a time. I am only going to have to fight it later, and it is not going to get any better. I think the thing to say is, "this is a matter being considered by the Committee and I am not going to comment on it." I don't want to get into the business of taking each charge that comes up in the Committee and commenting on it: "It is being considered by the Committee. It is being investigated and I am not going to comment on it."

D   That is exactly the way I have drafted these. I have checked them generally.

P   I will just cut them off. I think, John, if I start breaking down, you see like I have done the Court thing on the Watergate stuff, I am not going to comment on it. I know all of these questions. I am not going to comment on it. That is a matter for the Committee to determine. Then, I will repeat the fact that as far as the Watergate matter is concerned, I am not going to comment on it, on anything else. Let the Committee find out. What would you say? You don't agree with that?

D   Well, the bottom line, on a draft that (unintelligible). But if you have nothing to hide, Mr. President, here at the White House, why aren't you willing to spread on the record everything you know about it? Why doesn't the Dean Report be made public? Why doesn't everything come out? Why does Ziegler stand up there and bob and weave, and no comment? That's the bottom line.

P   Alright. What do you say to that?

D   Well, . . .

P   We are furnishing information. We will . . .

D   We have cooperated with the FBI in the investigation of the Watergate. We will cooperate with the investigation of, the proper investigation by the Senate.

P   We will make statements.

D   And indeed we have nothing to hide.

P   All this information, we have nothing to hide. We have to handle it. You see, I can't be in the position of basically hunkering down because you have a lot of tough questions on Watergate, and not go out and talk on their issues because it is not going to get better. It is going to get worse.

D   I would agree. I think its cycled somewhat. I think after the Gray thing takes one course or the other, there will be a dead period of news on Watergate until the Ervin Hearings start again. This has obviously sparked the news again.

P   Well, let me just run over the questions again. If it is asked, what about Mr. Haldeman, Mr. Segretti, etc., etc. that is a matter being considered by the Senate Committee and I am not going to comment on it.

D   That is correct. That is specifically in their resolution.

P   I am not going to comment on something being investigated by the Committee. As I have already indicated, I am just not going to comment. Do you approve such tactics? Another question—?

D   Did Mr. Chapin's departure have something to do with his involvement with Mr. Segretti?

P   (inaudible) What about Mr. Dean? My position is the same. We have cooperated with the Justice Department, the FBI—completely tried to furnish information under our control in this matter. We will cooperate with the Committee under the rules I have laid down in my statement on Executive Privilege. Now what else?

D   Well, then you will get a barrage of questions probably, in will you supply—will Mr. Haldeman and Mr.

Ehrlichman and Mr. Dean go up to the Committee and testify?

P   No, absolutely not.

D   Mr. Colson?

P   No. Absolutely not. It isn't a question of not— Ziegler or somebody had said that we in our executive privilege statement it was interpreted as meaning that we would not furnish information and all that. We said we will furnish information, but we are not going to be called to testify. That is the position. Dean and all the rest will grant you information. Won't you?

D   Yes. Indeed I will! John,

P   My feeling, is that I better hit it now rather than just let it build up where we are afraid of these questions and everybody, etc., and let Ziegler go out there and bob acd weave around. I know the easy thing is to bug out, but it is not . . .

D   You're right. I was afraid. For the sake of debate, but I was having reservations. It is a bullet biter and you just have to do it. These questions are just not going to go away. Now the other thing that we talked about in the past, and I still have the same problem, is to have a "here it all is" approach. If we do that . . .

P   And let it all hang out.

D   And let it all hang out. Let's with a Segretti—etc.

P   We have passed that point.

D   Plus the fact, they are not going to believe the truth! That is the incredible thing!

P   They won't believe the truth, and they have committed seven people!

D   That's right! They will continually try to say that there is (unintelligible),

P   They hope one will say one day, "Haldeman did it," and one day, one will say I did it. When we get to that question—they might question his political savvy, but not mine! Not on a matter like that!

D   I have a thing on Sullivan I would like to ask you. Sullivan, as I told you, had been talking with me and I said Bill I would like for my own use to have a list of some of the horribles that you are aware of. He hasn't responded back to me, but he sent me a note yesterday saying John I am willing at any time to testify to what I know if you want me to. What he has, as we already know, he has something that has a certain degree of a dynamite situation already—the '68 Presidency, surveillance of Goldwater.

P I thought he said he saw that the '68 bugging was ordered, but he doesn't know whether it was carried out.

D That's right.

P But at least he would say (inaudible).

D Well, I have never talked with Bill about it. I have never gone into details, because he has always been very close about it, but he is now getting to the point if we wanted him to do this, someone—and I don't think the White House should do it—should sit down with him and really take down some notes of what he does know, how strong it is, what he can substantiate.

P Who the hell could do it if you don't?

D Well, probably there is no one.

P That is the problem.

D Now the other thing, if we were going to use a package like this: Let's say in the Gray hearings—where everything is cast that we are the political people and they are not—that Hoover was above reproach, which is just not accurate, total (expletive omitted). The person who would destroy Hoover's image is going to be this man Bill Sullivan. Also it is going to tarnish quite severely . . .

P Some of the FBI.

D . . . some of the FBI. And a former President. He is going to lay it out, and just all hell is going to break loose once he does it. It is going to change the atmosphere of the Gray hearings and it is going to change the atmosphere of the whole Watergate hearings. Now the risk . . .

P How will it change?

D Because it will put them in context of where government institutes were used in the past for the most flagrant political purposes.

P How can that help us?

D How does it help us?

P I am being the devil's advocate . . .

D I appreciate what you are doing. It is a red herring. It is what the public already believes. I think the people would react: (expletive deleted), more of that stuff! They are all bad down there! Because it is a one way street right now . . .

P Do you think the press would use it? They may not play it.

D It would be difficult not to. Ah, it would be difficult not to.

P Why is Sullivan willing to do this?

D I think the quid pro quo with Sullivan is that he wants someday back in the Bureau very badly.

P   That's easy.

D   That's right.

P   Do you think after he did this, the Bureau would want him back? Would they want him back?

D   I think probably not. What Bill Sullivan's desire in life is, is to set up a domestic national security intelligence system, a White House program. He says we are deficient. He says we have never been efficient, because Hoover lost his guts several years ago. If you recall he and Tom Huston worked on it. Tom Huston had your instructions to go out and do it and the whole thing just crumbled.

P   (inaudible)

D   That's all Sullivan really wants. Even if we could put him out studying it for a couple of years, if you could put him out in the CIA or someplace where he felt—put him there . . .

P   We will do it.

D   I think that is a simple answer. Let me just simply raise it with him.

P   There is no problem with Sullivan. He is a valuable man. Now would the FBI turn on him (characterization deleted) ?

D   There would be some effort at that. That's right they would say he was disgruntled. He was canned by Hoover. He is angry, he is coming back. But I would think a lot of that would be lost in the shuffle of what he is laying out. I don't know if he has given me his best yet. I don't know whether he's got more ammunition than he has already told me. I will never forget a couple off-the-cuff remarks.

P   Why do you think he is now telling you this? Why is he doing this now?

D   Well, the way it came out when TIME Magazine broke on the fact that it charged that the White House had directed that newsmen and White House staff people be subjected to some sort of surveillance for national security reasons. I called, in tracking down what happened, I called Sullivan and I said, "don't you think you ought to come over and talk to me about it and tell me what you know." I was calling to really determine whether he was a leak. I was curious to know where this might have come from because he was the operative man at the Bureau at the time. He is the one who did it. He came over and he was shocked and distraught and (unintelligible). Then, after going through with his own explanation of all what had happened, he started volunteering this other thing. He

72

said John this is the only thing I can think of during this Administration that has any taint of political use but it doesn't really bother me because it was for national security purposes. These people worked with sensitive material on Vietnam that was getting out to reporters.

P   Of course, the stuff was involved with the (expletive deleted) Vietnam war.

D   That's right. Then he told me about going to (location and name deleted) and all that, and he said, "John that doesn't bother me, but what does bother me is that you all have been portrayed as politically using"—

P   And we never did.

D   And we never have! And he said the Eisenhower Administration didn't either.

P   Never.

D   He said the only times that he can recall that there has been a real political use has been during Democratic tenure. I said for example, Bill, what are you talking about? Then he told me of the Walter Jenkins affair, when DeLoach and Fortas, etc.—

P   The Kennedy's, let me say, used it politically in that steel thing. That was not national security was it?

D   I asked somebody about that and they told me what happened. They were being defensive of Kennedy, and so he was saying that Kennedy had given Hoover orders and Hoover, being typical in his response, tried to get it yesterday as far as the answer for the President. And that is why sending people out in a plane in the middle of the night really fell on Hoover. This might be rumor over there, who knows?

P   It is still wrong!

D   Sure.

P   (expletive deleted) Can you imagine if a steel company or an automobile company had raised hell about something Ruckelshaus does, and we send FBI agents out to arrest? (expletive deleted) Does he know about the bugging in '68?

D   Yep! I think he would tell everything. He knows!

P   You do?

D   Uh huh. That's what I am saying he is a bomb!

P   You think we could get him to do this?

D   That is the real problem. How it could be done, how it could be structured. He sent me this note and I called up and said, "Bill, I appreciate getting that note very much. It takes a lot of guts to send a note like that to me." He said, "it has been a pleasure to see a man

73

standing up blowing up a little smoke up him and the like." He said, "well, I mean it! I am perfectly willing to do anything you want. If you want me to go up and testify, I will." I said, "well how much, you have just given me some tidbits in our conversation and I would really like to again repeat: can you put together what you do know; just for your own use, put it together on a pad—just your own recollections; and also tell me how you can substantiate them;—what kind of cross-examination you might be subject to on it if you did testify." So he is doing that. The question I have had is, how in the world can we program something like this? I just have a feeling that it would be bad for one Bill Sullivan to quietly appear on some Senator's doorstep, and say, "I have the information you ought to have." Well, "where did you get it?" "Why are you up here?" "Well the White House sent me." That would be bad! The other thing is, maybe this information could be brought to the attention of the White House, and the White House could say to Eastland, "I think you ought to call an executive session and hear his testimony. This is quite troublesome, the information that has been presented to us. It is so troublesome, we can't hold it here and hope to be less comfortable."

P Why couldn't we have him just present it to Eastland? Why an executive session? That doesn't serve—

D Well, the first approach would be enough of the story, not to tarnish the names, but it would leak out of there quite obviously. If it doesn't we could make sure it did.

D If Sullivan went up to Eastland cold, say, or Hruska, I think they would say, "go on down back to the Department of Justice where you work, and let's not start all this."

P Suppose, another thing, Pat Gray knows anyone, or Hruska on the Committee, who is a tiger on our side on the committee—

D Gurney has been good. He was good on the ITT Committee. He will study, he will get prepared.

P Could we go after the Bureau? I don't know whether we could or not.

D Not quite after the Bureau. What they are doing is taking the testimony of somebody who is going after the Bureau.

P I know that. I am just thinking. They will look down the road and see what the result of what they are doing is, won't they? I would think so. Would they go af-

74

ter Johnson? Let's look at the future. How bad would it hurt the country, John, to have the FBI so terribly damaged?

D   Do you mind if I take this back and kick it around with Dick Moore? These other questions. I think it would be damaging to the FBI, but maybe it is time to shake the FBI and rebuild it. I am not so sure the FBI is everything it is cracked up to be. I am convinced the FBI isn't everything the public think it is.

P   No.

D   I know quite well it isn't.

P   If we can get Jerry Wilson in there—What is your feeling at the moment about Gray? Can he hang in there? Should he?

D   They have an executive session this afternoon to invite me to testify.

P   Sure.

D   There is no question, they are going to invite me to testify. I would say, based on how I handle: (1) the formal letter that comes out of the Committee asking for information, and I programmed that if they do get specific as to what in the hell they do want to know, that I've got to lay it out in a letter sent down here so I can be responsive, fully responsive.

P   Respond to the letter in full!

D   I feel I can respond to the letter in full. I feel I have nothing to hide, as far this issue Gray raised.

P   Would you respond under oath?

D   I think I would be willing to, yes, give it under oath.

P   That is what I would say: that is, what I would prepare in the press thing. He will respond under oath in a letter. He will not appear in a formal session. They might then say, "would he be willing to be questioned under oath?"

D   That is not what the question is. Yes, I would be willing to be questioned under oath, but we are not going up.

P   No, no! Here?

D   No. I think that would be a hell of a bad precedent.

P   Just so we don't cross that bridge. I agree, but you would respond in writing. That's it. OK.

D   After that, if we have been responsive, their argument for holding up Gray's confirmation based on me should be gone. Sure, it can raise more questions than answers, but it should work. The effect of the letter we have taken the central points that they want answers to, given them the responses, given them something in Eastland's hand. And he can say, "alright, it is time to vote. And Eastland says he has the votes to get Gray through. Now, what happens on the Senate Floor is something else, because Byrd is posing very perceptive, and controlling that Southern bloc.

P Uh, uh! October! Byrd is running for leader of the whole Senate.

D But Mansfield, on the other hand, has come out and said he would support Gray's confirmation.

P My feeling is that they would like to have an excuse not to. And maybe they will use not you. But about these hearings—

D Well if they say they have to hold up Gray's confirmation until the Watergate Hearings are completed—

P That's great!

D That's the vehicle.

P That's a vote really for us, because Gray, in my opinion, should not be the head of the FBI. After going through the hell of the hearings, he will not be a good Director, as far as we are concerned.

D I think that is true. I think he will be a very suspect Director. Not that I don't think Pat won't do what we want—I do look at him a little differently than Dick in that regard. Like he is still keeping in close touch with me. He is calling me. He has given me his hot line. We talk at night, how do you want me to handle this, et cetera? So he still stays in touch, and is still being involved, but he can't do it because he is going to be under such surveillance by his own people—every move he is making—that it would be a difficult thing for Pat. Not that Pat wouldn't want to play ball, but he may not be able to.

P I agree. That's what I meant.

D Pat has already gotten himself in a situation where he has this Mark Felt as his number two man. These other people have surrounded him. He could have gotten a Wilson in there you know. Like this: saying, "Gentlemen, I am putting my own team in, and I am going to put in a team I have met around the country who are good office directors; Sacks out of Chicago," or whatever, and just put his own team together for the Headquarter's Office.

P That's the way it should be done.

D Gray should have walked in and made these major

76

personnel decisions. I wouldn't be surprised if death of his nomination occurs if they say they cannot go forward with Gray's hearings because of the Watergate.

P   Where would that be done, John, at what point?

D   It would simply be voted first in the Judiciary Committee. The question is, then, whether it will be put on the calendar by the leadership.

P   The leadership might determine that we will not put it on the calendar until after the Watergate Hearings. Then Gray would, in turn, say that he will not wait that long.

D   "Gentlemen, this is damaging to the leadership of the FBI, and I will have to withdraw based on this." What would be nice for all is to get Gray voted out of the Committee, with a positive vote, enough to get him out of the Committee, and then lock him in limbo there.

P   What is Moore's judgment about Sullivan? What does he think?

D   He said it speaks dynamite. And we both feel that it is the way it would be done, that would be the secret. How it is done? Whether it is the sort of thing that you leak out and do? It would have to be very carefully thought through. We would have to decide, should the White House not be involved or should we be involved? If we are going to play with it, we are probably going to say that we are involved and structure it in a way that there is nothing improper with our involvement.

P   The difficulty with the White House being involved is that if we are involved in this (expletive deleted), that is why it ought to be that he just . . .

D   I suppose the answer is to say to him, "you have intimated a few things to me, the proper place to take that information is to the Senate Judiciary Committee or to the Attorney General, possibly." And then have him take it to the Committee. Or is that too close to the President, still?

P   Well, he works for the Attorney General, doesn't he?

D   If he takes it to Kleindienst, Kleindienst is going to say, "Bill just don't do it because you are going to take DeLoach's name down with it, and DeLoach is a friend of ours."

P   (Expletive deleted)

D   Something I have always thought.

P   Nobody is a friend of ours. Let's face it! Don't worry about that sort of thing.

D   Something I can kick around with Dick Moore. But

first of all, it will have to be thought through every inch of the way. Either late yesterday afternoon—it wasn't when I talked with Bob—he was quite excited about it. Ehrlichman said, gave a very good, "uh huh." I said I am not going to rush anything on this. We have a little bomb here that we might want to drop at one time down the road. Maybe the forum to do it in is something totally out of context between the Gray hearings and the Watergate hearings. Maybe we need to go to the US News, sir. Who knows what it would be, but we ought to consider every option, now that we've got it.

P   Rather than going to a hearing, do "Meet the Press," and that will force the hearing to call him. That is quite the way to do it. Have him give an interview to US News, "Wires in the Sky" or something. A respected reporter—why not give it to Molenhoff?

D   Well that is interesting. Molenhoff is close, but our guy gets near Molenhoff. Molenhoff may not do anything.

P   No, and we are in a position with Molenhoff that he has been fighting us some. Maybe Molenhoff would be a pretty good prospect for this thing. It is the kind of a story he loves, but he digs on something. You couldn't call him, however, (inaudible)—The (characterization deleted) loves to talk too much, although he is a hell of a guy.

D   Ok. Can I call Clark and say "listen Clark, a guy has brought me a piece of dynamite that I don't even want in the White House?"

P   He will write that, won't he?

D   Yeah. Because that doesn't look like a set up deal. Well Clark Molenhoff is the first guy to uncover a shield of anything, and he will say no way—

P   But he would do it. That is very important piece. (unintelligible) Getting back, don't you feel that is the need here to broaden the scope?

D   The focus is right on us. That's the problem.

P   Nothing on the Democrats. —Nothing on what the previous three Administrations did?

D   Nothing. If Hunt is still a walking story we'll pull out of this thing. You can't find anybody who even knows what is happening. Although it has increased in the network coverage. That NBC thing last night, which is just a travesty as far and we're talking about shabby journalism, they took the worst edited clips out of context, with Strachan saying he was leaving. And then had a little of clip of Ron saying, "I deny that." And he was denying something other than what they were talking about in their charge. It was incredible. Someone is going through and putting that altogether right now and Ron ought to be able to (unintelligible) to that one on NBC. It was a very, very dishonest television reporting of sequence of events, but out of sequence.

P You see, John, when that Ervin gets up there—and a lot of Republicans even think he is a great Constitutional lawyer—it just makes us wonder about our even sending Gray up. Who knows?

D Who knows? That is right. If you didn't send him up, why didn't you send him up. Because he was—

P I know, but that is one thing: You send somebody else up to take them on, not a big clown. You know what I mean?

P I won't even announce any appointments. I think the problem of the Senate was with all this stuff hanging out there in the Ervin Committee.

D Well one thing, the saturation level of the American people on this story is cracking. The saturation level in this city is getting pretty high now, and they can't take too much more of this stuff.

P Think not?

D There is nothing really new coming out.

P I talked with some kid and he said I don't think that anybody incidentally would care about anybody infiltrating the peace movement that was demonstrating against the President, particularly on the War in Vietnam. Do you think so?

D No! Anyway, I don't care about that. What happened to this Texas guy that gets his money back? Was he—

D All hell broke loose for him that week. This was Allan

P No, no. Allan—

D Allan, not Duncan nor (unintelligible). All hell broke loose for Allan for this reason: He—the money apparently originally came out of a subsidiary of one of Allan's corporations down in Mexico. It went to a lawyer in Mexico who put it down as a fee billed to the subsidiary, and then the lawyer sent it back into the States, and it came back up here. But the weakness of it is that the Mexican lawyer: (1) didn't have a legitimate fee; (2) It could be corporate contribution. So Allan had personally put a note up with the corporation to cover it. Allan, meanwhile, is having problems with his wife, and a divorce is pending. And tax problems—

P (inaudible) Watergate—

D I don't know why that went in the letter. It wasn't used for Watergate. That is the interesting thing.

P It wasn't?

D No it was not. What happened is that these Mexican checks came in. They were given to Gordon Liddy, and said, "why don't you get these cashed?" Gordy Liddy, in turn, put them down to this fellow Barker in Florida, who said he could cash these Mexican checks, and put them with your Barker's bank account back in here. They could have been just as easily cashed at the Riggs Bank. There was nothing wrong with the checks. Why all the rigamarole? It is just like a lot of other things that happened over there. God knows why it was all done. It was totally unnecessary, and it was money that was not directly involved in Watergate. It wasn't a wash operation to get money back to Liddy and the like.

P Who is going to be the first witness up there?

D Sloan.

P Unfortunate.

D No doubt about it—

P He's scared?

D He's scared, he's weak. He has a compulsion to cleanse his soul by confession. We are giving him a lot of stroking. Funny thing is this fellow goes down to the Court House here before Sirica, testifies as honestly as he can testify, and Sirica looks around and called him a liar. He just said—Sloan just can't win! So Kalmbach has been dealing with Sloan. Sloan is like a child. Kalmbach has done a lot of that. The person who will have a greater problem as a result of Sloan's testimony is Kalmbach and Stans. So they are working closely with him to make sure that he settles down.

P Kalmbach will be a good witness, knowing what Kalmbach has been through.

D Kalmbach has borne up very well. In fact, I decided he may be—

P Kalmbach is somewhat embarrassed, as he is, they say lawyer for the President. Well, hell I don't need a lawyer. He and DeMarco, his other partner, handle our pay out there.

D He is sensitive on that point. He saw a transcript of a briefing where Ron was saying, "well he is really not, right nomenclature, 'personal attorney.'" Herb said, "well, gee whiz. I don't know whether Ron knows what all I do."

And I said, "well, don't worry about it."

P   What I meant is—I don't care about it, but I mean—it is just the fact that it is played that way, that he is in talking to me all the time. I don't ask him anything. I don't talk to him about anything. I don't know, I see Herb once a year when we see and sign the income tax returns.

D   That's right!

P   Now, true, he handles our San Clemente property and all the rest, but he isn't a lawyer in the sense that most people have a lawyer.

D   No, no. Although when you had an estate claim, he has some dove-tailing on it.

P   Anyway we don't want to back off of him.

D   No, he is solid.

P   He will—how does he tell his story? He has a pretty hard row to hoe—he and Stans have.

D   He will be good. Herb is the kind of guy who will check, not once nor twice, on his story—not three times —but probably fifty to a hundred times. He will go over it. He will know it. There won't be a hole in it. Probably he will do his own Q&A. He will have people cross-examine him from ten ways. He will be ready as John Mitchell will be ready, as Maury Stans will be ready.

P   Mitchell is now studying, is he?

D   He is studying. Sloan will be the worst witness. I think Magruder will be a good witness. This fellow, Bart Porter, will be a good witness. They have already been through Grand Jury. They have been through trial. They did well. And then, of course, people around here.

P   None will be witnesses.

D   They won't be witnesses?

P   Hell, no. They will make statements. That will be the line which I think we have to get across to Ziegler in all his briefings where he is constantly saying we will provide information. That is not the question. It is how it is to be furnished. We will not furnish it in a formal session. That would be a break down of the privilege. Period. Do you agree with that?

D   I agree. I agree. I have always thought that's the bottom line, and I think that is the good thing that is happening in the Gray hearings right now. If they send a letter down with specific questions, I send back written interrogatories sworn. He knows, the lawyer, that you can handle written interrogatories, where cross-examination is another ball game.

P   That's right!

D   You can make a person look like they're inaccurate even if they are trying to tell the truth.

P   Well now, really, you can't mean that! All the face-making and all that. Written interrogatories you can handle?

D   Can be artfully, accurately answered and give the full information.

P   (unintelligible)   Well, what about the sentencing: When the hell is he going to sentence?

D   We thought he was going to sentence last Friday.

P   I know he should have.

D   No one knows what in the world Sirica is doing. It is getting to be a long time now. It frankly is, and no one really has a good estimation of how he will sentence. There is some feeling that he will sentence Liddy the heaviest. Liddy is already in jail, he is in Danbury. He wants to start serving so he can get good time going. Hunt, he will probably be very fair with.

P   Why?

D   He likes Hunt—he thought Hunt was being open with him and being candid, and Hunt gave a statement in open court that he didn't know of any higher ups involved and Hunt didn't put him through the rigors of trial. Hunt was a beaten man who had lost his wife, was ill, and still they tried to move to have him severed from the trial. And Hunt did not try to cause a lot of problems. Bittman was cooperative, whereas Liddy played the heavy in the trial. His lawyer raised all the objections and the like, and embarrassed the Judge for some in-chambers things he had said.

P   But Liddy is going to appeal the sentence?

D   Liddy is going to appeal the decision, the trial. He will appeal that.

P   He will appeal the trial? He was convicted!

D   There is an outside chance that this man, this Judge, has gone so far in his zeal to be a special prosecutor—

P   Well some of those statements from the Bench—

D   Incredible statements!

P   To me, incredible!

D   Commenting on witnesses testimony before the Jury, was just incredible. Incredible! So there may be a mistrial. Or maybe reversible error.

P   What about the Cubans?

D   The Cubans will probably be thought of as hired hands, and receive nowhere near the sentence of Liddy, I would think. Not all of them. Barker, the lead Cuban, may get more than the others. It is hard to say. I just don't have any idea. Sirica is a strange man. He is known as a hanging judge.

P (unintelligible)

D That's right. He's tough. He is tough. The other thing, Sirica, there was some indication that Sirica might be putting together a panel. There is a system down there now, based on informal agreement, where a sentencing judge convenes a panel of his own to take advice from. If Sirica were being shrewd, he just might get himself a panel and take their recommendations.

P When will the Ervin thing be hitting the fan most any day, thinking from the standpoint of time?

D Well, I would say the best indications we have now is that public hearings will probably start about the first of May. Now, there will probably be a big bang of interest, initially. We have no idea how they will proceed yet. We do have sources to find that out, other than Baker. Incidentally, Kleindienst had called Ervin again, returned the call. Ervin is going to see him this week with Baker.

P Public hearings the first of May. Well it must be a big show. Public hearings. I wouldn't think though, I know from experience, my guess is that I think they could get through about three weeks of those and then I think it would begin to peter out somewhat. Don't you agree?

D No, I—

P ITT went longer, but that was a different thing, and it seemed more important.

D When I told Bob, oh, several months ago, I hope they don't think (unintelligible). He said the way they could have those hearings and do a masterful job on it, would be to hold one hearing a week on Thursdays, Thursday mornings, they cover it live. That way, you get live coverage that day; you get the networks that night; the national magazines that week; get the weekend wrapups. You can stretch this thing out by, really.

P Our members of the Committee at least should say, let's get it over with, and go through five day sessions, etc.

D Well you see, I don't think they are that perceptive. They just think they are.

P Well, so be it. I noticed in the news summary Buchanan was viewing with alarm the grave crisis in the confidency of the Presidency, etc.

D Well the best way—

P How much?

D Pardon?

P How much of a crisis? It will be—I am thinking in terms of—the point is, everything is a crisis. (expletive deleted) it is a terrible lousy thing—it will remain a crisis among the upper intellectual types, the soft heads, our own, too—Republicans—and the Democrats and the rest. Average people won't think it is much of a crisis unless it affects them. (unintelligible)

D I think it will pass. I think after the Ervin hearings, they are going to find so much—there will be some new revelations. I don't think that the thing will get out of hand. I have no reason to believe it will.

P Oh, yes—there would be new revelations.

D They would be quick (inaudible) They would want to find out who knew—

P Is there a higher up?

D Is there a higher up?

P Let's face it, I think they are really after Haldeman.

D Haldeman and Mitchell.

P Colson is not big enough name for them. He really isn't. He is, you know, he is on the government side, but Colson's name doesn't bother them so much. They are after Haldeman and after Mitchell. Don't you think so?

D Sure. They are going to take a look and try to drag them, but they're going to be able to drag them into the election—

P In any event, Haldeman's problem in Chapin isn't it?

D Bob's problem is circumstantial.

P Why is that? Let's look at the circumstantial. I don't know, Bob didn't know any of those people like the Hunts and all that bunch. Colson did, but Bob didn't. OK?

D That's right.

P Now where the hell, or how much Chapin knew I will be (expletive deleted) if I know.

D Chapin didn't know anything about the Watergate.

P Don't you think so?

D Absolutely not.

P Strachan?

D Yes.

P He knew?

D Yes.

P About the Watergate?

D Yes.

P Well, then, he probably told Bob. He may not have.

D He was judicious in what he relayed, but Strachan is as tough as nails. He can go in and stonewall, and say, "I don't know anything about what you are talking about." He has already done it twice you know, in interviews.

P I guess he should, shouldn't he? I suppose we can't call that justice, can we?

D Well, it is a personal loyalty to him. He doesn't want it any other way. He didn't have to be told. He didn't have to be asked. It just is something that he found was the way he wanted to.handle the situation.

P But he knew? He knew about Watergate? Strachan did?

D Yes.

P I will be damned! Well that is the problem in Bob's case. Not Chapin then, but Strachan. Strachan worked for him, didn't he?

D Yes. They would have one hell of a time proving that Strachan had knowledge of it, though.

P Who knew better? Magruder?

D Magruder and Liddy.

P Oh, I see. The other weak link for Bob is Magruder. He hired him et cetera.

D That applies to Mitchell, too.

P Mitchell—Magruder. Where do you see Colson coming into it? Do you think he knew quite a bit and yet, he could know quite a great deal about a lot of other things and not know a lot about this. I don't know.

D Well I have never—

P He sure as hell knows Hunt. That we know. Was very close to him.

D Chuck has told me that he had no knowledge, specific knowledge, of the Watergate before it occurred. There have been tidbits that I have raised with Chuck. I have not played any games with him. I said, "Chuck, I have indications—"

P What indications? The lawyer has to know everything.

D That's right. I said, "Chuck, people have said that you were involved in this, involved in that, involved in all of this. He said, "that is not true, etc." I think that Chuck had knowledge that something was going on over there, but he didn't have any knowledge of the details of the specifics of the whole thing.

P There must have been an indication of the fact that we had poor pickings. Because naturally anybody, either

Chuck or Bob, were always reporting to me about what was going on. If they ever got any information they would certainly have told me that we got some information, but they never had a thing to report. What was the matter? Did they never get anything out of the damn thing?

D I don't think they ever got anything, sir.

P A dry hole?

D That's right.

P (Expletive deleted)

D Well, they were just really getting started.

P Yeah. Bob one time said something to me about something, this or that or something, but I think it was something about the Convention, I think it was about the convention problems they were planning something. I assume that must have been MacGregor—not MacGregor, but Segretti.

D No, Segretti wasn't involved in the intelligence gathering piece of it at all.

P Oh, he wasn't? Who the hell was gathering intelligence?

D That was Liddy and his outfit.

P Apart from Watergate?

D That's right. Well you see Watergate was part of intelligence gathering, and this was their first thing. What happened is—

P That was such a stupid thing!

D It was incredible—that's right. That was Hunt.

P To think of Mitchell and Bob would have allowed—would have allowed—this kind of operation to be in the campaign committee!

D I don't think he knew it was there.

P I don't think that Mitchell knew about this sort of thing.

D Oh, no, no! Don't misunderstand me. I don't think that he knew the people. I think he knew that Liddy was out intelligence gathering. I don't think he knew that Liddy would use a fellow like McCord, (expletive removed), who worked for the Committee. I can't believe that.

P Hunt?

D I don't think Mitchell knew about Hunt either.

P Well Mitchell thought, well, gee, and I hired this fellow Fred Fielding who works for me. Look, he said, Magruder said to me, "will you find me a lawyer?" I said,

D Magruder says—as he did in the trial—well, of course, my name has been dragged in as the guy who sent

86

Liddy over there, which is an interesting thing. Well what happened they said is that Magruder asked—he wanted to hire my deputy over there as Deputy Counsel and I said, "No way. I can't give him up."

P Was Liddy your deputy?

D No, Liddy never worked for me. He wanted this fellow Fred Fielding who works for me. Look, he said, Magruder said to me, "will you find me a lawyer?" I said, "I will be happy to look around." I checked around the White House, Krogh said, "Liddy might be the man to do it—he would be a hell of a writer. He has written some wonderful legal opinions over here for me, and I think he is a good lawyer." So I relayed that to Magruder.

P How the hell does Liddy stand up so well?

D He's a strange man, Mr. President.

P Strange or strong?

D Strange and strong. His loyalty is—I think it is just beyond the pale. Nothing—

P He hates the other side too, doesn't he?

D Oh, absolutely! He is strong. He really is.

P Is it too late to go the hang-out road?

D Yes, I think it is. The hang out road—

P The hang-out road (inaudible).

D It was kicked around Bob and I and—

P Ehrlichman always felt it should be hang-out.

D Well, I think I convinced him why he would not want to hang-out either. There is a certain domino situation here. If some things start going, a lot of other things are going to start going, and there can be a lot of problems if everything starts falling. So there are dangers, Mr. President. I would be less than candid if I didn't tell you there are. There is a reason for not everyone going up and testifying.

P I see. Oh no, no, no! I didn't mean to have everyone go up and testify.

D Well I mean they're just starting to hang-out and say here's our story—

P I mean put the story out PR people, here is the story, the true story about Watergate.

D They would never believe it. The two things they are working on are Watergate—

P Who is "they?"

D The press, (inaudible), the intellectuals,—

P The Packwoods?

D Right—They would never buy it as far as one White House involvement in Watergate which I think there is just none for that incident which occurred at the Democratic National Headquarters. People here we just did not know that was going to be done. I think there are some people who saw the fruits of it, but that is another story. I am talking about the criminal conspiracy to go in there. The other thing is that the Segretti thing. You hang that out, and they wouldn't believe that. They wouldn't believe that Chapin acted on his own to put his old friend Segretti to be a Dick Tuck on somebody else's campaign. They would have to paint it into something more sinister, more involved, part of a general plan.

P Shows you what a master Dick Tuck is. Segretti's hasn't been a bit similar.

D They are quite humorous as a matter of fact.

P As a matter of fact, it is just a bunch of (characterization deleted). We don't object to such damn things anyway. On, and on and on. No, I tell you this it is the last gasp of our hardest opponents. They've just got to have something to squeal about it.

D It is the only thing they have to squeal—

P (Unintelligible) They are going to lie around and squeal. They are having a hard time now. They got the hell kicked out of them in the election. There is not a Watergate around in this town, not so much our opponents, even the media, but the basic thing is the establishment. The establishment is dying, and so they've got to show that despite the success we have had in foreign policy and in the election, they've got to show that it is just wrong just because of this. They are trying to use this as the whole thing.

D Well, that is why I keep coming back to this fellow Sullivan. It could change the picture.

P How could it change though? Saying here is another—

D Saying here is another and it happens to be Democrats. You know, I know I just—

P If he would get Kennedy into it, too, I would be a little bit more pleased.

D Let me tell you something that lurks at the bottom of this whole thing. If, in going after Segretti, they go after Kalmbach's bank records, you will recall sometime back—perhaps you did not know about this—I apologize. That right after Chappaquidick somebody was put up there to start observing and within six hours he was there for every second of Chappaquidick for a year, and for almost two years he worked for Jack Caulfield.

P Oh, I have heard of Caulfield.

D He worked for Caulfield when Caulfield worked for John, and then when I came over here I inherited Caulfield and this guy was still on this same thing. If they get to those bank records between the start of July of 1969 through June of 1971, they say what are these about? Who is this fellow up in New York that you paid? There comes Chappaquidick with a vengeance. This guy is a twenty year detective on the New York City Police Department.

P In other words we—

D He is ready to disprove and show that—

P (unintelligible)

D If they get to it—that is going to come out and this whole thing can turn around on that. If Kennedy knew the bear trap he was walking into—

P How do we know—why don't we get it out anyway?

D Well, we have sort of saved it.

P Does he have any records? Are they any good?

D He is probably the most knowledgeable man in the country. I think he ran up against walls and they closed the records down. There are things he can't get, but he can ask all of the questions and get many of the answers as a 20 year detective, but we don't want to surface him right now. But if he is ever surfaced, this is what they will get.

P How will Kalmbach explain that he hired this guy to do the job on Chappaquidick? Out of what type of funds?

D He had money left over from the pre-convention—

P Are they going to investigate those funds too?

D They are funds that are quite legal. There is nothing illegal about those funds. Regardless of what may happen, what may occur, they may stumble into this in going back to, say 1971, in Kalmbach's bank records. They have already asked for a lot of his bank records in connection with Segretti, as to how he paid Segretti.

P Are they going to go back as far as Chappaquidick?

D Well this fellow worked in 1971 on this. He was up there. He has talked to everybody in that town. He is the one who has caused a lot of embarrassment for Kennedy already by saying he went up there as a newspaperman, by saying; "Why aren't you checking this? Why aren't you

89

looking there?" Calling the press people's attention to things. Gosh, the guy did a masterful job. I have never had the full report.

P   Coming back to the Sullivan thing, you will now talk to Moore and then what?

D   I will see if we have something that is viable. And if it's—

P   You plan to talk with him again.

D   Yes he asked me last night to give him a day or so to get all his recollections together, and that was yesterday. So I thought I would call him this evening and say, "Bill, I would just like to know—"

P   You see, right after you talk to him it will become known. So maybe the best thing to say is that he is to turn this over and be maligned. But anyway, the Committee is going to say the White House turned over information on the FBI. I don't know how the (expletive deleted) we get it down there?

D   I think I can kick it around with Dick Moore. He and I do very well just bouncing these things back and forth and coming up with something. We would never be embarrassed about it.

P   To give it to a newsman, it would be a hell of a break for a newspaper, a hell of a story! The STAR just run a whole story on a real bomb on the FBI. Then the Committee member, the man you would use, for example, in this case would be to call Gurney, and to say, "Look! We are on to something very hot here. I can't tell you any more. Go after it, you'll get your other end this fall." Then he goes. It seems to me that's a very effective way to get it out.

D   Uh huh. It seems to me that I don't think Sullivan would give up the White House. Sullivan—if I have one liability in Sullivan here, it is his knowledge of the earlier (unintelligible) that occurred here.

P   That we did?

D   That we did.

P   Well, why don't you just tell him—he could say, "I did no political work at all. My work in the Nixon Administration was solely in the national security." And that is thoroughly true!

D   That is true.

P   Well, good luck.

D   Thank you, sir.

P   It is never dull is it?

D   Never.

Meeting: The President and Dean,
Oval Office, March 17, 1973.
(1:25 - 2:10 pm)

(Material relating to breakin at Dr. Fielding's office in California)

P Now on the Segretti thing, I think you've just got to—Chapin, all of them have just got to take the heat. Look, you've got to admit the facts, John, and—

D That's right.

P And that's our—and that's that. And Kalmbach paid him. And (unintelligible) a lot of people. I just think on Segretti, no matter how bad it is. It isn't nearly as bad as people think it was. Espionage, sabotage?

D The intent, when Segretti was hired, was nothing evil nothing vicious, nothing bad, nothing. Not espionage, not sabotage. It was pranksterism that got out of hand and we know that. And I think we can lay our story out there. I have no problem with the Segretti thing. It's just not that serious. The other potential problem is Ehrlichman's and this is—

P In connection with Hunt?

D In connection with Hunt and Liddy both.

P They worked for him?

D They—these fellows had to be some idiots as we've learned after the fact. They went out and went into Dr. Ellsberg's doctor's office and they had, they were geared up with all this CIA equipment—cameras and the like. Well they turned the stuff back in to the CIA some point in time and left film in the camera. CIA has not put this together, and they don't know what it all means right now. But it wouldn't take a very sharp investigator very long because you've got pictures in the CIA files that they had to turn over to (unintelligible).

P What in the world—what in the name of God was Ehrlichman having something (unintelligible) in the Ellsberg (unintelligible)?

D They were trying to—this was a part of an operation that—in connection with the Pentagon papers. They were—the whole thing—they wanted to get Ellsberg's psychiatric records for some reason. I don't know.

P This is the first I ever heard of this. I, I (unintelligible) care about Ellsberg was not our problem.

D   That's right.

P   (Expletive deleted)

D   Well, anyway, (unintelligible) it was under an Ehrlichman structure, maybe John didn't ever know. I've never asked him if he knew. I didn't want to know.

P   I can't see that getting into, into this hearing.

D   Well, look. No. Here's the way it can come up.

P   Yeah.

D   In the CIA's files which they—which the Committee is asking for—the material they turned over to the Department of Justice.

P   Yeah.

D   There are all the materials relating to Hunt. In there are these pictures which the CIA developed and they've got Gordon Liddy standing proud as punch outside this doctor's office with his name on it. And (unintelligible) this material it's not going to take very long for an investigator to go back and say, well, why would this—somebody be at the doctor's office and they'd find out that there was a breakin at the doctor's office and then you'd find Liddy on the staff and then you'd start working it back. I don't think they'll ever reach that point.

P   (Unintelligible?)

D   This was way, this was—

P   It's irrelevant.

D   It's irrelevant. Right.

P   That's the point. That's where—that's where—where Ervin's rules of relevancy (unintelligible). Now what the hell has this got to do with it?

D   It has nothing as a lot of these things that they should stumble along into is irrelevant.

Telephone conversation: The President and Dean, March 20, 1973. (7:29 - 7:43 pm)

P   John Dean, please.

Opr   Yes, Mr. President.

P   Hello.

D   Yes, Sir.

P   You are having rather long days these days, aren't you? I guess we all have.

D   I think they will continue to be longer.

D   The other witness they have now subpoenaed - there are two other witnesses - there is a Hoback girl from the Re-Election Committee - she was interrogated by Committee staff and counsel as a result of her confidential interviews with the FBI.

P   Hmph.

D   Alleging that that had been leaked by me to them and then, of course, that was not true.

P   That's not true.

D   And the other fellow they are calling is a fellow by the name of Thomas Lombard who is trying to establish a link between Dean on that one. Lombard did volunteer work for me in my office and did volunteer work for Liddy and at one time he saw Liddy in my office. Big deal. It was purely campaign, you know.

P   Well, is that what Lombard will testify to, or will he testify to -

D   Well he has written a very lengthy letter to the Committee declining to testify originally and saying this is all I would have to say and it is probably not relevant. I know nothing of Dean and Liddy's connection.

P   Right.

D   Other than the fact that they—

P   That's not bad then - maybe he will make a pretty good witness.

D   He might. He might.

P   What about the Hoback girl?

D   The Hoback girl should be broken down. She should come out in tears as a result of the fact that she is virtually lying about one thing and our people will be on the—

P   You mean—do our people know what to ask her?

D   Yes they do. Yes they do.

P   Uh, huh. Why is she doing it? Do we know?

D   She - ah—

P   Disgruntled? Somebody -

D   Disgruntled. She has been fairly disgruntled all along. She is a Democrat that worked over there in the Finance Committee. She professes a personal loyalty to Maury Stans but that is about the extent of it, any, of her loyalty.

P   Yeah.

D   I never have figured out how she got in there.

P They didn't bite the bullet with regard to subpoenaing you?

D No. I don't think there is any chance they are going to do that.

P That's rather interesting isn't it? Something ought to be made of that.

D Unless they get—they are taking more evidence on me. Obviously with these other two witnesses, not that I think anything will come out of this. It will just be more—I had a conversation with John Ehrlichman this afternoon before he came down to visit you. I think that one thing that we have to continue to do, and particularly right now, is to examine the broadest, broadest implications of this whole thing, and, you know, maybe about 30 minutes of just my recitation to you of facts so that you operate from the same facts that everybody else has.

P Right.

D I don't think—We have never really done that. It has been sort of bits and pieces. Just paint the whole picture for you, the soft spots, the potential problem areas

P Uh huh.

D and the like so that when you make judgments you will have all that information.

P Would you like to do that—when?

D I would think, if its not inconvenient for you, sir, I would like to sort of draw all my thoughts together and have a—just make some notes to myself so I didn't—

P Could you do it tomorrow?

D Yes, Sir. Yes, Sir.

P Uh, huh. Well, then we could probably do it, say, around ten o'clock.

D That would be fine, sir.

P Do you just want to do it alone? Want anybody else there?

D I think just—

P It is better with nobody else there, isn't it?

D Absolutely.

P Anybody else they are all partisan interest virtually.

D That's right.

P Right. Fine. The other thing I was going to say just is this—just for your own thinking—I still want to see, though I guess you and Dick are still working on your letter and all that sort of thing?

D We are and we are coming to—the more we work

on it the more questions we see—

P That you don't want to answer, huh?

D That brings problems by answering.

P And so you are coming up, then, with the idea of just a stonewall then? Is that—

D That's right.

P Is that what you come down with?

D Stonewall, with lots of noises that we are always willing to cooperate, but no one is asking us for anything.

P And they never will, huh? There is no way that you could make even a general statement that I could put out? You understand what I—

D I think we could.

P See, for example, I was even thinking if you could even talk to Cabinet, the leaders, you know, just orally and say, "I have looked into this, and this is that," so that people get sort of a feeling that—your own people have got to be reassured.

D Uh, huh.

P Could you do that?

D Well, I think I can but I don't think you would want to make that decision until we have about a—

P No, I want to know. I want to know where all the bodies are first.

D And then, once you decide after that, we can program it any way you want to do it.

P Yeah. Because I think, for example, you could do it orally, even if you don't want to make the written statement. You could do it orally before the Cabinet, the leaders and the rest. Lay it all out. You see, I would not be present. You just lay it all out and I just—See what I mean?

D Uh, huh.

P Now that is one thing. The other thing is that I do think there is something to be said for not maybe this complete answer to this fellow, but maybe just a statement to me. My versions are these: bing, bing, bing. That is a possibility.

D Uh, huh.

P What I mean is we need something to answer somebody, answer things, you know they say, "What are you basing this on," I can say, "Well, my counsel has advised me that"—Is that possible or not, or are—

D Well, you know there is that—and there is always the FBI report which we have probably not relied upon enough. There is not one scintilla of evidence.

P   I know. But I mean, can't you say that? Or do you want to put it out?

D   Ah, it could be said, and it is something we haven't really emphasized. Pat Gray is the only person who has said it and it has really never gotten picked up.

P   How would you do it then? What I meant, isn't that something that you could say? Do you want to publish the FBI report?

D   Oh, no, because at our own strictures we are trying to place an up - right—

P   But you could say, "I have this and this is that." Fine. See what I am getting at is that, if apart from a statement to the Committee or anything else, if you could just make a statement to me that we can use. You know, for internal purposes and to answer questions, etc.

D   As we did when you, back in August, made the statement that—

P   That's right.

D   And all the things—

P   You've got to have something where it doesn't appear that I am doing this in, you know, just in a—saying to hell with the Congress and to hell with the people, we are not going to tell you anything because of Executive Privilege. That, they don't understand. But if you say, "No, we are willing to cooperate," and you've made a complete statement, but make it very incomplete. See, that is what I mean. I don't want a, too much in chapter and verse as you did in your letter, I just want just a general—

D   An all around statement.

P   That's right. Try just something general. Like "I have checked into this matter; I can categorically, based on my investigation, the following: Haldeman is not involved in this, that and the other thing. Mr. Colson did not do this; Mr. so and so did not do this. Mr. Blank did not do this." Right down the line, taking the most glaring things. If there are any further questions, please let me know. See?

D   Uh, huh. I think we can do that.

P   That is one possibility, and then you could say that such things—and then use the FBI report to the Cabinet and to the leaders. It might just be very salutary. You see our own people have got to have confidence or they are not going to step up and defend us. You see our problem there, don't you?

D   And I think at the same time it would be good to brief these people on what Executive Privilege means, so they can go out and speak about it. Some of them are floundering.

P   And why it is necessary.

D   I thought about having someone prepare some material that can be put out by the Congressional people so they can understand, people can understand. It is tremendous to have a piece of paper that they know they can talk from.

P   Pointing out that you are defending the Constitution; responsibility of the separation of powers; and we have to do it. Distinguishing the Adam's case; ignoring Flanigan, which is one we should never have agreed to, but nevertheless—Anyway let's think a little about that, but we'll see you at ten o'clock tomorrow.

D   Yes, Sir.

P   Fine.

D   Alright, sir. Good night.

P   Take the evening off.

D   Alright.

Meeting: The President, Dean and Haldeman, Oval Office, March 21, 1973. (10:12 - 11:55 am)

P   Well, sit down, sit down.

D   Good morning.

P   Well what is the Dean summary of the day about?

D   John caught me on the way out and asked me about why Gray was holding back on information, if that was under instructions from us. And it was and it wasn't. It was instructions proposed by the Attorney General, consistent with your press conference statement that no further raw data was to be turned over to the full committee. And that was the extent of it. And then Gray, himself, who reached the conclusion that no more information should be turned over, that he had turned over enough. So this again is Pat Gray making decisions on his own on how to handle his hearings. He has been totally (unintelligible) to take any guidance, any instruction. We don't know what he is going to do. He is not going to talk about it. He won't review it, and I don't think he does it to harm you in any way, sir.

P   No, he is just quite stubborn and also he isn't very smart. You know—

D   He is bullheaded.

P   He is smart in his own way but he's got that typical (expletive deleted) this is right and I am going to do it.

D   That's why he thinks he is going to be confirmed. He is being his own man. He is being forthright and honest. He feels he has turned over too much and so it is conscious decision that he is harming the Bureau by doing this and so he is not going to.

P   We have to get the boys off the line that this is because the White House told him to do this and everything. And also, as I told Ehrlichman, I don't see why our little boys can't make something out of the fact that (expletive deleted) this is the only responsible position that could possibly be made. The FBI cannot turn over raw files. Has anybody made that point? I have tried to several times.

D   Sam Ervin has made that point himself. In fact, in reading the transcript of Gray's hearings, Ervin tried to hold Gray back from doing what he was doing at the time he did it. I thought it was very unwise. I don't think that anyone is criticizing your position on it.

P   Let's make a point that raw files, I mean that point should be made that we are standing for the rights of innocent individuals. The American Civil Liberties Union is against it. We are against it. Hoover had the tradition, and it will continue to be the tradition. All files are confidential. See if we can't get someone inspired to put that out. Let them see what is in one.

D   (expletive deleted) You—

P   Any further word on Sullivan? Is he still—

D   Yes, he is going to be over to see me today, this morning someplace, sometime.

P   As soon as you get that, I will be available to talk to you this afternoon. I will be busy until about one o'clock. Anytime you are through I would like to see what it is he has. We've got something but I would like to see what it is.

D   The reason that I thought we ought to talk this morning is because in our conversations, I have the impression that you don't know everything I know and it makes it very difficult for you to make judgments that only you can make on some of these things and I thought that—

P   In other words, I have to know why you feel that we shouldn't unravel something?

D   Let me give you my overall first.

P   In other words, your judgment as to where it stands, and where we will go.

D   I think that there is no doubt about the seriousness of the problem we've got. We have a cancer within, close to the Presidency, that is growing. It is growing daily. It's compounded, growing geometrically now, because it compounds itself. That will be clear if I, you know, explain some of the details of why it is. Basically, it is because (1) we are being blackmailed; (2) People are going to start perjuring themselves very quickly that have not had to perjure themselves to protect other people in the line. And there is no assurance—

P   That that won't bust?

D   That that won't bust. So let me give you the sort of basic facts, talking first about the Watergate; and then about Segretti; and then about some of the peripheral items that have come up. First of all on the Watergate: how did it all start, where did it start? O.K! It started with an instruction to me from Bob Haldeman to see if we couldn't set up a perfectly legitimate campaign intelligence operation over at the Re-Election Committee. Not being in this business, I turned to somebody who had been in this business, Jack Caulfield. I don't remember whether you remember Jack or not. He was your original bodyguard before they had the candidate protection, an old city policeman.

P   Yes, I know him.

D   Jack worked for John and then was transferred to my office. I said Jack come up with a plan that, you know—a normal infiltration, buying information from secretaries and all that sort of thing. He did, he put together a plan. It was kicked around. I went to Ehrlichman with it. I went to Mitchell with it, and the consensus was that Caulfield was not the man to do this. In retrospect, that might have been a bad call because he is an incredibly cautious person and wouldn't have put the situation where it is today. After rejecting that, they said we still need something so I was told to look around for someone who could go over to 1701 and do this. That is when I came up with Gordon Liddy. They needed a lawyer. Gordon had an intelligence background from his FBI service. I was aware of the fact that he had done some extremely sensitive things for the White House while he had been at the White House and he had apparently done them well. Going out into Ellsberg's doctor's office—

P   Oh, yeah.

D   And things like this. He worked with leaks. He tracked these things down. So the report that I got from Krogh was that he was a hell of a good man and not only that a good lawyer and could set up a proper operation. So we talked to Liddy. He was interested in doing it. I took Liddy over to meet Mitchell. Mitchell thought highly of him because Mitchell was partly involved in his coming to the White House to work for Krogh. Liddy had been at Treasury before that. Then Liddy was told to put together his plan, you know, how he would run an intelligence operation. This was after he was hired over there at the Committee. Magruder called me in January and said I would like to have you come over and see Liddy's plan.

P   January of '72?

D   January of '72.

D   "You come over to Mitchell's office and sit in a meeting where Liddy is going to lay his plan out." I said I don't really know if I am the man, but if you want me there I will be happy to. So I came over and Liddy laid out a million dollar plan that was the most incredible thing I have ever laid my eyes on: all in codes, and involved black bag operations, kidnapping, providing prostitutes to weaken the opposition, bugging, mugging teams. It was just an incredible thing.

P   Tell me this: Did Mitchell go along—?

D   No, no, not at all, Mitchell just sat there puffing and laughing. I could tell from—after Liddy left the office I said that is the most incredible thing I have ever seen. He said I agree. And so Liddy was told to go back to the drawingboard and come up with something realistic. So there was a second meeting. They asked me to come over to that. I came into the tail end of the meeting. I wasn't there for the first part. I don't know how long the meeting lasted. At this point, they were discussing again bugging, kidnapping and the like. At this point I said right in front of everybody, very clearly, I said, "These are not the sort of things (1) that are ever to be discussed in the office of the Attorney General of the United States—that was where he still was—and I am personally incensed." And I am trying to get Mitchell off the hook. He is a nice person and doesn't like to have to say no when he is talking with people he is going to have to work with.

P   That's right.

D   So I let it be known. I said "You all pack that stuff up and get it the hell out of here. You just can't talk this way in this office and you should re-examine your whole thinking."

P   Who all was present?

D   It was Magruder, Mitchell, Liddy and myself. I came back right after the meeting and told Bob, "Bob, we have a growing disaster on our hands if they are thinking this way," and I said, "The White House has got to stay out of this and I, frankly, am not going to be involved in it." He said, "I agree John." I thought at that point that the thing was turned off. That is the last I heard of it and I thought it was turned off because it was an absurd proposal.

P   Yeah.

D   Liddy—I did have dealings with him afterwards and we never talked about it. Now that would be hard to believe for some people, but we never did. That is the fact of the matter.

P   Well, you were talking with him about other things.

D   We had so many other things.

P   He had some legal problems too. But you were his advisor, and I understand you had conversations about the campaign laws, etc. Haldeman told me that you were handling all of that for us. Go ahead.

D   Now. So Liddy went back after that and was over at 1701, the Committee, and this is where I come into having put the pieces together after the fact as to what I can put together about what happened. Liddy sat over there and tried to come up with another plan that he could sell. (1) They were talking to him, telling him that he was putting too much money in it. I don't think they were discounting the illegal points. Jeb is not a lawyer. He did not know whether this is the way the game was played and what it was all about. They came up, apparently, with another plan, but they couldn't get it approved by anybody over there. So Liddy and Hunt apparently came to see Chuck Colson, and Chuck Colson picked up the telephone and called Magruder and said, "You all either fish or cut bait. This is absurd to have these guys over there and not using them. If you are not going to use them, I may use them." Things of this nature.

P   When was this?

D   This was apparently in February of '72.

P   Did Colson know what they were talking about?

D   I can only assume, because of his close relationship with Hunt, that he had a damn good idea what they were talking about, a damn good idea. He would probably deny it today and probably get away with denying it. But I still—unless Hunt blows on him—

P   But then Hunt isn't enough. It takes two doesn't it?

D   Probably. Probably. But Liddy was there also and if Liddy were to blow—

P   Then you have a problem—I was saying as to the criminal liability in the White House.

D   I will go back over that, and take out any of the soft spots.

P   Colson, you think was the person who pushed?

D   I think he helped to get the thing off the dime. Now something else occurred though—

P   Did Colson—had he talked to anybody here?

D   No. I think this was—

P   Did he talk with Haldeman?

D   No, I don't think so. But here is the next thing that comes in the chain. I think Bob was assuming, that they had something that was proper over there, some intelligence gathering operation that Liddy was operating. And through Strachan, who was his tickler, he started pushing them to get some information and they—Magruder—took that as a signal to probably go to Mitchell and to say, "They are pushing us like crazy for this from the White House. And so Mitchell probably puffed on his pipe and said, "Go ahead," and never really reflected on what it was all about. So they had some plan that obviously had, I gather, different targets they were going to go after. They were going to infiltrate, and bug, and do all this sort of thing to a lot of these targets. This is knowledge I have after the fact. Apparently after they had initially broken in and bugged the DNC they were getting information. The information was coming over here to Strachan and some of it was given to Haldeman, there is no doubt about it.

P   Did he know where it was coming from?

D   I don't really know if he would.

P   Not necessarily?

D   Not necessarily. Strachan knew it. There is no doubt about it, and whether Strachan—I have never come to press these people on these points because it hurts them to give up that next inch, so I had to piece things together. Strachan was aware of receiving information, reporting to Bob. At one point Bob even gave instructions to change their capabilities from Muskie to McGovern, and passed this back through Strachan to Magruder and apparently to Liddy. And Liddy was starting to make arrangements to go in and bug the McGovern operation.

P   They had never bugged Muskie, though, did they?

D   No, they hadn't, but they had infiltrated it by a secretary.

P   By a secretary?

D   By a secretary and a chauffeur. There is nothing illegal about that. So the information was coming over here and then I, finally, after—. The next point in time that I became aware of anything was on June 17th when I got the word that there had been this break in at the DNC and somebody from our Committee had been caught in the DNC. And I said, "Oh, (expletive deleted)." You know, eventually putting the pieces together—

P   You knew what it was.

D   I knew who it was. So I called Liddy on Monday morning and said, "First, Gordon, I want to know whether anybody in the White House was involved in this." And he said, "No, they weren't." I said, "Well I want to know how in (adjective deleted) name this happened." He said, "Well, I was pushed without mercy by Magruder to get in there and to get more information. That the information was not satisfactory. That Magruder said, 'The White House is not happy with what we are getting.' "

P   The White House?

D   The White House. Yeah!

P   Who do you think was pushing him?

D   Well, I think it was probably Strachan thinking that Bob wanted things, because I have seen that happen on other occasions where things have said to have been of very prime importance when they really weren't.

P   Why at that point in time I wonder? I am just trying to think. We had just finished the Moscow trip. The Democrats had just nominated McGovern. I mean, (expletive, deleted), what in the hell were these people doing? I can see their doing it earlier. I can see the pressures, but I don't see why all the pressure was on then.

D   I don't know, other than the fact that they might have been looking for information about the conventions.

P   That's right.

D   Because, I understand that after the fact that there was a plan to bug Larry O'Brien's suite down in Florida. So Liddy told me that this is what had happened and this is why it had happened.

P   Where did he learn that there were plans to bug Larry O'Brien's suite?

D   From Magruder, long after the fact.

P   Magruder is (unintelligible)

D   Yeah. Magruder is totally knowledgeable on the whole thing.

P   Yeah.

D   Alright now, we have gone through the trial. I don't know if Mitchell has perjured himself in the Grand Jury or not.

P   Who?

D   Mitchell. I don't know how much knowledge he actually had. I know that Magruder has perjured himself in the Grand Jury. I know that Porter has perjured himself in the Grand Jury.

P   Who is Porter? (unintelligible)

D   He is one of Magruder's deputies. They set up this scenario which they ran by me. They said, "How about this?" I said, "I don't know. If this is what you are going to hang on, fine."

P   What did they say in the Grand Jury?

D   They said, as they said before the trial in the Grand Jury, that Liddy had come over as Counsel and we knew he had these capacities to do legitimate intelligence. We had no idea what he was doing. He was given an authorization of $250,000 to collect information, because our surrogates were out on the road. They had no protection, and we had information that there were going to be demonstrations against them, and that we had to have a plan as to what liabilities they were going to be confronted with and Liddy was charged with doing this. We had no knowledge that he was going to bug the DNC.

P   The point is, that is not true?

D   That's right.

P   Magruder did know it was going to take place?

D   Magruder gave the instructions to be back in the DNC.

P   He did?

D   Yes.

P   You know that?

D   Yes.

P   I see. O.K.

D   I honestly believe that no one over here knew that. I know that as God is my maker, I had no knowledge that they were going to do this.

P   Bob didn't either, or wouldn't have known that either. You are not the issue involved. Had Bob known, he would be.

D   Bob—I don't believe specifically knew that they were going in there.

P   I don't think so.

D   I don't think he did. I think he knew that there was a capacity to do this but he was not given the specific direction.

P   Did Strachan know?

D   I think Strachan did know.

P   (unintelligible) Going back into the DNC—Hunt, etc.—this is not understandable.

D   So—those people are in trouble as a result of the Grand Jury and the trial. Mitchell, of course, was never called during the trial. Now—

P   Mitchell has given a sworn statement, hasn't he?

D   Yes, Sir.

P   To the Jury?

D   To the Grand Jury.—

P   You mean the Goldberg arrangement?

D   We had an arrangement whereby he went down with several of them, because of the heat of this thing and the implications on the election, we made an arrangement where they could quietly go into the Department of Justice and have one of the assistant U.S. Attorneys take their testimony and then read it before the Grand Jury.

P   I thought Mitchell went.

D   That's right, Mitchell was actually called before the Grand Jury. The Grand Jury would not settle for less, because the jurors wanted him.

P   And he went?

D   And he went.

P   Good!

D   I don't know what he said. I have never seen a transcript of the Grand Jury. Now what has happened post June 17? I was under pretty clear instructions not to investigate this, but this could have been disastrous on the electorate if all hell had broken loose. I worked on a theory of containment—

P   Sure.

D   To try to hold it right where it was.

P   Right.

D   There is no doubt that I was totally aware of what the Bureau was doing at all times. I was totally aware of what the Grand Jury was doing. I knew what witnesses were going to be called. I knew what they were asked, and I had to.

P   Why did Peterson play the game so straight with us?

D   Because Peterson is a soldier. He kept me informed. He told me when we had problems, where we had problems and the like. He believes in you and he believes in this Administration. This Administration has made him. I don't think he has done anything improper, but he did make sure that the investigation was narrowed down to the very, very fine criminal thing which was a break for us. There is no doubt about it.

P   Do you honestly feel that he did an adequate job?

D   They ran that investigation out to the fullest extend they could follow a lead and that was it.

P   But the way point is, where I suppose he could be criticized for not doing an adequate job. Why didn't he call Haldeman? Why didn't he get a statement from Colson? Oh, they did get Colson!

D   That's right. But as based on their FBI interviews, there was no reason to follow up. There were no leads there. Colson said, "I have no nowledge of this" to the FBI. Strachan said, "I have no knowledge." They didn't ask Strachan any questions about Watergate. They asked him about Segretti. They said, "what is your connection with Liddy?" Strachan just said, "Well, I met him over there." They never really pressed him. Strachan appeared, as a result of some coaching, to be the dumbest paper pusher in the bowels of the White House.

P   I understand.

D   Alright. Now post June 17th: These guys immediately—It is very interesting. (Dean sort of chuckled) Liddy, for example, on the Friday before—I guess it was on the 15th, no, the 16th of June—had been in Henry Peterson's office with another member of my staff on campaign compliance problems. After the incident, he ran Kleindienst down at Burning Tree Country Club and told him "you've got to get my men out of jail." Kleindienst said, "You get the hell out of here, kid. Whatever you have to say, just say to somebody else. Don't bother me." But this has never come up. Liddy said if they all got counsel instantly and said we will ride this thing out. Alright, then they started making demands. "We have to have attorneys fees. We don't have any money ourselves, and you are asking us to take this through the election." Alright, so arrangements were made through Mitchell, initiating it. And I was present in discussions where these guys had to be taken care of. Their attorneys fees had to be done. Kalmbach was brought in. Kalmbach raised some cash.

P They put that under the cover of a Cuban Committee, I suppose?

D Well, they had a Cuban Committee and they had—some of it was given to Hunt's lawyer, who in turn passed it out. You know, when Hunt's wife was flying to Chicago with $10,000 she was actually, I understand after the fact now, was going to pass that money to one of the Cubans—to meet him in Chicago and pass it to somebody there.

P (unintelligible) but I would certainly keep that cover for whatever it is worth.

D That's the most troublesome post-thing because (1) Bob is involved in that; (2) John is involved in that; (3) I am involved in that; (4) Mitchell is involved in that. And that is an obstruction of justice.

P In other words the bad it does. You were taking care of witnesses. How did Bob get in it?

D Well, they ran out of money over there. Bob had $350,000 in a safe over here that was really set aside for polling purposes. And there was no other source of money, so they came over and said you all have got to give us some money. I had to go to Bob and say, "Bob, they need some money over there." He said "What for." So I had to tell him what it was for because he wasn't just about to send money over there willy-nilly. And John was involved in those discussions. And then we decided there was no price too high to pay to let this thing blow up in front of the election.

P I think we should be able to handle that issue pretty well. May be some lawsuits.

D I think we can too. Here is what is happening right now. What sort of brings matters to the (unintelligible). One, this is going to be a continual blackmail operation by Hunt and Liddy and the Cubans. No doubt about it. And McCord, who is another one involved. McCord has asked for nothing. McCord did ask to meet with somebody, with Jack Caulfield who is his old friend who had gotten him hired over there. And when Caulfield had him hired, he was a perfectly legitimate security man. And he wanted to talk about commutation, and things like that. And as you know Colson has talked indirectly to Hunt about commutation. All of these things are bad, in that they are problems, they are promises, they are commitments. They are the very sort of thing that the Senate is

107

going to be looking most for. I don't think they can find them, frankly.

P   Pretty hard.

D   Pretty hard. Damn hard. It's all cash.

P   Pretty hard I mean as far as the witnesses are concerned.

D   Alright, now, the blackmail is continuing. Hunt called one of the lawyers from the Re-Election Committee on last Friday to leave it with him over the weekend. The guy came in to see me to give a message directly to me. From Hunt to me.

P   Is Hunt out on bail?

D   Pardon?

P   Is Hunt on bail?

D   Hunt is on bail. Correct. Hunt now is demanding another $72,000 for his own personal expenses; another $50,000 to pay attorneys fees: $120,000. Some (1) he wanted it as of the close of business yesterday. He said, "I am going to be sentenced on Friday, and I've got to get my financial affairs in order." I told this fellow O'Brien, "If you want money, you came to the wrong man, fellow. I am not involved in the money. I don't know a thing about it. I can't help you. You better scramble about elsewhere." O'Brien is a ball player. He carried tremendous water for us.

P   He isn't Hunt's lawyer?

D   No he is our lawyer at the Re-Election Committee.

P   I see.

D   So he is safe. There is no problem there. So it raises the whole question. Hunt has now made a direct threat against Ehrlichman. As a result of this, this is his blackmail. He says, "I will bring John Ehrlichman down to his knees and put him in jail. I have done enough seamy things for he and Krogh. they'll never survive it."

P   Was he talking about Ellsberg?

D   Ellsberg, and apparently some other things. I don't know the full extent of it.

P   I don't know about anything else.

D   I don't know either, and I hate to learn some of these things. So that is that situation. Now, where are at the soft points? How many people know about this? Well, let me go one step further in this whole thing. The Cubans that were used in the Watergate were also the same Cubans that Hunt and Liddy used for this California Ellsberg thing, for the break in out there. So they are aware of that. How high their knowledge is, is something else. Hunt and Liddy, of course, are totally aware of it, of the fact that it is right out of the White House.

P   I don't know what the hell we did that for!

D   I don't know either.

P   What in the (expletive deleted) caused this? (unintelligible)

D   Mr. President, there have been a couple of things around here that I have gotten wind of. At one time there was a desire to do a second story job on the Brookings Institute where they had the Pentagon papers. Now I flew to California because I was told that John had instructed it and he said, "I really hadn't. It is a mis-impression, but for (expletive deleted), turn it off." So I did. I came back and turned it off. The risk is minimal and the pain is fantastic. It is something with a (unintelligible) risk and no gain. It is just not worth it. But—who knows about all this now? You've got the Cubans' lawyer, a man by the name of Rothblatt, who is a no good, publicity seeking (characterization deleted), to be very frank with you. He has had to be pruned down and tuned off. He was canned by his own people because they didn't trust him. He didn't want them to plead guilty. He wants to represent them before the Senate. So F. Lee Bailey, who was a partner of one of the men representing McCord, got in and cooled Rothblatt down. So that means that F. Lee Bailey has knowledge. Hunt's lawyer, a man by the name of Bittmann, who is an excellent criminal lawyer from the Democratic era of Bobby Kennedy, he's got knowledge.

P   He's got some knowledge?

D   Well, all the direct knowledge that Hunt and Liddy have, as well as all the hearsay they have. You have these two lawyers over at the Re-Election Committee who did an investigation to find out the facts. Slowly, they got the whole picture. They are solid.

P   But they know?

D   But they know. You've got, then an awful lot of the principals involved who know. Some people's wives know. Mrs. Hunt was the savviest woman in the world. She had the whole picture together.

P   Did she?

D   Yes. Apparently, she was the pillar of strength in that family before the death.

P   Great sadness. As a matter of fact, there was a discussion with somebody about Hunt's problem on account of his wife and I said, of course commutation could be considered on the basis of his wife's death, and that is the

109

only conversation I ever had in that light.

D   Right.

D   So that is it. That is the extent of the knowledge. So where are the soft spots on this? Well, first of all, there is the problem of the continued blackmail which will not only go on now, but it will go on while these people are in prison, and it will compound the obstruction of justice situation. It will cost money. It is dangerous. People around here are not pros at this sort of thing. This is the sort of thing Mafia people can do: washing money, getting clean money, and things like that. We just don't know about those things, because we are not criminals and not used to dealing in that business.

P   That's right.

D   It is a tough thing to know how to do.

P   Maybe it takes a gang to do that.

D   That's right. There is a real problem as to whether we could even do it. Plus there is a real problem in raising money. Mitchell has been working on raising some money. He is one of the ones with the most to lose. But there is no denying the fact that the White House, in Ehrlichman, Haldeman and Dean are involved in some of the early money decisions.

P   How much money do you need?

D   I would say these people are going to cost a million dollars over the next two years.

P   We could get that. On the money, if you need the money you could get that. You could get a million dollars. You could get it in cash. I know where it could be gotten. It is not easy, but it could be done. But the question is who the hell would handle it? Any ideas on that?

D   That's right. Well, I think that is something that Mitchell ought to be charged with.

P   I would think so too.

D   And get some pros to help him.

P   Let me say there shouldn't be a lot of people running around getting money—

D   Well he's got one person doing it who I am not sure is—

P   Who is that?

D   He has Fred LaRue doing it. Now Fred started out going out trying to solicit money from all kinds of people.

P   No!

D   I had learned about it, and I said, "(expletive deleted) It is just awful! Don't do it!" People are going to

110

ask what the money is for. He has apparently talked to Tom Pappas.

P   I know.

D   And Pappas has agreed to come up with a sizeable amount, I gather.

P   What do you think? You don't need a million right away, but you need a million? Is that right?

D   That is right.

P   You need it in cash don't you? I am just thinking out loud here for a moment. Would you put that through the Cuban Committee:

D   No.

P   It is going to be checks, cash money, etc. How if that ever comes out, are you going to handle it? Is the Cuban Committee an obstruction of justice, if they want to help?

D   Well they have priests in it.

P   Would that give a little bit of a cover?

D   That would give some for the Cubans and possibly Hunt. Then you've got Liddy. McCord is not accepting any money. So he is not a bought man right now.

P   OK. Go ahead.

D   Let me continue a little bit right here now. When I say this is a growing cancer, I say it for reasons like this. Bud Krogh, in his testimony before the Grand Jury, was forced to perjure himself. He is haunted by it. Bud said, "I have not had a pleasant day on my job." He said, "I told my wife all about this. The curtain may ring down one of these days, and I may have to face the music, which I am perfectly willing to do."

P   What did he perjure himself on, John?

D   Did he know the Cubans. He did.

P   He said he didn't?

D   That is right. They didn't press him hard.

P   He might be able to—I am just trying to think. Perjury is an awful hard rap to prove. If he could just say that I—Well, go ahead.

D   Well, so that is one perjury. Mitchell and Magruder are potential perjurers. There is always the possibility of any one of these individuals blowing. Hunt. Liddy. Liddy is in jail right now, serving his time and having a good time right now. I think Liddy in his own bizarre way the strongest of all of them. So there is that possibility.

P   Your major guy to keep under control is Hunt?

D   That is right.

P   I think. Does he know a lot?

D   He knows so much. He could sink Chuck Colson. Apparently he is quite distressed with Colson. He thinks Colson has abandoned him. Colson was to meet with him when he was out there after, you know, he had left the White House. He met with him through his lawyer. Hunt raised the question he wanted money. Colson's lawyer told him Colson wasn't doing anything with money. Hunt took offense with that immediately, and felt Colson had abandoned him.

P   Just looking at the immediate problem, don't you think you have to handle Hunt's financial situation damn soon?

D   I think that is—I talked with Mitchell about that last night and—

P   It seems to me we have to keep the cap on the bottle that much, or we don't have any options.

D   That's right.

P   Either that or it all blows right now?

D   That's the question.

P   We have Hunt, Krogh. Well go ahead with the other ones.

D   Now we've got Kalmbach. Kalmbach received, at the close of the '68 campaign in January of 1969, he got a million $700,000 to be custodian for. That came down from New York, and was placed in safe deposit boxes here. Some other people were on the boxes. And ultimately, the money was taken out to California. Alright, there is knowledge of the fact that he did start with a million seven. Several people know this. Now since 1969, he has spent a good deal of this money and accounting for it is going to be very difficult for Herb. For example, he has spent close to $500,000 on private polling. That opens up a whole new thing. It is not illegal, but more of the same thing.

P   Everybody does polling.

D   That's right. There is nothing criminal about it. It's private polling.

P   People have done private polling all through the years. There is nothing improper.

D   That's right. He sent $400,000, as he has described to me, somewhere in the South for another candidate. I assume this was 400,000 that went to Wallace.

P   Wallace?

D   Right. He has maintained a man who I only know

by the name of "Tony," who is the fellow who did the Chappaquiddick study.

P   I know about that.

D   And other odd jobs like that. Nothing illegal, but closer. I don't know of anything that Herb has done that is illegal, other than the fact that he doesn't want to blow the whistle on a lot of people, and may find himself in a perjury situation. Well, what will happen when they call him up there—and he has no immunity? They will say, "How did you pay Mr. Segretti?" He will say, "Well, I had cash on hand." "How much cash did you have on hand?" Where does it go from there? Where did you get the cash? A full series of questions. His bank records indicate he had cash on hand, because some of these were set up in trustee accounts.

P   How would you handle him, John, for example? Would you just have him put the whole thing out? I don't mind the $500,000 and $400,000.

D   No—that doesn't bother me either. As I say, Herb's problems are politically embarrassing, but not criminal.

P   Well he just handled matters between campaigns. These were surveys etc., etc. There is no need to account for that. There is no law that requires his accounting for that.

D   Ah, now—

P   Sources of money. There is no illegality in having a surplus in cash after a campaign.

D   No, the money—it has always been argued by Stans that it came in the pre-convention primary for the 1968 race, and it was just set aside. That all can be explained.

P   How about the other probabilities?

D   We have a runaway Grand Jury up in the Southern District. They are after Mitchell and Stans on some sort of bribe or influence peddling with Vesco. They are also going to try to drag Ehrlichman into that. Apparently Ehrlichman had some meetings with Vesco, also. Don Nixon, Jr. came in to see John a couple of times about the problem.

P   Not about Vesco, but about Don, Jr.? Ehrlichman never did anything for Vesco?

D   No one at the White House has done anything for Vesco.

P   Well Ehrlichman doesn't have to appear there?

D   Before that Grand Jury? Yes he could very well.

P   He couldn't use Executive Privilege?

D   Not really. Criminal charge, that is a little different. That would be dynamite to try to defend that.

P   Use the Flanigan analogy?

D   Right! That's pretty much the overall picture. And probably the most troublesome thing is the Segretti thing. Let's get down to that. Bob has indicated to me that he has told you a lot of it, that he, indeed did authorize it. He did not authorize anything like ultimately evolved. He was aware of it. He was aware that Chapin and Strachan were looking for somebody. Again, this is one that has potential that Dwight Chapin should have a felony in this. He has to disprove a negative. The negative is that he didn't control and direct Segretti.

P   Wouldn't the felony be perjury again?

D   No, the felony in this instance would be a potential use of one of the civil rights statutes, where anybody who interferes with the campaign of a candidate for national office.

P   Why isn't it under civil rights statutes for these clowns demonstrating against us?

D   I have argued for that very purpose.

P   Really?

D   Yes, I have.

P   We were closer—nuts interfering with the campaign.

D   That is exactly right.

P   I have been sick about that because it is so bad the way it has been put out on the PR side. It has ended up on the PR side very confused.

D   What really bothers me is this growing situation. As I say, it is growing because of the continued need to provide support for the Watergate people who are going to hold us up for everything we've got, and the need for some people to perjure themselves as they do down the road here. If this thing ever blows, then we are in a cover up situation. I think it would be extremely damaging to you and the—

P   Sure. The whole concept of Administration justice. Which we cannot have!

D   That is what really troubles me. For example, what happens if it starts breaking, and they do find a criminal case against a Haldeman, a Dean, a Mitchell, an Ehrlichman? That is—

P   If it really comes down to that, we would have to

114

(unintelligible) some of the men.

D That's right. I am coming down to what I really think, is that Bob and John and John Mitchell and I can sit down and spend a day, or however long, to figure out one, how this can be carved away from you, so that it does not damage you or the Presidency. It just can't! You are not involved in it and it is something you shouldn't—

P That is true!

D I know, sir. I can just tell from our conversation that these are things that you have no knowledge of.

P You certainly can! Buggings, etc! Let me say I am keenly aware of the fact Colson, et al., were doing their best to get information as we went along. But they all knew very well they were supposed to comply with the law. There was no question about that! You feel that really the trigger man was really Colson on this then?

D No. He was one of us. He was just in the chain. He helped push the thing.

P All I know about is the time of ITT, he was trying to get something going there because ITT was giving us a bad time.

D I know he used Hunt.

P I knew about that. I didn't know about it, but I knew there was something going on. But I didn't know it was a Hunt.

D What really troubles me is one, will this thing not break some day and the whole thing—domino situation—everything starts crumbling, fingers will be pointing. Bob will be accused of things he has never heard of and deny and try to disprove it. It will get real nasty and just be a real bad situation. And the person who will be hurt by it most will be you and the Presidency, and I just don't think—

P First, because I am an executive I am supposed to check these things.

D That's right.

P Let's come back to this problem. What are your feelings yourself, John? You know what they are all saying. What are your feelings about the chances?

D I am not confident that we can ride through this. I think there are soft spots.

P You used to be—

D I am not comfortable for this reason. I have noticed of recent—since the publicity has increased on this thing again, with the Gray hearings, that everybody is now starting to watch after their behind. Everyone is getting their own counsel. More counsel are getting involved. How do I protect my ass.

P   They are scared.

D   That is bad. We were able to hold it for a long time. Another thing is that my facility to deal with the multitude of people I have been dealing with has been hampered because of Gray's blowing me up into the front page.

P   Your cover is broken?

D   That's right and its—

P   So what you really come to is what we do. Let's suppose that you and Haldeman and Ehrlichman and Mitchell say we can't hold this? What then are you going to say? What are you going to put out after it. Complete disclosure, isn't that the best way to do it?

D   Well, one way to do it is—

P   That would be my view.

D   One way to do it is for you to tell the Attorney General that you finally know. Really, this is the first time you are getting all the pieces together.

P   Ask for another Grand Jury?

D   Ask for another Grand Jury. The way it should be done though, is a way—for example, I think that we could avoid criminal liability for countless people and the ones that did get it could be minimal.

P   How?

D   Well, I think by just thinking it all through first as to how. You know, some people could be granted immunity.

P   Like Magruder?

D   Yeah. To come forward. But some people are going to have to go to jail. That is the long and short of it, also.

P   Who? Let's talk about—

D   Alright. I think I could. For one.

P   You go to jail?

D   That's right.

P   Oh, hell no! I can't see how you can.

D   Well, because—

P   I can't see how. Let me say I can't see how a legal case could be made against you, John.

D   It would be tough but, you know, I can see people pointing fingers. You know, to get it out of their own, put me in an impossible position. Just really give me a (unintelligible)

116

P Oh, no! Let me say I got the impression here—But just looking at it from a cold legal standpoint: you are a lawyer, you were a counsel—doing what you did as counsel. You were not—What would you go to jail for?

D The obstruction of justice.

P The obstruction of justice?

D That is the only one that bothers me.

P Well, I don't know. I think that one. I feel it could be cut off at the pass, maybe, the obstruction of justice.

D You know one of the—that's why—

P Sometimes it is well to give them something, and then they don't want the bigger push?

D That's right. I think that, I think that with proper coordination with the Department of Justice, Henry Petersen is the only man I know bright enough and knowledgeable enough in the criminal laws and the process that could really tell us how this could be put together so that it did the maximum to carve it away with a minimum damage to individuals involved.

P Petersen doesn't know does he?

D That's right. No, I know he doesn't now. I know he doesn't now. I am talking about somebody who I have over the years grown to have enough faith in—you constantly. It would have to put him in a very difficult situation as the Head of the Criminal Division of the United States Department of Justice, and the oath of office—

P No. Talking about your obstruction of justice, though, I don't see it.

D Well, I have been a conduit for information on taking care of people out there who are guilty of crimes.

P Oh, you mean like the blackmailers?

D The blackmailers. Right.

P Well, I wonder if that part of it can't be—I wonder if that doesn't—let me put it frankly: I wonder if that doesn't have to be continued? Let me put it this way: let us suppose that you get the million bucks, and you get the proper way to handle it. You could hold that side?

D Uh, huh.

P It would seem to me that would be worthwhile.

D Well, that's one problem.

P I know you have a problem here. You have the problem with Hunt and his clemency.

D That's right. And you are going to have a clemency problem with the others. They all are going to expect to be out and that may put you in a position that is just un-

117

tenable at some point. You know, the Watergate Hearings just over, Hunt now demanding clemency or he is going to blow. And politically, it's impossible for you to do it. You know, after everybody—

P   That's right!

D   I am not sure that you will ever be able to deliver on the clemency. It may be just too hot.

P   You can't do it politically until after the '74 elections, that's for sure. Your point is that even then you couldn't do it.

D   That's right. It may further involve you in a way you should not be involved in this.

P   No - it is wrong that's for sure.

D   Well - there have been some bad judgments made. There have been some necessary judgments made.

P   Before the election?

D   Before the election and in the wake the necessary ones, you know, before the election. You know, with me there was no way, but the burden of this second Administration is something that is not going to go away.

P   No, it isn't.

D   It is not going to go away, Sir!

P   It is not going to go away.

D   Exactly.

P   The idea, well, that people are going to get tired of it and all that sort of thing.

D   Anything will spark it back into life. It's got to be,—It's got to be—

P   It is too much to the partisan interest to others to spark it back into life.

D   And it seems to me the only way—

P   Well, also so let's leave you out of it. I don't think on the obstruction of justice thing—I take that out. I don't know why, I think you may be over the cliff.

D   Well, it is possible.

P   Who else do you think has—

D   Potential criminal liability?

P   Yeah.

D   I think Ehrlichman does. I think that uh—

P   Why?

D   Because of this consipracy to burglarize the Ellsberg doctors' office.

P   That is, provided Hunt's breaks?

D   Well, the funny—let me say something interesting about that. Within the files—

P   Oh, I thought of it. The picture!

D   Yes, sir. That is not all that buried. And while I think we've got it buried, there is no telling when it is going to pop up. Now the Cubans could start this whole thing. When the Ervin Committee starts running down why this mysterious telephone was here in the White House listed in the name of a secretary, some of these secretaries have a little idea about this, and they can be broken down just so fast. That is another thing I mentioned in the cycle - in the circle. Liddy's secretary, for example, is knowledgeable. Magruder's secretary is knowledgeable.

P   Sure. So Ehrlichman on the—

D   What I am coming in today with is: I don't have a plan on how to solve it right now, but I think it is at the juncture that we should begin to think in terms of how to cut the losses; how to minimize the further growth of this thing, rather than further compound it by, you know, ultimately paying these guys forever. I think we've got to look—

P   But at the moment, don't you agree it is better to get the Hunt thing that's where that—

D   That is worth buying time on.

P   That is buying time, I agree.

D   The Grand Jury is going to reconvene next week after Sirica sentences. But that is why I think that John and Bob have met with me. They have never met with Mitchell on this. We have never had a real down and out with everybody that has the most to lose and it is the most danger for you to have them have criminal liabilities. I think Bob has a potential criminal liability, frankly. In other words, a lot of these people could be indicted.

P   Yeah.

D   They might never be convicted but just the thought of spending nights—

P   Suppose they are?

D   I think that would be devastating.

P   Suppose the worst—that Bob is indicted and Ehrlichman is indicted. And I must say, we just better then try to tough it through. You get the point.

D   That's right.

P   If they, for example, say let's cut our losses and you say we are going to go down the road to see if we can cut our losses and no more blackmail and all the rest. And then the thing blows cutting Bob and the rest to pieces. You would never recover from that, John.

D   That's right.

P   It is better to fight it out. Then you see that's the other thing. It's better to fight it out and not let people testify. and so forth. And now, on the other hand, we realize that we have these weaknesses,—that we have these weaknesses—in terms of blackmail.

D   There are two routes. One is to figure out how to cut the losses and minimize the human impact and get you up and out and away from it in any way. In a way it would never come back to haunt you. That is one general alternative. The other is to go down the road, just hunker down, fight it at every corner, every turn, don't let people testify—cover it up is what we really are talking about. Just keep it buried, and just hope that we can do it, hope that we make good decisions at the right time, keep our heads cool, we make the right moves.

P   And just take the heat?

D   And just take the heat.

P   Now with the second line of attack. You can discuss this (unintelligible) the way you want to. Still consider my scheme of having you brief the Cabinet, just in very general terms and the leaders in very general terms and maybe some very general statement with regard to my investigation. Answer questions, basically on the basis of what they told you, not what you know. Haldeman is not involved. Ehrlichman is not involved.

D   If we go that route Sir, I can give a show we can sell them just like we were selling Wheaties on our position. There's no—

P   The problem that you have are these mine fields down the road. I think the most difficult problem are the guys who are going to jail. I think you are right about that.

D   I agree.

P   Now. And also the fact that we are not going to be able to give them clemency.

D   That's right. How long will they take? How long will they sit there? I don't know. We don't know what they will be sentenced to. There's always a chance—

P   Thirty years, isn't it?

D   It could be. You know, they haven't announced yet, but it—

P   Top is thirty years, isn't it?

D   It is even higher than that. It is about 50 years. It all—

P   So ridiculous!

D   And what is so incredible is, he is (unintelligible)

P People break and enter, etc., and get two years. No weapons! No results! What the hell are they talking about?

D The individuals who are charged with shooting John Stennis are on the street. They were given, you know, one was put out on his personal recognizance rather than bond. They've got these fellows all stuck with $100,000 bonds. It's the same Judge, Sirica, let one guy who is charged with shooting a United States Senator out on the street.

P Sirica?

D Yes - it is phenomenal.

P What is the matter with him? I thought he was a hard liner.

D He is. He is just a peculiar animal, and he set the bond for one of the others somewhere around 50 or 60,-000. But still, that guy is in. Didn't make bond, but still 60 thousand dollars as opposed to $100,000 for these guys is phenomenal.

P When could you have this meeting with these fellows at I think time is of the essence. Could you do it this afternoon?

D Well, Mitchell isn't here. It might be worth it to have him come down. I think that Bob and John did not want to talk to John Mitchell about this, and I don't believe they have had any conversation with him about it.

P Well, I will get Haldeman in here now.

D Bob and I have talked about it, just as we are talking about it this morning. I told him I thought that you should have the facts and he agrees. Of course, we have some tough problems down the road if we—(inaudible) Let me say (unintelligible) How do we handle all (unintelligible) who knew all about this in advance. Let me have some of your thoughts on that.

D Well we can always, you know, on the other side charge them with blackmailing us. This is absurd stuff they are saying, and

P See, the way you put it out here, letting it all hang out, it may never get there.

(Haldeman enters the room)

P I was talking to John about this whole situation and he said if we can get away from the bits and pieces that have broken out. He is right in recommending that there be a meeting at the very first possible time. I realize Ehrlichman is still out in California but, what is today? Is tomorrow Thursday?

H   (unintelligible)

D   That's right.

P   He does get back. Could we do it Thursday? This meeting—you can't do it today, can you?

D   I don't think so. I was suggesting a meeting with Mitchell.

P   Mitchell, Ehrlichman, yourself and Bob, that is all. Now, Mitchell has to be there because he is seriously involved and we are trying to keep him with us. We have to see how we handle it from here on. We are in the process of having to determine which way to go, and John has thought it through as well as he can. I don't want Moore there on this occasion. You haven't told Moore all of this, have you?

D   Moore's got, by being with me, has more bits and pieces. I have had to give him,

P   Right.

D   Because he is making judgments—

P   The point is when you get down to the PR, once you decide it, what to do, we can let him know so forth and so on. But it is the kind of thing that I think what really has to happen is for you to sit down with those three and for you to tell them exactly what you told me.

D   Uh, huh.

P   It may take him about 35 or 40 minutes. In other words he knows, John knows, about everything and also what all the potential criminal liabilities are, whether it is—like that thing—what, about obstruction?

D   Obstruction of justice. Right.

P   So forth and so on. I think that's best. Then we have to see what the line is. Whether the line is one of continuing to run a kind of stone wall, and take the heat from that, having in mind the fact that there are vulnerable points there;—the vulnerable points being, the first vulnerable points would be obvious. That would be one of the defendants, either Hunt, because he is most vulnerable in my opinion, might blow the whistle and his price is pretty high, but at least we can buy the time on that as I pointed out to John. Apparently, who is dealing with Hunt at the moment now? Colson's—

D   Well, Mitchell's lawyer and Colson's lawyer both.

P   Who is familiar with him? At least he has to know before he is sentenced.

H   Who is Colson's lawyer? Is he in his law firm?

D   Shapiro. Right. The other day he came up and—

H   Colson has told him everything, hasn't he?

D   Yep, I gather he has. The other thing that bothered me about that is that he is a chatterer. He came up to Fred Fielding, of my office, at Colson's going away party. I didn't go over there. It was the Blair House the other night. He said to Fred, he said, "well, Chuck has had some mighty serious words with his friend Howard and has had some mighty serious messages back." Now, how does he know what Fielding knows? Because Fielding knows virtually nothing.

P   Well,—

H   That is where your dangers lie, in all these stupid human errors developing.

P   Sure. The point is Bob, let's face it, the secretaries, the assistants know all of this. The principals may be as hard as a rock, but you never know when they, or some of their people may crack. But, we'll see, we'll see. Here we have the Hunt problem that ought to be handled now. Incidentally, I do not feel that Colson should sit in this meeting. Do you agree?

D   No. I would agree.

P   Ok. How then—who does sit on Colson? Because somebody has to, don't they?

D   Chuck—

P   Talks too much.

D   I like Chuck, but I don't want Chuck to know anything that I am doing, frankly.

P   Alright.

H   I think that is right. I think you want to be careful not to give Chuck any more knowledge than he's already got.

D   I wouldn't want Chuck to even know of the meeting, frankly.

P   Ok. Fortunately, with Chuck it is very—I talk to him about many, many political things, but I have never talked with him about this sort of thing. Very probably, I think he must be damn sure that I didn't know anything. And I don't. In fact, I am surprised by what you told me today. From what you said, I gathered the impression, and of course your analysis does not for sure indicate that Chuck knew that it was a bugging operation.

D   That's correct. I don't have—Chuck denies having knowledge.

P   Yet on the other side of that is that Hunt had conversations with Chuck. It may be that Hunt told Chuck that it was bugging, and so forth and so on.

D   Uh, uh, uh, uh. They were very close. They talk

123

too much about too many things. They were intimate on this sort of—

H   That's the problem. Chuck loves (unintelligible). Chuck loves what he does and he loves to talk about it.

P   He also is a name dropper. Chuck may have gone around and talked to Hunt and said, well I was talking to the President, and the President feels we ought to get information about this, or that or the other thing, etc.

D   Well, Liddy is the same way.

P   Well, I have talked about this and that and the other thing. I have never talked to anybody, but I have talked to Chuck and John and the rest and I am sure that Chuck might have even talked to him along these lines.

H   Other than—Well, anything could have happened. I was going—

D   I would doubt that seriously.

H   I don't think he would. Chuck is a name dropper in one sense, but not in that sense. I think he very carefully keeps away from that, except when he is very intentionally bringing the President in for the President's purposes.

P   He had the impression though apparently he, as it turns out, he was the trigger man. Or he may well have been the trigger man where he just called up and said now look here Jeb go out and get that information. And Liddy and Hunt went out and got it at that time. This was February. It must have been after—

D   This was the call to Magruder from Colson saying, "fish or cut bait." Hunt and Liddy were in his office.

H   In Colson's office?

D   In Colson's office. And he called Magruder and said, "Let's fish or cut bait on this operation. Let's get it going."

H   Oh, really?

D   Yeah. This is Magruder telling me that.

H   Of course. That—now wait, Magruder testified—

D   Chuck also told me that Hunt and Liddy were in his office when he made the call.

H   Oh, ok.

D   So it was corroborated by the principal.

H   Hunt and Liddy haven't told you that, though?

D   No.

H   You haven't talked to Hunt and Liddy?

D   I talked to Liddy once right after the incident.

P   The point is this, that it is now time, though, that Mitchell has got to sit down, and know where the hell all this thing stands, too. You see, John is concerned, as you know, about the Ehrlichman situation. It worries him a great deal because, and this is why the Hunt problem is so serious, because it had nothing to do with the campaign. It has to do with the Ellsberg case. I don't know what the hell the—(unintelligible)

H   But what I was going to say—

P   What is the answer on this? How you keep it out, I don't know. You can't keep it out if Hunt talks. You see the point is irrelevant. It has gotten to this point—

D   You might put it on a national security grounds basis.

H   It absolutely was.

D   And say that this was—

H   (unintelligible)—CIA—

D   Ah—

H   Seriously,

P   National Security. We had to get information for national security grounds.

D   Then the question is, why didn't the CIA do it or why didn't the FBI do it?

P   Because we had to do it on a confidential basis.

H   Because we were checking them.

P   Neither could be trusted.

H   It has basically never been proven. There was reason to question their position.

P   With the bombing thing coming out and everything coming out, the whole thing was national security.

D   I think we could get by on that

P   On that one I think we should simply say this was a national security investigation that was conducted. And on that basis, I think the same in the drug field with Krogh. Krogh could say feels he did not perjure himself. He could say it was a national security matter. That is why—

D   That is the way Bud rests easy, because he is convinced that he was doing. He said there was treason about the country, and it could have threatened the way the war was handled and (explitive deleted)—

P   Bud should just say it was a question of national security, and I was not in a position to divulge it. Anyway, let's don't go beyond that. But I do think now there is a time when you just don't want to talk to Mitchell. But John is right. There must be a four way talk of the particular ones you can trust here. We've got to get a decision on it. It is not something— you have two ways basically. You really only have two ways to go. You either decide that the whole (explitive deleted) thing is so full of problems with potential criminal liabilities, which most concern me. I don't give a damn about the publicity. We could rock that through that if we had to let the whole damn thing hang out, and it would be a lousy story for a month. But I can take it. The point is, that I don't want any criminal liabilities. That is the thing that I am concerned about for members of the White House staff, and I would trust for members of the Committee. And that means Magruder.

D   That's right. Let's face it. I think Magruder is the major guy over there.

D   I think he's got the most serious problem.

P   Yeah.

H   Well, the thing we talked about yesterday. You have a question where you cut off on this. There is a possibility of cutting it at Liddy, where you are now.

P   Yeah.

D   But to accomplish that requires a continued perjury by Magruder and requires—

P   And requires total commitment and control over all of the defendants which—in other words when they are let down—

H   But we can, because they don't know anything beyond Liddy.

D   No. On the fact that Liddy, they have hearsay.

H   But we don't know about Hunt. Maybe Hunt has that tied into Colson. We don't know that though, really.

P   I think Hunt knows a hell of a lot more.

D   I do too. Now what McCord does—

H   You think he does. I am afraid you are right, but we don't know that.

P   I think we better assume it. I think Colson—

D   He is playing hard ball. He wouldn't play hard ball unless he were pretty confident that he could cause an awful lot of grief.

H   Right.

P   He is playing hard ball with regard to Ehrlichman for example, and that sort of thing. He knows what he's got.

H   What's he planning on, money?

D   Money and—

H   Really?

P   It's about $120,000. That's what, Bob. That would be easy. It is not easy to deliver, but it is easy to get. Now,

H   If the case is just that way, then the thing to do if the thing cranks out.

P If, for example, you say look we are not going to continue to—let's say, frankly, on the assumption that if we continue to cut our losses, we are not going to win. But in the end, we are going to be bled to death. And in the end, it is all going to come out anyway. Then you get the worst of both worlds. We are going to lose, and people are going to—

H And look like dopes!

P And in effect, look like a cover-up. So that we can't do. Now the other line, however, if you take that line, that we are not going to continue to cut our losses, that means then we have to look square in the eye as to what the hell those losses are, and see which people can—so we can avoid criminal liability. Right?

D Right.

P And that means keeping it off you. Herb has started this Justice thing. We've got to keep it off Herb. You have to keep it, naturally, off of Bob, off Chapin, if possible, Strachan, right?

D Uh, huh

P And Mitchell. Right?

D Uh, huh

H And Magruder, if you can.

P John Dean's point is that if Magruder goes down, he will pull everybody with him.

H That's my view. Yep, I think Jeb, I don't think he wants to. And I think he even would try not to, but I don't think he is able not to.

D I don't think he is strong enough.

P Another way to do it then Bob, and John realizes this, is to continue to try to cut our losses. Now we have to take a look at that course of action. First it is going to require approximately a million dollars to take care of the jackasses who are in jail. That can be arranged. That could be arranged. But you realize that after we are gone, and assuming we can expend this money, then they are going to crack and it would be an unseemly story. Frankly, all the people aren't going to care that much.

D That's right.

P People won't care, but people are going to be talking about it, there is no question. And the second thing is, we are not going to be able to deliver on any of a clemency thing. You know Colson has gone around on this clemency thing with Hunt and the rest.

D Hunt is now talking about being out by Christmas.

H This year?

D   This year. He was told by O'Brien, who is my con-
veyor of doom back and forth, that hell, he would be
lucky if he were out a year from now, or after Ervin's
hearings were over. He said how in the Lord's name could
you be commuted that quickly? He said, "Well, that is my
commitment from Colson."

H   By Christmas of this year?

D   Yeah.

H   See that, really, that is verbal evil. Colson is—That
is your fatal flaw in Chuck. He is an operator in expedi-
ency, and he will pay at the time and where he is to accomplish whatever he is there to do. And that, and
that's,—I would believe that he has made that commitment if Hunt says he has. I would believe he is capable of
saying that.

P   The only thing we could do with him would be to
parole him like the (unintelligible) situation. But you
couldn't buy clemency.

D   Kleindienst has now got control of the Parole
Board, and he said to tell me we could pull Paroles off
now where we couldn't before. So—

H   Kleindienst always tells you that, but I never believe it.

P   Paroles—let the (unintelligible) worry about that.
Parole, in appearance, etc., is something I think in Hunt's
case, you could do Hunt, but you couldn't do the others.
You understand.

D   Well, so much depends on how Sirica sentences.
He can sentence in a way that makes parole even impossible.

P   He can?

D   Sure. He can do all kind of permanent sentences.

P   (unintelligible)

D   Yeah. He can be a (characterization deleted) as far
as the whole thing.

H   Can't you appeal an unjust sentence as well as an
unjust?

D   You have 60 days to ask the Judge to review it.
There is no Appellate review of sentences.

H   There isn't?

P   The judge can review it.

H   Only the sentencing judge can review his own sentence?

P   Coming back, though, to this. So you got that
hanging over. Now! If—you see, if you let it hang there,

you fight with them at all or they part—The point is, your feeling is that we just can't continue to pay the blackmail of these guys?

D I think that is our great jeopardy.

P Now, let me tell you. We could get the money. There is no problem in that. We can't provide the clemency. Money could be provided. Mitchell could provide the way to deliver it. That could be done. See what I mean?

H Mitchell says he can't, doesn't he?

D Mitchell says—there has been an interesting phenomena all the way along. There have been a lot of people having to pull oars and not everybody pulls them all the same time, the same way, because they develop self-interests.

H What John is saying, everybody smiles at Dean and says well you better get something done about it.

D That's right.

H Mitchell is leaving Dean hanging out on him. None of us, well, may be we are doing the same thing to you.

D That's right.

H But let me say this. I don't see how there is any way that you can have the White House or anybody presently in the White House involved in trying to gin out this money.

D We are already deeply enough in that. That is the problem, Bob.

P I thought you said—

H We need more money.

D Well, in fact when—

P Kalmbach?

D Well, Kalmbach.

H He's not the one.

D No, but when they ran out of that money, as you know it came out of the 350,000 that was over here.

P And they knew that?

D And I had to explain what it was for before I could get the money.

H In the first place, that was put back to LaRue.

D That's right.

H It was put back where it belonged. It wasn't all returned in a lump sum. It was put back in pieces.

D That's right.

P Then LaRue used it for this other purpose?

D That's right.

H   And the balance was all returned to LaRue, but we don't have any receipt for that. We have no way of proving it.

D   And I think that was because of self-interest over there. Mitchell—

H   Mitchell told LaRue not to take it at all.

D   That's right.

H   That is what you told me.

D   That's right. And then don't give them a receipt.

P   Then what happened? LaRue took it, and then what?

D   It was sent back to him because we just couldn't continue piecemeal giving. Everytime I asked for it I had to tell Bob I needed some, or something like that, and he had to get Gordon Strachan to go up to his safe and take it out and take it over to LaRue. And it was just a forever operation.

P   Why did they take it all?

D   I just sent it along to them.

H   We had been trying to get a way to get that money back out of here anyway. And what this was supposed to be was loans. This was immediate cash needs that was going to be replenished. Mitchell was arguing that you can't take the $350,000 back until it is all replenished. Isn't that right?

D   That is right.

H   They hadn't replenished, so we just gave it all back anyway.

P   I had a feeling we could handle this one.

D   Well, first of all, I would have a hell of a time proving it. That is one thing.

P   I just have a feeling on it. Well, it sounds like a lot of money, a million dollars. Let me say that I think we could get that. I know money is hard to raise. But the point is, what we do on that—Let's look at the hard problem—

D   That has been, thus far, the most difficult problem. That is why these fellows have been on and off the reservation all the way along.

P   So the hard place is this. Your feeling at the present time is the hell with the million dollars. I would just say to these fellows I am sorry it is all off and let them talk. Alright?

D   Well,—

P   That's the way to do it isn't it, if you want to do it clean?

H That's the way. We can live with it, because the problem with the blackmailing, that is the thing we kept raising with you when you said there was a money problem. When you said we need $20,000, or $100,000, or something. We said yeah, that is what you need today. But what do you need tomorrow or next year or five years from now?

P How long?

D That was just to get us through November 7th, though.

H That's what we had to have to get through November 7th. There is no question.

D These fellows could have sold out to the Democrats for one-half a million.

P These fellows though, as far as what has happened up to this time, are covered on their situation, because the Cuban Committee did this for them during the election?

D Well, yeah. We can put that together. That isn't of course quite the way it happened, but—

P I know, but that's the way it is going to have to happen.

D It's going to have to happen.

P Finally, though, so you let it happen. So then they go, and so what happens? Do they go out and start blowing the whistle on everybody else? Isn't that what it really gets down to?

D Uh, huh.

P So that would be the clean way—Right!

D Ah—

P Is that—you would go so far as to recommend that?

D No, I wouldn't. I don't think necessarily that is the cleanest way. One of the things that I think we all need to discuss is, is there some way that we can get our story before a Grand Jury, so that they can really have investigated the White House on this. I must say that I have not really thought through that alternative. We have been so busy on the other containment situation.

P John Ehrlichman, of course, has raised the point of another Grand Jury. I just don't know how you could do it. On what basis. I could call for it, but I—

D That would be out of the question.

P I hate to leave with differences in view of all this stripped land. I could understand this, but I think I want another Grand Jury proceeding and we will have the White House appear before them. Is that right John?

D Uh huh.

P   That is the point, see. Of course! That would make the difference. I want everybody in the White House called. And that gives you a reason not to have to go before the Ervin and Baker Committee. It puts it in an executive session, in a sense.

H   Right.

D   That's right.

H   And there would be some rules of evidence, aren't there?

D   There are rules of evidence.

P   Rules of evidence and you have lawyers.

H   You are in a hell of a lot better position than you are up there.

D   No, you can't have a lawyer before the Grand Jury.

P   Oh, no. That's right.

H   But you do have rules of evidence. You can refuse to talk.

D   You can take the 5th Amendment.

P   That's right.

H   You can say you have forgotten too can't you?

D   Sure but you are chancing a very high risk for perjury situation.

P   But you can say I don't remember. You can say I can't recall. I can't give any answer to that that I can recall.

H   You have the same perjury thing on the Hill don't you?

D   That's right.

P   Oh hell, yes.

H   And the Ervin Committee is a hell of a lot worse to deal with.

D   That's right.

P   The Grand Jury thing has its in view of this thing. Suppose we have a Grand Jury thing. What would that do to the Ervin Committee? Would it go right ahead?

D   Probably. Probably.

P   If we do that on a Grand Jury, we would then have a much better cause in terms of saying, "Look, this is a Grand Jury, in which the prosecutor—How about a special prosecutor? We could use Peterson, or use another one. You see he is probably suspect. Would you call in another prosecutor?

D   I would like to have Peterson on our side, if I did this thing.

P   Well, Petersen is honest. There isn't anybody about to question him is there?

D   No, but he will get a barrage when these Watergate Hearings start.

P   But he can go up and say that he has been told to go further with the Grand Jury and go in to this and that and the other thing. Call everybody in the White House, and I want them to go to the Grand Jury.

D   This may happen without even our calling for it when these—

P   Vesco?

D   No. Well, that is one possibility. But also when these people go back before the Grand Jury here, they are going to pull all these criminal defendents back before the Grand Jury and immunize them.

P   Who will do this?

D   The U.S. Attorney's Office will.

P   To do what?

D   To let them talk about anything further they want to talk about.

P   But what do they gain out of it?

D   Nothing.

P   To hell with it!

D   They're going to stonewall it, as it now stands. Excepting Hunt. That's why his threat.

H   It's Hunt opportunity.

P   That's why for your immediate things you have no choice but to come up with the $120,000, or whatever it is. Right?

D   That's right.

P   Would you agree that that's the prime thing that you damn well better get that done?

D   Obviously he ought to be given some signal anyway.

P   (Expletive deleted), get it. In a way that—who is going to talk to him? Colson? He is the one who is supposed to know him?

D   Well, Colson doesn't have any money though. That is the thing. That's been one of the real problems. They haven't been able to raise a million dollars in cash. (unintelligible) has been just a very difficult problem as we discussed before. Mitchell has talked to Pappas, and John asked me to call him last night after our discussion and after you had met with John to see where that was. And I said, "Have you talked to Pappas?" He was at home,

133

and Martha picked up the phone so it was all in code. I said, "Have you talked to the Greek?" And he said, "Yes, I have." I said, "Is the Greek bearing gifts?" He said, "Well, I'll call you tomorrow on that."

P   Well look, what is it you need on that? When—I am not familiar with the money situation.

D   It sounds easy to do and everyone is out there doing it and that is where our breakdown has come every time.

P   Well, if you had it, how would you get it to somebody?

D   Well, I got it to LaRue by just leaving it in mail boxes and things like that. And someone phones Hunt to come and pick it up. As I say, we are a bunch of amateurs in that business.

H   That is the thing that we thought Mitchell ought to be able to know how to find somebody who would know how to do all that sort of thing, because none of us know how to.

D   That's right. You have to wash the money. You can get a $100,000 out of a bank, and it all comes in serialized bills.

P   I understand.

D   And that means you have to go to Vegas with it or a bookmaker in New York City. I have learned all these things after the fact. I will be in great shape for the next time around.

H   (Expletive deleted)

P   Well, of course you have a surplus from the campaign. Is there any other money hanging around?

H   Well, what about the money we moved back out of here?

D   Apparently, there is some there. That might be what they can use. I don't know how much is left.

P   Kalmbach must have some.

D   Kalmbach doesn't have a cent.

P   He doesn't?

H   That $350,000 that we moved out was all that we saved. Because they were afraid to because of this. That is the trouble. We are so (adjective deleted) square that we get caught at everything.

P   Could I suggest this though: let me go back around—

H   Be careful—

P   The Grand Jury thing has a feel. Right? It says we are cooperating well with the Grand Jury.

D   Once we start down any route that involves the criminal justice system, we've got to have full appreciation that there is really no control over that. While we did an amazing job of keeping us in on the track before while the FBI was out there, and that was the only way they found out where they were going—

P   But you've got to (unintelligible) Let's take it to a Grand Jury. A new Grand Jury would call Magruder again, wouldn't it?

D   Based on what information? For example, what happens if Dean goes in and gives a story. You know, that here is the way it all came about. It was supposed to be a legitimate operation and it obviously got off the track. I heard—before, but told Haldeman that we shouldn't be involved in it. Then Magruder can be called in and questioned again about all those meetings and the like. And it again he'll begin to change his story as to what he told the Grand Jury the last time. That way, he is in a perjury situation.

H   Except that is the best leverage you've got with Jeb. He has to keep his story straight or he is in real trouble, unless they get smart and give him immunity. If they immunize Jeb, then you have an interesting problem.

D   We have control over who gets immunized. I think they wouldn't do that without our—

P   But you see the Grand Jury proceeding achieves this thing. If we go down that road—(unintelligible) We would be cooperating. We would be cooperating through a Grand Jury. Everybody would be behind us. That is the proper way to do this. It should be done in the Grand Jury, not up there under the kleig lights of the Committee. Nobody questions a Grand Jury. And then we would insist on Executive Privilege before the Committee, flat out say, "No we won't do that. It is a matter before the Grand Jury, and so on, and that's that."

H   Then you go the next step. Would we then—The Grand Jury is in executive session?

D   Yes, they are secret sessions.

H   Alright, then would we agree to release our Grand Jury transcripts?

D   We don't have the authority to do that. That is up to the Court and the Court, thus far, has not released the ones from the last Grand Jury.

P   They usually are not.

D   It would be highly unusual for a Grand Jury to come out. What usually happens is—

H   But a lot of the stuff from the Grand Jury came out.

P   Leaks.

D   It came out of the U.S. Attorney's office, more than the Grand Jury. We don't know. Some of the Grand Jurors may have blabbered, but they were—

P   Bob, it's not so bad. It's bad, but it's not the worst place.

H   I was going the other way there. I was going to say that it might be to our interest to get it out.

P   Well, we could easily do that. Leak out certain stuff. We could pretty much control that. We've got so much more control. Now, the other possibility is not to go to the Grand Jury. We have three things. (1) You just say the hell with it, we can't raise the money, sorry Hunt you can say what you want, and so on. He blows the whistle. Right?

D   Right.

P   If that happens, that raises some possibilities about some criminal liabilities, because he is likely to say a hell of a lot of things and will certainly get Magruder in on it.

D   It will get Magruder. It will start the whole FBI investigation going again.

P   Yeah. It would get Magruder, and it could possibly get Colson.

D   That's right. Could get—

P   Get Mitchell. Maybe. No.

H   Hunt can't get Mitchell.

D   I don't think Hunt can get Mitchell. Hunt's got a lot of hearsay.

P   Ehrlichman?

D   Krogh could go down in smoke.

P   On the other hand—Krogh says it is a national security matter. Is that what he says?

D   Yeah, but that won't sell ultimately in a criminal situation. It may be mitigating on sentences but it won't, in the main matter.

P   Seems we're going around the track. You have no choice on Hunt but to try to keep—

D   Right now, we have no choice.

P   But my point is, do you ever have any choice on Hunt? That is the point. No matter what we do here now, John, whatever he wants if he doesn't get it—immunity, etc., he is going to blow the whistle.

D   What I have been trying to conceive of is how we could lay out everything we know in a way that we have told the Grand Jury or somebody else, so that if a Hunt blows, so what's new? It's already been told to a Grand Jury and they found no criminal liability and they investigated it in full. We're sorry fellow—And we don't, it doesn't—

P (Unintelligible) for another year.

D That's right.

P And Hunt would get off by telling them the Ellsberg thing.

D No Hunt would go to jail for that too—he should understand that.

P That's a point too. I don't think I would throw that out. I don't think we need to go into everything. (adjective deleted) thing Hunt has done.

D No.

P Some of the things in the national security area. Yes.

H Whoever said that anyway. We laid the groundwork for that.

P But here is the point, John. Let's go the other angle, is to decide if you open up the Grand Jury: first, it won't be any good, it won't be believed. And then you will have two things going: the Grand Jury and the other things, committee, etc. The Grand Jury appeals to me from the standpoint, the President makes the move. All these charges being bandied about, etc., the best thing to do is that I have asked the Grand Jury to look into any further charges. All charges have been raised. That is the place to do it, and not before a Committee of the Congress. Right?

D Yeah.

P Then, however, we may say, (expletive deleted), we can't risk that, or she'll break loose there. That leaves you to your third thing.

D Hunker down and fight it.

P Hunker down and fight it and what happens? Your view is that is not really a viable option.

D It is a high risk. It is a very high risk.

P Your view is that what will happen on it, that it's going to come out. That something is going to break loose, and—

D Something is going to break and—

P It will look like the President

D is covering up—

P Has covered up a huge (unintelligible)

D That's correct.

137

H   But you can't (inaudible)

P   You have now moved away from the hunker down—

D   Well, I have moved to the point that we certainly have to take a harder look at the other alternative, which we haven't before.

P   The other alternative is—

D   Yes, the other choices.

P   As a matter of fact, your middle ground of Grand Jury. I suppose there is a middle ground of a public statement without a transcript.

D   What we need also, Sir

H   But John's view is if we make the public statement that we talked about this morning, the thing we talked about last night—each of us in our hotel, he says that will immediately lead to a Grand Jury.

P   Fine—alright, fine.

H   As soon as we make that statement, they will have to call a Grand Jury.

P   They may even make a public statement before the Grand Jury, in order to—

H   So it looks like we are trying to do it over.

D   Here are public statements, and we want full Grand Jury investigations by the U.S. Attorneys office.

P   If we said that the reason we had delayed this is until after the sentencing—You see that the point is that the reason time is of the essence, we can't play around on this. If they are going to sentence on Friday, we are going to have to move on the (expletive deleted) thing pretty fast. See what I mean?

D   That's right.

P   So we really have a time problem.

D   The other thing is that The Attorney General could call Sirica, and say that, "The government has some major developments that it is considering. Would you hold sentencing for two weeks?" If we set ourselves on a course of action.

P   Yep, yep.

D   See, the sentencing may be in the wrong perspective right now. I don't know for certain, but I just think there are some things that I am not at liberty to discuss with you, but I want to ask that the Court withhold two weeks sentencing.

H   So then the story is out: "Sirica delays sentencing Watergate"—

D   I think that could be handled in a way between Sirica and Kleindienst that it would not get out. Kleindienst apparently does have good rapport with Sirica. He has never talked since this case developed, but—

P   That's helpful. So Kleindienst should say that he is working on something and would like to have a week. I wouldn't take two weeks. I would take a week.

D   I will tell you the person that I feel we could use his counsel on this, because he understands the criminal process better than anybody over here does.

P   Petersen?

D   Yes, Petersen. It is awkward for Petersen. He is the head of the criminal division. But to discuss some of things with him, we may well want to remove him from the head of the Criminal Division and say, "That related to this case, you will have no relation." Give him some special assignment over here where he could sit down and say, "Yes, this is an obstruction, but it couldn't be proved," so on and so forth. We almost need him out of there to take his counsel. I don't think he would want that, but he is the most knowledgeable.

P   How could we get him out?

D   I think an appeal directly to Henry—

P   Why couldn't the President call him in as Special Counsel to the White House for the purpose of conducting an investigation. Rather than a Dean in office, having him the Special Counsel to represent us before the Grand Jury.

D   I have thought of that. That is one possibility.

H   On the basis that Dean has now become a principal, rather than a Counsel.

D   I could recommend that to you.

H   Petersen is planning to leave, anyway.

D   Is he?

P   You could recommend it and he could come over and I would say, "Now Petersen, we want you to get to the bottom of the damn thing. Call another Grand Jury or anything else. Correct? Well, now you gotta know whether Kleindienst can get Sirica to hold off. Right? Second, you have to get Mitchell down here. And you and Ehrlichman and Mitchell by tomorrow.

H   Why don't we do that tonight?

P   I don't think you can get Mitchell that soon, can you?

H   John?

P It would be helpful if you could.

D It would be better if he could come down this afternoon.

P It would be very helpful to get going. Actually, I am perfectly willing to meet with the group. I don't know whether I should.

H Do you think you want to?

P Or maybe have Dean report to me at the end. See what conclusions you have reached. I think I need to stay away from the Mitchell subject at this point, do you agree?

D Uh, huh.

D Unless we see, you know, some sort of a reluctant dragon there.

H You might meet with the rest of us, but I am not sure you would want to meet with John in this group at this time.

P Alright. Fine. And my point is that I think it is good, frankly, to consider these various options. And then, once you decide on the right plan, you say, "John," you say, "No doubts about the right plan before the election. You handled it just right. You contained it. And now after the election we have to have another plan. Because we can't for four years have this thing eating away." We can't do it.

H We should change that a little bit. John's point is exactly right. The erosion here now is going to you, and that is the thing that we have to turn off at whatever cost. We have to turn it off at the lowest cost we can, but at whatever cost it takes.

D That's what we have to do.

P Well, the erosion is inevitably going to come here, apart from anything and all the people saying well the Watergate isn't a major issue. It isn't. But it will be. It's bound to. (Unintelligible) has to go out. Delaying is the great danger to the White House area. We don't, I say that the White House can't do it. Right?

D Yes, Sir.

Meeting: The President, Dean, Haldeman and Ehrlichman, EOB Office, March 21, 1973.
(5:20 - 6:01 pm)

P Well, what conclusions have you reached up to the moment?

H Well, you go round and round and come up with all questions and no answers. Right back where you were at when you started.

P Well, do you have any additional thoughts?

E Well, I just don't think that the immunity thing will wash—

P In a Grand Jury?

E It may but (inaudible John's Grand Jury package was—

P To get immunity for some—

E For various witnesses.

P Who had to go before the Grand Jury.

E I think you have to figure that that is out of the picture. I just don't believe we can do that. It can't be carried off.

H Either the Grand Jury (inaudible special, or a special panel,

D A panel could investigate and report back on the whole thing. Immunized witnesses can be obtained.

P Will it be an indictment of people in the Presidential family?

D We have pending work on legislation to get immunity powers at the Department of Justice right now, asking them to assess this.

P Well, let's take the Grand Jury now, without immunity, and what are your ideas about getting out of it?

D Well, yes I think that is still a possibility, at least for some very drastic results (inaudible) statutes later on some (inaudible)

E Well, there could be people in and out of the White House indicated for various offenses.

P The other item I mentioned, I wouldn't spend too much time with that.

E The other item would be to pick out two papers and possibly three and say "(expletive omitted, you asked me about this. Here is my review of the facts." I think we disagree as to whether or not that is a viable. I

141

think you could get out a fairly credible document that would stand up, and that would have the effect of turning the scope, and would have the effect of maybe becoming the battle ground on a reduced scope, which I think is important. The big danger is the Ervin Hearings, as I see it, is the Committee will run out leads into areas that it would be better not to have them get into. And then Baker could come in this direction. And then you could put out a basic document that would come on in a limited subject that would rather consciously hit the target.

P   The imposing problem is this, Does anybody really think we can do nothing? That's the option, period. If he fights it out on this ground, it takes all summer.

H   Which it will.

P   That's it, whether or not today at the danger point.

H   Well, we have talked about that. We have talked about possible opportunities in the Senate. Things may turn up that we don't foresee now. Some people may be sort of playing the odds.

E   The problem of the Hunt thing or some of these other people, there is just no sign off on them. That problem goes on and on.

P   Well, that's right. If that's the case then, what is your view as to what we should do now about Hunt, et cetera?

E   Well, my view is that Hunt's interests lie in getting a pardon if he can. That ought to be somehow or another one of the options that he is most particularly concerned about. Now, his indirect contacts with John don't contemplate that at all—(inaudible)

P   He assumes that's already understood.

D   He's got to get that by Christmas, I understand.

E   That's right. And if he does, obviously he has a bigger defense crosswise.

H   If that blows—

E   If that blows and that seems to me, although I doubt if he is understood, he has really turned over backwards since he has been in there. However, can he, by talking, get a pardon? Clemency from the Court? Obviously he has thought of this. If he goes in there and tells this Judge before sentencing, if he says, "Your honor I am willing to tell all. I don't want to go to jail. I plead guilty to an offense. If I don't have to go to jail, I will cooperate with you and the government. I will tell you everything I know." I think that probably he would receive very favorable consideration.

P   Yeah. And then so the point we have to, the bridge we have to cross there, that you have to cross I understand quite soon, is what you do about Hunt and his present finance? What do we do about that?

D   Well apparently Mitchell and LaRue are now aware of it so they know how is is feeling.

P   True. Are they going to do something?

D   Well, I have not talked with either of them. Their positions are sympathetic.

P   Well, it is a long road isn't it? When you look back on it, as John has pointed out here, it really has been a long road for all of you, of us.

H   It sure is.

P   For all of us, for all of us. That's why you are wrestling with the idea of moving in another direction.

D   That's right. It is not only that group, but within this circle of people, that have tidbits of knowledge, there are a lot of weak individuals and it could be one of those who crosses up: the secretary to Liddy, the secretary to Jeb Magruder. Chuck Colson's secretary, among others, will be called before the Senate Committee. This is not solved by one forum. A civil suit filed by O'Brien which for some reason we can't get settled. They are holding on to it. They will have intense civil discovery. They may well work hand and glove with that Senate Committee. They will go out and take depositions and start checking for the inconsistencies, see what is in the transcript of one and see what people say in the other (inaudible)

P   Well, I am not going to worry about that.

D   Well, they, the people are starting to protect their own behind: Dwight, for example, hired himself a lawyer; Colson has retained a lawyer; and now that we are all starting the self-protection certainly.

P   Maybe we face the situation. We can't do a damn about the participants. If it is going to be that way eventually, why not now? That is what you are sort of resigned to, isn't it?

D   Well, I thought (inaudible) by keeping on top of it it would not harm you. Maybe the individuals would get harmed.

P   We don't want to harm the people either. That is my concern. We can't harm these young people (inaudible. They were doing things for the best interests of their country—that is all.

H   Well, we don't have any question here of some guy stashing money in his pocket.

143

P   It isn't something like this, for example, (expletive omitted) treason.

H   Well, like Sherman Adams, doing it for their own ambition or comfort.

P   Well, that is why I say on this one that we have to realize that the system is going to run and that is your problem.

H   The only problem (inaudible)

D   It is structured. That your concern about, "There is something lurking here." Now is the time to get the facts before Richard Nixon himself. Dean couldn't get all the information. People wouldn't give it to him. There are things, there are a lot of things. And if you would like to get all of this information and you lay it before the public, but it is not going to come because some people go to a Grand Jury and tell the truth.

H   Lie?

P   And it isn't going to come out of the Committee.

H   For those reasons,

D   It would not be fair. Go ahead, that's the point, or it may never come out. But now is the time to throw it all out.

H   They are not going to have the key witnesses.

D   So therefore you select a panel of the Attorney General, the head of the Criminal Division, head of the Civil Division—something like that. Call on everybody in the White House, and tell them we want them, we have been instructed by the President to tell him exactly what happened. And you won't be prosecuted for it because that is not the point now. The point is to get out this information. And then you will make a decision, based on what you learn, whether people can remain in the government or not. And if it is bad they will be removed or forced to resign. If it was something that is palatable, they'll go on with their job.

H   The hue and cry is that this is a super-Presidential Board. And now they realize that they have got guilty people, and they immunize them so that they cannot be prosecuted.

D   I am not so sure how many people would come out guilty.

H   The perception, as you put it.

P   The point is, we were talking—

D   Alright, is that better? Or is it better to have (inaudible) and things blow up and all of a sudden collapse?

144

Think about it.

H   After a little time, the President is accused of covering up that way.

P   That isn't the point.

E   Or is there another way?

P   Yeah, like—

E   The Dean statements, where the President then makes a bold disclosure of everything which he then has. And is in a position if it does collapse at a later time to say, "I had the FBI and the Grand Jury, and I had my own Counsel. I turned over every document I could find. I placed in my confidence young people and as is obvious now (inaudible)

P   (inaudible) It doesn't concern me. I mean as far as the policy is concerned. You as White House Counsel, John. I asked for a written report, which I do not have, which is very general understand. I am thinking now in far more general terms, having in mind the facts, that where specifics are concerned, make it very general, your investigation of the case. Not that "this man is guilty, this man is not guilty," but "this man did do that." You are going to have to say that, John. Segretti (inaudible) That has to be said. And so under the circumstances,

E   Could he do this? To give some belief to this, that he could attach an appendix, listing the FBI reports that you had access to: interview with Kalmbach, interview with Segretti, interview with Chapin, Magruder, and whoever and me. So that the President at some later time is in a position to say, "I relied."

D   And Dean cooperated on these things.

E   That's right.

P   It also helps with the Gray situation because it shows Dean's name on the FBI reports as reporting to the President. He can say in there, "I have not disclosed the contents of these to anybody else. Yes, I had access to the reports for the purpose of carrying out your instructions." And I know that that is true because you are the one I asked with regard to my report.

E   I think the President is in a stronger position later. The President is in a stronger position later, if he can be shown to have justifiably relied on you at this point in time.

D   Well, there is the argument now that Dean's credibility is in question. Maybe I shouldn't do it. Maybe someone else—

H This will rehabilitate you though. Your credibility—

P As a matter of fact, John, I don't think your credibility has been much injured. Sure you are under a test that they want. You are up there to testify. I don't think it is the credibility. They want you to testify. I would not be too sensitive about that. You are going to make a hell of a good impression.

E Beyond that, you can help your participation in the interviews by saying that, in addition to having seen the FBI synoposes, you were present at the time of the interviews.

P No. Not seeing. You were present at the time of the interviews and that you, yourself, conducted interviews of the following people. I am just trying to think of people, et cetera, that you can list.

D It will turn it all into a puzzle.

H Absolutely, yeah.

E I am doing this in furtherance of my role.

P Also, that there has been such a lot of—put out about what you have done without referring to the fact, without being defensive about it, you intended to—This should not be a letter to Eastland. I think this should be a letter to me. You could say that, "Now, now that hearings are going on, I can now give a report that we can put out."

H That is what you can say. In other words, he gives you a report because you asked him for it, regardless of the timeliness.

D I am not thinking of that. Don't worry about that. I have no problem with the timing. It is just that Liddy and McCord are still out on appeal. That is why I haven't tried to do this before.

H We are going to have a big period of that. I think you could say—

E You could say, "I have a report. I don't want to show it. I would not want it published because some fellows' trial of the case is still on."

P Let me say this. The problem with, is: I don't believe that helps on our cause. The fact that cover up—I am not sure. Maybe I am wrong. The fact that the President says, "I have shown Ervin." Remember we had nobody there. I think that something has to go first. We need to put out something.

H If we worry about the timeliness, and try to hang it on a sense thing, then we have to ignore the trial, and say

146

Dean has given you a report. We basically said it was an oral report. The thing is that Dean has kept you posted from time to time with periodic oral reports as this thing, as it becomes convenient. You have asked him now to summarize those into an overall summary.

P   Overall summary. And I will make the report available to the Ervin Committee. And then I offer the Ervin Committee report this way, I say, "Dear Senator Ervin. Here is the report before your hearings. You have this report, and as I have said previously, any questions that are not answered here, you can call the White House staff member, and they will be directed to answer any questions on an informal basis." (inaudible)

H   Yeah.

E   Let's suppose you did do that. You did as to the burglary, you did it as to Segretti and you made some passing comments to money, right? You send her up there. Let's suppose I am called at some time. Our position on that is that I wasn't a prosecutor, that he was sent out to do an investigation on Ellsberg. And when we discovered what he was up to, we stopped him. Now, I suppose that lets Ellsberg out, because there are search and seizure things here that may be sufficient at least for a mistrial, if not for—

P   Isn't that case about finished yet?

E   Oh, it will go a little while yet. Let's suppose that occurred. That it was a national security situation. The man exercised bad judgment, and I think it is inarguable that he should never have been permitted to go to the Committee after that episode, having reflected on his judgment that way. But beyond that, the question is did he completely authorize (inaudible)

P   Yeah. Getting back to this, John. You still tilt to the panel idea yourself?

D   Well, I see in this conversation what I have talked about before. They do not ultimately solve what I see as a grave problem of a cancer growing around the Presidency. This creates another problem. It does not clean the problem out.

P   Well,

E   But doesn't it permit the President to clean it out at such time as it does comes up? By saying, "Indeed, I relied on it. And now this later thing turns up, and I don't condone that. And if I had known that before, obviously I would have run it down."

P   Here's what John is to. You really think you've got

to clean the cancer out now, right?

D Yes sir.

P How would you do that? Do you see another way? Without breaking down our executive privilege.

D I see a couple of ways to do it.

P You certainly don't want to do it at the Senate, do you?

D No sir, I think that would be an added trap.

P That's the worst thing. Right. We've got to do it. We aren't asked to do it.

D You've got to do it, to get the credit for it. That gets you above it. As I see it, naturally you'll get hurt and I hope we can find the answer to that problem.

E Alright, suppose we did this? Supposing you write a report to the President on everything you know about this. And the President then, prior to seeing it, says "Did you send the report over to the Justice Department?" When it goes he says, (unintelligible) has been at work on this. My Counsel has been at work on this. Here are his findings."

P Where would you start? I don't know where it stops. Ziegler? The Vice President?

H Well, re Magruder over at Commerce. Obviously you would send a report over that said Magruder did this and that. Well, that is what he is talking about apparently.

P And then Magruder. The fellow is a free agent.

H The free agent.

P Who according to the Hunt theory, could pull others down with him.

H Sure. What would happen? Sure as hell we have to assume Dwight would be drawn in.

D Draw numbers with names out of a hat to see who gets hurt and who doesn't. That sounds about as fair as you can be, because anyone can get hurt.

P Strachan. This wouldn't do anything to him would it?

D Strachan? I would say yes. About the same as Jeb.

H Do you think so?

D Yes, I think he has a problem.

P What is the problem about?

H He has a problem of knowledge.

D Magruder has a problem of action, action and perjury.

H Well, Strachan handled the money. That is the problem.

D The thing that I would like to happen, if it is possible to do it, is—Hunt has now sent a blackmail request directly to the White House.

P Who did he send it to? You?

D Yes.

P Or to me?

D Your Counsel.

H That is the interesting kind of thing, there is something there that may blow it all up that way and everything starts going in a whole new direction.

E That he would hurt the Eastern Asian Defense. Right there. That is blackmail.

H For example, where does that take you? That takes you to your support, the other people who are not fully aware of the DC end of it. But then we didn't know about it either.

D That's right. Well, then you have to get the proper people to say—

H Well, see if we go your route, you can't draw the line someplace and say—

D No, no you can't.

P You see, if we go your route of cutting the cancer out. If we cut it out now. Take a Hunt. Well, wouldn't that knock the hell out from under him?

D That's right.

H If you take your move and it goes slightly awry, you have a certainty, almost, of Magruder going to jail, Chapin going to jail, and you going to jail, and probably me going to jail.

P No, I question the last two.

H Certainly Chapin. Certainly Strachan. No, not really. Chapin and Strachan are clean.

E I think Strachan is hooked on this money.

P What money was that?

E He is an accessory on undeclared campaign funds.

H That's not his problem. The only man responsible for that is the Treasurer. I am sure.

D I don't know under the law.

P That undeclared was money from before 1970, that was 1968.

E Yeah. But then it got back into the coffers and was used in this campaign.

D Let's say the President sent me to the Grand Jury to make a report. Who could I actually do anything for? As a practical matter, firsthand knowledge, almost no one. All I could do would be to give them focus point leads.

P   Right.

H   Then they would start calling the leads.

D   That's right and whether all of them would come down or be served. There again, we don't have anybody who could talk to somebody who has learned how to process that sort of thing on the outside. I was talking outside with Bob about Henry Peterson. We need to have someone talk to Henry Peterson, who can say to Henry, "What does this mean in criminal justice? What kind of a case could be made on this? What kind of sentences would evolve out of that?" He would have a pretty good idea of most of the statutes that are involved. There is so much behind the statutes.

P   Do you want to recommend that? That you talk to him?

D   Well, you are putting in his knowledge.

P   I see.

D   There're a couple of points—

H   It would be even much better. Yes. I have this brother-in-law in school.—

D   He wants a wild scenario.

H   My friend is writing a play, and he wants to see how—

D   It bothers me to do anything further now, sir, when Hunt is our real unknown.

P   Do you think it is a mistake to talk to him?

D   Yes, I do.

P   It doesn't solve anything—it's just one more step.

H   The payment to Hunt does too.

D   The payment to Hunt does. That is why I say if somebody would assess the criminal liability.

H   Maybe we are mis-assessing it?

D   Well, maybe. We don't know.

P   Would you reply to him?

H   I think I would.

E   How else would you do it? You could start down that road. Say, "I want to talk with you about some questions that arise in the course of my own investigation, but I would have to swear you to secrecy."

H   If he will take it on that basis.

D   The answer is, of course, in the course of this investigation I don't know whether he would talk to me off-the-record.

H   What are your options?

E   Boy, if you could eliminate the option by taking a

legal position. You knew nothing about it.

P So you don't see the statement thing helping insofar as in any way sparking the start? You think that over some more.

D Yes sir. You see it is a temporary cancer.

P I agree with that. And the point is,—but you see, here is the way I would see the statement that we would put out: Everything we would intend to say in a general statement that I have already indicated with regard to the facts as we send them in, we say people are to cooperate, without executive privilege, et cetera. Statement, it is true, is temporary. But it will indicate that the President has looked into the matter, has had his Counsel report to him and this is the result of the matter. We tell the Committee "we will cooperate." The Committee will say no. And so we just stand right there.

D Well, really I think what will complicate the problem will be Sirica giving a speech from the Bench on Friday when he sentences. Where he will charge that he doesn't believe that the trial conducted by the lawyers for the government presented a legitimate case and that he is not convinced that the case represents the full situation.

H In other words—

D It will have a dramatic impact coming from the Bench.

P That's right.

D I may say in Sirica's defense, it has been charged that there are higher-ups involved in this. He may take some dramatic action like, he might appoint a special prosecutor. Who knows?

P Can he do that?

D Sure.

P He would appoint a special prosecutor, for what?

D For work in the field of investigating. He is the Presiding Judge.

H You know he can pick the Grand Jury. Or he said he could.

P The government is going to do that for a while.

D A week after sentencing they are going to take all of the people who have been sentenced before a Grand Jury—

P These same ones?

D These same ones. And see if they will now want to talk. When it comes to Sirica and sentencing, he may be giving the ones who talk a lesser sentence. If they don't

151

talk, he will probably leave these long sentences stand.

P Suppose he does that. Where does that leave us, John?

E I don't think that is a surprise to the defendants. I think their counsel has advised them of that.

P Right, right. However in terms of this, what about a solution? We are damned by the courts before Ervin even gets started.

E The only thing we can say is that we have investigated it backwards and forwards in the White House, and have been satisfied on the basis of the report we had that nobody in the White House has been involved in a burglary, nobody had notice of it, knowledge of it, participated in the planning, or aided or abetted it in any way. And it happens to be true as for that transaction.

P John, you don't think that is enough?

D No, Mr. President.

E Let's try another concomitant to that. Supposing Mitchell were to step out on that same day to say, "I have been doing some investigation at 1701 and I find—so and so and so and so."

P Such as what?

E I don't know what he would say, but that he wanted to be some kind of a spokesman for 1701.

P What the hell does one disclose that isn't doing to blow something? I don't have any time. I am sorry. I have to leave. Well, good-bye. You meet what time tomorrow?

H I am not sure. In the morning probably.

Meeting: The President, Haldeman, Ehrlichman, Dean and Mitchell, EOB Office, March 22, 1973. (1:57 - 3:43 pm)

P Well, John how are you? It is good to see you.

M Mr. President, I am just great—how are you?

P You're a big Wall Street lawyer—you do have to admit you're rich—

M Not in front of all these people who help collect taxes. But I can report that the firm is doing quite well.

P Are they?

E There isn't any reason why it shouldn't.

M I would agree.

E (first part not audible) Eastland is going to postpone any further hearings on Gray for two weeks and allow things to cool off a little bit. He thinks Gray is dead on the Floor.

P He's probably right—poor guy.

H Gray, the symbol of wisdom today and future counsel for tomorrow.

D Maybe someone will shoot him.

Laughter

P How's that?

H He said yes he thinks John Dean did lie to the FBI when he said he wasn't sure whether Howard Hunt had an office in the White House.

D I said I had to check it out—what happened is that the agent asked if he could see the office. It occurred right after an interview and I said I would have to check that out. And now it has been interpreted that I was lying to the FBI about the fact that he had an office or didn't have an office here.

H Which wasn't the question—

D Which wasn't the question—right.

H But the headline for tonight will be GRAY SAYS DEAN LIES.

P Gray apparently didn't know what the testimony was—

D He never really sought to find out the facts on the question.

P Or the question, perhaps was put in a way that—that he misunderstood the question.

H (something inaudible)

M Another factor—those agents may not have reported it exactly.

D That's right.

H Gray says it is a matter of the FBI interview with Dean on (inaudible)—Dean said I will have to check it out when asked if Hunt had a White House office—he wasn't asked that—he was asked if they could see the White House office Hunt had, and Dean said I will have to check that. So then they say did Dean lie to the agents and perhaps to Gray? Looking back I would have to say that you were absolutely correct.

D It's such an irrelevant point even—that is the funny thing.

P As a matter of fact though—(inaudible)

D They are working on it right now and we should have it in the next hour.

H Wasn't Gray responsible for (inaudible)

D Well, (inaudible) has it right now. I just talked to

153

him. He would like to sit down and have the Senator talk to you right now because Byrd has indicated that he would like to have all the records of all the conversations we have had since the hearings started. It seems to me you had called me—you had initiated the calls—to report on the hearings.

P Well—What's that all about?

D He's a very down man right now—I might say.

H (Inaudible) Did you check—

D They are trying to find it over there right now. They are trying to find a copy of the transcript.

H (Inaudible)

D In fact that is a good point for Ziegler to say—that is what it reminds me of too.

H (Inaudible)

H (Inaudible)

P Well he may be feeling sorry for himself (inaudible)

D He sounds down—he realized after our conversation he sounded down—and I said, well I will talk to you later Pat and I needed conversion. He sort of paused and said, "boy I'm tired—keep the faith."

H (Inaudible) Has he been coached?

D I don't think so—Dick Moore is talking with him right now to get his feeling.

P What did Dick have to say? He won't be able to get a solution.

D (Inaudible) on the specifics.

H Here they go—they all get on the wire right quick.

D They got material—what they wanted—the information they wanted was in the office.

P It was in the office?

D To this day I don't really know where Hunt's safe was hidden.

H I don't think there was one—was there?

H John has been with Ziegler this morning.

D Yeah, I left them to come over here.

P You did. What are they working on?

D They are trying to get all the facts right now. The transcripts, the hearings, and the frame up.

P Is that true that (inaudible) or the Grand Jury? (Inaudible)

D In about fifteen or twenty minutes I will shoot back over there and (inaudible)

P How long will it take?

D   About fifteen minutes.

H   John had this (inaudible) he had lunch with Howard Baker's Administrative Assistant at the Administrative Assistant's request.

P   The same one who called Colson?

H   I don't know that it was the same one Bill had suggested. This fellow wanted to get guidance from Timmons as to what the President was expecting out of the hearing and he was talking about this executive privilege business and where we were going to stand on that. He expressed the personal view that the President could waive executive privilege. He did not think Ervin would accept the written interrogatories and that they would probably go to the subpoena.

P   (Inaudible)

H   Nothing was raised about Baker being concerned that he didn't have contact—nothing on the earlier request was raised at all. He did say that Baker was a little pissed off at Kleindienst because he had not met with him at all. He had one meeting scheduled—on Wednesday—and Kleindienst cancelled it. And it has not been rescheduled—so Baker has had no communication with Kleindienst. The day it was scheduled was the day you had your press conference and announced that under executive privilege neither Dean nor anyone else could go up which caught Baker unawares. This (inaudible)

P   Well, then

M   Plus the fact that they have impeachment and all Weicker does is (inaudible)

H   Oh yeah—

P   Don't get worried—but find John a lawyer right quick.

H   Well he is objecting to the agreement that Ervin made with Kleindienst—he is going to demand that they subpoena the Attorney General and the Director of the FBI to produce all the files, and materials they have on it.

D   I talked to Kleindienst last night—he raised that, and said he is working it out with Weicker but that Weicker was not dissatisfied with the hearings and so he thinks the views of the Chairman of the Senate Minority will bear the consequences.

P   (Inaudible) In a letter to (inaudible)

P   It is Baker's idea—he wanted to talk with Kleindienst and didn't want to talk to anybody else. That's the way we left it.

D   I think that Kleindienst ought to be aware of the fact that Baker is distressed that he hasn't made a greater effort to see him.

P   You tell him that will you?

D   I will.

P   Follow through—

E   Could I suggest that you call Kleindienst? You had the other conversation with him. Could you call him and say that you have a rumor that Baker is unhappy?

P   Oh yes, I will call him and tell him that.

H   I don't think he (Baker) is standing on his tippy-toes.

E   Well, with all the publicity Baker is not going to be in any position to talk with anybody in the White House.

P   He doesn't want to talk with anyone, he doesn't want to collaborate.

H   He wants to cooperate—this guy Abrams says he wants to be helpful, he wants to work things out. He told the President he wanted to do that through the Attorney General.

P   That's right but he said he didn't want to talk with anybody but Kleindienst.

D   Does Kleindienst know that?

P   Yes, of course.

H   Yes he told the President—the President then called Kleindienst and told him.

P   Were you there?

H   Yes.

M   What are they going to collaborate on?

P   Oh, I suppose on such matters as whether Gray wants the FBI (Inaudible)

E   Well, again, . . .

P   Ok, all done.

H   Well, again I go back to the fact that Baker says Kleindienst cancelled their meeting. He should be called—

P   OK—you do it. I would think Kleindienst—

H   (something about broadcast)

M   Well that's another thing . . .

M   Well let's suppose—(inaudible)—do you think you can get anything accomplished with Sam Ervin?

H   Yeah, but we needn't be concerned about Baker's (inaudible) with Ervin.

P   Well let's talk about Gray—the problem with him is I think he is a little bit stupid.

P   Frankly, I think too maybe Kleindienst doesn't help him any.

D   He has up to this point. John Ehrlichman talked to Kleindienst last night and asked whether he had been giving Gray guidance.

H   The trouble is Dick has been giving him guidance to bear down—something like this comes along and Gray overreacts—almost spasm reaction. We had to really lay on Gray not to give them access to the FBI files. This is literally the opposite of what Kleindienst told him.

P   You shouldn't have even needed that. It should have been second nature. He should have known you never turn over raw files to a full committee.

E   I talked to Dick Saturday night and he was beside himself with the failure of Gray to follow any advice. He said, "Hell we covered this situation carefully. We had a real session on it."

P   Well, Ok. I'll help.

H   Well what words of wisdom do we have from this august body at this point?

E   Our Brother Mitchell brings us some knowledge on executive privilege which I believe—

M   (Inaudible)

P   I wish Byrd would come out and state—I believe it would be well worthwhile to—

M   Well there certainly could be stronger people in Washington.

P   There may be some

Telephone call taken by the President

Hello
Oh Dick, I wanted to tell you on Baker that his Administrative Assistant was talking to Timmons and they (inaudible) there has not been any move to have any discussion (inaudible) Well, I just wanted to tell you that the point is nobody here can talk to Senator Baker with any justification at all.
Really, uh, uh
Today?
Well, the point is we are counting on you to be the man there Dick and I want to keep everybody else out of it so—and I told Baker—if you want to talk with someone here—who would like to talk with—he said you. I said fine, he is running down here—
Yeah.
How about this—why don't you get him on the telephone—and get him down there. It is sort of a line with

157

Baker saying he doesn't have any contact with the White House. Well, of course, he didn't want that—that is his fault—not our fault. We have to accept that would not be the right thing—on the other hand, it is essential for you to give him guidance. I get it, he wanted everybody to come back in public session.

Yeah

Yeah. No way, etc.

Well, we will keep in touch with you, Dick—basically (inaudible) that would be the best way—in terms of what (inaudible) and in our guidelines but then I think you really have to be our Baker handholder too. That's a hell of a tough job—you have to have him move in with you to do it, huh? Yeah, yeah,—the way, yeah, yeah, I understand. Postponed—right, right, yeah,

Yeah, yeah

Right,

Yeah

(Inaudible)

Yeah, some of these open—I understand you were as shocked as I was that some of the raw files had already been made available to the Committee.

Did he?

Oh, he said so, huh?

Yeah

Well do what you can.

Incidentally, with Weicker did you work that thing out with him? He said he had written a letter you know—yeah. Why don't you talk to him? Yeah, I expected that. Yeah, yeah. Right. You don't—you never have done that before. No—that is for the birds, right, you were doing it to try to get him cleared. Alright, let's leave it this way—you will handle Baker now—you will babysit him starting like in about ten minutes? Alright.

(End of telephone conversation)

P He says he has called Baker a dozen times—he is either busy or out of town—but he says he will try. He talked with Weicker for an hour on the phone. Well, anyway, he says he has the picture now. I thought Kleindienst—

H I would guess

P Oh, yes, he said he talked with him for an hour—I talked to Kleindienst—Maye it's not Kleindienst, maybe its Baker.

158

H   I would guess that is right. I have always said—they are always down here bitching about nobody calling them—nobody giving them anything and all that.

P   Yet his Administrative Assistant called Colson—or that is what Colson informed me.

H   That is a casual pitch.

D   They were looking for some—Baker was looking for some such room—sort of link with the White House.

P   It's got to be Kleindienst. Go ahead on executive privilege. How would you handle it?

M   All I have worked out was—in the form—what we discussed—

P   Well, I guess under the situation with the statement that we have, we are in a position to negotiate with the Committee on the how, but we are not in a position to cross the bridge and just to say Hunt and Liddy will go down—say this one will go down and testify in open—in a public session—and to say the White House staff will not. But you've got a lot of other things?

M   Oh, no.

P   Incidentally, that is what I told Baker too. We begin with that proposition and see what is there and what we can get by with.

M   On executive privilege, Mr. President, they already have something waived. (Inaudible) The point being is that this seems to be the only way to be involved. I would lay out the formula with Sam Ervin or negotiate it through Baker—or however else we can do it. And I would also put together a damn good PR team thing. The facts can be produced—what about this—what about the President's team? The team is important.

E   OK, I have written it. I can see that Chapin, for instance, could figure, without in any way bringing in the name of the President; so I am going to discuss right now with Baker that—

P   Not Baker.

E   Who else would you talk to? I've got a report here and I think I see where the danger points are and where they aren't. I would want to observe obviously any questions that may be asked. I can pinpoint some people now that really wouldn't make any difference.

H   John, you admit you are seeing danger points. If you send any one member of the White House up to testify it is no danger point for him but if some other one can't because it is a danger point then what you are saying is that the President was involved.

159

E   I didn't say danger from the sense of their being provocative—

M   Well, gentlemen for the sake of discussion (inaudible) the normal procedure for the Segretti matter and the like based on the evaluation of the FBI made (inaudible) or whether it is based on the Grand Jury and the trial transcript or whatever the record could have been available to me—investigation of the past memorandum would indict him. (inaudible) (two memorandum that the courts have public records)

P   We tried that move, John—

M   Well, I did too—before Mr. President. But now that the indictment has come out (inaudible) has the feeling that they have the documentation back of it. Now that the bag has come out.

D   I think the proof is in the pudding, so to speak—it is how this document is written and until I sit down and write that document. I have done part of it so to speak. I have done the Segretti thing and I am relatively satisfied that we don't have any major problems there. As I go to part A—to the Watergate—I haven't written—I haven't gone through the exercise yet in a real effort to write such a report, and I really can't say until I do it where we are and I certainly think it is something that should be done through.

P   What do you say on the Watergate (inaudible)

D   We can't be complete if we don't know, all we know is what, is what—

P   It is a negative in setting forth general information involving questions. Your consideration—your analysis, et cetera. You have found this, that. Rather than going into every news story and every charge, et cetera, et cetera. This, this this,—put it down—I don't know but

D   I don't think I can do it until I sit down this evening and start drafting.

H   I think you ought to hold up for the weekend and do that and get it done.

P   Sure

H   Give it your full attention and get it done.

P   I think you need—why don't you do this? Why don't you go up to Camp David?

D   I might do it, I might do it.

P   Completely away from the phone. Just go up there and (inaudible) I want a written report.

E   That would be my scenario. He presents it to you at your request. You then publish—(inaudible)

E   I know that but I don't care.

H   You are not dealing with the defendants on trial. You are only dealing with White House involvement. You are not dealing with the campaign.

D   That's where I personally . . .

P   You could write it in a way that you say this report was not comment on et cetera, et cetera, but, "I have reviewed the record, Mr. President and without at all compromising the right of defendants and so forth, some of whom are on appeal, here are the facts with regard to members of the White House staff et cetera, et cetera, that you have asked me about. I have checked the FBI records; I have read the Grand Jury transcripts—et cetera, et cetera.

E   As a matter of fact you could say, "I will not summarize some of the FBI reports on this stuff because it is my understanding that you may wish to publish this." Or you may allude to it in that way without saying that fact. Just say that I do not summarize all the FBI documents and so forth.

D   It is my understanding that all the FBI reports have been turned over to the Ervin Committee.

H   Not everything. He has only seen half of them.

D   Another vehicle might be, take the report I write and give it to Ervin and Baker under the same terms that they got the FBI reports. You could say, "Now, this has innuendo in it—and from this the press might assume things that shouldn't be assumed, but I want you to know everything we know." And publicly state that, "I have turned over a Dean Report to your Committee." Then begin to say that, "You see that various people have various ingredients which may be of assistance in testifying. But it is not worth their coming up here to be able to repeat to the Committee what is here in this report in some forum where they are going to be treated like they are in a circus. But I am also willing, based on this document, to set some ground rules for how we can have these people appear before the Committee."

H   In case of that the Committee would issue a warrant on our phone calls. Bully!

P   That's right.

H   That is all I know about the damn thing is that the Secret Service at some point has been bugged.

D   And that could go on forever with you on that tack. I could draw these things like this Staff into this report and have Kleindienst come get it and give it to Ervin in confidence—I am not talking about documents you see. I am talking about something we can spread as facts. You see you could even write a novel with the facts.

P   Inaudible

D   Inaudible

P   Inaudible

E   My thought is—

P   In other words, rather than fighting it, we are not fighting the Committee, of course—we are fighting the situation thing.

E   And I am looking to the future, assuming that some corner of this thing comes unstuck, you are then in a position to say, "Look, that document I published is the document I relied on, that is, the report I relied on."

P   This is all we knew.

H   That is all the stuff we could find out—

E   And now this new development is a surprise to me—I am going to fire A,B,C and D, now.

D   John, let me just raise this. If you make the document public the first thing that happens is the press starts asking Ziegler about it, expecting the document every day. "Well, why did Ehrlichman receive the call? How did they happen to pick out Ehrlichman? What did he do with the information after he got it?" Keep in mind every item, there will be a full day of quizzing. It will keep up day after day after day.

M   (Inaudible) I think there should be a concerted judgment about when and under what circumstances this is put out.

P   Another thing, let me say, that while Ziegler should be in on this stuff, I think Ziegler should (inaudible)

D   Well, you have said you are going to cooperate with the proper investigation.

P   But I am not going to comment on it while it is improper.

D   Well, why not put ourselves in a framework where you are way out above it? You are cooperating with the Committee, turn over the report, and no further comment.

P   I think you could get off of having Ziegler have to comment—I was trying to pull Ziegler off that for my own sake, too. We will give the Committee full cooperation, but we are not going to comment while the matter is being considered by the Committee—unless the Committee does this and that—

H   As John says for that reason don't publish the complete report. Only hand it over to the proper legislative committees.

P   Well, then we just turn it over to them. Can we get anything else out to the public? Putting out a statement to Republicans—we got a report from the White House?

E   I just got a report which bears out the—

H   Ron can make the statement.

E   Another way to do this would for you to have a meeting with Ervin and Baker.

P   Yeah. We have thought of that and decided against it.

E   Well we would have a reason for the meeting. This meeting would be for the purpose of turning over the document and discussing ground rules and before you did that you would have to have it all agreed in advance as to what the ground rules would be—namely, you've got quid pro quo here because you could come to Baker or to the Committee directly and say, "look, I will turn over the Dean report to you, providing we can agree on how witnesses will be treated up there."

You could even screw executive privilege.

P   John—for example, if you were talking about executive privilege this really gets down to specifics. What you do about executive privilege. What about Colson—does he go or not?

D   I think Colson has to go.

P   He has to go?

D   Oh, yes.

H   Everybody goes under John's plan including Ehrlichman and me—everybody except John Dean, who doesn't go because he's got the client/lawyer privilege.

M   I think you and John could be negotiated out.

P   Should we negotiate it now?

M   I think the Court would show that a very simple thought, involvement with the (inaudible)

D   Well the trouble is—one of our arguments—

H   Let us go John—I don't see any argument against our going if you are going to let anybody go.

D   That's right.

H   You've got less to hurdle with us than you have with some of the others. Sure if you get the big fish out there in front of the television cameras I think you fellows would be tough. I think Strachan wouldn't get them nearly as excited as John and me going out there.

P   Strachan and Chapin.

H   Well, Chapin wouldn't have to go before them.

H   If you could do it in Executive Session,

D   Then we would have no reason not to go—

H   Then why hold us back?

P   These Executive Session things always appeal to me—Now of course you could always say (inaudible)

D   Maybe we could invite the Committee down to the Roosevelt Room or Blair House.

H   Maintain informality.

H   I don't know what Hunt will do—

P   Would Executive Session help?

E   Well, Executive Session I suspect would at this point—(inaudible) I really think these guys are concerned about this Mexican standoff and I think they will all—I do think that Ervin's crack on television about arresting people who cross the line about (inaudible) crossing the line—litigation

M   In addition to that you have a long—really lengthy

P   This thing could go on for a hell of a long time.

H   Sure it is going to be a long time.

D   Better take it on the counsel thing.

H   That's what he doesn't want.

D   I know, but—

H   Someone like Dwight Chapin—that's the easy one—you did that with someone who had no contact

P   As bright as he is (inaudible) As long as Dean—they didn't test it. We asked them to. They didn't bite that one very fast did they John?

H   Chapin is the guy to ask on. You try to go to a federal judge on Chapin and that will be a good Court opinion. He is a former employee. He had no policy role, he had no major contact with the President.

M   (inaudible)

P   Chapin?

M   He is no longer employed.

H   He is the object of a subpoena. He's been called to testify at the Gray hearings, and what not. But he knows he's done nothing.

M   They could get him up there and—

E   Well, the precedent on this frightens me.

P   We have a precedent problem. In the case of a present White House employee there will not be a precedent problem.

M   In the case of a present one it does not—

P   Then they would have to go in front of the cameras and show how it would not become an important first.

E   Of course we have the anomoly of Clark Mollen-hoff running up and trying to give testimony in a civil service ceremony here now—saying, "ask me a question—ask me a question, This is a Kangaroo Court." The guy running the hearing is telling him to sit down and shut up, and what is happening here is that the government is asserting the executive privilege.

M   No, they are not. That is not executive privilege.

E   It is the closest thing to it. The point is, who's privilege is it to assert? What do you do with a Chapin? I think—I don't know want you to think this is the reason I called you—to figure out a scenario but I assume that immediately a subpoena issued, that on behalf of the President you would immediately go over to the Committee saying that the Executive asserts privilege.

P   Let me ask this. This question is for John Ehrlichman and Dean. You were the two that felt the strongest on executive privilege thing. If I am not mistaken, you thought we ought to draw a line here. Have you changed your mind now?

D   No, I think it is a terrific statement. It puts you just where you should be. There is enough flexibility in it.

P   Well, all John Mitchell is arguing then, is that now we use flexibility in order to get off the coverup line.

E   And as I told him, I am so convinced that we are right on the statement that I have never gone beyond that. He argues that we are being hurt badly by the way it is being handled. And I told him, let's see—

H   I think that is a valid evaluation on the individual point, but that is where you look like you are covering up right there. That is the only active step that you have taken to cover up the Watergate all along was that.

P   Even though we have offered to cooperate?

H   On legal grounds, precedence, tradition, constitutional grounds and all that stuff you are just fine, but to the guy who is sitting at home who watches John Chancellor say that the President is covering this up by this historic review blanket of the wildest exercise of executive privilege in American history and all that—he says "what the hell's he covering up, if he's got no problem why doesn't he let them go talk."

M   And it relates to the Watergate—it doesn't relate to Henry Kissinger—foreign affairs or anything. The President and all that business they don't know what the hell you are talking about.

P   Maybe we shouldn't have made the statement.

H   We should have because it puts you in a much better position. They were over here. That is what Ervin wanted. He wanted all of us up there with unlimited, total, wide open. The statement in a sense puts us over here. Now you move back to about here and you probably can get away with that.

E   You can get away with it in the Watergate context. You said executive privilege and then you applied it in the first instance to Gray. I wouldn't change that, and that is exactly right. At the same time you are in a position to say, "Oh, now there is this other case and what I regarded there consistent with my statement is so, and so, and so."

H   It is very clear—that the questions once properly asked don't have any bearing on these people's relation to the President. Which they don't. The President had nothing to do with it.

M   I don't know.

E   There again, it would be hard to get proof. You are right and we are going to need some of that for our campaign. The argument will be that the President has backed off his rock solid position on executive privilege and is now letting Chapin, Colson, Haldeman and everybody testify.

P   (inaudible)

E   They are saying that there are PR problems.

P   People don't think so—Several—That's right.

H   They don't think—they think you clamped down an iron curtain and won't let anybody out of here ever. It was my understanding—I talked to you or maybe someone else—that the Committee's operating rules do not permit witnesses to have Counsel.

D   That is Grand Jury. I have never heard that about the Committee.

H   About the Committee?

D   No—not the Committee.

P   On the contrary the committees—ever since the days I was there they have always allowed counsel.

D   I can't imagine their not allowing counsel.

P   No sir, committees allow counsel.

H   It seems to me if we are going to do this that it becomes important to any White House staff members who testify that they should not only have private counsel, personal counsel, but that the President's Counsel should be there because you are under oath, as his waiver of executive privilege and the President's Counsel should be there

166

to enforce the limitation and the witness should not have to be in the position of saying, "That is one I can't answer because it is outside the grounds."

E You are appealing that someone should do it then for us?

P How would it be with the Executive Session thing?

H They would probably have television at that. What do you do when something comes up that is top secret?

P How do you handle that PR wise?

M You handle that only with the Executive Session. Otherwise you come up with another Roman holiday like we have had with Kleindienst and Gray. A fact-finding operation is there to get the facts and not to put on a political circus as they have in the past.

D If there were no cameras up there, there would be no reason to have the Executive Session because—

H Well then you come back to arguing for an open session with no television cameras.

P (Inaudible) I forgot about the formal session. It is a formal session.

E I think that is the least personal—

D That is correct we have said—no debate and there shouldn't be.

M Well that won't wash.

E Yeah, I probably think it would.

P We ought to see about it.

D I think it is arguable. They are interested in eliciting information and I think (inaudible)

H Is there an executive session of a Senate Committee where other Senators can come in, where any Senator has the privilege of submitting questions? Senator Kennedy would want to sit there I am sure.

P He can't ask questions.

H He can't?

D Not unless (inaudible)

P All the members (inaudible) but we shall see. But it is normal practice that no one can ask questions but members of the Committee.

H But Teddy could still sit there in the audience and then go out to the TV camera and say (inaudible) look this is what is being said, et cetera.

P Oh, well we are going to have that.

D I think if he did that he would be terribly criticized.

H I was just thinking in the membership of the Committee. We are in reasonably good shape and that the people we have on the Committee are not as bad as some Senators who would turn the use of TV afterwards for their own purposes.

P Not as spectacular.

M (inaudible) Could I point out (inaudible)

D (Inaudible)

H When do they start hearings now?

D (Inaudible)

P The topic—here—we have plenty of time for those hearings, but what Bob is concerned about the PR. We don't have much time.

D PR is going to start being better right away with the termination of the Gray hearings for ten weeks that will let some steam out of that—

P The PR. What I meant is, and anyway that the main thing is to do the right thing. Don't rush too fast with the PR but it takes time to write, et cetera. John has to have time to write this report. Do we broach this whether we have a report or not? (Inaudible voice and answer)

P Let me ask you this: On the broaching of that, should we get Kleindienst to be the broacher?

(Inaudible)

P The point is, who else? I can't.

D That's right. Kleindienst in his conversations with Ervin and Baker—Ervin indicated that he would like to talk with Kleindienst about the executive privilege question. Maybe it is now time to get that channel re-opened again.

M Let me make this suggestion.

H Write it out both chapter and verse—some exhibits. You are gonna—

M Let me something first. I think one of you mentioned having a meeting with the Committee. It might be well say you want to discuss the executive privilege point with the Chairman. But don't discuss it with the Chairman until you get up there. At least this advises them that the discussion of the matter is available.

E And then ask him not to take a Committee move on the subject either until—

H Until he has talked to them, or the Committee has talked about it.

P Would this be the time (inaudible)—

P Who is going to talk to him?

E Who is going to be there?

M   Kleindienst talks to—

P   In other words to Baker and Ervin. The conversation could occur like tomorrow. We have to move in this direction, regardless of the report. We have to move to start the negotiation.

M   Well, I think there is too much lead time. It will get into the press before the Committee meeting. What is Wally Johnson's status?

D   That's funny—because he is still here regardless of the fact that he has been announced apparently. I gather he will be in with the Attorney General. I was thinking maybe to preserve my Counsel role with Ervin and Baker that I ought to be present with Kleindienst.

P   I agree, and the four of us sit down and talk about executive privilege—we won't get into any of the substance.

P   The thing about your being there with Kleindienst they might be skeptical—

D   I must say they were pretty good when they were dealing with me as Counsel—that is one of the reasons I am not one of the—(inaudible)

M   I think it would be appropriate for your Counsel to be present.

D   That's right.

P   Alright. Now that that is done let's get down to the questions—

D   I think that possible Kleindienst ought to call today and let Ervin and Baker know that he would like to meet with them early next week to talk about executive privilege and indicate that I would be present to see if we can find—

P   A formula for them to get all the information that they desire.

D   That's right.

H   This would be an unpublicized meeting.

D   Unpublicized.

P   That seems to me to be a sensible way.

H   I wouldn't say early in the week I think he better say Monday so you can get them before they change.

P   (Inaudible) What is your position on Dean having to testify?

H   He might.

P   We would have to draw a line there, wouldn't we John?

M   I would agree wholeheartedly (inaudible) To have

169

your Counsel testify would be a mistake.

H   Even if Dean would have to, it would be a mistake (inaudible)

P   Well on the Dean thing—you simply say well that is out. Dean has made this report and here is everything Dean knows.

E   I think John on Monday you could say to Ervin if the question comes up, "I know the President's mind on this and he is adamant about my testifying as such. At the same time he has always indicated that the fruits of my investigation should be available to you." And just leave it at that for the time being.

D   One issue that may come up as the hearings go along is the fact that the focus on this book is that Dean knew—as you all know I was all over this thing like a wet blanket. I was everywhere—everywhere they look they are going to find Dean.

P   Sure.

H   Well, I don't think that is bad.

E   I don't either. You were supposed to be.

P   You were our investigator. You were directed by the President to get me all the facts. Second, as White House Counsel you were on it to assist people in the Executive Branch who were being questioned. Say you were there for the purpose of getting information. That was your job.

D   That's right.

P   But the main point certainly is that Dean had absolutely no operational activity. The wonderful thing about your position is that as far as they are concerned—your position has never never been as operative.

H   That is true—that even in the private sessions then—you volunteered to give them a statement on the whole question of your recommendation of Liddy which is the only point of possible kind of substantive culpability that you could have and now you can satisfy all of those actions—that is if you want to.

P   At the President's direction you have never done anything operational, you have always acted as Counsel. We've got to keep our eye on the Dean thing—just give them some of it—not all of it. I don't suppose they say John—no—we won't take it. (inaudible) Just take the heat of being—on the other hand you've got Chapin going and you've got Colson going.

H   No, he doesn't.

P   You've got (inaudible) and (inaudible) going.

M   You can't keep them out of all these sessions, Bob. I will get back to (inaudible) on the basis of Chapin's talk to Segretti last week.

D   They can subpoena any of us. There is no doubt about that. If they don't serve it here because they can't get in. They can serve you at home somewhere. They can always find you.

H   We move to Camp David and hide! They can't get in there.

P   Well, go ahead.

D   The question is once you are served and you decline—then you have a defense situation. Now I would say that it would get very difficult to believe that they will go to contempt on people who are present White House employees.

P   They would on a Colson wouldn't they?

D   That would be a good test case for them to go on. The other thing though is they could subpoena Colson to come up there and Colson could then say, "Well, I decline to testify on the grounds that I think it is privileged communication, or privileged activity." Again you get a little fuzzier.

M   If they ask some unusual questions—

D   Yes, that's right.

D   Then it will get much fuzzier as to whether or not they would cite him for contempt or not.

P   Suppose the Judge tomorrow orders the move when he opens up the Grand Jury and says I want them to call Haldeman/Ehrlichman and everybody else they didn't call before.

D   They would send them all down.

P   Then do you still go on this with the Ervin Committee—the point is—if the Grand Jury decides to go into this thing, what do you think of that?

E   I think you say, "Based on what I know about this case, I can see no reason why I should be concerned about what the Grand Jury process is about." That's all.

P   Then they would have to do both—appear before the Grand Jury and the Committee?

D   Sure.

E   You have to bottom your defense, your position on the report. And the report says nobody was involved, and you have to stay consistent with that.

M   Theoretically, I think you will find the Grand Jury is not about to get mixed up with that sort of thing.

H   (Inaudible) Well, there is danger in a Grand Jury.

D   Well, there are no rules.

P   Well, Grand Juries are not really very fair some-times—

D   That's right.

M   (Inaudible)

H   What would happen? Would Silbert be the prosecutor on this?

D   Unless the court appointed a special prosecutor.

H   Which he could do.

P   We better see tomorrow about that—but—if that is the case who is to move now on the first one? Who is to call Kleindienst?

D   I am to follow through with Kleindienst, Sir. I am going to call him and tell him to call Baker first and then Ervin and tell them that you would like to meet with them on Monday to discuss and to explore—a formula for providing the information they need that in a way that does not cause a conflict with general policies on executive privilege.

P   Yet meets their need for information. Right?

D   Right.

P   They have requested that kind of a talk already, haven't they?

D   Yes.

M   You will sit down with Dick, Mr. President?

P   Yes, yes. I don't want you to talk about this report with anyone.

D   Well, we are going out over the weekend (inaudible)

H   Also write out a thing for Kleindienst so that—

P   I think you can talk to Kleindienst. I think you can do most of the talking. You can do it.

D   I don't think we ought to read anything in this first session but I think we ought to let them know that we are thinking about reaching some sort of—

P   Saying, "What would you think here?"

H   Stay loose.

P   We want to see what can be worthwhile with regard to this—we will talk about informal sessions. Has Ervin's position been he insists on formal sessions? Is that his position?

D   Well, we don't know. We have never really discussed it.

H   His response to your position—naturally that is what you have now—that is Ervin's response—that written stuff isn't any good, "I want the body, we really can't ask a piece of paper questions." Now, what we are saying is that . . .

P The written thing was in which?

E That was a Ziegler (inaudible) I believe, not a statement.

H But it is a general thing. That was in your press conference. You, they will provide written—I think you said it—

P I may have said it.

H I think you did in the press conference and Ervin's response is to that. Your statement could have been, "these people will be happy to provide written answers to appropriate questions."

P Are you sure it wasn't in a statement?

E No, I am sure we used informal —

D It came up the third time when I responded to Eastland's invitation to furnish information, and you said we would furnish written information and then it was repeated after that—that we would be happy to supply information in writing.

H Then Ervin responded—he specifically rejected that only on the grounds that you can't ask questions of a piece of paper. So we are giving him that opportunity. He hasn't said that the processes of the Senate require that those questions be answered in (inaudible).

P What is the argument that you give John to people as to why Executive Session rather than an open session?

D Well, I—

P You can't really give—you can't really attack the Committee's guidance. What do you say?

D Well, I think what I would do is to talk a little about the position in our mind—with the position he took so vocally in the Gravell case.

P That's right.

D Where he came out and said that a Lesislative Aide could not be called to question for advice they give their Senator or Congressman. He just went on and at great length cited executive privilege, etc.

P He will say this is not advice to the President. Go ahead.

D Then I will say that these are men who do advise the President and we have to draw the line.

P And that's the principle involved and to have that principle discussed in open session forum is the kind of thing where you have to go off to the Bench where the Jury doesn't hear it.

D Well—

H I don't think, John or Dick, if they're in a Monday meeting should tip their hand and offer to appear in Executive Session and get them on to the Executive Session wicket.

D No, no, I agree.

H We should openly indicate a willingness to listen to ideas as to what would be done and an open-mindedness to try to work something out. If that is going to become the issue it seems to me that that is an issue we could win publicly where we may not be able to win it with the Senate.

E Where if we go in with the idea of expressing the President's concern about the protection of his people is expected.

P I am also concerned about frankly having matters of seniority debated publicly. That is a matter that ought to be debated privately.

D That's right.

P And the fact that it is raised does not indicate guilt. That is part of his argument for Gravell, too. That fact that it is raised does not indicate guilt. That is what we are really talking about here. But having it in public session, those—

D I will work out a complete negotiating scenario and have thought it through before I go up.

H Your objective in that meeting is simply for you to indicate to them a willingness to discuss. It is not to have a proposal for them to accept or reject.

D I agree. The scenario is for myself and for Dick (inaudible)—it is a record for the future.

P It is the record for the future. Maybe you can tell Ervin on the mountaintop that this is a good way to set up a procedure for the future. You know what I mean, where future cases of this sort are involved. We are making a lot of history here, Senator.

M And the Senator can be a great part of it.

P A lot of history. We are setting a stirring precedent. The President, after all, let's find out what the President did know, talk about the Hiss Case.

D Ervin away from his staff is not very much and I think he might just give up the store himself right there and lock himself in. You know I have dealt with him for a number of years and have seen that happen. I have reached accord with him on legislation—

H   If he holds out for anything you may get an answer from him—(inaudible)

P   Suppose now he just takes the adamant line—nothing?

D   Doesn't sound like Richardson's information— sounds like him sitting and saying nothing.

P   Well, if he just says, "We are going to have public sessions. It's got to be that or else."

E   Then we say, "Maybe we have a law suit Senator and it is going to be a long while before legislative hearings and what not."

P   If you want your hearings—then that is the other thing. The other point is would it not be helpful to get Baker enlisted in some way in advance. If that could be done not begging him. Could we put Kleindienst to that thing?

M   On the second step—not on the opening step.

P   Even on the opening step the problem that I have here is that if Baker sits there and just parrotts Ervin's adamant statement—"Hell no, there can't be anything except public sessions," you have nothing to do.

M   You know how these Senators act—Baker will lay the whole thing out on the table.

P   Yes, I guess you are right. Baker, on the other hand, Kleindienst should at least call and say look Howard, "Why don't you try to work something out here?"

H   Baker could in effect say—we want to work something out—what can you give us?

P   You can't be tough. Right now, Howard is just going for a law suit.

H   Give us a hand and try to open this up. Baker could find that much better there, to be positive this time around.

D   Don't lock yourself in—we will have another session or so on it.

P   Yeah, the other point is if they insist (inaudible) it becomes essential, then than this be forgotten and then have a law suit.

E   You say well then ok, why don't we now discuss are we going to go legally and perhaps we can at least agree on what apparent legal issues there are, so instead of being three years it will only be a year and a half.

H   Get it settled before this Administration moves, or gets kicked out.

D   They know it is many months, who they are going after and under the circumstances that they know they have a tough law suit ahead of them. They have to hire counsel. It is going to cost money to freeze it on their side; they don't have money. They don't have Department of Justice to handle their case; they have to bring in special counsel who probably know nothing about executive privilege, will have to be educated. Get the Library of Congress clanking away getting all the precedence out and the like.

H   We've got all that.

D   It is a major operation for them to bring in. They have to get a resolution of the Senate to do it—

E   Of course Ervin is a Constitutional expert himself. Any Constitutional expert might want to do that.

P   Yeah. Have you considered any other possibilities? John, you are the one who is supposed to know the bodies.

D   That's right. I think we have had a good go-round on the things now.

P   Do you think we want to go this route now? Let it hang out so to speak?

D   Well, it isn't really that—

H   It's a limited hang out.

D   It is a limited hang out. It's not an absolute hang out.

P   But some of the questions look big hanging out publicly or privately.

D   What it is doing, Mr. President, is getting you up above and away from it. That is the most important thing.

P   Oh, I know. I suggested that the other day and they all came down negative on it. Now what has changed their minds?

D   Lack of candidate or a body.

H   Laughter.

M   (Inaudible) We went down every alley.

P   I feel that at a very minimum we've got to have this statement. Let's look at it. I don't know what it—where in the hell is it—If it opens up doors, it opens up doors— you know.

H   John says he is sorry he sent those burglars in there—and that helps a lot.

P   That's right.

E   You are very welcome, sir.

176

(Laughter)

H Just glad the others didn't get caught.

P Yeah, the ones he sent to Muskie and all the rest; Jackson; and Hubert, etc.

E I get a little chill sitting over there now thinking of those people.

P Yeah. I would hate to be those fellows at the moment.

P Incidentally, we don't plan to have a press briefing today do we?

E We hadn't planned it—it wouldn't hurt.

H Well, I have a meeting upstairs with John at 3:30—with (inaudible)

E Alright he is going to top our press tomorrow.

P Let's let it go.

E Qk.

P OK suppose you take care of it now and I won't come over there. If you get any more soundings let me hear Friday. It would be my thought then that I would tend to break it off at 4:30 or 5:00 p.m.

M 4:00 p.m. will be the minimum—I have to get to New York.

P Yeah, then its done. Yeah. I understand. Bob—what time is my take-off scheduled for Florida? Are you ready?

H Yes, sir.

P Well we won't rush.

E It is 3:16—how about 15 or 20 minutes from now?

Meeting: The President, Haldeman, Ehrlichman and Ziegler, EOB Office, March 27, 1973. (11:10 am - 1:30 pm)

P I don't believe that I should go out on national television tonight or tomorrow and go out on the Watergate Commission and then come on the next day on national television on Vietnam. I don't like the feel of that. I don't think you—can it ready by that time? My view is to get the Vietnam thing out of the way, and then get this right as you could. In other words, that gives you time.

E The picture of the Congress having an inquiry going on and the Grand Jury in session, the Judicial branch—

P Right.

E It seems to me it gives you a good opening for you

177

to step in and say there doesn't seem to be anybody except me in position with all this. I have talked with the Chief Justice of the United States; I have talked with Senator Ervin, Senator Baker and I, after that consultation, have posed this three-branch—

P   For an inquiry to start with the proposition of Ervin and Baker, where you don't come a cropper right there at the beginning on whether you can get the three branches. What's your view of the three-branch, John?

E   Well, I am not sure you could get it either.

P   What,—well, that's it. Suppose you couldn't. Then I still think that it is good possibly that I—but we've got to have somebody other than me that could broker it. The problem you've got to recognize is that Haldeman can't, you can't, and Dean can't. Mainly because you possibly could, but its also the (unintelligible) about the whole White House. What we might have to do—I hate to assign this to anybody, but I might have to use Rogers on this to be the broker.

E   Yep.

P   Rogers can be a good broker at times. I don't know whether you could get a—

(Knocking on door -)

P   Oh, hi. How are you?

Z   Thought we would just check in.

P   Sure, sure. Right, right. In position, right—

Z   We have the patient rehabilitation veto today and the (unintelligible) to Thieu in South Vietnam, preparations—.

P   Right.

Z   I talked to Dean and to Moore this morning in terms of whether or not we say anything (unintelligible) the Grand Jury.

P   Right.

Z   And Dean's feeling is that we should not today.

P   That is my feeling.

Z   And Moore's feeling is that we should not today, and I concur in that.

P   Yeah. My view is today, unless you've got something more to say, I would simply say I have nothing to add to what (unintelligible) I think that would be better, just get out there and act like your usual cocky, confident self.

Z   Then if I am asked a question about whether or not

Dean would appear before the Grand Jury, if I am asked that question—

P   Yeah.

Z   How should I handle that?

P   That's tough.

Z   I could—Two options: One would be to say that (unintelligible); the other would be to say the (unintelligible).

P   (unintelligible) Well, if you say (unintelligible) permission—What do you think, John? You tell him. Well, it is easier to get out of it if you say well that is not a matter (unintelligible)

Z   I am inclined to think that today my best position is just to say that this was discussed yesterday. We are willing to cooperate.

P   Why don't you say, "We have indicated cooperation and when we see the form of the request, or whatever it is—"

Z   "These matters must proceed in an orderly manner and I am not going to get up here and comment on the possibility of—"

P   "of future action" (unintelligible)

E   The other thing you might do is—this would put our friend John Dean III in a tough spot—say, "while there have been some accusations against him, he's really in the poorest position to defend himself of anybody in the government."

(Material unrelated to Presidential actions deleted)

E   I don't know whether it would add anything, really, from our standpoint to say this, but the point is here that the poor guy is under disability to step out and defend himself because of his position. Because he is Counsel to the President, and that in a way—

P   That helps—

E   inhibits him. Well,—

P   But (intelligible) for Ron to get into that?

E   Well, but it is in the saying, would he appear before a Grand Jury?

P   Why don't we just say, "Well, this is a matter that is not before us." Point out that he is Counsel to the President, Counsel to the White House—use the White House. Say, "He is the White House Counsel and therefore, his appearance before any judicial group, therefore, is on a different basis from anybody else, "which is basically what

I - you know when I flatly said Dean would not appear but others would. You know, I did say that, and of course—

E   It was on a different basis. And at the same time, a man in any position ought to be given a chance to defend himself from these groundless charges.

P   "Mr. Dean certainly wants the opportunity to defend himself against these charges. He would welcome the opportunity and what we have to do is to work out a procedure which will allow him to do so consistent with his unique position of being a top member of the President's staff but also the Counsel. There is a lawyer, Counsel—not lawyer, Counsel—but the responsibility of the Counsel for confidentiality."

Z   Could you apply that to the Grand Jury?

E   Absolutely. The Grand Jury is one of those occasions where a man in his situation can defend himself.

P   Yes. The Grand Jury. Actually if called, we are not going to refuse for anybody called before the Grand Jury to go, are we, John?

E   I can't imagine (unintelligible)

P   Well, if called, he will be cooperative, consistent with his responsibilities as Counsel. How do we say that?

E   He will cooperate.

P   He will fully cooperate.

E   Better check that with Dean. I know he's got certain misgivings on this.

Z   He did this morning.

P   Yeah. Well, then, don't say that.

E   Well, I think you can pose the dilemna without saying flatly what you are going to do.

P   Yeah. We—But maybe you just don't want to. You better not try to break into it, Ron.

Z   You get into posing the dilemna—

P   Then they are going to break into questions. I would simply stall them off today. Say that is not before us at this time, but let me emphasize, as the President has indicated, there will be complete cooperation consistent with the responsibilities that everybody has on the separation of powers. Fair enough? And, of course, consistent with Mr. Dean's other responsibilities as a Counsel. See? How about just saying it that way? Well, John, do you have doubts?

E   No. But if Zeigler opens, Ziegler has to answer something. About the only thing that occurred to me when I read this thing yesterday was somehow or another, he should be introducing the fact that Dean is going to get a chance to clear his name.

P Yeah.

E Eventually there is going to be an opportunity for that in some forum, at some time, in some way. But maybe you get into—

P I don't think this is the day to do it.

Z I think that is right. Give them more than a day to see how we approach the whole matter (unintelligible— R Z exit).

(Material unrelated to Presidential actions deleted)

E On the FBI, we will start moving some names to you. I hope you will look into that guy that (unintelligible) mentioned - we are trying to get a resume and some background.

P A judge with a prosecuting background might be a hell of a good thing. I have decided when we move on it, it must be simultaneous. Gray comes in and says, "I am sorry, I can't get confirmed. I don't want to be confirmed in a way in which there is any division. There must be unanimous support for whoever is, and support for and trust in, the Director of the FBI. As a result of the hearings to date, it is obvious that I am not going to get that kind of support in the Senate, even though I believe that I may be confirmed under the circumstances, I respectively request that you withdraw my name." We withdraw his name and send somebody else down. That is a very sound basis. I am thinking of doing that. I would hope next week right after (unintelligible).

E Ah, what would you think of doing that simultaneously with the appointment of a Commission. We could make it in the same announcement. Could say, "here is a fine man who has been unfortunately splattered by this thing. It is a case study in how bystanders can get splashed by this sort of thing. It's not a fight where he came in."

P You think, also, John, or at least you probably gave somebody the idea, that we should get Kleindienst out, too, at this point?

E Yeah, yeah.

P How do we do that?

E Well, I am going to see him today, and Bob's going to talk to him, and we will hit him from two directions.

P Get Kleindienst to resign?

E   Oh, no, no. Get him out front.

P   Oh, I thought you said get him out of the office.

E   Oh, no. I hadn't talked about that. That's Bill Rogers.

P   Oh, I am sorry, John.

E   No. We talked this morning about getting him out front.

P   I am afraid its (unintelligible) of canning him right away. Let's see. Let's see about that. Maybe we can. Well, what have you got to report. John and I have just started on (unintelligible).

H   All I have is Dean's report. I did not talk to Mitchell, because this thing changed what you might want from Mitchell. He had a long conversation again today with Paul O'Brien. Everybody has been talking (unintelligible) this, that, and all that. Of course, O'Brien is very distressed with Mitchell. The more he thinks about it, the more O'Brien comes down to Mitchell could cut this whole thing off, if he would just step forward and cut it off. He said the fact of the matter is as far as Gray could determine, Mitchell did sign off on it. And if that's what it is, the empire will crack.

E   You said, "Gray."

P   What's that? I am sorry.

H   O'Brien, not Gray. As far as O'Brien can determine Mitchell did sign off and Dean believes that to be the case also. Dean doesn't think he can prove it, and apparently O'Brien can't either, but they both think that.

P   That's my—

H   And the more O'Brien thinks about it, the more it bothers him with all he knows, to see all the people getting whacked around in order to keep the thing from focusing on John Mitchell, when inevitably it is going to end up doing that anyway and all these other people are going to be so badly hurt they are not going to be able to get out from under. And that's one view. Now to go back on the Magruder situation as O'Brien reports it, having spent several hours with Magruder, yesterday afternoon, O'Brien and Parkinson. Jeb believes, or professes to believe, and O'Brien is inclined to think he really does believe, that the whole Liddy plan, the whole super-security operation, super-intelligence operation was put together by the White House, by Haldeman, Dean and others. Liddy, Dean cooked the whole thing up at Haldeman's instructions. The whole idea was the need for a super-intelligence operation. Now there is some semblance of, some validity

182

to the point, that I did talk, not with Dean, but with Mitchell, about the need for intelligence activity and—.

P   And Dean recommended Liddy?

H   Yes. But not for intelligence. Dean recommended Liddy as the General Counsel.

P   Yeah, but this is where Magruder might come—well, go ahead.

H   That Mitchell bought the idea that was cooked up at the White House for a super-intelligence operation, and that this was all set and an accomplished fact in December of 1971, before Liddy was hired by the Committee. But then Liddy was hired by the Committee to carry it out and that that's why Dean sent Liddy over to the Committee. Then there was a hiatus. There were these meetings in Mitchell's office where Liddy unveiled his plan. And the first plan he unveiled, nobody bought. They all laughed at it. It was so bizarre. So he went back to the drawing board and came back with a second plan and the second plan didn't get bought either—that was at the second meeting—and everything just kind of lingered around them. It was sort of hanging fire. Liddy was pushing to get something done. He wanted to get moving on his plans. And at that point he went to Colson and said, "Nobody will approve any of this, and, you know, we should be getting going on it." And Colson then got into the act in pushing to get moving with the Colson phone call to Magruder saying, "Well, at least listen to these guys." Then the final step was—all of this was rattling around in January—the final step was when Gordon Strachan called Magruder and said Haldeman told him to get this going, "The President wants it done and there is to be no more arguing about it." This meaning the intelligence activity, the Liddy program. Magruder told Mitchell this, that Strachan had told him to get it going on Haldeman's orders on the President's orders and Mitchell signed off on it. He said, "OK, if they say to do it, go ahead."

P   Was that this bugging?

H   The whole thing, including the bugging. The bugging was implicit in the second plan. He doesn't seem to be sure whether it was implicit or explicit.

P   Well, anyway—

H   He doesn't think that particular bug implicit, but that the process of bugging was implicit and, as I didn't realize it, nor did (unintelligible), but it was also in the Sandwedge going way back—the early plan. That, incidentally, is a potential source of fascinating problems in that it involved Mike Acree, who is now the Customs Commissioner or something, Joe Woods, a few other people.

P   Nothing happened?

H   It wasn't done, activated, but these—At some point, according to Magruder, after this was then signed off and put under way Mitchell called Liddy into his office and read him the riot act on the poor quality of (unintelligible). That's basically the scenario or summary of what Magruder told the lawyer. Dean's theory is that both Mitchell and Magruder both realize that they now have their ass in this thing, and that they are trying to untangle it. Not necessarily working together again, but they are. In the process of that they are mixing apples and oranges for their own protection. And that they are remembering various things in connection with others, like Liddy and Hunt.

(Material not related to Presidential actions deleted)

H   He says for example, Magruder doesn't realize how little Dean told Liddy. He thinks that Dean sent Liddy in (unintelligible) Liddy (unintelligible) frankly to satisfy Dean. His screaming to Liddy was that he was General Counsel over there and also take as a side activity the political intelligence because we do need information on demonstrators and stuff like that. That they are not doing anything about, but he never got into any setting up an elaborate intelligence apparatus.

P   Ok.

H   Dean says that as a matter of fact, in contrast to Magruder's opinion, at the first meeting where a Liddy plan was presented, everybody at the meeting laughed at the plan on the basis that it was just so bizarre that it was absurd and completely funny.

P   Yeah.

H   The second meeting, Dean came into the meeting late. He was not there during most of the presentation, but when he came in he could see that they were still on the same plan of orbit and he says in effect, I got Mitchell off the hook because I took the initiative in saying, "You know it is an impossible proposal and we can't, we shouldn't even be discussing this in the Attorney General's office," and all that Mitchell agreed, and then that is when Dean came over and told me that he had just seen this wrap-up on it, and that it was impossible; that they shouldn't be doing it; that we shouldn't be involved in it and we ought to drop the whole thing. Then as Dean said, "I saw a problem there and I thought they had turned it off and in any event I wanted to stay ten miles away from it," and did." He said the problem from then on, starting somewhere in early January probably, was that Liddy was never really given any guidance after that. Mitchell was in the midst of the ITT and all that stuff, and didn't focus on it, and Magruder was running around with other things and didn't pay much attention, and Liddy was kind of bouncing around loose there.

E   Well, now, how do you square that with the allocation of money to it?

H   Well that presumably was the subject in focus by somebody. Who signed off on that?

E   Magruder, possibly Mitchell, possibly Stans, certainly—

P   I don't know that they can say that the allocation of money for this super-intelligence operation, I don't think I ever—that's what Magruder said—

E   Someone was paid to focus on—

H   Yeah, someone focused and agreed that there had to be some intelligence and that it would take some money and that Liddy should get it.

E   And against the background of the two plans being presented and rejected, the logical question that would arise is, well, what are you going to do with the money? You don't have an approved plan?

H   Yeah.

E   So that doesn't put anything together.

P   Well, it doesn't hang together, but it could in the sense of the campaign—

H   Well, what he thinks, he thinks that Mitchell did sign off on it.

P   My guess is Mitchell could just say, "Look," he says, "this, that and the other thing," and he says, "alright go ahead but there was no plan of this."

H   Except if you support Dean's opinion (unintelligible)

P   So -

H   Now O'Brien says that Magruder's objective in holding at the moment is a meeting with Micthell and me. And that what he has told the lawyers, that will be a shot across the bough and tear down the meeting place. O'Brien doesn't really believe Jeb, but he's not sure. O'Brien is shook a little bit himself as he hears all this. But he does see very definitely and holds also to the theory of mixing of apples and oranges. He's convinced that Jeb is linking together things that don't necessarily fit together in order to help with (unintelligible). And, again, he's very disappointed in Mitchell. He feels that Mitchell is the guy that is letting people down. O'Brien made the suggestion that if we wanted to force some of this to a head, there is one thing you might consider is that O'Brien and Parkinson, who are getting a little shaken now themselves, are retained by the Committee. That is by Frank Dale. He is the Chairman of the Committee.

P   Does that still exist?

H   Yes. They are—

P   They aren't involved in the damn thing are they? O'Brien and Parkinson?

H   Yes.

P   They ran this all from the beginning?

H   Oh, no.

P   Well, that is what I thought.

H   But they are involved in the post-discovery, post - June 17th.

P   (expletive removed)! (unintelligible)

H   O'Brien says, "Everything with the Committee— what you might want to consider is the possibility is to waive our retainer, waive our privileges and instruct us to report to the President all of the facts as they are known to us as to what really went on at the Committee to Re-Elect the President."

P   For me to sit down and talk to them and go through—

H   I don't know. He doesn't mean necessarily personally talk to you, but he means talk to Dean or whoever you designate as your man to be working on this. Now, other facts. Hunt is at the Grand Jury today. We don't know how far he is going to go. The danger area for him is on the money, that he was given money. He is reported by O'Brien, who has been talking to his lawyer, Bitman, not to be as desperate today as he was yesterday but to still be on the brink, or at least shaky. What's made him shaky is that he's seen McCord bouncing out there and probably walking out scot free.

P   Scot free and a hero.

H   And he doesn't like that. He figures here's my turn. And that he may go—

P   That's the way I would think all of them would feel.

H   And that he may decide to go with as much as is

186

necessary to get himself into that same position, but probably would only go with as much as is necessary. There isn't a feeling on his part of a desire to get people, but a desire to take care of himself. And that he might be willing to do what he had to do to take care of himself, but he would probably do it on a gradual basis and he may in fact be doing it right now at the Grand Jury. He feels, in summary, that on both Hunt and Magruder questions we're not really in the crunch that we were last night. He is not as concerned as he was when he talked with you last night. We are now going with Silbert—

P   Who's that?

H   The U.S. Attorney is going to Sirica seeking immunity for Liddy so Liddy can be a witness. Liddy's lawyer will argue against immunity, for he does not want it. Dean's judgment is that (unintelligible) will probably fail. Sirica will grant it. Sirica's clear disposition—

P   If he doesn't talk, then he gets contempt. Is that it?

H   Liddy, if he gets immunity, his intention, as of now at least, is to refuse to talk. And then he would be in contempt. The contempt is civil contempt and it only runs for the duration of the Grand Jury which is limited. And as long as he is in jail anyway, it doesn't make a hell of a lot of difference to him.

P   I will almost bet that is what Liddy will do.

H   Well that's what Dean will also bet. Dean has asked through O'Brien - Maurolis for Liddy to provide a private statement saying that Dean knew nothing in advance on the Watergate, which Liddy knows to be the case. To his knowledge, Dean knew nothing about it. Dean would like to have that statement in his pocket and has asked Liddy for such a statement. Dean feels that he would want to get it. O'Brien raised the question whether Dean actually had no knowledge of what was going on in the intelligence area between the time of the meetings in Mitchell's office, when he said don't do anything, and the time of the Watergate discovery. And I put that very question to Dean, and he said, "Absolutely nothing."

P   I would—the reason I would totally agree—that I would believe Dean there (unintelligible) he would be lying to us about that. But I would believe for another reason—that he thought it was a stupid damn idea.

E   There just isn't a scintila of hint that Dean knew about this. Dean was pretty good all through that period of time in sharing things, and he was tracking with a number of us on—

P   Well you know the thing the reason that (unintelligible) thought—and this incidentally covers Colson—and I don't know whether—. I know that most everybody except Bob, and perhaps you, think Colson knew all about it. But I was talking to Colson, remember exclusively about—and maybe that was the point—exclusively about issues. You know, how are we going to do this and that and the other thing. (unintelligible) mainly, the labor bill, how do we get this, how do we get aid to the Catholic schools.

H   Getting that aid to Catholic schools, you know, was a—Colson's fight was with (unintelligible).

P   Right. That was what it is. But in all those talks he had plenty of opportunity. He was always coming to me with ideas, but Colson in that entire period, John, didn't mention it. I think he would have said, "Look we've gotten some information," but he never said they were. Haldeman, in this whole period, Haldeman I am sure—Bob and you, he talked to both of you about the campaign. Never a word. I mean maybe all of you knew but didn't tell me, but I can't believe that Colson—well—

H   Maybe Colson is capable of—if he knew anything out of that, but not telling you what we were at least—

P   Well, at least, nothing of that sort because as a matter of fact I didn't even know—I didn't know frankly that the Ellsberg thing, etc. - electronically thing - you know what I mean?

E   (unintelligible)

P   And I guess there you deliberately didn't want me—

E   Well, sir, I didn't know. I didn't know what this crowd were up to until afterwards.

P   Right.

E   And I told you, afterwards we stopped it from happening again.

P   Right.

E   In that setting—

P   That was in the national security?

E   That was in the national security leak thing. But the interesting thing about Colson, corroborative of what you say, is that when I got a phone call from Secret Service saying there had been this burglary - the first guy I called was Colson.

P   Yeah.

E   And his response, as I recall it, was one of total surprise and he could have said then, "Oh, those jerks,

188

they shouldn't have"; Or, "I knew about it earlier"; Or, referred to it by saying, "It would have been a meaningful leak," but he didn't. He was totally nonplussed, the same as the rest of us.

P   Well, the thing is too, that I know they talk about this business of Magruder's, saying that Haldeman had ordered, the President had ordered, etc., of all people who was surprised on the 17th of June—I was in Florida—was me. Were you there?

E   No, I was here.

P   Who was there?

E   I called Colson, Haldeman and Ziegler and alerted them to this.

P   And I read the paper. What in the name of (expletive removed) is this? I just couldn't believe it. So you know what I mean—I believe in playing politics hard, but I am also smart. What I can't understand is how Mitchell would ever approve.

H   That's the thing I can't understand here.

P   Well, Magruder I can understand doing things. He is not a very bright fellow. I mean he is bright, but not— he doesn't think through to the end. But Mitchell knows enough not to do something like that.

H   Yeah, but I will tell you what could have happened very easy there. Mitchell was Attorney General. He was using, legally, and sometimes officially he was using his great, great capacity to pull irons out of (unintelligible) every day and you get into a mine center and you get used to that.

P   Could be. Could be.

H   You don't regard it with the same kind of feeling that—

P   Yeah. Could be. Could be. Well, anyway.

H   Dean says—he says—I did see Liddy roughly five or six times during that period of January 5 to June, and it was always on campaign legal matters. You know.

P   Well, I know. Dean—remember you always told me Dean made all these studies of it and—

H   I believe that. He said at one of those meetings I went to, I said to Liddy something about how is it going? He said he started to say I am having a hell of a time getting Magruder going on this operation and Dean said, "I told you, Gordon, that is something I know nothing about and don't want to know anything about, as a matter of fact."

P   That's right.

E   That was prior to June of 1972. Right?

H   Right. Yeah. Here's another factor, now that we know he is following up that point. He said as a matter of fact, the reason I called him on June 19—I said, "Now wait a minute. You called Liddy on June 19?" He said, "Yes. The reason I did, because Kleindienst told me that Liddy had come to see him on the 18th at Burning Tree. That was the day after the discovery on Sunday, we, ah—the purpose of that was to tell Kleindienst he had to get his men out of jail and all that. Kleindienst said I wish that damn Liddy would quit talking to me about this stuff. At that time, Liddy told Kleindienst that Mitchell had ordered it.

P   Oh.

H   That's true. You know though, Liddy was using that as his means for trying to get to the (unintelligible)

P   You know Mitchell could be telling the truth and Liddy could be too. Liddy just assumed he had abstract approval. Mitchell could say, "I know I never approved this damn plan. You've got to figure the lines of defenses that everybody's going to take here. That's Mitchell's. Right? What's Haldeman's line of defense? Haldeman's line of defense, "I never approved anything of the sort. I just"—you know that—What's Ehrlichman's? There is no doubt he knows nothing about it. The earlier thing—yes. We did have an operation for leaks, etc. What would you say if they said, "Did you ever do any wiretapping?" That is a question they will ask. Were you aware of any wiretapping?

E   Yes.

P   You would say, "Yes." Then, "Why did you do it?" You would say it was ordered on a national security basis.

E   National security. We had a series of very serious national security leaks.

P   As you were saying on the—

E   Let me go back and pick up this business about taps. I think—I have done some checking and I want you to get the feel for what I would say if this Hunt thing slopped over on me.

P   Incidentally, my view is—I don't know Hunt—I don't think Hunt will do that.

E   I don't think he will either, because—

P   You don't think he is going to have to take a fall for (unintelligible) any burglary? If he does—

E   The, the line of response would be this as I see it. Starting back in the days when I was Counsel to the President, we were very concerned with our national security leaks and we undertook at that time a whole series of steps to try and determine the source of the leaks. Some of this involved national security taps duly and properly authorized and conducted. We had three very serious breeches. After I left the office of Counsel, I continued to follow this.

P   Yeah. At your request.

E   We had three very serious breeches. One was the whole Szulc group; one was the Pentagon Papers and the other was the Pakistan-India situation; but there were leaks all through there and so we had an active and on-going White House job using the resources of the Bureau, the Agency and the various departmental security arms with White House supervision. In this particular instance, Hunt became involved because at the time of the Pentagon Papers break we had dual concerns. We had concern about the relationship of this particular leak to other security leaks that we had across the government—Rand, etc.—and so we moved very vigorously on the whole cast of characters in the Pentagon Papers thing. Some of our findings have never come out. It was an effort to relate that incident to the other national security breaches we had, and also to find out as much as we could about this. We put a number of people into this that we had at work on other things. One was Hunt and he in turn used Liddy. I didn't know—and this is fact—I checked this two or three ways. I didn't know what they were doing about this operation in Los Angeles until after it occurred and they came to me and told me that it had been done and that it was unsuccessful and that they were intending to make a re-entry to secure papers that they were after. I said no, and stopped it at that time. Young and Krogh operated that, the whole operation. From the beginning as a matter of fact with the Szulc leaks and so on they laid it out perfectly. And Krogh is very frank in saying, "I authorized this operation in Los Angeles, no two ways about it." He says, "If I am asked, that's what I will say and I will resign and leave the Department of Transportation and get out of town." He said, "I thought at the time we were doing the right thing and—"

P   Should he?

E   I don't think he will have to. Number one, I don't think Hunt will strike him. If he did, I would put the national security tent over this whole operation.

P   I sure would.

E And say there are a lot of things that went on in the national interest where they involved taps, they involved entry, they involved interrogation, they involved a lot of things and I don't propose to open that up to (unintelligible) just hard line it.

P I think that is what you have to do there. But I wanted to get that one out. O. K. Go ahead.

H All right, now. One information idea in talking with Dean that he proposed last night—he says he still thinks it is possible and has a good possible approach—he has been trying to take it apart. He says the approach, as he sees it, is that the President says here's what's been charged about the White House and about the Committee to Re-Elect the President. He puts it all in perspective in terms of political, you know, this kind of stuff goes on, this is all (unintelligible) about.

P Yeah.

H But we are now at a point where fact and fiction are becoming badly confused. We are involved in an intense political situation with the press, with the Senate Committee, you know, and others are prejudging this case—(unintelligible) then Weicker and others who are.

P Various people will—defendants that are guilty, known to be guilty, are making charges.

H Right.

P Which should, of course, be—

E The FBI is being falsely charged with inadequate investigation activity and duplicity and so forth.

P (unintelligible) Justice.

E The Department and the U.S. Attorney's office are being—

P They're (unintelligible) questionable.

H Now, no man is above the law and that is a basic principle we must operate on, but under these circumstances there's no possibility of a fair hearing and every man is entitled to the protection of the law and the public is entitled to the facts in the matter. But the people who are in charge and are involved are entitled to fair treatment. People who are involved, well wasn't any (unintelligible) in being involved. So, I've created a super panel which will have the cooperation of all investigative agencies. All the people who have been charged in this matter have volunteered to submit their entire—their facts—to this panel.

P Be questioned by it.

H   And be questioned by it. They've agreed to waive their right to trial by jury.

P   What (unintelligible)

H   And the panel is empowered to act to remove anybody that it sees fit because of involvement, to level fines and to impose criminal sanctions. The defendants in the Watergate trial, the men who have already been—can also submit any information that they want.

P   Right.

H   Anyone who does not submit to the proceedings of this committee under these conditions—

P   Resign.

H   Will be faced with the fact that all information developed by the committee and all other sources will be turned over to the Justice Department for criminal prosecution. There will be no judgment until all the facts are received by the commission and then the commission will make public all of its findings and the reasons for all actions taken. They will proceed in secret and their decisions will be final and not subject to appeal. And the people appearing before them will voluntarily submit to that. What (unintelligible) is appeal.

P   How's that (unintelligible)

H   I don't know.

E   That's—that sounds like a little bit simpler than that—than what I originally thought he had in mind. He says—

P   Wonder if the President has the power to set up such a thing. Can he do that sort of thing? You know, that's the whole point. I don't think so.

E   Executive process.

H   By voluntary—

E   You get the (unintelligible) away. Yeah but it isn't—it isn't that guy. It's the fellow who doesn't submit who in effect is being denied due process.

P   You're right.

H   The information on him will be turned over to the criminal—might be he'd be subpoenaed.

P   No then you see you sort of condemned him by—

E   Negative inference.

P   Negative inference.

H   We're all condemned by negative inference right now.

E   I appreciate that, but that's—

P   You're not condemned in a court.

E It's a little different. Well, I—that isn't, that isn't a salient point at all in this thing.

H He feels that there are a lot of advantages on this and two major internal ones. It will take the panel a long time to get set up, get its processes worked out, get its hearings done and make its findings and then you'll probably be past the '74 elections which'll be desirable. Secondly, the President maintains the ultimate stroke on it, because he always has the option on January 19 to pardon anybody who (unintelligible) a pardon. So the potential ultimate penalty anybody would get hit in this process could be about two years. His view would be to put—you need to get someone on the panel who knows politics.

E Former Governor, or something like that.

H But if you would want Earl Warren, he'll do it but it's not (unintelligible). What could that matter to the people. I said what do you do about Ervin. Well, you call Ervin down. You tell him the plans and explain why you're doing it, that justice is not being carried out now, there's finger pointing and a lot of problems. And you ask him to hold his hearings in abeyance until the panel serves its purpose.

P And what if Ervin would say, well I'll hold my hearings in abeyance on Watergate, but not on other things. I'm guessing here.

P That's their problem.

H Then you ask,—

P Oh, that's not theirs.

H Then, I said, what if I asked Ervin to serve on the panel. He said he thought that was a pretty good idea. He said he probably wouldn't do it, but it'd still give him an awkward stand on a stickly position. The only other idea he comes up with is he said, "One thing you might want to consider is the President calling Mitchell in for a one-on-one talk. The President now has all the facts on this—(unintelligible) tell us. But I, Dean, don't know the facts on Mitchell." He said, "I think that Mitchell would not pull any punches with the President and if the President—that would be a way to find out what Mitchell's true perception of what did happen."

P And that's probably the only way.

H Supposing—

P Suppose now, the fact that (unintelligible) took my time. Suppose you call Mitchell and say to him, will you—what do you learn—for what. And Mitchell says, "Yes, I did it." Then what do we say?

H   Its greater knowledge that we possess right now—if he would only confess.

E   I was just going to say, maybe if Rogers said it to him—

P   Mitchell?

H   Bill thinks—

P   Mitchell? Mitchell despises him.

H   Yeah, I know he does. That's all it is - I didn't call Mitchell because I need (unintelligible) but we should go ahead with Magruder, I think.

E   Right now?

P   Oh, I agree.

H   (unintelligible)

P   (unintelligible)

E   I say any idea of a meeting between you and Mitchell ought to wait until the Magruder, Haldeman, Mitchell meeting.

P   Oh, really?

E   And see what transpires there. Maybe the idea that Magruder says he (unintelligible)

P   What about the other way around. How about me getting Mitchell in and say, look (unintelligible) you've got to tell us what the score is, John. You have to face up to where we are. What do we say? How do we handle (unintelligible)

H   My guess is Mitchell would turn on you. I think Mitchell would say, "Mr. President, if it will serve any useful purpose for you I would come—"

P   Isn't it just as well for me to call and ask him to meet with Magruder? Or what do you think, John? I have not really had from Mitchell but I have had from Haldeman, I have had from Ehrlichman, I have had from Colson cold, flat denials. I have asked each of you to tell me, and also Dean. Now the President, therefore, has not lied on this thing. I don't think that yet has been charged. Liability has been charged, but they haven't charged the President with any offense. They are (unintelligible) in trying to protect his people who are lying. But I don't—doesn't anybody suggest that I (unintelligible) this whole damn thing?

H   As of now it is all saying that you being ill-served by (unintelligible).

P   By my people. But I don't know about Mitchell. I never asked him.

H   (unintelligible). It can't hurt anything. (unintelligible)

P I should get Mitchell down rather than ask him, don't you think?

H Yeah.

P What I've got to do is think in terms of my own plans. I will spend my day today on this, but I will have to clear the deck for tomorrow (unintelligible)

E You could say, considering legislative legal insurance, they tell me that according to the information they have, they need some assurances where you are concerned.

P Here is what Magruder is saying.

E Magruder is saying?

P I think I will tell him here is what Magruder is saying. I don't know really know what he is saying about the White House, but I understand he is saying that you signed off on it. Is that what Magruder is saying?

H If Magruder goes public on this, then you know—

P Incidentally, if Magruder does that, let's see what it does to Magruder.

E It depends on how he does it. If he does it under immunity, it doesn't do anything to him.

P All right—except ruin him.

H Well, yeah. It ruins him in a way he becomes a folk hero to the guys—

P He becomes an immediate hero with the media. You know, in terms of—I know how these things work.

E Mike Wallace will get him and he will go on "Sixty Minutes," and he will come across as the All American Boy who was doing, who was just doing—who was serving his President, his Attorney General and they misled him.

P Yeah.

E And he can do it.

P So—

H And look at the alternative that he now sees. It is either that or he goes to jail on perjury.

P How are they going to prove it?

E With other witnesses, not through his own mouth.

P What other witnesses?

H Beats me. I don't know how they can prove perjury.

P Hunt?

H He has to be a great big gamble because he knows —let's assume—he knows he did perjure himself and, if you know that you are guilty, you have to be pretty concerned about someone's ability to prove it.

P That's right.

E   And Liddy and McCord, and Sloan and that little thing in McCord's letter about Sloan has to worry him.

H   If its about Sloan. That's another thought. It may be about Barker.

E   Is he (unintelligible)

H   And it is more likely because Barker worked for him.

E   I see. Well—

H   Barker said he couldn't remember who he delivered the tap reports to.

(Material unrelated to Presidential actions deleted)

P   Well, what is Mitchell's option though? You mean to say—let's see what he could do. Does Mitchell come in and say, "My memory was faulty. I lied?"

E   No. He can't say that. He says—ah, ah—

P   "That without intending to, I may have been responsible for this, and I regret it very much but I did not realize what they were up to. They were—we were—talking about apples and oranges." That's what I think he would say. Don't you agree?

H   I think so. He authorized apples and they bought oranges. Yeah.

P   Mitchell, you see, is never never going to go in and admit perjury. I mean he may say he forgot about Hunt/Liddy and all the rest, but he is never going to do that.

H   They won't give him that convenience, I wouldn't think, unless they figure they are going to get you. He is as high up as they've got.

E   He's the big Enchilada.

H   And he's the one the magazines zeroed in on this weekend.

P   They did? What grounds?

H   Yeah. (unintelligible) has a quote that they maybe have a big fish on the hook.

P   I think Mitchell should come down.

E   To see you, me, Magruder.

P   Yeah. We'll have him come down at 5:30. (unintelligible) I would like to talk with him. You, Magruder and he and Dean—no, no.

H   Well, Magruder said he would be happy to have Dean sit in. Its my view, I don't think we want Dean to sit in.

P   (unintelligible)

H   I don't think so.

P   Magruder has got to know—I just don't—my own feeling is, Bob,—the reason I raise the question of Magruder is what stroke have you got with Magruder? I guess we've got none.

E   I think the stroke Bob has with him is in the confrontation to say, "Jeb, you know that just plain isn't so," and just stare him down on some of this stuff and it is a golden opportunity to do that. And I think you will only have this one opportunity to do it.

P   (unintelligible) said it isn't so before.

E   That's all the better, and in his present frame of mind I am sure he will rationalize himself into a fable that hangs together. But if he knows that you are going to righteously and indignantly deny it, ah—

P   Say that he is trying to lie to save his own skin.

E   It'll bend—it'll bend him

H   Well, but I can make a personal point of view in the other direction, and say, "Jeb, for God's sake don't get yourself screwed up by—solving one lie with a second. You've got a problem. You ain't going to make it better by making it worse.

P   Hero for the moment, but in the minds of—

H   Well, then you've got Magruder facing all—

P   Let me tell you something—let me tell you something. I have been wanting to tell you this for some time. (unintelligible) always dealing with foreigners. Good causes are destroyed. Chambers is a case in point. Chambers told the truth, but he was an informer, obviously because he informed against Hiss. First of all, it wouldn't have made any difference whether the informer (unintelligible). First of all he was an (unintelligible) Hiss was destroyed because he lied—perjury. Chambers was destroyed because he was an informer, but Chambers knew he was going to be destroyed. Now, they've got to know that this whole business of McCord going down this road and so forth. I don't know the (unintelligible)

E   McCord is a strange bird.

P   Trying to get out. I have never met him. Ever meet him?

E   Nope. But Dean—

P   Tell me about him.

H   Let's go another one. So you persuade Magruder that his present approach is (a) not true; I think you can probably persuade him of that; and (b) not desirable to take. So he then says, in despair, "Heck, what do I do?

198

Here's McCord out here accusing me." McCord has flatly accused me of perjury - He's flatly accused Dean of complicity." Dean is going to go, and Magruder knows of the fact that Dean wasn't involved, so he knows that when Dean goes down, Dean can testify as an honest man.

P   Is Dean going to finger Magruder?

H   No, sir.

P   There's the other point.

H   Dean will not finger Magruder but Dean can't either—likewise he can't defend Magruder.

P   Well—

H   Dean won't consider (unintelligible) Magruder. But Magruder then says, "Look, if Dean goes down to the Grand Jury and clears himself, with no evidence against him except McCord's statement, which won't hold up, and it isn't true. Now, I go down to the Grand Jury, because obviously they are going to call me back, and I go to defend myself against McCord's statement which I know is true. Now I have a little tougher problem that Dean has. You're saying to me, 'Don't make up a new lie to cover the old lie.' What would you recommend that I do? Stay with the old lie and hope I would come out, or clean myself up and go to jail?"

P   What would you advise him to do?

H   I would advise him to go down and clean it up.

P   And say I lied?

H   I would advise him to seek immunity and do it.

P   Do you think he can get immunity?

H   Absolutely.

P   Then what would he say?

E   He would say, "I thought I was helping. It is obvious that there is no profit in this route. I did it on my own motive. Nobody asked me to do it. I just did it because I thought it was the best thing to do. Everybody stands on it. I was wrong to do it." That's basically it.

H   Magruder's viewpoint that to be ruined that way which isn't really being ruined is infinitely preferable to going to jail. Going to jail for Jeb will be a very, very, very difficult job.

E   (unintelligible) he says he is a very unusual person. The question now is whether the U.S. Attorney will grant immunity under the circumstances.

H   Well he would if he thought he was going to get Mitchell.

E   Yeah, that's right.

H   The interesting thing would be to watch Mitchell's

face at the time I recommend to Magruder that he go in and ask for immunity and confess.

P   John, what about this Commission?

E   The first step on that it seems to me is to sell Bill Rogers on the idea, if it's a good idea.

P   But the other thing first is to talk with Bill Rogers and see whether he comes up with a decent committee.

E   Well I would say first we've got to be convinced that it is a good idea. If the President's satisfied that it is a good idea, then we get Bill Rogers to—

P   Well you see to make it is—the problem that we've got here as everybody there felt at the time (unintelligible)—

E   There's glory in this for Bill. This is his idea.

H   You see you are saying Bill would publicly be the father of this.

E   Bill would be the father of this. He would go to Ervin and say I am terribly concerned about this whole business.

P   He would be the broker?

H   He came to the President and said this is what you must do.

P   Go to Warren?

E   He would go to Ervin and say I see this impasse developing between the Grand Jury and (unintelligible).

P   Might go to Judge Sirica?

E   I don't think he would. He's not really smart.

H   I know that, but why not see him? That's fine.

E   Either that or go to Burger, (unintelligible) somebody in the Judicial branch and have them designate two senior judges from around the country who have retired—trial judge types. And just designate them at random. It takes it out of your hands. Ah, they represent the judicial and—

P   And not have Warren?

E   And not have Warren. No.

P   Warren is so old, you see.

E   He scares me to death.

H   Then you'd have to ask the Speaker—

P   The Warren thing.

H   and the Majority Leader—

P   No, I don't think the Congress.

E   No. They've already done that. I think you are off the hook on that.

H   You mean invite Ervin and Baker?

E   You invite Ervin and Baker and they decline. Then

that is the whole story of the Congress.

P   Then just have the two senior judges.

E   The senior judges and—

P   Why don't we have a panel of senior judges rather than try to get—you talk about the former Attorney General and so forth—

H   I would take your senior judges.

P   You see, if we had the Chief Justice and a panel of three senior judges, or four—maybe Clark/

E   Maybe Clark as the Chairman.

H   Yeah.

P   Clark is a Democrat and a former Attorney General. He'd be the Chairman. A panel of three I think would make a lot of sense. Now they have to have a staff. How do we finance that? The Justice Department?

E   Of course (unintelligible). He's got an office over here in the Federal Building.

P   They would hire legal counsel—

E   What that does is tend to rob Ervin and the Grand Jury with yet a third investigatory group. It seems to me though, if it is just senior judges, you miss the genius of the fact that it's got to be executive, legislative and judicial.

P   Speaking of—why do that?

H   Executive is what's on top.

E   Executive in a sense that you have citizen members. You know, the public is represented. The government, the whole question of integrity—

P   By this (unintelligible) you forget Congress if you get just Judges. I think a panel of judges isn't all that bad either. A good standing panel of three judges.

E   I don't think it sells, though. That's the trouble. Then you look like you are dragging a red herring across the trail. You have to have some kind of rationale—

H   Bill, last night, had some ideas on too—

P   Prominent Americans???

H   But then it has a reason for being and a reason for pre-empting.

P   What about making Clark chairman?

H   He could be called both an executive and judicial type, and then have two senior judges plus Ervin and Baker. There's a panel.

P   Well, anyway, let's (unintelligible)

E   I think in principle, though, getting a line around this whole subject is terribly important at this point rather than just bleeding this every day for hours at a time.

201

H   Sending down people to the Grand Jury—

P   Oh, I understand. I understand that. My point is, John, I don't think—people say, you have to get it out tonight for example. It isn't going to be done tonight or tomorrow night. We can't get it done that fast.

H   I don't think you want to anyway. I think you want to end the war and freeze food prices first and then do this.

P   I wish it were Friday.

H   Friday is the time to do it.

P   Good, that means we better get going today. Alright. Who talks to—should John Ehrlichman and you talk to Bill Rogers, or is that a waste of time?

H   As of now John should not, as Bill is very concerned about not talking to people about it. I already have, and I think I should.

P   Alright. Fine. You get Bill to come over. Say you want to talk to him first and that I want to talk to him. Fair enough? But you will say he comes over to see me. The second point is to call Mitchell. Maybe you better make these calls on this phone so I will know what the hell my schedule is this afternoon.

E   I am going to meet with Kleindienst—

P   Yeah.

E   on these other subjects.

P   Alright. What do we want Kleindienst to do?

E   We want to raise this thought with him in a hypothetical way.

P   (Characterization deleted). The only thing I would say on Kleindienst at the moment is to tell him we are going to have to break with Gray who is killing us. We need to know what Gray's going to do. Can we handle it that way?

E   How are we run the Bureau—

P   Who runs it, etc. etc. I don't know what Kleindienst knows or believes about this damn business. I once said to John or to Kleindienst, you know the man they are really after is John Mitchell. He said, "Oh, no, they are not after John Mitchell." I said, "Did you ever talk to him about it?" He said, "Oh, no." He has never discussed the damn thing with Mitchell. I wonder—

H   Well, damn it, he talked to Weicker. Now Weicker is out today with another statement.

P   What did he say today?

H   He has absolute proof that it goes to the White House staff and he is not going to name names until he gets his evidence in hand but something will turn up eventually.

P   Well, what—Kleindienst—well, raise that with him again.

E   Well Weicker (unintelligible)

H   He ought to say, "Well, I talked with the Senator and he told me he didn't have any. Now he is back out in the press again. I don't understand that."

P   Well, who is Weicker. Who does he think he is talking about?

H   I have no idea. I don't know. I don't know who it can be.

P   Maybe it's this - ah—has Magruder talked to Weicker?

H   I don't think so.

P   Where is Weicker getting this?

H   Porter talked to everybody he can, including Mary McGrory.

P   McCord at the present time only fingers—his present finger is pointed only at two people, Dean and Magruder, so far.

E   And of all people McCord would be in a position, I think, to involve Mitchell. He spent all that time with Mitchell and Martha.

P   But the question is whether McCord has got anything on the White House staff.

E   No, no. Hell, nothing.

P   Have you talked to McCord? I do think Kleindienst has got to take up the leading oar on this business of Weicker right away.

E   Right, Again.

P   Again—he got him in today—

E   Did Weicker have much to do with Gray?

H   Yes. He's a friend of Gray.

E   Might have come from Gray. I don't know.

H   Weicker has very much to do with Gray. Weicker is Gray's sponsor. Weicker was against the White House before they sunk Gray and Weicker has issued a very vicious statement about us. This doesn't reach to the President but it sure gets to those sons-of-bitches around him, and I think he almost uses the words sons-of-bitches. It's as close to it as he could get. Those terrible people around him, evil men.

P   Have you thought about Colson?

H   That's what Dean thinks.

P   Dean thinks Weicker is talking about Colson?

H   Yeah, I think he does. He thinks it is Chuck.

P   Do you think Gray would talk to Weicker? John, has Gray ever talked with Colson?

E   Not to my knowledge—

H   I don't think he has.

P   John, you would have no problems to talk to Pat Gray and ask him what the hell Weicker is up to. Do you mind?

E   Not at all.

P   I think you should. "We can't understand what you are doing here on this. If there is anybody, the President wants to know."

H   Why the hell does he tell the newspapers instead of (unintelligible)?

P   And ask him, as the Director of the FBI, to ask Weicker what it is. He, as the Director of the FBI, is supposed to get all the information he can now. If there is anybody, the President wants the information. Let's try to get to Weicker through Gray. Do you mind trying that? I would like you to try that very soon, like one o'clock.

E   Right away.

P   You go find out about Weicker. What time do you get to see Kleindienst?

E   I don't know. They were setting it up when I came over here.

P   Alright. We're going to set up a meeting with Magruder—not right now. Mitchell first. Get him first.

H   Mitchell? Alright.

P   You know John, let me add, there is one other thing here that Kleindienst might look into. I was pointing out that (unintelligible)—Of course, you have to change Gray. You know that. Kleindienst, I think you have to ride with that a while. I don't think you can just kick the Attorney General out like that, you know. He was going to go anyway at a certain time, so he can go. Beyond that the point is to say that members of the White House staff who are indicted, etc., they would have to take a leave of absence—suspended—leave of absence. Say that you and Bob would have to in the event you were named. I think they have to mention cutting off at the pass some place here and I believe—put it this way, (unintelligible the spectacle of their just taking the whole damn White House staff up. There is someplace where you've got to cut them off.

H   Once you establish it, that you are following that route, if they were smart they would just start naming ev-

204

erybody just so you'd have no choice.

P   There is no way except that, Bob.

E   What I am getting at here and, maybe that isn't the way to do it, I don't know, is to insulate you, number one.

H   Well, that doesn't bother these people.

E   To make you appear to be ahead of the power curve and also to have some symbolic act of absolution after the thing is over, by being able to take them all back on. And say, "Alright, we have been through the whole thing. They fired the worst they had, but didn't make the case. I am taking this fellow back and reinstating him with full status." So obviously that is the reason. I can see the practical problem you would be faced with: you've got an awful lot of guys around here who like to—

H   Hold each other off, you know.

P   That isn't the problem. The problem is not the fact that we can't run the shop. We can run the shop, maybe not as well, but we can run it. But on the other hand, you say—like—let's—suit yourself—let's use Haldeman, because Haldeman could really beat these charges. Say Haldeman wanted to leave then—

H   (Telephone rings) (Haldeman answers telephone) Hi, John: Any chance of your coming down? That's ok. Ah, could you come down first thing in the morning? Tonight? Which would you rather come? Yeah, Yeah. Ok. Well, this is to see me and also the other fellow. Good. Check out a couple things again. You mean that Commission thing. Yeah, what's your feeling on that? She goes a little far on this thing about your baiting Marquis Childs and all that sort of thing. And not necessary. Just set up the Commission and let them report out their findings with the idea that criminal law and prosecution will evolve. It is a blue ribbon, four star grand jury. That's really what it is. Ah, one other thing that—delay in your coming down would be bad. Did he tell you that Jeb wants to meet with you? Oh, he is. Ok. That's the—I thought, well—the last I heard he wanted to get together with the two of us and now it is the next thing we are going to take a stab at down here. If he is there, you will have covered that ground with him. Ervin? Full Committee. No, no. That's a weak reed. Nothing. Yes. Well, we'd be glad to do it. There has been specific follow up on specific items, but he does. If you call and say, "Call somebody and say this," he calls somebody and says exactly that and calls back says, "Well, I didn't get any answer and that is the end of that." There is no initiative and

205

there's no stuff beyond the vegetable. But Dean says we aren't getting that either. I'll—do you think I should talk to Kleindienst? You do? Ok, ok. On any of the Committee and indeed the Grand Jury. Ah, what will you do, have the office call what time you will be here? Ok. Right. Thanks. Yes, sir. Sure, sure. Ok.

H   Magruder is with him right now.

P   What did he say about a meeting?

H   He is coming down the first thing in the morning.

P   Don't wait. What I meant is, I would like to get a report on his conversation with Magruder. Would you call him back on that?

H   Sure.

P   Do it this afternoon.

H   (unintelligible). It's worth a try, though.

P   Keep trying. It is now one o'clock, so probably—

H   Secretary of State, please. Yes, please.

(Telephone rings

P   Will he do it - what did he say?

E   The only thing he knew was that Kleindienst had reported to him briefly that he had had a very amicable meeting with Weicker, but he didn't go into any of the details of the meeting. I suggested to him that he talk with Kleindienst first to find out what Weicker had said to Kleindienst before he, Gray, contracted him.

P   I don't want to—

E   Then I suggested to him—

(Telephone rings)

H   Bill - could you come over this afternoon to meet with the President? What's your time? We we ought to get together for a few minutes ahead of—give your some background on what we have done. What's the earliest convenient time for you? Two o'clock? Is that alright? Is it? Ok. Make it that you have an appointment with the President. Wait a second.

P   Bob, I've got Mrs. Boggs at 3:00, so make it 1:30 so that I see him at 2:30.

H   How about 1:30? Good. With me, because the President is tied up for a few minutes at three and we could go over at 3:15. I think I would say with the President. Yeah, and just drop in my office on the way. I

think your record ought to be a meeting with the President. Ok.

E   So Gray is going to do this. He is going to check
with Weicker and then I left it with him that he either report through me if it were appropriate, or if not, to you
direct, so that—

P   Is he going to call Weicker in?

H   He is going to Weicker?

E   He is going to see Weicker.

P   That's good.

H   Yep.

E   Today. I don't know where Weicker lives but
mostly he (unintelligible) here—

P   What the hell makes Weicker tick?

E   Nobody's been able to figure that out.

H   He sure must be mad at one of us. I don't know
who or why.

P   I am anxious to get his report. You know what I
mean. I don't know.

E   I don't know of any specific spies of his down here
at all. I have heard that he is just establishing his indepen-
dence at this point against the upcoming Committee hearings.

H   Undoubtedly he's meeting with Jeb Magruder.

E   Oh, really?

H   He could have done it.

E   How about that?

H   That isn't why he's been at Weicker's office too. He
says he could come down later.

P   He says at the market house?

H   I think he said market house. I don't know. I
think—

E   I know what he means!

P   I really think I should not try to do that speech
Thursday night. There are more important things.

H   No, sir!

E   That's the most important thing, that you keep the
momentum of the business going—

P   I know, I know. I just meant though—I am just
thinking—having this long seance with Mitchell tomorrow
is going to be very difficult. Well, I will get it done.
I will try to do—At least let's not have this difficult a
schedule on Thursday. Keep one day of personal preparation. Although I feel pretty well.

(Material unrelated to Presidental actions deleted)

P Anybody else that you can think of to mull over this plan? Rogers is coming in at three. Well—

E I will see Kleindienst. That's settled—

P You'll see Kleindienst? When?

E This afternoon at three o'clock.

P Three o'clock, and then I think, when—huh?

H Should I also see Kleindienst? Should I, or should John be the only one?

P John, you do it.

H That's what Mitchell was asking. Mitchell is very distressed that Kleindienst isn't stepping up to his job as the contact with the Committee, getting Baker programmed and all that (A), and (B) that he isn't getting—see Dean got turned off by the Grand Jury. Dean is not getting the information from Silbert on those things said at the contact with the Committee, getting Baker programmed and all that (A), and (B) that he isn't getting—see posed to be sending us—

P Ask Kleindienst, John, put it on the basis that you're not asking nor in effect is the White House asking; that John Mitchell says you've got to have this information from the Grand Jury at this time and you owe it to him. Put it right on that basis, now, so that everybody can't then say the White House raised hell about this, because we are not raising hell. Kleindienst shouldn't—where are you going to see him, there or here?

E In my office.

P Have a session with him about how much you want to tell him about everything.

E Ah—

P I think you've got to say, "Look, Dick, let me tell you, Dean was not involved—had no prior knowledge—Haldeman had no prior knowledge; you, Ehrlichman, had none; and Colson had none. Now unless—all the papers writing about the President's men and if you have any information to the contrary you want to know. You've got to know it but you've got to say too that there is serious question here being raised about Mitchell. Right? That's about it isn't it?

E See Magruder is playing—the game is interesting here. McCord is throwing off on Magruder and Dean. Why he picked Dean, I don't know.

P Why did he pick Dean to separate? Dean was in the news I guess.

E   Now wait a minute. Alright, not as much as Magruder. Magruder, too. What is shocking to me is his blowing off against the one fair guy you wouldn't think he would cut up, against Haldeman.

H   Yeah. Yeah, because he had thought—

P   He didn't pick Strachan. Nobody would care about Strachan—

E   But they care a hell of a lot about Haldeman.

P   And then Magruder was made by Haldeman.

E   Yeah.

P   And he also knows it's not true.

E   Oh,—

P   I can't figure it out.

E   Well, I wouldn't be surprised if McCord has been led by Committee counsel. You see all the stuff about—

P   Dash.

E   Yeah. All the stuff about Dean comes in the *LA Times* story. It doesn't come in the McCord letter.

P   Yeah.

E   And Dean is the logical target of the Committee.

P   Bob, how do you analyze Magruder tossing it off to you rather than to Mitchell? That startled you, didn't it?

H   Well, he hits Mitchell too. He is just trying to wrap me because he wants to get you in. I think my view is that what Magruder was doing here was firing a threat to the President and intends to say it—I don't think he intends to use that so much as he intended—he is trying to get people shook up.

P   He isn't asking to see me is he?

E   Oh, no. He is trying to get a line around you for his own protection.

H   In other words, if all Magruder is going to do is take the dive himself, then we are not going to hear about it. If he makes us worry that he is going to get Mitchell and you and me—

P   John, do you see any way though, any way, that Magruder can stick to his story? No.

E   Yes, because he's an ingenious—

P   Stick to his story?

E   He is an ingenious eitness. I think, I am told, if he is really as good as they say he is as a witness, it is possible that he could get away with it. Ah, it's arguable.

P   It's his word against McCord.

E   And he is flowing with the stream, you see. He is saying the things they want him to say.

P   No, no, no. I don't mean if he says—

E   Oh if he sticks to his old story - I see, I see. I thought you meant the story he is laying out here.

P   Oh, no no. This story. They would take that in a minute.

E   I tell you I am to the point now where I don't think this thing is going to hold together, and my hunch is that anybody who tries to stick with a story that is not susceptible to corroboration is going to be in serious difficulty.

P   So, what do you feel then?

E   Well, that is why I said I thought he ought to move to a real and immune confession of perjury if he can do it. There's too many cross-currents in this thing now.

P   Yeah. This is my view. If Magruder is going to lie about it, you know, I am sure he checked it out. If Magruder is going to say then—then what the hell is in it for him.

H/E   Immunity.

P   Well, if he gets immunity—do we have—can't the U.S.—Who grants immunity? The judges?

E   Sirica grants immunity in the Grand Jury proceedings; Ervin grants it in Congressional proceedings; the Attorney General can grant it in anything.

P   Could the Attorney General grant it in the Congressional?

E   No, but what he does there is informally work out with the Congress the pendency of Justice Department action.

(Material unrelated to Presidential actions deleted)

P   This is a bad rap here. We are not going to allow it. Our real problem is Mitchell. Now what about this? What are you going to do about it? He knows damn well Mitchell is right. Of course, we ought to know—can't the Attorney General call Silbert, or is that too dangerous for him?

E   Well he doesn't have to do that - Henry Petersen follows that thing on a daily basis.

P   Henry Petersen?

E   Henry can let Dick know, and that's all there is to it.

P   Alright. You just tell Dick. You see the problem is, there, that Dick thinks I am—if he says he has furnished the Grand Jury things to the White House that there is a problem.

E   It's a tender problem. I think what he has to do—

P No one could say this. Our need—our interest here—you could say is whether there are any White House people involved here and we will move on them.

E That's right. And the President wants to know.

P That is the purpose. Not to protect anybody, but to find out what the hell they are saying.

E Absolutely. That is the only basis on which to go.

P What have you today? Get every day so that we can move one step ahead here. We want to move. We are not going to wait until a Grand Jury drags them up there.

E Ok, I will let you know as soon as that is done.

P I wonder if we aren't in a position to talk with Rogers and so forth, and get all the evidence in.

E Judge Sirica. That's, in effect, what you would do if you sent everybody down to the Grand Jury. I think the Judge does not have—

P You don't think sending them to the Grand Jury is a viable option?

E This idea doesn't appeal to me.

P I am just thinking. I know picking out these commissions are so difficult, so (unintelligible) as the good doctor says.

E Well, think about it in these terms. If you came out Friday and said, "Ok, I will get this thing cleared up, so I am going to send every man jack of the White House down to the Grand Jury to hang. Sure. Sure. You lay it out, directly or indirectly. I have talked to the Judge and he assures me it will be done very expeditiously and, ah,—

P What I was thinking, you see, as an alternative - the Judge has now come out as a white knight here. The judge is—and incidentally, we can say in a sense that the Judge has given a sentence of 55 years to somebody who had no former offense and so forth and so on—but the reason Sirica doing this is much deeper, is because he thinks there is a cover.

H Sure.

P I don't think you can hold that against the Judge. You know, I mean—I do in a way, but you know—

E He is the proprietor of the Court Room and he tries to conduct trial, to get publicity. That's what it is.

P Yeah. Another alternative that I thought of, rather than try to set up another procedure, call the Judge in and say, "Judge, we will carry out this investigation by sending them all down here and you can question them. I want everybody here and I want you to get to the bottom of this

thing. You will have my total backing." Now that is another way to do it.

E   That's ok, as long as you then get out front.

P   Well, I—

E   You say to the country, "I have now had this conversation with the Judge—"

P   Yeah. Well, that's what I mean. That's what I
would say.

E   The thing that I get over and over and over again
from just ordinary folks—

P   Right.

E   "Why doesn't the President," so and so and so and
so.

P   "Say something what's he done on it?"

E   Yeah. So symbolically you've got to do something.

P   That's right. Do something so that I am out front
on this every—they don't think the President is involved
but they don't think he is doing enough.

E   That's it. That's it.

P   No matter how often we say we will cooperate—as
you know we have done—and on and on and on—

E   They don't believe that at all—it is not getting
through. Ziegler is not sufficiently credible on this.

P   That's right.

E   In a sense, because—

P   What about the Judge business? Let's look at it that
way, rather than the Commission.

E   Well, then what you have done is you have said, "I
will send John Dean; I will send Haldeman; I will send
everybody to the Grand Jury. No immunity, just send
them down there to testify. Let it all come out.

P   What's that mean to the Grand Jury?

E   (unintelligible)

P   No, I mean I'm not going to—

H   On the Grand Jury strategy, do you say, "I am
waiving executive privilege?"

E   I think you do.

P   Yeah.

H   I think you do.

P   Now Colson disagrees with that one, doesn't he?

H   He says you're nuts.

P   No. I can say, consistent with that—when you say
executive hearings, you mean—

H   You instructed us to be as forthcoming as we
can—

P   All the facts that have to do with any of this thing,

this thing here, there is no—I consider no—

H   But you don't specifically say you are giving up executive privilege.

P   No privilege will be claimed unless it is absolutely necessary, or something like that. We will work out something.

E   That will be the following question, the minute that you say that.

P   For me to say that on all matters that relate to this particular matter, "Yes, that is what I would say executive privilege is waived on." I think you've got to say that, Bob.

E   You could say this. You could say I have never had a communication with anybody on my staff about this burglary—

P   Therefore -

E   Or about Segretti, prior to—

P   Segretti, Segretti is not in this court so that is no problem.

E   Well - then alright -

P   I have never had any—

E   Since I had no communication with anybody on the White House staff about this burglary or about the circumstances leading up to it, there is no occasion for executive privilege in this matter.

P   With regard to this, I want you to get to the bottom of it. So there will be no executive privilege on that. On other matters—

H   And that takes you up to the June 17th. What do you do after June 17th?

P   Use the executive privilege on that.

E   Yeah, but there would be questions like, "Did you ever discuss with the President, Mr. Haldeman, the matter of executive clemency for any of these defendants."

P   Both of them say no.

H   Or the payment of money. The payment of—

P   Haldeman and Colson would both say no, there's no question.

H   Since you want to waive privilege so that we can say no, rather than invoking it—

P   You can say that.

H   I think you've got to say that because basically their situation—Well, Colson will be very disturbed by that and he must have a reason why he would.

P   Well, why don't you get (unintelligible) in so that I can hear it clearly and I will know. What is it, Bob, as you recall at the moment, and then I will let you go. Colson says don't give anything away that you don't have to, but you don't have to, but you don't know what the hell is going to happen to you if you go in and lie.

H His thing is don't do any line to break your privilege, because if you get into (unintelligible) you may want it.

P But don't use my privilege. Why don't we just say, "With regard to this (unintelligible)?

H And then get a John Dean problem. What about all your lawyer/client privilege?

P Lawyer/client with me—

H Yeah.

P Well, that's fine. I said that is a matter that has to be decided upon.

H No lawyer/client with other members of the staff. Only pertains to his role as your (unintelligible) our role as your agents.

P Well, I think we can work something out. John, consider for a moment the play—not for the big thing—incidentally I should put this down - or I would just say "The place that this should be—"

E You see the argument that could be made.

P I know the Judge is tough and all that sort of thing. The argument could be made. There is an honest judge. He will get the facts. The argument could also be made by (unintelligible). When criminal charges are involved, the proper place for those to be considered is not in a kangaroo court of this Congress that drags on and on and on, but before a Grand Jury. And indictments, indictments would be heard before a Criminal Court. Under the circumstances (unintelligible)—

E Ervin's answer to that will be the President is trying to fight this battle on his battleground and it is obvious he wants his FBI, his Justice Department, his prosecutor—

P But not his Judge. You see the one strong point is—Rogers had raised, not in this connection but with Bob—is that the Judge out of this is the big white knight now. He is as clean as a hound's tooth. He is as clean as anybody you can find.

H You ask the Judge or direct the Judge or request the Judge—You can't direct a Judge.

P No.

H Request the judge and highly recommend to the Judge that he appoint a special prosecutor.

P That's right.

H   The President's Justice Department, therefore, the President's FBI, the President's Special Prosecutor—

P   Let me say the same thing is going to happen before a Commission in the long run. Let's face it. They'll have special prosecutors who will want to make a name for themselves. Everybody wants to make a name for themselves in this (unintelligible). They'll drag it on and on and on. The idea that a Commission might go through the '74 election, etc.—my view is I can't have this (unintelligible) I think the damn thing is going to come out anyway, and I think you better cut the losses now and just better get it over much sooner and frankly sharper. Let's just say, "Well Judge, let's go."

H   How come all the rush now? You're not committed to this route. You are not necessarily forced to come out now Magruder can stay with his own position if he wants to.

P   Of (unintelligible)

E   Anybody would say—

P   What I meant is, John, if you called the Judge in and say, "Look Judge, you recognize that—while we've never met - that I would strongly recommend a special prosecutor," if he doesn't have confidence in the present prosecutor, "but you can pick anybody you want. Now have at it. That I will—"

E   I think that is something to talk to Kleindienst about. I'll talk to him.

P   You talk to him and Bob I think you should talk to Rogers about this.

E   Special Prosecutors, as Rogers points out, is a slam at the Justice Department, which is already in trouble.

P   It needs to be slammed. The Judge, in other words the idea of killing—

H   It's the popular route—

P   The idea, the President gets the Judge and says, "Now you are an honest Judge. You are doing your job. Those special prosecutors have nothing to hide here. Alright, let's go.

E   I don't think the Judge appoints him. I think the Attorney General appoints him, as a matter of fact.

P   Well we can say, "if you want a Special Prosecutor, the Attorney General will appoint one. Kleindienst says he is a good friend of Sirica's, or whatever, so—

E   Yeah. He could work it out.

P   "He will appoint a special prosecutor if you request one."

H   Well, would it be acceptable to you even though he told you he wanted one? So that you get it out of the—

P   I am inclined to think that—I feel that kind of a move—of course if he names (unintelligible) we could do that right tomorrow.

E   Uh, huh. Well, would you want to on television tomorrow?

P   No, but the way I would do the television—I am not planning to do this before at 9:00 o'clock, on prime time. I would do this in the Oval Room; no make up at all. In other words, that's enough right there. What the hell, I could say I have done this, I have—I want to get to the bottom of this and what have you (unintelligible) Ok, John? Alright.

E   Surely nothing troubles me.

(Materials unrelated to Presidential actions deleted)

P   Well you have plenty to do at this point. Inform me as soon as you get something from Gray on Weicker? Inform me as soon as you've got something on Kleindienst. Alright?

E   Yep.

P   I would have a real workshed with him. Just say, "Mitchell is just damn disappointed, "and he will listen and he will jump up and down and shout. But what the hell, I am always kind. But you just say I want to level with you.

Telephone conversation: Ehrlichman and Kleindienst, March 28, 1973.

E   The President wanted me to cover with you. Are you on an outside Line?

K   I'm at my parents' house.

E   Oh, fine, OK, so it's a direct line? Number one, he wanted me to ask you those two things that I did yesterday about the grand jury and about Baker. He had me call Pat Gray and have Pat contact Lowell Weicker to ask Weicker about this second story that he put out yesterday to the effect that he had information about White House involvement. And Weicker told Gray that he was talking there about political sabotage and not about the Watergate.

K About the Segretti case?

E Yeah, and that he was quite vague with Pat as to what he had.

K I called him also, you know, after I talked to the President on Monday.

E Well, the President's feeling is that it wouldn't be too bad for you in your press conferences in the next couple of days to take a swing at that and just say we contacted the Senator because we continue to exercise diligence in this thing and we're determined to track down every lead and it turns out he doesn't have anything.

K I would really at this delicate point question the advisability of provoking, you know, a confrontation with Weicker. He's essentially with us, he and Baker get along good.

E Is he?

K Baker has had a long talk with him and told him to shut up and said that he would and I talked with him on Sunday after he said he didn't have anything but he's kind of an excitable kid and we just might not want to alienate him and I think that if he finds himself in a direct word battle with the White House and me and loses face about it I think in the long run we might need that guy's vote.

E I see. You don't think that this is evidence of alienation to the point of no return then?

K No. You mean by Lowell?

E Yeah.

K No I don't. He's pretty disenchanted with the whole concept of it. Connecticut politician—

E Well, use your own judgment on it, Richard.

K On TV I guess 7 or 8 times this Sunday when I finished my testimony before my appropriations committee all three networks I referred to the letter that I sent to Sirica and I also emphasized and repeatedly said (a) the President wants this investigated, let the chips fall where they will but secondly that if anybody has any information we not only want it we expect to get it so we can investigate it and if necessary indict other people and that anybody who withholds information like that is obstructing justice. But I did not refer to Weicker. And my judgment right now is not to do so.

E OK, OK.

K If he gets to that point, the hell with him.

E   Well, our uneducated and uninformed impression was that he was trying to develop an attack line here on the White House or the President.

K   If that . . . if we would conclude that that is what he's up to that he is completely alienated then I say we've got to take him on.

E   Well, keep track of that and you'll be talking to Baker and you get a feel of it. OK, now, the President said for me to say this to you. That the best information he had and has is that neither Dean nor Haldeman nor Colson nor I nor anybody in the White House had any prior knowledge of this burglary. He said that he's counting on you to provide him with any information to the contrary if it ever turns up and you just contact him direct. Now as far as the Committee to re-elect is concerned he said that serious questions are being raised with regard to Mitchell and he would likewise want you to communicate to him any evidence or inferences from evidence on that subject.

K   With respect to them, unless something develops with these 7 people who were convicted all those people testified under oath before a grand jury and their testimony was not contradictory and until something comes along I think this fellow McCord if he has something besides his own testimony in addition to that to refute the sworn testimony, then you'd have to do it. The comment that I made yesterday about McCord was that it takes—

E   Take him for what he is.

K   He's facing a long jail sentence and he has all kinds of motives to say all kinds of things but I also pointed out that most of the people, well, these people who were involved were interviewed by the FBI and they testified under oath before a grand jury to the contrary of what McCord is saying. But I understand the President's direction.

E   He's concerned about Mitchell.

K   So am I.

E   And he would want to have a private communication from you if you are possessed of any information that you think he ought to have with regard to John.

K   Now he ought to think about John—McCord or Liddy or Hunt or any of these 7, you know, testify under oath specifically to their knowledge they have a basis for saying so that Mitchell or any of these guys knew about it; we have a very serious problem. Possible perjury, possibility of going back to the grand jury, they have a grand jury determine when anyone should be indicted. When you talk about Mitchell and me that really creates the highest conflict of interest. And we want to give some thought to having in such an event having a special prosecutor.

E   What is the procedure for that?

K   Well, I don't know. I think that the President could appoint somebody as a special prosecutor to direct the FBI to cooperate with him, giving them an opportunity to hire some attorneys, you know, on his staff and then just have complete authority to have his own investigation and if there's evidence that comes out that there were acts of criminal behavior have them presented to a grand jury then proceed with it.

E   Could you have somebody brief out how that's done? Just so we know? And the question would be whether the President or Sirica or you or you know who actually does it?

K   Well it wouldn't be the judge. The judge has no jurisdiction. I think it would be the President.

E   OK.

K   But it has its own problems that by doing that you in effect say publicly well OK the Department of Justice and the Attorney General the U.S. Attorney and the FBI all corrupt. I've now found that out and have got to get myself a new—

E   Of course we've resisted that right straight through.

K   I think that we have to do it in the event that it appears that Mitchell himself is going to be involved in any further litigation because all the men are doing this who have worked for him been appointed and I think if it came down to him that that's what I would seriously start thinking about, recommending.

E   Also this business of the grant of immunity to witnesses before the grand jury, is that peculiarly in the province of the court?

K   No, that's the Department of Justice.

E   That is?

K   In almost every criminal case of any consequence when we convict somebody the next thing to do is haul them back in before a grand jury to find out what they know. You have to do it in this case—always going to do it. Quite a limitation posed on us John is that—who couldn't cut it (inaudible). But you have two really distinct situations here. You have the Watergate inquiry by Senator Ervin, that's the political side of it. And then you have the obligation imposed upon us to investigate criminal conduct. Two separate distinct operations. They're getting all fuzzed up.

E What progress are they making right now, have you had a reading on it?

K Well, the last time I talked to Henry Monday because of Sirica's sentencing procedures it got a little boxed up. Sirica is really lousing this thing up. I don't know. I'm going to talk to Petersen this morning and I'll call you back.

E OK, great, that's all I had on my list.

K Thanks, John

E Now, he said that there was a possibility he'd like to see you in San Clemente Saturday morning first thing. So you might just keep that in the back of your mind. Don't rearrange any of your schedules or anything but I'll let you know if that materializes. We'd send a chopper up to LA for you. Thank you.

K OK.

Meeting: The President, Ehrlichman and Ziegler, Oval Office, March 30, 1973. (12:02 - 12:18 pm)

Someone left the room after having a picture taken

E We have, I think, a useful statement that has been cleared by Dean and Mitchell and is directed with the cover-up charge.

P Do you want me to read it?

Z I think you probably better.

P I can read it (unintelligible) discuss and so forth. Or do you want to read it?

Z No, well it's not a statement, Mr. President, it's some talking points for me.

P Yeah - O.K.

E The brackets at the top go to the end.

P Could we say—could we add one thing here? Say this for the last. Every—I've called for an investigation on the White House staff—is that? And—every—every. This is a statement of the President?

Z No - no—I would make it.

P Yeah - yeah—the President called for—fine. Every member of the White House staff who has been men-

220

tioned (unintelligible) mentioned as a—has submitted a sworn affidavit to me denying any knowledge of.

E   any prior knowledge.

P   any knowledge of or participation in. Could we say this?

E   No—I wouldn't.

P   Why? Not true? Too defensive?

E   Well, number one—it's defensive—it's self-serving. Number two—then that establishes the existence of a piece of paper that becomes a focal point for a subpoena and all that kind of thing.

P   (unintelligible) something.

(long pause)

P   Members of the White House staff would welcome an opportunity—Are we going too far and urging the Grand Jury to do it?

E   Well—that's—we were farther over and we've come back to welcome. I don't know. Maybe that's still too strong.

Z   We should tell the President about the framework which will be giving this. There's a leak out of the Committee—

P   Oh.

Z   for the Re-Election of the President and the suggestion that you have waived the - the restriction on—on Dean being

E   The Dean thing. See, we cleared it with Mitchell, we cleared it with Magruder and with Dean's lawyer.

E   And Dean thinks it was Magruder that leaked it.

P   Members of the White House staff. Well, (pause) I don't know whether you can say "would welcome the opportunity." Why don't you say, members of the White House staff will, will appear before the Grand Jury in person at any time the Jury feels it's relevant and furnish any information regarding that individual's alleged knowledge. You see what I mean? I don't think you say would welcome. Will appear—will appear before the Grand Jury if the Jury feels it is relevant. Furnish any information of an individual's alleged knowledge. (pause) Have you got it in hand?

Z   Well, except for that it is only for me, as a talking piece.

P   Yeah. Have you had it? If the Grand Jury feels it's relevant, members of the White House staff, by direction of the President, will—will appear before the Grand Jury.

221

I think that's a little better than the idea that members of the White House staff would welcome. Don't you think so John?

Z   By direction of the President

E   Right.

P   By direction of the President will appear before the Grand Jury and furnish any information regarding that individual's alleged. I like that a little better.

E   OK.

(pause)

P   I would say it is not the objective of the White House however to draw a curtain down over this matter, to cover up this matter, cover up this matter, and to withhold any information.

(long pause)

P   Why don't we say that we admit there are, of course, other informal ways that could be used. We are ready—we are ready to—say—we are ready to discuss those procedures with the Committee. No, and we are ready to cooperate with the Committee to work out the procedure—to work out a proper procedure—be proper to work out a proper procedure. How's that, John? Is that all right?

E   That's all right. You want to say, we continue to be ready?

P   No—just say, we are ready—let's—that's a little.

E   All right.

P   We are ready—we are ready to work out—to work out—that's right. Let them see that we are backing down a bit.

E   All right.

P   Ready to work.

Z   And then who should we get to say this?

P   We get.

Z   Well, John?

E   Well, now, you've given Kleindienst the franchise.

P   Yep.

E   You—we've got to get word to him which we were going to do Saturday. That we were going to shift courses.

Z   Let's say.

P   We are ready—we are ready—we'll say the—let's leave it with the Timmons' office.

E   Well why say it?

P   Yeah - just say it—well with members—the appropriate members of the staff.

222

E   Why not say this? This is going to be done without publicity.

P   Yeah.

E   And.

P   No—it's going to be done informally without publicity—by whatever.

E   Period.

P   This will be done informally.

Z   We can do it but we just have one problem to dwell on. If you give the name, like, if you say,

P   Yeah.

Z   well Timmons' office would be.

P   That's right. Then they go after him.

Z   Prepared to do that. Then—no - then you do solidify your point, you see.

E   Yeah, but the problem is that there's always—there's already a lot of complaint on the Committee, and particularly with Baker, that there's too many people running this show.

P   That's right.

E   And if we introduce Timmons or we introduce somebody else.

P   Yeah. don't give them a name. The - the, why don't you just say the President will name a—no.

E   You could go this far.

P   Yeah.

E   You could say we've been in touch with the Committee.

P   Yeah. Yes.

Z   Have you?

E   And—yeah—I've talked to Baker.

P   We have been—we have been in communication with members of the—no—well, then you see—you've only been in touch with one member.

Z   When we're dealing with.

E   Well, why don't you say communications have been opened and will proceed.

P   Communications have been opened with members of the Committee. What members? That's—I'm not going to discuss that. I can't go into that. Communications have been opened with the Committee—why don't you say with the Committee—Committee—communications are handled with the Committee to—for the purpose of working out a proper, informal procedure.

Z   And that has taken place?

E Yeah—I talked to Baker yesterday.

P That's right. Well, we've had lots of talks with him. He talked to Baker at length, Ervin's gone. Is that all right, John?

Z If I could say, John is - has.

E You see, we got an Attorney General problem.

P We got—we got Kleindienst.

E Let's not force this.

Z All right.

E If you want to, you can say, well I may have something more to say about this later.

P That's fine. Damn well. Just say. I'm not going to discuss it because these are informal negotiations at this point—informal discussions are taking place at this point.

Z Right.

P As soon as something is formalized we will let you know.

Z Good.

P That's really true and say if something is worked out we will let you know. The, some informal discussions have already taken place. That's right—some informal discussions. I'm not going to go into the.

Z All right—I've got it.

P How's that?

(pause)

P Oh, it'll be a little long

(pause)

P Within the framework of our judicial system. You might say of our system. Don't you think so?

E Read the phrase.

P Yeah. It is our position today and in the past that if these charges are to be tested it should be done within the legitimate framework of our judicial system. Don't you think so?

E That takes it out of the Congress, then.

Z But the legislative.

P Yeah—well then—just say system. And you don't—and then you're not using the last—the bracketed thing at all?

E The bracket at the top goes at the end where he says,

Z   Not going to apply it specifically. But he's referring to the bracket at the end.

E   No - no - we're not going to use that.

P   You're not going to use that?

E   No—it's got a lot of problems associated with it.

P   Yeah—because you're taking the Committe on.

E   Yeah—well we worked with a lot of different variations of that and just decided really it was better to leave it out.

Z   Give the Committee—And give the Committee back into the start there by saying.

P   I question. (pause) I don't know. Well, anyway, it's all right. Do you think it helps some?

E   I think it does. And I think. Ron's going to get some questions—Ron's going to get up there—well Ron, you're not going to apply this to specific instances. What are you trying to say to us? And he again could come back and say, what I am saying to you is that the mistake that people are making—there's a mistaken impression that the White House is trying to cover up in this matter—is just a mistake.

P   Listen—I'd almost start this thing—I just want to lay to rest what I think is a—what is a - I'm not making any charges of how it happened. I want to lay to rest a massive misapprehension that has been created in the press, created in the country with regard to the White House position on the Watergate matter. The aftermath. That is, because of—because of our—and that is—we are attempting, the position is to withhold information and to cover up—this is totally true—you could say this is totally untrue. I think I'd start right out that - massive misapprehension and so forth and so on.

Z   Cover up and withhold information.

P   Cover up withhold information.

Z   And then bang into it.

E   Mm huh.

Z   Part of the case is built on the fact that fellows love this room, and your press of course - is no place to work this out.

P   Yeah - yeah. That's it exactly.

E   And our refusal to—our refusal to try this case in the newspapers.

P   Yeah

E   Has led to.

P   Yeah - Yeah - now—I'd say our—now—a part of that, I must say, due to the fact—our refusal to try the case in the newspapers—to try this matter in the newspapers—and the position of maintaining the constitutional—the President's necessity of maintaining the constitutional separation of powers. But as the President, I'd say, as the President made crystal clear in his press conference on August 2, the purpose of his insistence on the separation of powers is not to cover up. There will be total and complete cooperation with the agencies of government to get at the facts. And the facts can be obtained and still maintain the principle of separation of powers—and all the facts can be obtained. Something like that.

E   That's in there I think pretty good. (dishes or walking around)

P   You don't want to make a sworn statement, huh?

E   I would just as soon not—I think we are better off not, oh, doing up a stream. Look at the -

P   The only position that I am concerned about is this. I wonder if you could take whatever Ron says and—

E   We're going to hypo it—we're going to get it around.

P   Get it to the Congress.

E   Right.

P   Get it to George Bush.

E   Right. I'm going to see the guys that are going to do that and I'll do it now.

P   All right, fine. If you could work on that between now and three o'clock I think it would be very helpful.

E   I shall.

P   Fine—you work on it and I'll take off.

Press Briefing: Ziegler, March 30, 1973.

(Excerpt from Ziegler's Press Briefing)

* * *

With regard to the Grand Jury, the President reiterates his instructions that any member of the White House staff who is called by the Grand Jury will appear before the Grand Jury to answer questions regarding that individual's alleged knowledge or possible involvement in the Watergate matter.

This is a re-statement of a policy which has been in effect. If the Grand Jury calls any member of the White House staff, that person, by direction of the President, will appear to testify regarding that individual's alleged knowledge of possible involvement in the Watergate matter.

* * *

Telephone conversation: The President and Ehrlichman, April 8, 1973. (7:33 - 7:37 am)

P Oh, John. Hi.

E I just wanted to post you on the Dean meeting. It went fine. He is going to wait until after he'd had a chance to talk with Mitchell and to pass the word to Magruder through his lawyers that he is going to appear at the Grand Jury. His feeling is that Liddy has pulled the plug on Magruder, and that (unintelligible) he thinks he knows it now. And he says that there's no love lost there, and that that was Liddy's motive in communicating informally.

P Uh, huh.

E At the same time, he said there isn't anything that he, Dean, knows or could say that would in any way harm John Mitchell.

P But, it would harm Magruder.

E Right. And his feeling is that Sirica would not listen to a plea of immunity at a (unintelligible) I should say. And that (unintelligible) from him. He would be much better off to go in there and have an informal talk and that's what he wants to do.

P Right.

E So obviously we didn't tell him not to, but we did say that it is important that the other people knew what he was doing.

P Well, Mitchell, of course, was going to be put to the prod on this one.

E That's right.

P Mitchell has got to decide whether he's going to tell John Dean, "Look here, I don't think you ought to say a word or you've got to go down and lie." Well, John is not going to lie.

E He says John Mitchell is sort of living in a dream

227

world right now. He thinks this is all going to go away.

P   He thinks that?

E   Yeah.

P   John Dean thinks that John Mitchell is living in a dream world?

E   Yeah. He thinks that that's Mitchell's frame of mind on all of this. For instance, he hasn't bothered to obtain counsel. He hasn't really done much about preparing himself or anything of this kind. So—

P   But what does Dean think about it?

E   Well, Dean says it isn't going to go away. It's right on top of us and that the smartest thing that he, Dean, could do is go down there and appear cooperative.

P   Right.

E   So, he'll be around all day tomorrow and we'll see how this unfolds during the day.

P   What does he—Do you have any feeling about the Magruger thing as to what he ought to do?

E   Yes. And he said, "Well, the thing that I didn't understand was that Magruder was the target of the long Liddy discussion" . . . and there wasn't anything that he, Dean, could add.

P   No, no, no no. But what about the theory of your idea that Magruder ought to come in and say, look, my recollection has been refreshed and so forth.

E   Well, yeah, but he said that he's satisfied that they are not really after Magruder on perjury. They are after him—

P   On Watergate.

E   They are after somebody as the instigator of the plot.

P   I see.

E   And that, cleaning up the—

P   What does he think Magruder will do? Whether Magruder will—

E   Well, nobody knows.

P   Magruder could be the loose (unintelligible) of the whole plan.

E   He's entirely vulnerable and nobody knows.

P   Uh, huh.

E   But Dean's very strong feeling is that this is a time when you just have to let if flow. And that's his . . .

P   I tend to agree with him, you know. Do you?

E   Yes, I do. I do.

P   Basically, Mitchell must say—go in and hard-line

it, John, etc. We cannot, we can't claim privilege for Dean on this kind of matter, can we?

E   I don't believe on acts prior to the investigation, no.

P   That's right, and that's what they're asking for and Dean says, look, I'll be very careful, etc., but. . . . So, where do we go from there then? Then, he pulls the plug on Magruder, but then the point that John Mitchell has got to be concerned about is that Magruder pulled the plug on him.

E   Well, that's right. That's right. That's correct.

P   But the next question, John, they are going to ask Magruder is, "Who told you? Did you clear this with anybody? Who gave the final approval?"

E   Yeah. Uh, huh. Obviously.

P   I don't think, strangely enough. . . . If he's going to pull the plug, he's going to pull it on Mitchell rather than on Haldeman.

E   Well, that's right . . . and . . . and that's the reason that we felt that not only out of fairness, but also in order to make sure that nobody felt that the White House is buying them . . . that John ought to talk to these fellows and let them know what it is that he's intending to do.

P   When does he have to decide this?

E   Well, he has to get in touch with them tonight.

P   Uh, huh.

E   And he thought that he would probably see them tomorrow night.

P   Uh, huh.

E   You see, they prepare their case at night and work the jury during the day.

P   So—he'll tell them that tomorrow night I'll talk to you and . . . . tonight, he says—what's he going to say tonight?

E   Well, he just says, give me an appointment tomorrow night.

P   So. . . he'll go over and see them.

E   Yeah.

P   Right.

E   I think he has to do that.

P   That's right.

E   All right, sir?

P   But he's got to let it off pretty hard with Mitchell . . . he hasn't got any choice on it, that he will not testify to anything after the fact. And that he'll not testify except

229

. . . and then he'll be damn careful he's protective about it. Is that what he's going to say? We don't want Mitchell, you know, popping off.

E   Well, he's going to just say to John that he certainly is not going to look for . . . But then, he, Dean, doesn't really know anything that jeopardizes John. Which is true.

P   Now, who is going to talk to Magruder?

E   Ah, Dean's lawyer is going to talk to Magruder's lawyer and . . .

P   What the hell is he going to tell him, though?

E   He'll tell him that John has been invited to come down for an informal conference and that he is going to have to go.

P   That's right. So what does that do to Magruder?

E   Well, that undoubtedly unplugs him but . . . but it also alerts him in the most orderly kind of way.

P   Right.

E   And, . . .

P   But John Dean says Magruder can't get off by going in and confessing to the perjury.

E   No, no, he says that's not really what they're after.

P   They want to convict him for Watergate.

E   Right.

P   Well, if he confesses perjury, he's going to be convicted for Watergate, right?

E   Both.

P   They'll get him for both?

E   Yeah.

P   Under the (unintelligible) version of the law.

E   Well, I'm afraid that if he comes down and testifies, I would guess what he will try to do is plead some sort of a constitutional protection, Fifth Amendment, or something.

P   Yeah. That's what I would think. He had better plead the Fifth Amendment. I don't think he's got any other choice.

E   It doesn't sound like it to me.

P   Right. OK, you'll let me know tomorrow . . . after Ervin.

E   I'll let you know after Shultz.

P   Yeah. Yeah. Ok.

E   Bye.

Meeting: The President, Haldeman and Ehrlichman, EOB Office, April 14, 1973. (8:55 - 11:31 am)

(Material unrelated to Presidential actions deleted)

P   Did you reach any conclusions as to where we are.

E   No conclusions. Dick Wilson, I think, has an interesting column this morning (unintelligible) It's all a money problem. unintelligible) It's all a money problem. (Unintelligible) Well, yes—

P   Wilson's in the Star.

E   (Unintelligible)

P   So what—?

H   (Unintelligible) is really the essence of this whole thing is too much money. Too much was spent. And so I—

P   Yeah. My point, everybody—

H   No not everybody. Let's say, one group, pieces that (unintelligible) has on that side and more like (unintelligible) says that his, you know, solving Watergate doesn't take care of it.

P   Lots of people, I think want the President to speak out on the whole general issue of money and campaign and all that.

E   Generally, but he gets specific on this. He says also (unintelligible)

P   Is that what you think, go out and make a speech?

E   I'll tell you what I think. I think that the President's personal involvement in this is important. And I know—

P   I don't think it's a speech. Well, that's a point. I think there are other ways you can get. at it. Now I was thinking of the—before we get into that though let's get back. I'd like to go in, if I could, to what your conversation with Colson was and in essence, what did he and the lawyer tell you about?

E   That visit was to tell me that Hunt was going to testify on Monday afternoon.

P   How does he know that? How does he get such information?

E   Undoubtedly through Bittman,

P   Right.

E   or Bittman to Shapiro (?)

231

P Now why is Hunt testifying? Did he say?

E He said, I'll tell you what he said and then I'll tell you what I think the fact is. He said Hunt was testifying because there was no longer any point in being silent. That so many other people were testifying, that there was no—he wasn't really keeping any (unintelligible)

P Yeah.

E It wouldn't add much. My feeling is that Bittman got very antsy.

P Why?

E This grand jury started focusing on the aftermath and he might be involved.

H Exactly.

P What did he say?

E He went to the U. S. Attorney and he said, "Maybe I can persuade my client to talk."

P What do Colson et al, Colson and Shapiro, think we ought to do under these circumstances? Get busy and nail Mitchell in a hurry?

E Yes

P How is that going to help?

E Well, they feel that after he testifies that the whole thing is going to fall in in short order.

P Right.

E Mitchell and Magruder will involuntarily be indicted. Both will say you have lost any possibility of initiative for participation in the process.

P What does Colson want us to do?

E He wants you to do several things. He want you to persuade Liddy to talk.

P Me?

E Yes, sir. That's his—I didn't bring my notes, but, basically

P Oh. Last night you didn't mention that.

E I thought I had.

P Maybe you did, maybe you did. I would need to let—bring Liddy in and tell him to talk?

E You can't bring him in. He's in jail.

P Oh.

E You would send, you send word to him, of course through a spokesman or in some way you would be activist on this score.

H There's no, that doesn't involve any real problem. As Dean points out, he is not talking 'cause he thinks he supposed not to talk. If he is supposed to talk, he will. All he needs is a signal, if you want to turn Liddy on.

232

P   Yeah. But the point—that Colson wants to call the signals. Is that right?

E   He wants you to be able to say afterward that you cracked the case.

P   Go ahead. What else?

E   Well I forget what else. You remember, Bob, when I was busy (unintelligible). He feels that the next forty-eight hours are the last chance for the White House to get out in front of this and that once Hunt goes on, that's the ball game.

P   But you've got to be out in front earlier?

E   Well,—

P   But, I mean to go public—

E   Either publicly, or with provable, identifiable steps which can be referred to later as having been the proximate cause.

P   He's not talking because he thinks the President doesn't want him to talk? Is that the point?

E   He's—according to them, Mitchell's given him a promise of a pardon.

P   Bittman?

E   According to Colson and Shapiro.

P   I don't know where they get that. Mitchell has promised Liddy a pardon?

E   Yes, sir.

P   Another point that Colson may not have mentioned, I have an uneasy feeling that that Magruder story may have been planted.

H   No.

P   Is it true?

H   There is a third Magruder phone call which I have heard that says—

P   That he did talk to the reporter?

H   Says he did talk to a reporter on Monday, and did not say any of the things he is reported to have said; that what he, that it wasn't an important conversation. He said he gave the reporter the same line.

P   Yeah.

H   That you know. In listening to Magruder's thing, I was convinced he wasn't completely telling the truth (unintelligible) what he was saying. As you get into it, I'm convinced that its, (unintelligible) that part was pretty much (unintelligible). However—

P   Yeah. But you come—all these people you put together now. But if you come to Magruder, where in the hell does Colson get such a thing? Or is Colson a liar or—

E   Shapiro says he has a very good press contact who has proved very reliable to him. He says his practice in this town depends on his knowing what is going on. And he's told his press contact, This is one of the

P   Has says he's talked to Magruder. Magruder said—

E   And they've now told us—we'll never get the chance—(unintelligible)

P   Does Magruder know about—

E   Magruder may have talked to some of the press and that that was (unintelligible)

P   But in a great detail, Colson (unintelligible) that he nailed Bob Haldeman. The way Colson said, he said he had Colson and two, but not any way that's particularly bad. Right?

E   Well I think, I think like on so many things this got, this got planted as a little seed by Shapiro with Colson and that it grew and apparently

P   Uh, uh.

H   I would guess what's happened is he's got this report from, Colson does, from Danny Hofgren that at the bar in the Bahamas with (unintelligible), someone (unintelligible) one night said to Hofgren everybody was involved in this. He didn't—

E   Everybody knew about it?

H   Mitchell, Haldeman, Colson, Dean, the President

P   Magruder—

E   He said, he specifically said the President.

P   Magruder does believe that, does he?

H   No. I've got it—

P   I just wonder if he believes (unintelligible). Does he believe it, John?

E   No. He tape recorded this thing. Higby handled it so well that Magruder has closed all his doors now with this tape.

P   What good will that do John?

E   Sir, it beats the socks off him if he ever gets off the reservation.

P   Can you use the tape?

E   Well no. You can use Higby.

P   Why not—

E   Well, it's illegal.

H   No, it's not. It is not.

P   Don't you have to tell somebody—

E   Put a beeper

H   There is no beeper required. Check the Washington law.

234

P   Yeah.

H   District of Columbia is under federal law and the federal law does not require disclosure to the other party of the recording of phone conversations. The phone call was made to Magruder's lawyer's office which is also in the District of Columbia so both ends of the conversation were in the District of Columbia and there is no law requiring disclosure.

E   (Unintelligible)

P   Well, anyway—

H   It cannot be admissible, but it's legal.

P   That's interesting. That's a new one. (Unintelligible) now and then, any way. I never heard anybody beep and I know that—

H   No. It all depends on where you are. The basic law in most states is that you must disclose to the other party that you're recording the conversation.

P   Yeah. What is the situation—I'll get past this in a hurry. What is the situation, John, in your opinion on what was Colson's and/or Shapiro's motive in building up the Magruder story? Maybe they believe it?

E   Their innuendo is that Mitchell has put Magruder up to this.

P   I guess not. OK. There is the motive. Now, let me come to something else.

H   I don't believe that Magruder's—

P   I don't either. Not at all.

H   I believe Mitchell has tried to.

P   Huh?

H   I believe Mitchell tried to. To keep Magruder's faith because he refers to Mitchell and says now that I have decided to talk I am going to have to tell Mr. Mitchell and he's going to be very unhappy with me because he's told me not to.

E   (Unintelligible) Magruder's an emotional fellow ready to crack. I have no doubt that he's ready to talk.

P   What is it? He hasn't been subpoenaed, has he?

E   Well, he won't be. But he's already been there.

P   But they won't give him a chance to

E   He doesn't think they'll give him a chance to go back unless he comes running at them and strokes them.

H   Let's say they don't call the suspects and and (b) they don't recall perjured witnesses.

P   What would you do if you were his lawyer? Wouldn't you advise him to go in and try and purge himself? At least gets rid of one charge, doesn't he?

E I'm not sure he's rid of it, but it certainly reduces it when he comes in voluntarily.

P The way I understand it under the law, John, if he were to under the—

E Well, you don't—you see there's contrary evidence already here—

P I see.

E In other words,—

P Strachan—Strachan got in before there was contrary evidence.

E Exactly. Exactly

P John, -

H I want to talk to Magruder.

E And you take the circumstances, now

P They better have—

E If it's known, if it's known, for instance, that Hunt is going to come in and testify then Magruder comes rushing in and says I want to tell all, it's, you know,

P Magruder's got no hope now?

E Yeah, but I think he could improve it. I think he really could help and purge himself.

P Turn Bob on him. I come to the other things that you talked to Colson about. I was going to talk—what is Hunt going to say? Do we have any idea?

E Yes—

P He says, for example, will he say that Colson promised him clemency?

E No. Apparently not.

P You see the only possible involvement of the President in this is that, now apparently John, either you or Bob or Dean, somebody told me they said, told Colson not to discuss it with me.

E I did.

P You did? How did it get to you then John? How did you know that the matter had to be discussed with Bittman or something like that?

E Well, I—

P When did this happen? As I remember a conversation this day was about five thirty or six o'clock that Colson only dropped it in sort of parenthetically, said I had a little problem today, talking about Hunt, and said I sought to reassure him, you know, and so forth. And I said, well. Told me about Hunt's wife. I said it was a terrible thing and I said obviously we will do just, we will take that into consideration. That was the total of the conversation.

236

E   Well, I had, we had had a couple of conversations in my office—

P   With Colson?

E   I had with Colson. Yeah.

P   Well how was, who was getting, was Bittman getting to Colson? Was that the point? Who—

E   Hunt had written to Colson

P   Oh?

E   Hunt wrote Colson a very, I think a I've been abandoned kind of letter.

P   When was this, John?

E   I am sorry—

P   After the election?

E   Oh yes. Yeah.

P   Oh. And Colson, you knew about this letter?

E   Colson came in to tell me about it. And he said, "What shall I do?" And I said, "Well, better talk to him." I thought somebody had better talk to him, the guy is obviously very distraught.

P   Right.

E   And has a feeling abandoned.

P   Right.

E   And he said, "What can I tell him about clemency or pardon." And I said, "You can't tell him anything about clemency or pardon." And I said, "Under no circumstances should this ever be raised with the President."

P   (Unintelligible). Well, he raised it, I must say, in a tangential way. Now he denies that, as I understand it, that he said they'd be out by Christmas. He says—

E   I've never talked to Chuck about that, have you?

P   What did he say he said? Well, I'll tell you what I, what Dean, or somebody, tells me he said he said. He said that he didn't. He just talked or saw Bittman casually—were off on (unintelligible) or something of that sort.

E   Bittman?

P   That was it.

E   Oh.

P   And he said to Bittman, he said, "I—

E   Well, now, that—

P   He said, "I, I had given," he said, "I know about Hunt's concern about clemency. I, Chuck Colson feel terrible about it, 'cause I knew his wife." And he said, "I will go to bat for him and I have reason to believe that my views would be listened to." Well its the last part that might in any way remain, although—

E   He says he talked with Bittman, that he was very

skillful in avoiding any commitment. He says that Bittman was pitching him, but that he wasn't catching 'em. And he might have a tape of that meeting or a tape of the conversation or some such thing.

H   That's where he lost his thread, then. He said you and Dean told him to promise clemency, but that he was smarter than you and didn't.

P   He doesn't say you and Dean promised?

H   That Ehrlichman and Dean told him to promise Bittman.

P   Well, anyway. I better change my (unintelligible). Let me ask the question.

H   This is a little strange.

P   Well, just so you—let's see, does he indicate that Hunt's going to talk to that subject, for example? The promise of clemency?

E   He didn't say that. He didn't say that. I didn't ask him.

H   Well we've got to go on the basis, John—as I recall, they don't have anything to indicate—we don't know how they know what Hunt's going to testify. We assume that Bittman told them.

E   Right.

H   We don't, they don't have any indication based on their knowledge that Hunt's going to testify, of what Hunt is going to testify to, except on the basis of Shapiro's meeting with Hunt—

E   The other day.

H   The other day. And that is assuming what Hunt told Shapiro is what he will tell the Grand Jury, but I don't know why they'd have any reason to assume that.

E   Shapiro's general comment was that Hunt would corroborate a lot of McCord's hearsay.

P   Yeah.

E   But that it also would be hearsay.

P   All right. Hunt, however, and this is where Colson comes in right? Hard. Hunt could testify on Colson's (unintelligible).

H   Yeah—but what they said he said,

P   Has it—

H   On the coverup, what he said.

P   Now wait a minute. I'm talking about something else. We're talking about when he and Liddy are in the office with Colson. Colson picked up the phone and calls Magruder. All right?

H   Sure.

P   Now, Colson says that they didn't discuss the (unintelligible) then. But Hunt could say, I went in and I showed this whole thing to Colson and Colson told me—picked up the phone and talked to Magruder. Does Colson realize his vulnerability there?

E   Well, Colson claims he has no vulnerability, because when Hunt and Liddy came in to talk to him they talked in very general terms.

P   I understand that.

E   So, he doesn't acknowledge that there's any possibility.

P   I understand that, but I am just simply saying,

E   I think you're right.

P   That Hunt and Liddy could assert, could charge that—that's the point. If they talk, I would assume they would get into that point with them, any cross-examiner.

E   I've asked Colson specifically about that conversation and he maintains that they were talking in general terms about intelligence and when they said intelligence he meant one thing and apparently they meant another.

P   Question, for example, is Hunt prepared to talk on other activities that he engaged in?

E   Well, I think, I couldn't derive that.

P   You mean is he going to blow the White House on the—

E   I couldn't get that at all.

P   The U.S. Attorney, I would assume, would not be pressing on that.

E   Ordinarily not. McCord volunteered this Hank Greenspun thing, gratuitously apparently, not—

P   Can you tell me is that a serious thing? Did they really try to get into Hank Greenspun?

E   I guess they actually got in.

P   What in the name of (expletive deleted) though, has Hank Greenspun got with anything to do with Mitchell or anybody else?

E   Nothing. Well, now, Mitchell. Here's—Hughes. And these two fellows, Colson and Shapiro, Colson threw that out.

P   Hughes on whom?

E   Well, you know the Hughes thing is cut into two factions—I don't even know—but they're fighting.

P   Yeah.

E   Bennett, Senator Bennett's son, for whom Hunt worked,

P   Oh?

E   Represents one of those factions.

P   So he ordered the bugging?

E   I don't know. I know the (unintelligible) say it's a bag job.

H   They busted his safe to get something out of it. Wasn't that it?

E   No. They flew out, broke his safe, got something out (unintelligible). Now as they sat there in my office—

P   Other delicate things, too. You've got apart from my from my poor brother, which unfortunately or fortunately was a long time ago but, more recently, you've got Hubert Humphrey's son works for him and, of course, they're tied in with O'Brien I suppose. But maybe they were trying to get it for that reason.

E   I don't know why. The two of them put on a little charade for me in the office.

P   Shapiro and Colson?

E   Yes, we talked about this and it may have been genuine and it may not.

P   But they didn't know anything about it?

E   No. They said, one said to the other, "Say, that may have something to do with the New York Grand Jury," meaning the Vesco Grand Jury which is a runaway and which is into—

P   You think Colson knew about that?

E   I don't know. I don't say he knew about it. I said, he says he doesn't know even who Hank Greenspun is.

P   (Unintelligible)

E   I'll take him at face value on that one.

P   You didn't know that either?

E   I know very well who he is.

P   All right. Let me just take a minute further and run out the Hunt thing, and then the Grand Jury, I want to get all the pieces in my mind if I can.

E   Sure.

P   Hunt's testimony on pay-off, of course, would be very important.

E   Right.

P   Is he prepared to testify on that?

E   Apparently so, that's what they say, that he will, and that he will implicate O'Brien and Parkinson. And then, of course,—

P   O'Brien and Parkinson?

E   The lawyers.

P   Were they the ones that talked to Hunt?

E   Well, he says they were and that they handed him

the money. He in turn handed it to his wife and she was the go-between for the Cubans.

P   Yeah. For what purpose?

E   Well, I think he'll hang 'em up on obstruction of justice.

P   Can Hunt do that?

H   How can he do that? Why would he simply—why doesn't he accomplish his purpose simply by saying they gave them money to handle their legal fees?

E   Well, (unintelligible) out there apparently.

P   Now this is—I don't think you—this is what Colson tells you guys?

H   Right.

E   I don't have any other information on this.

P   Hunt then is going to go. Now that raises the problem on Hunt with regard to Kalmbach. He has possible vulnerability as to whether he was aware, in other words, the motive, the motive,—

E   This doesn't add anything to do with Kalmbach's problem at all.

P   What happened on that? Dean called Kalmbach? And what did Dean call Kalmbach about?

E   He said we have to raise some money in connection with the aftermath, and I don't know how he described it. Herb said how much do you need, and

P   It was never discussed then?

E   Presumably Dean told him, and Herb went to a couple of donors and got some money and sent it back.

H   Dean says very flatly that Kalmbach did not know the purpose of the money and has no problem.

P   Dean did know the purpose? Hunt testifies—so basically then Hunt will testify that it was so-called hush money. Right?

E   I think so. Now again, my water can't rise any higher than source.

P   I understand.

E   But that's what—

P   Where does that serve him, let me ask?

H   John,—Would it serve him?

E   The only thing it serves him is to—

P   Would it reduce his sentence?

E   Have his sentence reduced.

H   He'd be served the same purpose by not saying it was hush money, by saying it gave it to these guys I had recruited for this job and I

P   I know.

E   I agree.

H   —was concerned about their family—

P   That's right, that's what it ought to be and that's got to be the story that

H   Unintelligible.

P   Will be the defense of these people, right?

E   Only defense they have, (unintelligible) and so forth.

H   That was the line they used around here.

P   What?

H   That was the line they used around here. That we've got to have money for their legal fees and family.

P   Support. Well, I heard something about that at a much later time.

H   Yeah.

P   And, frankly, not knowing much about obstruction of justice, I thought it was perfectly proper.

E   Well, it's like—

P   Would it be perfectly proper?

E   The defense of the—

P   Berrigans?

E   The Chicago Seven.

P   The Chicago Seven?

H   The have a defense fund for everybody.

P   Not only a defense fund—they take care of the living expenses, too . . . Despite all this about legal fees, they take care of themselves. They raise—you remember the Scottsboro case? The Communist front raised a million dollars for the Scottsboro people. Nine hundred thousand went into the pockets of the Communists. So it's common practice.

E   Yeah.

P   Nevertheless, that Hunt then saying there was a pay-off. All right. Hunt, on other activities—Hunt then according to Colson was not—I don't know what Colson meant about the door of the Oval Office.

E   I'll have to get back on that. Shapiro was there and I didn't want to get into it.

P   Right.

H   (Unintelligible).

P   No, not. It was an earlier conversation about the Magruder conversation when Colson—I think the Magruder conversation from what I have seen related—

H   Magruder doesn't go to the door of the Oval Office. He doesn't even come to visit me in the White House.

P   I know. But he—it is Colson's view that Magruder's

talking would have the effect of bringing it there because of the—I think what he is really referring to, John, is that by reason of Colson, by reason of Magruder nailing Haldeman and Colson, that that's the door of the Oval Office. I don't know what else because there's nobody else around, nobody physically around.

H Magruder isn't going to nail Haldeman and Colson.

P Well, let's see. I don't think so either but.

H (Unintelligible)

P Well that, that tape is invaluable, is it not?

E Then I would suggest, Bob, that you keep it.

H And I'd disregard (unintelligible)

P Let me just say a couple of things that we have to get there.

H When we come to that, he'd say.

P With regard to your, regard to your views, and so forth, John, now I was told the other day, last night, John, you and Bob or somebody—I guess you and I were talking about somebody going to see Mitchell. You suggested Rogers. Got any other better names?

E Well, I've been up and down the list.

P Why did you suggest Rogers?

E Well, I suggested Rogers because—

P First let me tell you—the purpose of the mission and tell me what it is.

E The purpose of the mission is to go up and bring him to a focus on this: The jig is up. And the President strongly feels that the only way that this thing can end up being even a little net plus for the Administration and for the Presidency and preserve some thread is for you to go in and voluntarily make a statement.

P A statement (unintelligible)

E A statement that basically says—

H He's got to go beyond that.

E "I am both morally and legally responsible."

P Yeah.

E Now, the reason for Rogers is that he is clean, number one. He has been both Attorney General and has this other investigatory and Senatorial background. And there isn't anybody that Mitchell trusts, except Haldeman.

P He hates Rogers.

E I understand.

H Doesn't trust Rogers but he would know if Rogers came that it was you.

E Now, the only other alternative, going up and down the list.

H   From a public viewpoint Rogers is the dean of the Cabinet and is the logical man as an attorney, and former Attorney General.

P   From a public viewpoint, that may be but also

E   Take the reasons not to do this—

P   You thought of those?

E   Oh, yeah. Yeah. There have consistently been—you go back to the history of this—

P   I know, now is the time to do something. I agree with you.

E   Now is the only time, probably, and I am persuaded by that argument.

P   Oh, I am too. I am not arguing about not doing it. I am just saying, what about the names?

E   OK. In going down the list, John Alexander is the only other one that I have come to that in any way could bridge it. Garment can't do it.

P   Let me give you another name.

P   Ken Rush. He is a fine lawyer, utterly clean. A longtime friend of Mitchell. Not a close friend, but he's known him, you know, in New York and that group, up there you know, they sort of ran together. Rush would understand it all. Mitchell does not hate him.

E   I just don't know how able Rush is. You've got—I just don't know. Another name, there are two other names that have occurred to me that I'll throw out. One's Elliot Richardson and the other is Kleindienst. There is another possibility and that's Henry Petersen. That, of course, well,

H   But he's in the prosecutorial end.

P   That's right. And so is Kleindienst.

E   Yeah.

P   Kleindienst revealing to Mitchell that he had contact with the Grand Jury and all of that is wrong.

E   I must say I am impressed with the argument that the President should be personally involved in it at this stage.

P   Right. I agree.

E   Old John Dean had an interesting—got a phone call from him about twelve-thirty,

P   And you were here—

E   Oh, no. I was working on something I'll tell you about here.

P   What did you do?

E   Well, not much last night.

P   You mean another subject?

E   Oh, no.

H   There is no other subject!

E   No. I'll tell you. Last night I got home I decided that I would sit down and try to put on paper a report to you what I have been doing since you asked me to get into this.

P   Right.

E   I am concerned about the overall aspect of this and I want to talk about that before—I don't know what your timing is like.

P   No problem.

E   We'll probably get back to it.

P   Got plenty of time.

E   But Dean called and he said, "All right, here's a scenario which we've all been trying to figure out to make this go." He says, "The President calls Mitchell into his office on Saturday. He says, "John, you've got to do this. And here are the facts: bing, bing, bing, bing." And you pull this paper out here. "And you've got to do this." And Mitchell stonewalls you. So then, John says, "I don't know why you're asking me down here. You can't ask a man to do a thing like that. I need a lawyer. I don't know what I am facing—you just really can't expect me to do this." So the President says, "Well, John, I have no alternative." And with that the President calls the U.S. Attorney and says, "I, the President of the United States of America and leader of the free world want to go before the Grand Jury on Monday."

P   I won't even comment on that.

H   That's a silly—

P   Typical of the thinking of—

E   We're running out every line. So that was 12:30 this morning. I, but I—

P   I go before the Grand Jury. That's like putting Bob on national television,—

H   With Dan Rather.

P   What?

H   With Dan Rather.

P   Well by putting it on national television, period. (unintelligible)

E   Let's take it just as far as you call Mitchell to the oval office as, a

P   No.

E   I'm essentially convinced that Mitchell will understand this thing.

P   Right.

E   And that if he goes in it redounds to the Administration's advantage. If he doesn't then wer're—

P   How does it redound to our advantage?

E   That you have a report from me based on three weeks' work; that when you got it, you immediately acted to call Mitchell in as the provable wrong-doer, and you say, "My God, I've got a report here. And it's clear from this report that you are guilty as hell. Now, John, for (expletive deleted) sake go on in there and do what you should. And let's get this thing cleared up and get it off the country's back and move on." And—

H   Plus the other side of this is that that's the only way to beat it now.

P   Well,—

H   From John Mitchells personal viewpoint that's the only salvation for John Mitchell. I see no other way. And, obviously, once you've had it, you've got to admit—

P   How can he make it, anyway.

H   Another factor, in that, to consider, for what it's worth, is the point Connally made to me in that conversation we had.

P   I ought to talk to Mitchell?

H   I don't know whether he said that to you or not. He made the point that you had to get this laid out and that the only way it could hurt you is if it ultimately went to Mitchell. And that that would be the one man you couldn't afford to let get hung on this.

P   Even worse than (unintelligible) thought.

H   He thought so.

P   That's true. Yeah.

H   It seemed to me, because he's the epitome of your hard-line.

P   I think he's wrong about that. I think this is the worst one, well, due to the closeness to the President at the time of the crime. Would you agree, John?

E   (unintelligible) the

H   But, what Connally also said was unless it's the President himself who nails him. Then the President is (unintelligible)

E   Can I put in a larger picture on this? We kind of live day to day for these things, and forget

P   Yeah.

E   the perspective then will be put on this period

H   Yeah.

E   three months later.

P   The point is whether or not, I think I've got the

larger picture, alright, and I mean, in this regard, the point is this that we need some action before, in other words, is like my feeling about having the Grand Jury do it and the court system do it rather than Ervin Committee. Now we want the President to do it rather than the Grand Jury.

E   No.

P   And I agree with that.

E   Well, you're doing it in aid of the Grand Jury.

P   No. I didn't mean rather than the Grand Jury but I mean to worm the truth, now look, the Grand Jury doesn't drag him in, he goes in as a result of the President's asking him to go in.

H   Ok—but while you're on that point could I argue a contrary view for a minute? Because I don't agree with that.

P   Yeah.

H   I strongly feel, thinking it through, with all the stuff we talked about last night, that we don't want the President in it, and that the solution here, if we can find it—maybe it's impossible—

P   Is for (unintelligible) to come voluntarily?

H   Well, or for Magruder to come voluntarily and nail it. But if the solution is - I agree with some—

P   Where does Magruder come to? To me?

H   No. The U.S. Attorney.

P   Why does, what if I urged Magruder to—I mean, let me look at this. The urging of Liddy to testify, the urging of Magruder to testify and Mitchell. John run those by. I didn't mean to to stop your analysis but I think I know what you're—isn't that really the essence of it?

E   I'm trying to write the news magazine story for next Monday.

P   Right.

E   "Monday week. And if it is that "Grand Jury indicts Mitchell.

P   Right.

E   "The White House may have its cover up finally collapse last week when the Grand Jury indicted John Mitchell and Jeb Magruder"

P   Right.

E   "Cracking the case was the testimony of a number of peripheral witnesses who, each of whom contributed to developing a cross triangulation and permitted the Grand Jury to analyze it" and so on and so forth. The final straw that broke the camel's back was the investigators discovery of this and that and the other thing." That's one set of facts. And then the tag on that, is "White House Press Secretary Ron Ziegler said that the White House would have no comment."

P   I know. I know. It can't be done.

E   The other one goes: "Events moved swiftly last week, after the President was presented with a report indicating for the first time that suspicion of John Mitchell and Jeb Magruder as ringleaders in the Watergate break-in were facts substantiated by considerable evidence. The President then dispatched so and so to do this and that and maybe to see Mitchell or something of that kind and these efforts resulted in Mitchell going to the U.S. Attorney's office on Monday morning at nine o'clock, asking to testify before the Grand Jury. Charges of cover-up by the White House were materially dispelled by the diligent efforts of the President and his aides in moving on evidence which came to their hands in the closing days of the previous week."

P   I'd buy that.

E   OK.

P   You won't, so get down to the tactics?

E   Now, I've been concerned because since the end of March, I have turned up a fair amount of hearsay evidence that points at this (unintelligible). Now just take

P   So did Dean.

E   So did John.

P   So did Dean.

E   Now taking this

P   Yet he tried, very honestly, he tried to look it at the best way he could. Maybe he could and maybe he really didn't know.

E   Well, its hearsay. And so, you don't hang a guy, you don't hang a guy—

P   And, also, we are going to remember Mitchell has denied it.

E   But I sit over there in Bob's office and listen to that tape of one of the co-actors saying flat out on the tape that he was guilty and that Mitchell was (unintelligible) going to force our fall, and—

P   Did he say that? Did he say that?

E   Yeah.

P   Well, we can't—

E   And I said to myself, "My God. You know, I'm a

United States citizen. I'm standing here listening to this, what is my duty?"

P Well the point is you've now told me. That's the problem.

E That's correct. That's correct.

P See the difference is that the problem of my position up to this time has been quite frankly, nobody ever told me a damn bit of this, that Mitchell was guilty.

E That's right.

H Well we still don't know. I will still argue that I think the scenario that was spun out, that Dean spun out on Mitchell is basically the right one. I don't think Mitchell did order the Watergate bugging and I don't think he was specifically aware of the Watergate bugging at the time it was instituted. I honestly don't.

E That may be.

(Material unrelated to Presidential actions deleted)

P What did he say? What did he tell Moore?

E Well, remember I asked Moore to find out what Mitchell had testified to.

P Yeah. Moore heard the testimony and said well you're not—

E He was never asked the right questions. Now, as far as he

H He probably didn't to the Grand Jury, either.

E That's right. As far as the quality of the evidence is concerned—

(Material unrelated to Presidential actions deleted)

E Well, to go back to the

P All right. I only mentioned (unintelligible) because, let me,—go ahead with your—

E Well, all I was going to say is that—

P All right. I now have evidence that—

E You don't have evidence if I

P I'm not convinced he's guilty but I am convinced that he ought to go before a Grand Jury.

E What I did last night and this morning was to write out what would in effect be a report to you.

P Right.

E Of this (unintelligible) deliver it to you.

P John,

P I know. All right. Let's come around again, though. You know the case. You conducted the investigation for me. You have reported to me, and I have asked you to go up and lay it on the ground to Mitchell and to tell Mitchell, look, there is only one thing that can save him. I think John's got to hear that kind of talk and I think he's got to hear it from somebody that doesn't have—I was thinking of bringing Rogers in and telling him all of this stuff, but Mitchell will wind him around his finger. Well, there's our problem.

E If you want me to go I'll go.

P (unintelligible) But the message to Garcia has got to be carried.

E Bob has a pretty good feel of Mitchell's attitude toward me that I don't have.

P Well, Mitchell's attitude toward you is not going to be hurt—it isn't going to be any better for Rogers. It would be toward Rush, but how can you—Rush is smart and he is tough. He's a good man and he's a man, incidentally, that we can consider—

E He can't argue the facts of this case.

P The point is, Rush, is a man that if you need a special man in the White House. I was thinking last night that he is the best man I can think of to bring over to advise the President on this thing and examine all the White House things, to look at all the FBI files, to look at the Jury report, Dean report, FBI files and give me a report. He is articulate, he's (unintelligible), he's respected. He's one of the towering figures in the Ambassadorial world and in the bar. He's no slouch.

P And an outsider, it's going to take so long. Rush, I trust. Rush is a friend. He is a total White House man, yet he is not tied in to this.

E He's exactly the kind of guy we need. Now, I don't know how he—he hasn't practiced law for a long time and that's not an immediate drawback, but—

P He has the lawyer's mind.

E You got to get him somebody to help him like

H Haven't events overtaken that project?

P No. No. Bob, the point that I make is let's suppose they get Mitchell. They're going to say now what about Haldeman, what about Chapin, and what about Colson and the rest? I've got to have a report indicating—you've got all those Segretti projects. I want somebody to say, now look, here are the facts. Of the White House people (unintelligible). There are no other higher-up. The White House (unintelligible). Put a cap on it. And second, then face the Segretti crap. In forcing this out, Dean remains a problem and here's—let me just read you what I've come to on that. "John Dean has not involved himself in this matter as your counsel for several months and properly so. I should not continue to fill in for him," meaning me, "for several reasons, including the impermissable demands on my time that were involved. You need a full time special counsel to follow these related problems who can advise you of the legal niceties from his experience in constitutional, criminal and (unintelligible) law practice. I'll be happy to continue to consult with him, etc. I do not recommend that Dean take a leave. That is neither in nor out. He has involved himself to the extent described above. Either that requires dismissal, or it does not. And that choice should be made at once. If he is discharged, the U.S. Attorney and the Grand Jury should be (unintelligible)." But I think you've got to bite the bullet on Dean, one way or the other, pretty quick.

H All right, but recognize that that kills him. Dean's reaction, basically he says that that kills him.

(Material unrelated to Presidential actions deleted.)

P Well, let's see what does Dean say when you tell him that?

E He doesn't agree with that.

P I know he doesn't agree, but what does he do?

E He wants to stay and just disconnect himself from this case. And he says, yes, that's right. Make your decision now, but make your decision that I should stay. He needn't decide that right this minute; I would encourage him not to. But in talking about Rush, that relates to this general subject. I think I would pass it for the moment.

P But the only thing that I was—I agree.

E And get back to the Mitchell thing which really is

P Like today. I know.

E Like this morning.

P I don't think there's anybody that can talk to Mitchell except somebody that knows this case. There's one of two people. I can verse myself in it enough to know the thing, but I am not sure that I want to know. I want to say Mitchell, look, I think that the attorneys for the Committee, O'Brien, and I found this out, and I found out that, and I found out that, and the Grand Jury has told me this that—I just don't know, you know what I mean. They talk about my going out—I am not trying to duck it. I just, John—and, I'll take this one on. The thing, John, is that there's nobody really that can do it except you. And I know how Mitchell feels. But you conducted this investigation. I would, the way I would do it—Bob, you critique this—I'd go up, and I'd say the President has asked me to see you. That you have come today with this report; that these are the total facts indicating, of course, that the Grand Jury is moving swiftly; Magruder will be indicted, you think. Under the circumstances, I am suggesting—can't be in a position—that you (unintelligible) the Grand Jury and say I am responsible. I did not know, but I assume the responsibility. Nobody in the White House is involved, etc., and so on. We did try to help these defendants afterwards, yes. He probably would not deny that anyway. He probably was not asked that at an earlier time. But the defendants are entitled to that—

E   But you're glossing it. I don't think you can do that.

P   All right.

E   I wouldn't want to—

P   All right.

E   I wouldn't want to have you—

P   All right. Fine. Fine. What would you say to him?

E   I'd say, ah—

P   (unintelligible.)

E   I'd say, you know, face up up John. And, you know, I've listened to Magruder, and he's, in my opinion he's about to blow and that's the last straw.

P   And, also, Hunt is going to testify, too, Monday, we understand.

E   We've got to think of this thing from the standpoint of the President and I know you have been right along and that's the reason you've been conducting yourself as you have.

P   Right.

E   It's now time, I think, to rethink what best serves the President and also what best serves you in the ultimate outcome of this thing.

P   Right.

E   I think we have to recognize that you are not going to escape indictment. There's no way. Far better that you should be prosecuted on information from the U.S. Attorney based on your conversation with the U.S. Attorney, than on an indictment by a Grand Jury of 15 blacks and

3 whites after this kind of an investigation.

P Right. And the door of the White House. We're trying to protect it.

E If the Grand Jury goes this way you've been dragged in by the heels. If you go down first thing Monday morning or yet this afternoon, and talk to the U.S. Attorney, and say Ok, "I want to make a statement." Then, two things happen. One, you get credit for coming forward. Two, you serve the President's interest. And I am here in behalf of the President—

H Well, and, three, you have the dignified opportunity to discuss this in the office of Earl Silbert instead of in the (unintelligible) watching (unintelligible).

E And I'm here at the President's request to ask you to do that.

P Yeah.

E He has reviewed the facts now.

P That's right.

E He has no alternative, John, but to send me here and ask you to do this.

P Right. If you want to hear it personally—

E Pick up the phone.

P No. Come down and see him.

H I have a couple of modifications to that. One, a minor change not to what you say but in setting it up. It would be helpful in doing that if I call Mitchell and said that the President wanted you to talk with him. Then there's no question on his mind that you're operating unilaterally.

P Right. Right.

H And, secondly, that if at all possible, come down here. My reason for it is—A—you get him here under your circumstances. B—if you make your case which you may be able to do—in his mind he may be on the same track, maybe at the same point.

P Yeah.

H If he is you might be able then to swing a let's get Silbert right now and go on over. See, he may say, I've got to talk to the President before I do this."

P Yeah.

H And then (unintelligible) to do it.

P Let me say this. I've run through my mind the thoughts. Believe me the idea of Rogers, as you, John—as Bob will tell you, is not one that I don't think is potentially good. I had hoped to get him in. But I know Rogers like the back of my hand and Rogers does not like real,

253

mean tough problems and will not do it.

H   The trouble with Rogers is that Mitchell will over-run him. Mitchell will say, "Here, Rogers, we've got this problem. You know what I think? Those kids over at the White House are really on the (unintelligible).

P   What if you knew when I know. What about then?

E   Well, he'd roll his eyes and Rogers wouldn't know one way or the other.

P   You see, John, somebody has to talk to him who knows the facts. That's the point.

H   (Unintelligible) one part of your scenario really worries me. You say I listened to Magruder.

E   Well, I can't say it quite that way.

H   You can say what Magruder is going to do.

E   I can say—

P   We have learned that Magruder is going to testify.

E   I can say—well I can start out by saying, "Look, I can't vouch for any of this first hand. A tremendous amount of what I know is second-hand, like my conversation with Paul O'Brien, but I have every reason to think that Magruder is in a frame of mind right now to go down there and tell everything he knows."

P   "That Hunt's going to go Monday."

E   "Hunt's going to go Monday."

P   And Liddy—well you can't say Liddy. Maybe Mitchell has a feel—

E   I have reason to think Liddy has already talked.

H   You know (unintelligible) so they're obviously moving on the cover-up.

P   Yeah.

E   If Mitchell went in, that might knock that whole week into a cocked hat.

P   Why?

H   Well, I'm not sure then they care about the cover-up any more.

P   Well, they might.

E   If Mitchell gave them a complete statement—

P   I wish they wouldn't, but I think they would, Bob.

E   If Mitchell gave them a complete statement.

P   They shouldn't. You're right. The cover up, he said that—well, basically its a second crime. Isn't that right, John?

E   Yes.

P   Do you think they would keep going on the cover up even if Mitchell went in?

E   Well, I would assume so. I would certainly assume

so. You see, they've got to explain to the Ervin Committee some day why they do things and they've got a hell of a lead. They're really not in shape to stop them at this point. They would certainly be diverted.

H   Everything relating to this and all the fringes of it and all the—well, maybe other—

E   I think they're in a position to—I just don't know.

P   Yeah, that's right. But the point is what they have that they're relating to primarily is Dean.

H   I don't know about (unintelligible).

P   Dean. I have to bite the Dean bullet today.

E   I didn't say that. I didn't say that. But I think it is a dependent question, and if you are in a situation where Mitchell stonewalls you, and walks out and says, "To hell with you guys, I've got to live my own life."

P   Let's say—we could—when I look at my watch, it's not because of an appointment.

H   You've got a dentist appointment.

P   I've been here since 8 o'clock this morning.

E   That's why?

P   (Unintelligible) Don't worry about that. No, that's no problem. (Unintelligible) John out to the Grand Jury.

E   Let me get around that by suggesting what I think his response would be.

P   Yeah.

E   His response will be, "Look, Ehrlichman, you're supposed to be a lawyer. You know better. Somebody who is a target in an inquiry of this kind and tries pressure into giving up his rights is sort of antithesis of what rights I would have if I were a defendant. You're in the executive branch, a government official. You're supposed to tell me that I have a right to counsel and read me the Supreme Court thing and so forth. Instead of that you just suggested that I divest myself of all my rights and you asked me down here for a' highly improper conversation. You haven't even suggested that I bring my attorney. And I think that what you are doing, you're acting as the prosecutor in this case."

H   How do you come off doing that?

P   He won't do that, in my opinion. He is more likely to say, "Oh, damn it. Look John, you know that there are people in the White House who are deeply involved in this and you know that Colson and Haldeman"—he may say this—"pressured this poor boy over here." I think Mitchell will take the offensive. Don't you agree, Bob?

H   You see, I am not at all sure but what Mitchell

may think I am involved. I am sure he probably thinks Colson's involved, because Magruder has used that. I would guess that's the line Magruder has used with Mitchell, and you might have to play Magruder's tape recording for him.

E   Well if John thinks—I don't think that will happen. I just don't.

P   Is Magruder planning to go see Mitchell?

H   Yes, sir, if he decides to go, if he decides to talk.

P   If he decides to talk—

H   And he is about on the verge. I just assume from that conversation that what he has decided, he is either going to talk or he's going to take the Fifth. He's not going to lie.

P   You're not (unintelligible). They may not call him back.

H   That's correct. (Unintelligible.)

E   He says, I know I'm going to be arrested. I know I'm on my way to jail. If Mitchell comes back with a line like that, "You're not serving the President, well, that if you made any kind of investigation surely you know people in the White House are involved."

P   What do you say?

E   I say, "Look, John, we're past the point where we can be concerned about whether people in the White House are involved. We're not protecting the President by hoping this thing is going to go away."

P   The people in the White House are going to testify.

E   "The thing is not going to go away, John, and by your sitting up there in New York pretending that it is, is just making it worse. And it's been getting steadily worse, by your sitting up there for the last couple of months. We're at the point now where we had no choice but to ask you to do this."

H   And you could say, "We have a whole series of people who have remained mum in order not to create problems for you, who, it's now clear, can no longer remain mum. They don't intend to create problems for you but, I mean—

P   Who do you mean? Liddy?

H   No. I mean his calls to Dean.

E   I could say that, "When I got into this I discovered that there were all kinds of people sitting around here who had bits of information. They were hanging on to them, because they didn't know where they led."

P   Well—

E   "And because they were afraid they would hurt John Mitchell. And I've had to put this whole thing together. And, now, having put it together, you guys know there's no escaping from it.

H   There's no escape. It's got to be proved whether—

P   Confident as a lawyer—

H   There's nobody that can do it that would be able to persuade anyone else.

P   There's nobody else that can do it. Also. Let me digress a moment before we get to the (unintelligible). Another indication of the problem we've got here is, which is related to what we talked about last night on getting out a statement (unintelligible). I just think we are in an impossible position, frankly, with regard to White House people on the Segretti thing. Now you've gone over that with Zeigler and he still thinks we should stonewall it?

H   Yes, sir.

E   I have not talked with him at length for a day.

P   Now here you've got the—I was just looking in the paper this morning. Saxbe, Mathias, Johnny Rhodes, John Anderson, other persons. Two or three of those names are not new, but they're all there. They are trying to build that up as a chorus of Republicans and more to come.

E   It'll be five a day until next month.

H   But they don't.

H   But it's interesting. It is not a universal chorus he must appear before the Committee.

P   Well—

H   If you've got some saying they've got to set up a way to take secret testimony—(unintelligible) and John Williams says

E   Or, else, even Baker.

P   Yeah.

E   But Baker does not say (unintelligible) him. He's protecting us on that.

H   (Unintelligible) and look into it.

P   Everybody's for himself. Then of course our own people are out saying we are having a hell of a time (unintelligible) May 9th dinner. I think that's—

E   I think a lot of that is bull, frankly, on the money thing.

P   We heard that at the time, you know, when we did Cambodia. They said, you remember (unintelligible).

H   But that's not true. We've had no problem. Even the papers are saying it's not true.

P   What in the name of—Bob, let me ask you quickly

a rather curious question. I thought our relations with MacGregor were not strained. I thought he felt pretty good.

H   He does.

P   Why does he go out and say that it cost a million and a half votes? And what did you want to win by? Want to win by 20 million?

H   No, that's—They say, well—

P   But, you realize that that plays?

P   The question that I have, there John, and let's come back to the Congressional Committee, what is Ziegler's—what does Ziegler suggest as an alternative? Stonewall the Committee?

E   Well, when you get to that with him, he recognizes that there's a problem.

P   You see the point is, the point is, I believe that cooperation with the Committee might at least indicate no cover up. That's what I'm trying to do.

E   Well, and that story will come out. We're going to go through a period now where we take some gas. For instance, Kilpatrick was on my radio this morning just taking Kleindienst apart something terrible on executive privilege.

P   Yeah.

E   Now that was a tactic. Kleindienst took a hard line up there

P   Yeah.

E   because if he had softened at all, that would have really hurt our negotiations. And so we are going to take some temporary gas on this. But I think in the long haul, it'll come out OK. Now I may be wrong on that, but I think it will.

P   What do you think Bob?

P   You think we should continue to negotiate?

H   Yep.

P   What is your view, John, as to how the Committee and how do you want it to come out during the negotiation? I'm going to be a little busy tomorrow.

E   I know that. I am going to see a draft Monday. And then, I have already reserved Blair House and I'm

P   What do you want?

E   Going to call a meeting.

P   What are you going to (unintelligible)

E   Well, I am going to go to our executive session and

P   And set this up for a historic way that we can do it for all these

E   Right.

P   Cover Kissinger—

E   And take the poison out of the relationship and so on. They're going to say to me, "Well, it's been nice meeting with you and we appreciate your courtesy, and the hors d'oeuvres have been great. We're now going to go up and write our own set of rules. You understand we can't be bound by your point of view."

P   Right.

E   "And then you guys at the White House are just going to have to decide whether you can live with our rules or not. Take it or leave it."

P   Then you'll say—

E   "Well, let's then talk about procedures for a law suit. Cause I think that's where we're headed." Let's "—I'm going to gig them about Mr. Lipschitz and soften him up a little bit if I can, but then I am going to say," Let's not—

P   What will you say about Mr. Lipschitz?

E   Well, I think we'll have quite a lot of fun with that in terms of double standard.

P   Yeah. And misdemeanor.

E   But I'm going to—

P   And, incidentally, Dash knew it.

E   Yeah. I am going to try to work out a process where Dash to Garment, if they want a test case, we'll frame a test case. They will serve a subpoena, we'll either move to quash it or they can go through the contempt process. But I think the motion to quash is the best way to go.

P   Right.

E   And figure out how we can go stipulated record.

P   And do it fast.

E   And do it before the Federal District Court. Now I think they'll agree with that. We certainly have not given them any reason to be antagonistic. That may be the one -

P   What—

E   Way to agree on process.

P   I know, but do we want to -

E   Well, now, here's the—

P   We don't want a Court case—

E   Well, now, here's what I'm getting at. The Court case will delay any appearance by any White House people. We'll agree that we'll abide the outcome of the case. Then if Mitchell does get indicted, Mitchell's lawyers are going to somehow move to stop the Ervin hearing.

P   Who is—that's your analysis isn't it or is that Colson and Shapiro?

E   That's Shapiro's analysis, also, and I have respect for his ability.

P   Do you quash the—on what ground?

E   On the point that they can't get a fair trial.

P   Yeah. What if they say, "Well, how about Mr. Segretti? What about him?"

H   Why can't they limit their—why can't they—

P   Say nothing about Watergate.

H   Leave out Watergate, but let them go with everything else but—

E   How could you do that?

P   Well, the problem you've got here is that they've got Mitchell and the other people.

H   Sure (unintelligible) all that they've got is the press says "inextricably linked." Of course.

E   And all they have to do is take a look at their big, long resolution. "Let's go." And the Judge would take a look at that and say, "I can't let this go on while (unintelligible) investigates your charge."

P   John, is that better than just caving?

E   Well, we've got the option of caving at any time.

P   You don't want to cave now? Let me put it this way—

E   Yes I do.

P   Let me put it this way. I can't watch (unintelligible). Mitchell—this is going to break him up.

H   As to Watergate

P   Oh, I know, I know and I don't think so. My idea is—it would be better, frankly, after Mitchell is indicted and then if we care—I don't think that is very good. I think it is a lot better for us to be forthcoming before he is indicted, not after. That problem for you to consider.

E   You asked me, "Do I want to cave now?" My feeling about this whole thing is that we ought to be looking at every nook and cranny for every device that there is to be forthcoming.

P   Right.

E   And this is a place where we could do it. My sense of this whole case is that our best defense is that the President always wanted this to happen, and that we weren't being cute about this at all.

P   All right—let's come to this. Ah, regarding the other side—he said, "well, see our heads up there on the dock, and act like convicted criminals and it'd be bad for

260

the White House. You're going to have that continuing thing— "cover-up, cover-up, cover-up."

H Rape is inevitable.

P That's the problem.

H Well, I'm not so sure you are going to have a continuing thing in cover-up when you bust—The Ervin thing goes on. They got a procedure and all that. But, you are down to a different level of staff if you busted the Watergate case. You're down to a level of "Who hired Segretti?" and I think I've got to get out in front on that before it goes up there.

P Well, I think Chapin gets out in front on that.

H No sir because I think—

P Do you think you can make a statement? How does that come along with Henry's thing? What do you think? Can I digress a moment to Segretti? I would like to get that out of the way, but what would you do? What's you're—

H I think, just turn it out. If the Mitchell thing breaks, like on Monday, and if (unintelligible) and that starts breaking and you get into a big bottling up of Watergate. It seems to me that's the best possible time, place and atmosphere for my statements to come out debunking Dean. "Obviously, I couldn't go out publicly and say that I've been sitting here wanting to tell my story waiting for the Senate Committee to get off its ass and nothing's happening here. And I couldn't go out unilaterally and do this while the process was running at the Grand Jury. But now they've come to their conclusions and the people in Watergate are done. Now, let's get the rest of this story covered too, because that doesn't—the rest of it doesn't involve criminal stuff to my knowledge."

P Except you've got—

E There's a problem.

P That's it.

H You've got a kid that's taken the 5th on that.

E Here's what you might do. Let's assume that Tuesday the Ervin Committee comes up with its rules. They will also set their date for hearing on Tuesday—the first of May, 5th of May, whatever it is.

P Do you think they will do that?

E This is their last regular meeting until after recess.

P Fine.

E You could come out then in response to that—and say, "Well, now that they have announced they are not going to have their meeting until May, I have been sitting here waiting. I can't wait any longer. Here's my statement." Send it all to the Grand Jury.

P   I wouldn't (unintelligible) the Grand Jury thing and so forth.

E   That makes it look like it was dragged out of you.

P   Also it gets it all into—the one says, "And also today Bob Haldeman admitted that he was behind the Segretti thing." I'd rather have the story separate, Bob. That's my problem with the other one. Don't you agree?

E   Yeah, I don't feel comfortable with his relating it to the Grand Jury at all. It sounds like, "Well, this is all coming out anyway so now I'm going to make my statement."

P   What's your reason—in other words, you'd relate it to the Committee and the Committee is not going to hear us until.

E   I want an early hearing—I want it.

P   Why can't Ehrlichman get out and say, "Haldeman et al has urged early hearings?"

E   As soon as we get (unintelligible) or why don't they kiss me off and publish their rules.

H   Ehrlichman doesn't have to get up. I can get up, quote my statement and say that, that I had urged early hearings, that there had been, that these—(unintelligible)

P   I'd like to get that story out right now, frankly, that Ehrlichman is urging early hearings.

E   Well, but you see—

P   We don't want early hearings, huh?

E   No, Number one, I don't want 'em. Number two, I have a commitment to Ervin and Baker.

P   That you won't discuss that?

E   And I won't discuss these negotiations until they're over. And it'll unless I want to blow 'em sky high, I shouldn't do that.

P   All right. Well we just take the gas on that. And coming back to, I think John's scenario, Bob, is better. I'd like to separate the two cases and I'd get the Segretti thing out.

H   Wednesday may be the day next week, because they meet Tuesday.

P   Oh, I see. In other words, the Ervin Committee says (unintelligible) you feel it's not time, that's too long. You could put out a statement which says, "I had nothing to do with Watergate." I think in this instance I would say—"but, second, I want to say what we did. I had this to do with Segretti." I wouldn't worry about the fact that he'd come back and say well now what did you do about this or that at this point. I just think this making a forthcoming statement that we present to everybody. That'll buy us some time and you need to buy a little time now and then.

H If you do it under the umbrella of the Mitchell indictment—

P His will come later. Indictment will come, I don't mean indictment,—

H But I'll tell you it could go quite fast. If Mitchell, today, agrees to do this and he and O'Brien and his lawyers went over to see Silbert this afternoon and made a statement, we'd put it out. He could get this thing get this cleared up. Silbert could file an information as early as Monday or Tuesday, you wouldn't have to get an indictment from the Grand Jury.

P We don't even know yet what Magruder is going to do.

E Does it really matter? If once you're possessed of this information.

P Yeah, I see. But, my Gosh. I'm not a mind reader. I'm thinking of those, whether Mitchell gets—you're bargaining with Mitchell. Mitchell's going to say, "Well, I don't know whether Jeb, how do you know Jeb's going to do that?"

E I don't. I don't. But it doesn't matter.

P Yeah. They've got other information?

E That's it.

P How do you know that John?

E Well, we've got some sources inside the U.S. Attorney process.

P That's right.

E I don't know how good they are, John.

H You can say, "John, I am sure you do too."

E You undoubtedly do, too. But everything that I can—

P You think John's had sources? For that problem; they are trying to give him a little bit of (unintelligible). We don't know what our sources are. Our sources are Shapiro, right?

E Oh, no. Dean and his lawyers have sources in the U.S. Attorney's office.

P Silbert, right.

H   Well, then, you've got the other two Grand Juries. How about those?

P   Tell me. Can I spend a minute? That's the thing that I wanted to know. I knew about the New York Grand Jury. What in essence is that? Vesco—

E   It's a, it's a runaway Grand Jury.

P   Yeah.

E   It started out as an SEC action against Vesco for violations of the Securities Act. They then bumped into this two hundred and some thousand dollar donation to the campaign.

P   Right.

E   They have been on that

P   Right

E   since. And they've had Stans up and they've had Mitchell in and they're working on the question of whether or not Vesco procured an appointment with the Attorney General of the United States in consideration of a two hundred thousand dollar campaign contribution.

P   Oh, my God. And Harry Sears charges that?

E   Violation of section 201. Now they have a witness, who was sitting in the room with Vesco and Stans.

P   Yeah.

E   Vesco came in and said, "Mr. Stans, how does a guy get to be a big contributor around here." And Stans said, "Well, the word big means two hundred thousand dollars." And Vesco said, "Cash or check?" And Maury says, "either one." And he—

P   This was after my poor brother was up there?

E   I'm not sure. I don't know, before or after. I just don't know. But in any event, he said, "Well, how does one work out a quid pro quo?" And Maury said, "Well, what's your problem?" And he said, "Well, I'm afraid the Justice Department is after me on an SEC violation." And Maury said, in effect, "I don't know what I can do about that. Let's see." Vesco then got a phone call, allegedly, from John Mitchell. Now, that's enough to indict.

P   It is?

E   They tell me it is. Because Vesco, as a result of the phone call got an appointment.

P   (unintelligible) My God that's dumb. You know what I mean. I can imagine all those (unintelligible) in here trying to get—

E Now that may not be enough to convict, but it's enough to indict.

(Material unrelated to Presidential actions deleted)

P We've come full circle on the Mitchell thing. The Mitchell thing must come first. That is something today. We've got to make this move today. If it fails, just to get back our position I think you ought to talk to Magruder.

H I agree.

P And you tell Magruder, now Jeb, this evidence is coming in you ought to go to the Grand Jury. Purge yourself if you're perjured and tell this whole story.

H I think we have to.

P Then, well, Bob, you don't agree with that?

H No. I do.

P Because I think we do have to. Third, we've got the problem

H You should talk to (unintelligible) first though.

E What really matters, Bob, is that either way—

P Yeah.

E Who is ever (unintelligible)

P You see the point is—

H But don't use Jeb as a basis for the conversation.

P Yeah. Say that the evidence is not Jeb. I'd just simply say that these other people are involved in this. With Jeb, although he may blow—

E I can say that I have come to the conclusion that it is both John and Jeb who are liable.

P Yeah. But no, I meant. Yeah, go ahead. I was simply going to say that we are not talking to John because Jeb is going to crack or that Dean is going to the Grand Jury. It's past that point. They've got the case made.

H That's right.

P He'll say, "Well, I think they're bluffing here." What'll you say?

E It isn't a question of bluffing. Nobody's made any representations to us at all. Nobody's tried to bluff us. It justs a question of putting together all the facts and any time someone, if the U.S. Attorney's office goes through the process that I've gone through, he'll have all the facts. And there'll it'll be. And you don't get it all from any one person. It's some from this one, some from that one.

H It's a typical, it's a typical case.

P How was Dean's—Incidentally, what is the—is the

265

liability of Hunt—I am thinking of the payoff thing.

E Yeah.

P This business, somebody in—Dean, Dean. Dean asked, told me about the problem of Hunt's lawyer. This was a few weeks ago. Needed sixty thousand or forty thousand dollars or something like that. You remember? I said I don't know where you can get it. I said, I mean, I frankly felt he might try to get it but I didn't know where. And then, he left it up with Mitchell and Mitchell said it was taken care of and after (unintelligible). Did he talk to you about that?

E He talked to me about it. I said, John, I wouldn't have the vaguest notion where to get it.

P Yeah.

E I saw him later in the day. I saw Mitchell later in the day—

P What happened?

E And he just said, "It's taken care of."

H Mitchell raised the problem to Dean and said, "What have you done about that other problem?" And Dean said, he kind of looked at us, and then said, "Well, you know, I don't know." And Mitchell said, Oh, I guess that's been taken care of." Apparently through LaRue.

P Apparently who?

H LaRue. Dean told us, LaRue. Dean talked with LaRue and LaRue said this whole thing is ridiculous now. He said, yeah—He said, "If I were in charge of this now what I would do I'd get a large bus, and I'd put the President at the wheel and I'd tell everybody we've got around here in it and I'd drive up to the Senate and I'd have the President open the door and, say, 'you all get out and tell them everything you know and I'll be back to pick you up when you're through.'" He said, "It's all out now and there's nothing we can do about it." He said LaRue also said, "You know I can't figure out how I got into this, to begin with, but it seems to me all of us have been drawn in here in trying to cover up for John."

P For Mitchell?

H Yeah, which is exactly what's happened.

P LaRue said this?

H Yes.

P He's right.

H And if LaRue is called, LaRue intends to tell the truth about it.

P Is he?

H Yeah.

P   Well

H   I don't know.

P   What instructions?

H   I don't know. I don't know any of that. He doesn't have—

P   No, but his instruction will be, LaRue, that I was helping to get—

E   The way Dean talks LaRue wasn't even thinking about the message.

H   I don't think LaRue cares. I think LaRue figures that the jig is up.

E   I had a bit of incidental intelligence that McCord dropped yesterday with regard to Mardian. Just a small—

P   (unintelligible) back in Phoenix.

E   I heard a cover story which he fed to the *New York Times* which would lay it all back at the White House. The trouble with that is, sir, (unintelligible) It will only stand so long as Mitchell stands. (unintelligible) at the White House.

E   That's all. I just don't know any other fact and—

P   But he could lay it to the White House?

E   But bear in mind Shapiro was giving me this in a whole litany of things that were persuasive (unintelligible) what he said to me (unintelligible).

P   The point on Mardian, well, let me say I don't think that Mardian or LaRue or Mitchell or Magruder or anybody want to hurt the President.

H   No, sir.

E   I feel that way. Colson? How about Colson?

H   He - of course, I just think he will do everything he can not to hurt the President.

P   Yeah. That has got to be true of everybody because it isn't the man, it's the office.

H   Sure.

P   But also it happens to be true. I wish I knew about the (expletive deleted).

H   They will have asked that doesn't apply and they could, I think rationalize to themselves that hurting or getting anybody else could be

P   That's right.

H   Good for the President rather than bad.

P   In other words,

H   And that includes Ehrlichman, Haldeman, Dean

P   Yeah.

H   Certainly Colson. Colson will be at the top of

267

that—Colson first, then Haldeman, then Dean, then Ehrlichman.

P   You see I think a Mardian story to the *Times* will be frankly that Colson put the heat on. Maybe

H   But he said at the White House. That could where he—

P   Maybe Haldeman?

H   Mardian. No, Mardian, I don't think has any personal desire to get me. I think, I know he hates Colson

P   Does he?

H   They all do. And anything that Mitchell does is—

P   You see you can make a hell of a circumstantial case on Colson. He's the guy that you know he's Dean's buddy, and Liddy he knew well—apparently knew well—

H   Wasn't Dean's buddy

P   I'm sorry. I meant Hunt's buddy.

H   Yeah. Right.

P   Of course. Right. Right. You know, but Colson is closer to this crew of the robbers than anybody else. That's the problem with Colson Colson's got a very—

H   He has no tie to Liddy.

P   Oh, no. No. No OK

H   That is the (unintelligible), but he has no string on this. His string is to Hunt.

P   Well, then Hunt—

H   Some others—the central background figure—

P   Is it Hunt? Hunt takes this money? He took it for what? To cover up?

H   Immunity. Bet Bittman's given immunity.

P   They're going to give Hunt immunity?

E   I don't know, I suppose—

H   Bittman says there dealings were standard.

P   How do you give him immunity for additional crimes.

E   He's convicted now, you see, so there would be for additional. (unintelligible)

P   So they could give him immunity for, ah—they could cut his sentence and give him immunity for the cover up; the hush money; clemency. How do you handle the problem of clemency, John?

E   (unintelligible)

H   Well, you don't handle it at all. That's Colson's, cause that's where it comes from.

E   That was the line of communication—

P   Colson to Bittman. I guess that's the only thing we

have on that—except Mitchell, apparently had said something about clemency to people.

H   To Liddy.

P   And Mitchell has never, never—Has he ever discussed clemency with you?

E   No.

P   Has he ever discussed it with you?

H   No.

P   (unintelligible) We were all here the room.

H   Well, may have said, "Look we've got to take care of this."

P   But's he's never said, "Look you're going to get a pardon from these people when this is over." Never used any such language around here, has he, John?

E   Not to me.

H   I don't think so.

P   With Dean has he?

E   Well I don't know. That's a question I can't answer.

P   Well, but Dean's never raised it. In fact, Dean told me when he talked about Hunt. I said, John, "where does it all lead?" I said, what's it going to cost. You can't just continue this way. He said, "About a million dollars." (Unintelligible) I said, John, that's the point. (Unintelligible) Unless I could get them up and say look fellows, it's too bad and I give you executive clemency like tomorrow, what the hell do you think, Dean.

P   I mean, you think, the point is, Hunt and the Cubans are going to sit in jail for four years and they are not being taken care of?

H   That's the point. Now where are you going to get the money for that?

P   That's the reason this whole thing falls apart. It's that - It's that that astonishes me about Mitchell and the rest.

E   Big problem.

(Material unrelated to Presidential actions deleted)

P   The word never came up, but I said, "I appreciate what you're doing." I knew it was for the purpose of helping the poor bastards through the trial, but you can't offer that John. You can't - or could you? I guess you could. Attorneys' fees? Could you go a support program for these people for four years.

E   I haven't any idea. I have no idea.

P   Well, they have supported other people in jail for years.

E   Sure, the Berrigan brothers

P   Huh?

E   I say, I don't know how the Berrigan brothers and some of those—

P   They all have funds.

E   Operate. I think they use them.

P   Yes there are funds if you are (unintelligible). I guess that's true.

E   So that they—

P   But not to hush up.

E   That's right.

P   That's the point. All right. One final thing. Dean. You don't think we have to bite it today?

E   Well, I'm not so sure. I'd be inclined. When you say bite it isn't simply a matter of making a decision, in my opinion—

P   I have made a decision. He's to go.

E   Well, I'm not sure that's the right decision. By forcing the issue, I don't mean to imply that

P   Oh, I see. (Unintelligible)

E   Uh, (unintelligible)

P   When you said you didn't think you agreed with the decision, I thought that was one of the recommendations you made.

E   No, my recommendation is that you recognize that there's a go no go decision that has to be made because—

P   Oh, I see

E   Here's your situation. Look again at the big picture. You now are possessed of a body of fact.

P   That's right.

E   And you've got to—you can't just sit here.

P   That's right.

E   You've got to act on it. You've got to make some decisions and the Dean thing is one of the decisions that you have to make. You may decide—

P   Bull, please. Steve Bull. All right, fine, fine. Then you're not—

E   Then you've got to dispose of it one way or the other.

P   Put that thing with Haig, what time you got now? Quarter after? I'll be there at EOB.

E   I'll tell you, I am still heavily persuaded that we af-

270

fect the Grand Jury and U.S. Attorney treatment of Dean favorably by keeping him on.

P   Ok.

E   And that that's important. Now—

P   Why is that? - because they like him?

E   No, no. No, no. Because they can treat him differently as the President's Counsel than as a dismissed person.

E   Exactly.

P   Yeah.

E   It's a very heavy psychological factor.

P   Well this will be done because there is another reason too. It isn't like, Dean is not like Mitchell, now, let's face it.

H   That's right.

P   Dean is not like Mitchell in the sense that Dean only tried to do what he could to pick up the pieces and everybody else around here knew it had to be done.

E   Certainly.

P   Let's face it. I'm not blaming anybody else—

E   No, I understand that. I have great trouble in (unintelligible) in the light of the known involvement that he had in the

P   Aftermath?

E   Right, but—

H   But the known involvement he had in that was for what was understood here to be the proper system

P   The question is motive. That's right.

E   That number one. Number two, there is nothing new about that. As I have developed this thing—I want you to read this—

P   Yeah.

E   There were 8 or 10 people around here who knew about this, knew it was going on. Bob knew, I knew, all kinds of people knew.

P   Well, I knew it. I knew it.

E   And it was not a question of whether—

P   I must say though, I didn't know it but I must have assumed it though but you know, fortunately—I thank you both for arranging it that way and it does show the isolation of the President, and here it's not so bad—But the first time that I knew that they had to have the money was the time when Dean told me that they needed forty thousand dollars. I had been, frankly, (unintelligible) papers on those little envelopes. I didn't know about the en-

271

velopes (unintelligible) and all that stuff.

E   The point is that if Dean's, if the wrongdoing which justifies Dean's dismissal is his knowledge that that operation was going on, then you can't stop with him. You've got to go through a whole place wholesale.

P   Fire the whole staff.

E   That's right. It's a question of motive. It's a question of role and I don't think Dean's role in the aftermath, at least from the facts that I know now, achieves a level of wrongdoing that requires that you terminate him.

P   I think he made a very powerful point to me that of course, you can be pragmatic and say, (unintelligible) cut your losses and get rid of 'em. Give 'em an hors d'oeuvre and maybe they won't come back for the main course. Well, out, John Dean. On the other hand, it is true that others did know.

E   But more than that. We've made Dean a focal point in the Gray process.

P   Right.

E   And he will become a focal point in the Ervin process.

P   We'll have to—yes, except, yes, if he goes down.

H   And if you dismiss him he'll still be a focal point.

E   He'll be a focal point. He'll be a defrocked (unintelligible)—

H   With with less protection, that's right.

E   And with less incentive.

P   Well the point that I think, I think—

H   What Dean did, he did with all conscience in terms that the higher good.

P   Dean, you've got to have a talk with Dean. I feel that I should not talk to him.

E   I have talked to him.

P   I mean about motive.

E   I have talked to him.

P   What's he say about motive. He says' it was hush-up?

E   No. He says he knew, he had to know that people were trying to bring that result about.

P   Right.

E   And he says, you know, the way I got into this was I was I would go to meetings in campaign headquarters and we'd get through the meeting and Mitchell and LaRue would say to—Mardian and LaRue would say to Mitchell. "You've got to do something about this." And Mitchell's stock answer was, to turn to John Dean and say, "What are you going to do?" And so John said, "I got to be kind of a water carrier. I'd come back from these meetings and I'd come in to see Bob," or me or somebody else, and say, "Well Mitchell's got this big problem." And then he'd say, "They'd say to me, 'well I don't know what I'll do about it.'"

P   When he came in to see Bob and you what would he say was the problem?

E   He'd say, "These guys, Hunt's getting jittery, and says that he's got to have umpty-ump thousand dollars, and Mitchell's terribly worried about it," and it was never expressed, but it was certainly understood—

P   On the question of motive then, though, I guess in those conversations with you with respect to motive was never discussed.

E   Never discussed with me in those terms.

P   Right. The motive was to help defendants who were, by golly who had worked for the campaign committee

E   It never really got that far because, we, at least my conversation with John always was, "Well, you know that's interesting, but I just don't know what to do for you."

P   Yeah. He may have gone further with you, Bob. Did he?

H   No. We referred him to Kalmbach. You aimed it at Kalmbach, I aimed it at Mitchell. I said, "John, you can't come here and ask for help, we don't have it." The one thing where it did go further, if you want to argue about it, it was in the sense that the 350,

P   That we had.

H   Which was not our money, we did move back over there.

P   For this purpose?

H   (Unintelligible). Yeah, yeah.

P   Who asked for it?

H   Nobody.

P   I mean how, who asked for the move on the 350?

H   Hunt did.

P   How did you know? Somebody came to you?

H   Gordon Strachan came to me after the election and said you have three hundred and fifty thousand dollars in cash. What do you want to do with it.

P   This was not requested by LaRue?

H   No.

P   Of Gordon?

H   No the problem was getting them to take it back.

They wouldn't take it, cause they didn't know how—

P   Well, that money—

H   LaRue wanted it but Mitchell wouldn't let him take it.

E   They just didn't know how to account for it.

P   Well, then, frankly, he wouldn't have to account for it, in my opinion.

H   Well but he didn't—he was

P   Nineteen seventy money.

H   He will have to account for it now, because Fred LaRue is in personal receipt under Grand Jury knowledge of three hundred and twenty-eight thousand dollars in cash delivered to him at night at his apartment by Gordon Strachan. The witnesses to that transaction were Strachan and LaRue.

P   LaRue testified—

H   But Strachan just testified that that's what happened. Well LaRue's got a problem. What did he do with it? At that point, it's income to him. He's got an IRS problem if he can't get that accounted for.

P   He'll use it—what does he say? He says, I used it for hush money?

H   I don't know what he'll say. He'll probably say I packaged it up—

P   That help? but that certainly doesn't help us.

H   Doesn't help anybody but, you know

P   The other thing he says, well, I just—I have retained it in a fund for future campaigns.

H   I'm sure he doesn't have it.

E   I am not sure, either, but I assume it went right out to pay these people. That's my assumption.

P   You know he used it—

H   Not all of it.

E   Now Dean says this. He says we have only two problems that we have to manage in the White House. One is the fact that we made a referral to Kalmbach, and he said that can be explained. And need not be a major problem, if it's clearly explained. And we have no problem with the aftermath.

H   I'm running the three fifty into my statement, but the question is whether we want it in.

P   Oh yes. Put it in there.

H   Nobody knows about it, but that's another bombshell.

P   I think there's been something written about it.

H   Yeah, but not that I had it. It is eleven o'clock.

P   All right. Eleven o'clock and the armistice is signed so off we go.

E   Mitchell is roughly two hours away, at best.

P   I think, I think he's going to come down and do it today. I think, Bob, I think you have to go out and call him now. And ask him if he can come down.

E   Tell him we'll send an airplaine for him.

H   (Unintelligible)

P   Yeah.

H   By the time we get a plane mobilized and up there it takes longer. We'll send it if he is playing golf or something.

P   I know. He may be gone. But the Point that I made was this, if he's out to play golf, just say we have an urgent message, and just say there have been (unintelligible) on the Watergate things.

H   (Unintelligible) him immediately.

P   Tell him he should come down but have him (unintelligible) can you come down? If he says, I can't come then Ehrlichman should go up.

H   Then say John will come up. Where'll you be.

P   Yes. If he says well I've got a dinner tonight and I've got—say, John, John this is very important. The President considers this of the highest urgency that you be aware of these developments.

E   Something that just can't be postponed any longer.

P   Can't be postponed and we—Harder than firing Hickel.

E   Oh, about the same.

P   That it?

H   Yes, sir.

E   Ok—anything new? Our last conversation? Can you give it to me now? Ok. I'll see you in a little while.

P   Colson?

E   No, that was Dean.

H   What did he say?

E   (Unintelligible) I think we're going to be—Well, you can put

P   We did not cover up, though, that's what decides, that's what's decides.

H   (Unintelligible) to go testify.

P   My point is that if three of us talk here, I realize that, frankly—Mitchell's case is a killer. Dean's case is the question. And I do not consider him guilty. Now that's all there is to that. Because if he—if that's the case, then half the staff is guilty.

E   That's it. He's guilty of really no more except in degree.

P   That's right. Then others

E   Then a lot of

P   And frankly then I have been since a week ago, two weeks ago

E   Well, you see, that isn't, that kind of knowledge that we had was not action knowledge, like the kind of knowledge that I put together last night. I hadn't known really what had been bothering me this week.

P   Yeah.

E   But what's been bothering me is

P   That with knowledge, we're still not doing anything.

E   Right.

P   That's exactly right. The law and order. That's the way I am. You know it's a pain for me to do it—the Mitchell thing is damn painful.

E   Sure.

P   Is he coming?

H   Yes, sir. I said, "Do you want to let us know what plane you're on so we can pick you up? He said, no let me (unintelligible)

P   Run over this. Do you delay your meeting with Magruder until you see him.

E   I don't think it really matters. It runs over this whole thing and having knowledge and having to act on it.

P   My point is that I think you better see Magruder before you see him. No. I guess you're

E   It doesn't matter, in my opinion

P   You should see Magruder, today. That's the main thing.

E   I think we ought to make a similar call to Magruder.

H   I should do it. I should call Jeb and say that things have developed and all this and—

P   Yeah.

H   Well, I didn't say that to Mitchell.

E   It doesn't matter.

P   Oh, Mitchell. He knows better. Say that to Jeb.

H   When I say it to Jeb it'll take probably thirty-seven seconds for him to turn up on your doorstep.

P   Oh, that's all right. It's all right. I think we should do it before you see Mitchell. Or you, do you feel uncomfortable about telling him?

E   No. As I say I think it's almost immaterial as to

which I see first. It's the fact of doing it rather than any particular sequence.

H Mitchell won't be here, he can't be here until (unintelligible)

P Yeah. I think, in my view, John, you can't wait to act. You can see Jeb Magruder and say now, Jeb, you're to testify (unintelligible)

E I wouldn't quite say it that way. I'll say, "I don't know if you know what I've been doing here the last three weeks. I have been ranging over this whole subject matter trying to bring to the President something more than John Dean has turned.

P Can you tell him as you talk to him that what he says is attorney-client? No? You can't tell him. Ok.

E I'll simply say that as you know Dean did an investigation which determined whether or not the White House was involved. My responsibility was greater than that. It was to range over the whole thing and try to bring to the President a new body of information on what actually happened, for example, first of what transpired. And from what I have been able to put together I have advised the President and he—this morning—and he has directed me immediately to contact you. Having found a highly accepted point of view in all of this that people should not disclose what they know because it somehow serves the President. It involves, apparently, considerable criminal jeopardy. (Unintelligible) what to do from your own standpoint, I now want you to have as a message from the President. He does not in any way view it as serving his interests for you to remain silent. Decide what to do from your own personal standpoint, and I haven't any right to interfere in that decision. If there ever was an impediment to your coming forward by reason of your impression, assumed or otherwise, of what the President wanted you to do I think it's my job to impart to you what is actually the case.

P I would, also, though, I'd put a couple of things in and say, Jeb, let me just start here by telling you the President holds great affection for you and for your family. I was just thinking, I was thinking last night, this poor little kid

H Yeah, beautiful kids.

P Lovely wife and all the rest, it just breaks your heart. And say this, this is a very painful message for me to bring—I've been asked to give you, but I must do it and it is that: Put it right out that way. Also, I would first put that in so that he knows I have personal affection. That's the way the so-called clemency's got to be handled. Do you see John?

E   I understand.

H   Do the same thing with Mitchell.

P   Oh, Mitchell? Well you could say to Mitchell, I think you've got to say that this is the toughest decision he's made and its tougher than Cambodia,—May 8 and December 18 put together. And that he just can't bring himself to talk to you about it. Just can't do it. And he directed that I talk to you. You see, what I am doing, John, is putting you in the same position as President Eisenhower put me in with Adams. But John Mitchell, let me say, will never go to prison. I agree with that assumption. I think what will happen is that he will put on the damndest defense that—the point you have, your suggestion is that he not put on a defense. You're suggesting he go in and say look I am responsible here? I had no knowledge but I am responsible? And nobody else had—that's it. Myself. That's it, and I want to. This thing has got to stop. Innocent people are being smeared in this thing.

E   He will understand, however it comes out. Once you are possessed of a reasonable body of knowledge, you have an obligation to do something and, rather than simply to turn it over to the U.S. Attorney, the thing that you are doing, in the first instance, is giving him an opportunity to come forward.

P   Rather than having a special prosecutor, say that he comes to a special prosecutor. The President rejects that. The idea that we turn it over to the U.S. Attorney. Call him in, which I could do. Or call in the Attorney General, which I could do, but I think its (unintelligible) to do this because I cannot have this. Now, of course, he's going to ask, "Well, now, John what knowledge do you really have, except hearsay."

E   "I don't have any knowledge, except hearsay, John."

P   But I do know that Magruder

E   I know that John Dean said

P   (Unintelligible) there is no question about what is going to happen.

E   That's right.

H   You won't have to appeal to him on that because he's made the point you know that if Dean testifies it's going to unscramble the whole omelet.

P   That's why I don't want to leave it at the point that

278

Dean's or Magruder's or anyones testimony is essential to Mitchell's—

E   That's right.

P   You see that's the point of that. On the Dean thing, I wouldn't say that the President has stood, frankly, John, on executive privilege thing, because it's up to (unintelligible) and so forth.

E   "It isn't my purpose to prove to your satisfaction you're guilty of that you're going to be indicted, but—it's my purpose to say that the President is now in possession—

P   That I believe we should come to you. What are you going to suggest that he do, John?

E   Well, if he asks me, what do you want me to do? I am going to say, "If you will do what I ask you, what I would suggest, you would pick up the phone or you would allow me to pick it up, and call Earl Silbert and make an appointment today and go over and talk with the U.S. Attorney about this case with counsel."

H   I'll see the President and tell him you're going to go.

E   No.

H   OK

E   "Well, you're asking me in effect to go down and enter a guilty plea." And I would say, "Look, John, you're the only who knows the basic (unintelligible) to go and to decide whether there's any room with what you know and the ultimate action of the jury through which you might pass unpunished. I can't make that judgment for you and I don't have any right to make it for you. All I'm saying is that if we're looking at this thing from the standpoint of the President, today is probably the last day that you can take that action, if you're ever going to take it to do the President a bit of good."

P   "Do you realize, John, that from the White House, I mean, Colson, maybe Haldeman are going to get involved in this thing too?"

E   Well, here again, we're looking at this thing not from the standpoint of any other individual. "We are looking at it from the standpoint of the Presidency and that's the only way I think you and I can approach this."

P   And I'd go further and say, "The President has said let the chips fall where they may. He will not furnish cover for anybody." I think you ought to say that.

E   That's right.

P   Don't you agree, Bob? That isn't it?

H He may go. He may get Chuck. He may get you. We asking—

P We are asking on this thing (unintelligible) Get the White House. You see on the other hand, he may do something else, Bob. I think he would think the latter.

H That's the thing we've worried about all along, that somebody will get (unintelligible) what we do but we can't live by whether we (unintelligible) the (unintelligible).

P (Unintelligible)

E And this is one that will permit him, one that might help the Presidency rather than damage it.

P Bob, do you think there's something to be said for having John wait to talk to Magruder until after he sees Mitchell? Suppose you get stone-walled with Mitchell.

H Well, I think John's in a stronger position if he's talked with Magruder than if he hasn't but I, maybe I.

E I tell you, it is not what Mitchell says that matters today. It is the fact that you have acted on information you have today.

P Yeah.

E Now, let's suppose Mitchell turns us down cold, and says I'm going to preserve all my rights. I'm going to fight every inch of turf and so on and so forth. OK. That's right. But at least you, having accumulated all this knowledge this week, have tried to get this thing out, so that sometime two months from now, three months from now, a year from now when there's a panic you can say on the 14th of April—

P It's the 13th.

E 14th - 14th day of April.

P This is the 14th - Saturday.

E Yeh. Friday was the 13th, yesterday. On April 14th—

P No, seriously, as I have told both of you, the boil had to be pricked. In a very different sense—that's what December 18th was about. We have to prick the boil and take the heat. Now that's what we are doing here. We're going to prick this boil and take the heat. I - am I overstating?

E No. I think that's right. The idea is, this will prick the boil. It may not. The history of this thing has to be though that you did not tuck this under the rug yesterday or today, and hope it would go away.

P Now. In the scenario. I sort of go out and tell people that I have done this.

E   I don't know. It depends on how it all turns out. If he does not go to the U.S. Attorney, if Magruder decides to stay clammed up—

H   What would you do?

P   Well, that, well, let's suppose they still indict. You don't want them to indict and then have to say that on Saturday, the 14th of April, you, John Ehrlichman—

E   Yeah. But you see the problem there is—

H   (Unintelligible) at least you got the record now.

E   The problem is that if you were to go out on this kind of hearsay and say we know who did it, then you've prejudiced their rights.

P   Then you're thought is to get out beforehand.

E   No, no.

P   Your thought is just to make a record of the decision?

E   When somebody comes to (unintelligible) what the hell was the White House doing all this time? Then you're in a position to say well, we began to investigate personally the external circumstances and we came to some conclusions—we acted on those conclusions.

P   John Ehrlichman conducted an investigation for the President.

E   And we made an effort. Now, it may be that what should happen here is that if they both stonewall, I ought to sit down with Silbert and just say now I don't have a lot of evidence.

P   I agree with that.

E   But I have an accumulation of heresay—

P   And the President wants you to go forward on this.

E   And I'll turn over to you the report that I made for the President for whatever it's worth. And I want to tell you that I have had contact with two of your targets to make clear to them that nobody in the White House wanted them in any way to be reticent. Beyond that, I don't have anything to say to you.

P   Well, then, let's see what happens.

E   Well, let's see what these guys go. But I think maybe like, tomorrow, I ought to see Silbert.

P   I agree. I think the record should be made we have talked to him so that he knows that the President has moved on this.

E   And that's, that puts—

P   And we saw the U.S. Attorney and turned over our information to him. All the information we had.

E   I would like a record of my conversation with both

281

Magruder and Mitchell. I think personally that maybe I ought to get my office geared up so that I can do that.

P   (unintelligible), or do you remove that equipment?

E   Yeah.

P   I do here for my meetings with Henry but I don't know.

E   I think it's better if I do it over there.

P   Why don't you just gear it up? Do you know, do you have a way to gear it up?

E   Yeah. I've done it before.

P   Well go gear it. No, no. Well, wait a minute. No, I think that's too—

H   (Unintelligible)

P   Who will? I would just have it so that you will know that what we've got here. I don't want to hear the record, I want to say. So these guys, don't have me hear the record.

H   (Unintelligible) I don't know whether to tell you or not, but there is certainly a purpose for me to sit in on the meeting.

P   I think you should.

H   Maybe that's it. That would give you a witness for one thing. If either of those people were questioned and you don't have anybody else, you've got a problem.

P   And then when Mitchell says, Bob, you know you were in this too. What's Bob Haldeman say?

E   Well, he won't. He won't.

P   I think, Bob, shouldn't sit in because Haldeman is. No. I think, so. That gives you the witness. And also Mitchell feels he's got a friend there. And he knows that you're not just doing this on your own, freewheeling it. Bob says we talked it all over. The President said we can't sit on information that's of this nature. Get any information on the White House stuff. It's going to be exactly the same procedure. I think you ought to move on the Jeb thing, Bob.

H   I get him in my office.

P   Give your report to me on it. When you finish your conversation with Jeb, I'll be over.

(Material unrelated to Presidential actions deleted.)

Meeting: The President and Haldeman, Oval Office, April 14, 1973. (1:55 - 2:13 pm)

P   Well, you chatted and decided not to take (unintelligible)

H   Yes sir, he said stay on standby—It may be better if it looks like a good idea for you to be there if you can just be available because I may want you to come up fast so I am on standby.

P   Magruder

H   He has had him in there for forty-five minutes, but he still (unintelligible). I called Magruder - it took a long time to get him - he was not available - and I was trying to get him through his office but his lawyer said he could reach him in about an hour which he did and had him call me. Jeb said - I started out by saying now there have been some developments and we have reviewed this whole thing with the President and he thought it was important to have you and your lawyer meet with John Ehrlichman right away and get up-to-date on where things stand from this side. He said - fine, I can do that, I can't make it until about four o'clock. That was the way it was left - but he then said - you know this whole thing - I don't know the situation but it is all done now. I said, what do you mean? He said I decided late last night with my lawyers that I am going to go ahead - you told me to do what my lawyers told me to do. You said you couldn't advise me.

P   Is that what you told him?

H   Yes. You see he called saying, what does Bob want me to do? I told Larry to tell him that I was not in a position to tell him what to do, that that was last week, that that was a decision he had to make and work out with his own advisers. You know - that I wasn't cutting him off - it was simply that it was his area. Well anyway, he said they had decided last night that he would have to tell all and his lawyers met with Silbert today and informed Silbert that Magruder was ready to tell all and requested an opportunity for him to do so. He doesn't know what the timing is but the plan is that he will meet first with Silbert and review what he is going to say and then Silbert will take him to the Grand Jury. Now, the kind of a deal - first - Jeb said I did not ask for immunity - I did not feel

283

I was entitled to it. He said the reason that I tell everything is because they are going to get it anyway. They have witnesses on witnesses now and there is no reason for me to be quiet because they've got everything anyhow.

P How does he know that? Did Silbert tell him?

H I guess Silbert told his lawyers.

P Uh, huh.

H It is a damn good prosecuting lawyer like Silbert to get a key witness to tumble, but—

P Immediately?

H Sure, they've got the facts - they may not be able to prove them but they've got them. Magruder is set to give them the proof. He says the only thing I gain out of this is the hope that I don't go up for all the counts they've got me. He says they've got me for six or eight counts perjury, two counts of conspiracy and two counts of obstruction of justice essentially and that ends up with sentences of 135 to 160 years in jail. He says my lawyers feel that if I open up on this and they have had discussion - they haven't made a deal apparently with Silbert - as to what they will do - that he has been told the way the process will work is that he will give his information and they will determine from the information what counts they will seek to indict him on. They will then take him before the Grand Jury and go forward with Grand Jury indictments on a limited number of counts and they will try to work on cooperation and that sort of stuff to lighten his load and he will then plead guilty on all counts. He will not stand trial - he will not testify in public court - he will only testify to the Grand Jury and whatever they bring as indictments he will take guilty pleas on and go to jail.

P It isn't a fair trial is it?

H He told me that whole thing in a broken voice and showed more strength than I thought he had, to be perfectly frank. He obviously groped his way through in his own mind.

P It is terribly hard.

H It is awfully hard - particularly if you are very sharp.

P You don't know what is involved—

H He understands it - he said the other thing that you have to understand, Bob, is that this whole thing is going down the drain - he said everybody is going to crumble. At this point I would suspect these lawyers have talked to each other. He said LaRue, everybody involved here is going to blow with the exception of John—

284

P   Mitchell?

H   Unfortunately, I had this conversation just as John Mitchell was driving up the driveway - I held Mitchell—had him go up to John Ehrlichman's office but then Ehrlichman heard all of this before he went into Mitchell. Jeb has not told Mitchell of his decision yet - he said, I want to make my decision and then my lawyers are working it out with Silbert this morning and then my next step is to tell John Mitchell which I want to do.

P   How the hell can John Mitchell deny it? He was right on the (unintelligible) spot.

H   Jeb says unfortunately I will to a degree implicate John Dean and to possibly to some degree Bart and I hate to do it, but he said where I am now there is nothing - I can't pull any punches. He said there is no way that anything I do will get to you.

P   John Dean will have to testify (unintelligible)

H   Well, John Dean - that doesn't trouble me - I don't think it troubles Dean - where he gets John Dean is on his attendance at those meetings.

P   That meeting Saturday night?

H   No - the problem there is that the discussion at those meetings clearly and specifically did involve bugging.

P   Oh, Dean never denied it as it has turned out. That's John Dean's stand - but what about the aftermath? Does the aftermath hold on Dean?

H   I don't think Magruder knows about the aftermath.

P   Where does he get to Gordon Strachan?

H   He says he gets Gordon on—

P   Sending material to him—

H   He still implies at least that Gordon know about it before you know - he knew everything they did. Larry tells me he did not.

P   He will testify that he sent materials to the White House?

H   If he is asked, he will, yes.

P   He'll be asked - is that something he will say he sent to the White House. What would Strachan say?

H   Strachan has no problem with that. He will say that after the fact there are materials that I can now surmise were what he is referring to but they were not at the time identified in any way as being the result of wiretaps and I did not know they were. They were amongst tons of stuff. Jeb makes the point. He said, I am sure Gordon never sent them to Bob because they were all trash. There was

285

nothing in them. He said the tragedy of this whole thing is that it produced nothing.

P   Who else did he send reports to - Mitchell?

H   I don't know. The thing I got before was that he sent them either to - that one went to him and one went to Strachan.

P   What our problem there is if they claim that the reports came to the White House - basically to your office - what will you say then?

H   They can. This doesn't ever have to come out.

P   I know, but they will ask it in the Grand Jury.

H   If they do ask it in the Grand Jury - the Grand Jury is secret. The only way it will come out is if they decide to indict Strachan and put him up for trial. He, Jeb, is totally convinced that they have no interest in Strachan at all - and they have all this stuff. And I can see how they feel - Strachan is like a secretary - he is useful as a witness.

P   (Unintelligible)

H   Yeah, he implies - or has in earlier stuff - he doesn't now directly. He doesn't say anything now directly - but did in the earlier stuff that Strachan knew about it beforehand. That Strachan knew they were bugging the Watergate. Strachan says he didn't. Jeb has implied a lot of things that I know aren't true, but I know that a lot of things that other people are saying aren't true so I would have no idea whether he believes now that—one of the problems Jeb has is that he's not sure what is true at this point.

P   He tells you this?

H   He tells me that he is sorry about this because it will probably hurt Dean and it may hurt Bart. You see that is the kind of thing - you know - from his judgment - he is looking at things a little different now.

(Material not related to Presidential actions deleted)

P   Has anything come out yet - something implies that there are copies of a bill from the Watergate to the White House or not or has that not been said? He could have had - but I suppose not (unintelligible)

H   I am sure that it is the thing that follows—all of them had access to everything - involvement - implication is clearly there.

P   Everybody is sure trying to get in the act now. I see a message here from Steve that John (unintelligible) had

thought about the Watergate and had some ideas he
would like to pass along.

Meeting: The President, Haldeman and Ehrlichman, Oval Office, April 14, 1973.
(2:24 - 3:55 pm)

P   All finished?

E   Yes sir. He an innocent man in his heart and in his
mind and he does not intend to move off that position. He
appreciated the message of the good feeling between you
and him.

P   He got that, huh?

E   He appreciated my—

P   How did you get him here? Give us a little chapter
and verse.

E   Well, I started out by saying that the subject was so
difficult for you to talk to him personally about that you
had asked me to do this.

P   What did you next say?

E   That you had had me doing this. That I had
presented you with a set of conclusions that were admittedly hearsay, but that pointed in the direction of his
ex-soldier and Jeb's and other people and that you were
having me systematically talk to these people because in
the course of this investigation we had discovered a frame
of mind on the part of some people that they should stand
mute in order to help the President, and that your sense
was that the Presidency was not helped by that, and that
it was not my purpose to tell anybody what he should do,
but only to tell him that as far as your view of the interest
of the Presidency were concerned, that they were not
served by a person standing mute for that reason alone.
Now, there might be plenty of reasons why a person
might want to stand mute to put the government out to
prove it. And that wasn't the question. Then he said,
"Well, what you say to me is that the President is reserv-
ing to me all my options," and I said, "Of course he is,
John. The only thing that he doesn't want you to feel is
that you don't have the option of going in and copping, if
you want to do so. You have completely every option to
go in or not to go in." And he said, well he appreciated
that but he had not been taking the position he had for
the reason that he thought he was necessarily helping or

287

hurting the Presidency, but he said, "You know, these characters pulled this thing off without my knowledge." He said, "I never saw Liddy for months at a time." And he said, "I didn't know what they were up to and nobody was more surprised than I was. We had this meeting," and he lobbed mud balls at the White House at every opportunity - it was very interesting how he dragged it in. One after the other. But first he said, "There were these meetings. These characters came over to my office and Liddy put on this million dollar presentation which was perfectly ridiculous. The origin of that, of course, was in the White House where Bob Haldeman and I talked about something called the Operation Sandwedge that was really the grandfather of this whole thing." He said, "Of course, that was never put together because we couldn't get the right people to do it." They were talking about Joe Woods and people of that kind and so he said, "It never happened."

P   What is Operation Sandwedge?

H   He is right. Jack Caulfield came up with that back in 1971, said we need some fellows to set up our own detail.

E   So then he went on to say that there were only those meetings - he is still hung up on there were only three meetings thing. He made it very clear to me that he did never believe there was a fourth meeting. He said that, of course—

H   He wasn't in the fourth meeting, John. There was no fourth meeting as far as he was concerned.

E   No, no, but he didn't refer to three or four, he referred to the meetings themselves. He argues that there was no meeting after the million dollar meeting.

H   Well, it wasn't that way.

E   Right. That is the sense of what he was saying. I didn't press him on it and I tried to play him with kid gloves. I never asked him to tell me anything. He just told me all this stuff. He says that actually Magruder is going to have a problem with all of this because Dean talked Magruder into saying the wrong things to the Grand Jury, and so Magruder's got a problem.

P   My God, Mitchell was there?

E   Yep.

P   Is that Dean they are referring to?

E   Sure

H   Sure

P   Mitchell was there when Dean talked him into saying the wrong things?

E or H That's what he says. That is what Mitchell says.

P What does Dean say about it?

E Dean says it was Mitchell and Magruder. It must have been the quietest meeting in history everybody's version is that the other two guys talked -

P Go ahead.

E Well it goes on like that. His characterization of all this is that he was a very busy man, that he wasn't keeping track of what was going on at the Committee - that this was engendered as a result of Hunt and Liddy coming to Colson's office and getting Colson to make a phone call to Magruder and that he, Mitchell, was just not aware that all that happened until Van Shumway brought Liddy into Mitchell's office sometime in June and that's the first he had knowledge of it. It was much later in the conversation before—

H Before the discovery?

E I don't know. I don't know. You can listen to it. I've got it taped. Forgive me. But in any event, much later I said that the Grand Jury, or the U.S. Attorney, felt that they had John wired. And he said, "Well, what possible evidence could they have to feel that way?"

P John Dean or John Mitchell?

E John Mitchell, Well I said I understand that one version of the fact is that Magruder brought you a memo with a number of targets on it, and that you checked off the targets that you wanted. And he said, "Why nothing could be further from the truth than that."

P That was John Dean's version.

H That's right.

P That's what he said to Mitchell.

H Right. Then what Mitchell said to me was that he did not - he said I checked - I signed off on it.

P Go ahead.

H I said you mean you initialed it and he said no.

E Then I said they had testimony saying Hunt and Liddy, having a conversation, and Liddy saying to Hunt, "Yes, I know how you don't like this stuff, but we have to do it because Mr. Mitchell insists on it." He said, "I never saw Liddy for five months. From February to June, I never laid eyes on him." He said, "I think Liddy is the source of a lot of my problems here, using my name, etc. So it is very much of (unintelligible) thing. He said, "If I am indicted, it is going to be very hard but," he said, "I have to think of my reputation. I can't let people get away with this kind of thing," and he said, "I am just going to have to defend myself every way I can." He said, "Obviously I can't get a fair trial in the city of Washington by any stretch of the imagination. We'll just have to see how that all comes out." He said, "I am sorry to hear that so much of this is going to come to the White House because it certainly is not in the President's interest to have all this kind of thing come out." He made a great point of the $350,000. He says that his recollection—and he said, "You want to check this because," he said, "I am very vague on the facts of this." I told him about Strachan, because Strachan used to work for him. And I told him that Strachan had been, and has to go back and correct the $350,000 to $328,000. He said, "I wasn't the only (unintelligible) for that money." And I said, "Oh?" And he said, "No, you would have to check with John Dean on this but," he said, "it is my recollection that Dean had Strachan draw other money out of that fund for payments to these defendants." I said, "Well, that is the first I have heard of that. I understood that Strachan had gone to Bob and said this fund and Bob had said send it back to the Committee and that Strachan had taken it to LaRue as a representative of the Committee." He said, "Yes, I think that's the way it all went, but not until some of it had been tapped by the defendants." And I said, "It was not known to anyone over here who was going to receive it." I said, "Was that before the money got to LaRue?" And he said, "Yes, I am sure it was." I said, "Well, who would know about that because I have never heard that before?" He said, "Well, Dean." So—

P   The $328,000 is wrong, too, then?

E   Well if Mitchell is to be believed, that's right that is the inference. But you don't know of any other withdrawal do you, Bob?

H   Well, I told you the $328,000 was not returned in one trip, but it all went to LaRue.

P   (unintelligible)

H   Here is the sequence on that. We wanted to get the money back to the Committee. The Committee wouldn't take it. Mitchell wouldn't let LaRue take it. I said give it all back. Mitchell said no. Then they got desperate for money, and being desperate for money took back—I think it was $40,000. That is all they would take. I still said, "Take it all back, not just a segment of it, and made the point that I didn't see what the problem was. If they needed money and we wanted to get rid of money, it seemed to me it was of mutual interest in working it out. And that, then, was what happened. The balance—

P Tell Strachan on Monday that he better be clear that he didn't give—

H Right.

P Strachan has testified apparently that he gave the whole bundle at once.

H No, he wasn't asked that.

P He wasn't asked?

H His testimony in that area is not wrong.

P Good.

E Now, John kept referring to, using the phrase, protecting the rights of people. One of the ways that he used that phrase was in response to my question about what he thought I ought to do with the information that I had collected in the last several weeks. And he said, "Well, you have to first of all consider the rights of individuals." I said, "Yes. At the same time here is the Presidency hindered now with a body of hearsay and not absolute knowledge. Ah, my inclination is to give it to Kleindienst." And he thought about that awhile and he said, "Yes, I guess that is the best thing you could do." I said, "Now you should know that Kleindienst has said that if you in any way get cracked in this case that he is going to step aside, regardless of the case. I understand Henry Petersen also will." And I said, "That the thing Kleindienst is pushing for is a special prosecutor." John said, "That would be a grave mistake because it would be subversive to the orderly process of justice if everytime you had an important case you strive to put the matter in an ad hoc process."

P Well, I particularly - the present prosecutor (unintelligible).

E So I said, "At least, he thought he should step aside." He got a very wide smile on his face, and he said, "Well, its great to have friends isn't it?" He says, "Especially the way we stuck by them"—meaning the ITT business, I assume, because of Kleindienst. So that was an interesting little aside. He said, "I would be very grateful if you would all kind of keep me posted," and I said, "Fine." He knew that we were talking to Chappie Rose. I told him no decision had been made about a Special Counsel, but we were inclined not to appoint a Special Prosecutor; that you were—

P He doesn't mind a Special Counsel?

E He thinks it is a good idea to have a Special Counsel. He suggested that maybe the Special Counsel should be the one to go talk to Kleindienst, rather than somebody from the White House staff.

P I'll be darned.

E And so that was his only reaction to that. I told him again that I thought he ought to be represented, and that Paul O'Brien was now a target of this Grand Jury and that I thought he really had to think about getting representation. He said he had given it a lot of thought, but that he didn't think that he would want to make a change yet. He thought he would wait and see how O'Brien got along.

H Which confirms he considers O'Brien to be his attorney.

E Right.

H That's interesting.

E He asked me how he was involved; what I heard about the prosecutor's view of Mitchell's involvement in the obstruction of justice suit. I said that I really had not been able to find anybody who was in a fishing net, who really went to a defendant and said, "Don't talk" or so and so. And he said, "Well I really wonder if you ever will, other than their lawyers." He said, "My impression of this is that they are the ones who are worried about their fees and who will really be coming to us rather than for any of us going to them to bring about a change in testimony. As a matter of fact," he said, "the same that—

H Dean has been saying that all along. He said, "The thing - that we were talking to Dean about," he says, "I wasn't really worried about what they testified to. I was worried about what they would say to the press."

H Exactly what Hunt made the challenge.

E Yep.

H But somehow Dean doesn't see that that way.

he said, "Yes, I am sure it was." I said, "Well, before?"

E Well, we've got to talk to him some more. He, Mitchell, did not mention Martha at all and I didn't raise it. That was just not even in the conversation. I told him that the only way that I knew that he was mentioned, insofar as the aftermath was concerned, was that from time to time he would send Dean over saying, "Hey, we need money for this," and he said, "Who told you that?" And I said, "Well, John, that is common knowledge, and Dean will know that you told him that." I said, "Dean has not been subpoenaed. He has not testified and, as a matter of fact, the way they are proceeding down there, it looks like they are losing interest in him." I said this to John because I wanted him to be impressed with the fact that we were not jobbing him.

P   Oh. I get the point. Now does he know that Magruder is going to confess.

E   I said that in the course of calling to invite people to come talk with me today, and I indicated that there were more than two, that the persons who called was told that Dean intended—pardon—that Magruder intended to make a clean breast of it and that was first party information and very reliable, and that that would tend to begin to unravel the saint from the sinner in both directions. And he agreed with that. Now he said, "Which version is it that Magruder is going to testify to? Is it the one that he gave Bob and me in Bob's office, or is it some other version?"

H   That's not true.

E   I said—

P   What was the version he gave Bob? Was it another version?

E   Well, let me tell you what Mitchell said. It was another gigging of the White House. He said, "You know in Bob's office, Magruder said that Haldeman had cooked this whole thing up over here at the White House and—"

P   Had he said that?

E   Well that is what he said, and that he had been sort of—

P   Now wait a minute. Your conversation with Mitchell is the one where—

H   I've got my notes on it.

P   where Mitchell (unintelligible) is one where—Mitchell does—it's good you have the notes, too, but—

E   Mitchell's theory—

P   Whatever his theory is, let me say, one footnote—is that throwing off on the White House won't help him one damn bit.

E   Unless he can peddle the theory that Colson and others were effectively running the Committee through Magruder and freezing him out of the operation which is kind of the story line he was giving me.

H   Did he include me in the others?

E   Yep.

H   That I was freezing him out of the operation?

E   That you, in other words, he didn't say this baldly or flatly, but he accumulated a whole bunch of things: it's Colson, Dean and Bob working with Magruder, and that

293

was sort of the way the line went.

P No. The White House wasn't running the campaign committee.

H He's got an impossible problem with that. The poor guy is pretty sad if he gets up there and says that. It is a problem for us, there is no question about it, but there is no way he can prove it.

E He had a very, very bad tremor—

P He has always had it.

E Well, I have never noticed it as bad as this.

P So, you've done your (unintelligible)

H The next question is whether you see Magruder or not and you are now set to see him at 4 o'clock, and if you are going to cancel him, why don't you do it right now.

E I see no purpose in seeing him.

P Why because Magruder is aware of the fact that -

H Magruder is already going to do what John is going to tell him to do, so we now know—

P Our purpose, as I understood it—what I mean Bob, was for making a record.

E Alright. For that purpose maybe I should. Maybe what I should do—

H Ask him to tell you what he told me, and then you say, "Good."

P We would like to get the hell what he is going to say.

E Alright, alright.

P I would particularly like to get what the hell he is going to say about Strachan.

E Alright.

P You could say, "Look, Jeb, I have to conduct this investigation on the White House. "Tell me what you are going to say," If he says Strachan knows, ask him how he knows he knows.

E Alright.

P Do you think we should ask him that or do you not want to dig him on that?

H That's O.K.

E Once he tells me he intends to go forward to tell the truth, he has nothing to lose in talking to me.

P Without guiding or leading him, you can at least maybe get that out tonight.

H Well, his lawyer will be there.

E Right.

P The other thing is what about—of course, you realize that if he says something about Strachan then of

294

course that puts an obligation on us to do something about Strachan doesn't it?

E Well at least to corroborate it or investigate it or go forward on it.

H Question, John,—

E Well, if it ends up that way, why then you have a sort of a dog fight.

H Let me say this. I don't think Jeb wants to hang Strachan. I think Jeb is worried about the fact that in going through this, he is going to reveal things that will implicate Strachan. That is the same kind of thinking as Strachan and Chapin, who were both very concerned about getting me into the Segretti thing. In other words, they see any involvement, any mentioning of the name as being a problem.

P Yeah.

H I don't think Jeb sees it or understands the question of whether he really got Strachan in or not, and I am not sure how far he intends to go with Strachan.

E He didn't say, didn't really make it clear?

H No. He just said unfortunately this whole thing is going to come up and if it comes up, Bob,—I said, "What is the problem with Gordon?" And he said, "Well, I don't know. That depends on what other people say."

P Other people, you mean like a secretary, you mean, or someone like that?

H Could be.

P Typing a memorandum. To a degree I think one of the nice things in Strachan's case is the—the other possibility, of course, would be—maybe they are very likely, they might do this Bob, that they are going to ask the question, "Who told you to do this Jeb, or Mr. Magruder?"

H He stoutly denied that Strachan told him to do it. Larry brought back the exact story that he insists—

P What about the Colson (unintelligible.)

E He says that he is going to have to hurt Mitchell.

H He says, "The ones I am going to hurt is Mitchell, and to some degree, John Dean and maybe Gordon.

P He's obviously thought this through. Isn't it worthwhile to find our—I think we owe it to ourselves to find out about John Dean, for example, what he—now understand that he thinks (unintelligible) this is true from (unintelligible).

H Alright.

E I think that's right. This is probably a golden opportunity in a way.

P   Right. to find out—let me put it this way. You've got to find out what the hell he is going to say. (unintelligible) which is frightening to me, (unintelligible) rather than (unintelligible)

H   Right.

P   The interesting thing is—did Bob tell you—are you prepared to say that he says that he, Magruder, says they will indict him and not Mitchell. That's a hard damn thing. Isn't that what you told me, Bob? Bob, didn't you tell me that?

H   No. He said everybody is going to fall on this. He wasn't meaning indictments. He was meaning going to talk.

P   Oh.

H   Himself, LaRue, everybody is going to drop but John. He didn't mean that Mitchell was going to be indicted.

E   That's correct.

H   He meant that Mitchell was the only one to who was going to continue to hardline, because everybody else had given up. And that is why he has given up. His point is that his keeping quiet now or lying now serves no purpose because all it is going to do is get him on a perjury counts as well as everything else. If he can clean up anything he can live with himself better. He faced the fact that he has had it.

P   Uh, uh. So that means LaRue, O'Brien. Is that right?

H   Depends on how far they go.

E   That's right.

H   Jeb doesn't know—I don't think - much about that.

P   It's under cover. They'll push him. I think he can put up a pretty good fight on the thing don't you?

H   I would think so.

P   If they indict him, it is going to be a damn hard case to prove. You've got to prove motive there, don't you, John?

E   Yes. Dean argues that in a conspiracy such as they are trying to build they may not have to prove the same kind of (unintelligible) of some of the participants but only that they were in it. I would have to read the cases. I just don't know what the law is.

P   Of course, you've got there the defendants. They're the same way, too.

H   That's right.

P   In fact, the key witness there is Hunt.

E   Well there are the defendants and the defendants' lawyer, Bitman.

P   Hunt and Bitman. Hunt is to testify tomorrow.

E   My guess is that a fellow like Bitman has probably negotiated immunity for himself, and has—

H   Dean strongly feels they wouldnt give it to him.

P   They would.

H   Will not—

E   He is going to tell them about a lot of conversations he had with a lot of people.

P   Bitman is?

E   Yeah.

P   Do we know that?

E   I dont' know that but I know, for instance, that Bitman had a conversation with Colson that was a Watergate conversation. And I know what Colson says about it—that he was brilliant and adroit, avoided any—

H   And he says Bitman's recollection of it would be exactly the same as Colson's—his recollection of the specific conversation—but he says Bitman may draw conclusions from it.

P   This is the clemency conversation? And his conclusion would be that he felt the President had offered clemency?

H   No. His conclusion he, Colson, will have Hunt out by Christmas. He says you know what kind of pull I have at the White House. I will be able to work that. That's what he would have thought. That by saying—

P   How does Colson handle that?

E   He says he has a paper or a memo or something that says exactly what he said.

P   Just a minute.

H   He wrote a memorandum of the conversation immediately after the conversation. That's all it is—his side of the story.

P   You don't think this would lead to an indictment of Colson do you?

E   I don't know. Dean thinks everybody in the place is going to get indicted.

H   They're all doing the same thing. Look, Dean said just looking at the worst possible side of the coin that you could make a list of everybody who in some way is technically indictable in the cover-up operation. And that list includes, in addition to Mitchell, Haldeman, Ehrlichman, Colson, Dean,—

P Because they all discussed it?

H Strachan, Kalmbach, Kalmbach's go-between, Kalmbach's source, LaRue, Mardian, O'Brien, Parkinson, Bitman, Hunt and you know just to keep wandering through the impossibles, maybe for everybody on that list to take a guilty plea and get immediate—what do you call it—

E Clemency

H Clemency. That shows you the somewhat incredible way of some of John Dean's analytical thinking.

E No way.

P It's a shame. There could be clemency in this case and at the proper time having in mind the extraordinary sentences of Magruder, etc. etc., but you know damn well it is ridiculous to talk about clemency. They all knew that. Colson knew that. I mean when you talked to Colson and he talked to me.

E The Magruder thing is 4 o'clock and it is still on.

H I think I have to go confirm it.

E Alright. Now the question is whether I ought to get hold of Kleindienst for, say 5 o'clock, and get this thing all wrapped up.

P Have you determined it should be Kleindienst rather than Silbert?

E Yeah. Dean's right about that I am sure.

P How do you know?

E I asked him for his advice on this. He said Silbert would ask you to wait a minute and he would stop out of the room and he would come back to get you and walk you right into the Grand Jury.

P Oh.

E And you see, he doesn't dare handle a communication like that personally from the standpoint of the later criticism. He says the better out would be to go to Kleindienst who will probably step aside and refer you to Dean. Dean would in turn say to Henry Petersen they have done this little investigation over at the White House. They have collected a bunch of hearsay. There doesn't seem to be much new but they've got it there if anybody wants it. Petersen would in turn inform Silbert who would say, "I've got more than I can handle here now. We'll wait and interview that guy later."

P The purpose in doing this is what?

E The purpose of doing it is—

P The White House has conducted an investigation and has turned it over to the Grand Jury.

E   Turned it over to the Justice Department.

P   Before the indictments.

E   Right.

P   How much are you going to put out?

E   I think I would let them drag it out of me in a way. I don't know I just really haven't thought that part through.

P   Because if they say why did the White House wait for Justice Department to do all this—

E   Did the White House know is probably the way this would in turn come.

P   Yes, as a matter of fact.

E   We had been at work on this for some time. President first ordered it.

P   Independent investigation.

E   Needed it known.

P   I had ordered an independent investigation at the time McCord had something to say. Right.

E   Alright.

P   At that time you conducted an investigation.

E   And that a—at the time I was ready to report to you my tentative conclusions, and they were no more than that, you felt that they were sufficiently serious—well, you felt that one overriding aspect of the report was that some people evidently were hanging back feeling that they were somehow doing the President a favor. That the President had me personally transmit to them his views that this ought to be a complete open thing; that may or may not have played some part in—

P   Jeb Magruder's subsequent disclosures to the Grand Jury?

E   In any event, rather than for us simply to hold the information in the White House, we turned it over to the Justice Department for whatever disposition they wanted to make of it.

P   If Mitchell is indicted here, you think he is going to be convicted?

E   Yeah, I think so. I can't guarantee it, but I would be amazed once Magruder goes in there.

P   Well, that's only one man.

E   Well, that is plenty.

P   Is it?

E   Oh, yes, sir.

P   What about the law?

E   Well, with all the other stuff they've got, they—

P   All the other stuff they've got?

E   They have a way of corroborating -

P   Alright. So let's go down the road. If Mitchell is indicted, when do you think this is going to happen? With Magruder going in today, it could come sooner.

E   Could be. Could be, although Dean feels it will not be before May 15th at the earliest and now with the glut of people coming in, it may be even later than that.

P   Because they want to make a show.

E   They will want to do it all at once.

Steward   Yes, Sir?

P   I will have some consomme.

E   I might have Dick and Jeb come over at 5 o'clock.

P   Yeah.

E   And tell them what we have done, tell them that I will reduce the report to typewriting, which it is not now.

H   He could probably be over sooner if you wanted him. He is at his lawyer's office.

E   Why don't we do it as soon as we can?

H   3:30?

E   No sense of sitting around here. Make it 3:30. It looks like we always have a drum on the lawn when these things are going on. We had a band out there when Hickel came in.

H   Oh, really? Would you check Jeb and see if they—why not have it held here?

E   Yes, sir.

P   What is the situation then with Mitchell? Undoubtedly, he will have a change of venue?

H   If he could come at 3:30 it might be even better. Here.

E   Well, I think he would have maybe a better chance of getting a judge in a different venue—concerning the witnesses—than he would certainly here in Washington who would feel the political heat of letting the Senate go on. I don't know how to calculate that. That's—It's a good question. I mean, you would have to have it in a place like Missoula, Montana.

P   It is a national story.

H   Place like Pascagoula Mississippi might even be better.

E   Yeah, that would be better. Miami would a pleasant place for it.

P   With you here, you men and Dean, without building stars—well, we have a pretty big bag.

H   Right. (unintelligible) his opinion is that they will not reach him. He does not think he is a target and he

300

doesn't think he will be. He thinks he might be but he doesn't think he will and if he's not, that means they are just going to be targeting on the White House.

E Well, I am not so sure of that.

H That's right. He said they may be after bigger targets.

E Yeah. The same names are kind of pealing off, like yours truly.

H Yep. I think he is trying to get attention with that John.

E He does believe me.

P I don't think though—as a matter of fact I can't see that. John Dean has said that we all have to keep our thinking in perspective, - but the potential relationship Magruder had with John is nothing compared to Dean's. He sat in on the damn meetings.

H That's right. As however even at a somewhat higher level—if he can establish himself in a similar role as that of Gordon Strachan - and say that he was merely a messenger, a conduit, an agent.

E Boy, Mitchell sure doesn't agree with that. I assume Mitchell will never testify. That would by my assumption.

H Well one thing that you know we haven't talked about, but I am sure you have thought through and I have talked to him and told him I was reporting to the President is that the outcome of the Magruder thing is that there will never be any published Magruder testimony.

E That's right.

H So the question of what Magruder's testimony amounts to is only—

E That's not right, Bob. He will be indicted and he will plead guilty and be sentenced.

H That's right.

E Then he is available so the Committee or to the Court as a witness in somebody else's case.

P Oh, he is?

E He will be brought in his prison denims, change into a business suit and be put on the stand.

P Oh.

H Really?

E Sure.

H Why doesn't he take the Fifth on additional possible self-incrimination?

E He's already been doing it.

H (unintelligible) must - go on anyway. This stuff wasn't hanging on any of those things anyway and we just have to face that fact that whatever the story is it is going to be out anyway.

E They will have the entire story out, plus probably two other stories that two other guys make up.

H That's right.

E And that anything and everything that is said will be believed.

H And at least some of which will be enormously damaging to us.

E There would no way—

H Not provable, but damaging—

E No way to deny it.

P It is terrible when they get such a big bag.

H Yep.

P What does all this mean with regard to the—our posture here. Would you say let's take the gaff?

H No, or do you deny it?

P And cooperating with the committee and so forth. You are now looking at another month of it.

H I don't think we should take that chance. See if we can—a month or more.

P I don't want to. I don't want to. Bob, you see the point. I don't want to cooperate with the committee unless I could get a resolution of the entire Republican Caucus in the Senate. We can't do that. (Unintelligible) based on the (unintelligible) situation. Do you not agree?

H Well, I don't know, but I think what happened there—

E Look, what should I say to Ervin and Baker on Monday?

P That's exactly why I am raising this point.

E One thing, it's a live actors show. I think Magruder and Mitchell and others—

H If they show up at the Senate—

E Will not be witnesses at the Ervin hearings.

P They will not? You just told me a moment ago that they could be witnesses at the trial.

E Well, they can but the point is that—after the trial and their sentencing.

P Yeah. Of Mitchell.

E They could be subpoenaed.

P Yeah

E And they would be delivered up to the committee.

P But by that you mean until Mitchell is tried they can't be.

302

E That's right. Until they stand trial, well, it would prejudice their rights.

P Not only they—but he's already given—pled guilty.

E Ah. Well then Magruder could be a witness after he's been sentenced. If he wanted to be and—

P Wanted to be?

E Here's the tricky point. Whether or not Ervin can grant immunity to someone who has been sentenced and is serving a sentence is something that I don't know, whether that would make any difference or not. I have no doubt that a judge can, but I don't know whether the Senate can. I think Ervin's best bet is to suspend as soon as these indictments are announced. If he were smart that's what he'd do, and then just let this thing (unintelligible) and then come around afterwards and punch up places that they missed. Just go around the battlefield and get the croix de guerre.

P Well after they get through, this—this kind of indictment—there isn't going to be that much gas in the Ervin Committee. I mean, they'll go ahead, but I mean they'll say well, now, what the hell. Still Segretti—too small. (Unintelligible.)

E Just take the leavings.

P What?

E He gets the leavings. That's all.

H They'll delve into it because their whole pitch is that this isn't the Watergate. It's the use, the misuse, of money and all that sort of stuff. They're going to run that money (unintelligible) down. Where did it come from.

H Where did it go?

E Mitchell said, incidentally—

P (Unintelligible) million dollars?

H Well, yeah.

E Mitchell said that we should take great care to establish that three fifty came from the pre-'72 campaign money.

H Right.

E I asked. "Any questions in your mind about that?" And he said, "No. My impression is that that is where it came from," but he said, "Maury Stans and Herb Kalmbach spent a week together trying to tie all these various funds down as the source and that's a big loose end."

P Well you better—let's get that one. Well, there's no question about that was there Bob?

H   Not in my mind.

E   Well, but you see Maury and Herb—

H   Was that, there was—well, (unintelligible) the question was how much of it would we set aside. (Unintelligible) to three fifty.

E   Maury—

P   (Unintelligible) over here? Maury?

H   No. Gordon Strachan went over there and got it. Well, either Sloan brought it over here or Strachan went over there. I'm not sure which. Strachan took delivery from Sloan.

P   (Unintelligible) this was before the campaign started, in other words?

H   April sixth.

P   April sixth?

E   That may make a problem.

P   After the date of—

H   The day before the seventh.

P   (Unintelligible) it was April seventh. But it was (unintelligible) before.

E   Yeah it was cash that had been—John (unintelligible) but John implied that they had bigger problems and that they had to use this money to make up shortages some place else or something. I don't know. He didn't get into all this, but he said—

H   They never told me that.

E   They had problems with making their accountings all come out even—Kalmbach and Stans.

H   Kalmbach assured me all the time that the cash from seventy was intact, except for some that we knew had been used. But what was intact was—there was supposedly about two million. What was intact was about a million six and the question—there was way more than three fifty in other words. Many times that. And the question was how much of that million, six—and they convinced me that you don't want a million six—or it could have been restored to two million (unintelligible) but you don't want that because under the new laws and everything there is no way that you could find to spend it. There isn't that much stuff you can spend on that wouldn't be traceable. And so somehow a figure of three fifty was negotiated as being a reasonable figure that might be, you know, would cover what might come up that wouldn't be impossible and wouldn't put exactly a hole in the campaign. So it was (unintelligible). That was money that was not really—

P   Didn't belong to the Committee?

H   Belonged to the Committee. What happened really is that it did. We made a contribution to the Committee.

E   Yeah. That's what it was.

H   The friends of Nixon in seventy.

P   Yeah.

H   Made a million three contribution to the Committee and kept three fifty of what it had of its carry over funds.

E   That's the way to argue that.

H   That's the way it was.

P   I wonder if you'll (unintelligible) then—(unintelligible) I think, Bob.

H   I can't reach Magruder. There's no answer (unintelligible) over something. If he arrives here they'll let us know.

P   We better get the other things out of the way. I think we're going to be—I don't want to be hammered—(unintelligible) I don't want to—I don't (unintelligible) they'll hammer the hell out of us anyway, but I don't (unintelligible) that's a—that's just a (unintelligible) all here. We'll take—we'll take a hell of a beating (unintelligible) in the next thirty days, a lot of heat, we'll take with regard to why we aren't appearing, why we aren't going to appear before the Committee. Now, how do we answer that? Do we answer that by saying the Committee won't agree to our—to the proper ground rules? Is that correct?

E   We say we don't want to turn it into a circus. We want our testimony received in a judicious and probitive way. We are willing to have our people go, but only under the right circumstances.

P   Well.

H   You get it by the Kissinger thing we are releasing the record of your negotiations down channel.

P   Yeah.

H   Simply say that this is what we offer.

P   Yeah.

H   We stand ready to meet this offer whenever the enemy is willing to talk.

E   Seriously.

P   The question would then arise.

H   Tell 'em we'll resume the bombing.

E   I think it will probably not in the light of the heat from the Grand Jury and so on.

H   I still think you can. Maybe it can't be done, but

there ought to be a way to turn the Grand Jury thing strongly our way, which is that this proves the rightness of the President's approach of full cooperation with the proper process of justice which is bringing people, even at the very highest level, to account.

P   You (unintelligible) cooperation.

E   Yeah. I think we should do that.

H   And cooperating on the (unintelligible). And the value of that.

P   (Unintelligible) first man out on it should not be favored. You understand the importance of that and so forth and so on. Then I've got to (unintelligible) and get (unintelligible). Trying to think of how to use you effectively in this too, John, is a—

E   I have to be—I have to be unwilling to tell the press what I discovered because of the rights of individuals.

P   Yeah.

E   Unless we want to get Mitchell and Magruder off. I could sure as hell give them an iron clad defense.

P   Oh. Oh, I meant (unintelligible).

E   Just don't defend 'em huh?

P   The time the Grand Jury has indicted.

E   I could prejudice their rights in such a way that they could—will never get a fair trial.

P   I guess you're right. You can't do it. See, Bob, very little you can do (unintelligible) Grand Jury.

E   Well, how about a—

H   What's wrong with prejudicing their rights?

E   Well, I don't know. How about if I were to do this.

H   Get your indictment, but you don't get anybody in jail.

E   I could say that I made a report. I could say that I made a deal. I could say that you instructed me to do certain things. One of the things you instructed me to do was talk to Magruder. Another thing you instructed me to do was to talk to the Attorney General. And I did all those things.

P   And you did, but not Mitchell.

E   And then I wouldn't mention who else. I could say I talked to other people.

P   "Did you talk to Mr. Mitchell, Mr. Ehrlichman?"

E   I am not going to get into any other names of any people.

H   Then why get into Magruder?

P   Cause he's testifying. That's the only difference. I

don't know. You always come up with what not to do to those people.

E   (Unintelligible) right.

P   Does (unintelligible) know Bob. Aren't we really sort of in a position where it would be better to know whose (unintelligible) in that damn Grand Jury. At least, pull the (unintelligible) on something there. I really think you do. And, they're (unintelligible) happy. It seems to me that a hell of a lot of the issue about do something involves our inability to (unintelligible) back that we're willing to cooperate. That we're willing to waive executive privilege and keeping our people silent. Now that's what I'm really trying to (unintelligible).

E   We will get—

H   I've always heard that that's the right—that's the point—that kind of argument.

P   Is that (unintelligible).

H   (Unintelligible) one day plus story.

P   Yeah.

H   The price for which is weeks of—

P   Disaster.

H   Disaster.

E   But the thing that's wrong with that is that while it's a one day plus story, it's also the illumination of ninety days of negative stories.

P   Before you ever get there. That's the point.

H   And it's setting up ninety days of other negative, more negative stories.

E   Well, maybe. Maybe. That's a very good question.

P   The question is how much more negative is there.

E   You could have—

P   Then have the Senators go out and characterize it and all that.

E   You could have peace with honor if we could get them to agree, as I believe they will, that executive privilege is reserved at the time of questioning.

H   They've pretty much stipulated that, haven't they?

E   That's right.

P   What do you mean reserved?

E   I mean—

P   Negotiated?

E   No.

H   You (unintelligible) regarding the individual question—

E   Right.

H   Evaluate privilege as to appearance.

307

E   Right.

H   But you also (unintelligible) the merits of each individual question as to whether it relates to privilege or not and ask you question by question. It will be by your representative (unintelligible). And Connally's happy dream that I go up there charging away at the Senate doesn't work.

P   I think Henry has a good point here too and the thought about it is, he doesn't want to go out and be the first witness and if there is an overrule (unintelligible). I think makes sense. Although, let me say I do think that we still ought to consider—are we still considering the possibility of getting out the Segretti story?

E   Yes.

P   No way we could do it?

E   I think getting out the Haldeman story would be more useful in the light of Magruder and others going down to testify.

P   In other words you'd get that out before they testify?

E   If possible.

E   Well, (unintelligible) yeah.

H   The best (unintelligible) story you'd get out would be a White House story.

P   That's right.

E   About how we've been working at—

H   Which meets Henry's objections. Well, it's the Haldeman story, but you add to it—the whole thing. It's the—

E   You say (unintelligible) I have investigated. (Unintelligible) up the whole.

P   What—what I, basically, is having an Ehrlichman report. We've got some of the Dean report. That would be simply we have an Ehrlichman report that he makes and here is the situation with regard to the White House involvement. I haven't gone into the Committee thing.

E   Now the current (unintelligible) the current (unintelligible) on White House involvement primarily are Haldeman's (unintelligible).

P   That's right.

E   Well, I didn't go into White House involvement. I assumed that—

P   No. I (unintelligible).

E   That what you needed to know from me, and this would be what I would say, "What the President needed to know was the truth or falsity of charges that were leak-

308

ing out with regard to—Committee for the Re-election personnel and any connections to the White House that might exist. That was the area of inquiry rather than whether anybody in the White House was involved."

P (Unintelligible) trying to get you out there in a way that you didn't have to go into all that stuff, you see.

E I know. I understand. I understand.

P The fact that you are going to go before the indictments.

E Well, I'd do it before the indictments and say, look, we have great confidence in the Grand Jury process.

P That's right.

E And I don't want to do anything that is going to in any way impair that process.

P That's right. A number of people have been called before that Grand Jury, and I'm not going to—

E The—

H Say everything I have found has been turned over to the Justice Department.

E Check.

H Relating to that.

P Everything that the Grand Jury is considering.

E And I doubt seriously that I discovered anything new. What I probably did was simply bring into the White House for the first time a body of information that otherwise was available. Other investigators undoubtedly could do the same thing that I did and maybe a lot better. But we had had no occasion, previously, to bring all that information before us. I talked to Kleindienst, so I got what the Justice Department had. I got stuff from all over and we brought it in and we tried to assemble it in a way that it was meaningful for the President and—

H Did you review the FBI files?

E No.

H Why not? That's the original source you said was the most extensive investigation in history. Why the hell didn't you look at it?

E I didn't look at it because I didn't need to look at it. I got a summary.

P Dean (unintelligible) the summary.

E No, and the Justice Department—

P Yeah, go ahead.

E And—

P I think that's easy enough (unintelligible).

H I do too.

E I didn't, I didn't try and duplicate the work of the

U.S. Attorney. What I tried to do was simply determine for the President's use—and for the President's use only—whether or not there was substance to charges that we were hearing, and whether or not there was White House involvement with relation to those charges. And to determine whether or not the White House ought to be doing anything about its own personnel or about others that it was not doing. We were not trying to determine what the U.S. Attorney should do or the Grand Jury should do or the Justice Department should do. At the same time it would be. (unintelligible) for us to withhold anything from the Justice Department in the thought that some of this information might not have been previously available to them. So I am not going to go into it. I am not going to tell you what I found.

P Well, but here's the Haldeman story (unintelligible).

E But—no. I'm not going to tell you specifically what I found because obviously the purpose of my work was simply for the President to form judgments—as the basis for the President to form judgments—with regard to White House personnel and other government personnel. And to determine whether or not the White House was actually in any way impeding the progress of the prosectorial effort by anything that we were inadvertently doing. And, so that—that's not very fancy and I'd want to think that through.

P So (unintelligible) what I'm trying to get is how you get his story out. That's what I'm (unintelligible).

E Oh. I see. I think you just put that out—just flat put that out. And do it—hang it on the peg of the Ervin Committee setting a date for their first day of hearings.

P You mean you'd ask for an early date?

E No. They will, they will Wednesday, they will Wednesday.

P Right.

E Their hearing schedule.

P And then Haldeman will make his statement—

E Haldeman makes his statement and says, well I have been sitting here waiting for a chance to be heard. It's obvious now that it's going to be umpty-ump days before—

P We think the dates (unintelligible).

E Well, first of May is the earliest.

H When they start.

E Yeah.

310

H   And they—then when they hear McCord and (unintelligible) witnesses before that.

E   Yeah.

H   Before us.

E   So he could say it now looks like it will be several months before I would get a chance to be heard before the Ervin Committee at best, so I would like to make a statement at this time going into a number of charges that have been—

P   That have been bandied about.

E   Right.

P   Then you—the way I would handle that, I would say, "Now let's take the Segretti matter"—no—"First, let's take Watergate." You say, "I had no knowledge—" (unintelligible). "Let's take the Segretti thing. Now, here are the facts."—Then I would point out—(unintelligible) point out (unintelligible) incrimination?

H   No.

E   Well, we don't know that.

H   Huh?

P   (Unintelligible) OK, John. (Unintelligible). with Segretti?

H   Well, he was clearly (unintelligible) which is totally (unintelligible) that Segretti—Segretti's instructions were that he was to do nothing illegal. And, well then answer the question how could you launch a guy out—

P   Yeah.

H   And (unintelligible)

P   Yeah.

H   (Unintelligible) that's one of the reasons that they—

P   Now, well, yeah.

H   (Unintelligible)

P   Now—here's my (unintelligible) then, and there are charges of money—cash.

H   I have a whole list of the general charges.

P   Well, the point is on the money, now I'd (unintelligible). I would say, "(Unintelligible) money—yes, there was three hundred and fifty thousand dollars left over from the campaign in 1970. It was delivered to the White House.

H   You see that ties to the same fund that Kalmbach —see you get a question, how could I authorize the expenditure of money to Segretti?

P   Yeah.

H   Well, I've already established in the Segretti thing

that Kalmbach had these funds left over for the campaign and that's what I would assume he would use.

P   Right. Right.

H   He was to cut—

P   He decided that these funds were made available for private polling and so forth and so on. "They were used only for—twenty-eight thousand dollars was used for—twenty-two thousand dollars for advertising and the balance of three hundred and twenty-eight was returned.

H   They are going to get very excited about that advertising when, as soon as they find that out, they are going to track that down. And that, we have (unintelligible).

P   Vietnam?

H   It was "Tell it to Hanoi."

P   Hmph.

H   It was a "Tell it to Hanoi" ad countering Vietnam anti-Vietnam veterans.

P   (Unintelligible).

H   Wasn't (unintelligible).

P   That's good.

H   It went to Baroody which was the—

E   Bill or another Baroody?

H   No, Sam or Charlie.

E   Sam.

H   Or Edgar or somebody. One of the others.

P   "Tell it to Hanoi" ads (unintelligible).

H   Whatever it was, it wasn't—I was scared to death it might be something.

P   Yeah.

H   A Colson ad but it wasn't. At least that's according to (unintelligible).

E   Mitchell kept lobbing out little tidbits about Colson's operation.

P   Hmmm.

E   About sending rioters up to the Capitol steps and other things that he knew about.

P   Well, that was separate from all of Mitchell's stuff, though, wasn't it? What Colson did?

E   Well, he was saying it's really too bad that all this is coming out because there's so much sordid stuff that will be (unintelligible) to the White House.

P   But sending rioters to the Capitol steps. What do you mean?

H   They weren't rioters for heavens sake.

P Well, they named demonstrators. Why do you tell me?

E No, tell it to John Mitchell.

H I don't think anybody (unintelligible) Colson can (unintelligible) rioters.

P The point is—that is the (unintelligible) my thought with Bob, though, is not to make the counter-charge in his—in this (unintelligible).

E That's right.

P I think he should save that for the Committee. Now do you agree with that, Bob?

H I don't know.

H It's weak. It's weak if I don't.

P Yeah. You've got to say—

H I think I've got to make it in—I don't mean make it—

P Put it in general terms, but hold the white paper.

H I say—cite some examples—and say, "All these were done by the others," but I hold off on the thing that I have requested the Committee to look into, and when I'm up there I can say it's a matter of fact, you know, (unintelligible)

P I do feel that we should get this ready and really bounce it and I think that's the day to do it and I'd say (unintelligible) and I'd say—

H It's ready. Oh, no, it isn't ready but it's close. But it's awful long.

P Will it be alright?

H I'm not so sure that (unintelligible).

P Perfectly alright. Grand Jury. (Unintelligible) the damn (unintelligible) down to it. And if it says if the Committee doesn't, I cannot allow—I cannot allow—the (unintelligible). I mean the—"my effectiveness as an Assistant to the President will be seriously damaged." "Eroded by false charges and so forth and consequently I am making this statement now. I will make this statement under oath. (Unintelligible) I will make this statement under oath and answer questions under oath when the Ervin Committee finally gets around to hearing me." How's that sound to you, John?

E Sounds pretty good.

P All right. Now I think—I will say—point out—(unintelligible) it is (unintelligible)—"I do not suggest that—"I have only tried to cover in this statement questions of charges to date. That's what I have said and it has

313

not been—and I am sure that others will be made." And
(unintelligible)

H But I can't possibly anticipate what they—

P "I cannot anticipate them. I do not—I cannot anticipate them, but I'd be prepared to answer them." He
won't thereby have answered through me questions why
(unintelligible). Now the only question that you have left
is, I suppose, sort of the peripheral (unintelligible) Dean
rumbling around here and asking you and Haldeman how
about getting us some money for Watergate defendants.
Damn. I can't believe it. I can't believe they'd (unintelligible) you for conspiracy if you were asked for that. Maybe
they could.

H I—technically, I'm sure they could. Practically, it
just seems awfully remote, but maybe that's wishful thinking.

P Incidentally, could Strachan—I think—be very
helpful for him to say what that twenty-two thousand dollars was for before the Grand Jury. Why not?

E He will have to. I can't imagine that they would—

P Well, they haven't asked him yet.

E Yeah, but they will. Because—

P Twenty-two thousand dollars in (unintelligible).

H That makes sense.

P To be sure, you just tell what happened, you mean?
Huh?

H Yeah.

P Yeah, let's be sure. Well, you could say (unintelligible), it was my (unintelligible).

E I probably better get up and get set up for (unintelligible).

H Let me ask you if this—has that been—there was
something else on Gordon.

P Gordon (unintelligible).

E I'm supposed to ask Gordon whether it was delivered in pieces?

H Oh, yeah.

P (Unintelligible) forty thousand dollars to (unintelligible) why did he deliver it (unintelligible) actually it
was—it was a large—that's a large amount of money.

E No, they've already got him on that.

P Oh, that (unintelligible).

E It all fit in a suitcase or something and (unintelligible) of support.

H The reason they were in pieces because there was

314

difficult for them obviously that (unintelligible) to receive back all this cash.

P   Yeah.

H   And they requested that it not be.

P   Requested it in two installments?

H   (Unintelligible) part of it at the time (unintelligible) balance. My interest was delivering all of it as quickly as possible. I don't know what their (unintelligible) was.

P   At the suggestion of (unintelligible) Magruder (unintelligible) everything you can.

H   He's bringing two lawyers.

P   (Unintelligible).

H   What we'll do—the point here—if you want Jeb (unintelligible).

P   Well, as you know (unintelligible) they want Strachan and they want Dean. Right?

H   (Unintelligible)

P   Just trying to get the facts and that's all there is to it.

E   I'll get back to you when—

P   Be sure you convey my warm sentiments.

E   Right.

H   I think I ought to get Strachan squared away.

P   Sure.

H   And if he (unintelligible).

P   Well, we'll see what this finally come down to here (unintelligible). I firmly think—frankly I should say I don't know, but based on what Ehrlichman tells me about (unintelligible) and that removes him from some other things he said. That's what makes (unintelligible) here. (Unintelligible) is the important thing.

H   Well (unintelligible) Dean. I can't understand because it's in his interest, as well as everyone else's, to see the motive grow with loyalty.

P   I guess we're not surprised at Mitchell, are we?

H   No. It's partly true.

P   Hmh.

H   What he's saying is partly true. I don't think he did put it together.

P   He shouldn't—he shouldn't throw the burden over here, Bob, on you. Now, frankly, Colson I understand, Colson certainly put the heat on over there. I don't think John seriously (unintelligible) unless you put them up to this thing.

H (unintelligible) I didn't. He knows I didn't. No question of that.

P I should think he knows it. (Unintelligible) himself. So his (unintelligible), huh?

H That's what he says.

P You know he'll never—he'll never (unintelligible). What do you think about that as a possible thing—does a trial of the former Attorney General of the United States bug him? This damn case!

H I don't know whether he (unintelligible) or not.

P He'll have to take the stand at some points. (Unintelligible) all this has happened now.

H That's exactly the point. He's got no defense witness that can deny it.

P You know in one sense, Bob, it's better to (unintelligible) a couple of these small things but it's much better to hand it to the Grand Jury. McCord may move on the theory that Mitchell will be sorry and the others too (unintelligible) the damn thing—and the Ervin Committee get credit in the Watergate thing?

H Yeah.

P I don't know. Am I seeing something (unintelligible) that really isn't (unintelligible) or am I?

H No, no. That was the thing I was trying to get at this morning. That what that proves is the President's, in my view, the President's course was right. The President wasn't covering up. The President was cooperating with the proper place and the proper place has come to the proper result, which is to find out in an orderly manner without tarring innocent people, to find out what's going on.

Meeting: The President, Haldeman and Ehrlichman, EOB Office, April 14, 1973. (5:15 - 6:45 pm)

(Material unrelated to Presidential Actions deleted)

E Well, he and his two lawyers who are very bright young guys came in. So I said, "Evidently, judging by your phone call earlier this is moot." He said, "Yes we have just come from our informal conference with the U.S. Attorney." He proceeded then to voluntarily give me his whole testimony.

P (unintelligible)

H (unintelligible) sticky wickets, but no new ones.

E That's right.

P Your definition of their (unintelligible)

H On the other side (unintelligible)

P On Dean, he told him to lie?

E Oh, no. He's been a participant, an active participant in this thing right from the very beginning.

H Talked about the case in the most coherent way we've ever had.

E And I must say—

H We finally will know what happened.

E This has the—this has the ring of truth about it. He is a convincing witness. So, you know. But at the same time it has—

H It also is not in conflict with anything else you've got, and almost totally corroborates everything else you've got except you get to end of it this time.

E This all starts back in September of seventy-one, when Dean, Caulfield and Magruder met and contrived an intelligence effort called Sandwedge. Two months later, Dean had been unable to find the right people to make that thing work. (unintelligible) and Dean had approved of Liddy. And later ah, and Dean, Liddy and Magruder met. Liddy, after having some contact with Dean, and Magruder is a little vague on this, came forward with a million dollar proposal. Magruder says that Dean says that a million dollars was the right figure. And that's why he picked that figure. And so the four of them met. They went over it and Mitchell rejected it. A week later, Liddy came back with a budget half as big, the half-million dollar budget. And that was also rejected—

P By Mitchell?

E by Mitchell. Dean went on and said "These kinds of things shouldn't even be run by Mitchell. He's Attorney General of the United States. He is sitting over here in his parochial office and he shouldn't even (unintelligible)" Liddy and Magruder then went off to try and develop a satisfactory project proposal. A quarter million dollar level. Magruder said he was never satisfied with it. He kept sending Liddy back to the drawing boards. Finally, Colson called with Liddy and Hunt in his office—talked vigorously. Finally, although he, and he felt Mitchell, too, were nervous about it and didn't feel comfortable about it, he said, "Well all right, I'll start this moving."

P (unintelligible) that he doesn't say that Colson

chewed him out? Specifically about this proposal?

E He said, Gordon Liddy's projects. He did not say wire taps. He used the word "projects" In fact, there was in being a budget for this quarter million dollar proposal. It was in writing. A copy of it had been furnished to Gordon Strachan. And it was very specific in terms of the kinds of equipment to be used.

P It was furnished to Strachan?

E Yes sir. There was no follow-up from Strachan. That is he informed Strachan that he was going to go ahead with the so-called Liddy proposal and, "I read his non-response as OK from higher-up. I am not able to say of my own knowledge that there was any knowledge of anyone higher-up." In point of fact the—(unintelligible) was insisting upon was information on Larry O'Brien. That was the thing he called about and that was the thing that he had been driving at. Around the end of March, Magruder and LaRue went to Key Biscayne where John Mitchell was.

P Magruder? LaRue? Right.

E They presented to Mitchell Liddy's final proposal. Which was bugs in three places—Watergate—

P They were on the phone?

E They were in person.

P Magruder and Mitchell—and LaRue. Presented it to Mitchell?

E Yes, sir.

P In three places, huh?

E It involved bugging three places—Watergate, McGovern Headquarters and the Fontaine Bleau

E In the conversation, Mitchell orally approved it. Now it involved other things besides taps, and he was not specific. He said, "In all honesty this was a kind of a non-decision. Nobody felt comfortable in this thing but we were sort of bull-dozed into it." was the way he put it. Ah—

P By Colson?

E That's the inference. (unintelligible) Liddy's project. I said, "Well now, clear up for me just how well informed was Strachan?" He said, "I informed him orally of it. He had the budget."

P The budget he prepared himself—

E Parts started to come out of that thing were junk. We got synopses in the log. He said, "I got the only copy. I, Magruder, got the only copy of that synopses."

P Mitchell a copy?

318

E He thought they were all junk too. "furnish a junk store." The one copy that Magruder had had pictures of the kinds of papers that you'd find around with campaign headquarters. He sent a synopses of the pictures to Mitchell. He thought it was so bad he picked up the phone and called Liddy and chewed him out. He called 'em "(expletive deleted)" "I told Strachan that the synopses were here. He may have come over and read them." and as I pressed him on that he got less and less sure of that. He says, "I told him they were there."

H Strachan says, "I stopped reading the synopses, and they were—we had 'em here."

E Now I've got to skip back a ways and then I'll come back to Mitchell.

H You sure he made that claim to Strachan?

E I think March, about the time of the meeting down in Key Biscayne. Liddy threatened Magruder's life. He said he was transferred to the Stans' operation.

P Yeah.

E LaRue approached Magruder and said, "We need that operation. You ought to take him back with us. It's dead in the water without him." In fact, from the White House to the headquarters, he says he told the U.S. Attorney, convinced him that they needed the operation. Back to the quality of the work. They—what they were getting was mostly this fellow Oliver phoning his girl friends all over the country lining up assignations. And Flemming, and discussing their young leaders' conference. Liddy was badly embarrassed by the chewing out he got. He met in a meeting with him, and said to John Mitchell, "Mr. Mitchell I'll take care of it." That was all that was said. So the next break-in was entirely on Liddy's own notion. Magruder says neither Mitchell nor Magruder knew that another break-in was contemplated. I said, "What—after the firing of Liddy?" Magruder was very nervous about him. He phoned John Dean and asked Dean to talk to Liddy and try and settle him down because he was acting erractic. I asked, "Who in the White House is involved in this whole thing?" He gave me the names I gave you: Dick Howard, some of Colson's people, and a lot of the secretaries in the EOB, have various information about a lot of different projects, they had pickets—all kinds of things that will come pouring out in the process of this whole thing. Well I said, "Back to the burglary, who else?" He said, "No one else." He said, "The U.S. Attorney is hot after Colson:—they know he was close to

Hunt. The only thing they have him on right now is the phone call to Magruder," so far as Jeb knows. But his attorney then chimed in, and said, "I think the U.S. Attorney has a good deal more because the U.S. Attorney told the lawyer that Hunt had re-perjured himself with respect to Colson."—when he was called back in under immunity and testified as to the break-in, and the capture of the burglars, and the cover-up. Mitchell, LaRue, Mardian and the lawyers basically—

P   Plus Magruder.

E   Dean divised a cover story, in concert with these other people, and enlisted Bart Porter who went to the Grand Jury and perjured himself in concert with the cover story. Dean prepared Magruder and others for the testimony at the Grand Jury, cross-examining and getting them ready. Likewise, he leaked out information from the Grand Jury to the people at the Committee for the Reelection. The U.S. Attorney knows that he did that. It is illegal to do so.

P   Did he say where he got it?

E   He got it from a higher-up. Now, I assume that's Henry Petersen, but I don't know. OK, with Magruder and Mitchell in the operation of their - this cover story about these meetings. And they worked out a deal where they had cancelled one meeting—the million dollar meeting—and the second meeting which was the half-million dollar meeting—they told the grand Jury they—

P   He's testified to all this?

E   Yes. They talked about election laws. Yeah, he's just told the U.S. Attorney all this. He (unintelligible) destroyed his diary, but he couldn't do that. There's a million and a half dollars in cash that was distributed.

P   (expletive deleted)!

E   LaRue and Stans know about it. There is "the famous list" of where that money went. I don't know. I am going to have to check my notes with O'Brien. O'Brien may have told me about that. He may have given some idea of where that went. The three fifty is a part of that. Mitchell says to Magruder, "Don't talk."

P   Discouraged him. What about Haldeman?

E   Haldeman's very much a target of the U.S. Attorney. So far they indicated that he was implicated only by association with other people—meaning Strachan presumably. And the attorney gave me his private evaluation, that it was a little puffing on the part of the U.S. Attorney. He did not think that they had anything. Reisner and

Powell Moore—Powell Moore is somebody on Timmons' staff who was at the Committee and who accompanied Liddy on what are called "The Saturday events." The Saturday events are the events that took place the day after the break-in. Liddy went out to find Kleindienst at Burning Tree and told him to get them out of jail on orders from John Mitchell. And LaRue, of course, and Mardian, largely on obstruction. They are developing many counts of obstruction of justice. One of the attorneys then, in winding up, I told - I gave Jeb your good wishes and felicitations and so on and one of the attorneys said "Well, you know, in all this there is not a scintilla of evidence that the President was in any way aware of any of these transactions." And he said, "Well I didn't say that for any purpose except just to express to you an impression I have about the way this thing's going." He said, "Literally tens of dozens of people down there crying to be heard by the U.S. Attorney. And he said, "This thing is rapidly deteriorating." But he said, "In all of this I don't see any evidence of the involvement of the President." So that was that and I thanked them and sent them on their way. Now I have the Attorney General of the United States sitting at home waiting to go to this dinner party and I have the Deputy Attorney General out of town. But as Bob points out, there isn't anything in my report that isn't pretty well covered and expanded on in what we just got from Magruder. But I think what I can do is call the Attorney General, tell him what I was going to tell him, tell him that Magruder has just disclosed to me what he has shown to the U.S. Attorney and that I really don't have anything to add, but that I did want him to be aware of the fact of the work that was done, and what I have done today. And, ah—

H   Meetings which you had with Mitchell and Magruder.

E   Yeah.

H   Purpose of your meetings was to make the point to them that they should not go on—on the misguided assumption that that was for the Presidency, which is what Mitchell is saying.

E   Right. This says that the meetings in Key Biscayne existed long after—

P   What is, what about Strachan? Strachan says you did not know about this.

H   Can I give Strachan a report on this?

P   Sure. What is your view about his perjury?

E   I don't know.

H   He's going to the Grand Jury Monday morning. That's why it's better that he be given this information so he doesn't perjure himself.

P   Right.

H   I don't think he's testified on any of this so I don't think he has any perjury problem. What he has to do is prove the defense that—

P   Meets these points.

H   Meets these points and—

P   Good.

H   And he could—he can keep himself as an office boy, which is what he was. An office boy. If he lied about a thing—he persuaded Gordon to keep Liddy on—Jeb to keep Liddy on—I would think he would argue back that—"Jeb said to me, 'well, what should we do?' and I said, 'I think you better keep him on—he's getting good stuff.' " Don't you think so?

E   I think Gordon knows how to deal with that if you give it to him.

H   Now, I went back to Gordon today on this (unintelligible) and he said, "Absolutely, there was no other money." That the only deal was for a fella to handle that according to what Howard told him—that's who they sent the money over to.

P   For (unintelligible).

E   Well, we got Magruder, now, in this pickle. He's still on the government payroll in the Commerce Department.

P   In Commerce?

E   I think it is Commerce. I thought he was.

H   Now, this has been his second time around. Let me tell you what my concerns are. When he got down to it, he told the truth. And when he is talking about us, at least, he is bringing us into it. He will, for instance, he will want to elaborate on the Sandwedge and say I was involved in it. Now, to the extent that I listened to a presentation, I was. But I, at the time said, "This is something I don't want to be involved in. Something that should not be handled in here. Don't come to me any more with it," and they didn't. And then he will say I was involved in the meetings. That he came to me after that second meeting and said, "They came up with, ah, plans, with a preposterous plan." I told him that, "It can't be done." They shouldn't even be talking about it in the Attorney General's office. I said, "John, get out of it. You stay out of

322

this, too." And he did. He said he would stay out of it from then on, and I suspect he did. They'll tie me in that way—by indirection in a sense but, the problem, he'll, I think, I think, is people with him. Maybe that sounds like "everyone go down with the ship" but, ah, when it comes to this cover up business—

P Expanding on, ah?

H Yes, he has a feeling—the three fifty. I am not uncomfortable with that, but Dean, Dean is.

P What do you do about Dean? In other words, John—

E The U.S. Attorney's got to—

P But Dean has been—

E I think this all has broken since. I think they were probably playing their cards closer.

P And, now - Magruder testifies.

E I think that's their analysis.

P Yeah.

E I think they are after Colson, you, me and by me, I say to the highest level provable—objective.

P Let me say that this tends to—ah—with the Ervin Committee overhanging—

H One, with these each day, occurred for months.

E Well, looking at the time. I should call Kleindienst to be sure I catch him before he gets out.

P Why don't you call him?

E If I can find him.

P All right.

E That's the only thing I'm thinking about—is that, with the thing on—.

P I see.

E If it turns out I call him (unintelligible)

P I don't see how McCord can be put on now without prejudicing the cases of the defendants.

E That's right.

P I mean - I would try to go to Ervin and tell him not to do it.

E Ah, Jeb's attorneys felt that they would do so, and they say that there are cases that would require it.

P What about negotiations with Ervin on Monday?

H I have a feeling that Ervin would be delighted. This would give him a chance to prove his case better. "You will have more than you have here."

P Yeah.

E He would be delighted to. He's going to think it solves all this stuff.

H   I'm not sure it does this. At least it should get them to the ribbon.

P   Yeah.

E   (telephone call) Hi, General. How are you?

E   How was the golf?

E   First half good?

E   I want to bring you up to day on what I have been doing. For about the last three weeks—well, since I saw you, before I saw you out in San Clemente—the President has had me trying to gather together, as you know, a certain amount of law and facts to be in a position to kind of substitute for Dean, and to advise him on the White House involvement, but even broader involvement, in this whole transaction. Yesterday, I gave him my summary and, admittedly, it was hearsay, but some of it pretty reliable. And the whole thing fit together pretty well as, at least, a working hypothesis. One of the things that I told him was that I had encountered people who appeared to be reticent to come forward because they somehow felt that the Presidency was served by their not coming forward. So he had me today, in a series of conversations with people, to straighten them around of that point. The first one I talked to was your predecessor. Then I talked to Magruder, and—

E   Well, as it turns out, I was just a little late in talking to Magruder, because he had just come back from telling everything to the U.S. Attorney. He has decided to come clean.

E   Yep. He had his informal conference minutes before he came in to see me.

E   Dramatically inconsistent.

E   And he implicates everybody in all directions up and down in the Committee to Re-Elect.

E   Yep, cold turkey. My instructions after I had completed—well I might say I also talked to a couple of other people who are around here just to pass the word to encourage them to testify, if the only reason they were not testifying was some concern about the Presidency. Also, being very careful to say that I recognized everybody had rights, and that it didn't mean in anyway to indicate that they should not avail themselves of their full rights. Now, Magruder then—

E   Yep.

E   Yep. No question.

E   More than just a participation in a conspiracy, Dick.

E   Yes, they are principals.

E   Well, I must say that my conversation with him was reassuring in that regard. He is very steadfast in his protestations of innocence.

E   Well, the Magruder case is not only testamentary but is circumstantial—is persuasive to me.

E   I saw Mitchell first. I didn't have all of this Magruder business. Now, here I am a citizen of the United States and the designated inquirer of a body of information. My purpose and intent was to advise you of this when I got finished with this process and tender this information for whatever purpose it would serve, recognizing that up until just a few minutes ago it was almost entirely hearsay. Magruder has just unloaded on me the substance of his conversation with the U.S. Attorney—informal conversation. And I find that I now have very little to add to what Magruder had already given the U.S. Attorney.

E   I felt that I should go forward and at least advise you of this and to—

E   Let me spoil your afternoon completely, will you? One of the things Magruder told me was—and his attorney who was with him corroborated—was that they are very concerned about Dean's facility for advising people at the Committee of the proceedings of the Grand Jury.

E   Well, he was apparently informing Magruder and others of what the Grand Jury was saying and doing.

E   And Silbert or someone else said to his attorney, well, we know the source of Dean's information and it was from higher up.

E   Well, anyway, there—

E   there's that. In any event, I remember what you told me before, and I originally had thought that perhaps something would be served by you and Sneed coming in and the three of us visiting, but this thing has taken the Magruder bounce, and I am inclined to think now that you ought to just tell Sneed the substance of this conversation.

E   That is probably just as well, don't you think?

E   Yep.

E   He can make the decisions that need to be made from here on.

E   Well, I think the President's feeling is that Sneed could do that.

E   Well, I think he is pretty firm on that.

E   OK, I think you should on Monday.

325

E Alright.

E I understand.

E OK. You give it some thought and we will too, and then we should talk on Monday.

E Uh, huh.

E Alright.

E Rogers passed those along to me.

E Yeah. A list. Ok, my boy. I just wanted you to have a nice time this evening.

E Don't forget my tender that if there is anyway that any of this hearsay of mine that I have collected is in anyway useful, I would be glad to make it available. My present thinking is that it could add very little to what Magruder just told me.

E Prejudicing anybody's rights.

E That is why I am calling you, my dear.

E Well you are my favorite law enforcement officer.

E Do you want me to give you anything additional on Monday?

E What do you mean? Mitchell and Magruder.

E Well, no I have been talking to people for three weeks. I have talked to everybody but the milkman.

E And outside, and people's lawyers, and every damn thing.

E Yes.

E Alright.

E The President

E You know I have talked to him.

E Well, I have talked to them and in some cases they know I have talked to other people.

E Well, they know that because they knew the source of my leads, etc.

E Dean, LaRue, Mardian, Porter.

E No. He is largely implicated on the obstruction of justice.

E Yeah.

E From stem to stern.

E Yep.

E He just was having a terrible time living with it, and he didn't see any point in waiting any longer. His attorneys said they analyzed it very carefully, and see no advantage to getting in and out.

E A couple of very bright guys. I have their names over there, but I can't tell you now. Bernbaum and somebody else. Sears, I think is the other guy. I don't have the names right now.

E Pardon?

E Sure.

E Sure.

E Alright, let me know.

E Thanks, Pal. I will see you there.

E Oh yeah. I am going to go and see Bernstein and what's his name, get their awards.

E Alright.

P Let me ask you, John, about Colson. Everything that has been said, despite the fact of how accurate—it would be consistent with Colson's not knowing the Watergate defendants?

E Magruder doesn't lay a glove on him.

P But he says they're hot after him. Of course, the only thing They would be hot after him is on the—ah—Hunt.

E His connection with Hunt. Their premise apparently is, according to their lawyers, that everything Hunt knew, Colson knew.

P But Hunt—then Hunt therefore will—they'll try to get him to come in and lay a glove on Colson.

H It would be Colson's role (unintelligible)

E Well, Kleindienst says—for reasons—I have to be very careful about who I communicate with, for the next little while.

P OK

E He wants me to meet with Henry Peterson tomorrow. I'm possessed of information establishing the commission of a crime. And I've got to be darn careful about who I talk to.

P Sure. On—ah—things that you've found out.

E Yeah

P Ah—as to who?

E He says Sneed was detached from Watergate—was in a perfect position to act on it, but he wishes we'd get a special prosecutor.

P (unintelligible)

E He wants to talk about it Monday and

P Do you still think that's a bad idea?

E I think it would be very bad. All these people—prosecutor

P I want you to say that to him tomorrow.

E I sure will.

P I have just decided against it. Well, if you could hear me—Why raise this—"he's considered it. Thought it through. He doesn't want a special prosecutor because

327

there's no question with the people you've got. They're doing a hell of a job here. As the cases will point out. And we should throw them out, we'll throw them out now. Let them continue—" Correct?

E   Yeah. I agree. Interesting, the interesting fact—The U.S. Attorney for the District of Columbia has just had Magruder in the office and can sew up the case.

P   Yeah.

H   (unintelligible)

P   Yeah. John, when you get to that, would you let him resign?

E   Well I don't think—

P   I don't think he has to.

E   I think he may want to, and if he does want to, I think he should.

P   If he does want to you could put Sneed in the job?

E   As acting and you get somebody damn good.

P   You wouldn't keep Sneed in the job?

E   I don't think he's, he's—

P   You'd rather have our friend over at HUD?

H   Somebody like him - yeah.

P   Well, we need somebody that's good.

E   You should have a spokesman.

P   Where?

E   Yeah.

P   Ehrlichman should get out the facts that he has made this investigation, that we weren't drug kicking and screaming into this thing. I don't know.

E   I may have a legal problem. I'll talk to Dick tomorrow.

P   Yeah—it may be a real problem.

E   And if it's not a legal problem, I'll have a question Monday for Ziegler on what Mitchell was doing at the White House. "Just say he was here talking to me."

P   "The whole matter has been referred to the proper authorities."

E   Yeah, he'll have to.

P   And he'll say, "Oh that's been given to the proper authorities." That's what I would think.

H   All he has to say is—why can you just say—

E   Huh?

H   Unless you want that authority to say you've been investigating.

P   That's the whole point.

E   Gives you an opportunity to say you've been investigating

328

P With regard to the hearings, shouldn't we—and at least put this one out? First, the hearings when they eventually come are going to be anti-climatic in my opinion

E Could be anti-climatic. The networks might just not want 'em.

P Because of the fact that the big fish have been indicted?

H Can't tell.

P And so forth.

E Or you may have Weicker saying "Why haven't these guys indicted him? And you could say—

P I think I have reached the conclusion, just the two of you—I know Ziegler will disagree with the conclusion, but it's a loser for us to continue trying to say that—I think you've got to say, "I think we ought to go, to go on that. What do you think Bob? Let's be forthcoming on that and get that out fairly soon. I've got to get some appearance of cooperation. You agree, Bob, or not?

H I do.

P Now the question is what do you do about Dean. That may be moot. For that reason I would say—I—

H Does Magruder guess that Mr. Dean's going to be indicted?

E Magruder does not link Dean with the break-in and the bugging.

P No, but he says he was there—

E He's in the inception.

P Yeah.

E But they have that on him.

H But he's in a wholly (unintelligible) all he had to do—reject this plan—

E Sir? And he is not a participant in the Liddy, Magruder quarter-million—take it to Florida—plan. He is no link at all to the plan that was carried out.

P All right then—so they get him for what? They get him for the aftermath, the aftermath, and the obstruction. He has have a chance. Not much. They'll say that he believed that he has a constructive immunity on that

E But he doesn't have it any more.

P No - (unintelligible) This would tend to bear out the Colson story that—It sounds like the story that he gave me.

H (unintelligible) But Colson's interested, too, (unintelligible) tell us that Magruder had nailed him.

P That's right.

E It's established that what he told me was substantially what he told the U.S. Attorney.

P I understand.

H Anyhow you see we are interested in giving you all the information.

P (inaudible)

E I doubt it. Completely relaxed in this. A smile on his face. He wasn't shaking. He wasn't going to fight it.

H Every time I've seen him—

E He just said "I hope this isn't going to be for too long."

P It's the right thing. We all have to do the right thing. Damn it! We just cannot have this kind of a business, John. Just cannot be.

H According to Magruder—Magruder said the same thing. Of course, they think I'm just more trapped—

P I think Mitchell is beyond belief or do you think (unintelligible)

E Well, that's true. What it basically comes down to, of course, what, sure the circumstances—

P But LaRue?

H If LaRue tells the same story about—

P and Liddy. Liddy, Dean—

H Well, Liddy can't talk because Liddy's susceptible—

E But Mitchell says I can see that Liddy has done so and so and so and so. And Liddy says, "Boy, that's crazy, look here -" I saw him on this day, and this day, and this day—

P How about Dean? One other question. About the Haldeman statement: should it be made now?

E Can't hurt anything, not hurt anything. It would have to be broader on Strachan.

P The point that I am wondering, you see, I don't know. What does he say of Haldeman?

H Said that (unintelligible) Strachan did anything.

E No.

P Did participate?

E I suspect Strachan is not going to corroborate anything. "My relationship with the committee was to (unintelligible)

P Yep. No harm in putting that out. What the hell. You've got to get it out. What do you think, Bob?

H I don't think it does, but I am somewhat, you know puzzled by it, in my own assurance that it's a good idea. It's the feelings of the Kissingers and Zieglers that it's a disaster for me to be out front.

E   You're not about to be out front.

P   I—the point is Bob that, you have—

H   to be that far out front before this hits. And then this hits. It puts me in the league with it, is what they would argue.

E   The story of the new found freedom he's made, will run around and tell everyone in town. He just launched into this, you know, I didn't ask him—

H   You can understand that. A guy that says—he's been constipated for eight months and all of a sudden was able to take a crap is going to enjoy it.

P   Why don't you make a deal on Monday for this. That because, it'll be (unintelligible) and we'll take all the people, any members of the White House staff, with any privilege, any executive privilege waived reserved to be decided in executive session. How does that sound to you?

E   Well, my position would be that they don't get to decide the question of executive privilege. We decide that.

P   Oh you—you would say—(unintelligible)

E   We say we are going to send our people up there and we don't care if you have television or a night in a damn circus tent. You can send them up there and every question is subject to research under objection for executive privilege. We are not going guilty.

H   What do you do with my knowledge of hearsay—I just throw it all out now?

E   No.

P   You don't do it? Well—

E   I have gone into that in great detail with Ervin and he agrees with the concept that we are conduits to the President, that anything that was given to us is privileged.

P   He agrees with you, in other words.

H   If anything is given to the (unintelligible).

P   I would say, "We will give you Dean in Executive session." How does that stand up? Or, start with Dean.

E   I did.

P   But you see, you get in a position where you can say, they claim precedent because of the nature of the situation—to make the substance part public.

E   I must say that I think part of the trouble with our agreement—

P   Yes.

H   John Dean may be into this where they can't call him anyway.

P   That's what I'm thinking about.

E   Yeah.

P You see I'm, I'm just thinking it through on this one. It appeared to be forthcoming and that I wouldn't let the Dean thing be a fracas, if not necessary. I just think that that's one move you can make now at the present time. I just go—I think I'm a proponent of the idea that "buy a good headline for a day" and invite Dean back for later on. But we're going to get beat on the head and shoulders. Let's face it. We're going to get it until the Grand Jury indicts and then, that would be maybe another three weeks. After that, when they do indict, then they'll say, "Mr. President, what the hell are you going to hold Dean to the (unintelligible)?" I think we've got to do that. I just feel it's one of those things. To announce it, that I make it tomorrow night. Would you do that?

H To repudiate that today, you know, that means Tuesday.

(Unintelligible).

P Maybe we should. I think, I think we've got to get bouncing. There's another thing I'm thinking of, Bob. I'm thinking of the fact that this is here now, may make the hearings a hell of a lot less interesting and also a lot— they sure as hell can't—

P Sure.

H I hate to see that stuff keep getting obstructed by Watergate. That isn't the problem. All of this stuff is going to make Watergate. This makes Watergate look a lot worse than it really used to look.

P This does? Oh, I say it does because it involves many people. And in that way—

H That's our problem. Shouldn't people leave before this gets out? Is that—Dick was saying before it was going to be made by Dean, but now it's Magruder's on the apple sauce. "What, can they sit around—"

P Well, for one thing they want to get all the others; if you want to get all the obstructions, you've got to hear all these people.

E Not all of them, but they have got to, they got about five people—they got Hunt up.

P Who, who?

E They make their case from the time that they vote on indictments. They may recess the Grand Jury for a couple of weeks.

P Well, you have the—a little later we've got the (unintelligible). Say you're not going to do it because of Dean.

H If the situation's going to get worse, then you

332

maybe have to do something. If this is as bad as it's going to get, then, if this is going to change in a different direction, maybe you're better off not doing anything. Of course, the alternatives are, it's going to get worse. In other words, if you think you're going to swing, there is an actual danger, then the Republican House will meet and pass a resolution calling on the President, and probably a unanimous resolution.

P   I think it's very close to that right now. I think this would trigger it, without question. They would be so horrified about that—

H   Could be. He says it's not going to satisfy them. He says this pretty much establishes the Watergate thing and then you say to people like Goldwater, the people that want this done with are going to—You've got to look at the other possible boxes to say, "Well, thank God, it's all been cleared up now. Let's forget all this other—" And some will say, "It's now clear the White House wasn't involved, and thank God they weren't. And it's clear the President wasn't involved and thank God he wasn't. It's a tragedy that that great man, John Mitchell, was."

P   And that so many people at the Committee were.

H   And then, everybody will dwell on that.

P   Except that you've got a fair chance that Dean will go. A fair chance that someone will break.

E   I would spotlight it as the umbilical cord at the White House and the Committee and the question will be, "What is the other end of those umbilical cords?"

P   Then, you don't think—You don't think there's much—Dean, no, Dean's high enough.

H   The believable mess of it is being answered by this. "There is—somebody higher than Gordon Liddy had to have agreed to spend a quarter of a million dollars to bug the Democratic National Committee."

E   Now you've got that somebody.

P   That's Mitchell.

H   Now that you've got somebody who was, you've got a believable case where you can now say, "Well, so there was some other stuff going on but this was where the problem was."

P   I don't know what the stink—

H   Maybe the answer—

P   I'd just like to get Segretti out in our formal—Don't you think so?

H   Yes, you've got to get it out. (Unintelligible)

P   Haldeman. Just say that Haldeman (unintelligible)

and let's see what they say. Huh?

H   If it says Haldeman commits guilt.

P   I know.

H   What I want to do—

P   Yeah.

H   The Ziegler or Kissinger view is very strongly that that's what I shouldn't do. I'm the last guy to decide who to—should do it.

P   Yeah. What do you think, John?

·H   John thinks I should.

E   I think we should come out.

P   You come out like I do. Several of the Republicans—

E   Now as I say, I haven't heard Henry's—

P   No, I've—several other Republicans and the like will come out after that and say, "Haldeman should resign because of his involvement in the Segretti matter."

H   You have to say I do have to resign or you defend it.

P   All right. Defend it.

H   Or you defend it. You can't, I don't think you can ignore it. If I've done that you've either got to—you've got to make the judgment that that was sufficient to cause me to resign or it wasn't. That's the first question of the first person. (Unintelligible)

P   You think that Haldeman ought to resign, you mean?

E   Yeah. Ziegler can, the next day. "His connection to this was very remote, was very benign." And he helped unwrap it, knowing that—stepped forward—we established that a crime was committed by Segretti.

P   I would not be as strong for your taking it out, except for his having said "self-incrimination," the fact that that made him—

H   You've got a really - a punchy decision which is whether you want me to resign or whether you don't. That's one you've got to figure out. The problem with that is if I go on the basis of the Segretti matter, you've got to let Dean go on the basis of his implication, which is far worse.

P   Yeah.

H   Strachan's already out of the White House so that's no problem. If he's going to ring Ehrlichman in, you are going to have to let him go.

E   He's got sort of a hypothesis in that he is developing in our conversation that—that—referring him to

334

Kalmbach—which is actual. As a matter of fact, I didn't refer him to Kalmbach. He came to me and said, "May I go to Kalmbach." (Unintelligible)

P   Go to Kalmbach for the purpose of—

E   For the purpose of getting Herb to raise some money. For the purpose of paying the defendants. For the purpose of keeping them "on the reservation."

P   Right. With that they could try to tie you and Bob in a conspiracy to obstruct justice.

E   That's his theory.

P   It's rather questionable.

E   Well, I'm not so sure that makes any difference at this point. The coloring is—the key was in their pocket.

P   Well, (unintelligible).

H   Strachan's position is totally true—without giving him any help.

P   I know. The way you have to handle that, let's face it, it is there, of course. You've got the whole business of the aftermath, as to motive. And there, if you or Bob were asked, what do you say?

E   Well, as far as I can read obstruction and I may be putting favorable (unintelligible) concerned about what these fellows are going to testify to. The Grand Jury (unintelligible) so that they could go out, sell their stories to one magazine or another.

P   Sure, John, you are not particularly concerned about that?

E   I was concerned about that, particularly Hunt who is a kind of an author type and would be inclined to do that kind of thing.

H   And that is no part of who was or wasn't guilty or where the thing led.

P   I see.

H   That's exactly right. We weren't protecting anybody.

E   I'm even willing to buy that.

H   I know, and I said that to John, and John didn't agree with me.

P   I wish we could keep Dean away from that. Magruder—we don't have to get that (unintelligible). Let me say—let's sleep on what we do with the—ah—My view is though, I think that the odds are, that the interest in the Committee is less. What they are after is some of the big fish. The second thing is going to be—

H   "A lot of people are going to say, you solved the Watergate—now, forget it." And not come to this.

P   Some of our people can say, "That's tough, now what do you want to investigate?"

H   To folks out there just say, just give an answer and get it out of the way. That's all. They don't care.

P   It's really such a bad thing. And he'll come in, plead self-incrimination, and clear him.

E   Be lively—copy when they start bringing in all these people from around the country. What they did or who were victims, you know—

P   It'd be lively copy, John, but it's so spongy.

E   Yeah.—Lively.

P   It's not good stuff.

?   (Unintelligible)

P   Well, let me explain my analysis. The—In my opinion, Bob, the forthcoming thing which I think. I tilted against—I think. I am now tilting for. I think any move right now—

H   I think you've got—if you're going to do it, though, I think you've got to face the likelihood that Magruder or somebody is going to call for my resignation. I hired Segretti. I did hire Segretti.

P   You and Strachan.

H   Yeah. The stuff over a period of time will have come back with these—

P   This is the first time?

H   You've got a couple of others who should have been caught.

P   We've got to face that.

H   You might want to try to tie it to a resignation at the time I do it. On the basis that, "Well, here is a mistake, and I have no problem with it. But I'm also not going to—not troubled with—don't want to shut down—without my sticking around—"

P   (Unintelligible) ought to resign which I (unintelligible).

H   I'm not suggesting—I'm not suggesting I'd like to resign. I would not like to.

P   Yeah.

H   I'd be willing to, without creating any sticky problems.

P   The duty of our, all our, the duty of our whole staff though is to play their role—

H   I'm free from some other things that I can cut loose, which I could do. The problem that is there on the other side is, there is some pluses to it. What about that?

P   With an Attorney General added in? —And a White House Counsel, possibly.

H   Pretty big bag, John.

E   The biggest.

P   Policy, that's the point.

H   Yeah.

P   As far as equal protection, perspective, but it'll take some time.

H   Assuredly (unintelligible)

P   I see.

H   Well, fire some people, because you cannot—

P   I have given them leave. If they should not fall under indictment, they can continue their duties.

H   If they intend to plead innocent.

P   You know in the United States the chances are, you're going to plead innocent or guilty. And if you're going to plead guilty—innocent—Fine, you are suspended, I'll tell you when you can concentrate on the—

E   Sit out the Ervin negotiations and how we get out the investigation and all this.

P   Well this—as I say—I want to keep Ervin at the (unintelligible) but I kind of feel myself that (unintelligible)—

E   With that being the case, and the Dean material—not to wait for him, to come in—maybe there's no need to grapple with it.

H   If he breaks off, you could be affirmative with the Committee—

P   I think—

E   My exponent—

P   Yes, and what would you say? You could say, "The President is directing this—he's not into (unintelligible)." Say, "Look here." (Unintelligible) I don't think that's needed tomorrow. I think that, I think you ought to meet with Ervin and cut the deal and then even though there isn't much of a compromise. You could say, "We worked on a compromise under which there is an Executive session. Dean goes—

H   Dean goes free.

P   Dean in Executive session is a very nice way to cut a loss, huh?

H   (Unintelligible)

P   Oh, that's not to you, Bob.

P   We put a story out which will keep the enemy a little cool for awhile, huh?

337

E   Not only that, but you can date it back to negotiations commencing two weeks ago, three weeks ago, whatever it was.

P   Yeah. Yeah.

H   You put it out my statement at the same time?

P   The next day.

H   Wednesday.

E   Wednesday. You should put my statement out on Wednesday also, or wait until Thursday for my statement. I think we better be right out in the open—

P   That's right. I'd put yours out right with it. You're going to have the next day to build it up a little.

H   No—you don't want to build it up.

P   Put it right out. The problem here, let me say, in your case, is not Segretti. I think we should go with the Segretti stuff and then—The problem in your case is Strachan. I mean the—keeping the (unintelligible).

H   (Unintelligible)

P   Oh, yes, you will testify on that.

E   Sure, and it's secret. The question is whether Strachan is indicted or not.

P   If he is indicted?

H   I think I've got to cover myself on the Strachan thing, as you say, in such a way so that if anything does happen it's covered and you can go back and see I said this guy—should not be built up as a central figure, nor should I start to explain his every action. I can't. Some of his actions were obviously carried out unilaterally. I think that's overly objective.

P   I think some of Magruder's stuff could be pretty lively. I think it's probably basically true. How do you remember back that far? Think of that—

H   You can't be that precise—

P   You can't be that precise—You remember the things that you want to remember, pretty much.

H   Well, especially when you've lived through a whole series of varying, very heated drives—

P   Careers.

H   Like he has.

P   Careers. You've got to remember now, Magruder is going to be as potent a witness, and again—

H   Strachan will be a strong witness too, and they're going to—

P   And they will say, "And who's going to lie? I mean, here's a guy who has a record of lying. He lied. Are you going to take his word against Strachan who did not lie.

338

He came back to the U.S. Attorney."

H   We can produce people around here who can give you five different stories that Magruder's told.

P   Who?

H   Don't you think so?

P   What do you think Mr. Colson is going to be doing? You're not going to tell him this, are you? I wouldn't think so.

E   Colson is undoubtedly sending all kinds of signals to Mr. Hunt—

H   And that Chuck is overkill. He is his own worst enemy. Where the hell do you quit?

P   (Unintelligible)

E   He says that the *New York Times* has a story that he was here for a meeting with me yesterday.

H   He acts like it was the first time he has ever been into the White House—

(Unintelligible)

P   Well, you fellows need a rest.

H   Rest? There's that damn dinner.

E   We'll grin at the White House Correspondents.

H   That's no rest, that's work.

P   Well, a year from now. It will soon be different.

E   Oh, yeah.

P   Nope, seriously—

E   Six months.

P   Nope, sooner than you think. Let me tell you, John, the thing about all this that has concerned me is dragging the damn thing out. Dragging it out and being—and having it be the only issue in town. Now the thing to do now, have done. Indict Mitchell and all the rest and there'll be a horrible two weeks—a horrible, terrible scandal, worse than Teapot Dome and so forth. And it isn't—doesn't have anything to do with Teapot.

E   Yeah.

P   I mean there is no venality involved in the damn thing, no thievery or anything of that sort of thing. Nobody got any papers. You know what I mean?

E   Yeah. That's true.

H   Glad to hear it.

P   The bad part of it is the fact that the Attorney General, and the obstruction of justice thing which it appears to be. And yet, they ought to go up fighting, in my view, a fighting position on that. I think they all ought to fight. That this was not an obstruction of justice, we were simply trying to help these defendants. Don't you agree on that or do you think that's my—is that—

E   I agree. I think it's all the defendants, obviously.

P   I know if they could get together on the strategy. It would be pretty good for them.

E   Well, I think, undoubtedly, that will shake down.

P   I would think that the U.S. Attorney's (unintelligible)

H   Thank you, sir.

E   Yes, sir.

Telephone conversation: Ehrlichman and Kleindienst, April 14, 1973. (Approximately 6:00 pm)

K   Hi, John

E   Hi, General. How are you?

K   Pretty good, how are you?

E   How was the golf?

K   Half good and half bad.

E   First half good?

K   Well, the middle was good and

E   I want to bring you up to day on what I have been doing. For about the last three weeks—well, since I saw you, before I saw you out in San Clemente—the President has had me trying to gather together, as you know, a certain amount of law and facts to be in a position to kind of substitute for Dean, and to advise him on the White House involvement, but even broader involvement, in this whole transaction. Yesterday, I gave him my summary and, admittedly, it was hearsay, but some of it pretty reliable. And the whole thing fit together pretty well as, at least, a working hypothesis. One of the things that I told him was that I had encountered people who appeared to be reticent to come forward because they somehow felt that the Presidency was served by their not coming forward. So he had me today, in a series of conversations with people, to straighten them around of that point. The first one I talked to was your predecessor. Then I talked to Magruder, and—

K   It's pretty hard to talk to those two when they have testified under oath before a Grand Jury.

E   Well, as it turns out, I was just a little late in talking to Magruder, because he had just come back from

340

telling everything to the U.S. Attorney. He has decided to come clean.

K No kidding? Magruder?

E Yep. He had his informal conference minutes before he came in to see me.

K Would that be inconsistent with his testimony before the Grand Jury?

E Dramatically inconsistent.

K (expletive removed)!

E And he implicates everybody in all directions up and down in the Committee to Re-Elect.

K Mitchell?

E Yep, cold turkey. My instructions after I had completed—well, I might say I also talked to a couple of other people who are around here just to pass the word to encourage them to testify, if the only reason they were not testifying was some concern about the Presidency. Also, being very careful to say that I recognized everybody had rights, and that it didn't mean in anyway to indicate that they should not avail themselves of their full rights. Now, Magruder then—

K Let me ask one thing—

E Yep.

K As a result of what you just told me, it would indicate there is a substantial case of perjury against Mitchell and Magruder in the first instance.

E Yep. No question.

K So, complicity in the overall conspiracy?

E More than just a participation in a conspiracy, Dick.

K They would be principals?

E Yes, they are principals.

K Uh. I can't believe John Mitchell would have ever known that and let it go on.

E Well, I must say that my conversation with him was reassuring in that regard. He is very steadfast in his protestations of innocence. Well, the Magruder case is not only testamentary, but is circumstantial—is persuasive to me.

K But Mitchell denied it?

E I saw Mitchell first. I didn't have all of this Magruder business. Now, here I am a citizen of the United States and the designated inquirer of a body of information. My purpose and intent was to advise you of this when I got finished with this process and tender this

341

information for whatever purpose it would serve, recognizing that up until just a few minutes ago it was almost entirely hearsay. Magruder has just unloaded on me the substance of his conversation with the U.S. Attorney—informal conversation. And I find that I now have very little to add to what Magruder had already given the U.S. Attorney.

K   That's not good.

E   I felt that I should go forward and at least advise you of this and to—

K   John, at this point, it seems to me that you are going to have to be very careful.

E   Let me spoil your afternoon completely, will you? One of the things Magruder told me was—and his attorney who was with him corroborated—was that they are very concerned about Dean's facility for advising people at the Committee of the proceedings of the Grand Jury.

K   (unintelligible)

E   Well, he was apparently informing Magruder and others of what the Grand Jury was saying and doing.

K   (unintelligible)

E   And Silbert or someone else said to his attorney, well, we know the source of Dean's information and it was from higher up.

K   That is pretty speculative, because I don't think Henry Peterson would have told him.

E   Well, anyway, there—

K   I couldn't have because I didn't know.

E   there's that. In any event, I remember what you told me before, and I originally had thought that perhaps something would be served by you and Sneed coming in and the three of us visiting, but this thing has taken the Magruder bounce, and I am inclined to think now that you ought to just tell Sneed the substance of this conversation.

K   He and I have kind of agreed to stay out of Watergate things. He knows nothing about it, has participated in no conversations.

E   That is probably just as well, don't you think?

K   I think we better have one son-of-a-bitch in that Department—

E   Yep.

K   who's got—

E   He can make the decisions that need to be made from here on.

K   Yeah. I think at this point we ought to think very

342

hard on the suggestion I made to you when I was out in San Clemente.

E   Well, I think the President's feeling is that Sneed could do that.

K   Sneed could do that, but you wouldn't have any credibility with it.

E   Well, I think he is pretty firm on that.

K   I would sure like to talk to him about it.

E   OK, I think you should on Monday.

K   I really would, John.

E   Alright.

K   Because there is no question but that Sneed can do it, not knowing about it. He was never there during any material period of time. He is, however, the Deputy Attorney General - a Presidential appointee.

E   I understand.

K   He is my subordinate. OK?

E   OK. You give it some thought and we will too, and then we should talk on Monday.

K   I've thought of Sneed in this role because he has stayed out of it up to now.

E   Uh, huh.

K   And I think that is why you might need a guy on the outside.

E   Alright.

K   Incidentally, there are two or three people who are suggested for that role. The Chief Justice contributed—

E   Rogers passed those along to me.

K   It's got (unintelligible)

E   Yeah. A list. Ok, my boy. I just wanted you to have a nice time this evening.

K   (expletive removed)

E   Don't forget my tender that if there is anyway that any of this hearsay of mine that I have collected is in anyway useful, I would be glad to make it available. My present thinking is that it could add very little to what Magruder just told me.

K   Thinking of Magruder as a primary witness type. You better be very careful what you do from here on out, John. Don't put yourself in the position of—

E   Prejudicing anybody's rights.

K   With respect to the Commission—

E   That is why I am calling you, my dear.

K   Your's is a very God damn delicate line as to what you do to get information to give to the President and what you can do in giving information to the Department

343

of Justice, you know, to enforce the law.

E   Well you are my favorite law enforcement officer.

K   (unintelligible)

E   Do you want me to give you anything additional on Monday?

K   Who did you talk to, John?

E   What do you mean? Mitchell and Magruder.

K   Those are the only two?

E   Well, no I have been talking to people for three weeks. I have talked to everybody but the milkman.

K   People on the President's staff?

E   And outside, and people's lawyers, and every damn thing.

K   Until today, when the Magruder came up, did you come across any direct evidence that in your opinion amounted to conduct that violated the law?

E   Yes.

K   You did. Let me talk to Henry Peterson and see what line we ought to follow here.

E   Alright.

K   Who else have you talked to about this besides myself?

E   The President

K   But also the person that you talked to who would give you information about the commission of a crime, who did you tell that to?

E   You know I have talked to him.

K   No - you talked to people that gave you this information.

E   Well, I have talked to them and in some cases they know I have talked to other people.

K   Yeah.

E   Well, they know that because they knew the source of my leads, etc.

K   Who else does Magruder implicate besides himself and Mitchell?

E   Dean, LaRue, Mardian, Porter.

K   Magruder will say that Mardian knew about this before the discovery?

E   No. He is largely implicated on the obstruction of justice.

K   After the happening?

E   Yeah.

K   He puts LaRue in?

E   From stem to stern.

K   Did he make any statements with respect to the use

of campaign monies to pay these guys off? What do you know about that? Fred LaRue is going to go to jail. I guess you know that?

E   Yep.

K   What persuaded him to do that?

E   He just was having a terrible time living with it, and he didn't see any point in waiting any longer. His attorneys said they analyzed it very carefully, and see no advantage to getting in and out.

K   Who is his attorney?

E   A couple of very bright guys. I have their names over there, but I can't tell you now. Bernbaum and somebody else. Sears, I think is the other guy. I don't have the names right now.

K   Are you going to be in town Monday?

E   Pardon?

K   Are you going to be in town Monday?

E   Sure.

K   Are you going to be in town tomorrow?

E   Sure.

K   I might want Henry and I to get together with you, just so we don't make any mistakes.

E   Alright, let me know.

K   Have a nice evening!

E   Thanks, Pal. I will see you there.

K   Are you going to that same dinner?

E   Oh yeah. I am going to go and see Bernstein and what's his name, get their awards.

K   See you tomorrow.

E   Alright.

Telephone conversation: The President and Haldeman, April 14, 1973. (11:02 - 11:16 pm)

(Material not related to Presidential actions deleted)

P   One thing that occurs to me Bob is this and, as I reflect a little on Magruder's stuff—

H   Uh, huh.

P   I'll be damned if I don't think some of that could be, you know, exaggerated. But I don't know—

H   That's right.

P   I don't know. I can't tell. He is obviously flailing

around like a wild man at the present time.

H   No, no, he's not really. I think he was earlier. He was frantic, but once he figured out where he was going, I think he—

P   He thinks this is what he remembers now?

H   Yep. Uh, huh.

P   I am not sure that his interpretations on various things—they could be interpreted either way you know, like his interpretation on Dean, his interpretation on Strachan, for example.

H   Yep, yep.

P   Certainly—

H   That's right and there—

P   I just don't know how it is going to come out. That is the whole point, and I just don't know. And I was serious when I said to John at the end there, damn it all, these guys that participated in raising money, etc. have got to stick to their line - that they did not raise this money to obstruct justice.

H   Well, I sure didn't think they were.

P   Huh?

H   I didn't think they were and I don't think they did.

P   Well—

H   With maybe some exceptions.

P   Right, right. Of course, I suppose there they will say, like McCord has said, that that was the purpose. That somebody told him that. That doesn't mean anything.

H   Yeah.

P   The question, of course, is Liddy and the others. But we shall see. It is the word of the felons against the word of the men that raised the money, huh?

H   That's right. Well, you just—You don't know how much will come out in what way either. I mean that—

P   No, we, at least I think now, we pretty much know what the worst is. I don't know what the hell else they could have that is any worse. You know what I mean. Unless there is something that I don't know, unless somebody's got a piece of paper that somebody signed or some damn thing, but that I doubt.

H   It doesn't appear that there is such a thing. I mean there has been no hint to that. What you hear is all stuff that has been hinted at. It goes further than what was in some areas, but it's obviously totally consistent, basically, with everything John has developed.

P   Let me ask you this: I wonder if it is not only fair, but in our interest, for either you or John without going

346

into too much detail to fill him in on Magruder? I mean, having in mind Colson could—

H Who's (unintelligible)

P Colson. I mean we have no interest—you know what I mean—in getting him up there, you know, guilty on a perjury charge.

H Of course there is nothing Jeb said that is inconsistent with anything that Chuck has said.

P Oh, that could be right. Chuck could say, yes, the Liddy project, sure but I thought the Liddy project was something else.

H That's right. That's what he does say.

P He does, huh?

H Yeah. And as Ehrlichman said—under questioning, they specifically said that he didn't get into any specifics on it, and they have nothing that hits him on any specifics. And I think he's probably clear on it.

P I think he believes that, Bob. I know—

H I do too.

P I think he believes that.

H I have thought that all along.

P Well, we will sleep on the damn thing and, what is the situation tomorrow? Is Ehrlichman going to sit down with Ziegler again, or something?

H Yeah

P I do think that PR thing we've got to sort of make up our minds on what the hell—

H Sir, I want to get at getting the statement done.

P And we've got to get at sort of make this decision with regard to this damn Committee. I don't know—

H Yep.

P I still have mixed emotions on it. I don't know, I don't know. I have been one way one time one way another.

H Well, it's a mixed bag. It has pluses and minuses, and it is hard to be sure which outweighs the other.

P One more scenario would have been to say they will all come up. Everybody will come up in Executive Session including Dean. Just say that. Make that offer, and that's flat.

H Yeah and that gets turned down and then we're standing on the question of—The way it will be played is not that the Committee is being unreasonable by insisting on television, but that we are being unreasonable by insisting against it.

P Well, that would be true unless you go out and

hammer that the whole record could be made public.

H   Yeah.

P   It's only that we want information, not a show—

H   Yeah.

P   And that we think it is reasonable.

H   The question then is that you lose something obviously by doing that, and do we really gain enough to make it worth it? How bad is it if we go on television? I am not at all sure it is all that bad. In the first place, it is going to be in the daytime. In the second place, as of now it is not going to be carried live by the networks.

P   Yeah.

H   Now it might be, but I would guess it won't be after this other stuff breaks, it isn't going to be that important anymore. The networks don't want to carry it. It would cost them money. What will probably end up happening is, it will be carried on the public broadcasting which has virtually no audience in the daytime.

P   Uh huh. I suppose what happens there is that every new break is carried for five or ten minutes in the evening news.

H   That's right.

P   That's the point.

H   It is going to be carried anyway. It is a question of whether it is carried for five minutes with one of us on camera for a couple of those minutes, or whether it is carried for three minutes with—

P   Weicker—

H   Weicker and John Chancellor and Dan Rather, saying: "trembling with fear and obviously trying to hide the truth, ah, . . ."

P   I wonder if you would do this? Did you discuss public or private thing with two people whose judgment is—Rogers and Connally? What did Connally think? Public?

H   I am not sure.

P   Would you mind?

H   I would have to reopen that

P   Would it be alright for you to call him tomorrow and say, "Look. We've just got to make a command decision on this—"

H   Sure

P   And I think you should tell—would you tell him about the Magruder?

H   Nope.

P   No, I guess not.

H   I can say the whole thing looks like it is coming to a conclusion—

P   Before the Grand Jury

H   Yeah.

P   That's right.

H   Without saying anything specific.

P   Now, the other fellow whose judgment would be pretty good would be Bill Rogers on that.

H   Yeah. I agree.

P   I wish you would give him a call.

H   Right. I will.

P   I think with Bill, though, you could tell him, don't you think?

H   Nope. I don't think I should. In the first place, I am not supposed to know.

P   This isn't from the Grand Jury, Bob.

H   No, I know. But Kleindienst is worried about John giving the information to anybody, and that—

P   I see. You're right.

H   I don't see anything to be gained from telling him, anyway.

P   But you can tell him that our investigations indicate that the Grand Jury is hot on the trail of breaking the thing now.

H   Yeah.

P   And that is the way it is going to come. That—but if you wouldn't mind giving a call in the morning to both of those fellows, and tell them you are calling for the President and that he would like to have their considered judgment, should you be on television.

H   Right. Will do.

P   And it may be on the Dean thing, I am almost inclined to think we ought to give on that. What do you think? The idea of backing down—they are going to take it back down anyway, so what's the difference?

H   That has never bothered me, but I guess I am wrong on it, because it sure bothers other people.

P   It bothers Ziegler and the rest, but—

H   I think we gain more by backing down than we lose. I don't think you have any problem of being the President. We're fighting enough battles anyway.

P   I would just say, because of all of these charges that have been around these men are entitled to be heard in public.

H   That's right.

P   And I want them heard in public, and I want them

to tell their story in public. I am almost convinced that that is what we ought to do with the whole damn bunch and not try to stand on the Dean thing and the rest. Get a settlement that way. Well, that's my present view, Bob, and we can go on it. Another point. You do, one person you do tell and I—and he can still say that he just told him to tell the truth. You ought to tell Strachan, but tell him—

H   John is telling him.

P   John is, but not in a way that Strachan indicated that he knows what the other fellow said.

H   That's right

P   Is Strachan smart enough to do that?

H   Yes.

P   He has to be prepared that he is going to be asked this and is going to be asked that. John should put him through a little wringer there.

H   Yep.

P   John is the one who should do it. He is conducting an investigation for the President.

H   Well, and he's got the information. I don't. I can reconstruct—

P   No.

H   part of it.

P   That's right. I agree. But John will know the questions too.

H   The specific points is what he needs to cover.

(Material not related to Presidential actions deleted)

Telephone conversation: The President and Ehrlichman, April 14, 1973. (11:22 - 11:53 pm)

(Material not related to Presidential actions deleted)

P   I just wanted to see what your plans were for tomorrow?

E   I am going to come in about nine o'clock.

P   Right.

E   And see Strachan.

P   Strachan?

E   And, I have a couple of calls coming in. One from Kalmbach's lawyer and I want to see Dean in the morning also. I've got him coming in and I thought I would see Ziegler if I can work it in.

P   Uh, huh.

E   I would kind of like to cover several bases.

P   Let me say with Ziegler - the more I think about this, John, I think we ought to give him the full court. I don't think it makes a hell of a lot of difference to say hold on Dean. I would say since these charges have been made I think that the men in the White House staff that have been charged, etc. have a right to be heard publicly and that's that - under certain proper ground rules.

E   Ok - let me run that by Ron in the morning and get him accommodated to it, the coverage of it.

P   I know, but isn't that really what we should do?

E   I feel it is.

P   Then you should sort of separate out everything - haggle around and then maybe you could settle the damn thing tomorrow with him.

E   Alright - I am sure I can on that basis.

P   Say because these charges are just flowing around and leaking etc. - give him hell about that - and that we just can't have that thing.

E   Alright.

P   I was talking to Bob - and Bob made the point - he said, well just look at what will happen here. In a sense it will be the evening news basically - you know what I mean - they are not going to run it live - not now on the nets. And also there are chances of how much the committee can do, particularly with Mitchell, if he hires somebody - an attorney enjoining -, it could go on for a while. But the point is - Bob says you will have either seven minutes of John Chancellor and Weicker interpreting what was said in a secret session or do you want four minutes of that and maybe three minutes of Haldeman?

E   Well, that is a good point.

P   Is that something to be considered?

E   It

P   It sure is. At least we get a little piece of it that way.

P   You know - you see a man looking honest and earnest etc., denying it in a public forum—

E   Yeah, yeah

P   where he just—you know I just have a feeling—

E   There is something to be said for splitting the time with them.

P   Yes and -

E   Are you planning to work tomorrow?

P   Well I tell you, - sure, - what I plan to do - I have to do church.

E   Sure

P   And I have to be around on that in the morning and so I may not get there in the morning. Well, anyway you will be busy all morning.

E   That's right. I've got Kleindienst.

P   So I will be there in the afternoon around 2 o'clock or so if you want to chat with me, I will be around.

E   Ok - I'll leave word.

P   We'll see. We'll see. Do your other business, etc. John, too, I wonder if we shouldn't reconsider, if you shouldn't, I mean you have to consider this - rather than having Colson go in there completely blind, give him at least a touch up - or do you think that is too dangerous.

E   Say that again - I didn't quite hear it.

P   Colson rather than just saying nothing to him, if it isn't just as well to say - look you should know that Magruder is going to testify, etc., or is that dangerous according to Kleindienst?

E   I'm not so sure. I have to call him anyway tomorrow. He has an urgent call in for me. Ah, I don't think I want to say anything at all to him about John. John, incidentally, I understand, was on CBS News and just hard-lined them.

P   Oh, I agree on John.

E   Yeah.

P   On Magruder that is what I meant.

E   Well, I can say something very brief. I don't need to indicate that he said anything to me.

P   Yeah, that you understand that he has talked. I mean, not to the Grand Jury but to -

E   Yeah, I think I could safely go that far.

P   And say that he should know that before he goes, and be prepared.

E   Friday—I will call him in the morning.

P   Let me put it this way: I do think we owe it to Chuck to at least—

E   Sure

P   So that he doesn't, I mean, go in there and well frankly on a perjury rap—

E   I understand. I don't think he is in any danger on that but—

P   Why wouldn't he be in any danger, because he's got his story and knows pretty well what he is going to say?

E   Yeah, I think he is pretty pat, but I will talk to him in the morning and give him a cautionary note anyway.

P   This urgent call may be just what we know, or it may be more of something on our friend—

E   Uh, huh.

P   What's that other guy - Hunt?

E   Yeah

P   There isn't a damn thing you can do about that either.

E   No. I will tell you, I am going to probably see Kleindienst sometime tomorrow and for any reason you don't find me there, that's probably where I am.

P   And with him on the Special Prosecutor, say, look Dick, in view of the fact that the U.S. Attorney is now doing such a thorough job and since there is going to be definite results from it, it would be a terrible reflection on the system of justice.

E   Right.

P   And this Administration would be in effect admitting that the Justice Department was so corrupt that it couldn't prosecute.

E   Uh, huh.

P   But if they prosecute a former Attorney General John, what more can you ask?

E   Pretty loose, pretty independent.

P   I really feel that—

E   Yeah

P   and that the Special Prosecutor thing can only open other avenues potentially. I don't mean that there is anything you want to cover up, but you know. He will just go through and—

E   I think it is folly

P   Don't you think so?

E   Yes sir.

P   Dick could just say that there is a difference of opinion, but this is it. That I have decided it, and that he—

E   He wants to talk to you about it, but I think I can take care of it tomorrow without any problem.

P   But if it is necessary for him to come in and for me to tell him that, I will tell him.

E   Well, I think I can handle it.

P   Now wait a minute. I am not adverse to it. My feeling frankly is this: that you know I was just thinking tonight as I was making up my notes for this little talk, you know, what the hell, it is a little melodramatic, but it is totally true that what happens in this office in these next four years will probably determine whether there is a chance and it's never been done, that you could have some sort of an uneasy peace for the next 25 years.

E Uh, huh.

P And that's my—whatever legacy we have, hell, it isn't going to be in getting a cesspool for Winnetka, it is going to be there.

E Yep, yep.

P And I just feel that I have to be in a position to be clean and to be forthcoming, etc. This is why I think that on the—

E I totally agree with that.

P Committee, out, etc. etc.

E I totally agree with that.

P Re-think a little bit more about that Haldeman thing. My present thinking,—he raised it himself you know, this business—but I just think you've got to fight for somebody. I don't know. But what is your feeling at the moment?

E I don't think he is in that bad shape. I may be kidding myself, but I—

P The only thing that concerns me is what they said about Strachan, and

E Yeah, well—

P You don't think that relates that closely?

E Let me talk with him tomorrow, and just see how much of that we have to swallow. He may object to some of that, and with good basis. So—

P You've got to figure this too on Magruder. If I could suggest it, Magruder probably believes he is telling what he knows.

E Yeah.

P On the other hand, this happened a long time ago, and Magruder is a very facile liar.

E Yes.

P And he could well be thrashing around a bit here and drawing conclusions, etc. etc.

E He believes his own story.

P Yes, what do you think? Because some of this—

E Well, I'll tell you. They told me that he was an extremely credible witness.

P Oh, definitely.

E And I can see why. He comes across very sincere, very earnest and very believable. But of course, now you have to balance a lot of what he says. What he says I have no way of corroborating or not corroborating.

P You have to balance what he says by the fact that he was very believable when he lied.

E Yeah. That is what I say.

P Now the question is, how much of this is the truth and how much of it is something he believes to be the truth?

E About the only thing I can say is that it sounded credible, but I can't vouch for it obviously. And that's one of the reasons I want to get Gordon in.

P One last thing. How do you see the Mitchell scenario rolling out, John. Put yourself in his position and just sort of ruminate a bit, and tell me how you see it rolling out.

E Well, I would—

P First, you are convinced he will be indicted, are you?

E Yes.

P You are?

E I don't think there is one chance in fifty that he won't be.

P Alright, now.

E The court will open and publish them and he will probably arrange to come down and take delivery of the—

P Indictment?

E indictment, and I would guess he will hire F. Lee Bailey. That would be my hunch.

P Not a bad idea.

E He's got one problem in that the firm represents one of the other defendants, but he may be able to get around that.

P Uh, huh.

E Whoever he gets will immediately move for a change of venue and file 89 motions.

P Right. Motions to quash—

E Sure, sure and—motions to disqualify the judge, attacking the legality of the Grand Jury and everything you could imagine.

P Won't that take a little time?

E Yes sir, you bet it will! My hunch is that the soonest you could get a case like that to trial would be the Fall. September or October—

P Really?

E Something of that kind.

P That leaves the Committee hanging for a while, I

suppose. I don't know whether that is good or not.

E   Well I don't think they would let the Committee proceed in the meantime.

P   You don't really?

E   They would use every effort to stop it, and I am just guessing, but just common sense tells me they could stop it. I don't know the law.

P   One long shot, should you talk to Ervin?

E   Should I?

P   Yes.

E   Confide in him?

P   (Characterization deleted)

E   Oh, I don't think so. I can't trust him

P   (Characterization deleted)

E   No, I can't - I just wouldn't dare. Kleindienst might at some time later.

P   He should make the deal. I think, frankly, let's get off of the damn executive privilege.

E   Get a little ride on it huh - while we can?

P   Well at least I do think it would cool a little of the Congressional stuff, you know.

E   Uh, huh.

P   I really do. As I read the Congressional stuff, they say - they can't understand this or that or the other thing. Alright now we are—basically, also, its bold. The President just says there is enough of this nonsense? We are going to fight. You see what I mean?

E   Uh, huh, I get you. Ok, it suits me.

P   It puts the President in the position of being as forthcoming as we can—want the facts out,

E   Yep

P   And that's that. And I am not concerned about the word backing off, etc. So, sure, we back off and that is the story for about two days.

E   Yeah.

P   Really.

E   I think that is great.

P   We have won lots of things with the Congress. We lose one. But you, in interpreting it, would say we have reached a compromise with the Committee, that we limited it to this, to charges of wrongdoing.

E   Uh, huh.

P   Right?

E   And they came along orally on the rules.

P   And the rules now provide adequate protection for

executive privilege and so the President says, let them all go.

E   Yep. I think that's great.

P   But putting in the point that the President directed it and I think the idea that the President has stepped into this thing and has said, let's get this thing done.

E   Yep.

P   And you go out and say the President says, look we have had enough talk, enough—

(Material not related to Presidential actions deleted)

P   But when you are in a battle, if you are going to fight a battle, you are going to fight it to the finish. And the thing about Bob, as I say, is this: I get back to a fundamental point. Is he guilty or is he not? In my view, he is not, you know.

E   Yep.

P   And if he isn't—even if it means that the whole country and the Congress and all the members of the Senate and House say resign, resign, the President says, No. I will not take a resignation from a man who is innocent. That is wrong. That is contrary to our system, and I am going to fight for him.

E   Uh, huh.

P   If evidence is brought out to the contrary, fine. Then we will take a look at it.

E   Well, that is another reason for putting his statement out, it seems to me. It is the standard that we are flying, so to speak. Sure, they will shoot at it but if they never hit it, why then there is no room for argument.

P   We can get that statement broadly circulated. What about, incidentally, now, about the drill of frankly telling our own leaders that and getting them maybe charged up a little on this?

E   Well, I have been doing a little thinking on that. I am not so sure until we wind out the whole judicial process here, that is the Grand Jury process, that you are really going to be in much a position to do that. I will give that some more thought, but—

P   You mean because something is going to come out of the Grand Jury?

E   Yeah - you have sort of a half-told tale.

P   Well you can say, look, I am speaking just for the White House staff, and they are going to go up and tes-

357

tify. Now fellows, give them a chance. That is what I meant.

E   Uh, huh, I get you. Well that at least—sure.

P   And give them a chance. Then you say, they have all given sworn statements on this thing, and we feel that we are due our day in court, etc., etc.

E   Here's a copy of Haldeman's statement—

P   That's right. Uh, huh.

E   Yeah. We could certainly do that without making reference to the other.

P   Including Agnew, etc.

E   And you could trace the history of our attempt to cooperate with Ervin. Tell them about that.

(Material not related to Presidential actions deleted)

P   Fine. Well, John, you have had a hell of a week— two weeks. And of course poor Bob is going through the tortures of the damned.

E   Yeah. That family thing is rough.

P   I know the family thing. But apart from the family thing, you know, he is a guy that has just given his life, hours and hours and hours you know, totally selfless and honest and decent. That is another thing! Damn it to hell, I am just about to say. Well you know you get the argument of some, anybody that has been charged against, you should fire them. I mean you can't do that. Or am I wrong?

E   No, you are right.

P   Well, maybe I am not right. I am asking. They say, clean the boards. Well, is that our system?

E   Well that isn't a system. You know, that is a machine. That's—

P   That's right. I feel, honestly,—I mean, apart from the personal feeling we both have for Bob, don't you? But you know, I raised this myself. One way out is to say, well look, as long as all these guys have been charged, out they go and they can fight this battle and they can return when they get cleared. It is not good, is it?

E   You know I don't think it is. I don't think that is anyway to run a railroad. I think—

P   I suppose that would probably be the deal of purists. What does Len think on that? Does he think that, or—

E   I don't know. I think you have to show—

P Well, that is irrevelant—

E some heart on the thing.

P Well, the point is, whatever we say about Harry Truman, etc. while it hurt him a lot of people admired the old bastard for standing by people

E Sure—

P who were guilty as hell

E Yep

P and damn it I am that kind of person. I am not one who is going to say, look, while this guy is under attack, I drop him. Is there something to be said for that, or not?

E I don't think, number one, I don't think you would gain anything by it. The problem doesn't go away.

P No they will say, oh, that Nixon's top person, closest man to him, in the office four or five hours a day, and out he goes. Everything must be wrong!

E Yep - that is it. That is liking separating Siamese twins.

P We have done so many good things, you know, which Bob has worked on so arduously, and damn it, so there will be fragments here and there. Well, people make mistakes, but you don't fire a guy for a mistake do you?

E No.

P Not for a well-intentioned mistake. But my whole view of drawing up the line. One point, you are going to talk to Dean?

E I am.

P What are you going to say to him?

E I am going to try to get him around a bit. It is going to be delicate.

P Get him around in what way?

E Well to get off this passing the buck business.

P John, that's—

E It is a little touchy and I don't know how far I can go.

P John, that is not going to help you. Look he has to look down the road to one point that there is only one man who could restore him to the ability to practice law in case things go wrong. He's got to have that in the back of his mind.

E Uh, huh.

P He's got to know that will happen. You don't tell him, but you know and I know that with him and Mitchell there isn't going to be any damn question, because they got a bad rap.

P You say that Dick was really shaken?

E Yeah, he was.

P Damn it, I told him once, I said, Dick, the real target here is Mitchell. He said, oh, no, it can't be! He's got sort of the idea that probably it is Haldeman or Colson.

E Well I am sure he is going to call me the first thing in the morning.

P Yeah, but with him I would be very tough. I would say Dick—just don't mess around—they are after Mitchell, and they are going to get him at the present time. At least, that's what our information indicates and so here is where we go.

E He is probably doing a little checking with his U.S. Attorney tonight.

P Would he do that?

E Oh sure, sure. He has to make the ultimate prosecution decision, or else he has to delegate it to somebody, so he is entitled to—

P Your point is that he would delegate it to Dean. I think the Dean is the best one to delegate it to, rather than, John, the suggestion that he resign and then we will put in another Attorney General. That would be a hell of an admission that, that we thought—

E He isn't going to want to do that would be my guess. He isn't going to want to resign at this point.

P He shouldn't. Well, you know, when I come to think about it, basically, he should for other reasons. If we could get the Ellsberg case over, I would just like to get that FBI fellow. Is there anyway at all—you are going to talk to Ziegler—that you can get out the fact that you have conducted a thorough investigation?

E We will work on that. I think there is.

P I think we have to get that out. Don't you?

E I think so.

P The President is calling the signals.

E I suspect that somebody is going to put it together. My hunch is the *New York Times* will. You see, they have the story that Colson was in yesterday.

P They know that Mitchell was in.

E And, of course, all the wires have that Mitchell was in today. So, somebody is going to start stringing all this together.

P So what would happen? You'd have Ziegler or yourself go out and say yes I have seen them? Or you haven't thought that through yet?

E   I think I wouldn't have to say that I have seen them. We could just say that we have had a job of work going on for several weeks.

P   Well you could say that the President, because of the charges that have been made, wanted an independent investigation made and he directed you to make it. You have made an independent investigation of the situation because the President wants it. If there is anybody who is guilty in this thing, he must through the judicial processes be brought to the bar. Is that what you would say?

E   Or simply to aid you in analyzing the steps that ought to be taken here. You are being asked to do a lot of extraordinary things—

P   You could say the President wants this matter cleaned up, once for all.

E   Right.

P   It has been hanging around and yakked about. Innocent people have been hurt in the process. Charges have been going around. Now we have a judicial process, and we want this thing finished.

E   Beyond that, you have had all kinds of Senators and Congressmen calling for the appointment of a Special Commission and all that kind of thing.

P   So you're it.

E   For you to come to any sort of a judgment on those kinds of proposals, you have to have a pretty clear understanding of the facts.

P   Right. Well, with Dean I think you can talk to him in confidence about a thing like that, don't you? He isn't going to—

E   I am not sure—I just don't know how much to lean on that reed at the moment.

P   I see.

E   But I will sound it out.

P   Well you start with the proposition, Dean, the President thinks you have carried a tremendous load, and his affection and loyalty to you is just undiminished.

E   Alright.

P   And now, let's see where the hell we go.

E   Uh, huh

P   We can't get the President involved in this. His people, that is one thing. We don't want to cover up, but there are ways. And then he's got to say, for example?

You start with him certainly on the business of obstruction of justice.

E   That's right.

P   Look, John - we need a plan here. And so that LaRue, Mardian and the others - I mean,

E   Well, I am not sure I can go that far with him.

P   No. He can make the plan up.

E   I will sound it out.

P   Right. Get a good night's sleep.

E   Thank you, Sir.

P   I'll bet you do. You know in a way it is a curious thing—not curious at all—but, John, while it is terribly painful, of course, to go to that dinner tonight—while it is painful, I just feel better about getting the damn thing done. Or do you agree?

E   Absolutely.

P   I mean, after all, it is my job and I don't want the Presidency tarnished, but also I am a law enforcement man.

E   Yeah.

P   Right.

E   Yeah, and you have to move on to more important things.

P   Yes, that's right. Ok, boy, see you tomorrow.

E   Right, sir.

Meeting: The President and Ehrlichman, Oval Office, April 15, 1973. (10:35 - 11:15 am)

(Phone ring)

P   Who all have you seen this morning?

E   Well, I have Strachan up there right now.

P   Yeah. I had a call from Kleindienst.

E   Yeah. I heard you did and I thought you ought to take it. He—

P   O sure, sure, I did. I didn't refuse. He said "I should see you, and I'd like to see you alone this afternoon. Today." I said fine. He's coming to the church service.

E   Yeah.

P   I'm going to see him in the EOB. He said he had been up most of the night with Titus. Who is Titus?

E   U.S. Attorney in the District.

P   And what's the other fellow's name?

E   Silbert.

P   No not Silbert.

E   Glanzer?

P   Petersen.

E   Oh Petersen.

P   See if he wants (unintelligible) together. So I would see what he has to say.

E   OK.

P   I assume it's the special prosecutor thing, among other things, but what else I don't know.

E   I don't know either. He obviously got Titus in to find out what the progress is in the Grand Jury; so he's now—he's now better posted than he has been I'm sure, and he's probably a little bitter with Titus for not keeping him better posted if in fact he wasn't.

P   With regard to (unintelligible) this special prosecutor thing, what line do you want to take?

E   Well—let's think about it. He wants a special prosecutor so that he . . .

P   He can stay on as Attorney General.

E   He can stay on and so that he doesn't have any—so that he personally doesn't taint the process by reason of his closeness to Mitchell. And that makes sense. Sneed does not have that problem, and Sneed is controllable within limits, and I think he is credible. I may be wrong about his credibility.

P   I agree with this, I think he's credible. The reason I think he's credible is something else—is that the Grand Jury I assume (unintelligible) come through with some indictments. I mean, suppose they just indict Magruder and Mitchell (unintelligible).

E   Yeah.

P   Well, that's the fish.

E   Yeah.

P   The big fish.

E   Yeah.

P   Damn it, what more do they want? Now what's the problem with the special prosecutor? As I see it, it just puts another (unintelligible) loose (unintelligible) around there.

E   Well the special prosecutor . . .

P   Reflects on

E   will second-guess Silbert. I assume will feel that his mandate is to . . .

P   Tear hell out of the place?

E   Yeah - yeah.

P   That's right.

E   And—that's just an additional risk which you wouldn't have with the Dean whose been a part of the process. I just—I don't think.

P   (Unintelligible) with him (unintelligible) myself (unintelligible). If not then, let's face it, he hasn't been very helpful throughout this thing.

E   That's right. (Unintelligible) he stood as far away from it as he could get.

P   And Mitchell let it get away from him. A little (unintelligible). Is that what he said to you?

E   Yeah. He expressed real bitterness.

P   You didn't get Colson yet?

E   Not yet. No. He's at church apparently. Ziegler will be here at Church. He's coming over. So I'll see him while you're seeing Kleindienst.

P   I suppose Colson is (unintelligible) Hunt, and Bittman which, of course, could tie Colson in, right?

E   Yeah.

P   Up to his navel. There's not a damn thing you can do about that is there John?

E   No, really not, not at this point. You have to depend on Hunt's natural secrecy and secretiveness.

P   John, there is nothing in it for Hunt. Let me ask this, (unintelligible) go back over everything he's done prior to that time.

E   Well . . .

P   There might be something?

E   Well, he's up on, apparently, he has perjured himself a second time. Gee, he perjured himself at the trial, then he was granted immunity, came back into the Grand Jury, and perjured himself again. The U.S. Attorney is looking down his throat and could say to him look, I can forget some of these counts if you're a good boy now.

P   Yeah, but the point that I make is this—is really, of course, you know, its the limits of his testimony.

E   mmhuh-mmhuh.

P   If he testifies just on Watergate that's fine. He isn't going to get a damn thing more than anybody else.

E   I don't see any incentive for him to broader, and I haven't heard a whiff of that.

P   (Unintelligible) give him immunity for that? I suppose, or would they?

E   I don't know. I don't think they can give him immunity at this point.

P   (Unintelligible) talked with Strachan?

E   Yes, sir, just about ten minutes ago. And I've been doing all the talking so far.

P   (Unintelligible) trying to talk (unintelligible).

E   What Magruder had said about him and so forth. So.

P   (Unintelligible) any (unintelligible) for removing him?

E   Not yet. Not yet.

P   He's a good man—good man.

E   I think he, I think he'll do fine. You see . . .

P   (Unintelligible) you expect anyone (unintelligible) I was cogitating last night, and we've got the people that can—I mean on the obstruction of justice thing, which I think is our main problem at this time—well of course it is the main problem because it involves the other people.

E   Yeah.

P   Otherwise it's just Chapin

E   Yes, Chapin

P   and Mitchell.

E   Yeap

P   Magruder

E   Yeah.

Possibly Dean, but a . . .

E   Mardian and LaRue

p   (Unintelligible) on the (unintelligible) of the case?

E   LaRue

P   They got him on that too?

E   Yeah. Yeah.

P   You mean Magruder has?

E   Yeah.

P   That's going to be hard. This fellow's lied twice to (unintelligible)?

E   That's right. That's true.

P   The people you've got with obstruction are Hunt and Goldblatt and Bittman, right?

E   Oh, Rothblatt the lawyer.

P   Rothblatt?

E   Yeah, right. Well, I don't think Bittman is going to testify. I would be very surprised if he did.

P   Why?

E   Well.

P   Get him involved in obstruction of justice?

E   Well I just don't think—I think, I'm just guessing here, my guess is that he's worked himself out a haven in all of this.

365

P   Wouldn't serve his interests to get involved in the obstruction of justice. He's basically almost a bag man, not a bag man, but a message carrier, isn't he?

E   No. No.—was an instigator—He was concerned about his fee. And a . . .

P   Oh really John?

E   Yeah. Yeah. So he was one of the active promoters of that as near as I can tell.

P   (Unintelligible) me what you and (unintelligible) say on the obstruction thing. What was involved? I mean, from our side, our guys.

E   Well you had defendents who were concerned about their families. That's understandable. You had lawyers who were concerned about their fees and that's less understandable.

P   Oh, yes. It's understandable.

E   Well I mean in terms of the end result. You had a campaign organization that was concerned about the success of its campaign . . .

P   Yes

E   and didn't want these fellows to say anything in public that would disrupt the campaign.

P   Is that legitimate to want people not to say it out in public which (unintelligible)?

E   I think so. I think so. And then you had a . . .

P   No, but I mean, say something in public that would disrupt the campaign or because it would embarrass people?

E   Sure.

P   Cover up, you mean?

E   It would impeach the campaign in effect. But at the same time a lot of those same people who had that legitimamate motive—Hello (unintelligible) [Voice: Hello, sir. (door opens and closes)] they had the same people who had that legitimate motive had an illegitimate motive because they were involved in protecting their own culpability and here we're talking about LaRue, Magruder, Mitchell possibly.

P   (Unintelligible) they wanted the defendents to shut up in court?

E   Certainly, certainly.

P   So you would say, you could say . . .

E   You have.

P   in other words you have Dean we'll say, now let's take Dean

E   All right.

P   As a case in point. This says something that Dean was not—we could get him out of it—he could weasel out. I say weasel out; he says he's not involved in the prying.

E   Well see Dean's problem is that he was in touch with these committee people who could to Dean express a benign motive and at the same time had a corrupt motive. If I were Dean, I would develop a defense that I was being manipulated by people who had a corrupt motive for ostensibly a benign motive. And in point of fact . . .

P   Some did have benign motives.

E   That's right. You take a fellow like Shumway over there for instance . . .

P   Yeah.

E   who has to think about the PR of the campaign.

P   Making statements. Well for example it's the—it's like in the very tangential, and it's only tangentially that it touches you and Bob. You know what I mean that somebody came to you.

E   Yeah.

P   I mean you said go talk to Kalmbach. If you were talking about keeping (unintelligible) if you know the defendants were guilty, and if you didn't know who else was (unintellingible)

E   That's correct.

P   And you just thought that they (unintelligible).

E   Well you know, the thing that ran through my mind . . .

P   Yeah.

E   was Howard Hunt has written 40 books, and

P   Yeah.

E   Howard Hunt was worried about the support of his family. And I could see Howard Hunt writing an inside expose of how he broke into the Democratic National Headquarters at the request of the Committee to Re-elect the President.

P   Yeah.

E   Now, if I had a choice between getting contributions for the support of Howard Hunt's family.

P   Yeah. And that's . . .

E   And that was pretty easy.

P   And I suppose they would say though that . . .

E   Oh, didn't care what Howard Hunt said to the Prosecutor. He can say anything he wanted to the prosecutor in a secret—in a secret session. That didn't hurt us.

P   It was all secret then.

E   The Grand Jury was secret.

P   The Grand Jury was all operating at that time.

E   Sure.

P   It hadn't come to trial?

E   Sure—it didn't come to trial until after the election.

P   Yeah. (Unintelligible)

E   So.

P   I think (unintelligible) it was—nobody was trying to keep him from telling the truth to the Grand Jury—to shut him up to the Grand Jury?

E   I can say in truth and candor that Dean never explained to me that there was any kind of a deal to get these guys to lie or to change their stories or to refuse to testify to the trial of the action or anything of that kind. That was just never discussed. So I don't feel too uncomfortable with this.

P   Another (unintelligible) if Kleindienst resigns.

E   If Kleindienst resigns, that says there is something wrong with the Justice Department.

P   So you would keep him?

E   At this point.

P   Even if he disqualifies himself?

E   That's right—which wouldn't be anything too new.

P   Sure.

E   Now he may have some . . .

P   Other information?

E   Yeah, or technical reason or something of that kind.

P   (Unintelligible) may have some information aside from the Grand Jury that I don't know if (unintelligible)

E   I have a call in for him and the operators left it over here. The reason that I do is that he never did pin down for me what it is that he wants me to do. Now I've tended to him as I think I had to.

P   Good.

E   And he said well I'll check it and be in touch with you tomorrow. So fine. I left word over there that I am here. That's the only, the only reason for my call. And you might ask him if there is anything we ought to do here in the light of developments, but I do feel that—thank you (coffee dishes clattering)—I do feel that there is nothing new in what I have beyond what Magruder has already told me, so I think it's largely academic.

P   (Unintelligible)

E   Yeah.

P   (Unintelligible)

E Titus would have told him last night what Magruder said, and so he will, this morning, have I think as much knowledge about this thing as we have. There may be one or two—one or two details that.

P But Magruder said they are hot after Colson

E Suspicion

P or Magruder's attorneys say that. Magruder had nothing on Colson.

E No. The one phone call is the only incident that he has to relate.

P His attorney says I think they're hot in going after Colson.

E Yeah.

P The reason there of course is Hunt.

E Right—the association.

P Yeah.

E And that's natural. You've got a guy in the case that . . .

P Well Hunt (unintelligible) Colson.

E Yeah. Hunt has to know it.

P What do you do about Colson, John?

E I don't think there's much to do at this point. He's

P Yeah.

E he's building his own defenses. I assume that he's doing whatever has to be done with Hunt—that only he could do.

P So, but, but . . .

E Well you know he's, I'm sure, has had surreptitious contact with Hunt.

P Yeah. He says (unintelligible) take care of your kids.

E And I think Chuck's natural proclivities will

P Do everything.

E do anything we can possible do.

P See (unintelligible). There isn't a hell of a lot more they can tell us that Magruder hasn't told (unintelligible)

E That's right.

P In other words, there isn't a hell of a lot they can gain by . . . what was the, what could Liddy (unintelligible) to corroborate Magruder?

E That's all he could do. At this point Magruder gives them everything they could have hoped to get from Liddy.

P (Unintelligible)—How do you get Liddy's sentence cut down? (Unintelligible)

E It may be too late for him.

P I wonder if it is. Huh? Or is it?

369

E   Yeah. He was only . . .

P   Why didn't he talk (unintelligible)?

E   I don't know. I really don't.

E   I don't understand him at all and Magruder paints him as really weird—really weird.

P   (Unintelligible) guy.

E   And all kinds of things. And there are all kinds of Liddy stories running around.

P   Well I (unintelligible) down. I want to see what Kleindienst told (unintelligible) and since he's asked I will.

E   I'll be here and if you want me for anything why just holler.

P   Well look, I'll just listen to him. He has come in so often.

I can say on ITT, of course, we didn't—my basic responsibility (unintelligible) McClaren settled this case or something like that, and a

E   Yeah.

P   (Unintelligible)

E   No, that wasn't to settle a case.

P   No, not settle

E   That was not to file an action. You remember they were about to file a law suit and

P   How did we know about it?

E   Flanigan found out about it.

P   You came and told me?

E   I came and told you about it.

P   Why

E   (Unintelligible) may have forgotten the details.

P   Why didn't we think they should file an action?

E   Well

P   I am sure it was a good reason.

E   Yeah. We had a run

P   (Unintelligible) we had a runaway anti-trust division at that point.

P   Yeah, and I had been raising hell with McClaren

E   That's right.

P   on all this, and I said now this is a violation of my policy—

E   not on.

P   (Unintelligible) a violation of rules that I had laid down with McClaren.

E   And I will testify to my dying day that our approach to antitrust cases has (unintelligible) virtually

370

without variation, on policy rather than the merits of the individual case.

P Wasn't that case (unintelligible)?

E There was one exception to that and that was that Granite City Steel case where we criticized their analysis—the Council of Economic Advisers did.

P Yeah.

E And we went back on them on the specific case rather than just the general policy. That was on a factual issue.

P What the hell was it, John, that (unintelligible) Kleindienst. Here's this guy, you know, who is really good hearted and worked hard and all that sort of thing and went down to the wire and so forth. His advice has been just wrong.

E I think he felt, and I have not talked to him about this, but I think he felt that if he involved himself in this case at all in Mitchell's behalf, that eventually it would have tainted the whole proceeding and maybe redounded to Mitchell's disadvantage—

P Right

E and—

P Oh I suppose that's (unintelligible).

E and that Mitchell's best chance—

P I'm not speaking in Mitchell's behalf but I am just thinking of—just so that we would be (unintelligible), or try to know how (unintelligible).

E Well—yeah—that's true.

P (unintelligible)

E He.

P All you were ever asked was the general question, what's going on.

E Yeah. He—well, this is kind of interesting. I may have told you about this, but the U.S. Attorney now feels that Dean overreached them by providing information out of the Grand Jury to the Committee for the Re-election. I think that may be legitimate criticism if he in fact did that. On the other hand, for him to provide us with information inside, for the orderly operation of the government, is another matter. That's two quite different things. If you peddle information from a Grand Jury to the outside, or if you peddle it inside to people who are responsible.

P (Unintelligible)

E Oh that was, let me think.

P   (Unintelligible) Grand Jury at that point.

E   He had information on who was going to be called as witnesses so that apparently Mardian was able to get around and coach witnesses.

P   Did Mardian coach them?

E   In some cases Mardian, I guess, was very heavy-handed about it, and—

P   Well, is there anything wrong with that?

E   Yeah, well there's something wrong with—

P   He was not their attorneys is the problem?

E   Well, no, the problem—the problem is he asked them to say things that weren't true.

P   Oh.

E   When I say coach I use the word loosely, and—

P   (Unintelligible)

E   Well no, a fellow over there named Porter—Bart Porter for one.

P   Where is he now, in jail?

E   No, he's in business somewhere, and he will probably be indicted.

P   They coached him to what, did he say?

E   Say.

P   Was he—he was one of the buggers over there?

E   No - no. Oh no, he worked for the Committee, worked for the Committee, but they asked him about higher-ups and about whether there was any (unintelligible) and so on and so forth.

P   How was he in the deal? How would he know about it?

E   He worked over there in Magruder's office, and he apparently passed money to Liddy from Sloan and was privy to quite a lot of the information.

P   I though John (unintelligible) Liddy to take money for that (unintelligible).

E   Apparently he did. Well I don't mean after—I mean to pay for equipment and to.

P   Oh (unintelligible)

E   That's right.

P   Why the hell didn't the Grand Jury indict him?

E   Well because they didn't have the, they didn't have the evidence. There was a cover story which Mardian and others cooked up, and Porter, who corrorborated the cover story, is now indictible for perjury. He is a little fish who got caught in the net.

P   Poor son of a bitch. It's wrong. It's wrong.

E   The whole thing is just monumentally tragic.

P   It is. Now don't let it get you down.

E   Well that's right, that's right, and it'll pass.

P   Dean is concerned, and concerns me.

E   Yeah.

P   I don't think he could have been that active in the pre—the post yes—the pre things. Magruder, Magruder may be (unintelligible) a little (unintelligible) in some of that stuff.

E   Well, I've got to get him in, and I hope to see him today.

P   He would not (unintelligible) Dean (unintelligible) According to Dean's story about those meetings which he told me is about (unintelligible) Magruder's.

E   That's right. That's right.

P   He says, he says look we shouldn't be talking about such things

E   I know

P   particularly in the office of Attorney General. Magruder says he approved the million dollars—that's about right.

E   And that Mitchell was the one who disapproved it.

P   Well this would (unintelligible) Magruder/Dean (unintelligible)?

E   Cause Dean shows up very prominently in the whole Magruder thing.

P   And Dean was in Florida you said on some occasion? Remember the Florida trip you told me about?

E   No, No. The three people there—Mitchell was already down there—Magruder and LaRue went down.

P   For what purpose?

E   Brought him the final Liddy proposal.

P   The two fifty?

E   With the Watergate and the Fontaine Bleau and the McGovern headquarters spelled out.

P   How did Dean find out? Dean find out that there was a three—three things on a list? He knew that, and went up and told Mitchell about that.

E   Yeah, and I.

P   How did Dean know that?

E   I don't know. I don't know how he knew that. I assume that at some point in time Magruder told him that.

P   I see. Magruder talks pretty much doesn't he?

E   Mmhuh.

P   (Unintelligible)

E   Yeah. And in a lot of these things, of course, he had a lot of different versions of everything, but I think it's reasonable to assume that he passed that along to Dean.

P   Sure.

E   Mitchell phoned me this morning to say that Daniel Schorr had been on the shuttle when he rode back to New York.

P   CBS caught him?

E   Yeah, and, well no, they saw him here.

P   Yeah.

E   and then they sent somebody out to the airport.

P   (Unintelligible)

E   And so, he said to Schorr he didn't know anything about the Watergate, and he didn't think anybody cared about the Watergate and he had just been down to the White House and he hadn't seen the President. That was all that he said. He is looking forward to testifying before the Ervin Committee, and so forth. So he called me this morning just to say that

P   (Unintelligible)

E   he wanted us to know what he had actually said in case there was any press report to the contrary.

P   Well Ziegler should simply say, yes he was here to see you (unintelligible) it's true (unintelligible).

E   Don't have any comment on that.

P   No comment—that's (unintelligible) What do you think?

E   I think that's the only way to handle it.

P   (Unintelligible) handle it (unintelligible). I have no information on the subject. I have no information on the subject.

E   Right.

P   Ziegler (unintelligible)

E   I'm glad you complimented him last night. That's

P   (Unintelligible) stay right at the (unintelligible)

E   (Unintelligible)

P   He is a good man. They know it. They know it. You've got to give them their stories. They respect him for it.

E   I thought you were going to go with the Biblical conclusion that the guy who serves two masters, but a

P   Yeah.

E   he will hate the one and love the other, but a—

(laughter).

P   Yeah. (unintelligible)

E   Yeah, that's the one.

P   (Unintelligible) turn around and (unintelligible).

E   We are at kind of an ebb tide right now in this whole thing, in terms of the media, as I see it. They are all a little afraid to get too far out on a limb on this 'cause they think something's going on with the committee negotiations, and there's no new news breaking, and so they are kind of.

P   Waiting.

E   waiting.

P   Yeah—they'll get a full tide when they get to the Grand Jury.

E   Well sure, but now is a good time for us to fill that vacuum.

P   Oh, yes—a little news.

E   Yeah.

P   Sure—let 'em know other things are going on.

E   Yeah.

P   I read (unintelligible) front page the Haynes Johnson (unintelligible) story today about—story on (unintelligible).

E   I haven't had a chance to read that. I saw the headlines.

P   It's not corroborated of course, but they said their survey of the country and all showed that the President's support that first the support regarding the war was not (unintelligible)—the economy is the problem (unintelligible) but the overriding issues that are (unintelligible) Watergate. (unintelligible), but John that is just not true.

E   Yeah.

P   Of course Gallup come up tomorrow and show—he'll show that (unintelligible) another poll out there (unintelligible). Look you can't go the the (unintelligible) you can't go to the—you've been around here.

E   That's right—that's right.

P   It's a pervasive issue (unintelligible). Go in and out of the hotel they've—

E   Yeah.

P   Yelling. Watergate, Watergate. Tell us about Watergate. Seriously, it's a hell of a Washington story.

E   And Haynes Johnson, of course, is notorious for finding what's he's looking for.

P   Of course.

E   You remember after the election and that great national survey.

P   Yeah. Yes, and also that he (unintelligible) practically killed him to do it; first, (unintelligible) in this same piece that these people were not (unintelligible).

E   Mmhuh.

P   Now—(unintelligible). But then, but it's, we have to—we go through these cycles too, John, I mean this is a little more—more—shall we say a bigger cycle than most because of the enormous—a combination of Watergate—it usually is a one issue thing.

E   Yeah.

P   Now it's a combination of the Watergate plus the—these guys say it's the Watergate—(unintelligible).

(Materials not related to Presidential actions deleted)

Meeting: The President and Kleindienst, EOB Office, April 15, 1973. (1:12 - 2:22 pm)

P   Well.

K   How you feeling?

P   Fine - fine - a little tired—I've been working very hard as you can imagine with everything

K   Last night after the White House Correspondents' Dinner, at midnight, Henry Petersen called me, quite agitated—after which he and Earl Silbert, who is the Chief Assistant U.S. Attorney who tried the Watergate matter and Harold Titus came over. Titus is the United States Attorney.

P   Like some coffee. Would you like coffee?

K   No, thank you sir.

P   Coca-Cola?

K   Nothing, thank you. I'd like a glass of water if I may.

P   Glass of water—and some coffee—Chief.

K   The purpose of it was to give me the benefit of what had transpired on Thursday, Friday and Saturday with Magruder, and then what had been transpiring for a week with John Dean and his attorneys.

P   They didn't negotiate with Dean I understand.

K   John has some attorneys—I don't recognize the names.

P   Attorneys?

K   Yes.

P   Good, good he's got one.

K   The posture that Dean and his attorney, that they're exploring the legal situation with the understanding if they don't work out some kind of a strong arrangement then anything that is said or represented by either John or the attorney will not be used.

P   Hhmm.

K   Kind of an exploratory situation.

P   Yeah.

K   I wanted to see you and why I wanted to see you immediately, by myself, is that.

P   No problems then—in seeing me by myself. If you want, I mean.

K   Yes, Sir.

P   I guess with Cabinet people and the rest they always can. I have other people in, Dick, as you know, so that nobody keeps the damned notes out of the Cabinet. My understanding is—

K   I talked to John Ehrlichman last night. Also.

P   Yeah—he told me that you wanted to come in, and I said "fine."

K   When I talked to him last week I didn't think there would be much necessity to be here today, Sunday.

P   This is Sunday, certainly.

K   Magruder's conversations and John's conversations with attorneys, with every absolute certainty that Magruder's going to be put on before the Grand Jury.

P   Are they going to call him back?

K   Yeah.

P   Oh, of course, because he's going to plead guilty.

K   He's going to plead guilty and he's going to tell everything he knows

P   Sure.

K   That kind of information is not going to remain confidential.

P   As you know, the—we have no,—I have not and I would not try to get information from the Grand Jury, except from you.

K   Right.

P   And we have not. But the reason—the reason that I am aware about the Dean thing—I have taken Dean off the matter, of course. I had to. As far as what he was reporting here at the present time. I put Ehrlichman on.

P   Ehrlichman's conducted his own investigation which I told him to give you. He says it's now not going to mean much because he says Magruder frankly corroborates everything that he thought (unintelligible)

377

K Yeah.

P Except that Magruder may—you can't tell, in his view, that you can believe everything Magruder says because Magruder's apparently got a—

K Got a self-interest involved.

P He's got his self-interest and you don't know whether he's going to drag this fellow or that fellow or whatever the hell is. You know that's the trouble when a guy starts lying and, you know—I mean—wondering whether Magruder is telling the whole truth on John Mitchell—you know, Mitchell—have you talked to Mitchell?

K No and I'm not going to. I don't think that I can talk to him.

P I think you should know, Mitchell insists—I didn't talk to him. You know, I have never asked him. Have you ever asked him?

K No sir. We have never discussed the matter.

P I never have either. I asked Bill Rogers about that. I said, Bill, should I ask him? No, John Mitchell. And so I asked Ehrlichman. I said, now I want you to ask him.

K Yeah.

P What I was going to say—the only information that we have is the Magruder information and the Dean information and that's enough.

K Yeah—that's what we have here. The difficulty as outlined by.

P The special prosecutors?

K No. No. The difficulty with respect to some of the information as outlined. I stayed up until five o'clock this morning with these people going over and over it again.

P Right.

K (unintelligible) basic things where Dean implies—(unintelligible). The basic problem that—it's possible that Dean might testify to, what Magruder will testify to, and then you've got Strachan or somebody like that. He was on Haldeman's staff. There is a possible suggestion that Haldeman and Ehrlichman ah, as yet—it looks that way—whether there is legal proof of it so far as that—that they.

P Indicating what?

K Well, knowledge in this respect, or knowledge or conduct either before or after the event. But that in any event, whether there's—

P Both Haldeman and Ehrlichman?

K   Yes. Whether it's sufficient to bring about an indictment as a result of the course the testimony implies. There will be statements made, circumstantial evidence depicted

P   Right.

K   That could raise a very serious question with respect to both of them. That is my primary reason for talking to you (unintelligible).

P   Sure - Sure.

K   I thought you ought to know.

P   Who told you this? Silbert?

K   Yeah.

P   So he says he gets his information from whom? Dean?

K   Dean with respect to some statements that Ehrlichman is supposed to have made after the event. There's no suggestion that John Ehrlichman knew anything about it before.

P   Yeah.

K   As to Bob, this fellow Stracken (pronounciation). Is that his name?

P   Strachan.

K   Strachan?

P   He worked for him. He's a guy who worked for Haldeman, down in the basement.

K   Well, we haven't really gone all the way with him yet. He's kind of fishing around, you know, as to what he's going to say and what's he's not—he's being a little bit suggestive but there will be the probability that Strachan might provide testimony that would—

P   Implicate Haldeman?

K   Would implicate Haldeman and it wouldn't be direct, precise testimony.

P   I have asked both Haldeman and Ehrlichman.

K   I know you have.

P   And they have given me absolute—you know what I mean. You can only—it's like—you would, you'd believe John Mitchell, I suppose, wouldn't you? I don't believe Haldeman or Ehrlichman could ever—you know—(unintelligible) hurt to be so close to people and yet I think of—

K   John Mitchell and I were a little off more by ourself. (unintelligible) But the difficulty with respect to Bob and right now they do not think that they are going to have the kind of legal evidence that would lead to indictment. However, they all feel that as a result of the closed testimony—a matter which is going to come out. It will be circumstantial, an association, an involvement, and it's going to be—

P Why don't you do something about it?

K Well, I think that that's part of the problem. The evidence with respect to those now who would have knowledge of this before June 17th, 'cause it's going to come out. You take some of the evidence with respect to Dean.

P Dean was in the meetings. Dean claims that he said no. And Mitchell does too. And that's what you've got to live with.

K But then they feel the serious aspect of the conduct thereafter came in the, according to this testimony, that, with respect to obstruction of justice

P Right

K —and that is the admission that LaRue, Mardian, Dean say that he was rehearsed and rehearsed and coached and coached by LaRue, Mardian, Mitchell, Dean, all for his initial testimony before the Grand Jury. Well, Magruder could testify that he believed that—there's two things—the obstruction of justice and suborning a witness of perjury.

P That could get them all on that.

K And if LaRue, Mardian, Dean, Mitchell said no we didn't do that but we were told what the story was—we did nothing.

P They would question that.

K Anyway, that's certain to be known to the prosecutor.

P That's right.

K With respect to the money that was available and used for attorneys supporting these defendants.

P Mm, huh. The motive I think you passed that on to Ehrlichman—after I raised the question. A motive was involved there huh?

K About the money?

P Yeah.

K You know.

P If the money was raised.

K If you plead guilty and he's guilty there's no crime committed.

P What's that?

K That's.—I don't know.

P Explain that legal point please.

380

K   Well, I inquired into it personally.

P   Of course I was thinking of the Berrigans and all the funds that have been raised through the years, Scottsboro, etc. Nobody ever raised any question about it. If you raise money for the defense and it's for support—and Ellsberg—(expletive removed) in Ellsberg, the defense—

K   And likewise in this case. If I had committed a crime and you know about it and you say, "Kleindienst, you go in the Court and plead guilty to the commission of that crime and here is ten thousand dollars, you know, to tide you over and so forth."

P   That isn't a crime?

K   No. On the other hand, if you know that I committed a crime.

P   Right.

K   And you say, "you go in there and plead guilty, and here is twenty-five thousand dollars on the condition that thereafter you'll say nothing. You must make the plea, take the Fifth Amendment, the judge cites you for contempt, you've got to continue to testify you don't. You do not take it." Then you are now in a position of obstructing justice.

P   Excuse me. If you'd explain that again. If you tell 'em—if you tell 'em—if you raise the money for the purpose of telling them *not* to talk.

K   After he's pleaded guilty. Let's take the—

P   Well, they were all before the Grand Jury at this point, Right?

K   And the judge says, "I'm going to give you immunity—I have ordered you to testify to what you know." He refuses, takes the Fifth Amendment and he's punished for contempt. And you give him twenty-five thousand dollars. (unintelligible)

P   There was some thought that—that was all after the election that that happened, huh?

K   I don't know but that happened after the conviction—after Liddy's conviction.

P   Oh, in other words, the obstruction they are talking about is what happened after the conviction?

K   Yes sir.

P   Rather than before the conviction?

K   Yes sir.

P   Well, who the hell would—you mean—but I can't see Haldeman or Ehrlichman or anybody in that (unintelligible)

K   Well.

P No—I'm just asking. Or Dean, ah, you mean that after that that they raised—they gave money for that purpose?

K For whatever they gave—let's say that money was given to Liddy in connection with—and.

P Let me say this—there isn't any question that money that they have had on that or whatever—Mitchell's defense frankly—it would be—you know—these people had worked for the Committee and they were provided with money for their legal fees and for their support. That is—this is before their conviction. Now comes the point of after their conviction. That's when the case may be, that's when you get the jeopardy.

K Or if people are up for trial, Mr. President, you say.

P NO - no - no - I'm sorry—not conviction—but after their indictment.

K Yes. After the indictment "here's fifty thousand dollars. You plead guilty and thereafter take the Fifth Amendment. If they offer you immunity, you know, not testify about anything." If that's.—

P And then you give 'em money?

K Yes.

P That's—I agree.

K Yes—obstruction of justice.

P Yeah. If the purpose of it is to get them not to talk. In other words, not to carry out what the judge said. I can see that. Sure.

K What the situation really is, and that's why I wanted to communicate with you immediately, today, to keep this general story off the streets.

P Oh, hell—don't they know about it?

K Tomorrow morning it's likely to be all over town. Tuesday noon.

P Involving Haldeman and Ehrlichman, too?

K Yeah—just generally. This Sirica, Judge Sirica, is not enforcing the strict requirements of law with respect to secrecy in Grand Jury proceedings.

P Certainly the one with regard to Mitchell—do they, let me ask you this—do they tell you flatly Mitchell will be indicted?

K Yes. They do—so will Dean.

P Will be indicted?

K Yeah.

P Even without his testimony—they're talking about it?

K   Magruder's testimony will be enough to indict him.

P   Strachan—will he be indicted?

K   They don't know yet. Incidentally, Dwight Chapin testified with respect to the so-called Segretti affair.

P   Yeah.

K   And said that Haldeman knew about it.

P   That's true. But that's not something they're in—because of Segretti—even though Segretti pleaded the Fifth. It's just bull—the Segretti thing—it's not this—it's just.

K   That has nowhere near the potential of this situation. The only thing it does with respect to Bob, it casts a little bit of a taint.

P   I know.

K   That reflects upon the rest of it.

P   Now what is your, what is your recommendation, then?

K   Well, first I have this situation. It seems to me that so long as I do anything at the Department of Justice I cannot hereafter be with Haldeman, Ehrlichman, Mitchell, LaRue. They won't believe that we didn't talk about the Watergate case.

P   Who can you have contacts with? Me? I shouldn't be

K   I think it is—I don't know whether I need contact anyone. Incidentally, there's a—there's a weak possible case on Colson.

P   What is that?

K   He knew about and was involved in a conversation pertaining to money for Liddy's projects. Called on Colson to make over there—to somebody else.

P   Yeah, I heard about that.

K   You know, "Where the devil are Liddy's projects?" So—

P   Colson denies this doesn't he?

K   Yes. He also did the unusual thing of hiring himself a lie detector test.

P   Oh (expletive removed)

K   Isn't that a terrifying thing I've ever heard?

P   Of course, I'm a great supporter of Colson's. He's been a brick as have all these people. But (expletive removed) that was a stupid thing.

K   Just stupid. Crazy. Secondly—

P   They consider there's a weak case on him at this point.

K   Yes—and a very, very peripheral, weak case—probably not an indictable case with respect to Ehrlichman and Haldeman.

P Yeah.

K Just learned that.

P O. K. You're point is that it'll break—that their names have been mentioned?

K You know—it'll come out in trial and testimony.

P What's your recommendation on it?

K Well.

P Let me tell you what concerns me, if I may. I want to talk to the special prosecution a little bit. You know, it's embarrassing and all the rest, but it'll pass. We've got to—we've got to just ride it through Dick.

K Yes

P Do the best we can. Right?

K Yes sir.

P We don't run to the hills on this and so forth. The main thing is to handle it right.

K Those are my inclinations Mr. President.

P Well you know—we've got to handle it right.

K That's right.

P And naturally because of your association with John Mitchell you would have to disqualify yourself.

K Mardian, LaRue.

P Oh—you know them all. Right - right - right. Now the difficulty with the special prosecutor—it gets a guy into the (expletive removed) thing. First it's a reflection—it's sort of an admitting mea culpa for our whole system of justice. I don't want to do that. I think what you ought to do—agreed—the Dean doesn't know probably anything about criminal law.

K He doesn't know anything about this case either.

P About this case—but I think that the Dean—the Dean is a decent, honorable man and you step aside, say that the Deputy Attorney General of the United States will be in charge of this matter. And you say to him and (unintelligible).

K Don't understand—I think he ought to (unintelligible)

P No question about Silbert and those guys going after it. And I—let me tell you. I have never—you know—I have never felt that—I have always told these people around here—I say (expletive removed) don't hold anything back. Just burns me that they did.

K Last summer the conduct of everybody over here Mr. President—really created great suspicions in the minds of Silbert and Petersen, you know.

P Right.

K Instead of being open and frank with you, trying to create an impression of trying to help out, getting things going

P This was basically the Dean problem. He was running it.

K And also I think—well everybody was just scared to death. They didn't know where the damn thing was going to end.

P They thought there was an election—you know— let's face it—that's why—why John.

K Why sure—I understand—I understand. It'll always be an unanswered question and for that matter they were simply set in motion thereafter you know so aggravating —you know, this little

P But after the election, I couldn't think what in the name of (expletive removed) reason did they play around then? Do you?

K No.

P You didn't know that they were doing this? I didn't know.

K No sir—I didn't know.

P I didn't—you know—as I was—one of the problems here—I have always run my campaigns. I didn't run this one I must say. I was pretty busy. Or—maybe—handling the Russian Summit. And you know, after the election—we were right in the middle of the December eighth bombing—and holding meetings—within the whole Administration. But I just can't imagine—at that point—after the election is when this is supposed to have happened.

K I think there are two paramount.—

P Understand—I mean the others—they were involved throughout. But I mean after the election (Expletive removed) to condone it.

K It seems to me there's two overriding considerations here. One is yourself and your Presidency and secondly is the institution. Both of which I think have to be protected and preserved by the institution of justice. For me to recuse myself and say the Deputy is now making all the prosecution statements. The thing I have against that Mr. President is that that Deputy is still your appointee. He's my deputy.

P Yeah.

K I could be removed until this is cleared up—well

385

that's just an attempt you know to cover his (expletive removed). As this thing goes into trial and when this testimony comes out somebody going to come to a crescendo real fast.

P   Of course.

K   Then Sneed is going to be under attack. Frankly I don't know enough about Joe Sneed—to know whether he's got the ability to sit there and take it or will he do it. A little bit differently than I and less than partisan for twenty years. He has no particular attitude to you, me or anybody else. He's a good lawyer, a decent man—probably got his future ahead of him but whether he thinks of himself—and I just don't know enough about him.

P   Yeah.

K   At the present time. For one thing whether he's got the ability.

P   Yeah.

K   In a tough situation to it out or whether he could.

P   Yeah—but you got anybody else?

K   Well that's why—and then on the other hand, with respect to the special prosecutor, Mr. President. I think when you come down.

P   I'm not going to appoint him. Who would make it? You would make it?

K   I would. This would be my special prosecutor.

P   Got anybody in mind?

K   The Chief Justice, Roger Goff (?) and several other lawyers. And incidentally the Chief Justice and I are very close friends. And I want to get his feeling about the concept of it and also who he would recommend. The one person that everybody kind of comes together on is a guy by the name of Barnabus Sears in Chicago. He is the attorney that was appointed to prosecute the killing of those blacks by the police—you know the thing in Chicago? And prosecuted in Chicago police officers who allegedly, you know, (unintelligible). Barney Sears is a past president of the House of Delegates of the American Bar Association, a "distinguished" lawyer and, you know, has all those—and credentials. He's a very, he's a very independent person. It has one aspect of it that you people realize, but Sears and I have been close friends for twenty-two years. (unintelligible) labor case with Motorola back in the early days. Barney Sears came in at one point and another guy.

P   So what would you do? He'd come in and learn the whole case?

K Yeah—what he would really do—he'd keep Silbert, Titus and Petersen in place and as they progress with the case instead of having the ultimate prosecutor responsibility in me he'd do that in this function in that way.

P What does that do to Mitchell?

K I would say Mitchell will be indicted.

P Oh, they're all going to be indicted. Well, that's my point. I thought, I think if the course just goes like it is they're going to be indicted. You mean you'd have a special prosecutor immediately? Here's my point, if they're going to indict anyway that sort of—that shows that (expletive removed) the thing does work. See that's the thing I wonder. These guys are crowding in—

P Silbert and the rest—they aren't taking any program—we're not giving them any. You're not giving them any are you?

K No.

P Another way you can do it—another way you can do this. I could call in—I'm just thinking out loud. I could call in Titus and Silbert I'd say, look—you are totally independent here and you are to tear this case up. Now go to it. See my point is, you call in a special prosecutor (expletive removed), he's got to learn the whole damn thing.

K You come down to.

P Yeah.

K Little fundamental questions—like do you have enough evidence to go on perjury indictment? When you got one against one, you know, through the ordinary rules of prosecuting policy suggest that you try people for perjury.

P Right.

K Even maybe with—and I think that's just because of the climate.

P Well let me ask you this. Let me think about it Dick.

K Oh sure.

P You would suggest Sears. I would say Dean—I mean not Dean but the Dean.

K Let's both think about it.

P But with the idea that I really feel that I ought to—that frankly I've got to take the leadership on the thing and I ought to go in and say, look—there's—got the facts and you are to go forward with this—and I don't care who it touches and that's it.

K Well with respect to the Presidency and I don't

387

presume to advise you with respect to that Mr. President.

P No—I want to know your input.

K But I think that you probably would want my views. You understand I have been up all night long and I might not be as (unintelligible). It seems to me that if, as a result of Magruder, Dean (unintelligible) and Hunt.

P In belief?

K (unintelligible)

P This would be direct. Is there enough evidence on Haldeman that I should, that I should say to him, "look Bob you take a leave of absence until this thing is cleared up?"

K Right now—no—might be any day—that's the question. I think that your options become reduced each day that this thing goes on.

P What I am getting at is this. Is it also possible that they don't get enough on Haldeman to indict?

K Well, he could be indicted but then at least his circumstantial participation will presume now with regard—

P What about—what about Ehrlichman?

K That's a close one—a situation that would occur after they were arrested based upon the possible projected testimony of Dean in the case.

P How would—I don't see how he would be in it—in what way?

K Well, at least now.

P What will Dean say about Ehrlichman?

K Keep in mind anything that Dean and his attorneys have told them is a conditional statement. If they don't work something out it's all withdrawn and it's not going to be used. Keep that in mind, Mr. President. But Dean intimated two things with respect to Ehrlichman. One, Dean had in his possession some documents that were taken out of Hunt's office—that's number one.

P He's told the U. S. Attorney this?

K Yes. Other item he issued a directive that—to get Hunt out of the country. Instances, standing by themselves—nothing more to say on one side or the other can constitute an obstruction of justice. They have the hard evidence right now that would lead to the indictment of John on those two counts. But it couldn't be tomorrow, two days from now away.

P With respect to Bob—Strachan. Did they tell you—

K They

P I thought on that?

K Yes sir. In fact, I've got some notes here—

P No—Ehrlichman?

K He's hooked.

P Dean?

K Deep six it and get Hunt out of the country.

P He said Ehrlichman, John (unintelligible)

K (unintelligible) before the indictments.

P Dean's testified that Ehrlichman told him to do that.

K Right.

P What Dean—Dean has told 'em, but he hasn't testified?

K Right—and that other point about Dean's posture with the United States Attorney—that's why I wanted to talk to you about this. That these are conditional statements. If Dean worked out an arrangement satisfactory to Dean the U. S. Attorney's office and Dean agree that they are not going to have knowledge of these statements.

P So what would happen?

K Well, in the event they don't work something out then Dean presumably wouldn't testify this way with respect to Ehrlichman or he might, depending upon what (unintelligible) If they work something out, probably it would be for the purpose of—no, no sir. There's going to be no immunity offered.

P Well, then why would he get it? Work something out—why?

K Well that's—that hasn't been resolved because Dean and his lawyers are being very, very careful there.

P I'm sure.

K (unintelligible) you get these people facing jail and you (unintelligible). The point is that.

P Haldeman?

K Haldeman—they believe this fellow Strachan is just about ready to (unintelligible)—on the face of it.

P Some of this—got some of the take in other words. Haldeman had—if Haldeman was furnished the reports.

K Either the reports or papers that would indicate that Liddy was doing something like this.

P Oh—papers?

K Apparently there was the sum of three hundred fifty thousand dollars.

P Yeah—I know about that.

K Transferred from the White House to LaRue.

P Right.

K That Bob indeed indicated that the transfer of that money. (unintelligible)

P I think (unintelligible).

K   Might have just thought that (unintelligible). That would implicate

P   That I would think would mean that he had some of it—the reports from the bugging.

K   Either the reports or budgetary or—

P   Oh—even budgetary?

K   Or program papers that on the face of it would indicate that Liddy was engaged in an eavesdropping operation and, you know, that Haldeman would have known about it? So he called and said something about it but that's yet another thing you've got to keep in mind.

P   I don't (unintelligible).

K   I don't think so either.

P   Huh?

K   I don't think he did either.

P   Haldeman could tell me though—he's a—I'm sure—Bob would tell me—he's a "don't give a (expletive removed) kind of a guy" anyway and Ehrlichman would tell me too. The deep six thing troubles me. Although—what was that? Oh. I know what that could be—that could be—you see Hunt's operations before—that's what that is. Hunt worked in the White House, you know, on some national security matters and I think that's what that's involved. Not the Watergate.

K   Let's get back to this concept of the Presidency, sir.

P   Right

K   What you do is the right thing to do and then when having done it then it would be recognized as the right thing.

P   Right.

K   And I know—I don't know—but I believe—feel that we should have—I think the options that you have to consider there are two. One do you, the President, what I have told you today, that might be forthcoming. And before that comes out would you ask 'em to step aside until this whole thing blows over? If it all blows over—maybe you're not indicted or culpable. Finally you come back and they do wind up having been indicted, you at least have off of your personal staff—those people who are going to be involved in the criminal justice system. If you don't take that step, and I—really don't pretend to advise you on it sir—and then if it comes out. it's leaked out and then you've got to do it after the disclosure is made publicly. you know, I think it.

P   Let me ask you this—if it should come to a critical

point—let us suppose—let's suppose the worst. That it does—that it does come out on Haldeman and Strachan with his testimony that he had papers etc. The question really is basically whether an individual, you know, can be totally, totally—I mean, the point is, if a guy isn't guilty, you shouldn't let him go.

K   That's right—you shouldn't.

P   It's like me—wait now—let's stand up for people if there—even though they are under attack.

K   I know.

P   In Haldeman's case though—I want to ask you—if you think—I just want to ask you your opinion. And the same on Ehrlichman based on this—do you think that—where he had no knowledge of Watergate.

K   I think neither one of them knew about it before. Just judging from leads around here and found himself in this fantastic situation. Could have as a result of his constant communication with John Dean—with John Dean looking for a way to save himself—could have by the remarks that John made that would either circumstantially involve him in or be the grounds for an indictment.

P   Increase the chances of their being indicted by letting them go? That's another (unintelligible). When I say let them go, give them a leave which—

K   That'd be all right—it's all right.

P   You find—you find them guilty before they have a chance to prove their innocence, don't you? And another way you could do it is this—you could say if that question is raised, you could move then instantly. You see the point is that—your suggesting I should do this based on information we have now.

K   Which is not very good, precise.

P   That's the point that I am making—can on the basis of this kind of information.

K   I don't suggest anything now—I'm just—

P   No—no—I know—No—I'm just trying—understand—I want to know what is the right thing to do and understand we are going to come out of this thing. The Justice Department and the Presidency are going to come out clean because I don't tolerate this kind of stuff. But the point is, Dick, I also. I can't—I can't let an innocent man down. That's my point.

K   I know that. What effect does it have on the discharge of let's say Bob's and Ehrlichman's duties as they'd be the object of speculation and attack in the press. What effect does it have upon their being able to discharge their duties?

P Well one thing. of course, Bob could put it out first.

K The three fifty?

P Right. (unintelligible) testimony and the Strachan work and so forth and so on. In other words, he puts out the story. That's another—one thing—and he puts out the Segretti story too. I really think that's what he has to do.

K Have him appear before the Grand Jury?

P Will he be asked?

K No—except a punitive defense might ask him.

P (unintelligible) here—you don't understand (unintelligible).

K The prosecutor doesn't subpoena a punitive defendant—his attorney doesn't—you know this stuff is going on—now does your guy want to come in and testify.

P You see, I realize that the fellows like up at the Ervin Committee and now the Grand Jury they're going to smash the likes of Haldeman all the time but you can't let a guy go—without a (unintelligible) if he's guilty, if you know he's innocent.

K Right. Let me say what I had to do with this Harry Stewart. Remember the United States Attorney in San Diego?

P Yeah.

K Was involved in my confirmation hearings. An allegation was made with respect to his obstructive conduct. It started as an administrative investigation by the FBI. While the investigation was going on, Harry Stewart just stepped aside as the United States Attorney. Then ultimately he went back. That whole judgment was a process on my part.

P Right.

K I sharply examined it and the hindsight of this stuff is fantastic.

P What's the name of your man in Chicago?

K Barnabus Sears.

P I can sure get that down. but I'm going to get that U.S. Attorney in one way or another.

K And I've thought for months that something was wrong.

P Sorry to hear you say that. No—that's my problem—what to do. Poor (expletive removed)—they're all—they've got a right to a fair trial.

K I've tried about two or three thousand in the last

twenty years and I did (unintelligible). The two aspects of this that have an overriding importance beyond them is the institution of (unintelligible) and also the criminal justice system.

P   Right. Only the people have got to have confidence (unintelligible) and frankly you could come out stronger.

K   Yeah.

P   You just prove that you will take on even your friends.

K   That's right.

P   That's what we'll (unintelligible). The only thing that troubles me about the Haldeman/Ehrlichman, Dick is that—I don't—I just wonder about—about—moving on them before.

K   The evidence (unintelligible)

P   See what I mean?

K   Sure, I understand.

P   That indicates that maybe I know something—which I don't.

K   That's right—nor do I—nor do—all that the government knows is what I have given you. I think, based upon what little is now known would be impeded in either. I don't think that John Ehrlichman should have as an assignment for you anything further to do with this, though.

P   Because of the deep six thing?

K   You know, if it turned out, either through circumstantial testimony or other testimony which could lead to a possible indictment that's part of the circumference.

P   Got to have somebody over here to do—the (expletive removed) thing—what the (expletive removed) do you do?

K   What do you do?

P   Garment? He's Mitchell's former law partner. That won't do, will it?

K   You know the burden of the (unintelligible) so far as you are concerned is that you and I would defend him. Anyone else (unintelligible).

P   Oh, I understand. Not going to—don't—job to do it—and this is (unintelligible) Chief Investigator for the Senate Committee—the (expletive removed) was charged with a felony, bargaining pleaded for a misdemeanor—got a suspended sentence.

K   Yeah.

P   For bugging!

K   Yeah—for bugging.

P   Same thing—that's what should have happened here.

K   As a matter of fact, looking at it again, without trying to determine the impact of it with respect to the election. simple (unintelligible) the obstruction of justice.

P   The obstruction of justice is what's bad.

K   And the perjury—the suborning of witnesses, the perjury and perjuring yourself.

P   You don't have Ehrlichman involved in that—you don't have Haldeman involved in any of that?

K   No—no. When you get Mitchell and Magruder and Mardian and, let's say, Dean all having one approach to this problem, and Magruder over there you're going to have a hard time convicting John Mitchell, Bob Halde-man, LaRue etc. One of the faults these lawyers find is that, you know, because they, if this is true, they will be a (expletive removed) difficult thing to prove.

P   There's a chance Mitchell could beat this?

K   Oh, sure.

P   You do?

K   Oh (expletive removed) yes. It all depends on how this other comes out but, Mr. President, if all you're talking about.

P   Suppose Liddy, suppose Liddy—what's he going to do?

K   Now that's something else—now if Liddy comes in and corroborates Magruder and incidentally they are bitter enemies. They are bitter enemies.

K   Magruder is afraid for his life.

P   Yeah?

K   Even tried to—

P   Liddy—you say Liddy has told all, has he?

K   No he hasn't—he hasn't said a word to anybody.

P   Is that right? Did these guys tell you that?

K   Yes sir. He's taken the fifth.

P   They said that he's come in and talked to them. They—that's what they're telling everybody.

K   That's not true, sir.

P   I mean—if Magruder says that—he hasn't?

K   To my knowledge—I'll check that.

P   Find out.

K   Find out but to my knowledge as a result of everything that was said last night Liddy has not said a word.

P   What about Hunt?

K   Hunt doesn't know anything.

P   He knows about the obstruction of justice—somebody gave him the money. Isn't that the one where Mrs. Hunt or somebody—I don't know what that is—I don't know.

K   You know as much about it as I do.

P   (unintelligible) say something (unintelligible) and I don't want to get so deeply involved.

K   Neither do I and you know from the outset, Mr. President, on this one, because of all of us who are involved—our relationship—I determined that I was going to have the broadest kind of an overview. It's just for this very reason I don't want to right now.

P   Yeah.

K   If Liddy doesn't corroborate Magruder—what Liddy does now in view of Magruder's case I don't know but inherent in Magruder's—

P   He and Dean are taking Liddy and Magruder. You've got two guys it's pretty hard for a jury, if you were a good criminal—an F. Lee Bailey—say, are you going to take the word of these two men against all these other men, gentlemen?

K   When you have something besides F. Lee Bailey, but you take LaRue and Mitchell—

P   Let me say—let me say—I only mention F. Lee Bailey because Mitchell is very close to him now, as you know.

K   I know that, yeah.

P   That's probably who he'll use.

K   I don't know.

P   I say probably—I'm just guessing—I haven't talked to him about it, but he and Bailey are—he's going to fight until the end. He's not going to—

K   I hope he does.

P   Would you—his relationship and former Attorney General.

K   And that would be—that would be a trial for him.

P   Sure. Pitch John Dean take (unintelligible). I was so surprised.

K   When Ehrlichman called me last night all he said, mentioned Magruder. And he said what about informing him if I had any notice that John Dean had initiated this. I really don't until his attorney can negotiate with them.

P   If Dean does not testify about deep sixing

documents and getting Hunt out of the country they have nobody else that can say that.

K   What they want initially.

P   Yeah—will they work out.

K   I think they'll honor their agreement between them.

P   Well, as you know, Dean put it out for press.

K   No—no sir.

P   They're decent men.

K   Yes they are.

P   Good.

K   Yes sir.

P   But Dean.

K   They raised questions whether or not I should even mention that to you because of the (unintelligible)

P   No, (expletive removed) you should tell me.

K   Oh (expletive removed) I didn't argue with them about that. That's not anything. I'm going to tell you what I have learned.

P   I could call them. Let me run this by you. I think I should call them and I consider it highest devotion. What I want you to have (unintelligible) it up here. I think we have—we haven't denied anybody, (expletive removed). Conducted the investigation. The FBI's conducted the investigation. I said I just want you to know that and you're on your own—on your own. And I am—because Dick Kleindienst was a close associate of John Mitchell's I want you to report to Dean Sneed. Now that's the way that I think I should approach it Dick rather than bringing in a special prosecutor.

K   I have no objection to that.

P   Well, without you being there—I don't think they should work through you anymore due to the fact, although we know you didn't have a (expletive removed) thing to do with it—nobody would ever believe—I don't think that.

K   I could make a fair decision on Mitchell.

P   On John Mitchell. Just like I wouldn't think I could probably make a fair one on Haldeman, but you see—don't you think that's true?

K   Yes sir.

P   And I'll—and the way I would do it—I will say, the Attorney General and I have talked and he recommends this. And I'll say, we have talked about it and this is the best way to do it. So we'll put Sneed.

K   And I think it's a very strong possibility.

396

P   You see my point?

K   The only—there's only two aspects of it that I'm not sure about. One of those I'm not sure about is Joe Sneed.

P   I know.

K   He's—you know.

P   Well, let's—what the hell—there's really nothing for him to do except just be honest. They're going to do the job. I know they're going to do the job.

K   Second thing, Mr. President, was the other argument that I'm thinking about. The more believable, more acceptable business, this other thing. The problem of this thing as the result of any appointment of you.

P   Yeah.

K   In favor that you might be able to provide later or whether I could. The credibility aspect of this thing on part of yourself soon.

P   Yeah—think it's best to handle it rather than doing it—escalating it—by nine o'clock then it should be done. I have thought about it and I have made—I have said this and that and the other thing and that's that.

K   One aspect of this thing which you can always take and that is, as the President of the United States, your job is to enforce the law.

K   In the case of any, of any investigations and trials—you know, I mean—now that the time has come as a result of blah, blah, blah, you know.

P   Special prosecutor immediately casts a doubt frankly, Dick, on the whole Justice Department.

K   Yeah—right.

P   I don't like that.

K   Neither do I.

P   But you have—there's not need—you understand, I just don't like that.

K   My feeling.

P   I think—you see the other line would be to say—put sort of a (unintelligible) you couldn't do this? You mean the Attorney General has asked—huh?

K   You might wait to have me recuse in this thing when the indictments come up. I think if they indict John Mitchell we can't be criticized for favoritism, you know.

P   Yeah—in other words, you stay in the job.

K   Until the trial. I don't know, I think this is something we ought to explore very carefully. In terms of (unintelligible)

P You see, there's where your special prosecutor comes in. You want the—you go to the special prosecutor for.

K No, the special prosecutor would not try the case, Mr. President. What he would do is substitute himself for the Attorney General. Silbert would try the case. What he would do would have overview with respect to what they were doing and participating in the prosecuting decisions that are made from time to time. (unintelligible) believe I (unintelligible) discuss with the—with (unintelligible) might not have it with the Deputy Attorney General and —so I support him. You know, I would do it myself.

P (unintelligible)

K And I fully realize by bringing this guy in it's—the effect has a bad reflection upon me, you know, I understand that—that is my recommendation.

P Yeah. I thought we would—I think we just ought to—after your hard lining the executive privilege I think we ought to make a deal with the Ervin Committee provided the ground rules are proper. Do you agree?

K Oh sure. Thing about my hard line is, you know,

P What you're saying is a bargain—the thing by which you are going to work that out. I thought we ought to get something out on that like Monday or Tuesday. That sound good to you? That's a good—a good way to be on the offensive.

K And I, I understand, Mr. President, you have some thought in mind with respect to John Dean. I would respectfully urge you not to accept—include John Dean in the package with (unintelligible) and those people you are.

P (unintelligible)

K Yes.

P Oh yes, (expletive removed) yes, it's better now.

K Negotiate with the United States Attorney—I'll tell you—I don't think.

P No—no. I'm putting him up. The only thing I would say is that—to him—I would say that as President's Counsel (unintelligible) executive (unintelligible) and all that—(expletive removed) I wouldn't even (unintelligible). The Ervin Committee though is going to be as— nothing by the time this thing.

K Oh by the time (unintelligible) we keep it in the criminal justice system where it belongs.

P Where it belongs.

K   The Ervin Committee.

P   And incidentally they ought to—whoever is—Silbert ought to get over there right now and tell the Ervin Committee not to go shouldn't he?

K   I don't know.

P   I (unintelligible). How—how can Mitchell, for example, get a fair trial with the Ervin Committee leaking all over the place and so forth and so on. I would—if I were the prosecuting attorney I'd say to the committee, now keep McCord and all these (expletive removed). Don't you agree?

K   Sure—if they'll do it.

P   I really think as a lawyer—as a criminal—as a—you know, a smart lawyer for Mitchell and the other defendants could move to quash.

K   Well they could get the cases dismissed as a result of this horsing around with the Ervin Committee.

P   Yeah.

K   (unintelligible) Ervin Committee going after—their Constitutional rights might be so impaired that they could have the indictments quashed. That's what. Any litigation concerning John Mitchell will probably take ten years—you know a couple of years before the trial, four or five years appeals, motions, trial. Well I think (unintelligible) and it could be with John Mitchell.

P   (expletive removed) I would want to appeal the Chicago Seven, the Berrigans, and the Ellsbergs and all those (expletive removed). And they've fooled around all this time. Well it's a hard thing, Dick, hard thing. These fellows, even the Cubans—or even perhaps they most of all. They were doing (unintelligible) they were helping the campaign.

K   That's right. Sure.

P   And they just—just showed incredibly bad judgment—right?

K   It's still a fact, Mr. President, it's been two or three months, you know, while you were getting your campaign organization going, and Mitchell was just a puppet. You know John was in a rather awkward situation being the Attorney General, having talked to those guys.

P   And having very troublesome (unintelligible)

K   Right. Had his own real leadership over there and got (unintelligible) the situation.

P   Yeah, Magruder—and Magruder's sort of a lightweight in a very heavy job.

K   Yeah—and also he had not experience in politics.

P   That's right. And then so they decided that—gee, this is great and this is real fun—(expletive removed)—they see.

K   Yeah.

P   And incidentally you got to—you see—if Haldeman had been running it it wouldn't have happened either. But look what the (expletive removed) he was doing, we were on our way to China and then we were on our way to Russia.

K   I know.

P   We weren't in the campaign—they were. We couldn't and that's why we had no control. Well, anyway, I'm not making excuses. The thing to do now is to.

K   Deal with the facts as you have them.

P   Go forward.

K   It would have to be by you, Mr. President.

P   There's (unintelligible). How about another man that we could bring down? How about a former Circuit Court Judge like Lombard?

K   Well the Chief Justice doesn't like that unless he has completely retired from the judiciary.

P   Says he can serve if we gave him an interim appointment?

K   Yes—yeah.

P   Seventy-one years of age?

K   No-no. What you are doing is having a Federal judiciary.

P   Well it seems to me that's the same.

K   The Chief Justice thinks this fellow Sears—he's the one who recommended Sears.

P   Thinks we should have a special prosecutor?

K   Yes. He does. Yes.

P   Now what does he say—now—I want to get some other judgments because I—I'm open on this. I lean against it and I think it's too much of a reflection on our system of justice and everything else.

K   Yeah—that's.

P   What is Petersen's reasoning?

K   Petersen's reasoning would be that I should recuse myself now that it looks like Mitchell and—

P   Yeah.

K   rest of the boys.

P   Yeah—you should do it right now.

K   And that—yeah—but.

P   You—now wait—you'd do this? You see, you do it now it's based on testimony.

K   When I would do it.

P   Well let me ask you though, you would do it before the story broke? Before the indictments or afterwards?

K   I don't know. We haven't gotten to that point.

P   Or is it the point that should be done before the indictments are drawn up so that the indictments are drawn up properly. Is that the point?

K   Yeah—just so that any aspect of the investigation, presentation to the Grand Jury and indictments could not possibly be changed by.

P   So what would Petersen say—you would withdraw?

K   Yeah—but that would not be in a public, you know, TV statement—

P   Yeah.

K   Internal—administrative.

P   And then—what would happen?

K   Well, I would.

P   What would he advocate?

K   I would do one of two things under that circumstance—would be to delegate the responsibility for the entire matter to Petersen, Assistant Attorney General of the Criminal Division.

P   Petersen is the fellow to approach?

K   Yes he is—yes he is.

P   Would the—would the country respect him on this?

K   Yes—he's a (expletive removed) of a guy (unintelligible)

P   I didn't—he was—he is a career man—I didn't appoint him in the first place.

K   He's the first career Assistant Attorney General I think in the history of the Department.

P   O. K.

K   So—but he.

P   Let's consider that one for a moment.

K   It could either be Petersen—or—Sneed.

P   Petersen would be better than Sneed.

K   (unintelligible). That would be initially handled by an administrative document from me to Petersen.

P   But you do it right now? What you should do in any event, what you should do right now—let me say, I still think my—I ought to consider—my suggestion that I call these people in—maybe with you as a matter of fact and say look I just want you to work with Petersen and

401

get everything done. Correct? But let me—let's think about that.

K   Let's think about that. I think we got to do something pretty quickly before this stuff gets out of hand. In view of the disclosure made to me last night and yesterday afternoon by Ehrlichman I think I've got to do something. I'm now on notice that Magruder, you know.

P   Yeah.

K   Testified to—that.

P   That's right—that's why I told Ehrlichman to tell you. I didn't (unintelligible). In fact he suggested it—he said, look I've got this stuff. This was even before Magruder talked to him. I think I should turn over to Kleindienst. I said "do it." And then the events caught up with us and Magruder came in, and said, look, I—almost irrelevant. I didn't think Magruder (unintelligible). So that's why, Dick, why we've been scrupulous and your record must show that. Been scrupulous, that Ehrlichman he called you, he called you before Magruder and afterwards. We didn't wait 'til Magruder—

K   That's right.

P   What I should do

(no more sound—tape runs out)

Telephone conversation: The President and Haldeman, April 15, 1973. (3:27 - 3:44 pm)

Opr   Yes, Sir,

P   Mr. Haldeman, please.

Opr   Thank you

Opr   Mr. Haldeman

P   Hello, I hope you are enjoying this lovely day.

H   No, I am afraid not. Got to get out and take a look at it. It really looks beautiful outside.

P   Are you working on your statement?

H   Yeah - and I talked to Bill and - haven't been able to reach—

P   Yeah. I got that message from Bill.

H   Did you talk to him?

P   John Ehrlichman's got it. He talked to you or to Bill, I don't know which.

402

H Rogers—I gave John a very quick rundown, but Bill wanted to think about it and talk some more and I think he has gone out to play golf or something. He doesn't seem to be around now, so he will call me later this afternoon. His view - he said it really depends on what the Grand Jury does. In other words, he doesn't come on strongly that we should go up there. He has some real reservations about whether we should. I think you got a real problem in the judicial proceeding with possibly prominent people under indictment and all that, and run a Congressional investigation at the same time. And the problem we have had up to now is the feeling that nothing is being done. This whole feeling is going to change, and if something is being done you don't have to start doing everything and he said if we can work out some safeguards that Congress would live up to, via capitulation and all that maybe we should consider going because people do want things cleared up. He said, I really, I think the Committee is handling themselves poorly. I think if the Grand Jury is going to come out fairly soon with their indictments, I would strongly vote the other way. I would hang tight for an offer to go up and speak to the Committee in Executive Session, but I wouldn't go up on camera. He said, I think your court room rules is basically a sound position and that people will see that.

P Uh huh. I just told Ehrlichman to the contrary, but I can change my mind. Ehrlichman had talked to Moore - and Moore says, "Well, hell, everything is really - there is going to be so much flying around it isn't going to make any difference." Moore tends to—well,—

H I don't think that is necessarily true either.

P Moore—I think is—

H If that is true then, why go up on television?

P It just makes it worse doesn't it? Well his point, I guess, Moore's point is at least have the President be forthcoming. But what does that do? Let the President be forthcoming and let them kill us.

H That's right. And Roger's view is if you—at least his preliminary view and he wanted to think about it a while—he said if indictments come down at high levels.

P Yes—

H Then you have been forthcoming. You have said all along that you would cooperate with the Grand Jury. Now if you cooperated with them, which you said you were doing, and nobody said you weren't, and they produce results, that is what the people are after. The people's concern is that nothing—that everybody is just sitting here doing nothing about the Watergate, which is what they think because they haven't seen any result out of the Grand Jury.

P Well, we are going to have some.

H He also made the point, I said - well we may be able to get a victory here without having to pay the price, in the sense that if we agree to go up and the Grand Jury comes down with indictments they will probably turn off the hearings for a time anyway. Then we would have the trials and that sort of stuff. So we would have appeared to be forthcoming but we wouldn't maybe have to go. And he said I don't agree with that because—

P Bill said what?

H Bill said I don't agree with that - but he said - he thinks it is inevitable that they have to stop the hearings if there are indictments at a high level.

P He's right. I agree with that.

H He says they can't go on with those hearings while those people are pending trial. Until they have been tried and sentenced - you cannot go ahead with the hearings. On that basis, you don't want to know how long that is going to take.

P Kleindienst just stopped in. He said it will take four or five years.

H Why in the world does he think that

P The trials, appeals, they'll go to the Supreme Court, you know Mitchell is in a fight and these other guys, what the hell?

H On that basis, you have the judicial process running who are these people. Bill feels strong on this.

P What about the other things they want to get into?

H If they can separate them, that's fine. They are the ones who have said they are totally tied together.

P Yeah, one thing too about the other things. They are going to be denied some of their principal witnesses. I mean Mitchell will not testify. He will never go up there, you know, before the Committee.

H Right.

P And Magruder. He won't go up.

H Nope. Now you are getting the White House people going up and not the other people. Where are you on that? And that is a question. Bill said, don't make a commitment now, you may have to meet in October or some-

404

thing when this thing runs itself out.

P   But he did think we could make the Executive Session commitment?

H   Yes

P   Puts us in a good forthcoming position.

H   That's his point, that that is a very sound offer, just as your offer to work with the Grand Jury was a sound offer that produced results. You say we will be perfectly willing to work with the Senate.

P   You indicated to Bill there would be indictments at a high level?

H   I said it looks as if they are going to be bringing indictments and that they are higher ups over at the Committee.

P   What did he say?

H   He didn't react at all, but a little later he said, "Well, if Mitchell is indicted, or something, you know." I didn't say that, but he did.

P   Ok

H   And—

P   You know, in a way—I mean in reading the Johnson/Witcover piece in the *Washington Post,* we are so low now we can't go any lower. Huh?

H   Yeah.

P   What did you think of that? Are they right? Not when they say today there is the over-riding concern today for Watergate. There will be when it comes out, obstruction and all that but—

H   Yeah. You can get that out by, you know, getting hold of a guy and say if President Nixon did the Watergate would you still vote for him and say No.

P   I wonder if they will use the Gallup Poll tomorrow if the damn thing comes out?

H   Well, I haven't seen the Gallup release. I don't know that it went out, but I often don't get it until after it comes out.

P   We did have a hard figure on it didn't we?

H   He said it was a hard figure. 60-33.

P   Anyway, we are glad to have that.

H   So, what does Kleindienst think now? Does he—

P   He's for a Prosecutor.

H   So is Bill.

P   Bill is? Who did he have in mind?

H   He didn't have anyone in mind and I didn't get into that question with him.

P   I have really come to that conclusion, too, Bob.

H   Oh, really?

P   For a reason. This is not to prosecute the case. A special Prosecutor, to look at the indictments to see that the indictments run to everybody they need to run to, so that it isn't just the President's men, you see.

H   In other words, he is above Silbert rather than replacing Silbert?

P   Oh no, Silbert runs the case and that's all. But he is just in there for the purpose of examining all this to see that the indictments cover everybody.

H   Uh, huh. Well that does protect you a lot, because if they don't indict some of us then you have a cover up problem. If you have that guy, then you have a basis—

P   Then he goes out and says, "I have examined all of this, and now let's stop all this. These men are not guilty and these men are not indictable and these are."

H   Yeah.

P   We are thinking about that. We haven't decided that yet. But I lean toward it now in order to just—we've got to get into the proper position there.

H   That would make sense, rather than having Sneed take over.

P   Yep, because he's compromsied too—I can do things for him in the future, see? I can for anybody, but—

H   Yeah, but he is your appointee which is a little different. Although any Special Prosecutor is your appointee.

P   Yeah. It is a little different if he is outside. This Wright from Texas is the guy I sort of lean to. You know, the Dean of the Texas Law School.

H   Well, I don't know. Did Dick have any reading on timing on indictments?

P   No.

H   Because that is—

P   He thinks a lot of the stuff may leak with Magruder running around, and—Strachan told an interesting thing to Ehrlichman on Magruder which makes the point that I am—two weeks ago Magruder talked to Strachan, and tried to get Strachan to concoct with him the story that he, Strachan, did walk across the street with Magruder and tell Magruder to go forward with the operation.

H   Which Strachan claims isn't true apparently.

P   No. My point is, don't you see, the devastating thing this is to Magruder, to his credibility?

H Yeah.

P I said to John, "Why the hell is he trying to do this?" Because Magruder's defense is that he is just doing it because of pressure from higher ups. You see the point?

H Yep.

P And Magruder—so I am not so sure that a hell of a lot of Magruder's stuff, even on Mitchell, may be open to serious question. Serious question.

H Ok. But yeah, on some things I think that is true.

P Some things, I think Mitchell is still in it.

H But I don't see how you—

P But I mean, anything Magruder says about you, for example, if he does, you know what I mean. I think, Bob, your analysis of Magruder once that he is a guy that doesn't know the truth, is really true.

H I really believe that—

P And I think now he has lied so much is he going to lie again and work with his attorneys and get himself separated from all this thing, etc. I think Strachan will be a damn believable witness when he goes down there. I really feel he will be.

H He will if he stays to the truth.

P If he just tells the truth

H If he doesn't try to tangle things up at all.

P Right. Hmm—Magruder was telling Strachan, "Look this should be the story that I would like to tell -"

H It is kind of ridiculous. Why would Strachan agree to that?

P Oh, he—it would implicate Strachan, but he is at the same level, too, see, so it wouldn't hurt him. The point of that would be simply—and he said Magruder told him about his family and his concerns and all that, made a great plea about how his personal problems were so serious. And he said, "Please, now, let's go along on this story."

H Yeah.

P That is interesting.

H Well Magruder was bouncing around in desperation, telling all different kinds of stories to different people.

P That's right. Remember you told me that—

H Trying to tie something together and I think what happened is he ran that string out and finally just gave up because that wouldn't work and decided to tell the truth, but in the process he probably doesn't know what the truth is. He has made up so many different stories. I can understand that. It is hard for me to remember what's true, having just heard all of these other people's stories. It is difficult to sort the stuff out. If you start lying yourself—

P   Bill may have a point there. I have sort of had this, and I don't think Ehrlichman and particularly Moore didn't agree with it, that—look, if they get a hell of a big fish, that is going to take a lot of the fire out of this thing on the cover up and all that sort. If they get the President's former law partner and Attorney General, you know. Do you agree or not? Am I—?

H   Yeah. What I feel is people want something to be done to explain what to them is now a phony looking thing. This will explain it.

P   Explain that they did it, and then of course the cover up comes in and they did that too.

H   And it all makes sense, it is logical, believable, because it's true.

P   Right

H   And there it is - I can't - it seems to me that there is at least a strong possibility, if not probability or certainty, that public reaction is going to be, well, thank God that is settled; now let's get away from it. Rather than the reaction of, "Ho, ho, ho, here is something pretty bad; let's spend a lot more time looking into it."

P   That's right. Well—

H   I think people want solutions; they don't want ongoing problems.

P   You know some of that so-called people-polling, and polling. Don't they say that Watergate, didn't you say that Gallup or, well, that its a concern, it worries them, etc.—considered it a caper, and they want the damn thing explained.

H   That's right. They want it explained and they want to get off of it. There isn't—

P   Kleindienst also comes in with the idea that sometime I've got to go out and make a Checker's Speech at 9:00 o'clock at night. I told him, "Now, Dick, I am not going to do that."

H   Oh, I think that would be crazy. I sure do.

P   I said, "Now, Dick, I am not going to. I am not going to elevate it that way. If its going to be elevated, let the press elevate it. I will go out and say it before the press, in the press room, you know."

H   Yeah. Unless there is—there is nothing now that indicates doing that.

P   But when (it comes out), I am going to have to say its rough, but that shows that our judicial system is—we, you know. The Special Prosecutor thing helps in another way. It gets one person between me and the whole thing. You see, the Dean report now has been totally discredited and, you see,

H   Yep. That's right, and I think that is a darn good route for it, especially if it can be done. I hadn't thought about it, or understood it at the level you are now talking about, and that would seem to me exactly what you are after.

P   Not somebody to prosecute Mitchell. I won't have that.

H   That is the other problem. What do you say when they indict Mitchell, and Mitchell doesn't plead guilty? You obviously can't say, I'm sorry.

P   Oh well, we will just say that I will not comment on the case. I'm—let's have the men work up a statement.

H   I won't comment and I have full confidence in the American judicial process.

P   In the process and I—

H   hope it will bring the guilty parties to account and clear the innocent parties.

P   He has pled innocent and I think he should have every opportunity to—(I don't know whether I can say I am confident in his innocence)—that will be the key question.

H   That is just what I was going to say. You cannot—

P   It is not proper for me to comment on that because there has been an indictment. It is not proper for me to comment, except that he is a fine man, he is entitled to it. I think we should not judge this case until it has been heard in the judicial process.

H   You don't want to get into the position that Hiss's character witnesses got in.

P   I can't do it. I know.

H   What you can do is express your faith in the system. You know there is a lot to be gained from this if the damn system comes out right.

P   That's right.

H   In restoring people's faith in the system, rather than in this jackass kangaroo court.

P Yeah. Ok. Incidentally, I wondered if you would talk to John Ehrlichman. I will get him but when you talk to him—

H I will be talking to him.

P Be sure to tell him that I think that the way I hear Bill's thing spelled out, that I think it makes a hell of a lot of sense. Ok?

H Yes, Sir.

P Alright.

H Alright.

Telephone conversation: The President and Kleindienst, April 15, 1973. (3:48 - 3:49 pm)

Oper Yes, please

P Attorney General Kleindienst, please.

Oper Yes.

P hello.

K Mr. President?

P Hi, Dick.

K May I bring Henry Petersen with me?

P Yeah. I want to ask him to do something.

K I'll be over there in a couple of minutes. Alright sir.

Telephone conversation: Higby and Haldeman, April 15, 1973.

P For Mr. Haldeman?

Opr Yes.

Opr Mr. Haldeman, Mr. Higby wants you.

LH Hello, Bob.

H Yeah.

LH John Dean just called me. He had a message he wanted to relay to the President through you. He would not speak directly to you.

H Alright.

LH (1) I hope you understand my actions are motivated totally out of loyalty to you, the President.

H   Wait a minute.

LH   totally out of loyalty to you and the President.

H   Yep

LH   And if it's not clear now—

H   Uh, huh.

LH   it will become clear.

H   Wait a minute.

LH   (2) Ehrlichman requested to meet tonight—

H   Heah.

LH   but I feel inappropriate at this time.

H   Just a minute. Ok.

LH   I am ready and willing to meet with you, meaning the President, at any time to discuss these matters.

H   Just a minute.

LH   (3) I think you, meaning the President, should take your counsel from Henry Peterson who I assure you does not want the Presidency hurt.

H   Hmph.

LH   That was the end of his message. He was calling you from his home, the operator said.

H   From his home?

LH   That's what the operator said.

H   How long ago was that? Just now?

LH   Yes, sir.

H   Ok. Thank you very much.

LH   Yes sir.

Telephone conversation: The President and Petersen, April 15, 1973. (8:14 - 8:18 pm)

Opr   Yes sir.

P   The Assistant Attorney General, Mr. Petersen, please - he is probably at home.

Opr   Yes Sir.

P   Hello.

HP   Mr. President.

P   Did you get on your boat?

HP   No, no, no - I just came on home.

P   Oh you did. Right. Anything further you want to report tonight before our meeting tomorrow at 12:30?

HP   Not anything that specially, that I didn't give you today.

P Nothing that adds to what we had earlier, huh?

HP That's right - they concluded the meeting with Dean. His counsel says he will not permit him to plead; that a—

P Permit him to plead? What do you mean by that?

HP To plead guilty. In other words, he will go to trial.

P He is going to plead not guilty, huh?

HP That's right, unless we come to some agreement with him. His counsel's position is that it would be a travesty to try Dean and not try Ehrlichman and Haldeman.

P Uh, huh.

HP That is the basic information to the extent that it developed in these preliminary negotiations isn't much more than I gave you.

P Well, let me ask you this. Based on this, though. you mean that inhibits you from using the information then, or do you use it, or how do you do it, or do you use it for leads, but you can't use it unless he pleads? right?

HP We cannot use it for any purpose unless he pleads.

P For no purpose?

HP That's right. That's incorrect, unless we strike some agreement with him.

P Hmp.

HP He had a call from Ehrlichman - Ehrlichman wanted to meet with him tonight

P I see.

HP about eight o'clock. We advised him he would have to make his own determination but suggested that he not.

P I see.

HP He, then, through his counsel informed us that he was writing a note to you in which he would say (1) that what he was doing was in your best interests and that that would all become apparent as this situation unfolded.

P Right. Let me ask you this—why don't I get him in now if I can find him and have a talk with him?

HP I don't see any objection to that, Mr. President.

P Is that alright with you?

HP Yes Sir.

P Alright - I am going to get him over because I am not going to screw around with this thing. As I told you

HP Alright.

P   But I want to be sure you understand, that you know we are going to get to the bottom of this thing.

HP   I think the thing that -

P   What do you want me to say to him? Ask him to tell me the whole truth?

HP   Yes, sir. And there is one other thing: that is a signal from you might bring out the truth from Liddy.

P   From Liddy?

HP   Yes sir.

P   A signal from me? What do I do?

HP   He went to John Mitchell, I am told, and indicated that he would do whatever he was told to do.

P   I never met the man. I don't know what I can do with him.

HP   Uh, huh.

P   How do I give him the signal?

HP   Well, I will do it for you.

P   He, Liddy has talked to John Mitchell and said a signal from the President?

HP   No, he said a signal from Mitchell.

P   From Mitchell?

HP   Yes, sir, and so indicated that he was going to stand firm.

P   Then, what I am trying to get at, how do I get—I then would go over Mitchell to you, Liddy and you're telling me that?

HP   No. We just go and say that we have discussed this situation with the President of the United States and he thinks it is vitally important that you tell us everything you know.

P   I get it. Uh huh. OK. Now you will be through with your things you think by 12:30. Right?

HP   Yes, sir.

P   OK. Well, get a good night's sleep, huh?

HP   I will, indeed.

P   As good as you can.

HP   Yes, sir.

P   Ok.

HP   And you too.

P   Fine.

HP   Good night, Sir.

**Telephone conversation: The President and Petersen,
April 15, 1973. (8:25 - 8:26 pm)**

P   Hello.

Opr.   I have Mr. Petersen.

P   Hello.

HP   Yes, sir, Mr. President.

P   I am trying to reach Dean - I think I may be able
to get him, I hope. He seems to be in transit from someplace to someplace. But I will report to you after I see
him.

HP   Very good.

P   In the meantime, on Liddy—I don't know the man,
of course, and have no control over him, but, hell, you
are to tell him the President wants everybody involved in
this to tell everything they know. Ok?

HP   Indeed so. I will get in touch with his lawyer first
thing in the morning.

P   You might do it tonight.

HP   Very good.

P   I don't want to stall around. Ok?

HP   Very good.

P   Don't you think that is the best thing to do?

HP   Indeed so.

P   Fine. One thing I want to be sure of Henry; you
understand as far as Liddy is concerned I have no control
over him—don't know the man at all and I just want,
since he has raised the question, that maybe not talking
because of me—

HP   No, no - I don't want to leave that impression.

P   Because of Mitchell, huh?

HP   He is taking orders from higher authority. The
decision is mine but since you are the highest authority he
will stand in line if we handle it discreetly.

P   I just want him to be sure to understand that as far
as the President is concerned everybody in this case is to
talk and to tell the truth. You are to tell everybody, and
you don't even have to call me on that with anybody. You
just say those are your orders.

HP   Yes, Sir.

P   Ok.

HP   Alright, thank you, sir.

Telephone conversation: The President and Petersen, April 15, 1973. (9:39 - 9:41 pm)

Opr   Yes, Sir

P   Mr. Petersen, please, you know, of the Justice Department.

Opr   Yes

P   Hello.

HP   Mr. President.

P   Henry I have been—I talked to John Dean and haven't quite finished, but he stepped out for a minute. I wanted to ask you this. He says that he thinks it is important that I tell Liddy's attorney—I don't know who he is —by the name of Maroulis do you know him, that what I told you a few minutes ago.

HP   Yes - I have already been trying to get in touch with him.

P   Let me say this. You tell him, if necessary, you haul him in here and I will tell him. Ok?

HP   Alright. Indeed so.

P   You know what I mean. You tell him I have called you directly tonight and that you have it direct from the President if he needs if from me, I will tell him.

HP   Very good.

P   Because you see, John felt that maybe he wouldn't take it from you. But I would think he would—or what do you think? What is your judgment?

HP   Well, we certainly will tell him. He and Liddy are very close friends and I am certain the word would get back to him.

P   Right. Ok you tell Maroulis that the President has directed that you are to talk to him and to tell him he is to tell everything he knows. He should have before but my point is, if necessary, if he has to come in to see me—but you come with him. I don't want any things where he comes in and makes any motions—you see what I mean?

HP   I understand.

P   Does this sound like good medicine to you or do you think I should not see him?

HP   I think we ought to reach that question after we see what the reaction is.

P   Right. I would prefer if you could handle it because it ought to be handled at your level rather than having me bring some attorney in and give him an order.

HP   I agree

P   So you do it on my direction. I think that will do the trick. If it doesn't I will see him myself.

HP   Very well.

Telephone conversation: The President and Petersen, April 15, 1973. (11:45 - 11:53 pm)

Opr   Yes, please

P   Would you get me Mr. Henry Petersen of the Justice Department - Assistant Attorney General.

Opr   I certainly will sir, right. Thank you

P   Hello

HP   Yes, sir.

P   I hope I didn't wake you up.

HP   No, not at all.

P   I wanted to tell you first, I have—apparently I've got the President of the Rotary International at noon tomorrow. Could you make it 1:30?

HP   Yes, sir.

P   That won't interfere with your lunch or anything?

HP   No.

P   Fine. Second, I have met with Dean. I got him in finally and heard his story and I said directly to him, "Now when do you want to resign?" And, he said, "Well I will resign but I would prefer to wait until I have testified." Now I want to ask your judgment on that. I can bring him in in the morning and tell him, "Look, I want your resignation."

P   But, what do you want me to do? I don't want to interfere with your process?

HP   Mr. President, I don't think that we ought to—

P   Tip our hand?

HP   Not yet. He is the first one who has really come

P   Oh, I see.

HP   He came in a week ago Sunday.

P   Right. Let me say this. The main thing Henry we must not have any question, now, on this, you know I am in charge of this thing. You are and I am. Above everything else and I am following it every inch of the way and I don't want any question, that's of the fact that I am a way ahead of the game. You know, I want to stay one step ahead of the curve. You know what I mean?

HP   I understand.

P   So - if you think on Dean -

HP   I think we ought to hold the line.

P   Alright and you will let me know.

HP   Yes, sir. I will indeed.

P   as soon as - then I will call him in and naturally he will have to resign.

HP   Yes, sir.

P   Now Haldeman and Ehrlichman - I have informed both of them of the charges that have been generally made and I have said that if they stand up, and I didn't have to say it. They said well, of course, we will, we don't want to be an embarrassment. They are good guys. But my feeling with both of them, and it is only a question, and we talked today of when—no, it is whether, also, but I think you've got to hear Strachan and I think you've got to hear Dean and then I suppose you would want to hear them or do you think we should move on them before? Or do you want to think of that overnight?

HP   We would like to wait. We would like to wait, Mr. President.

P   Because like today, you were suggesting that we call them all in and have them resign and I just wanted to be sure you didn't think I should do that because I am perfectly prepared to.

HP   That is really your judgment. I think ultimately that is going to have to be done.

P   Yeah. But your point is that as far as the case is concerned, you are telling me now that it is best to wait. Is that the point?

HP   On Dean, yes. And on Ehrlichman/Haldeman - I suppose until we hear their testimony, which is, well, we want to put them off until we can fashion all the—

P   All the others.

HP   things into a pattern.

P   How soon would that be, for my own planning, about a week?

HP   I don't think it is going to be less than a week and I would say two weeks or more.

P   Oh, you think it might be two weeks?

HP   I would say so. Yes, sir.

P   It will take that long, huh?

HP   I am afraid so because—

P   Well by that time, my view is that the damn thing will leak out and I - well be that as it may, we'll see.

HP   That conceals it.

P   Why don't you and I talk about that tomorrow?

HP   We will.

P   And we will look over the Haldeman/Ehrlichman thing to see what the facts are and maybe you could give me a little sheet of paper on both as to what you feel their vulnerabilities are so that I—could you do that?

HP   I will try indeed. Yes, sir.

P   I mean just say, for these reasons, etc. and then I will be in a position to act on it.

HP   Very good.

P   You understand, there isn't going to be any problem, of course not with Dean and neither Haldeman nor Ehrlichman. They are perfectly prepared to do whatever I say at a moment's notice because they put the office first. But the only thing I am concerned about is in the prosecution of a case like this, it may be that if you have them move it may have an effect on some of the others you are trying to get to testify. I don't know, but—

HP   That is certainly true with Dean.

P   Certainly true with Dean?

HP   Yes, sir.

P   Uh, huh. He is in a mood to resign right now but I will see. I will check him tomorrow.

HP   Are you seeing—

P   Uh huh. And Haldeman/Ehrlichman, you say we'll talk about it tomorrow. Or do you want to think about it?

HP   I want to think about it some more, yes, sir, because we are going to have to weave all of the facts with respect to them into a pattern. It is not going to come out neat and clean—

P   And clear—

HP   with respect to either one of them.

P   Because, in both cases they have a—basically in both of their cases, as I look at the thing since it is basically the obstruction of justice case for the most part, with the possibility of Haldeman of knowledge, although that is questionable to believe. But you have to hear Strachan before you decide that.

HP   Yes, sir.

P   But that's a matter which is going to involve your

hearing them too, what they know, I suppose, as well as hearing the others.

HP Oh, I think that is right and I think with respect to the obstruction of justice thing is concerned, it is easy for me to see how they fell into that, if you like.

P Yeah. Uh, huh. Rather than being directly conspirators?

HP That's right. That's right.

P And there is a difference in that respect, I suppose.

HP That's right. A difference, at least, in moral culpability.

P Sure. Motive.

HP In plain terms of ultimate embarrassment, I think that -

P The embarrassment is there, but in terms—basically in terms of motive which might be the legal culpability, they might be off but in terms of embarrassment they would have to be out of the government?

HP Yes, sir.

P I get your point and, frankly, either one is enough. I understand that totally because that was what was involved in the Adams' case, as you recall.

HP Yes.

P He was not legally guilty of a damn thing. Well, he might have been, might have been, I suppose, making the telephone call, if they had ever brought him to trial. But because of the possibility, we had to move on him. Well in any event, I am glad to get your view on it but I want you to know that having talked to Dean and told him to wait, I wanted you to know that I had told him to wait because I had agreed with him that I would not do it until I heard from him, but let me say I am going to wait until I hear from you then, on Dean. Is that fair enough?

HP Fine, yes, sir.

P And you will probably hear him Monday or Tuesday, tomorrow—well, you don't know yet.

HP We don't know yet. Now, it's not going to be that quick. We have Strachan, LaRue and O'Brien—

P Tomorrow?

HP Tomorrow. Let's say Monday and Tuesday.

P Yep. Huh, huh, What about Magruder? You have to get him in there some place, don't you?

HP We've had him in and we have to get his testimony in before the Grand Jury, and we are trying to work out with his lawyers as to whether or not—

P   Well, he will come in and plead guilty so you can. Because it seems to me, that your idea of getting him on and pleading guilty and beating the damn press and the Ervin Committee to it is a very good one.

P   Otherwise, you know, they are going to say they forced you to do it. And that is very important, don't you agree?

HP   There are negotiations underway with counsel now and obviously they are very much afraid of Sirica. They are afraid Sirica is going to clap him in jail immediately.

P   Oh.

HP   We have to see Sirica too.

P   Now, Sirica's got to see the point of this. My goodness because the point is Sirica's got to realize he is getting bigger fish.

HP   That's right.

P   Right?

HP   That is it exactly.

P   Alright. Good luck. Good bye.

HP   Thank you for calling, Mr. President.

Meeting: The President, Haldeman and Ehrlichman, Oval Office, April 16, 1973. (9:50 - 9:59 am)

JE   Did you get those—

P   I'm going to ask him which one he wants to sign. It seems to me that I don't want to pressure him or should I just have him sign effective today or not announce it. What is your advice? We've got plenty of time.

JE   Well, as I made it loud and clear that he ought to sign both of them. Then you could use whichever one he wanted or none, depending on how circumstances unfold.

P   (Unintelligible)

JE   Unless he won't. You know, you know what to do at that point.

H   You go to Petersen and ask him not to (unintelligible)

P   That is why, John, I want to nail down what Dean said about other bugs on the White House and so forth, and so on. I assume that is the Plumbers operation.

JE   No, no. What he is referring to is the FBI's bugs

on the journalists in the first year he was nominated.

P   (Unintelligible)

JE   Hold on. No, no. These were almost all FBI bugs. What I said all National Security—

P   But I was wondering what your advice if I should not tell him today that anything in that area is National Security (unintelligible)

JE   I think you should, and I think it should cover not only that but Plumbing operation and anything else of which he has knowledge that I am (unintelligible) that with Executive Privilege right now.

P   Executive Privilege—

JE   And I don't want to ever hear (unintelligible) discuss those matters.

P   Yeah.

JE   (Unintelligible)

P   I don't know whether he did. He might have.

JE   Well, he might have been if he has yet afterwards or before—

P   (Unintelligible)

JE   Now if you remember the whole operation was because you were afraid there were leaks out at the NSC and you were trying to find them.

P   I thought they were due to the FBI.

JE   Well, all the (unintelligible) were but there was one in Georgetown at somebody's house that actually was never put on. It was (unintelligible) but it was explored and how Dean knows about that, I don't know. The FBI files—

P   (Unintelligible)

JE   I can't say. I doubt it. I think it was before his time.

P   The reason that I made the call while in Dean's presence last night was that he said Liddy was saying how he knows Liddy had told (unintelligible) or something like that. I said he must (unintelligible). Well, he thought he ought to get ahold of his attorneys. Liddy said will not (unintelligible) higher authorities. (Unintelligible) not the President, (unintelligible) Mitchell. And I said, I called Petersen (unintelligible) where to go (unintelligible) Liddy's attorney. The President is not asking for any type of (unintelligible).

JE   He can't hurt anything at this point and it certainly (unintelligible) way the thing he had to do with Mitchell and Magruder.

P   (Unintelligible)

JE   Remove any impediment against their testifying by reason of misplaced loyalty to you.

P   (Unintelligible)

JE   Petersen, is obviously reacting to the whole (unintelligible).

P   I would like also a scenario with regard to the President's role, in other words, the President—

JE   Ziegler has just left my office. He feels we have no more than 12 hours. He's got some input from the *Post* and he estimates unless we take an initiative by 9 o'clock tonight it will be too late. Now, for that reason, I would suggest that Ziegler set a meeting with Petersen and if you and Ziegler can persuade Petersen the announcement has come from the White House—

P   I'll tell them.

JE   Otherwise the Justice Department will, of course, crack this whole thing.

H   Perhaps the whole thing, but I think it would be a good idea (unintelligible) Petersen alone.

JE   That is a very good point.

JE   Now you know how (unintelligible) around for sometime ahead of time you got this well thought through and well laid out and I think he is quite (unintelligible) about it and quite (unintelligible).

P   (Unintelligible)

JE   We'll do that while you are gone. There is one point before you talk to Dean that I heard last night that doesn't fit together. Maybe it doesn't matter. And that is that Dean said, last night, as I understood it, that Petersen had told you that Liddy has not talked. They can't get Liddy to talk.

P   Yeah.

JE   Dean told us that Liddy had told him everything. Told the U.S. Attorney.

P   I know that, I know that, but I—

JE   Petersen lying to you or (unintelligible)

P   Well, maybe a little both.

JE   Well, I think it is probably (unintelligible)

P   A snow job.

JE   Either that or Dean is (unintelligible) cover-up in case anything starts to seep out.

P   Cover-up—How strong (unintelligible)

JE   Ron thinks that it ought to be done from up here. That (unintelligible) I mentioned it to him the other day he thought you should do it here, if you did it at all.

P   I could do it right here?

JE   Yes. But he wants to get out the fact that Dean (unintelligible) you that the Dean report was inadequate (unintelligible) that several weeks ago you reinstituted an examination of the personal investigation and that this culminated in a whole series of actions over the weekend.

P   I spent the weekend working on it. (Unintelligible) got to say.

JE   The report did not. This is the week that Mitchell being here (unintelligible)

P   (Unintelligible)

JE   Well, now, if I am going to be splashed on this thing you are better off now having another scrap with Dean.

P   Well, somebody is going to be.

JE   Well, we could not (unintelligible)—

P   Investigation of the matters.

JE   I think that that is the way, the investigation of the matter.

P   But I didn't talk to Mitchell.

JE   Well, they say who did it, delegating him to do that. I mean that, that's—

P   (Unintelligible) look one damn thing

JE   Well, I think there is a full Ehrlichman report, unquote. (Unintelligible)

P   Would you mind talking to Moore to see Gray or (unintelligible) you can talk to him can't you? Time is of the essence right now. (Unintelligible)

JE   I understand.

P   (Unintelligible)

JE   No, no, I'll take care of it.

P   (Unintelligible)

JE   As a matter of fact, I have a problem. I'm going to get Moore to talk to Fielding also, and find out what was in there because I don't want to know.

P   Right (Unintelligible)

JE   And then Moore can advise you.

P   I don't know (unintelligible) when I get back (unintelligible) Justice Department drag it out of the White House. You (unintelligible)

JE   (Unintelligible) you do it. Petersen here is working with me on—

P   Yesterday. Yesterday, I talked to Mr. Kleindienst. He removed (unintelligible) people involved. I said, "Now, Petersen and myself. That's right, Petersen (unintelligible)

JE   Well, he's got a (unintelligible) So. Well, I'll be seeing Dean now.

P   Yeah, but—

JE   I think that the point is that in picking up these letters from him, it would be the agreement that neither he nor you would announce it immediately. So the announcement would be your discretion.

P   Right.

JE   And the decision would be at your discretion as to which way to go.

P   Right.

JE   And you might ask him whether he intends to plead guilty or not—

P   Yeah.

JE   Or not guilty.

P   Yeah.

JE   And that will weight in your own (unintelligible)

P   That's right. That's right. (Unintelligible)

(Material unrelated to Presidential actions deleted.)

Meeting: The President and Dean,
Oval Office, April 16, 1973.
(10:00 - 10:40 am)

The President/John Dean

P   Good morning, John. How are you?

D   Good morning.

P   Sit down, sit down. Trying to get my remarks ready to deliver for the building trades. You know I was thinking, get the odds and ends—(inaudible). You will remember we talked about resignations, et cetera, et cetera that I should have in hand. Not to be released.

D   Un, huh.

P   But that I should have in hand something or otherwise they will say, "What the hell. After Dean told you all of this, what did you do?" You see?

D   Uh, huh.

P   I talked to Petersen about this other thing and I said, "Now what do you want to do about this situation on Dean, et cetera?" And he said, well, he said I don't want to announce anything now. You know what I mean.

D Uh, huh.

P But what is your feeling on that? See what I mean?

D Well I think it ought to be Dean, Ehrlichman and Haldeman.

P Well, I thought Dean at this moment.

D Alright.

P Dean at this moment because you are going to be going and I will have to handle them also. But the point is, what is your advice? You see the point is, we just typed up a couple just to have here which I would be willing to put out. You know.

D Uh, huh.

P In the event that certain things occur.

D I understand.

P To put—just putting. What is your advice?

D I think it would be good to have it on hand, and I would think to be very honest with you—

P Have the others too?

D Yeah, have the others too.

P Well as a matter of fact, they both suggested it themselves so I've got that—I am sorry, Steve, I hit the wrong bell.

D (Half laugh)

P So I have already done that with them.

D Alright.

P They said look whatever—and I want to get your advice on them, too. And what I would think we would want to do is to have it in two different forms here and I would like to discuss with you the forms. It seems to me that your form should be to request an immediate leave of absence. That would be one thing. The other, of course, would be just a straight resignation.

D Uh, huh.

P First, what I would suggest is that you sign both. That is what I had in mind. And then we'll talk about after—you don't know yet what you're. For example, if you go in and plead guilty you would have to resign.

D That is right.

P If on the other hand, you're going in on some other basis, then I think the leave of absence is the proper thing to do.

D Uh, huh, I would think so.

P And that is the way I would discuss it with others, too. If you have any other thoughts, let me know. I am not trying to press you on the thing. I just want to be sure

John's got the record of anything that I should have here.

D   I think it is a good idea. I frankly do. But I think if you do it, for one, I think you have problems with others too Mr. President.

P   I already have the others.

D   That is what I am trying to advise you on—

P   But on theirs, both, it is all pending their appearance, et cetera. That isn't yours. Nothing is going to be said but I have to have it in hand by reason, as I told them as a matter of fact after our talk last night. I told them that I have to have these in hand so that I can move on this if Petersen is going to report to me everyday. I said now Petersen, "If you get this stuff confirmed, I need to know." He said, well, I asked him specifically, "what do you do? Who is going to be today?" And he said, "well, Strachan." There are three today I think. Who is the third one?

D   I don't know.

P   That's right! You're not supposed . . .

D   (Laughter)

P   Then, OK.

D   What I would like to do is draft up for you an alternative letter putting in both options and you can just put them in the file. Short and sweet.

P   Alright. Fine. I had dictated something myself. All my own which, if you can give me a better form, fine. I just want you to do it either way. Do you? Or do you want to prepare something?

D   I would like to prepare something.

P   Good. Alright. Fine. Why don't you take this? You can take those as an idea and have something. I've got to see Petersen at 1:30.

D   Alright.

P   Understand I don't want to put anything out because I don't want to jeopardize your position at all. You have a right to, just as everybody else has. You have taken a hell of a load here but I just feel that since what you said last night that we've got to do it and with Haldeman and Ehrlichman I have leave of absences from them. Which, however, I will not use until I get the word from Petersen on corroboration which he advised himself. I talked to him after you left—about 11:45 and let [him— characterization omitted] know how hard we work around here.

D   Well, you will have something within a couple of hours.

426

P   I won't be back. Yes, you draft what you want me to. In other words you can—

D   And if you don't like what I draft, you can tell me and I will change it in any way that you want.

P   Oh sure, oh sure. But I can't make the decisions, of course. You see and also, well, put it this way: you draft what you want and if I have any concern about it I'll give you a ring. You can be around, et cetera. But you would agree that nothing should be put out now?

D   I would agree. I was thinking about that.

P   You see we got that problem today that the thing may break. You know with Magruder, et cetera and I. You know that is what I wanted to run over with you briefly. You know to get your feeling again as to how we handle it. You were saying the President should stay one step ahead of this thing. Well, we've got—the only problem is what the hell can I say publicly? Here is what we have done. I called in Kleindienst. I have been working on it all week. As soon as I got the Magruder thing I got in Kleindienst and then at 4:00 p.m. we got in Petersen. Kleindienst withdrew and assigned Petersen. I said, "Alright, Henry, I don't want to talk with Kleindienst anymore about this case. I am just going to talk to you. You are in charge. You follow through and get to the bottom of this thing and I am going to let the chips fall where they may." We have covered that all the way down the line. Now I had to follow him to a certain extent on the prosecution side. On the other hand on the PR side I sure as hell am not going to let the Justice Department step out and say look we dragged the White House in here. I've got to step out and do it, John. Don't you agree?

D   That's right.

P   Again, I don't want to walk out and say look John Dean's resignation has been accepted. (Expletive omitted) That isn't fair.

D   Nor would it be fair to say Ehrlichman and Haldeman's have.

P   You see, they haven't been charged yet. As soon as they are charged it's a problem. But in your case you haven't been charged with anything yet.

D   No, I have not.

P   That is my problem. The only reason I am doing this is because of what you said about them and that is why I am getting from them too.

D   Well there is a chance today when LaRue goes

427

down that Haldeman. Ehrlichman's name are going to be right down there before the Grand Jury.

P   Well, the name may be in but the point is you don't just throw somebody out because their name comes forth. You understand.

D   I understand.

P   You could also, if you would, I would like for you to prepare a letter that you would have for Ehrlichman and Haldeman. Would you do that?

D   Yes sir.

P   Then I will give them the form and let them work out something that is appropriate. Would you prepare that for me?

D   Yes, I will.

P   But they told me last night orally, just as you did, that

D   They stand ready?

P   With head erect, they said, Look, we will leave in a minute. We will leave today, do whatever you want." I said, "No, you are going to have to wait until we get some evidence." You know what I mean?

D   Uh, Huh.

P   I gather you agree with me.

D   That is what I do and the question is timing and—

P   Let's get Dean's advice as to how we handle this from now on. What is your advice?

D   Well, I would say you should have the letters in hand and then, based on what you learn from Petersen, you can make a judgment at the time. I think you are still five steps ahead of what will ever emerge publicly. I don't think—

P   I think they caught (inaudible) somebody told me that the *Post* according to Ziegler has something they are running tomorrow. Magruder talking around and everything. I don't know.

D   Well, I know some of the things Magruder said. He said that the prosecutors had asked him a number of questions about Ehrlichman and Haldeman. There is no doubt that that will be out on the street also.

P   Then the other will come out too.

D   Uh, Huh.

P   That's my point, see.

D   Fortunately, I am hoping that the ultimate resolution of this thing is that no one has any problems and that is possible.

428

P   Legally?

D   Legally.

P   That's right, which I hope is your case too. In other words when I say anything about the White House Staff—not you, not Colson, or Haldeman because—(expletive omitted). Let me make this point again. I need—we know there is. Ziegler has always said it was oral.

D   That's right.

P   Right. But you remember when you came in, I asked you the specific question "Is anybody on the White House staff involved in it?" You told me, "No."

D   That's right. And I have no knowledge—

P   You still believe that—

D   Yes sir, I do.

P   But you did tell me that in the aftermath there were serious problems.

D   That's right.

P   Right. And, I said, "Well, let's see what they are."

D   And now you are beginning to see what they are. They are potential, technical, obstruction of justice problems.

P   I talked to Petersen last night and he made exactly the same point. He said the obstruction was morally wrong. No, not morally. He said it may not have been morally wrong and it may not have been legally wrong, but he said from the standpoint of the Presidency you can't have it. So, he seems to think that the obstruction of justice thing is a (expletive omitted) hard thing to prove in court.

D   That's right.

P   Which I think should be some comfort to you.

D   Well, my lawyer tells me, you know, that, "legally you are in damn good shape."

P   Is that right? Because you're not—You were simple helping the defendants get their fees and their—What does he say?

D   In that position, I am merely a conduit. It is very technical, very technical. I am a conduit to other people. That is the problem.

P   What was the situation, John? The only time I ever heard any discussion of support for the defense fund was (inaudible). I guess I should have assumed somebody was helping them. I must have assumed it. But I must say people were good in a way because I was busy. Was when you mentioned to me something about hard-hitting problem. But that was handled by Mitchell. Was that true or what?

D The last time we had a request was the week before sentencing.

P He hit you at a dinner or something?

D No, no. O'Brien, who was one of the lawyers who was representing the Re-Election Committee, was asked by Hunt to meet with him. He came to me after the meeting and said that Hunt asked that the following message be passed to you. I said, "why me?" He said, "I asked Hunt the same question."

P You, Dean—or me, the President?

D Passed to me, Dean.

P He had never asked you before?

D No.

P Let me tell you. What did you report to me on though. It was rather fragmentary, as I recall it. You said Hunt had a problem—

D Very fragmentary. I was—

P I said, "Why, John, how much is it going to cost to do this?" That is when I sent you to Camp David and said (expletive removed) "Let's see where this thing comes out."

D That's right.

P And you said it could cost a million dollars.

D I said it conceivably could. I said, "If we don't cut this thing—"

P How was that handled? Who handled that money?

D Well, let me tell you the rest of what Hunt said. He said, "You tell Dean that I need $72,000 for my personal expenses, $50,000 for my legal fees and if I don't get it I am going to have some things to say about the seamy things I did at the White House for John Ehrlichman." Alright I took that to John Ehrlichman. Ehrlichman said, "Have you talked to Mitchell about it?" I said, "No, I have not." He said, "Well, will you talk to Mitchell?" I said, "Yes I will." I talked to Mitchell. I just passed it along to him. And then we were meeting down here a few days later in Bob's office with Bob and Ehrlichman, and Mitchell and myself, and Ehrlichman said at that time, "Well is that problem with Hunt straightened out?" He said it to me and I said "Well, ask the man who may know: Mitchell." Mitchell said, "I think that problem is solved."

P That's all?

D That's all he said.

P   In other words, that was done at the Mitchell level?

D   That's right.

P   But you had knowledge: Haldeman had knowledge; Ehrlichman had knowledge and I suppose I did that night. That assumes culpability on that, doesn't it?

D   I don't think so.

P   Why not? I plan to be tough on myself so I can handle the other thing. I must say I did not even give it a thought at the time.

D   No one gave it a thought at the time.

P   You didn't tell me this about Ehrlichman, for example, when you came in that day.

D   I know.

P   You simply said, "Hunt needs this money." You were using it as an example of the problems ahead.

D   I have tried all along to make sure that anything I passed to you myself didn't cause you any personal problems.

P   John, let me ask you this. Let us suppose if this thing breaks and they ask you John Dean, "Now, John, you were the President's Counsel. Did you report things to the President?"

D   I would refuse to answer any questions unless you waive the privilege.

P   On this point, I would not waive. I think you should say, "I reported to the President. He called me in and asked me before, when the event first occurred, and passed to the President the message that no White House personnel in the course of your investigation were involved." You did do that didn't you?

D   I did that through Ehrlichman and Haldeman.

P   I know you did because I didn't see you until after the Election.

D   That's right.

P   Then you say, after the election when the McCord thing broke, the President called you in. I think that is when it was, wasn't it?

D   No. It was before the McCord thing, because you remember you told me after Friday morning that McCord's letter—you said, "you predicted this was going to happen." Because I had oh, in the week or two weeks—

P   Why did I get you in there? What triggered me getting you in?

D   Well, we just started talking about this thing.

P   But I called you and Moore together for a Dean Report, didn't I?

D   On a Wednesday morning—

P   Oh, I know what was involved. It was involving that damn executive privilege and all that.

D   The Gray things were popping. On the Wednesday morning before I asked—

P   We had three conversations to my recollection.

D   Well, sir, I think we had more than that. But, of course, we have a record of that through those people.

P   Yeah.

D   I think we had more than that.

P   I have to read this. Go ahead.

D   But the one report where I finally called Bob and said, "Bob, I don't think the President has all the facts."

P   That's right and then you came and sat in this chair and that is the first time that I realized the thing.

D   That's right.

P   Now the question: well Mr. Dean, is: "Why didn't you tell the President before?" And your answer there is, "I didn't know." That's what you told me last night. You see, I don't want you, John, to be in a position and frankly I don't want the President to be in the position, where one of his trusted people had information that he kept from him.

D   I did not know.

P   Fine. You did not know. How did you find out then? But you can handle that.

D   That's right.

P   But I did ask you and I think you should say the President authorized me to say this—I won't reveal the conversation with the President—he asked me this question. I told him this, that nobody in the White House was involved. And in addition to that to the best of my ability I kept, I guess, or how do you think you should handle this Presidential advice? Maybe you better—

D   Well, I think the less said about you, I think you say anything you want to say anything about it.

P   Well, let me tell you I am going to handle that properly and I just wanted to be sure that it jives with the facts. I can say that you did tell me that nobody in the White House was involved and I can say that you then came in, at your request, and said, "I think the President needs to hear more about this case."

D   That's right.

P   Then it was that night that I started my investigation.

D   That's right—that was the Wednesday before they were sentenced. Now I can get that date—

P   Would you do this. Get your chronology of this. Wednesday you came in and told me that, et cetera. That would be helpful for me to have. That is when I frankly became interested in the case and I said, "Now (expletive omitted) I want to find out the score." And set in motion Ehrlichman, Mitchell and—not Mitchell but a few others. OK?

D   Sure.

P   One other thing. On this privilege thing—nothing is privileged that involves wrongdoing.

D   That is correct.

P   On your part or wrongdoing on the part of anybody else. I am telling you that now and I want you when you testify, if you do, to say that the President told you that. Would you do that? Would you agree to that?

D   Yes Sir.

P   Fine. However, let me say with regard to what we call the electronic stuff they heard, and what I have now found is in the leak area of the national security area. That I consider privileged.

D   I do too.

P   And I think you should say, for example, on that. What I mean is I think in the case of the Kraft's stuff what the FBI did, they were both fine. I have checked the facts. There were some done through private sources. Most of it was done through the Bureau after we got— Hoover didn't want to do Kraft. What it involved, apparently, John, was this: the leaks from the NSC. They were in Kraft and others columns and we were trying to plug the leaks and we had to get it done and finally we turned it over to Hoover. And then when the hullabaloo developed we just knocked it off altogether. But in my view, I consider that privileged.

D   I have no intention of raising that in any conversation.

P   Have you informed your lawyers about that?

D   No.

P   I think you should not. Understand, not because it would cut anything but I do think it is privileged. But it is up to you.

D   No—I think it is privileged also.

P Support your own—and this was necessary to do. If we had had Hoover under more control, as Lyndon Johnson did, it would have been better. Now, your guess is when will you be called? Perhaps Tuesday or Wednesday or—

D I would think sometime this week.

P You don't think the thing is likely to break today?

D No, I don't.

P I wonder what Ziegler's got. He must, he seems to think something is going to break. He hasn't been in to see me and I will have to get him in later. Well, I will ask Petersen. Don't you agree with me that it is better that we make the first announcement and not the Justice Department.

D Yes I do. On your own staff.

P Oh hell, I am going to make the announcement on Magruder too. (expletive omitted) It was our campaign. I am not going to have the Justice Department—we triggered this whole thing. Don't you agree? You helped to trigger it. You know what I mean.

D When history is written and you put the pieces back together, you will see why it happened. Because I triggered it. I put everybody's feet to the fire because it just had to stop.

P That's right.

D And I still continue to feel that.

P You put Magruder's feet to the fire. Where did you see Magruder?

D I didn't. In fact, I refused to see him. That was one of the problems.

P Oh, and that's why—

D I started to talk with—I met with him in one of these outer offices at a meeting.

P What got Magruder to talk? I would like to take the credit.

D Well.

P I was hoping that you had seen him because—

D He was told, one, that there was no chance.

P As a matter of fact, he made a statement about (inaudible) around the White House. I guess this was pre-primaries—it was all committed.

P But on Magruder, come again.

D The situation there is that he and Mitchell were continuing to talk. Proceeding along the same course they had been proceeding to locking their story, but my story

434

did not fit with their story. And I just told them I refused to change, to alter my testimony. But would repeat it just as I had given it. This had to do with a number of meetings in the Department of Justice.

P   Oh yes, I remember. You told me that. I guess everybody told me that. Dean said, "I am not going down there and lie," because your hand will shake and your emotions. Remember you told me that.

D   Yes, I said that. I am incapable of it.

P   Thank God. Don't ever do it John. Tell the truth. That is the thing I have told everybody around here. (expletive omitted) tell the truth! All they do John is compound it.

P   That (characterization omitted) Hiss would be free today if he hadn't lied. If he had said, "Yes I knew Chambers and as a young man I was involved with some Communist activities but I broke it off a number of years ago." And Chambers would have dropped it. If you are going to lie, you go to jail for the lie rather than the crime. So believe me, don't ever lie.

D   The truth always emerges. It always does.

P   Also there is a question of right and wrong too.

D   That's right.

P   Whether it is right and whether it is wrong. Perhaps there are some gray areas, but you are right to get it out now.

D   I am sure.

P   On Liddy I wanted to be sure. You recall our conversation. You asked me to do something. I have left it with Petersen now and he said he would handle it. That's the proper place. When Liddy says he cannot talk with peers it must be higher authority, I am not his higher authority. It is Mitchell.

D   Well, he obviously is looking for the ultimate, but I think he is looking for the ultimate. He has the impression that you and Mitchell probably talk on the telephone daily about this.

P   You know we have never talked about this.

D   I understand that.

P   I have never talked to Mitchell about this except when whether we got the executive privilege thing.

D   Right.

P   He came in and said everyone should testify in executive session except you. Which I think, I think it should not be with executive privilege.

D   I think, Mr. President, the earlier, it will be a fizzle,

435

when Petersen finishes with his—

P   You don't think we can hold to executive privilege anyway do you, John?

D   To hold on executive privilege?

P   Tell me your version what should we do?

D   I think if there are indictments down there in that court room, none of us will be able to go up to testify. I think the Watergate is just going to be totally carved out of the Ervin Hearings.

P   That's Watergate and then the other stuff is not that important, Segretti and all that?

D   Segretti and all that stuff is not that important. They will try. They can have a lot of fun with it, but it is not very meaningful.

P   So you think that Liddy thought thay my calling Mitchell would be typical. Well, we covered that last night. You were there. Is that enough?

D   Petersen will tell you if it doesn't—

P   You tell me if you don't think it is enough—

D   No, I think it is enough.

P   I am going to expect you—after all, you are still the Counsel around here—

D   Laughter

P   No, I am serious. You've got to advise me the same with Haldeman and Ehrlichman as long as you are around here, we've got to—

D   Well, I want to lay one thing out. I think there is a mythical belief—Now, I have not talked to Bob or John about this—they don't have a problem Mr. President. And I am not really sure that they do, but I am telling you, they do.

P   A problem? There is no question about it. Petersen made the point. I said, "Tell me what the facts are." And he said. "The problem is that they are going to get splashed, and when they get splashed, you've got a problem, Mr. President." Now then he goes on to say that as far as the legal form of obstruction is concerned and he covers all three of you here, it is a very difficult case to prove. Do you agree with that?

D   Uh, huh. That's fine.

P   You see that is the point. I know it would work. I am speaking not in personal terms.

D   It is a technical case and it is a tough case.

P   It's a tough one to prove. What does he mean by that?

D   Apparently, my lawyer said, "Now, I have won

436

cases on this with tougher facts than you've got I will assure you." It would not be a—

P So that is their real culpability, both Ehrlichman and Haldeman are in on the obstruction, is that your point?

D It would be a very good idea if they had counsel.

P I told them last night they ought to get lawyers so I am one step ahead of you there. Is there anything else you think I should do? You don't think I should—I am not going to let the Justice Department break this case, John.

D I understand. You've got to break it. You are breaking it. Well, (expletive omitted) that is what we have done.

D That's right.

P I could have told you to go to Camp David and concoct a story couldn't I? And you have never heard that said, have you?

D No Sir.

P In fact, I think I covered a little of that (inaudible). But on the other hand, it was your job to tell me, wasn't it?

D Uh, huh.

P And you have. Basically what you have done—no, you told me the truth though. You've told me the truth. It was your job to work for the President, the White House staff and they were not involved in the pre-thing. But then you thought the post-thing. You thought about it and that is why you decided, as you said,

D I thought we should cut the cancer right off because to keep this whole thing—

P Look, one thing I want to be sure. When you testify, I don't want you to be in a position, and I don't want the President to be in a position, that his Counsel did not level with him. See my point?

D There is no point that I have not leveled with you, as you should know.

P Now when they say, "Now Mr. Dean, why didn't you tell the President—did you know about this? Why didn't you tell the President?"

D That is a PR situation Mr. President. The U. S. Attorneys are not going to ask me questions asking what I said to the President and what I didn't.

P Well, I frankly think—I would hope you can help on the PR there by saying—

D I will be happy to help on it.

P I would like for you to say—and you are free to talk. You are to say, "I told the President about this. I told the President first there was no involvement in the White House. Afterwards, I told the President that I—" And the President said, "Look, I want to· get to the bottom of this thing, period." See what I am driving at—not just the White House. You continued your investigation, et cetera, and the President went out and investigated on his own. Which I have done, believe me. I put a little pressure on Magruder and a few of

D   Uh, huh.

P   And as a result of the President's actions this thing has been broken.

D   That's right.

P   Because also I put pressure on the Justice Department—I told Kleindienst—(expletive omitted)

D   No, I think you are in front right now and you can rest assured everything I do will keep you as far as—

P   No, I don't want, understand when I say don't lie. Don't lie about me either.

D   No, I won't sir—you—

P   I think I have done the right thing, but I want you to—if you feel I have done the right thing, the country is entitled to know it. Because we are talking about the Presidency here.

D   This thing has changed so dramatically. The whole situation since I gave you the picture

P   Since you sat in that chair—

D   In that chair over there and gave you what I thought were the circumstances, the potential problems. You have done nothing but try to get to the bottom of this thing, and—

P   I think so. Well, I said, "Write a report." But my purpose was you write a report as I said, "I want the Segretti stuff. Put everything else. Was the White House involved? You know, et cetera." How about—one last thing. Colson. You don't think they are going to get him into something?

D   I think he has some technical problems close also. I don't know if he has any. To the best of my knowledge, he had no advance knowledge of this thing. ·

P   Right. I suppose the key there is Hunt. He was so close to Hunt. I just want to know for my own benefit. As I told you last night, I don't want to get out there in front and have someone say "What about Chuck Colson?"

D   Chuck swore up and down to me—

P   I have got to say—to you John Dean—was Colson involved?

D   I have no information that he was at all.

P   Post? The two things you mentioned last night.

D   That and let's face it the other technical jobs, you know.

P   Yeah.

D   All the obstruction is technical stuff that mounts up.

P   Well, you take, for example, the clemency bit. That is solely Mitchell apparently and Colson's talk with Bittmann where he says he will do everything I can because as a friend.

D   No, that was with Ehrlichman.

P   Hunt?

D   That was with Ehrlichman.

P   Ehrlichman with whom?

D   Ehrlichman, and Colson and I sat up there. Colson presented his story to Ehrlichman regarding it and then John gave Chuck very clear instructions on going back and telling him, "Give him the inference he's got clemency but don't give him any commitment."

P   No commitment.

D   Right.

P   That's alright. No commitment. I have a right to say here—take a fellow like Hunt or a Cuban whose wife is sick or something and give them clemency for that purpose—isn't that right?

D   That's right.

P   But John specifically said, "No commitment," did he?

D   Yes.

P   And then Colson went on apparently to—

D   I don't know how Colson delivered it—

P   To Hunt's lawyer—isn't that your understanding?

D   Yes, but I don't know what he did or how—

P   Where did this business of the Christmas thing get out, John? What in the hell is that all about it? That must have been Mitchell, huh?

D   No, that was Chuck again.

P   That they would all be out by Christmas?

D   No, I think he said something to the effect that Christmas is the time the clemency generally occurs.

P   Oh yeah. Well, I don't think that is going to hurt him. Do you?

D   No.

P   Clemency is one thing. He is a friend of Hunt's. I am just trying to put the best face on it, but if it is the

439

wrong thing to do I have to know.

D   Well, one of the things, I think you have to be very careful. And this is why the issue should be very good is, if you take a set of facts and let the prosecutors who have no PR judgment but they will give you the raw facts as they relate to the law, and it's later you have to decide what public face will be put on it.

P   Oh, I understand. You can help on that, John.

D   Yes sir. Wherever I may be I will be available to help on that.

P   Well, I hope you are right—You think you testify when? Well, Petersen will decide that.

D   Yeah.

P   Do you want me to say anything to him about it?

D   No. I think my lawyers and the U. S. Attorneys office ought to continue to work in the same manner—

P   You see, I am having him report to me daily now. Which I think I should do.

D   Right.

P   So all I will say is that I am going to tell him that we have talked today and that I went over again the various materials—

D   What would be the best thing in the world is if they decide that they've got nothing but technical cases against people at the White House and they chuck them all out. That is not impossible.

P   Should I telephone him?

D   No sir.

P   That's what they ought to do.

D   That's right.

P   It may be a tough case for them to prove John.

D   Well, they started out not to do it and none of the events are even released. It could very well happen.

P   Well that's what I hope and I understand. The reason I have to have that is in case there is a break tonight. I don't want to have to call John Dean in and say, "Look, John, can I have it?" It looks like I was, like a cramp in my plans. I've got to know because I do have some knowledge there might be more involved here. All that I am saying of this, as you know, is that I have heard things from the U. S. Attorney, and from John Dean and from my own people that indicate that there could be a technical violation. Under the circumstances, I feel that it is my duty to have your resignation in hand. Of course, the President always has a resignation. How does that sound to you?

D   Well, that's right. Well, the thing is in phrasing the letter is important. You don't call anybody involved when it is their problem, so that is why I would like—

P   Well, understand those are my dictations. They are only a form for you. You work it out and work it out so that it would be one that would apply to you and work out the answer to Ehrlichman and Haldeman's letter. Just a form that I can give anybody—Strachan—

D   He has gone to USIA.

P   Well, that doesn't come to me does it?

D   Well, the whole Executive Branch—is

P   No, no I mean just let him submit his resignation to Krogh. I will get his resignation. I will tell those guys—

D   I don't think you ought to tell Strachan. I think

P   No, no, no—tell Krogh he ought to ask for his resignation.

D   I think Bob ought to do that though.

P   Bob Haldeman? Good. I will tell Bob to get Strachan and Magruder. That's your advice. Also if you do have any random thoughts on how many more we could do on the presentation of this thing, sit over in your office and think. You know what I mean, the President is in front.

D   I will give you some notes on it which I think will help.

P   Would you do that?

D   Sure I will.

P   The record. Here is what I have done—here is what I have done—here is what we think the President ought to do and when, you see what I mean? And then if we have to use these things, I pray to God we don't, you guys don't deserve them. You don't deserve them.

D   Well, the important thing is not them, it is you.

P   No—well, I know maybe it isn't me personally, it is this place.

D   It is this office and the campaign office as well.

P   Remember, be back.

D   Alright sir.

P   I would just sit there. Hang tight.

D   I couldn't be more objective Mr. President.

P   What

D   I say, don't think I have lost my objectivity at all in this. Do you know why? (unintelligible)

P   Laughter. Ok John.

Meeting: The President, Haldeman and Ehrlichman, Oval Office, April 16, 1973.
(10:50 - 11:04 am)

P Come in.

H Do you want John too?

P Yes, John too.

H The scenario worked out pretty well. Yeah—

P Well, John, let me say this is quite the operator. We first talked about the work he did before this began. I said that I wanted him to know that it is national security work. He said I consider it so. I said, "Have you told anybody about it?" He said, "No. I don't intend to. I don't intend to say a thing more than I need to say in answering questions with regard to this matter, and I will not comment on anything else of course. I will not comment on any conversation I have had with the President." So far as he is concerned, that operation will not be discussed. Of course, the problem I suppose is as far as others are concerned or were involved. But if they do John, I would play it straight out. Damn it, of course we do this.

JDE Well, I have been thinking about this a little bit. If I ever got a question like that at the Grand Jury I would have to step out and ask the U. S. Attorney to step out and tell him that its under Executive Privilege. Since it is a National Security matter, I can't answer; that I would be happy to refer it to the President for his decision as to whether I should answer that or not, but that I am in no position to respond. If he says, well then we will have to go talk to the Judge, I will say that is what I think we should do.

P Fine. And then you get to the Judge and say this involved—

JDE a highly sensitive national security—

P national security investigations involving leaks. Would you say that?

JDE No.

P No? You would not tell them what area?

JDE No. I am just not at liberty, and the procedure we have in government for a thing like that is for the witness who is put a question like that to refer it to the President for his personal review.

P   That's right.

JDE   And I would like an opportunity for that to be done.

P   I can see you being asked the question.

JDE   I kind of think that is right, but that is the process that I would have to follow.

P   I told him I would like to have that letter and he said, "What about Haldeman and Ehrlichman?" I said they have already told me that they will resign in case—naturally nobody is going to resign around here until somebody—until I get better information, until I can satisfy myself with Petersen, etc. And he said, "Well, do you mind if I take the letters and I prepare them? I would like to prepare them so that in the event I have to go to trial they won't prejudice me in that." I said, "Fine, fine. Prepare me what you think your letter of resignation should be." So there it is. So he is thinking in both terms, apparently. I am just guessing and I think that it is altogether proper, because he should have a letter of that sort. But I told him, as I told Haldeman and Ehrlichman last night, there is no question about people resigning around here. I've got their letters of resignation in hand anytime I want them. Wasn't that the proper thing to say to him?

JDE   That's fine.

HRH   He doesn't give you any indication how he is going to plead?

P   No. He said my lawyers have to work that out. But he also hits this again, John: that his lawyers think that his possible criminal liability is limited. You know what I mean, damn hard to prove. Now maybe he said basically when I see what is involved here—he mentioned something like, "sort of a (unintelligible) facing me, but it is a damn hard case"—and he said what his lawyers have told him is that the Justice Department could well come out of this without any indictments against anyone on the White House staff. I said, "What about Colson?" And he said, "Well there are three areas." He mentioned Bittman. He mentioned call to Hunt, etc.

H   The call to Magruder.

P   Oh, yes. Call to Magruder, but that's previous. I hit him hard and I said, "Now look here, John. We had received this report? What about his call? Was that true? And he said, "Yes." I said, "Do you still believe that?" And he said, "Yes." He said as far as anyone getting any (unintelligible) out, nobody got anything out of it. As for the legal side of this, John, he has some sharp lawyers and they think this is a damn hard case to prove.

JDE   For the government to prove?

H   Government thinks so, too, doesn't it?

P   As I told you today, Petersen said that the legal end is just terribly difficult.

H   It is our moral thing and the pressure. Basically it is a PR job.

P   We have to decide this and decide it in terms of many things. But I, at least, felt a little better about it than I did last night.

H   Apparently.

P   Well, now when do I receive Rogers?

H   Anytime you want. I talked to him. He is on standby.

P   How about four o'clock? Get him over here.

H   That is fine. Whatever you want.

P   Well, I will just call him and tell him to be on standby this afternoon. It may be earlier. Well, no, it is just as well. Get him over here at 4 o'clock.

H   4 o'clock.

P   E.O.B.

E   He is helping us to find counsel.

P   Good, good. How has the scenario worked out? May I ask you?

H   Well, it works out very good. You became aware sometime ago that this thing did not parse out the way it was supposed to and that there were some discrepancies between what you had been told by Dean in the report that there was nobody in the White House involved, which may still be true.

P   Incidentally, I don't think it will gain us anything by dumping of the Dean Report as such.

E   No.

P   What I mean is I would say I was not satisfied that the Dean Report was complete and also I thought it was my obligation to go beyond that to people other than the White House.

E   Ron has an interesting point. Remember you had John Dean go to Camp David to write it up. He came down and said, "I can't."

P   Right.

E   That is the tip off and right then you started to move.

P   That's right. He said he could not write it.

H   Then you realized that there was more to this than

you had been led to believe. (unintelligible)

P How do I get credit for getting Magruder to the stand?

E Well it is very simple. You took Dean off of the case right then.

H Two weeks ago, the end of March.

P That's right.

E The end of March. Remember that letter you signed to me?

P Uh, huh.

E 30th of March.

P I signed it. Yes.

E Yes sir, and it says Dean is off of it. I want you to get into it. Find out what the facts are. Be prepared to—

P Why did I take Dean off? Because he was involved? I did it, really, because he was involved with Gray.

E Well there was a lot of stuff breaking in the papers, but at the same time—

H The scenario is that he told you he couldn't write a report so obviously you had to take him off.

P Right, right.

E And so then we started digging into it and we went to San Clemente. While I was out there I talked to a lot of people on the telephone, talked to several witnesses in person, kept feeding information to you and as soon as you saw the dimensions in this thing from the reports you were getting from the staff—who were getting into it— Moore, me, Garment and others.

H You brought Len Garment in.

E You began to move.

P I want the dates of all those—

E I've got those.

P Go ahead. And then—

E And then it culminated last week.

P Right

E In your decision that Mitchell should be brought down here; Magruder should be brought in; Strachan should be brought in.

P Shall I say that we brought them all in?

E I don't think you can. I don't think you can.

H I wouldn't name them by name. Just say I brought a group of people in.

E Personally come to the White House.

P I will not tell you who because I don't want to prejudice their rights before (unintelligible)

E   But you should say, "I heard enough that I was satisfied that it was time to precipitously move. I called the
Attorney General over, in turn Petersen,"

P   The Attorney General. Actually you made the call
to him on Saturday.

E   Yes.

P   But this was after you heard about the Magruder
strategy.

E   No, before.

P   Oh.

E   We didn't hear about that until about three o'clock
that afternoon.

P   Why didn't you do it before? This is very good
now, how does that happen?

E   Well—

P   Why wasn't he called in to tell him you had made a
report, John?

H   That's right. John's report came out of the same
place Magruder's report did—

P   No. My point is

E   I called him to tell him that I had this information.

P   Yeah but, why was that? That was because we had
heard Magruder was going to talk?

E   No. Oh, I will have to check my notes again.

H   We didn't know whether Magruder was going to
talk.

E   That's right.

H   Magruder was still agonizing on what he was going
to do.

P   Dean—but you remember you came in and said
you have to tell him about it politely. Well, anyway—

H   I will tell you the reason for the hurry up in the
timing was that we learned that Hunt was going to testify
on Monday afternoon.

E   The President is right. I didn't talk to Kleindienst.
Remember, I couldn't get him.

P   Yeah.

E   I didn't talk to him until he got home from Burning
Tree, which was the end of the day, and I had already
talked to Magruder.

P   Right. But my point is when did we decide to talk
to Kleindienst? Before Magruder?

E   Oh, yes. Remember, early in the morning I said I
will see these two fellows but I've got to turn this over to
the Attorney General.

P   Which two fellows were you going to see?

E   Mitchell and Magruder.

P   With what your conclusions were?

E   I had this report and I tried all day long to get the Attorney General who was at the golf course and got him as soon as he got home for—

P   Do we want to put this report out sometime?

E   I am not sure you do, as such.

P   I would say it was just a written report.

E   The thing that I have—

P   The thing they will ask is what have you got here?

H   It was not a formal report. It was a set of notes.

P   Handwritten notes?

E   Yeah. There are seven pages, or eight pages. Plus all my notes of my interviews.

H   And then Magruder came over. Well, you don't want to put that out. You don't want to specify who came, but then you called in other individuals. Then the President met with the Attorney General and the Prosecutor and got the Head of the Criminal Division on Sunday. You met with him twice actually didn't you?

P   No, I met Kleindienst on Sunday at 1 o'clock, and then at 4:00 p.m., and then I met with Dean, Ehrlichman, you. And I also talked to Henry Petersen on three different occasions that night on the telephone.

H   Yeah.

Meeting: The President and Haldeman, Oval Office, April 16, 1973 (12:00 - 12:31 pm)

(Material unrelated to Presidential actions deleted)

P   Now we got a plan on how we stage this damn thing in the first stages. Ron's got it all worked out. We've gone over, and then he's got the use of this Advisory Group and—

P   What does this amount to Bob?

H   Well the trouble is, you can't leave that out because you get into invariables of whether you do it before or after the Magruder story is out. He feels, and they all feel, I guess, that you have to establish your position and what you have done and the scenario works pretty well on that.

P   Yeah, but you don't do a backgrounder on that.

H It works out pretty well on that. The ideal time to do it is when you break the case. Get Petersen over here. You run your backgrounder, tell your story. You know, I got into this and this is what I have done. Or Ziegler does, or however you do it. I guess you will do it. And then you say this has led, as we fully suspected it would, to the next major step. That Mr. Petersen here will describe which is the status of the case today. And then Petersen says "As the President has reviewed these steps, and I can tell you today that we have broken the case and that Jeb Magruder, one of the principal figures in this, has given us a full report on exactly what did transpire. It clearly establishes by his own testimony his own guilt as a high official of the Re-Election Committee and provides charges against others which we are pursuing with the same diligence that we have up to now, and I will not discuss the others. We will get to that and report to you periodically as developments take place. But this is following up proper processes and I am not going to jeopardize the rights of others. He could say that I am not going to say anything, and nothing should be said, that will jeopardize the rights of the defendants, but I also am not going to say anything that will jeopardize our prosecution because we are moving on people and we are going to get them." Ron will mention to you, and Steve chatted with me, Len Garment, as you would expect, has followed your orders that he steep himself in Watergate. He has steeped himself in the Watergate and now says it is imperative that he meet with you for at least five minutes, preferably prior to 2 O'clock today, to report to you. And what he will say to you is that it is clear to him that you are in possession of knowledge that you cannot be in possession of without acting on. And that your action has to include cutting cleanly and that you've got to remove me and probably Ehrlichman, although he has an interesting thesis, according to Ron—I have not talked to Len—which is at least worth considering, which is that I move ahead of the game now, put out my whole story, including the factual details without pulling any punches of my, you know, that $350,000 fund. Yes, I sent it back to the Committee—and I go into specifics. That I understand that Mr. Strachan delivered it to Mr. LaRue and that my motive was not to provide funds for the defendants. My motive was to move these funds back where they belonged, but I have to agree that I fully recognized that LaRue's motive in accepting

448

money was, as I had been told at least, was a need to provide money for the defendants, to provide legal fees and to provide support for their families. And I acted at all times at the instigation of and through John Dean. In other words I didn't do any of this. John Dean came to me and said we need this and I knew I wanted to get rid of the money and said this is the way to do it, etc. And I must say that John Dean, the President's Counsel, through whom I was working and who was my only contact in this matter, at no time advised me that I was involved in doing anything that was illegal or improper and I would assume and have to act on the assumption that Dean got away with it.

P Now, look. I don't want to get into the position of—

H Hanging someone else? Well, but he is going to have hung himself at that point in time.

P But the whole point is whether he then gets off and gets on other things. See what I mean? I don't want him —he is in possession of knowledge about things that happened before this. I told him that was all National Security.

H OK. Len makes a rather interesting case which is that we have to look at this in terms of the President and the Presidency.

P Right. I'll see him.

H That is what we all say.

P Does he know what I have already done?

H I don't know.

P Peterson and all the rest?

H I don't know. Ehrlichman and Ziegler feel you shouldn't see him and that Ron should just assure him that you have all these facts and that you are moving and what he wants done is in the process of being done.

P Why don't you call and tell him (unintelligible) in and tell him that now—

H I don't think I should tell him that. John should.

P I see your point, because he is asking for you to be fired?

H Well he is suggesting a route. He mentioned a case that is a better route for me and is a better route for the Presidency.

P But you would be the first one to go out?

H Yeah. I go out and I resign. I resign and tell my story publicly. Not to the jury, but do it publicly in some fashion and tell the whole story, all the details. And say that I am absolutely clear in my own mind that I have done nothing legally or morally wrong; that that might be up to the Grand Jury to determine. Then his argument is that I am in a position—he thinks that I can bring something like that off. He feels that Ehrlichman should not try to do it because he doesn't think he can bring it off and he thinks, therefore, you've got to cover up and try to hold Ehrlichman in but if you get a problem you will just have to let him go. But at that point it is a pretty rough spot anyway.

P   Yeah - we just don't know what the situation is on Ehrlichman, on what there is.

H   No. And there are more potentials there than there are on mine. Mine I think we have them all out and we know them all and Ehrlichman's—

P   Well, there may be more potentials. I think Dean, frankly, is more inclined to give Ehrlichman a screwing than anybody else. I have that feeling.

H   Well, and if Colson gets hung up anywhere, he will go on Ehrlichman and not on me. He can't get me because I didn't work with him on any of that stuff. John did.

P   What would this be, Bob? Would this be before I said anything?

H   I don't think so. I don't know. Ron just raised this at the last minute. He wasn't even going to raise it and then he said, "Well, you might as well know how Len spins it out."

P   What the hell information has Len got that I don't have?

H   None.

P   Is he just basing this on minutia, this, that or the other thing?

H   He doesn't have anything you don't have. All he says—he says it isn't a question of the legal thing. He said there is no question but that you could get through the whole legal thing but then look up the damn road you have to go through all these trials and everything. They are going to get back into it again there—

P   That's right.

H   They are going to get into the money and where the money went. If we haven't told them by then, they are going to drag it out of us drop by drop.

P   That's right.

H   I can see it is a weak appearing case in terms of what did I think I was giving the money back to them for. Where did the money go? Now there is no question about that, some of it. I don't think all of it did. But I knew where some of it was going to go.

P   But again you guys have to see what in the hell, again what LaRue testifies. What the money was for; to shut them up, or was it to provide help for their families.

H   You see, that is the whole point. In my viewpoint it wasn't to shut them up, but that is a hard case for anybody to believe I suppose.

P   Yeah, they will say it was to keep them quiet.

H   Well, absolutely. But that - so they can't make the legal case.

P   Does Ron like this scenario of your going out?

H   No. He is opposed to it. He thinks it is wrong, but he says you know I am biased so that is a judgment call that I probably shouldn't even try to make.

P   Rogers. I will see him this afternoon.

H   I haven't raised that with Rogers.

P   Rogers has not said that either you or Ehrlichman should leave has he?

H   But he doesn't know the facts.

P   Well—could you, you know really, so that—

H   Want me to meet with him and Bill and try to fill in the facts?

P   I really think you—as to what the points of vulnerability are, and you can just do this cold turkey. Say I just wanted him to know this as I haven't made notes. I just want him to know this, all cold turkey. I have just made a few. Say that is what I want to talk to him about. Could you do that? And point out that it is my view, and others, that this is a damn arguable, damn hard, case. Would you mind doing that? Have him come over, I should say at 3:30 and I will see him at 4:00 PM.

H   Sure.

P   That would be very helpful.

P   I would just say, so that Len doesn't think that I don't want to see him, I just don't want him to tell me the obvious. That is the point. Could Ehrlichman just let Len know that the events have overtaken us? Is that dangerous? No, we better tell him.

H   He knows pretty much on that.

P   He knows about Magruder and the rest?

H   I don't know that he knows it in specific terms, but

he has come up with the same information that John did and anybody that was looking into the picture.

P Well, the reason is I think I know everything Len would be telling me -

H Oh, yeah.

P hell you know, we talked about this a week ago. You know how you handle it.

H On the way to San Clemente I made the pitch for my going out ahead, but not going into it in as much detail. If I do it now with what they've got, if I do anything I have to do everything. That's Ron's point and I think he is right on that.

P Yeah. What does Ron think about this, leaving out the PR: does he think we should try to tough it through? I am going to ask Rogers that, frankly.

H I am not sure. I think Ron would say just wait and see. You see his point is that there is no question that I will be tarnished.

P The question is whether your useability, basically,—

H And you have to evaluate that at that point and it seems to me at that point you have the option of my saying to you that I have concluded and I will. I haven't, but I will sure say it—that I have concluded that I am tarnished to the point where I can't be useful.

P Right. Your usefulness has been impaired and, therefore, we can't be useful. That's the way you put it.

H Sure, then I go out. Garment's statement is that then I go out and hit this, use the position that I have established that way from the outside to—

P To fight?

H Yeah, somehow or other. I don't exactly know how. I think he spells that out but Ron didn't get into it with me. And a—

P Let me get some (unintelligible). Was it Ron and John Ehrlichman who said they did not think I should see him? They did not think I should bother seeing Len? On what grounds?

H No. Ron is the one who saw Len.

P I was up so late last night. Go ahead.

H Yeah. Ron thought you had to see him just for internal reasons. You know, Len's so concerned about things that you almost have to see him just to keep the—

P Why don't I see him after I see Rogers? How would that be?

H That you could do easily.

P   In other words, I will have a plan in mind. I'm going to set some thoughts in my mind. I am not going to have any trouble with them.

H   Ziegler has been meeting with this group of Chappie Rose and Moore and they have been running out of there with (unintelligible).

P   Could you ask Ziegler to have Len put it on a piece of paper before I meet? That would be helpful. Tell him I am meeting with Rogers at 4:00 o'clock and would just like his recommendation on a piece of paper before that. How does that sound to you?

P   Let me say that I can move the Rogers thing up or down.

H   Can you move him up to three?

P   Well, wait a minute. 1:30 PM. I've got to get some rest this afternoon.

H   Yeah. Still, leave it at four. You might know something by then.

P   Have you filled Henry in, Bob?

H   Nope.

P   You haven't? He's got enough problems in Laos. I haven't. Somebody else—he seems to know of it.

H   Well, Garment took it upon himself to go meet with Henry and Al Haig to discuss his concern about the whole situation, apparently.

P   Well, what the hell did he do that for?

H   ON the basis that he thought there was a real danger and threat to the Presidency and that—

P   Maybe I don't want a memo from him first. What do you think? Maybe he just better do it orally.

H   Well, John thought he should have written to you. That that is what he should have done at the beginning. Maybe you have a problem with that. That means the Secretaries got to write it up.

P   Yep, yep. Well just say, tell him that I am meeting with Rogers this afternoon. I think somebody should say that. Who has he put the request through? Through John?

H   No, he just sent it up through Steve Bull. Ron knew he was. He is working with Ron now, rather than John.

P   Ok.

H   You know, it is impossible. That is why I hope Rogers can stay cool and sort of above it. It is impossible for any of us—

P   All the concerned people. If we could get a feel. I just have a horrible feeling that we may react.

P   Reacting like Dean?

H   Yes. That we are way over dramatizing.

P   That's my view. That's what I don't want to do either.

H   As I say, that is self-serving too, so its—

P   Well, as you know of course, that would be the tendency. That is the trouble with Garment. I wanted him to get into this on the legal side. I didn't mean, I must say, I really didn't mean for him to get into the problems of each day and all that, because Len always reacts to things. Am I right that we have got to do something to restore the credibility of the Presidency.

H   Of course you know the credibility gap in the old days. Len is the panic button type. If we had reacted in Garment's way in other things, we wouldn't be where we are. That doesn't mean he isn't right this time, incidentally.

P   I know. It would be very helpful to me if you could see Rogers yourself. I would get him in at 3:00 o'clock, give him an hour on the whole damn thing. I wonder if you and John shouldn't see him together?

H   I would like to if that is ok with Bill.

P   Yeah. Will you ask him?

H   I will ask him. Say that we want to give him a full run before he meets with you.

P   I have suggested, John, too, because he has made a study and we want you to come in. In balance, he can meet with just you, but I prefer he meet with the two of you and then I want to see him at 4:00 o'clock.

H   Ehrlichman makes a strong case that on my making a statement or anything, that as of now that my potential—

P   Guilt?

H   Well, not guilt, but that I should not do anything without my lawyers.

P   That's my inclination. I don't think you can say a thing—

H   What can the lawyers tell me?

P   I think the time has outrun that, because Peterson has told me that you, Ehrlichman are going to be called to the Grand Jury soon. He has told me that. Under the circumstances, I could not advise you with my limited knowledge of the law. I could not advise anybody to make a statement. You know what I mean?

H   Check.

P   Because, basically, when you get in there they are going to question you on your damn statement.

H   Of course, for my dough, that is alright, because whatever I say in the statement is exactly what I say in the Grand Jury. So—

P   But, nevertheless, I wouldn't give them that opportunity. I'd keep that.

H   I think Len's view is that what you need is a bold, new, you know, really some kind of a dramatic move. Henry feels that, but Henry feels that you should go on television.

P   I know, 9:00 o'clock.

H   Which is his solution to any problem.

P   Do you believe I should do the 9:00 o'clock news?

H   On this, no.

P   I don't think so either.

H   I said, we are all steeped in this, but look at the newspaper. Where is the Watergate today?

P   Well in the country it is not that big. It is just a little bit in the evening news and it should be handled as a news story. I am not going to go on and say, look, we are in a hell of a shape. It will be a big news story, it will be a big story for a couple or three weeks. Let's face it,—

H   Yep, that's right.

P   But it is not going to be at the moment. We are going to have one hell of a time.

Meeting: The President and Petersen, EOB Office, April 16, 1973. (1:39 - 3:25 pm)

Door opening—walking
Inaudible
Inaudible

P   Yeah—I always come here in the afternoon (inaudible) tied up.

HP   That's (inaudible) great.

P   Well—I always run upstairs—that's why I'm a little panting.

HP   (Inaudible) stopped smoking

P   I get my exercise. Sit down—sit down.

HP   Four months ago I couldn't run the stairs.

P   Really?

HP   Yeah.

P   What's your age (inaudible)?

HP   52, sir

P   My, my you've got some great years ahead of you. (Inaudible)

HP   (Laughter) I stopped smoking about six years ago.

P   Right.

HP   And it didn't make any difference then. I didn't feel

P   Yeah. Let me get to two quick questions before you give me whatever you've got. Three questions—one very fundamental that (inaudible) perhaps the first two are related. I (inaudible) Dean, first Magruder, with the information that I know, it seems to me that I've got to tell the (inaudible) something about that's been done (inaudible) where it would be worse. What's your reaction to that? We got to be sure that when people ask us later that we didn't—these people that are out (inaudible).

HP   I think so. We're

P   Would that affect your case at all?

HP   I'd like that not to be done until we conclude the (inaudible)

P   With respect to?

HP   Plea.

P   Depending on the plea now (inaudible)

HP   We are trying to get the plea down. His lawyers are—reluctant on two grounds. One, whether Judge Sirica is just going to lower the boom on him.

P   Yeah.

H   And clap him in jail immediately.

P   Right.

HP   So we'll have to see Judge Sirica and see if we can't reach some understanding of that. All we would request is that he not be clapped in jail before the others against whom he's testified.

P   Like Mitchell and (inaudible)

HP   Go to jail. Secondly

P   LaRue

HP   Yes

HP   Secondly, his lawyers are most concerned about what action the—Senator Ervin and his Committee will take. And I instructed them to tell his lawyers that I'll go talk to Senator Ervin.

P   Is that your intention?

HP   Well that is - yes sir, I think we can make very persuasive arguments on a fair trial and a free press with a man whose pleading guilty and a potential witness.

P   How about the others?

HP   You can't guarantee success.

P   What about the others? What really can you do in this case? I would think you'd have a hell of a problem on—like getting a fair trial for Mitchell on this—and if—in case the Ervin Committee moves forward.

HP   I think this.

P   (Inaudible? What are you going to do?

HP   Oh I—that would—in effect we'd have to—what I propose to do is to ask Senator Ervin to hold up.

HP   To get him . . .

P   He won't agree with it.

HP   If he doesn't agree we'll just have to go our separate course.

P   There's nothing we can do to—try to enjoin the committee?

HP   I don't think so. Judge Sirica's even instructed all those people to cooperate with the Senate Committee—(laugh)

HP   (Inaudible) very far with him.

P   That's (inaudible)—that's before (inaudible).

HP   Ah.

P   Yeah.

HP   And if we go to - if we file an injunction action you know, we're going to have another constitutional confrontation between the judiciary and the committee.

P   But you've got to tell Senator Ervin that his continued investigation will jeopardize the rights of the defendants and also will jeopardize the possibilities of prosecution.

HP   That's right.

P   Understand—not on a case of (inaudible) but (inaudible) I'm speaking of a case of a Mitchell.

HP   Precisely right.

P   It would well—I would think, seriously jeopardize your chances on the prosecution. If I were Mitchell's attorney, I would raise holy hell about that, wouldn't you?

HP   Precisely right; yes sir.

P   I think he will.

HP   Yes sir.

HP   And of course, the Delaney case and you probably remember it, (inaudible).

P   Oh yeah. The Irish.

HP   Yes sir.

P   What happened there?

HP   Well (inaudible) we requested a Committee to hold off and they did not and as a consequence of all that the case was reversed on the basis of prejudicial publicity and (inaudible) a fair trial.

P   What was the name of that? Knowland? Or

HP   Delaney.

P   Delaney?

HP   Yes sir.

P   He was an Irishman. (Inaudible) First, (inaudible) —I shouldn't convict him—probably not.

HP   I honestly don't recall, Mr. President . . . I think that their (inaudible) . . .

P   Now, the second—The second is this then (inaudible) that I think well just is just to say we discussed it so we got the record clear. Use the—my now charge representing me in this thing. In other words—you understand now, you're talking only to me

HP   Yes, Sir.

P   and there's not going to be anybody else on the White House staff.

HP   Yes, Sir.

P   In other words, I am acting counsel and everything else. I don't want it from anybody else (inaudible). The only other person I possibly could think of would be Dick Moore but I he's a damn good guy.

HP   He's a valuable man,

P   Huh (?)

HP   He's a valuable man,

P   I might say that I—if I find some day—maybe something that I want to get to you but I am just so tied up I may ask him to do it. Will that be all right with you?

HP   Yes sir.

P   You have confidence in him?

HP   Yes sir.

P   Now you understand he's a friend of Mitchell's and a friend of everybody around here, but I think totally trustworthy and I don't think you've got him involved in the—with this damn thing.

HP   There's one reservation . . .

P   He might tell somebody else?

HP   No sir. . . . and well, I'll have to check it out. Yesterday, last evening, at my home when I was talking to

458

Silbert, we went into the . . . One of them mentioned Dick Moore. It was just a slip of the lip—no place in the conversation, and I meant to go back at them and ask them why 'cause they should not know him. I'll have to check that out with.

P   Well then don't (inaudible)—let's just—better keep it with me then.

HP   All right.

P   I need caution—I don't want to—I don't want any question raised on this. All I—you have told me now that you do not want Magruder's (inaudible) to have him canned today. Correct?

HP   Today.

P   That's right.

HP   I'll get back to you on that.

P   Because I told you that he has to go.

HP   Yes, Sir.

P   All right, but you think it might jeopardize your chance to bargain with the plea? Is that it?

HP   Yes, Sir.

P   How could we it do that? He knows he's going to have to go, and (inaudible)

HP   We haven't tied that down yet

P   Hmm?

HP   You see, I mean if he thinks we're being—if we pull the string too tight on him before these other things are tied down. We may be (inaudible).

P   Now but you've got all this information (inaudible) you can say that other people now as well as Dean—I (inaudible) Dean—what we do about him. I got him into (inaudible) this morning and I said look I think I've got to have in hand your resignation. He's writing it now.

HP   Right.

P   And I will get it from him later today and I don't want to (inaudible) him. I said I don't want to—he wanted to spend a week (inaudible) write one that would not be harmful to (inaudible). Well I know—I've got to have it—and obviously he can't continue as Counsel. Do you have any problems with that?

HP   I don't have any problem with that. But you do, because that is one of the reasons that I wanted you to see Dean. What you do between you and Dean is something else with a—other than what the prosecution does—

P   My point was . . .

HP   . . . The prosecution has a relationship where if

we as the prosecution were requesting you . . .

P Oh.

HP to can Dean as a pressure tactic.

P O (inaudible). I see. Why?

HP But, I have no objection to your reaching an agreement and (inaudible) are the alternatives.

P Yeah. I—see I had a different impression last night. Remember we talked and I—you left the clear impression to me that you didn't think—you said (inaudible) I said wait.

HP I, yes, because I need a lot more to—recommend to you that he be—he be canned.

P Whatever (inaudible). Suppose—put yourself in my position now—now put yourself in that your Counsel to the President now—now don't be on the prosecution side—(inaudible) our side. Dean, I think, wants to have his resignation effective after he has made his deal with you. Now (inaudible) the prosecution.

P Now—query—should I allow him to do that? I'm President and I know what the—I know what his situation is. If you were President (inaudible).

HP As President I would take his resignation and

P You would

HP Yes. As prosecutor I would do something different. But from your point of view I don't think you can sit on it. I think we have the information under control but that's a dangerous thing to say in this city.

P Ah

HP And if this information comes out I think that you should have his resignation and it should be effective. We both just (inaudible).

P There's this. This is something that we're going—you know—probably great difference of opinion in the Department of Justice (inaudible). More important for the Department of Justice is (inaudible). Presidency have (inaudible) as a result of some diligent efforts its own (inaudible). Now with (inaudible) I don't have to announce the (inaudible). We have a situation where the U.S. Attorney, in effect, the (inaudible) thing when the President has to go in and explain (inaudible).

HP (Inaudible) for a purpose.

P Yeah but I've got to say it before he pleads. sure (inaudible).

HP Yeah. The.

P Yeah. See what I am getting at is this. The only

things that I would say—I can say that I (inaudible) and I've got this information and the case has been broken and I've got to say that and if the Department of Justice is going to (inaudible) I've got to.

HP   Well what I'd do.

P   I've got to be able to say this.

HP   And we don't have any objection to that.

P   All right.

HP   A - a

P   When do you want me to. When can I say this?

HP   (Inaudible) always say shy. But what we want to tie it to is the Magruder plea.

P   Yeah but I've got to say it before he pleads. I've got . . .

HP   Can't you say—yes—but can't you make the announcements?

P   Well why don't you (inaudible) Magruder (inaudible)

HP   It depends upon the negotiations.

P   They're going to believe this (inaudible) if it breaks today. I don't want—you and I don't want the *Washington Post* to break it.

HP   No sir.

P   And after all—we have broken this—you, the Department of Justice, damn it—you see—demonstrated that the judicial system does work—isn't that right?—sometimes it takes time.

HP   I'd say that's correct.

P   But it does work.

HP   A - a.

P   You see I can't have Magruder go into open court and then I come in laying (inaudible) out of this and that the other thing. I'd like to explain (inaudible).

HP   No - that's not what I had in mind.

P   I've got to (inaudible). Before Magruder—as a matter of fact, why not today? What I had in mind is that I would—would go out with you—and at that point answer any questions. And I would say (inaudible) and talk about any individuals and so forth and so on—that are—broad ranging—and you know—proceedings going on I can't furnish you right this (inaudible) in your own minds 'til you see what you come up with, what we can do. Now then, of course, after that (inaudible) they aren't going to object to that I'm sure—there will be plenty of kudos and glory (inaudible) just fine.

HP   (Inaudible).

P (Inaudible) something, but the need, as you see, we've got to show that the President takes the initiative. When I get backed up here as this, Henry, I can't be here (inaudible).

HP You're absolutely right, and my only hesitancy is that's what you sense is this—what we do can't be counter-productive. If it serves to put us out in front and serves also to cause cooperating witnesses to withdraw them it's counter-productive.

P Which is (inaudible). You're talking about (inaudible)?

HP And Magruder and Dean and who could tie it down.

P Yeah.

HP You know with Dean and Magruder. You know we have two potential witnesses—only one who has agreed to be a witness and . . .

P On Dean, I guess perhaps you have mixed emotions on that as to (inaudible)—that might—my getting his resignation today might affect to tie it down too.

HP Yes sir.

P You feel very strongly about that.

HP Yes sir.

P Well let me put it this way—suppose I get his resignation dated today and he hands it to me and I'll say, John, this resignation is accepted the moment that you put any (inaudible) with this (inaudible). That - that—you see if I . . .

HP I have no objection to your taking his resignation immediately.

P Yes.

H My problem is with the announcement.

P Oh—we couldn't announce it to (inaudible)

HP I could tell him and I could tell his counsel. Well on that sort of relationship between you and the President of the United States. And I don't even intervene in that. You've got no right to sit down here, talk to us and expect me not to ask for your resignation. That doesn't bother me. It's the announcement part that bothers me, because . . .

P All right, fine what now? How do you see—how do you visualize all that we can get to keep ahead of the curve with regard to the announcement on this—on the Magruder thing and so forth. Can we make any announcement today about your activity—your position and—well I—no that'll tip everybody off—is that the problem?

HP   Well I think so. The meeting could (inaudible) seems to me is—what about Kleindienst?—it's an expression of dissatisfaction on your part (inaudible).

P   O that's right—that's right. You've got to . . .

HP   How do you handle it?

P   (Inaudible) where he wants them to (inaudible). Get it done(?) and get it done today.

HP   I'll call him.

P   (Inaudible) out.

HP   Oh I can't say he's with 'em. We're all outside in a storm.

P   But this—what's (inaudible) think of this?

HP   Personally, (inaudible) well I've been (inaudible) and have advised the Jury of that fact and two that Gray, from what Titus who has (inaudible) of the (inaudible) over there has to go in to see Sirica.

P   I don't think (inaudible) that (inaudible).

HP   That's (inaudible). I don't think he will do anything unless it's in the current (inaudible) of proceeding he's in (inaudible). I can't conceive a point which of Titus and—if there.

P   This timing thing I think is terribly important you know.

HP   I think it is.

P   Can't have the President—after all—after all these months and what we've gone through and now once I have learned something of it I say "bah."

HP   No - no. Well

P   Better we.

HP   I think we ought to talk of alternatives in general terms.

P   We can't. No, the announcement—what I had in mind would be (inaudible) announcement—still to the (inaudible) going to name several other people who were involved . . . (inaudible) because of the people named (inaudible) language used. (Inaudible) some people (inaudible) judgment (inaudible) matter for the President (inaudible) special, I'm going to call him special counsel (inaudible) this case (inaudible) possibility before he walks into that open court (inaudible) can't get to that today (inaudible) meeting with (inaudible)?

HP   (Inaudible) question. (Inaudible) I told him one, I would be willing to go (inaudible) and advise his lawyers of that fact and two that they—and by that I mean Titus who has the best relationship with Sirica over there—is going to have to wait and see Sirica, ah—

P (Inaudible)

HP That's a problem. That's risk we would have to take. I don't think he will. I don't think he will do anything unless it is in the context of a proceeding in his court. I can't conceive of him urging the (inaudible) of Titus and (inaudible).

P (Inaudible) timing on this is terribly important you know, because

HP I understand it is

P You can't have the press—after all these months and what we have gone through and all. Once, I find something out—I say— ACT!

P Better we . . .

HP Well, I think we ought to talk of (inaudible) in more general terms, Mr. President.

P You can't. No—the announcement—what I had in mind would be—the announcement—stick to developments and if he's going to name—several other people were involved (inaudible) other people—then my concern—were wrong and (inaudible) abuse and something has been charged. And that the President (inaudible)— I'm going to tell them that the (inaudible) Counsel has resigned.

HP Why can't you not have Ziegler make a statement that—a—well—that you as the President have taken it upon yourself to personally inquire into the Watergate situation.

P All right - what else?

HP And.

P That I designated Henry Petersen as my special counsel?

HP That's fine—and that—particular (inaudible) been made that I am not in a position to disclose, but there have been major developments.

P Say that the President has done (inaudible)—Sunday—but I've been in it for two weeks actually now and it's (inaudible) happened there (inaudible) incidentally, (inaudible)—a month ago I got Dean in and said (inaudible) a report (inaudible) Camp David and write a report. The report was not frankly accurate. Well it was accurate but it was not full. And he tells me the reason it wasn't full, was that he didn't know. Whether that is true or not

I don't know. Although it wasn't I'm told. But I am satisfied with it and I think I've read enough in the (inaudible) (inaudible) papers up here. So then I put Ehrlichman to work on it. Ehrlichman then worked for two weeks and he got materials together which—virtually—this is before—he got together a case basically hypothetical—based on—without orders—without knowing what the hell Magruder was going to say, which is (inaudible) what led to these same conclusions. Get my point? (Inaudible) called Kleindienst on Saturday, (inaudible) before Kleindienst (inaudible) and said look I've got this. Saturday afternoon Magruder, as you know came in. So we've seen—we got the wire about the same time but I—if it—it's a pretty good record in that respect. Because I had worked (inaudible) I said now damn it get these facts.

HP   It was Friday, you say, sir?

P   (Inaudible) Friday—Friday the thirteenth I guess.

P   Friday the thirteenth—but was it Friday?

HP   Yes sir.

P   Are you (inaudible)

HP   Yes sir, because I was down on my boat (inaudible)

P   Well—what could—(inaudible)—I could say that in the past (inaudible) the President—the President for the past two weeks conducted a personal investigation into this (inaudible) have used Ehrlichman, and a, where as Ehrlichman is involved in a way that you might be (inaudible) absolutes (inaudible)—absolutely impeccable going after facts.

HP   Well I'm concerned about that because of a . . .

P   If John is not . . .

HP   (Inaudible) Ehrlichman

P   Huh?

HP   In connection with Ehrlichman, I've got to point out something to you.

P   Yeah.

HP   You'll recall, one of the things that Dean says about Ehrlichman and—he was instructed by Ehrlichman to deep six certain documents that he found in Hunt's office.

P   Yeah.

HP   And that he thought better of that and gave it to Pat Gray.

P   Right.

HP   Well—several months ago I asked Pat Gray—a

very casual conversation—did you ever receive any documents from John Dean. (Inaudible) Gray tells me was that he did not and he said no. And I just let it go at that.

P   My God.

HP   Thereafter I heard he had also told Fred Fielding that he had given certain documents to Gray.

P   Who told you—Dean?

HP   Dean told me he also had told Fielding—Fred Fielding. When I leave here I'm going to stop by Fred's office and talk to him. Today I went up to see Gray. Well I asked him, he said that was absolutely untrue. He said I have never received anything from Hunt's office except through the Agency. Dean never gave me anything. So I'm going back to Dean on it, and I'm gonna leave here and talk to Fielding, and see what his story is on it. Incidentally, I have no (inaudible) that Fielding is involved. I just want to know what Dean told him about this.

P   Well I don't know, but you better ask Ehrlichman, too.—Dean (inaudible)

HP   We will ask all of them . . .

P   He was the one who was supposed to have (inaudible) and then told me I said what the hell's the story on this. He said that was never done. He said we were just talking about—what the hell is this? In fact, let me point out what I know—for whatever it's worth because I did conduct my investigation after I got this from you. I said what is this for what is this stuff. He said—basically, let me just say, what's been done and the wiretapping material and all that business—all of that was, of course, turned over to the (inaudible).

P   (Inaudible) in the safe also, were documents—documents that had no relation to the Watergate whatever. They were what they call political documents.

P   They said—he said we just sealed that up and,

HP   (Inaudible) Gray

P   (Inaudible) then you have both Ehrlichman and (inaudible). Word against Ehrlichman's and Dean's

HP   Maybe Dean—maybe Gray has to stimulate his recollection—maybe he got an envelope that he never opened. Strange as that may seem. But he said categorically no.

P   Well he's right in saying any documents about this case apparently.

HP   That's right and I explained to him that these

were not documents relating to Watergate, and he said I never got a thing. In this crisis, atmosphere that denied it, he denied it (inaudible) two months ago when I asked him casually. I don't know (inaudible) to reconcile that, but . . .

P How do you reconcile that? How the hell are you going to reconcile that?

HP Well, I guess we (inaudible). Ehrlichman, at some stage (inaudible). under oath on it. For one thing, we'd better get Fielding (inaudible)

P (Inaudible). Call the Director of the FBI?

HP We may have to.

P (Inaudible) it's worth, because Ehrlichman tells me the same story. I think Gray did get something. And probably destroyed it.

HP Probably (inaudible) he did.

P My suggestion is that—I mean—I have alerted—I have a suggestion—I think you better talk with Ehrlichman.

HP All right.

P Because Ehrlichman's recollection is that—he—I think he thinks he (inaudible)—you better tell him—better tell him what Gray has told you though.

HP (Inaudible).

P (Inaudible) now this is what he says and it may be that Gray just hasn't any recollection of what the hell it was and thought this was—well if it's not related to this case and fearful there is no place for political stuff in the FBI—that maybe was what he was thinking of. I don't know—I don't know what the hell the justification was—he could have—then he might be a rationale if there is a rationale.

P Gray says he didn't get anything?

HP Gray said he didn't (inaudible).

HP I think that (inaudible) all this down in this notebook

P Oh.

HP I don't think there's anything here that I didn't tell you yesterday except Strachan came in this morning.

P Yeah.

HP And he was warned of his rights and despite considerable fencing he didn't want to answer any questions. So they've sent him out and told him to get a lawyer and come on back this afternoon.

P Oh he pled self-incrimination?

HP   No—they didn't meet in Grand Jury. It was just a pre-appearance interview and they sent him out to get a lawyer. He didn't want to talk about it.

P   OH.

HP   So he is coming back—supposed to come back this afternoon with counsel.

P   He's not talking? I thought he was going to testify.

HP   Whether or not he—well, he may testify—but at this point.

P   Why didn't he have his lawyer with him this morning?

HP   Apparently he didn't think it was necessary—You see he appeared before the Grand Jury last week.

P   Yeah.

HP   And the questions asked were very easy—frankly, they were about political contribution violations and whether or not—Hunt and Liddy and (inaudible) expected to be more of the same.

P   All right, the point . . . (inaudible) Take this situation about this deep six thing.

HP   Yes, sir.

P   Is that enough to hang Ehrlichman on?

HP   No sir—I don't think it is. Well (inaudible) my point . . .

P   Well Ehrlichman says deep six it. I mean, he says we were talking about this and Dean says (inaudible) put it in. (Expletive removed) all it is (inaudible) is just a (inaudible) with the damn Bureau again. (Expletive!)

HP   Well, that's a . . .

P   (Inaudible) I pray to God (inaudible). Don't let me judge between these guys—these two guys?

HP   Okay. The second thing I wanted to mention to you, Mr. President, you asked whether or not there was any problem about having the (inaudible). I don't think there is. But there is this situation you should be aware of.

P   Yeah.

HP   Part of Magruder's testimony goes to the obstruction of justice—subordination of perjury, and he says that lawyers were involved, and Mardian was involved and that he cultured his testimony, cross-examined him on it. Dean was (inaudible).

P   Yeah.

HP   Ah

P   Pardon me, Dean coached him too?

HP   Yes sir.

P   On that

HP   Both of them

HP   Then, after he appeared Dean called and said you know what went on? And I said, well, (inaudible) a good witness in his own behalf, but, the jury just was unable to swallow . . .

P   The story . . .

HP   That he or anybody else was (inaudible)

P   You told (inaudible)

HP   The amount of money. Yes, Sir.

P   Now why the hell didn't Dean tell me that?

HP   That—but in any event I guess—the Grand Jury did believe him on that.

P   (Expletive)

HP   At that point—that was in the course of the in-quiry, because he was allegedly developing for you as President's Counsel to keep you informed of what was going on.

P   He said that—he (inaudible).

HP   But Magruder says then Dean called Magruder and said—you passed. I have talked to Petersen—you passed in your Grand Jury appearance. Now the . . .

P   What did you tell Magruder (inaudible)?

HP   Dean?

P   Dean—I'm sorry.

HP   I told Dean that he made a good witness in his own behalf.

P   But the Jury didn't believe him?

HP   But the Jury had some difficulty in accepting the story with respect to the money—that is—that anyone could . . .

P   Oh you mean the money for the bugging.

HP   (inaudible) hundred thousand dollars and not ask what the hell Liddy was doing with it, which is what Magruder was testifying to.

P   OK—go ahead.

HP   Dean then calls Magruder, according to Magruder, and says Petersen says you've passed. Now that has great relevance in terms of the subornation of perjury charge. And the possibilities are . . .

P   Well, when (inaudible) after—Dean said, you passed?

HP   Yeah—the possibility is that I could be witness.

P   Dean told Magruder—you passed. That's what Magruder says.

HP   That's right.

P   So you—and that—how's that involve subornation and perjury? Oh, I see.

HP   See they previously could engage in the cultured story—then go in. Dean was party to that. After he testifies, Dean calls me and says how did he do? I tell him. Dean then passes it on to Magruder, in effect—and "I told you it would be all right if you just testify the way we said, Petersen says you passed." I—conceivably, I could be a witness on that issue.

P   But

HP   Silbert

P   Is?

HP   No, no sir—he is not (inaudible). (Inaudible) it.

P   (Inaudible not supposed to talk to you—and you were not supposed to tell Dean (inaudible).

HP   I didn't tell him(inaudible).

P   He's conducting an investigation for the President.

HP   That's right.

P   Damnit, I'm entitled to know this.

HP   And I can tell under the rule.

P   Yeah.

HP   Those that (inaudible) to the extent that it's necessary to discharge my obligation

P   Yeah.

HP   And I didn't tell him any testimony in any event.

P   I see.

HP   I told him what occurred, that is to say the Grand Jury didn't believe his story—yes he was a good witness on his own behalf.

P   That's right.

HP   But I don't think. That's

P   You characterized it rather than give him the substance of it.

HP   That's right. That's right.

P   OK. (Inaudible) on—may I have that piece of paper please.

HP   Yes sir

P   This is on Haldeman and Ehrlichman?

HP   Yes sir

P   Right?

HP   And incidentally, you asked for Colson. We have very little on Colson. Colson's alleged to have been putting pressure on as a member of the White House staff,

P   Yeah. I know—I have heard that part of it

HP   But that's all.

P   Well listen I know all that, but I don't know whether it's bull. But everybody put pressure on, but the point is whether or not Colson and/or Haldeman put it on for money

HP   We don't know that.

P   That's the point.

HP   We don't know.

P   Colson denies it—and Haldeman denies it. Haldeman says he wanted it for one purpose and Colson wanted it for another purpose. Colson used the word O'Brien at one time I understand.

HP   I don't know—we don't know that. If we learn that that's going to be very damaging piece of information because our information is that O'Brien was a specific target of—

P   Hhm?

HP   The Liddy operation.

P   See—I don't know—I don't.

HP   But we don't know that.

P   O'Brien—what the hell—(inaudible) another—or Colson—it must be—I have heard that O'Brien—you told me that I think—you must have told me that—or (inaudible)—about somebody had said get (inaudible). Mitchell—Dean said—or Dean—it must have been Dean then—Dean said that—said Magruder had said that Mitchell said get the stuff on O'Brien. Is that correct? Does that have a (inaudible)?

HP   I don't know that.

P   Does that ring a bell?

HP   I don't know that. No, Sir.

P   Well put it down—if it's relevant—somebody ought to think—I heard something about O'Brien.

HP   Is it—it is true in this sense that O'Brien was allegedly the target of the Liddy operation which was being financed with the blessing of Mitchell and Magruder and Dean. It's true in that context.

P   Oh I see.

HP   But I don't have it specifically from anyone of them.

P   Hhmm. You don't have it on Colson—I hope not.

HP   No sir—I don't have it on Colson—now we are going to interview Howard, who is a—

P   Dick Howard?

HP   Yes sir.

471

P   What do you have him on?

HP   Just on Colson's activities—you know—whether we can tie any of this down with respect to—

P   He's a clean guy I think—I think—I hope so.

HP   Well—only as a witness—we have nothing against him—we look (inaudible).

P   So, as far as thing thing you don't have that on Colson?

HP   No sir.

P   Well who is it? I saw so many people over the past (inaudible) I was sure that you told me or maybe Dean did—Dean—Dean speaks rather freely at the moment. I guess he may have told me about—he seems to know everything about Magruder and this kind of thing. Now (inaudible) telling me about what they have on Colson. You sure you didn't talk to someone about that?

HP   Yes sir. At that point that's all I know. And I just discussed this with Earl Silbert before we came up here.

P   Nothing afterwards on Colson—nothing on the aftermath.

HP   No sir.

P   Nothing on?

HP   Allegations that Colson's involved but we have nothing specific.

P   No, no, no—I understand that. What's the situation on one other thing here. (Inaudible) I want to get to the bottom of it if I can, so.

HP   If it weren't for the subject, then, otherwise we could—

P   I want to get to the bottom of this. What is the situation on—come to—let me come to Magruder again. You don't think you could get new evidence—you would not mind—would you mind that release you talked about—with Ziegler in working out—see if he could work out some sort of a statement or do you prefer to go on (inaudible) not work work out a statement? It's gonna involve you, that's the point. (inaudible) I got the point that you feel that you could say that. There have been some major developments in the case, and the past few weeks, the President has been conducting his own investigation.

HP   I think that's fine, and I wholly support that.

P   Yeah.

HP   The only reservation I have.

P   You don't want to put your name in it yet.

HP   Well I don't have—that's up to you.

P   I thought you said Sunday.

HP   I don't have any objection to that.

P   Sunday. Because—

HP   I don't want the—

P   Because—

HP   I don't want the (inaudible) defendants named.

P   What?

HP   I don't want the putitive defendants named.

P   Oh, of course not.

HP   (Inaudible), and I don't

P   Wait a minute—then how do I get you into it?

HP   You just—

P   And Kleindienst out? Because of allegations that have been made, Kleindienst has removed himself from the case, can we say that?—Well How you want me to handle Kleindienst?

HP   Well I think that's terribly sensitive, Mr. President.

P   How do we.—What do I say then about you? That Henry Petersen is acting as the President's Special Counsel? Can I say it that way?

HP   Yes, you can say it that way.

P   (Inaudible).

HP   And I think just refuse any direct questions with respect to Kleindienst.

P   Then Sunday—Sunday—he has met at great length with Henry Petersen who is acting as Special Counsel at this time.

HP   I think.

P   Huh? No?

HP   I think they—that my concern is (inaudible)

P   First, your concern is—

HP   Concerns are: One, if you say there are major developments and then you—you leave the innuendo

P   Yeah.

HP   That Kleindienst was out—it looks like Kleindienst is a defendant.

P   I get it.

HP   So we ought to avoid that. The second thing is that we can't—we can't expound on that.

P   All right (inaudible)

HP   Why Kleindienst has refused.

P   For two weeks the President has conducted—conducted a personal investigation. (Inaudible) about that. He has nothing more to say at this point. (Inaudible) add something.

HP   I think (inaudible) plusses in that.

473

P   Then at least you're covered. Would you mind if I got Ziegler over and you and I go over this?

HP   (Inaudible). No sir not at all.

P   Have Ziegler come over please (Into phone) All right. Getting back to the nuts and bolts here. La Rue—did he testify today (inaudible)?

HP   He is coming in this afternoon (inaudible). He is coming without a lawyer.

P   But he is going to (inaudible) interrogatories to him. As I understand you are going to get him to (inaudible).

HP   We anticipate that's the reason he's coming without a lawyer—but we don't know. He'll be in this afternoon. And O'Brien, the lawyer, is coming in. He's very much concerned about the potential subornation charges. He's coming in this afternoon.

P   Subornation is the charge made by Magruder?

HP   Yes sir.

P   Questions there is again (inaudible) want to prove (inaudible).

HP   Well I suppose that's right. He says Dean corroborates it to a certain degree.

P   How does Dean come out on this thing? Well—Oh, I see. If you—you can negotiate—you can negotiate him out by when he talks? Is that basically it? I mean—

HP   The decision isn't made. His counsel says we want a deal. This man was an agent. This man didn't do anything but what Halde—

P   Haldeman and Ehrlichman told him to do.

HP   and Mitchell, and if you insist on trying him we, in defense, are going to try Ehrlichman, Haldeman, Nixon and this Administration. That's going to be our defense.

P   He'd try it—the President too?

HP   It's a goddamned poker game. Yes sir.

P   Yeah.

HP   (Inaudible) we spoke yesterday—it's just awful tough to offer John Dean immunity at this point. (Inaudible) both of his lawyers last night after you called.

P   The only point that I want to be sure we understood on that is that I don't claim to be his higher authority. Mitchell is his higher authority—I don't know who he is referrring to.

HP   Oh I understand that.

P   But I just want to be damned sure that.

HP   When I use that term—Liddy's a nut you see.

P I have never met the man. I don't know.

HP He's a—he's kind of a super patriot—

P I understand.

HP In a sense.

P (Inaudible)?

HP (Inaudible)—No—we called—I called Tom Kinnelly, who I know very well and told him—he's co-counsel—local counsel. Then Maroulis his principal lawyer, called me and I told him also, and I told him in these terms. That a report had reached the government that Liddy out of a misguided sense of loyalty to the President of the United States was refusing to cooperate, and that I had been instructed by you—

P Yeah.

HP to inform his lawyer that the President wanted everybody to cooperate

P Exactly

HP subject only to the qualification that no one of us wanted to be construed that the President was putting undue pressure on him, and—

P Good. You told the lawyer that?

HP I've got it written down. I've made memorandum for the file so that it protects you and—

P Right—right (inaudible) influence?

HP Yes sir.

P You got that report. I guess Dean was the one who made it clear that I told him while you were—while he was here.

HP I told you that we'd received it but Dean also gave you the same report. Now, Maroulis, who's Liddy's lawyer, flew down from New York last night and we had Liddy brought over to the jail so that Maroulis could interview him and give him this information, and we will see what develops.

P How did—now let's see—this would be your corroborating witness for Magruder?

HP Basically. This man is crazy, Mr. President. He's burning him arms. He showed the prosecutor and said, I will stand up to anything. I've made myself endure this to prove to myself that I can take anything. Jail will not break me and what have you. You've got to be a crazy man to sit there and burn yourself to see if you can withstand the pain.

P I feel, among others, I feel for the Cubans—they probably—they probably recruited them (inaudible)

'cause they were doing it for Castro or something.

HP   I think they did, I don't—

P   Do you see how anybody would do such a silly damn thing like that otherwise?

HP   Mr. President, the great mystery about this thing is—there's no rationalization for—

P   That's how (inaudible) puts it—I agree. I couldn't believe. I said (inaudible) got to be a joke—

HP   There's no rationalization at all.

P   When I heard it.

HP   Oh, incidentally, I have—there's one other item that I wouldn't put down. That in the course the negotiations, in the course of trial preparations, it became clear that Hunt had recieved certain documentation from CIA. He also received the loan of a camera and what have you.

P   Yeah - yeah - yeah.

HP   We anticipated that they might—the defendants might—try and defend by attacking the CIA. We asked the CIA people—we were told that they were simply responding to a routine request from another government agency to help out Hunt who was on a special assignment, and they—

P   This was (inaudible) the White House?

HP   Yes sir.

P   That was perfectly proper. He was conducting an investigation from the national security area for the White House at that point.

HP   They also said—

P   That wasn't bugging equipment I trust that they got from the CIA.

HP   No—it—

P   Camera?

HP   Camera, a thing to disguise your voice, credentials.

P   Yeah.

HP   What have you. We are also told that the request for that came from Ehrlichman. First we asked what agency and they said the White House. Then that the request came from Ehrlichman.

P   Right. That is not involved in this case, is it? (Inaudible) This came before.

HP   Came in the course of trial preparation.

P   But—what I am asking is—is it relevant to this case? Is it a matter (inaudible)—

HP   Well it's relevant in this with respect to Ehrlichman

P   Yeah.

HP   The question is did Ehrlichman—

P   Depends on what he was doing.

HP   facilitate Hunt's obtaining equipment that was used in conjunction with the Watergate caper?

P   That's right. Or was it—it's a question of time there as to when (inaudible). Do you know the time mode?

P   What else?

HP   Check that camera—they had some pictures developed for him. I'll have to check the dates for you, Mr. President.

P   Right—come in. (Ron Ziegler comes in.)

Z   Hi - how are you?

P   Henry Petersen

Z   Yes indeed.

P   Let me tell you the problem, Ron, that we have here. You know a few weeks—now do you think Henry that you'll get—that you could—you don't know what—about the Dean thing—you don't know when you are going to negotiate that?

HP   No sir.

P   It seems to me

HP   The simple fact of the matter is the man has just agreed to plead. Now it's only a question of time.

P   He's agreed to plead.

HP   He's agreed to plead—it's a question of time.

P   Plead what - guilty?

HP   Plead guilty—yes sir—Magruder has agreed to plead guilty.

P   No - no - no—Dean?

HP   Oh Dean. The negotiations on Dean are still wide open.

P   Dean isn't going to plead guilty?

HP   No sir.

P   He's got this defense of being an agent? Right?

HP   That's right.

P   Is that defense?

HP   Well it's a tactical defense—

P   It's tactical defense?

HP   Well, you know, the jury appeal unless you—in a sense jury notification of sympathy—that the jury will not convict because they think he's the fall guy.

P   Oh I see—well (inaudible)—the Cubans.

HP   Depends on how sympathetic an appeals is made.

P   That's my point.

HP But Dean's appeal's much more sympathetic. Dean's out for anyone on instructions, and he hasn't gone out and committed an overt criminal act. He hasn't broken any thing the Cubans did—which is what detracted from their attempt to do this. Dean has done—performed neutral acts which in the circumstances they were performed take on the trace of criminality, and he excuses that with, one—he wasn't fully informed; two he was only an agent; three, he didn't have enough authority to countermand Mitchell - or he told Haldeman and Haldeman didn't countermand. Dean was impotent in the circumstance. That will be his defense.

P I see.

HP (Inaudible) try it—the jury—you believe—

P Also told you that unless you grant him immunity he's going to attack everybody including the President. Is that right?

HP But you can't use that.

P Huh?

HP You can't use that

P Who can't?

HP Because Dean didn't tell us that.

P The attorney?

HP His lawyer said it.

P No I didn't—I didn't—I just thought—

HP But his lawyer said that in the course of negotiations. And he doesn't say that as a threat. He says this is what I am going to do. This is my defense. You're taking unfair advantage of this man.

P Oh I see. Going to go out as an agent?

HP Yes sir.

P No agent for the President that's for sure, because—

HP He's agent for Haldeman and—

P He hasn't testified that's he an agent for the President in any of this has he?

HP No sir.

P If he has, I need to know it.

HP Yes sir - I know.

P (Inaudible) see Dean until a month ago. Never even saw him.

HP That has great significance on your executive privilege argument with the Congress. He said narrower construction and I'm told your construction—

P Yeah.

478

HP   is not necessarily narrow

P   Yeah.

HP   It's the narrow construction of the doctrine which is applicable only to those who are agents for the President.

P   Yeah. So he, being an agent.

HP   That—and to the extent that it's invoked with Dean—he is per se an agent.

P   That wasn't what you just told me in that memo you gave me?

HP   That he is an agent for the President and Haldeman and Ehrlichman,

P   Yeah.

HP   and the court take judicial notice, for example, that the Chief Executive invoked executive privilege with respect to him. It's an argument that can be made with respect—your argument—

Z   I thought that was already done.

HP   Pardon?

Z   It's been done.

HP   (Inaudible), statements have been made in the press that it would be.

Z   Oh I see

P   (Inaudible) basically this—they haven't made a (inaudible)—Dean—but you are trying to made a deal, aren't you?

HP   Yes sir.

P   And the problem is that what kind of a one you can make won't do a (inaudible). I would assume that we (inaudible) to Dean—all Dean wants is immunity from indictment.

HP   Yes sir

P   You're prepared to give it to him? The judicial one?

HP   Yeah. We're not going to like it.

P   What?

HP   And only as a last resort. And only if—

P   (Inaudible) going to get

HP   Only if we have—

P   Other evidence?

HP   other evidence that could be used to convict higher-ups. Now it may only be John Mitchell but if so, why a—

P   But you could use Dean on Mitchell—that's the point.

HP   Yes sir.

P   You see with Magruder you end up with one man—he's already lied once.

HP   That's right

P   I know a little perjury—and with Dean—you've got two men.

HP   That's right.

P   Correct?

HP   That's right.

P   If you get Liddy you've got three.

HP   That's right.

P   That will be a tough (Inaudible) that's why you're considering giving him immunity?

HP   Yes sir.

P   You think it's a good decision.

HP   (Inaudible)—I haven't made it yet and I'm pondering it—and I don't want to make it. I think it's going to look terrible if we immunize Dean 'cause he is a ranking official and we're still bargaining for a plea. If we can get a plea, we won't do it. If we have to—

P   What kind of a plea would you be getting, Henry? I don't know the operation of it.

HP   Well I don't know—we might a—

P   Suspended? That sort of thing?

HP   Well.

P   He wants a plea that doesn't disbar him.

HP   He wants a plea that doesn't disbar him—he doesn't want to plead at all to be perfectly honest, but he'll want a plea that doesn't disbar him I'm sure.

P   Here's the situation. You see they're still bargaining with Dean. Second the Magruder thing—they're still bargaining with him. Is that correct?

HP   Yes sir—to determine a time.

P   But you think that might come—not today now with Magruder?

HP   Well I don't think that we can satisfy his counsel's concerns today. They may say, well you go see Senator Ervin first.

P   Well let's think about the Ervin Committee and—

HP   And Judge Sirica.

HP   His counsel said he ought not go to jail before the others. And it's conceivable that they'll say you go to see Senator Ervin first. He's wrote the whole (inaudible).

P   Hhmm.

HP   Ok.

P   So with Magruder you've got the (inaudible) then.

480

HP   That's it.

P   However, he suggests that we could say this for the—he says that—he said—and I would get from John Ehrlichman—the amount of time—it's either two weeks—I think perhaps we could say for the past such and such in talking to—Remember when I first saw Dean—called him in and sent him to Camp David. I think that was before we went to (inaudible).

Z   It was March 21st

P   March 21st? All right—fine. March 21st. Since March 21st the President has been conducting a personal investigation into the entire Water matter. There have been as a result of that investigation (inaudible) significant developments. The purpose of that—I have been thinking—I have been talking with—he said—Henry agreed with me that the President should be out in front.

HP   Yes sir—that's the reason we were so insistent on seeing you again.

P   Yeah—

HP   Yesterday.

P   Second—and the result of that is that—that's going to—that's going—that's why I run it by you is this—at least if Magruder or Dean are summoned by the Grand Jury today—go in or talk or something or we just don't know. But the *Washington Post* with all the stuff it has. Whenever they move we're a step ahead. How's that sound to you?

HP   Can we add to that Mr. President—

P   Yeah.

HP   in terms of your suggestion last night?

P   Yeah.

HP   That there had been some speculation that individuals involved in this thing are protecting, out of a misguided sense of loyalty the office of the Presidency, and that you want to make it clear and you asked members of your staff and everyone involved that you expect their full cooperation with the prosecutors.

P   (Inaudible) the problem is that we said that before you know and it never—I don't think it gets through. What do you think Ron about that? The President has again directed, I would say, has again directed that everyone, that all individuals on his staff and in the campaign committee, cooperate fully in this investigation with the U.S. Attorney's Office—with the U.S. Attorney—The United States Attorney. I think I would put in that and

481

keep it out of the Ervin Committee—you see?

Z   Yes sir.

P   And that—and that—you see the misguided sense of loyalty thing—has there been an article in the newspaper?

HP or Z   (Inaudible)

P   You see I am afraid—afraid to throw that out there—I think you better leave it right there—has directed—the misguidance of loyalty we can handle in an individual (inaudible)—but this message will get through.

HP   All right.

P   I don't want to admit—dammit—that anybody's so dumb to say that the—which they are, of course. Now Ron, brainstorm that for us—what do you think—that's—

Z   First of all, the way to do this, and I think we should do this, but the way to do this—the feeling that something is happening in town and you (inaudible).

P   What you could say is that I'm not going to comment on developments because it could prejudice—it could prejudice the rights of—

HP   of the prosecution or defendants.

HP   Well, shall we say, the (inaudible). They could prejudice the rights—it could prejudice the prosecution or the rights of defendants and innocent people. Cause you see they are not all defendants.

HP   Yeah.

Z   Doing this puts it (inaudible) that paragraph.

P   (Inaudible).

Z   (Inaudible).

P   Developments? That the major developments that are now being—can I say major developments that are now considered by the Grand Jury?

HP   Yes.

P   Major developments that are now being considered by the Grand Jury. As a result of this investigation there have been some major developments that are now being considered by the Grand Jury.

Z   (Inaudible) you said that? We face a situation where—

P   They'll run to—

Z   they will—have you said this?—we will face the situation number one (inaudible) conclusions about the scope of this (inaudible). Those people who are holding information will be under great pressure to move quickly with whatever they have.

P   Oh—then maybe you don't want to do that.

Z   Then—thirdly, doing this in this form, would very likely have—could have—a tendency to (inaudible) further to have McCord issue statements in behalf of others or

P   You're probably right.

Z   Anyone. That could be the result of a statement like this. Then fourthly, I suppose, we would receive extensive questioning in terms of well how was the President conducting this investigation? Is Dean involved in it? And you know—

P   Hhmhp. He was (inaudible) the time.

Z   Well I understand, but by a story of this sort

P   (Inaudible)

Z   You would have to cut Dean out of the pattern. We would almost be forced to, in response to questions, to cut Dean out of the pattern. We would have to say no Mr. Dean was not involved in this which would lead to substantial speculation with regard to Dean's role and I don't know that John's state of mind at this point could lead to an open production on his part. I think—what I am saying is there is a tendency—(Inaudible).

P   Maybe we should say nothing then—what do you think? (inaudible) asking public relations questions (inaudible) not your job.

HP   (Inaudible)—the only thing I'd want to do—

P   It crosses the line?

HP   there is an undercurrent going through this investigation now

P   Yeah.

HP   and it's getting through to the participants and potential witnesses. They've heard all the arguments and they are moving—there's a lot of movement—and nobody wants to be the last one in. They're all trying to get in first to talk and get the best deal they can. Those who have not been contacted are nervous and waiting.

P   Yeah.

HP   Something like this (inaudible) makes a good point, could precipitate them to run up there to Sam Dash and then we're in great difficulties.

Z   In other words, if there's a summons—

P   No—I don't think we can do it—we'll just have to cover it Ron in terms of—that the damn thing—we've also have this understanding, I do want to have this understanding, but—

HP   OK—but can't (inaudible) Mr. President?

P   And Magruder—but Magruder—what?

HP   Can't we go at it in another way?

P   How's that?

HP   Well an awful lot of your friends in the Congress are saying unkind things—

P   Yeah.

HP   about the Watergate investigation. How—how—if you have—maybe bring a half a dozen of them over here —from both sides and talk.

P   Ahh—no—they'd—that just breaks the story bigger—if we did—it would be the same story. I'd rather have it come out if we're going to do it—you see they'd go and say there have been some major developments.

Z   See, of course, what you're doing this for will—of course, it does put the President immediately out in front.

HP   (Inaudible) have much more at stake in this than I have. I think that's terribly important. I don't want to exaggerate but it seems to me that the—

P   May—may be it's just as well to let the *Washington Post* and the rest (inaudible)

Z   (Inaudible)—I wanted to raise those factors to see what—

P   (Inaudible) put some pressures on and so forth but it isn't going to prejudice the prosecution is it, if I say this?

HP   No sir, (inaudible)

Z   I don't know—know who he is, but what if someone who's sitting there waiting for a phone call and sees this bulletin—

P   I lean to doing it and—I think I've got to get out in front and let's get out right today.

HP   Personally, I think you have to too.

P   Right—I've got to get out and I've got to get it out today.

Z   This would be (inaudible).

P   (Inaudible). Can I also say that I've—can I say that—we don't want to get into the business—for example, say that I met today with Henry Petersen and that—

Z   that would add an awful lot of questions.

P   I met yesterday—that he's—that—these—the— (inaudible) no let me say this. First, on Friday the President—I think we should say which we have—that Ehrlichman and all—Friday the President gave the (inaudible) the Attorney General the results of his own investigation.

Would that be a fair account of that?

HP   An overstatement.

P   It overstates it, because you see the Ehrlichman thing really states everything that Magruder (inaudible) corroborated the next day. We don't want to overstate a damn thing. All right—we'll just say this—that we have had discussions over the weekend—why don't we say that? Has had intensive discussions over the weekend with the Attorney General, Mr. Henry Petersen, (inaudible) and has continued to have discussions over the weekend and today—extensive discussions.

HP   That's all right.

P   You better get out a.

HP   I do think it's important.

Z   Let me add to this sentence. The President was conducting personal (inaudible) into this matter and to see (inaudible). (Inaudible) press (inaudible) conducted a personal investigation of the Watergate matter.

P   A personal investigation—after all—that was after the—this was after the McCord—In other words, because of allegations that have been publicly made.

HP   I would say, "As a result of developments in the past several weeks the President has found it necessary to—"

P   Yeah—the President has—the President on March 21 has undertaken a personal investigation—you know, has undertaken his own personal investigation.—intensive investigation. Whose handling it? He is—done personally. I'd just say he—just—let's say—all the facilities that are available to him—with all the facilities that are available to him. How's that sound to you Ron? And better say FBI (inaudible). say, over the weekend he has met extensively with the Attorney General, Mr. Henry Petersen. (Inaudible) Helpful (inaudible) it really (inaudible). It'll knock true—let me say this—I think—put it this way. I think maybe the fact that I finally—when we get Dean—let's face him—face the fact, that the very fact that I kept asking him what the hell is this? Go up to Camp David and write it. And Dean says I can't write a report. I think he then became convinced the moment of truth had arrived. And that's why he began to talk to you. That's what he told me yesterday. So you see that at least is something we can—the Dean thing is.—Now, as a matter fact I—I must add that I didn't know he was not coming fully clean.

Z   Should we express concern?

HP   The questions are going to (inaudible).

P   What?

HP   Obviously the President was unsatisfied with the report he got from Dean.

Z   Is that correct?

P   That's correct - yes. It was all based on—based on what, you know, based on the information that has been—

Z   (Inaudible) concern (inaudible) White House

P   I—just—you know—I'm not going to

Z   Is the President concern with the over all developments. Should we have a line that the President is conducting a personal investigation.

HP   The President is concerned with the evidence. The evidence will determine where we go.

P   Yeah—but I would say—gentlemen, any comments upon this would be harmful to the people—could jeopardize getting the truth—could jeopardize the prosecution—the rights of defendants or of innocent people. The rights of potential defendants—the potential defendants or of innocent people. And therefore, there can be no further comment upon it. I'd just (inaudible) it right out there and that puts a shot across the bow. Let (inaudible) scream out—let McCord go on—that doesn't help any. They don't have what we have. Let's put it this way, Ron. We know what we've done. We've got Magruder and Dean. There's also LaRue and a few others. I'd take that—and see whether—you want to run that by somebody and talk to Dick Moore or—

Z   (Inaudible) Moore and—

P   Yeah—okay fine—and then let me know right away. I want to finish with Henry—get him back to (inaudible). Fair enough?

Z   Yes sir

P   It's my inclination to go with that today, though, I—

HP   We have no problem.

Z   I think I'll be inclined to handle this on the basis of providing it to, in other words, what has the activity been around the White House and so forth.

P   (Inaudible) saw me to leave the church service and I—

Z   Give it to a wire service story—the wire services can confirm it later instead of calling (inaudible).

P No, no, no, no—I wouldn't call—I'd just give It to the wires.

HP That's right - yeah.

P Just give it to the wires. Say gentlemen you wonder what the President has been doing?—where is he today?—he's in the EOB. But I want them to know that since the 21st I've been working my tail off, which I have,—I—I'm so sick of this thing.—I want to get it done with and over, and I don't want to hear about it again. Well I'll hear about it a lot, but I've got to run the country too. (Ziegler leaves)

P Come back can I, for a moment now, to our—our subjects of Haldeman and Ehrlichman. As I—let's be sure we understand (inaudible). As I understand it—and I don't (inaudible)—what we were saying last night—from a legal standpoint the case against them may be quite difficult to prove.

HP That's certainly true with respect to Ehrlichman.

P Yeah.

HP But Haldeman and Dean are much more difficult position from the purely theoretical legal point of view.

P Right—because of the money?

HP If Strachan confirms that he

P That he got the money?

HP That he got the budget report.

P Oh the budget report—yeah.

HP If Strachan confirms that—

P Strachan—Strachan's going to testify (inaudible) right?

HP If he confirms then that he gave Ehrlichman or Haldeman a summary of—

P Yeah.

HP The intercepted conversations.

P Right—right.—That shows that.

HP And he.

P That shows he had prior knowledge—right.

HP and Dean testifies that he told Haldeman about the second meeting in Mitchell's office where these things were discussed.

P Yeah—I asked Dean today. I said did Haldeman have any knowledge. He said No. Did Ehrlichman have any knowledge? He said No. I said did you have any knowledge? Dean said No. He said, "I went to the meetings."—Dean gave me the same story. He hasn't changed his story in that (inaudible). I went to the meeting but we thought we had it turned off. That was—that was his line. But he said that's before. But it's afterwards, he says, that both Haldeman and Ehrlichman have problems. That's what Dean tells me for whatever its worth as to whether—Did he tell you something different?

HP Well—that's perhaps what (inaudible). He said in Mitchell's office we ought not to be discussing this in the office of the Attorney General.

P Yeah.

HP All right—that's one thing. Now maybe he just figures that was turning it off. It didn't turn it off. He goes back to Haldeman and he says—we ought not to be involved in this—that's the way it was stated. And Haldeman says—right. But so far as we can ascertain nobody did anything.

P So.

HP So from a—

P Pretty hard—pretty hard to convict—I was just going to say—just looking at Haldeman. In the public mind, in other words, I think as you said last night on the phone very perceptively—in the public mind—

HP That's right.

P But legally.

HP That's right.

P It's still tough.

HP It's a very difficult case because it rests on inaction. But in any event with respect to Haldeman, that is a theoretical case, and with Ehrlichman next to nothing.

P All except the deep six.

HP O I wouldn't agree with that.

P Huh?

HP We'll have to go back to Gray—I'll talk to Fielding and I'll stop by and talk to Ehrlichman, too.

P Chance is you're going to hear that they—I don't know—you mean they turned it over—turned over a packet to Gray?

HP Yes sir.

P Ehrlichman I think you said, believes that? (Inaudible) include Gray? Let's don't get the Bureau back in this. One thing we talked about protecting—you know this—Gray is going to be leaving, as you know. I am trying to find the man who's beyond reproach—who can get a hundred votes in the Senate. Let's a—now we are not talking about protecting an individual. Gray is (inaudible) this weekend. (Inaudible) him out. Does this (inaudible) you?

HP (Inaudible) remarkable man, Mr. President.

P Huh?

HP I think Pat Gray's a remarkable man.

P But you see, his memory might be faulty on this. The point is—my point is I don't—if you feel this—his train has left the station you've got to (inaudible).

HP Well I don't think—

P I'm not telling you not to do anything stronger.

HP I don't think that it's especially germane.

P It's not relevant.

HP That's right. But it's important to determine whether or not Dean's telling the truth. (Inaudible) of the fact—it's a neutral fact but if it can be established that he's telling the truth.

P All right. Suppose you find that Ehrlichman corroborates Fielding that they did turn this over to him whatever it was—to Gray. Then what do you do? You call Gray in and ask him, where is it?

HP Well I'll go see him again and then (inaudible) we will want to pursue it.

P Yeah. You see Gray's—Gray's, if I can just suggest it, Gray's reaction, if he didn't get it, would be, in my opinion, (inaudible) didn't get it, or get something, and they told him this is political stuff. (Inaudible) I don't want it. That's what I would have said wouldn't you? Not drag in the Bureau. Not Watergate. I don't know.

HP Can't second-guess a man.

P (Inaudible)

HP The other (inaudible) if Kleindienst called me up and said, "look, there's this aspect of this investigation. I've got this stuff here. It's all co-mingled but it's clear that this doesn't relate. Why don't I just give it to you?" I'd probably take it. I think it's very understandable— what I can't understand is the denial. Well, (inaudible) to corroborate,

P Well if he got it—you see—the point is he doesn't have it now. That's the point.

HP Apparently hasn't.

P So he's flushed it.

HP Well there's a possibility that Dean threw it in the river (inaudible).

P (Inaudible) I have a recollection myself. I say a recollection that Dean told me that unequivocally, and I believe Dean on that.

HP We're going to go back to him again.

P (Inaudible). I'll get you out of here. (Inaudible) yet.

HP By the way Mr. President, I think that.

P (Inaudible) evidence—not evidence? (Inaudible) explain that the evidence was not evidence—is that right? The stuff out of his safe?

HP Well—that's.

P What would you get after him on this—destruction of evidence?

HP Well you see the point of it is—there are two other items that—according to the defense—Hunt's defense—that were missing. Both of which were notebooks.

P Hunt's notebooks?

HP And we can't find those notebooks. Dean says, Fielding says, and Kehrli says, they have no recollection of those notebooks.

P Yeah.

HP Hunt says they were there, and—

P So—

HP So only to the extent that the notebooks are missing which Hunt says they're germane.

P (Inaudible) does he tell us very much, huh?

HP No sir

P Is he going to?

HP Ah

P Or is he?

HP (Inaudible) before the Grand Jury.

P (Inaudible) anything in it for him, I suppose that's the thing.

HP He was testifying under compulsion. Came in immunized—we're going to have him back, particularly with respect to the fees. His testimony with respect to Dorothy Hunt was unbelievable.—"We were once in trouble with the income tax bureau and ever since then we've been sticking hundred dollar bills in the top of our closet and that's where the ten thousand dollars came from."

P You mean he gave to the Cubans?

HP That he gave to his wife, Dorothy, which she had on her when the plane went down and she was killed. She's alleged to be the intermediary that was carrying—

P Carrying the money to the (inaudible) that's what I heard—I read that in the paper.

HP So that he lied on that issue. And we'll have to have him back.

490

P   Do you think you can break him?

HP   I think, his lawyer is very concerned, and the lawyer got a hundred and fifty-six thousand dollars in fees.

P   Bittman—Bittman is his name?

HP   Yes sir.

P   I've heard of him—good lawyer?

HP   He's a good friend of mine, Mr. President, and a good lawyer. He prosecuted the Hoffa cases.

P   But Bittman's problem—his problem is (inaudible)

HP   He's very—he's very upset about it and—

P   Doesn't he know what the hell the (inaudible)? Does he think he was paid off?

HP   Does he think?

P   Does he, Bittman, think that his fees—Hunt's (inaudible) the purpose of getting his client to—

HP   Well I don't think he cares where his fee came from. That fee went in. He's concerned about the allegations that McCord makes based on (inaudible) Dorothy Hunt.

P   One thing that's got to be—one thing about Colson—wondering if—that I would be concerned with here—that is if—according to Hunt whether you've got a circumstantial problem as to whether Hunt may have told Colson. If what (inaudible) if Colson had not done a damn thing. According to Colson, he's sworn under oath that he didn't know anything about it. You would have him on perjury.

HP   Yes sir. And we don't have any evidence against him.

P   Well—the point here.

HP   It's—you know a very funny story

P   If you crack Hunt.

HP   to come out of this.

P   About whom?

HP   The *New York Times* when they interviewed or the *Los Angeles Times* when they interviewed Baldwin and they took a taped statement from him. In the course of the interview, Baldwin told them that he had taken the logs and just labeled the envelope and delivered it down to 1700 Pennsylvania Avenue. Then as he told us he couldn't remember the name and they went through a whole series of names, you know, whoever they were, and each one he kept saying no. And finally they said Murray Chotiner? And he said no. So they, after they concluded all their questions and names and what have you, they went back and then as just a flyer, Judge Sirica when he—in connection with the subpoena issue—hears part of the tapes and hears is Chotiner's name. He says to Silbert, I want these people subpoenaed and that's Murray Chotiner and others. And Silbert says, well he's been to the Grand Jury and this name has nothing to do with it. He's been calling about it ever since—subpoena. Now the *LA Times* told me—

P Chotiner?

HP that they had talked to Chotiner—

P Doesn't know a damn thing.

HP I know that.

HP (Inaudible) item of evidence.

P I know Murray like the back of my hand. He's too smart.

HP Well, that's what he told the *LA Times*. He said if I had done it, it would have been done well.

P Yeah, I know that, but he would never have done anything like that.

HP No sir. And he—we have no evidence against him.

P And I can assure you, I know that. I may not know other things but I know that.

HP It's become a matter of principle with us. We will not subpoena him. We have no reason to subpoena him.

P No, no, no.

HP And Sirica wants us to subpoena him just I think for the hell of it.

P Yeah.

HP The only way his name is mentioned is because they were trying to determine who, and I talked to the *LA Times*. We did go that far,

P Yeah.

HP and they say absolutely none.

P Listen, if you are going to answer it at all (inaudible) the big fish start flopping around. Well—coming back to Haldeman—I digressed—we went off. La Rue potentially then today has confirmed the money thing from Strachan. So today you're putting the net on that money at least,

HP Well Strachan (inaudible) and La Rue is due in this afternoon.

P Who did you get this morning then?

HP Oh we had Strachan in this morning.

P But he didn't talk?

HP But he didn't talk. I went through that earlier.

P   Okay. All right come to the Haldeman/Ehrlichman thing. You see you said yesterday they should resign. Let me tell you they should resign in my view if they get splashed with this. Now the point is, is the timing. I think that it's, I want to get your advice on it, I think it would be really hanging the guy before something comes in if I say look, you guys resign because I understand that Mr. Dean in the one instance, and Magruder in another instance, made some charges against you. And I got their oral resignations last night and they volunteered it. They said, look, we want to go any time. So I just want your advice on it. I don't know what to do, frankly. (Inaudible) so I guess there's nothing in a hurry about that is there? I mean I—Dean's resignation. I have talked, to him about it this morning and told him to write it out.

HP   (Inaudible).

P   It's under way—I asked for it. How about Haldeman and Ehrlichman? I just wonder if you have them walk the plank before Magruder splashes and what have you or what not. I mean I have information, true, as to what Magruder's going to do. (Inaudible) nothing like this (inaudible).

HP   Or for that matter, Mr. President.

P   Yeah.

HP   Its confidence in the Office of the Presidency.

P   Right. You wouldn't want—do you think they ought to resign right now?

HP   Mr. President, I am sorry to say it. I think that mindful of the need for confidence in your office—yes.

P   (Inaudible) basis?

HP   That has nothing to do—that has nothing to do with guilt or innocence.

P   What basis—how would you have them submit their resignation then?

HP   Well—when we say they—I'm much more concerned about—about—

P   Haldeman?

HP   Ehrlichman than I am about Haldeman, because Ehrlichman, we have much less, you know, in terms of potential involvement.

P   Yeah. Yeah.

HP   (Inaudible) the deep six it (inaudible), it goes to the quality of the information. Maybe it was trash and he said, get rid of the damn stuff, it's no good.

P   And then maybe Gray did.

HP   That's right. And the other thing with respect to Hunt. That's a little more sensitive. That—

P   How does it seem so?

HP   Someone, you know, who's closely associated with you, who tells Hunt to get out of the country is I think a tremendously sensitive piece of information.

P   Did he? But he didn't go?

HP   But he didn't go because the—

P   They changed their minds.

HP   Countermanded—the orders were countermanded. Now—

P   Well I would think that his defense on that if I— my guess would be—that he was trying to (inaudible) what happened (inaudible) maybe the best thing for him to get out of the country, you know what I mean? But your point—Dean tells it as if Ehrlichman ordered him out of the country. Right? Is that what you have?

HP   That's right—and that's the way it comes through Liddy. Hunts tells us that's the way Liddy stated it.—my principal.

P   My principals?

HP   My principal said.

P   Tell you what?

HP   Get out of the country Hunt. It doesn't seem to me that if that fact reaches light of day that it can be anything else but (inaudible) impact on the White House.

P   (Inaudible) message.

HP   (Inaudible) nothing to do with justice or injustice.

P   I know that it's because of the Presidency which, of course,

HP   Yes sir.

P   is what we are thinking about. I appreciate what you say, because, I'm thinking about that too. I'm trying to be fair.

HP   Well let me put it another way. If I were Ehrlichman I would feel like I have to go under the circumstances.

P   You would? Even Ehrlichman? Haldeman too?

HP   Both of them.

P   How do you feel about Haldeman (inaudible)?

HP   Well (inaudible).

P   You feel even more strongly?

HP   Yes sir, assuming, now remember what we have,

P   Yeah.

HP   Dean says he discussed this with Haldeman.

P   And?

HP   Haldeman didn't say stop.

P   I see.

HP   I can tell you—if one of my prosecutors came in and said another prosecutor was out bugging somebody in organized crime, I would not say we ought not to be involved in it—

P   Dean told me.

HP   I'd go to him and say stop it.

P   Excuse me. Did Dean say he discussed the bugging with Haldeman?

HP   He discussed the substance of the budget proposals which included the bugging operation. Operation.

P   Haldeman or Strachan?

HP   with Haldeman. And said we ought not to be involved in this and Haldeman agrees but nothing happens. Neither one of them stopped it. Now, maybe they both thought they were outranked by John Mitchell. I don't know.

P   Dean now says that he discussed the bugging operation—that's what I want to know. I didn't understand he said that. I thought he said he did that with Strachan.

HP   Magruder—Margruder says.

P   I get it.

HP   (Inaudible) goes through Strachan. Dean says when he came back from the second meeting he told Haldeman, "This is terrible, we ought not to be involved in this."

P   Right—right.

HP   And nobody does anything about it.

P   He hasn't been too damn forthright has he?

HP   Well.

P   I mean, he should have told me about Haldeman.

HP   It's awful hard to debrief a man, Mr. President, in an hour or two as you know.

P   Yeah—when I asked him specifically did Haldeman know and so forth—and he said no. And I guess maybe he was being perfectly honest. Told me that just this morning. And I said, he had no knowledge before, and neither did Ehrlichman, and he said neither did he. But I guess what he meant was that—you could reconcile that only by saying—that he had told Haldeman about it and Haldeman didn't know that it went forward. Maybe that's what he (inaudible).

HP   That's—

P   That would not make Haldeman liable in this case—the very fact he didn't stop it. He didn't have the responsibility. I am looking at it just from a legal standpoint. Now understand, from a public standpoint it's devastating. You think he would be liable for not issuing an order to (inaudible). I suppose if Dean was his subordinate. (Inaudible)

HP   (Inaudible) a subordinate. It depends on who has authority to act with respect to the budget proposals?

P   Haldeman (inaudible).

HP   He did not have any authority?

P   No sir—none, none—all Mitchell—campaign funds. He had no authority whatever. I wouldn't let him (inaudible).

HP   Then you're left with the fact that he has knowledge of

P   That's right.

HP   but he doesn't act upon.

P   Knowledge of a proposal?

HP   that comes out as a misprision of a felony.

P   Huh?

HP   That comes out to a misprision of a felony. Misprision is a statute that is hardly ever enforced. You could put everybody in jail I suppose if you tried to.

P   Knowledge and so on?

HP   That's right.

P   Knowledge it's being considered.

HP   That's right. (Inaudible) type of thing—

P   (Inaudible) say specifically that he discussed the budget proposal with Haldeman? Well I'll be damned!

HP   I think I have in those notes there that Dean came back to the White House after the meeting, told Haldeman about these proposals that were being discussed in the office of the Attorney General, and said we ought not to be involved. And Haldeman agrees, but nobody stopped the operation.

P   Dean says—

HP   (Inaudible) told him so the only thing I'm saying (inaudible)

P   Should we do it—should we do it from the top? Well, I'm going to talk to Bill Rogers a little later—I'll get his judgment about—on this—(inaudible) Haldeman. Dammit, I'm afraid that—I don't want Haldeman to go and then have to get (inaudible) and then have Ehrlichman go and get caught. Get my point? That's what I'm concerned about. I think they both—look if they're going to go they both got to go, don't they? They ought to go together?

HP   I think so, yes sir. Mainly because I don't know how that looks to you, but from the outside, they are almost a team.

P   That's right.

HP   But to let one go and the allegations with the other being (inaudible). The next day it might develop that (inaudible)

P   Well (inaudible) my judgment on this after I talk to Rogers. It's a very close call. The real question is to get—whether you let Magruder strike the blow and then they go. That's the point.

HP   Great responsibility and I know how—

P   Oh, I'll move on it.

HP   heavy it is.

P   Oh, I'll move on it. I'm just trying to think about whether—before Magruder strikes.

HP   I'm bothered, you know because this may be a terrible injustice to both of those men.

P   I know that (inaudible) but my point is (inaudible) how it is (inaudible) whether they go before Magruder. Let me tell you—let me put it this way—I really am in a pretty poor position to have them go before Dean goes.

HP   Well that's correct—I agree with that.

P   I can't announce Dean going today—that would jeopardize your prosecution. Or can I announce it? I am very seriously thinking.

HP   You're your own agent on that. As long as I can say—

P   No—I'm going to get his—I'm going to get—but you don't want me to—you told me earlier you don't want me to make that public

HP   I don't want—want to be in a position to say to John Dean—John, I did not recommend that the President take your resignation.

P   Fine. All right.

HP   As long as I could say that Dean's been here, he's talked to you. It's between the two of you. You're timing on that is okay with me.

P   I see. Even announce Dean today?

HP   Yes sir.

P   That wouldn't jeopardize your prosecution?

497

HP Well, we still have to bargain with him. But I don't—I don't see that—he's trying to use that, but I don't see that. As long as I can say, the prosecution team can say, we did not recommend that.

P How is he trying to use it? You mean—you say that—I'm a little concerned about Dean's or his lawyers—that he's going to attack the President and so forth. Other than that, I mean Dean above all else—

HP Well I don't think the President personally—the Presidency as an office as the Administration.

P Because of?

HP Because of Ehrlichman and Haldeman.

P It's Ehrlichman and Haldeman he's really talking about?

HP That may be his guts poker in the course of negotiations. That's what they say.

P Try the Administration and the President. (inaudible) affairs, (inaudible) huh?

HP That statement that's made in the heat of argument. Charlie Shaffer, a very committed, emotional, able lawyer. Stand up and say, goddammit. I'm not going to plead him. If I have to do this, I'll do this in return. That's the way he comes out.

P (Inaudible).

HP All right you ask him about that point specifically, about reporting to Haldeman on the—

P Yeah.

HP on the budget proposal.

P Yeah—I will. I need to know that. Dean this morning told me something I need to know (inaudible)—that he (inaudible) going to go testify to (inaudible). It seems to me the important thing that you should get your (inaudible) him as soon as you can.

HP That's right.

P But I guess you got problems there. You got to go to Ervin, you got to go to the Judge, and with Dean, you've got to make a deal with his—isn't that what you feel you (inaudible). You've got to give him something don't you?

HP Well.

P That's the problem you've got, (inaudible), Henry, (inaudible) him off with the others.

HP We can't give him too much because it will impair his credibility. That's another factor.

P (Inaudible). Now—I can get any—I need to know

if any further—I've got to keep on top of this thing, if any further breaks occur.

HP   Yes sir.

P   And perhaps by tonight we will know whether Strachan did testify.

HP   Yes sir.

P   I may call you around say eight o'clock—how's that?

HP   I would say not before eight.

P   I'll call you at nine—how's nine?

HP   Nine is fine.

P   Nine will be fine.

HP   That'll give me a chance to get my kids off the phone.

P   Yeah - nine o'clock. You (inaudible) Strachan and LaRue?

HP   Yes sir.

P   They both (inaudible) testify today?

HP   Yes sir. (Inaudible) All right—thank you sir.

P   Thank you.

Meeting: The President, Ehrlichman and Ziegler, EOB Office, April 16, 1973. (3:27 - 4:04 pm)

P   Yeah—did you make any progress on that thing? How does it stand? Fine.

E   I'd say that—

P   Gray denies to Petersen that he ever got the bundle. Oh, he's dumb. Well, Petersen tells me that he's told Haldeman—I mean Ehrlichman. He was very (unintelligible) Mitchell (unintelligible) this, Petersen being honest.

E   Dean informed Liddy that Hunt should leave the country.

P   (Unintelligible) the idea that Dean, you know. But you warned him didn't you?

E   Sure did. There (unintelligible) I was.

P   You didn't see it?

E   No, didn't know what was in it. Could have been shredded newspaper, as far as I know. So that, well it could be—

P   Well, Dean will say—

E   Dean will say what he put in it, I suppose. See,

499

Dean arrived at my office with a scotch-taped, sealed big envelope and handed it to Gray. What—I said, "Well,

P   There's the contents of (unintelligible) safe?

E   No. Dean had told me that before Gray got there, I think—I can't be sure of this—but in any event, I knew what it purported to be.

P   Where—when was Gray told that it was not really the Watergate?

E   I don't know. I don't know. It may have been told him in my presence or not, I just—

P   But, you think he was told?

E   He says he was, and I don't have any reason to doubt it, but I can't swear that I heard that said. Ah—and ah—again, I can't.

P   (Unintelligible)

E   Could say, you know, it may be that his story is I opened it and it was full of paper napkins or, you know, some damned thing. But if he says I was not in Ehrlichman's office and I did not receive a big manila envelope from Dean, then I'm going to have to dispute that. (Unintelligible) there and then do that.

P   (Unintelligible)

E   Yeah.

P   Has he testified to that, John, or do you think—?

E   He's told the U.S. Attorney that.

P   That what?

E   That he gave him an envelope there that was the contents of the Hunt safe.

P   (Unintelligible)

E   Dick Howard just got a subpoena from the Grand Jury.

P   Yeah.

E   The FBI agent who called said, "I'm coming over to serve you with a subpoena from the Grand Jury, Mr. Howard. You may want to go and talk to Mr. Dean while I'm on my way over there in case you want to get any advice."

P   Did he talk to Dean?

E   No, fortunately, he talked to Colson. Colson—I had told him that Dean was over the hill, cautioned him, and then he told me and said, "Boy, you got an outpost over there. Well, U.S. Attorney's having the FBI agents send everybody a subpoena—go talk to Dean."

P   Because he was (unintelligible) the practice.

E   Well, I hope that's what they thought, but more probably they'd like Dean to sit there and listen to every guy's story and then call over and let them know what's going on.

P (Unintelligible) Dean (unintelligible) talk to (unintelligible) apparently he's—

E I must caution you about that because it's certainly improper for him to be counselling any of our people.

P I've got to talk to him. He's got to quit counselling anybody right now.

E Let me finish this.

P Oh, sure, John. Did (unintelligible) tell you about the other (unintelligible) that he's coming to ask you about it? I'm not asking you to make up any story, but I'm just simply saying, I just can't—damned dumb Gray, Director of the FBI in the position of having two White House people say he got an envelope and he doesn't remember it. I heard you talked to him. What did he say to you last night?

E He said he can't say that.

P What did he say to you though?

E He said, I said—

P After (unintelligible).

E Dean say saying so and so, and he said he can't say that. And I said, he already has. But he said, I destroyed it. Well, that's it. You know, that's pretty tough (unintelligible) if he doesn't now. (Unintelligible) sure putting the best face on what they did to Strachan over there. Questioned by the prosecutors. Despite considerable fencing, he refused to discuss the matter and was excused by the prosecutor. According to Strachan—then they—you mustn't say anything to anybody about this because I suppose he wasn't supposed to call over here.

P Yeah, I don't.

E He called to get advice. He said they really worked him over, said stuff as, "Listen, Strachan, you're going to jail; think about your wife, think about your baby and how would you like to be disbarred, and—"

P I know. I know.

E You know, that kind of stuff.

P I knew they were going to work him over. He asked for a lawyer?

E No, they asked him to get a lawyer. They kept stressing it. They wanted him to get a lawyer and I think what they are doing is setting him up for (unintelligible).

P Well. That safe John, something about the damned notebooks—he said, notebook.

E Yeah, I know. He's said that right along.

P   And there were?

E   Oh, I don't know. I honestly don't. Now, Kehrli and the Secret Service agents were there when that safe was opened and (unintelligible). Never tried (unintelligible) appointments after that, so they are still on this.

P   That's your only vulnerability, John.

E   Deep six and the FBI business and Liddy. Well, that's interesting that Dean would take that remark and go out and act on it.

P   Deep sixing?

E   No, the Liddy deal.

P   Told (unintelligible).

E   Hunt, yeah, that it came through Dean.

P   But, apparently they didn't leave—in other words.

E   Oh, no. No, no.

P   You were discussing it. I told, I tried to tell Petersen, "Well, look, I can imagine them having a discussion—" he said, "He ought to leave the country—maybe we ought to deep six it."

E   Mmhuh.

P   And you didn't do any of those things. At least I think that's based on—Got any thoughts on this point?

(Ziegler enters.)

P   Who have you talked to?

Z   Yes, sir. I talked to Moore,

P   Yeah.

Z   Chappie Rose. Both of them are against it.

P   They're against it? All right. Because of the reasons you mentioned?

Z   Some of those. But Rose—their best lawyer is working on that—and—

P   OK.

Z   His concern.

P   We just won't try to get out in front. We got anything else you can say. Don't say, don't—we seem to, we've gotten into enough trouble by saying nothing so we'll say nothing today. You know, actually, thank God we haven't, thank God we haven't had a Haldeman statement. Believe me. (Unintelligible) thank God we didn't get out a Dean report. Right? Thank God. So, we've done a few things right. Don't say anything.

Z   (Unintelligible) made the point, looking at the statement, about comments and so forth that stampede.

P Well, I (unintelligible). I've got an understanding, John, with Petersen, and he wants us to move first and a—but I said, 'Well not before Magruder pleads." We've got to go out and—what I had in mind having you say quickly that—(unintelligible) statement. But in any event then, we're going to have to wait for the Magruder thing. The point is you've got the whole record. I just don't want to.

E He wants to wait until Magruder talks? Is that it? Petersen? No, I mean the others who—

Z Well, he didn't get into any discussion about Magruder talking. No.

E What was his objection?

Z His point is that, what Rose's point is, in the position of stampeding on (unintelligible) how this has been (unintelligible) this. But this point, the President is too closely tied in as an investigator and too closely tied in to the Grand Jury proceeding itself. In other words, he (unintelligible) in his view of this is to have the first (unintelligible) and suggests that the President is (unintelligible).

P (Unintelligible). I don't.

Z No, not affect. But the President is becoming as an investigator involved in knowledge and awareness of the Grand Jury proceedings.

P Oh, yeah. Yeah.

Z Which well could affect direction of those proceedings. He has contacted Petersen.

P Well, all the facts are going to show just otherwise though when it comes out, but go ahead. But this (unintelligible)

Z I think so.

P He didn't. John, I asked about Magruder today and they haven't got the deal with him yet because Magruder's attorneys insist on something with Ervin and something with Sirica. Magruder wants to go to the D. C. Jail (unintelligible) in there. They haven't worked that out yet. I asked about the timing on Dean. They haven't got a deal on him because—in fact his lawyers made an interesting comment. He said Dean shouldn't do anything to upset the unmaking of Haldeman and Ehrlichman and Mitchell, and if they don't get immunity they're going to try this Administration and the President. His lawyer, Schaffer. Petersen says that's quite common. Everybody shouts to everybody. I'm getting (unintelligible) difficult (unintelligible). After all, the business of the—about the Dean report, why end it that way? Dean will stick to the position. John, you can see how he's going to (unintelligible) Ehrlichman. You know, he did make some movement on his own in this thing. I've asked Dean a specific question. "Haldeman/Ehrlichman, did they know in advance?" He said, "No." I said, "I've asked you again, I've asked you." He told me that (unintelligible) Well Dean said after a second meeting over there he went over and saw Haldeman and said, "We oughtn't to be in this. Haldeman said, I agree. I said, "Well what's wrong with that." He said, "Well, Haldeman, by failing to act—"

E Yeah. That is true.

P Yeah.

E Dean states Haldeman agreed, but apparently no initiating of any instructions.

P Right. By failing to act. And then I said, I said, "Well how could he act? He wasn't in charge of the campaign and—(unintelligible) didn't he have (unintelligible) approval.?" "Why," I said, "He certainly did not. He had no responsibility at all. The campaign was totally out of the White House." But I suppose what he meant by that, Haldeman should—should have called Mitchell and said, "Knock it off." Is that what they're saying? Well, what does Haldeman say to that sort of thing?

E That's hard to get around, understand, because Dean's story, consistently, has been that at every one of those meetings, the plan was disapproved by Mitchell.

P Yeah.

E What's there to get out of?

P By going to Haldeman—

E Dean came back and said, "Well there was a proposal, and Mitchell disapproved it."

P You think he's making that up?

E I don't know. I—it doesn't make sense, in the context of those meetings, that everybody agreed on, that at all those meetings Dean attended it ended in disapproval.

P Yeah. "Well, why did he go to Haldeman?"

E So why? Yeah. Why is there a failure to act, when—

P Oh, he might—

E Everything is disapproved?

P Yes, but that is Dean's problem, but—

E Well, the suspenders.

P Huh?

E A guy says, I was thinking about going out—

504

P   Yeah.

E   and plugging a hole in your tire, but I decided not to.

P   Yeah the point is, I think you've got a very good point here. You say, "Well, look, what in the world is this? If the damn thing was disapproved, why does Haldeman get blamed for not disapproving it?"

E   Yeah. They need two disapprovals in order to make it stick?

P   That's what I was going to say, but—

E   Well, I don't know enough about it I guess. I'd sure like to see us come out sometime, and I suppose it has to be at a time that Magruder makes his deal.

P   Well, let me say, I'll—I've got Petersen on a short leash.

E   Ok.

P   Petersen or Dean. Keep that statement, regardless, and get this factual thing that John has worked up for you. You get that.

Z   I've had, I had that typed.

P   Fine. Because we've got to be ready to go on that instantly. We may go it today. We will survive it. I don't think it's very—

E   Not very appropriate news this morning.

P   Yeah, and that's it. They will get back to (unintelligible) I just think (unintelligible) their staff.

Z   (unintelligible)

P   It's obvious they will question him on this.

E   That's what matters though. The thing with the Ervin Committee, will, I don't know. A statement of rules, and the negotiations,

P   Right.

E   They adopted an awful lot of my stuff. Their rule on television is a very odd one. And it says "All still and motion picture photography must be discontinued before the witness commences his testimony. Television, however, may continue under the standing rules of the committee during the testimony of the witness."

P   So it must—that means what? It's live?

E   That my interpretation. Well, no. Tape would be motion picture.

P   Yeah.

E   Why not?

Z   That's electronic. See, the terminology is stills, motion picture or electronic.

E   That isn't the way they used it, and so I've got a

call in for Baker to try and get a clarification.

P   Right.

E   Because it may be their intent that if the networks will go live, then let them go, but if they tape, then they can't tape the testimony. And, if that's the interpretation, I think we ought to go for it.

P   Right.

E   Don't you?

Z   At ten o'clock in the morning? Well, you know, just—

E   If they run it at ten o'clock. Anyway, I'll get an interpretation and I'll be back to you on it for instructions. Well, there isn't much point in me going through the whole thing until—

P   I think the Ervin Committee, who (unintelligible) a break in this (unintelligible). Do you believe it would be at all helpful to be forthcoming with Ervin then?

Z   Well as we mentioned before, I think you have to have caution with the Ervin Committee (unintelligible). depends upon decisions. Whatever it is decided to check with (unintelligible) alternative here (unintelligible) or it may be to our advantage to analyze—

E   Well, my problem's Howard Baker goes to Russia tomorrow, so there's got to be action—or he goes Wednesday, excuse. There's got to be action tomorrow. The Ervin Committee's meeting up there now. Timmons thinks the thing they are meeting about is that somebody has pulled the plug on Dash, that he was nearly disbarred in Philadelphia—some unfortunate scandal—something about—He's been taken by surprise again and he's very unhappy and he's convened the Committee. The thing provides—well, they're kind of cute about this too. You can have a hearing in Executive Session. The Committee rules at the witnesses' request for the purpose of determining scope, in effect, what, where the witness should and should not testify.

P   Oh, I see. Well, that's good.

E   And that's good, I think. Then there's a lot of stuff in there about—they do prevail in making closing statements. They will.

P   What's your advice, John.

E   There's very little left to argue about except the television, and we could say we interpret this to mean that unless the television is live, there won't be any and that's satisfactory to us.

506

P Yeah.

E Now we might get the jump on them that way.

P All right. Fine.

E And then, let them come back and say, "No, that isn't what we mean. We mean it can be taped." And then we'll come back and say, "Well, that isn't satisfactory. By that time they're in a recess.

P Right.

E And the thing would be hung up until they get back.

P Yeah. And the other thing—we had to, you know, before it comes from the Ervin Committee. But I don't think before it comes to the Ervin Committee it's going to amount to a damn in the next four weeks.

Z The overall—

P Yeah.

Z decision, but—

P Don't you think at the present time we ought to be forthcoming here?

Z Yeah. I think—

E What you say, Ron, is that we intend to avail ourselves fully of the ground rule that permits the use of executive session and that undoubtedly the majority of the White House witnesses will be the subject of a request to the Ervin Committee for an executive session.

P That's right. Agree with that.

E Then, what we've done is gone to our high ground.

P Right.

E And let them pull us off.

Z Of course, what really is the Ervin Committee investigating?

P (unintelligible)

E They—it's probably moot. It's probably moot, but what we can say is we feel we can live with these ground rules.

Z Yeah.

E You know it's very—well, it is obvious that the negotiations were very worthwhile. We think the Committee has come up with a fine set of ground rules that we can live with. We are going to fully cooperate and then, on the side, you can say, "See this executive session provision."

P Well why don't we—frankly, frankly (unintelligible) executive (unintelligible).

E Maybe I ought to get them and have them for you, so that you can talk to Rogers about them.

507

P   Yeah. Later today you might just make your decision and go on that. We can settle the Ervin Committee.

E   Well, then, I'll have to get Baker's OK.

P   Well, why?

E   To make our announcement, because that's the way I have it set up with him. They've got a meeting tomorrow before we make any announcement.

P   Do you want to make an announcement tonight?

E   No, I thought that's what you meant, if you were going to go with the Ervin thing today.

P   Oh. We'll make it tomorrow then.

E   OK, well then I'll have a chance to talk to Baker tonight.

P   Baker, Baker will have left. He won't be at the meeting tomorrow.

E   Yes, he will. He won't go—he doesn't go until the next day. I misspoke.

P   Fine. You'll make the announcement tomorrow. Ok, Ron?

Z   Yeah, but—

P   Gives me time to think about it, that's the point. Go ahead. What is it?

Z   Well, I - if we make the announcement tomorrow, we could tie it into something.

P   Yeah. We have a general announcement. We want to (unintelligible) and with Chappie Rose and those guys. Do they realize that I've got to make this general announcement before the Magruder thing comes up?

E   Well, does he fear the President will look like he's interfering with the Grand Jury?

Z   No, it's a quote. He said, to which he (unintelligible) much contact with the Attorney General, the Assistant Attorney General—the President being investigator.

E   Well, bless his heart, those contacts are a matter of record.

P   That's right. I don't agree with him on that point.

E   That point's moot, you know. That was the President's only recourse.

P   That was it. I wouldn't worry about that (unintelligible). See, he's thinking as a lawyer. They probably like to see the President (unintelligible) this damned thing.

Z   No, I agree with that.

E   (Unintelligible)

Z   Well, I'm not arguing. Again, you see, can't argue. I'm just passing this point to you.

P   What would be your view about this kind of a statement? You don't want it tonight?

E   I don't want it tonight, but I'd sure like to see you go full breast on it tomorrow. See, Wednesday is the energy message.

P   Yeah.

E   And, we're going to be sort of saturating the press Wednesday with that.

P   Will they write and use it?

E   I don't know. I mean we're having briefings and all that baloney. And so, if possible, it would be best to go either tomorrow or Thursday with this and I prefer tomorrow.

P   We'll see how they get along with their negotiations. I suppose they're—

E   Seems to me like they're hard-nosing these negotiations. Dean doesn't really give them all that much. He let me look at that piece of paper you've got there and then he said, "Well, gee, did Hunt go out of the country? No, Well, what else is there?" "Well, he says, "I don't know about (unintelligible)."

P   Dean isn't corroborating Magruder in any way?

E   Yes.

P   That's what it looks like.

E   But can't they get that out of him anyway? You know.

P   (Unintelligible)

E   Well, let's think about that. If you were the prosecutor, what the hell do you care? You know, if you were Glanzer, you were sitting over there,—

P   The White House threatened, the President—

E   But what is, what is that he can say? You stop and figure.

P   That he's informed the President and the President didn't act? He can't say that can he? I don't think, I've been asking for his damned report, you know.

E   The fact that he put the chronology all together—he comes up with a hell of a lot of egg on his face.

P   I think he blames—he would blame you and Haldeman.

E   Well, he's going to have a little trouble with that.

P   Is he? Good.

E   And I put together my log today. And I have seen him on the average of five times a month since the Watergate breakin. See, Bruce Kehrli (unintelligible) you know

509

(unintelligible). I've seen none of his memos routinely. I don't supervise any of his work, so I think he's going to have a tough time making that stick. And some of those were on your estate plan.

P   Yeah.

E   Some of them were on the Library.

P   Good.

E   Some of them were on the leak scandal. So, he's not seen me five times a month on Watergate.

P   Well, listen, I've got to run. Let this go tonight. Fair enough?

Z   Yes, sir.

E   All right.

Z   Did you want to meet Garment for five minutes before you see Rogers?

P   No. I'll have to put that off. I've got Rogers (unintelligible) Garment's views and—you don't agree?

E   I agree totally. It's (unintelligible) for Garment is the reason, you see.

P   No, tell him, tell him that I feel very personally, but I want to get a little—that I've had a long talk with the U.S., with Petersen. There is a reason. Give him a little bull and tell him (unintelligible) had a long talk. There are reasons we can't say today, that there will be developments during the day. Going to be public. Some things that I have in mind (unintelligible) piece of paper on that, and I'll see him before. Well, is it going to be that much of a problem? You think I should see him? Maybe, you know, I don't. Wait 'til I see Rogers. Tell him to stick around.

Z   All right.

P   Tie it in with Rogers. Why don't you do that? How's that?

Z   The only advantage of (unintelligible) you have in your possession.

P   Well no. The point is—well, go ahead.

Z   Fifteen minute session (unintelligible) and bounce that off of Rogers.

P   I know what he's going to do is—(unintelligible) I mean the—this is a full court press, isn't it?

Z   That's right, so you don't need to tell him.

P   I know what the hell a full court press is.

Z   I understand that.

P   The thing you told me this morning.

Z   Yes, sir.

P   Well, I followed that already. He wants to go out and what? He wants Haldeman, Ehrlichman and Dean to resign. Right?

Z   Or just (unintelligible) You know, he has several variations (unintelligible) and letters.

P   Yeah.

Z   Suggesting that (unintelligible) they would step down.

P   They would (unintelligible) and then they would, and I would accept that. However the case breaks?

Z   Yes, sir.

P   Do that today?

Z   No, not today. You know, after the timing of the decision.

P   I'd prefer.

Z   I think it's—you have enough of that.

P   I think I want it to be a little clear in my mind with Rogers here.

Z   No (unintelligible) I'll put him off.

P   Tell him, that, look, that I got it and I'm just in the middle of this thing and that I, I'm thinking along those lines. Just say that, and that I'll, because of the talk, I cannot act today. Just say that. I just finished this long meeting. Didn't want to act, I can't act today, because it would frankly jeopardize the prosecution.

Z   Right. Ok.

P   And the right of the defendants. And that therefore, that I can't, that I've been told that by the Assistant Attorney General. That I cannot do that today. It will jeopardize the prosecution. (unintelligible) If the President (unintelligible) it will tip a lot of others off that they are working on at the present time, and that I had put the pressure on to get this so that I can be (unintelligible) And I have in mind all of those options. Tell him that I have met with all three of them today. The President met with all three of them and discussed this problem.

Z   Well, you may not want to see him.

P   Now, be sure—

Z   Be thinking about it.

P   Sure. Ask him if—

Z   Yes sir.

P   Right (unintelligible). Tell him I want to think about it; then, I'd like to talk to him. I want him to get his things in shape. I want a firm recommendation.

Z   He apparently has a statement.

511

P   Well, bring it in and I'd like to have that statement, if I could, by six o'clock tonight. You deliver it at six. I'll be with Rogers at six o'clock and I'd like to have that statement.

Z   I'll bring it in.

P   Oh, no. Should I have it before I see Rogers, that statement? Tell him I'd like to have it, that I've just gotten tied up here. Tell him I've been meeting with Petersen. I cannot act today, but I'll be ready to do something quite soon.

Z   Good.

P   Don't tell him about it.

Z   No.

Meeting: The President and Dean, EOB Office, April 16, 1973. (4:07 - 4:35 pm)

P   Hi, John.

D   Mr. President.

P   Well, have you had a busy day?

D   Yeah, I have been—I spent most of the day on trying to put together a statement that I think you could come out—apparently some other people have done some work on—I haven't been working with them. Presumably we are all kind of driving at the same point. I was working on a draft when you called.

P   Listen, I've got to see Rogers in just a few minutes so let me have (unintelligible)

D   Well, I think - I was calling Dick Moore in on it, but Dick is working on it with these others.

P   That's good. What would be best? Rather than giving it to me piecemeal, why don't you put one together?

D   It's got a strong thrust which puts you—

P   (unintelligible)

D   There is a tough question here - the degree of biting the bullet right at this hour. Now there is one paragraph—

P   There is a question of timing—

D   It is a question of timing but it is also a question— I have one paragraph in here that says what you are doing as a result of what has come to your attention and some of the things that Petersen has told you.

512

P Uh, huh.

D And one of the points is that it provides that all members of the White House staff will be called before the Grand Jury effective immediately. They will be on administrative leave until such time as the Grand Jury completes its work. Now here is the tough paragraph thus far: "In this connection, I have not spared my closest staff advisers and included in this action are H.R. Haldeman, Assistant to the President, John Ehrlichman, Assistant to the President, and John Dean, Counsel to the President." Now you can do that or leave that out and let them guess who is on administrative leave.

P Anybody called before the Grand Jury?

D That's right. That means that no man—

P You can bite the bullet on Dean, Haldeman, and Ehrlichman until then, huh? On the other hand, if (unintelligible) is lying—have you talked to (unintelligible)

D No, I haven't.

P I have a sensation that he is lying right now but the trouble with that is there might be some confusion. Petersen says, incidentally, on your letter—he thinks it is probably better to get a letter in hand and get the grievances out.

P I said, "Well, what do you think about it? I was considering your returning and I don't want to do anything to jeopardize your rights. He feels (a) that he wants to clear it. But he is not recommending it.—

D Uh, huh.

P He said - "Stand fast (unintelligible) However, public prosecution would not be harmful to an individual, you know, if we had the resignation in hand so we could act on it. (inaudible) other than let me say—let me see what you had in mind.

D I have a letter—

P I don't care about the letter but I thought it was fair - fair to everybody. (Inaudible)

D I wrote: "Dear Mr. President: Inasmuch as you have informed me that John Ehrlichman and Bob Haldeman have verbally tendered their requests for immediate and indefinite leave of absence from the staff, I declare I wish also to confirm my similar request as having accepted a leave of absence from the staff." Well, I think there is a problem—

P You don't want to go if they stay—

D There is a problem for you of the scapegoat theory.

P   You mean making use of it.

D   That's right.

P   Like Magruder being the scapegoat for Mitchell?

D   That's right. You know, everybody is appearing before the Grand Jury. This does not impute guilt on anybody.

P   Let me put it this way I think rather (unintelligible) I could say that you, as Counsel—that you have been responsible for the investigation. We already have said that about this case haven't we?

D   That's right. The only man you are dealing with and the only role I have is to help fill in any information I can to deal with the Public Relations of the problem. You know—

P   You can say it that way John. You can say the President sought your advice until it is cleared up.

D   That's right.

P   (unintelligible) I don't know that the letter (inaudible) and that goes out ahead, frankly, of the Magruder-Mitchell hitch doesn't it?

D   That's right. I wasn't counting on that—

P   We haven't made a deal with Magruder's lawyers yet. Magruder is turning from the Ervin Committee on Judge Sirica—

D   (Unintelligible)

P   I don't want you to talk to anybody else, understand? Except for (unintelligible)

D   I am not doing any investigative work or—

P   Well, that's right. (unintelligible)

D   Well, I turned that off three weeks ago.

P   Good. You haven't done any since three weeks ago?

D   That's right.

P   You haven't done any since March 21st?

D   Let me check back and see.

D   Necessity of the overall problems of the White House. Looks like we both talked to them about that.

P   Yes - yes it does. Tell me what you last talked with Haldeman about.

D   That Bob would like Dean to be the first to testify. It is very painful for me. (Inaudible)

P   (Inaudible) One thing you should all (inaudible)—Did Dean know? Did Haldeman know? Did Ehrlichman know? You may know. He said "Dean came over to Haldeman after that and told him about the plans for GEMSTONE."

P (Unintelligible) says you're right.. His point being that actually Haldeman then did know.

D No sir, I disagree with that interpretation—

P I didn't know, but if that was the case you see John then - I would have to—Dean would have told me something.

D No, because I have always put it to you exactly that, way because Bob has told me he didn't know. Now I know I didn't know but I feel—

P What about this conversation? (inaudible) If this had happened, wasn't Bob responsible for telling me?

D I think what happened is probably this - everyone assumed that John Mitchell would never have approved anything like this. I told him I was not going to have further dealings with Liddy or anybody over there on this and I didn't. I didn't have the foggiest notion what they were doing.

P That's what you told me, you know. (inaudible)

D Well, Bob tells me he did not know. Now I know the question is—the other thing is—I cannot, I couldn't describe twenty minutes after the meeting what Liddy was presenting was the most spectacular sales pitch you have ever seen in codes and charts and (unintelligible) operations.

P You mean Gemstone?

D Well, that is what I am told now later after the fact they called it. I told Bob, "They are talking about bugging. They are talking about kidnapping. They are talking about mugging squads, taking people south of the border in San Diego, etc."

P What did Bob say?

D He said, "Absolutely NO."

P You will so testify?

D That is right—absolutely. I don't know - I assumed - Bob has never told me anything to the contrary so I thought that nothing happened from the time of that meeting where he told me, "Don't do anything about it. You are to stay away from it. Don't talk to Hunt and Liddy." I said to Liddy, "I am never going to talk to you about this again, Gordo." So what I thought was that inaction was the result - of their not having produced something reasonable. Second, I don't know—

P You didn't get hold of Mitchell on it did you?

D I don't have the record on that—

P Magruder says that—but—(inaudible) Then I see.

515

Your statement is consistent with what you told me before. I wish you would tell (unintelligible) that Haldeman said, "Absolutely not."

D That's right. Bob and I have gone over that after the fact and he recalls my coming to the office and telling him about this crazy scheme that was being cooked up.

P Do you want to go and get together—

D I will work on this statement—they want to have something to (unintelligible) that they are going to go before the Grand Jury.

P Bill Rogers. We are going to have him available. Everyone needs help. None of us can really help another I really believe.

D That's right. All I am trying to think is how we can get you out from under.

P That's right. I tried to talk today about social issues, etcetera, and everyone is just interested in the Watergate Issue. My days are too short—

D Something about Magruder—they are going to take him to the courts.

P I know - he has agreed to (inaudible)

D I can't forsee what we would want to say about any investigation—

P "You see I make my own" How about trying that? "Let the White House Staff (inaudible)"

D Unfortunately it doesn't solve; your problem. Mine bother me but (unintelligible) Mitchell was making heavy comments that Liddy and Hunt will make heavier problems for the White House than he will. (unintelligible)

D Poor Bud Krogh is so miserable. Knowing what he knows—

P Need any help with him?

D There is no reason that he should be. The only evidence that they have (inaudible)

D It just got forced on him. When I was first talking to him—"Run these guys through the Grand Jury—" To be very honest with you, I have talked about it around here before I got in to see for many, many months. Then I thought I could not let it interfere with my work anymore so I thought I might as well forget it.

P That's right. That's when you came in to see me. Finally, that is when I came in to see you and got some answers.

D Now, they have their full investigation going—with subpoena power, investigative power, etcetera. It is all like a set of dominoes if one goes they will all go.

P Secretaries, etcetera

D I don't know (unintelligible) They are going to handle Ehrlichman and Haldeman. There is a potential prima facie situation right now (inaudible) which thereby makes it necessary for you to make a judgment that those people should leave the staff.

P Make it necessary for me to relieve them from any duties at this state.

D That's right.

P I don't have to discuss it with him—but just say, "You are all out"

D That is a tougher question because one that is putting you in the position of being the judge of the entire facts before all the facts are in necessarily.

P That is really my problem in a nutshell. So those fellows say that - this fellow says that—

D Maybe that is the way this ought to be handled. You say, "I have heard information about allegations about (inaudible) some publicly and some have not become public yet. I am not in a position to judge because all the facts are not in yet (inaudible)?

P (Inaudible) But you agree, John, don't you that the statement is fair to everybody? And frankly—(Balance inaudible—door closes.)

Telephone conversation: The President and Petersen, April 16, 1973. (8:58 - 9:14 pm)

P Mr. Petersen please, Assistant Attorney General. Henry Petersen.

Opr Oh, Henry Petersen.

P Hello

HP Yes, Mr. President.

P Did you get out with your kids?

HP Sort of. We got together with them.

P That's good.

HP They all just hollered, the President is calling, right at the nose at nine o'clock.

P Well, I wanted to get you in bed earlier tonight than last night, and I want to get to bed too. Let me say first, I just want to know if there are any developments I should know about and, second, that of course, as you know, anything you tell me, as I think I told you earlier, will not be passed on.

HP I understand, Mr. President.

P Because I know the rules of the Grand Jury.

HP Now—LaRue was in and he was rather pitiful. He came down with O'Brien and said he didn't want private counsel at all. He just wanted to do what he did. He told John Mitchell that it was "all over."

P He said he had told John Mitchell that?

HP Yes, He, LaRue, admits to participating in the (unintelligible) and obstruction of justice. He admits being present, as Dean says he was, at the third meeting, budget meeting, but—

P Who was present at that meeting Henry? I don't know.

HP He and Mitchell.

P He and Mitchell alone?

HP And he says, ah—

P LaRue and Mitchell? I didn't—that must be a meeting I seemed to have missed. Dean was not there at that meeting?

HP Dean tells us about it. Now I am not quite certain whether Dean was present or not. That meeting was down in Florida.

P Oh, some—oh, I heard about a meeting, but I think you told me about that.

HP He is reluctant to say at this point that Mitchell specifically authorized the budget for the electronic eavesdropping at that point. But I think he is going to come around. He is just so fond of John Mitchell. He admits that it could not have been activated without Mitchell's approval, however.

P Uh, huh.

HP O'Brien, they didn't get to. Strachan called back around five o'clock and said he was having difficulty in getting a lawyer. He finally got a lawyer. Colson's law partner.

P Oh? Colson's law partner?

HP The United States' Attorney's office took issue with this, and threatened to go to the Judge on a conflict then he—

P Got another one?

HP Got another lawyer. He'll be back tomorrow.

P All you got to today was LaRue?

HP That's right. Now, the other additional information from—

P LaRue said he had told Mitchell that it was all over?

HP Yes.

P When did he do that?

HP Just recently. Today, yesterday or the day before.

P I see.

HP You know, he had thrown in the sponge.

P I get it.

HP We talked earlier today about Ehrlichman. Now a little additional detail on that.

P Uh, huh.

HP Liddy confessed to Dean on June 19th—Dean then told Ehrlichman.

P Liddy confessed that he did the deal, or what?

HP That he was present in the Watergate.

P Uh, huh.

HP Ah, then you also asked about Colson. Colson and Dean were together with Ehrlichman when Ehrlichman advised about Hunt to get out of town and thereafter—

P Colson was there?

HP Colson was there so he is going to be in the Grand Jury. With respect to Haldeman, another matter. In connection with payments of money after—

P the fact.

HP June 17th, Mitchell requested Dean to activate Kalmbach. Dean said he didn't have that authority and he went to Haldeman.

P Uh, huh.

HP Haldeman gave him the authority.

P Uh, huh.

HP He then got in touch with Kalmbach to arrange for money, the details of which we really don't know as yet.

P Right.

HP So Kalmbach is also a Grand Jury witness to be called. And I think those are the only additional developments.

P Right. What is your situation with regard to negotiation with Dean and your negotiation with regard to testimony by Magruder?

HP Well the trouble is—

P   Trying to get the timing, you see, with regard to whatever I say.

HP   Magruder's lawyers are still waiting to get back to him.

P   I see.

HP   They are very much concerned about Judge Sirica and they are not so much concerned about Ervin. Now their immediate concern is Sirica and they want that ironed out first.

P   What do they want ironed out, that—

HP   That he won't go to jail before the rest of them.

P   Oh, I see, if he confesses?

HP   That's right. Thus, pending a meeting with Judge Sirica—

P   Which you've got to have, I suppose?

HP   Titus knows him better than any of us.

P   Sure.

HP   Probably Titus will handle that aspect of it.

P   Uh, huh.

HP   But that's got to be very delicately done. He is apt to blast us all publicly.

P   Sirica? Right.

HP   We'll see and then we will take up the Senator Ervin issue.

P   Doesn't seem to be the major issue, though. The main thing is Sirica, he is concerned about?

HP   Sure.

P   Sure, because the Ervin thing will become moot in my opinion.

HP   Now the other concern we have on that issue is how to charge.

P   How to charge?

HP   In terms of how we charge Magruder. In terms of the things we are concerned with, we don't feel like we ought to put Haldeman and Ehrlichman in there as unindicted coconspirators at this point, but we are afraid not to. If we don't and it gets out, you know, it is going to look like a big cover-up again.

P   Hmph.

HP   So we are trying to wrestle our way through that.

P   Whether you indict Haldeman and Ehrlichman along with the others, huh?

HP   Well we would name them at this point only as unindicted coconspirators, but anybody who is named as an unindicted coconspirator in that indictment is in all probability going to be indicted later on.

P So you have to make a determination as to whether—

HP Secondary issue is of course is whether we are going to have enough corroboration to make those statements, and—

P That statement would be made, as I understand it, as you were telling me, if—

HP It would be in Open Court.

P It would be made in Open Court, and then you would make a statement with the others. You would name them at that time?

HP Well, we wouldn't do it in those terms. We would simply do it in terms of feeding the facts to the Court.

P That would be done publicly. Would you name Mitchell then too?

HP Well, we would have to. You see the problem is—

P That would all be done in Open Court?

HP That's right. Once we do that, or even if we don't, Sirica's habit in Court, and he certainly is going to do it in this case, is to interrogate the defendant himself.

P Right.

HP And—

P The defendant who pleads guilty?

HP That's right. If he interrogates Magruder, that brings out the Ehrlichman/Haldeman facts and if we haven't mentioned them or included them in the conspiracy charge, then we are all going to have a black eye.

P I get your point.

HP These are the things we are trying to work out.

P You've got quite a plate full. You probably won't get it tomorrow then will you?

HP I doubt it. I doubt it.

P Uh, huh. What about Dean—in his case you are still negotiating, huh?

HP Well, we are still tying down facts with him and we want to get as much as we can.

P And basically with him, the point is you've got to get enough facts to justify giving him immunity? Right?

HP Enough to make the decision, yes sir.

P Depends on how much he tells you, is that it?

HP Right. And more than that, how much of it we can corroborate.

P   If you can't corroborate enough then he doesn't get off, is that it?

HP   Well, if we can't corroborate it, that's right. We can't very well immunize him and put him head to head against a witness who is going to beat him.

P   I see. Well his people are playing it pretty tough with you then?

HP   Yes sir.

P   I guess we'd do that too, I suppose.

HP   Indeed so.

P   I prefer them to do that. Let me see if I get the facts? You will hear Strachan tomorrow, perhaps.

HP   We expect he will be in. He will come in with his lawyer again.

P   My second point is that—let me see about the 19th—Dean says that—

HP   On the 19th.

P   Yeah.

HP   Liddy confessed to Dean.

P   Dean says that?

HP   Dean says that.

P   Liddy confessed to him and that he told Ehrlichman?

HP   Right. He told Ehrlichman.

P   Humph—that's new fact isn't it?

HP   It's at least—yes, sir, and that's a terribly important fact I think because there was no disclosure made by either one of them.

P   Either Dean or Ehrlichman?

HP   Yes, sir.

P   Humph. When did Dean say this?

HP   It got to me this evening. I am not quite sure when Dean said it. Silbert (unintelligible)

P   You see the point is. Dean didn't tell me that. That is the thing that discourages me.

HP   Well, Mr. President, you have to remember that we are debriefing him on what has transpired over the last eighteen months.

P   I see.

HP   It is very difficult, you know, to get it all in.

P   I know. I am not talking about you, but I am talking about what he didn't tell me, you see. That's a key fact that he should have told me, isn't it?

HP   Yes.

P   Uh, huh. Let's see, the 19th, and on the Haldeman

thing what did you have there again so I get that in my mind.

HP Let me go back over my notes. The principal thing that I wanted to point out to you on Haldeman is that Dean went to Haldeman to get authority to go to Kalmbach.

P Oh yes, yes, yes. That was it. When Mitchell told him to go to Haldeman.

HP Mitchell told Dean simply to activate Kalmbach to handle the money.

P I see.

HP Dean then went to Haldeman to get authority to contact Kalmbach. Thereafter, Kalmbach took care of the money. Now—details on the $350,000 which you indicated you knew about—

P I knew about the fund. I don't know how it all went—

HP This is how it developed. It developed, as related to us, as money over which Haldeman exercised control. That money was delivered to LaRue to be used for payments, at least a portion of it.

P Some of it. Right. I think Haldeman would say that's true. I think he would. I don't know, but we'll see. You should ask, I guess, Kalmbach.

HP The point of it is that it went to LaRue instead of going to the Committee directly.

P Uh, huh.

HP LaRue apparently did not give a receipt and Haldeman had requested it.

P Uh, huh. I think LaRue was loosely a member of the Finance Committee. I think that was the point Haldeman—I said, who did this money go to? He said, it went to LaRue was a member of the Committee or something like that or of Stans' committee. I don't know what that is. Is that correct, or do you know that?

HP I don't know that. All I know is that he worked for John Mitchell. I will check on that though.

P The money went to Mitchell?

HP No, I say all I know is LaRue worked for Mitchell.

P Yeah. I think he worked on the Finance Committee, but I don't know. You ought to check that out.

HP I will.

P O. K. the, The main thing I need, of course, is something—well, before, wait you are not going to have anything tomorrow in Court so I don't—

HP   I don't think so.

P   Tomorrow you just continue to develop the evidence.

HP   Yes, sir.

P   I think, therefore, no statement would be in order at the present time. We decided against one today. It just didn't seem to be—I thought it might—I just had to make my own determination. I thought it would jeopardize possibly the prosecution, you know. Who knows?

HP   Probably would raise more questions than it answered.

P   That's right. We don't want to say anything until—like if there has been a big break in the case and everybody starts—

HP   I will tell you one thing, Mr. President, that you ought to know. I had a call from (unintelligible) Ostrow of the L. A. Times, who is a decent man and a reasonably good acquaintance. A reporter of character, if there are any, and he said that they had a report out of the White House that—let me use his words—that two or three people in the White House were going to be thrown to the wolves. He asked if there was anything to it, and I said there is not a damn thing I can tell you about it. I just can't say anything about it one way or another. I don't want to confirm it and I don't want to deny it.

P   So they will probably write a story on that, huh?

HP   I don't know, but I mention it only because its—

P   It's beginning to get out. Yeah.

HP   Beginning to percolate.

P   It must have come from the U. S. Attorney's office you think?

HP   I doubt it, because I have not told them—unless they made their own conjecture.

P   U. S. Attorney - but they were thinking in terms of the Haldeman/Ehrlichman thing, and Dean, I suppose.

HP   I don't know what he was thinking about, and I don't—

P   Where does the Colson thing come in again? I want to get that one down too.

HP   Where does who fit?

P   Colson.

HP   Colson was present when Ehrlichman issued the order for Hunt to get out of the country.

P   I get it. Fine. O.K. So you will call him too?

HP   Yes, sir.

P   Right. O.K. Well if anything comes up, call me even if it is the middle of the night. O.K.?

HP   I will indeed.

P   Thank you.

HP   All right, Mr. President, thank you.

Meeting: The President and Haldeman, Oval Office, April 17, 1973. (9:47 - 9:59 am)

(Band Music)

H   Yes, Sir.

P   Oh, hello - sit down. I was thinking that we probably ought to use John Connally more to try to hammer out what our strategy is here on Watergate.

P   Rose, I am sorry I didn't intend to push your button now.

RmW   OK.

P   Thank you, Rose, I will call you later.

H   The only question there would be whether we ought to meet earlier on the basis that, well, we—

P   I understand I can't I have the Italian for a while. I could meet at 12:30. No, after that—1:00 o'clock.

H   The reason being, and the only reason, there is felt to be—and we may not want to react to it but we may—there is felt to be—Colson, for instance, called Ehrlichman this morning and said that his sources around town, department sources and everything, say that we've got one more day to act on our initiative.

(Material unrelated to Presidential action deleted)

H   And that all these breaks, this White House is all over town.

P   So we may have to go today.

H   And you have also seen or know the *Los Angeles Times* has the story.

P   About (unintelligible)

H   The White House has got to move, and the thought is that if we are going to move today we probably ought to meet earlier, so we are ready to move by three o'clock or 3:30 or something.

P Fine. Ok. If you just get together. I think we have to move today.

H Well, if we look like we have anything, we have to get out in front some way.

P Well you might have to give them the full report today the way it is breaking so fast. Let me say that the problem you've got here—I had quite a long talk with Rogers, etc.—of course he was much more rational than Len. Len's (unintelligible). On the other hand, you've got the problem of you and John sort of being nibbled to death over a period of time.

H Yep.

P And by not moving, having a situation where, frankly, the chances of your being—I mean of your being publicly attacked and also even the steam of the prosecution is greater. You know what I mean. It is a curious thing, but I am afraid that is the way it operates. You know every day there is some damn little thing that somebody touts around with, you see, so everything can be explained and try to defend and all that sort of thing. But I am not prepared to make that suggestion, but I want you to talk to John about it.

H Yeh. Ok.

P Dean met with Liddy on June 19th, must have been when he did it. He was in California in January but that is irrelevant. But they keep banging around and banging around. The prosecution gets out the damn stuff. Did John talk with you about it?

H Yeh, he mentioned it. Dean did tell us that story in Ehrlichman's office last week or two weeks ago.

P But not to go all through this.

H I don't think so.

P Yeh.

H I think I mentioned it to you. Remember I described the story to you in some detail (unintelligible) walked down 17th Street—

P This was all after we had started our own investigation.

H Oh, yeah.

P I mean it wasn't back then. It wouldn't indicate that we knew about all this, etc. Another thing, if you could get John and yourself to sit down and do some hard thinking about what kind of strategy you are going to have with

526

the money. You know what I mean.

H   Yeh.

(Material unrelated to President's actions deleted.)

P   Look, you've got to call Kalmbach so I want to be sure. I want to try to find out what the hell he is going to say he told Kalmbach? What did Kalmbach say he told him? Did he say they wanted this money for support or—

H   I don't know. John has been talking to Kalmbach.

P   Well, be sure that Kalmbach is at least aware of this, that LaRue has talked very freely. He is a broken man. The other thing is that this destruction of the (unintelligible) things is troublesome, of course. John tells me, too, and basically the culprit is Pat Gray. Does Colson know about that? Is that why they are calling Colson because Colson was in the room when it was handed to Gray?

H   No he wasn't. Well, apparently he wasn't.

P   He says he wasn't?

H   Colson thought, well there was a meeting before that, where they talked about the deep-sixing and all that supposedly.

P   He was in that meeting?

H   Which Colson was supposed to have been in.

P   Right, right, right.

H   Colson thought, well there was a meeting before flatly says that there was never anything where he was where there was a discussion of Hunt getting out of the country. Kehrli says the same thing. He was supposed to be at the same meeting. In fact, Ehrlichman has checked everyone who was at that meeting and nobody recalls that being said except Dean. And we now have the point that Dean is the one who called Liddy and told him to telephone Hunt to get out of the country and then called him later and said not to.

P   I would like a policy. I think, Bob, we have to think, I must say, we've got to think about a positive move. I think it ought to be today.

H   I agree.

P   I think it should be at 3:00 today. We have already, I hope the story doesn't break today in—

H   Even if it does you can get into cycle with it.

P   Yeah. Well, I don't want to be answering it.

H   No.

P That is the problem with this Italian here. I want a thing done today and you and John have got to think, frankly, in terms, let me say, not just in terms as a national group for the President and all that—but also you have to think in terms of having this damn thing continue to be dragged up bit by bit and answers dragged out bit by bit, anyway, I suppose. But the point is that Dean's incentive with the U.S. Attorney, incentive with everybody else will be this and that, you get my point?

H Yep.

P I am sure you and John can talk about it. You see what's happened, the prosecutor has been pretty clever. They got Magruder. Well Magruder just caved, but it had to come. It had to come, Bob. It was going to come.

H Yes I think so. I think it had to and should.

P That's right. The other point is the other element. The question now that is coming as far as Dean is concerned. He basically is the one who surprises me and disappoints you to an extent because he is trying to save his neck and doing so easily. He is not, to hear him tell it, when I have talked to him, he is not telling things that will, you know—

H That is not really true though. He is.

P I know, I know, I know. He tells me one thing and the other guy something else. That is when I get mad. Dean is trying to tell enough to get immunity and that is frankly what it is Bob.

H That is the real problem we've got. It had to break and it should break but what you've got is people within it, as you said right at the beginning, who said things and said them, too, exactly as Dean told them. The more you give them the better it will work out.

P I have to go. As a matter of fact, I am sure I will be ready by 1:00 o'clock.

H Ok.

528

Meeting: The President, Haldeman, Ehrlichman and Ziegler, Oval Office, April 17, 1973.
(12:35 - 2:20 pm)

(Material not related to Presidential actions deleted)

P   Where did we come out?

E   Well, we got two things, we got a press plan but it rests upon some decisions that you have to make on sort of an action plan.

P   Right, alright.

E   And, I just finished an hour with Colson who came over very concerned and said that he had to see you. That the message he had for you that he had to and wanted to explain in length is why Dean had to be dealt with summarily. His partner has a tie in with the U.S. Attorney's office and they seem to know what is going on there. Very simply put, I think his argument will be that the City of Washington, generally knows that Dean had little or no access to you.

P   True, that's quite right. Dean was just a messenger.

E   That knowledge imputed to us is knowledge imputed to you and if Dean is (unintelligible) and testified that he imputed great quantities of knowledge to us, and is allowed to get away with that, that, that will seriously impair the Presidency ultimately. 'Cause it will be very easy to argue - that all you have to do is read Dean's testimony - look at the previous relationships - and there she goes! So, he says the key to this is that Dean should not get immunity. That's what he wants to tell you.

P   Well, he told me that, and I couldn't agree more.

E   Now he says you have total and complete control over whether Dean gets immunity through Petersen. Now that's what he says. He said he would be glad to come in and tell you how to do it, why, and all that stuff.

P   I don't want Colson to come in here. I feel uneasy about that, his ties and everything. I realize that Dean is the (unintelligible), Dean, of course, let's look at what he has, his (unintelligible) and so forth about (unintelligible) go popping off about everything else that is done in the government you know, the bugging of the—

E   Well, the question is, I suppose is which way he is liable to do it most.

P   First of all, if he gets immunity he'll want to pay just as little price as he can.

E   Well, the price that - the quid-pro-quo for the immunity is to reach one through us to all of us. Colson argues that if he is not given immunity, then he has even more incentive to go light on his own malfactions and he will have to climb up and he will have to defend himself.

P   Now when he talked to me I said, "Now I understand John. I understand the tactic of all three resigning." I said, "all offered to resign." I told him that, you understand. I told him that you and John had offered to resign so he's aware of that.

H   Well, have they told him that the price of his immunity is that if we resign they'll give him immunity? Do they feel that makes their case? Or, does he have to give them evidence?

P   I don't know. He's going to have a tough time with that.

E   Well, to go on. My action plan would involve—

P   What would your plan be?

E   My action plan would involve your suspension or firing of Dean in the course of a historical explanation of your reliance on the Dean Report - his apparent unreliability -

P   But going out - you see the Garment guy got him in today - Garment says it's all going to come out anyway (unintelligible) etc., etc., etc., with the U.S. Attorneys. That's what Petersen's view is, of course.

E   What's that? The Garment deal?

P   That it is all going to come out, and Haldeman and Ehrlichman are going to resign. He told me that on Sunday. I asked him again yesterday. I said, "Now look it. That's pretty damned flimsy." He said, "Yes, I'm not talking about legal exposure. I'm just talking about the fact that as this stuff comes out they're going to be eaten, but eaten alive. Mr. President, the clamour is going to be something you cannot stand." I said, "Would it be better for them to get leave or something?" And he said, "No, this is the government. Rather to sit there and later as a result of this tid-bit and that tid-bit and so forth—he lied and I don't lie and so forth. Haldeman against Dean and Haldeman against Ehrlichman, Ehrlichman against Dean, who to hell is lying?" He said, "Definitely they'll say, (expletive removed), Mr. President, can't you let these fellas—" Now that's my point. That's what he said.

E   I understand.

P   That's an argument to be made. He said that to Rogers last night and that, of course, is Garment's argument. And I guess Rose, Chappie Rose agree with that, or whatever. My problem is, at the present time, I just don't want to have to talk to each of these side-line people individually, 'cause I don't know. I think some—Garment came in and was talking about the (unintelligible) story in the *Times*. Petersen told me about it last night. He said (unintelligible) had called. And I said, "That must have leaked out of your place." He said, "No, it didn't." Could it leaked out of here?

E   Could it have been Garment?

H   Could have been, but it isn't at all likely. It's a Justice.

P   But you see—what you say about Dean, I said to him (unintelligible). He supports the Garment plan. He's talked to Garment and Garment has talked to Dean.

E   Dean has talked to everybody in this place.

P   I told him not to talk to him any more. But you see Dean—let's see, what the hell—what's he got with regard to the President? He came and talked to me, as you will recall, about the need for $120,000 for clemencies—

E   You told me that the other day, I didn't know that before.

H   But so what?

P   What?

H   So what?

P   I said, what in the world John, I mean, I said John you can't (unintelligible) on this short notice. What's it cost (unintelligible) I sort of laughed and said, "Well, I guess you could get that."

E   Now is he holding that over your head? Saying—

P   No, No, No, I don't think Dean would go so far as to get into any conversation he had with the President— even Dean I don't think.

H   Well, he can't—you have both executive privilege in conversation with him.

P   Let's call it executive privilege, but on the other hand you've got to figure that Dean could put out something with somebody else.

P   That's the only thing I can think of he's told me but I've not got him in yet to ask about this thing about you—Liddy (unintelligible)

E   Oh well, they'll be one of those a day.

P   Well, the point is can we survive it?

E   Well—

P Can Haldeman and Ehrlichman survive it. The point that I—Let me say this. I know your (unintelligible) It's a hell of a lot different that John Dean. I know that as far as you're concerned, you'll go out and throw yourselves on a damned sword. I'm aware of that. I'm trying to think the thing through with that in mind because, damn it, you're the two most valuable members on the staff. I know that. The problem is, you're the two most loyal and the two most honest. We don't have to go into that. You know how I feel about that. It's not bull—it's the truth. The problem we got here is this. I do not want to be in a position where the damned public clamour makes, as it did with Eisenhower, with Adams, makes it necessary or calls—to have Bob come in one day and say, "Well Mr. President, the public - blah blah blah - I'm going to leave." Now that's the real problem on this damned thing and I don't think that kicking Dean out of here is going to do it. Understand, I'm not ruling out kicking him out. But I think you got to figure what to hell does Dean know. What kind of blackmail does he have? I don't know what all he does—

E Let me make a suggestion.

P Alright.

E You've got Dean coming in to you saying, "I've talked to the U.S. Attorney and I've told him a lot of things that I did wrong." So you put him on leave. He isn't charged with anything yet, but he's said them to you.

P I asked him that and he said I'll go on leave along with Haldeman and Ehrlichman.

E Well, he's not in any position to bargain with you on that. Now when the time comes that I'm charged with anything wrong—

P Well, John, you have been by a U.S. Attorney and by Petersen to me. Petersen is not charging you legal—

E That's what I mean. See I understand the difference. You see Dean has broken the law on the face of his (unintelligible) to you—

P Petersen has said to me, he says that there is—because of the evidence that has come in here—that Haldeman and Ehrlichman should (unintelligible) now I'm faced with that damned hardship.

P Hmmm. Say you get there. So you don't get immunity. Colson thinks it's in order not to give immunity, huh?

E Right.

P And tell him. Then he would say, "Well, what are you going to do about Haldeman and Ehrlichman?"

E What you have to say is nobody—

H He doesn't have to say that.

P Yes, he does.

E What you have to say is nobody in this White House—

P Dean isn't going to say it. I mean—Petersen—Petersen's the guy that can give immunity.

H Well, tell him not to give us immunity either.

P (unintelligible) that's a problem. Now, come on!

H Well, see, it's none of his business whether you suspend us or not. That's your decision.

P I know it is. The point is—let me put it candidly. If I do not suspend you, he will probably give him immunity. That's the problem (unintelligible) unbearable. If you do take a leave, I think he will—it's possible—well, it's possible that he would (unintelligible) even if you do leave—that he would (unintelligible) I agree. But Dean is the guy that he's got to use for the purpose of making the case.

H Yes, but, even Ehrlichman, which he already admits he doesn't have a case on (unintelligible) significance.

P Well, he says legally, yes, he does. In the case of Haldeman, it'll discuss—the Strachan things have—determine a lot to do with what Strachan says and what Kalmbach says—the 350 thing and that sort of thing.

H Kalmbach has no relation to me on that.

E That ah—

P Have you thought when you say before it gets to (unintelligible) thing out of the way. Have you given any thought to what the line ought to be—I don't mean a lie—but a line, on raising the money for these defendants? Because both of you were aware of what was going on you see—the raising of the money—you were aware of it, right?

E Yes, sir.

P And you were aware—You see, you can't go in and

533

say I didn't know what in hell he wanted the $250 for.

H   No - I've given a great deal of thought (unintelligible)

P   Well I wonder. I'm not—look—I'm concerned about the legal thing Bob, and so forth. You say that our purpose was to keep them from talking to the press.

E   Well, that was my purpose—and before I get too far out on that, ah, I want to talk to an attorney and find out what the law is—which I have not yet done.

P   Right!

H   That's just what I want to do too. This is only a draft.

P   Right. Good. The only point is I, I think it is not only that but you see that involves all our people. That's what I feel—it involves Kalmbach—

E   Well.

P   And what to hell Kalmbach was told.

E   Well, Mr. President, when the truth and fact of this is known, that building next door is full of people who knew that money was being raised for these people.

P   EOB?

E   Yes, sir, just full of them.

P   Many who know, but there were not so many actors. In other words, there's a difference between actors and noticees.

E   O.K. Well, apparently not, because I'm not an actor, ah—

H   The question there is testimony, I suppose.

P   I'm not trying to make any case—

E   No, but—

P   I'm not stating a case.

E   No, but I want you to think very critically about the difference here between knowledge of the general transactions going on, on the one hand, and being an affirmative actor on the other, because that's the difference between Dean and me. Now on this business on whether Dean should have immunity, I think you have to ask yourself really, the basic question, whether anybody in the White House who does wrong, ought to get immunity, no matter how many other people he implicates.

P   Strachan included?

E   Anybody—anybody. I just question whether in the orderly administration of justice, it looks right for anybody in the White House to get immunity.

P   I could call Petersen in (unintelligible) basic (unintelligible) public statement out at 3:00 p.m. is that right?

H   Well, yes—but you don't have to.

P   Well, Garment says we have to.

H   Well, yes, but isn't that what Garment said yesterday, the day before, and the week before that? Garment (unintelligible)—

P   Well, understand, I'm not panicking myself but they tell me there seems to be a considerable feeling that a—

E   Well, 1 agree with you.

P   (unintelligible) LaRue's been called, Strachan's been called, Dean might put up a story of the times. You never know. We don't need a Haldeman/Ehrlichman.

E   Yea, but you see it's typical Dean position. If Dean is treated different from us, he will go out and say he's a scapegoat for higher-ups.

H   That figures 'cause he knows Ostrow and Ostrow is the guy that covers Justice.

P   I see and Petersen told me that. He told about conversations with that wife of (unintelligible) apparently sat at some table with (unintelligible) libber they addressed, and the top guy, Rosenblatt or something like that, at the *Post* was talking to somebody else of the staff. "The Press is going to get out in front—we've got a hell of alot more—we've just held it back." They might be bluffing—I would doubt that they are at this point.

H   I would think they probably have more, but I would guess what they have more of is in the Committee. I don't think they got much more in the White House, unless, I don't know what it could be unless they got Colson stuff—that would be the only area.

P   (unintelligible)

H   Yeah, That's the only area where you have any jeopardy in the White House.

P   Let me say with regard to Colson—and you can say that I'm way ahead of them on that—I've got the message on that and that he feels that Dean—but believe me I've been thinking about that all day yesterday—whether Dean should be given immunity. The point is—I don't know that it can happen, but I can call Petersen in and say he cannot be given immunity, but nobody on the White House staff can be given immunity. And I—whether he'll carry that order out - that's going to be an indicator that that's Dean and (unintelligible). And then what do I say about Dean. Do I tell him that he goes?

E   Well, you see, the thing that precipitated Colson's coming over is that he found that Dean was still here.

535

You see, Dick Howard called Chuck and went through that business of the FBI men sending him into the arms of Dean. So, Colson called and says you've got an ass at your bosom over there, and so, today he checked again, apparently with Howard, and discovered that Dean was still here and he called and said, "I've got to see you." He came in and he says, "You guys are just out-of-your-minds," and said he wanted to see the President. He was fit to be tied about it.

P Colson was?

E Yes, because he thinks—

P But you see if I say, "Dean, you leave today," he'd go out and say, "Well the President's covering up for Ehrlichman and Haldeman" alright. There you are. Because he knows what I know." That's what he would say. I tried to put - I mean - I'm trying to look and see - John - what to hell we are really up against. First it was Liddy (unintelligible) scapegoat, now John Dean is.

H Well, the answer to that is that if he said it publicly, the President is not covering up for anybody, and will not tolerate—

P The way he's put it to me, Bob, very cute, as I have said, "Son of a gun (unintelligible) in view of what you have told me, if Haldeman and Ehrlichman are willing to resign, and so forth, I too, will resign." In other words, he basically put the shoe on the other - which of course is what led me to the conclusion that that's exactly what his attorney told him to do. If he can get Haldeman and Ehrlichman, that some way gets him (unintelligible) that's what you have here.

E Yeah, because then that will be argued back to the U.S. Attorney, "Well you see, the President thought enough of Dean's charges to let these guys go."

P I was trying to indicate to him that both of you had indicated a willingness to - in the event - that you know what I mean.

E And here's a guy that comes in and in effect, confesses to you the commission of crimes.

P And charges you.

E And charges us, that's right.

P That's right. And I said, "Now wait - these charges are not—" and you see he also has an alibi in the U.S. Attorney—

E Small wonders.

P He's asked (inaudible) Attorney General that the President should act—

E   Well, you see my point and—

P   Yeah

E   And you'd have to obviously, call us when—

P   Go ahead. Go ahead on the action—

E   Well, it would involve the suspension because it would involve a recounting of how you happened to get into the personal investigation of this by reason of Dean's being unable to reduce his full report to writing for you. And that that rang a bell, and you personally turned to and have spent a great deal of your time in the last several weeks on this—and have seen dramatic progress in the Grand Jury in the last several days. That would be Step 1. Now in addition to that you would say the Ervin Committee has come up with a good set of ground rules while do provide us with—

P   Well, did you work that out?

E   Well, you'd say this. I think you'll find that they are going to go on television under oath, pretty much regardless, but, the ground rules give you a toe hold. They do provide for Executive Session.

P   Is Executive Session considered executive privilege?

E   And they will consider—

P   And otherwise they will go into open hearings.

E   Yes, but there again executive privilege is reserved.

P   Executive privilege is reserved, fine.

H   At this point, the way we're in the soup now, we can lose nothing by going.

P   That's right.

H   I think we may gain.

P   That's right, I couldn't agree more. So if you can prepare me with at least that much, I'll agree. That I can say that today.

H   Well, that's a hell of a bomb shelter right there.

P   Yes, it is. But, let's get on with the rest of it.

E   That's it. That's all I have for today. But it gets you into the case—its you leading it. It notices the progress and the Grand Jury as related to your efforts and it doesn't say what they are.

P   Well, the point is though the story today is that John Dean is suspended, but—and then John Dean is going to be out there plastering—out saying the President has indicated that Haldeman and Ehrlichman too might go.

H   Let me suggest a different process, which is that you don't suspend John Dean, but that you instruct John Dean that he is not to come to work any more. He is in effect suspended, but not publicly suspended.

P He'll say, "What about Haldeman and Ehrlichman?"

H I would suggest to you that you do the same with us. And I was going to suggest, I was going to request that that action. For this reason—I've got to speak for myself. John's got to speak for himself. I have now concluded that my course is that I must put out my story. I must put it out in total and in my words, before I go to the—I don't know about the Grand Jury—before I—

P Before you go to the Senate Committee?

H go to the Senate Committee. I'm going to have to put it out there anyway.

P I don't think you're ever going to get to the Senate Committee. I don't think the Committee Hearings will ever go forward.

H I do. I don't think there is any chance of them not going forward. You think because of legal case (unintelligible) O.K. Great if they don't. Then maybe I never tell my story. But my view is that at some point in time I'm going to have to tell it.

P But you—the way—I would reserve, Bob, the right to tell that story until you felt you did have to go to the Committee Hearings. See what I mean? Or, unless you got to a point where you were nibbled to death.

H That's right. Or until a partial charge comes up. For instance, if the Grand Jury leaks or the Justice people leak the Strachan stuff, then that forces my hand.

P John?

E Well, subject to attorney's advice.

H That's what I was going to say. I will not make this statement until I have worked it out.

P Bill said he just couldn't remember.

H Well, we've got some leads. We're going to start on today, so we've got that, but my interest is served and I will also argue that the better off I come out of this, the better off you come out of it—vis-a-vis me. In other words, anything I do to my interest is to your interest.

P Let me ask you this, John.

E What's that?

P You said that you ought not to come for awhile. On what basis? I mean, we do this on an oral basis.

H What I'm doing now is requesting you, on an oral basis—

P Yeah.

H to not expect me to carry out any duties for awhile

because (inaudible) perfect this and get it ready—

P   Where would you do it, at home or in the office here?

H   I can do it wherever you want me to. I think I ought to do it in the office, but—

P   Alright.

E   If Dean says, "What about Haldeman and Ehrlichman?" You say "John, I'm talking to you about you. Now I'll take care of them my own way. I'm not going to have you bargaining with me."

H   I don't think the President can be in the position of making a deal with John Dean on anything.

E   Yeah. "I'll go if they go." Supposing I said, "I won't go unless Henry Kissinger goes!" Yeah, it's ridiculous. Let me speak to this. I have pretty much unplugged myself of my day-to-day stuff, because with this kind of stuff going on you just can't think about anything else.

P   Of course, it's been a little hard for me to also.

E   Sure. Now, I have a need to get into all kinds of records and my date books and these are volumes and volumes of correspondence and stuff. If I couldn't come into the office, I probably couldn't prepare a defense.

P   What about Dean coming in? Why not him? (unintelligible) I think I've told Dean he's to have nothing more to do with this case.

E   Well, he's sure not following out your orders, if that's the case.

P   You see what I mean.

E   Now, you'd have another problem, and I don't know what's been going on in the last week or so, but I imagine he's carted stuff out of here by the bale. I just don't know.

H   You don't know that.

E   I certainly—

H   If you suspend him or tell him to leave in any way, you also move in to take care of his files.

P   Could I say this, "John, both Haldeman and Ehrlichman have both requested the opportunity to be relieved of their duties—I mean their main duties, so that they can concentrate on this matter to prepare for their appearance before the Grand Jury." Could I say that?

E   Sure, well—

P   Wait.

H   The trap you're falling into there is that you're admitting to Dean that you regard the allegations that he has raised against us as of the same validity of his own criminal admission to you.

E   If that's the case then maybe that's what you should say.

P   No, no, no, there are two different levels.

E   Then that's the way it ought to be put. He brought in a lot of silly garbage about me which doesn't add up to a nickel's worth of a law suit. Ah, he's come in and told you that he's been involved in all kinds of stuff. It seems to be a very different qualitative problem. Here again, I hate to argue my case—it's very awkward.

P   You should argue, John. I wonder if whether or not I trapped myself (unintelligible) about this business when I said, "Look, John," I said, "both Haldeman and Ehrlichman have offered to resign."

E   Well, I offered to resign at your total and sole discretion. You don't have to have a reason—

P   (expletive removed) (unintelligible) Then I said—

E   Well—

P   Wait a minute. Wait a minute. Then Petersen said, he said, "We've got to have corroborative testimony." So you see what I mean?

E   Yeah.

P   Before we could get—Let me put it this way. He realizes that before he could try to give Dean immunity he's got to have corroborative testimony on the value of Dean's evidence. That's what he's trying to get at the present time. That's why he was calling Strachan, Colson, Kalmbach, et al. The purpose of it being, John, to get corroborative evidence that would say, well, Dean's evidence is so valuable as far as other people are concerned, that we can therefore give him immunity. Now I'm not a criminal lawyer, but does that make any sense?

E   I don't know.

P   But you see what his tactic is?

E   I put it.—I don't know what the previous commitment to him is, but he's not being fired, he's not being suspended, he's being directed to stay away from the office.

P   I might put it that since you are talking to a U.S. Attorney. If I could put it that way to him I might be able to make some hay. Bring the U. S. Attorney in. And I'll say don't give him immunity.

E   From a public policy standpoint.

P   Yeah, (unintelligible) And I'll tell you what Petersen did tell me. He did say this much. I said, "what about Dean?" and he said, "Well, we haven't made a deal with him yet." I think I told you about this—

E   Yep.

P   I said, "Why do you have to make a deal?" And he says "Well, he wants to make a deal." And I said, "What do you mean, let him off?" He said, "Well, that's what you do, Mr. President." I said, "Well," I said, "you're sort of (unintelligible)." We've had some real good talks. I mentioned this to Rogers. Rogers just shook his head and said. "That's right." And I said, "They have both said that." And I said "I will certainly have it under consideration."

E   Now there's another matter. If this is awkward for you, the best thing you should do is get rid of me, you know, once and for all.

P   Yep.

E   But if it is anything short of that—

P   Yeah.

E   Then it seems to be that you have to take into account qualitative differences.

P   Yep.

E   And if you don't want to make a formal suspension, then the thing to say is, "I want you to stay away from the office. Just don't come around, because I know everything that happens in this building is being funneled directly to the U. S. Attorney through you, or I have reason to think that, and I cannot have that situation." Now that's the way—Yeah.

P   So he isn't going to do it simply on the basis. He isn't giving Dean immunity simply on the basis of what Dean has already said.

E   I understand. Ah, my fear here is—

P   Dean getting immunity?

E   Dean getting immunity, or anybody in the White House getting immunity, it is in itself treatable as a cover-up. And obviously is we are put in a position of defending ourselves, the things that I am going to have to say about Dean are: that basically that Dean was the sole proprietor of this project, that he reported to the President, he reported to me only incidentally.

P   Reported to the President?

E   Yes sir, in other words—

P   When?

E   Well, I don't know when, but the point is—

541

P You see the problem you've got there is that Dean does have a point there which you've got to realize. He didn't see me when he came out to California. He didn't see me until the day you said, "I think you ought to talk to John Dean." I think that was in March.

E All right. But, but the point is that basically he was in charge of this project.

P He'll say he reports to the President through other people.

E Well, O. K. Then you see what you've got there is an imputation. He says then—as that kind of a foundation—"I told Ehrlichman that Liddy did it." What he is saying is that, "I told the President through Ehrlichman that Liddy did it."

H Which means that it was perfectly acknowledged as far as Ehrlichman was concerned and there was nothing that you were required to do about it anyway.

E That's right. But you see I get into a very funny defensive position then vis-a-vis you and vis-a-vis him, and it's very damned awkward. And I haven't thought it clear through. I don't know where we come out.

P Yeah. You see Dean's little game here (unintelligible). One of the reasons this staff is so damned good. Of course he didn't report to me. I was a little busy, and all of you said, "let's let Dean handle that and keep him out of the President's office." And maybe you didn't want him in there for other reasons too. But he did.

E Well, the case I'm going to make—

P Well, of course, he would then say who the hell did he report to?

E Well, in many cases, to no one. He just went ahead and did things.

P The other point is that they'll say (unintelligible) the first time he reported to the President—

E Well statistically, it's interesting. I'm now far enough in my records for last year.

P You probably had five meetings a month.

E Less than that. Matched against that, all the other things I was doing—substantive thing—and Dean becomes practically the least of my worries.

P How about you, Bob?

H I haven't any idea. I don't have a log. Unless Dean does.

P The only thing he doesn't have is the fact that should have come in to see me. Ziegler talked to him, I guess and so forth and so on.

E   Moore—frequently.

P   Moore—all right—Moore (unintelligible) but I haven't talked to Moore either, have I?

E   Well, I think, I've got to think this through. I just don't know where that leads.

P   (unintelligible) White House staff, John Dean, John Dean's highly sensitive information (unintelligible). Well, damn it, John Dean's highly sensitive information was on only one count. Believe me guys we all know—Well—the (unintelligible) stuff regarding Bob. Strachan has got to be worked out. I don't know how that's going to work out. Bob, did Strachan have a—the plan? What he says about whether he did have a plan—whether he did show it to you—remains to be seen.

H   He apparently said he did not.

P   All right. The other point is whether Strachan got information now that is the stuff that is clearly identifiable according to Petersen as being telephone taps. Strachan will probably say no it was not. - And so, that's that.

H   The discrepancy between Strachan and Magruder is because what Strachan got that could have been from that it turns out, was not. It was something else. When they get that, they'll get an interesting new problem, because Strachan would say it was Operations GEMSTONE, not Operation SEDAN CHAIR—and GEMSTONE wasn't Watergate so that will uncover that there was something else that they did. I don't know what it was.

P   Something else you mean?

H   I guess, 'cause there was an Operation GEM-STONE that Strachan got reports on.

P   They tell me that GEMSTONE was the code word for everything—GEMSTONE is for everything.

H   Well I thought SEDAN CHAIR was the Watergate thing, O. K. Well if GEMSTONE is the total thing, then what he got was reported from that. And it's a confidential sources indicate that that—It did not clearly identify, according to Strachan. I can't tell you anything else.

P   (unintelligible) I want you to know what he's told me.

H   All right.

P   John, I'm just trying to see what the options are on Dean—what we turn loose here.

E   Absolutely. Well, let's go back to the press plan. Maybe that will give us some guidance.

P Right.

E If you say in the press plan, "The President got concerned about this," the question, "why didn't he get concerned sooner because this has been in the paper for months and months?" Well, "the reason he didn't get concerned sooner is he was resting secure in the belief that he had the whole story."

P Right.

E Well, what made him insecure?

P Do I ever ask Dean in and ask him answers? The answer is no.

E No, but the point is that you were resting secure on his assurances.

P Go ahead.

E Well—

H Didn't you at some point get a report from Dean that nobody in the White House was involved.

E Didn't we put that out way back in August?

P I mean, I just said "Well, that's all I know now." It was never in writing. He never came in orally and told me Dean—John Dean I never saw about this matter. You better check, but I don't think John Dean was ever seen about this matter until I saw him, when John Ehrlichman suggested that I'd better see John Dean.

E You better check Bob, back in that period of time July - when we were in San Clemente - my recollection is that he did come and see you at that time - but we can check that.

P Oh - by himself? No.

E Well, by himself or with one of us. I don't know.

P He may have come in, but it was a pretty—I hope he did, hope he did. But he might have come in sort of the end, and someone said, "Look here's John Dean from Washington," and I may have said, "Thanks for all your hard work."

E Well—let's follow this line and see where it leads us. The President rested secure in the belief that his Counsel had investigated this and assured him that nobody in the White House was involved.

E O. K. Then, what moved him off of that belief and assurance? Well, what moved him off was the sequence of events leading to John Dean being sent to Camp David to write it all down.

P What moved him off first were reports that occurred in the court testimony.

E   That's right.

P   Charges were made by McCord—and other charges—Charges were made by McCord. I wouldn't say (unintelligible). Charges were made by McCord that, in open, before a jury committee. The President ordered a full investigation.

E   Well, the first thing you did—and maybe you can avoid saying this—but you're saying you ordered a full press investigation when Dean came back and said to Bob, "I can't write that down."

P   He told me that too.

E   Then that rang a bell. Because if Dean can't write that down, then we must have problems bigger than I ever thought. And so that's when you put on the full court press.

P   Well all right. Here's—you've got the dates on this. Well—

E   I have them in there, yeah. Let's see what Dean says on that. Well he says, "The reason I couldn't write them down is because Dick Moore and others said (unintelligible) said how could I write it down—draw the wagons up around the White House?" That phrase, remember that, isn't that a Dean phrase?

H   Sure. His line was that you could do that because there was no problem at the White House, the problems were at the Committee.

P   What did he tell you with that respect? What was Dean's line before he deserted?

E   Well, what he said—

P   My point is—you've got to watch out. He may say, "Well, they were trying to get me—conspired to get me to write a report that was untrue."

E   Well, I understand, except that he was sent to write it without anybody being near him.

P   Except Moore (unintelligible)

E   I'm sure that when he went through this exercise, it was impossible for him to write it down without it being a confession. And he said, "My God, I don't know how this case is going to break, but I'm crazy to have a piece of paper like that around."

P   Then I could say then that I ordered—who conducted the investigation?

E   The way we got it doesn't say—

H   You asked other staff members to explore this—you had Ehrlichman, Moore, Garment, Haldeman.

P   That's right. All right. And then—

E   Then you contacted some people and said, "Don't hold back on my account."

P   Yes, like Hunt—Liddy.

E   Like Mitchell and Magruder.

P   I passed the word to all sources that everybody was to talk, to tell the truth, which I had done previously. I reaffirmed. I reaffirmed specific terms to specific people.

H   Well, you had reason to believe that they might have a misapprehension on it.

P   Any misapprehension and so forth and so on—to all parties involved - who were those people. I should not say—

H   You can't list those people.

P   I should not say—well you can't list the people for a reason that would prejudice them. I talked to all parties concerned that if there was a shred of information which might in any way—which they might have on this case—I reaffirm what I had said publicly—that we must cooperate fully and tell the whole truth. Then, we come to the last weekend. On Saturday—a major development occurred—I can't say, "that as a result—" That would be an overstatement.

E   Nope.

P   Then on Sunday I can't say that I talked with Kleindienst. Just say on Sunday.

E   Except - remember I informed Kleindienst on Saturday - so you—

P   I informed Kleindienst. Then we'll get questions. "Did you inform him in person?" I can say I passed the information.

H   Say you passed the word to Kleindienst

P   I informed the Attorney General. At my direction Ehrlichman filled in the Attorney General completely on the information that we had found and on Sunday the Attorney General and (unintelligible). They indicated as a result, a major development in the case—these major developments in the case—we've got to get Petersen.

E   Then Ziegler or you could turn it over to Petersen, and let him say something innocuous.

P   And I directed Petersen to direct to me personally on my developments and any member of the White House staff or Federal Government was to be available to the Grand Jury and would testify - would be directed by the President to testify. Now you come to the next thing—

you see Garment's scenario here will be (unintelligible) "I have asked that any government people who have been—who might—who have been—who are directly or indirectly—subjects of the investigation, even though having—this is no indication of any guilt—will be relieved of their duties and until the Grand Jury (unintelligible) Anyone who refuses to cooperate will be dismissed. Anyone (unintelligible)."

H   Is that it?

P   Yes. (unintelligible). Anyone who refuses to cooperate will be dismissed. Anyone will be given leave until his until his trial is finished. He's had an opportunity to have his day in court. (unintelligible)

E   How about anyone granted immunity?

P   Anyone granted immunity will be—let me try Petersen on you today?

P   Your idea about Petersen would be to hit him (unintelligible) with that.

E   Trouble policy - I can't have it.

P   Until I do that, the President (unintelligible) follow it or (unintelligible) Petersen has - the President's—

E   Tying our hands?

P   Tying our hands. But we're not telling Dean not to talk. I direct everybody to talk, but nobody is to be given immunity.

E   In other words, you don't need—there are plenty of ways of proving a case around here.—besides granting some fellow immunity.

P   Yeah.

E   You don't need that, and it looks like what you are doing is letting somebody off scott free.

P   That's right. Also, it looks like a cover-up.

H   And particularly somebody - personally associated - in this case.

E   Maybe the point that Petersen is missing—maybe intentionally so, is that Dean is a major act in this thing. And big fish/small fish, nevertheless, if a major actor gets immunity and just walks away from the White House having committed 89 crimes - that - and it is your Justice Department, and the guy that runs it, reports daily to you, what does that say? That says—"Gee, I didn't want my Counsel to get hurt." The only question that remains is why didn't he grant immunity to everybody.

H   What it says is exactly the point - the Counsel knows more than—

547

P Now, should I have any more conversations with Dean?

E No. I don't think you should. I think you should send him a note and tell him what your decision is. Or have Kehrli or somebody call him and say, "Don't come to work anymore. You're not suspended, you're not fired, but you're not to come into the office until this matter is—"

P That's a good tough way. What can he do?

E I don't think he can do anything. If somebody says to him, "Well, did you get suspended?" He can say, "No, I really haven't. I'm just sort of not working until—"

H He hasn't been to work for a month anyway.

E He's been out talking to the U.S. Attorney the whole time.

H Well, he's been here because it serves his purpose to be the inside story. He's been out of the office for a month. He's been—

P I called him this morning and told him I wanted to talk to him later to ask him about that appointment June 19, but I don't think I better get into that any more.

E I don't either.

P And, and he's going to give me some song and dance.

E Well (unintelligible) for your private information, I have gone back to the participants in that meeting where I was supposed to have said, "send Hunt out of the country." To a man, they say it didn't happen. And two of them said, "Gee if either one of them—"

P What about the meeting?

E And they said, "If that had happened, it would have been burned into my recollection." The sort of thing like you ordering—

P You better damned well remember being—The main thing is this, John, and when you meet with the lawyers—and you Bob, and I hope Strachan has been told—believe me—don't try to hedge anything before the damned Grand Jury. I'm not talking about morality, but I'm talking about the vulnerabilities.

E Sure, good advice.

P Huh?

E Good advice.

P You guys—damnit—I know you haven't done a damned thing. I do know this—they've tried to track on perjury—you're going have that—

E   Fortunately I have good records—I know who was in that meeting and so, I was able to call—

P   (Unintelligible) attorneys that certain materials. The point is now they talked to people—somebody put those things in the bag—I suppose Fielding.

E   Fielding or Dean. I don't know. Let me just tell you—

P   Did he inventory? For example, who's going to testify what the hell was in that bag?

E   I don't know. May I just finish telling you about this - I think it is important—

P   (Unintelligible)

E   Well - it does - and also - Dean is the guy that made the call sending Hunt out of the country. But, the interesting thing about it all is that Friday, he called Colson and said, "Chuck, do you remember a meeting up in John's office where John said 'So and So and D-6' - and John said - 'send Hunt out of the country' - don't you?" And Chuck said. "I told him it never happened." And I didn't raise this with Chuck—he raised it with me. And said, "I had this funny phone call from this guy." So, he's out around planting his seeds.

H   He's playing the Magruder game - flying from flower to flower - planting his pollen.

E   So, I don't think—

P   I think those (unintelligible) you got very clever liars. I told you this before—very clever liars.

E   Yep.

P   (Unintelligible) I got to get out of this—

E   I think you can slide by that by just saying, "Stay home. Don't come in to the office."

P   Yep. I can say. "John, I think it's best that you don't come into the office."

E   I can tell you one way you might do it is to say, "I've had a report that an FBI man about to serve a subpoena on Dick Howard told Howard to come and talk to you. I can't have that. Because you cannot sit there as an agent of the U.S. Attorney."

P   I indicated that already.

H   Dean will say the same thing that you just said, that I can't prepare my case for the Grand Jury if I can't work with my files and so forth, and so if you are telling him not to come in, "I'll send a truck over and have my files brought to my home." That would take care of getting his files—

P (Unintelligible) his files subpoenaed?

H Well, there's a question on that—

E That's the position you ought to take on that.

H Damn right. All of the files are yours and they are not subject to any action that your files are subject to.

P Shall I tell him that?

E Nope. Let's wait until the question comes up.

P Well, how do I answer the question—Bob, what do I say, "I have to have your files?"

E Well, he's already made his statement. It's obvious to the U.S. Attorney. He's past that point.

P I don't think you can write him a note. It's going to anger him anyway. No sense in doing that. See what I mean? We've got to remember whatever he is doing—I don't mean that you can't—he's going to do anything to save his ass. That's what is involved. But on the other-hand—

E O.K. - I got an idea—

P You got to remember (unintelligible) he put this a lot higher. He could say, "Well, I told the President about $127,000, that we needed $127,000 and the President said, 'well I don't know where we could get it, I don't know.'"

H How could you do that though—that's true (unintelligible)

E Alright. I'll tell you how you might be able to handle that. The FBI has just served a subpoena on our WH police which asked that they produce the names of people cleared into the WH/EOB complex from 12:01 AM June 18, 1972 - to 11:00 PM June 18, 1972.

P Where were we then?

H What date?

P June 18.

E The day of the bugging.

H We were in San Clemente.

E Really?

H Yeah.

E Florida.

H I mean Florida. I'm sorry. That was the weekend that we flew directly to Grand Cay and you went to Walkers and we went over to Key Biscayne.

P Well, maybe that's an unsafe thing.

E The WH Police had notified Fred Fielding of the subpoena—

H See that's your other problem. You have a WH legal case and you have no WH lawyer—another interesting end to look at.

P Where's Fielding stand on all this?

H He's Dean's (unintelligible) lives next door to him. Dean sponsored him. That doesn't necessarily mean he goes Dean's way. Fielding is an honorable guy—provincially so—who may not like what Dean is doing any more than we do.

P Well, when I see Dean I'll say, "We're not going to publish this publicly or anything of that sort—but I do think that you should not—" What you want to do is get him out of the WH and yet Colson's recommendation is to get him out by firing him—

E Colson would like to discredit him.

P Well I know. But the question is what he could do to discredit us.

E Well.

P That's a problem.

H Yeah. But I think at some point, like you do on anything else, you gotta face up to the fact that the guy is either a friend or a foe—or a neutral. If he's a neutral you don't have to worry about him; if he's a friend you rely on him, if he's a foe you fight him, and this guy—it seem at this point—is a foe.

P When I talked to him I said, "Now John, any conversations are (unintelligible)." I said, "Anything (unintelligible) National Security are (unintelligible) you understand?" He said, "Yes (unintelligible) testified to it (unintelligible)."

H O.K. He said it and it was no problem for him to say it. But it was no problem for him to say a lot of things to us over the last couple of weeks too.

P The point is, if you break if off with him, then he could go out and say, "Screw the (unintelligible)."

H No he can't. It's not his privilege. It's yours.

P I know it's mine, but—

H If he screws the privilege—

P Well, I think you have to charge Henry Petersen or whoever is in charge here with protecting your privilege and then that's got to go down to Silberman and Silberman has to be cautioned that he is not to go into matters of executive privilege - he is not to go into matters of national security importance. Any matters involving a conversation with the President—or national security, anything like that, they can ask me.

E   Now, the question comes up—I don't know far this will run—but this caper in California for instance. Colson asked me this thing of Hunt's out there—the national security connected Ellsberg. Well Peterson knows about it I think. It's laying around someplace over there. But if the question comes up, Colson says, "How do I handle that?" I said, "Well Chuck, if I were asked that—I would say that that was a national security project and I'm not in the position to answer a question on that, because I would have to refer to the President for a waiver of executive privilege on that if he desired to do so." And he said, "Well, can I say the same thing?" And I said, "Well, I don't know whether you can or not. He said, "Well what would the President say if it's referred to him?" I said, "I don't know. I'll go ahead and ask him."

P   That's what we'd say.

E   Can I tell him that for you?

P   Yep. Anything on the (unintelligible) thing, the plumbing thing was national security, the ITT thing. No, I can't believe it was that—you know—the Hunt thing there. That will just have to handle the way it is. (Unintelligible) Colson about (unintelligible) Hunt thing?

E   I don't know. If anybody around here did, if anybody did it, was Dean.

H   I doubt if Dean knew about that. You see Dean and Colson never tracked particularly well together, I don't think.

E   Whoever operates this at the Justice Department has to be told that the inquiry must not jeopardize your privilege. Some day they're going to try and put you in a crunch spot.

P   Sure.

E   And they'll put a question to me and I'll say, "I can't take that question and then I'll be back to you and it's going to be hard."

P   No turning it off. It's national security—national security area—and that is a national security problem.

E   Or, if it is something that you and I have discussed directly.

P   (expletive removed) it.

E   I'll just (expletive removed) that—I'll just—

H   I don't think anybody is going to try to challenge that.

P   (unintelligible) conversations with the President (unintelligible).

552

E (unintelligible) just got to be told the background—

H Awful low before you get to that.

P (unintelligible) talk to the President about $127,-000 we had to get or were we able to get it or something. I don't know how—why it was at that point—that we were still working on money for Hunt—I don't know how the hell—

H That was the one that Bittman got to Dean on. He really cranked on it. He was very concerned—professed to be concerned because Bittman's threat was that Hunt said that, "If you don't get it to me I'm going to tell them all about the seamy things I did for Ehrlichman." And when Dean hit Ehrlichman on that, Ehrlichman's immediate reaction was let him go ahead—"There's nothing he can hang me on." Dean didn't like that answer and went on worrying about the money.

P Told me about it.

H Told you about it, told me about it. I was in here when he told you.

P Good. What did we say? Remember he said, "How much is it going to cost to keep these, these guys (unintelligible). I just shook my head. Then we got into the question—

H If there's blackmail here, then we're into a thing that's just ridiculous.

P He raised the point—

H (unintelligible) but you can't say it's a million dollars. It may be $10 million dollars. And that we ought not to be in this—

P That's right. That's right.

H We left it - that - we can't do anything about it anyway. We don't have any money, and it isn't a question to be directed here. This is something relates to Mitchell's problem. Ehrlichman has no problem with this thing with Hunt. And Ehrlichman said, (expletive removed) if you're going to get into blackmail, to hell with it."

P Good (unintelligible) Thank God you were in there when it happened. But you remember the conversation?

H Yes sir.

P I didn't tell him to go get the money did I?

H No

P You didn't either did you?

H Absolutely not! I said you got to talk to Mitchell. This is something you've got to work out with Mitchell—

not here—there's nothing we can do about it here.

P   We've got a pretty good record on that one, John, at least.

H   But there's a couple of complications he can throw in there (unintelligible) which would be of concern, but I just can't conceive that a guy—I can see him using it as a threat. I cannot see him sinking low enough to use that. I just—although I must admit the guy has really turned into an unbelievable disaster for us. People don't—he's not unAmerican and anti-Nixon. I'll tell you—during that period he busted his ass trying to work this out. It wore him to a frazel. And I think it probably wore him past the point of rationality. I think he may now be in a mental state that's causing him to do things that when he sobers up, he's going to be very disturbed about with himself.

P   Also, he's probalby got a very, very clever, new lawyer (unintelligible) I think that's part of the problem.

H   Could very well be. John, I can't believe, is a basically dishonorable guy. I think there's no question that John is a strong self-promoter, self-motivated guy for his own good, but—

P   But in that conversation I was—we were—I was—I said, "Well for (expletive removed), let's—"

H   You explored in that conversation the possibility of whether such kinds of money could be raised. You said, "Well, we ought to be able to raise—"

P   That's right.

H   "How much money is involved?" and he said, "Well it could be a million dollars." You said, "That's ridiculous. You can't say a million. Maybe you say a million, it may be 2 or 10, and 11"

P   But then we got into the blackmail.

H   You said, "Once you start down the path with blackmail it's constant escalation."

P   Yep. That's my only conversation with regard to that.

H   They could jump and then say, "Yes, well that was morally wrong. What you should have said is that blackmail is wrong not that it's too costly."

P   Oh, well that point (inaudible) investigation—

H   (inaudible)

P   You see my point? We were then in the business of—this was one of Dean's—when he was—was it after that we sent him to Camp David?

E   You sent him to Camp David on about the 20th. I think.

P   I would like to know with regard to that conversation, Bob—

E   I think it was about—his trip to Camp David—about the 23rd of March.

H   When was the (unintelligible) trip?

E   I haven't any idea. I have no idea.

P   Well,

E   Well, you'll know the date of your meeting here.

P   Well (inaudible). I suppose then we should have cut - shut it off, 'cause later on you met in your office and Mitchell said, "That was taken care of."

H   The next day. Maybe I can find the date by that—

P   Yeah. And Dean was there and said, "What about this money for Hunt?" Wasn't Dean there?

H   No, what happened was—Ehrlichman and Dean and Mitchell and I were in the office, in my office, and we were discussing other matters. And in the process of it, Mitchell said—he turned to Dean and said, "Let me raise another point. Ah, have you taken care of the other problem—the Hunt problem?" Something like that. I don't know how he referred to it. But we all knew instantly what he meant. Dean kind of looked a little flustered and said, "Well, well, no. I don't know where that is or something," and Mitchell said, "Well I guess it's taken care of." And so we assumed from that that Mitchell had taken care of it, and there was no further squeak out of it so I now do assume that Mitchell took care of it.

P   The problem I have there is—

H   Mitchell (unintelligible). LaRue was Mitchell's agent—

P   I understand that. What I meant is, I'm just seeing what Dean's lines of attack are.

H   You're saying, "Did I know about it?" I did. There's no question.

P   Say, "Yes, there was talk about it and so forth - and Mitchell took care of it." But you, on the other hand, you make the case that—

H   It's (unintelligible).

P   In this office, but not the other—not in your office.

H   In the other office the question of thing never arose. There again, Dean is the agent on it. Dean is coming in and saying what should I do. Dean's the agent on all this - that's where my money goes. All the input to me about the 350 came from Dean, and all the output came from Dean.

P   Then Dean was the one that said, "Look Bob, we

need 350 for or need the rest of this money."

H   No, they didn't even come that way. Dean said, "They need money for the defense, for their fees." And it was always put that way. That's the way it was always discussed.

P   Right - that's why I want that line. I think that's most important. You can work on—Get a lawyer.

H   And I said to Dean at that time, "Well, look, you've got a situation here. We've for the 350" I thought it was 350 - actually it was 328. "in cash that we need to get turned back to the Committee. Apparently they have a need for money - so we have a coincidence (unintelligible) now you ought to be able to work out someway to get them to take the cash - and that will take care of our needs and we help meet their needs." And he went back to Mitchell and Mitchell wouldn't do it.

H   And then they agreed to take 40 thousand of it which they did and shortly thereafter they agreed to take the rest, which they did.

P   You think - you check with (unintelligible) before the election in some—

H   It was not before the election.

P   Dean says it was before.

H   Strachan says it was in late November—30th or something like that.

E   Incidentally, remember you told me that Strachan had gone over there with Colson's partner and that the Judge wouldn't take him. It turned out that was Howard who went over. Dick Howard went over with one of Colson's partners. The U.S. Attorney kicked up a fuss about it. Saying that there might be a communication between the partner and Colson and so—

H   Strachan's lawyer is a totally (unintelligible) guy that he's acquired from somebody he knew in law school.

P   Good.

E   Now Colson has pitched me to retain his partner, which I think would be a mistake.

P   You

E   Yeah.

P   You can't retain his partner.

E   I don't think so. Be a big mistake because it would create identity between me and Colson that I don't feel comfortable with.

P   I don't want you—

H   You can't. You'd be out of your mind to do it.

P   Don't get in there with Colson. He'll defend himself.

H   Obviously Colson sees that as a way of getting in.

E   Sure.

H   We should not give Colson reason to get squeemish.

P   No.

E   I'm cultivating him.

P   No, sir.

E   I'm keeping him on the team. He feels that there is a coincidence of interest between you and me and him.

P   Right. Fine.

H   Consider (unintelligible) has to continue—

P   Right all the time. Let's go back now to the decision. First, should we make a statement today?

H   I would say yes.

P   I think so.

H   Ziegler should make it.

E   Well, if it is a carefully limited statement.

P   No questions.

E   I think—no. I think it should be a very tight statement—very conservative—well at least you should think it through so that you can stay away from the soft places. But I think broadly—across the country—people are waiting to see your face on the evening news talking about the Watergate case. And making more assurances.

P   Bill Rogers says this (unintelligible) first thought Ziegler—then as we left the boat last night (unintelligible) he totally rules out the 9:00. He says, "Don't make it the only story (unintelligible) 3 or 4 months (unintelligible)."

H   You know where the Watergate story is in the *Washington Post* today? Page 19.

E   (unintelligible)

P   I know. I know. And it'll be page 19 five months from now if we handle it right.

E   Now I suggested having Petersen stand by. You don't think that's a good idea.

P   No, no. I just think I should go out there and say, "O.K." John, let's come back to this business here—let's come back to the business of the—which is the play of the White House leaders (unintelligible) doesn't work.

E   Well, I think, in view of the foregoing, all that's gone and all that's been said, I think if you can get the results of having Dean out of his office, and I wouldn't worry about the files. I think you could put it on a basis that if he needs a file he could get it upon loan, so that at least you would be able to monitor what he was getting. I think that you would say to him, "In view of your relationship with the U.S. Attorney's office, I just don't think it is prudent for you to be on the grounds."

P   That's right.

E   And, you're going to have to work someplace else.

H   "I don't think there's any appearance problem, because you have been for a month anyway!"

E   Right. It won't be noticed. If we are asked in the press room—

P   That's right.

E   Ah, what your status is, we'll finesse it. And the question will come, "Has John Dean been placed on leave? No. Has John Dean been fired? No."

P   Alright.

E   And you could say to him, "If you don't bring it up, we won't."

P   Alright.

E   "If this leaks, it's going to leak from you because nobody is going—And, as far as Bob and John are concerned, I will make an appropriate arrangement with them."

P   I'm going to make an appropriate arrangement covering them. Course, it's something different—

E   "But, I cannot be in a position of having you dictate to me what it should be."

H   And you can't be in a position—

P   I can tell him, "I've made an appropriate arrangement, but it's got to be in my own way, depending upon what each is doing."

E   I think you could argue with him that the transition from John Dean being away from here and the transition being away from here is a very different kind of thing.

P   Yeah. That's right. We're not asking anybody to resign, John, because I think that would prejudice their rights.

E   Taking a formal leave—

P   Alright fine, you can do that, but you're rejecting the Garment proposal that everybody leave until everybody is clear that I talked with you a moment ago?

E   Well, I think a leave is the same as being fired in this context.

P   Do you Bob?

E   Prior to the charges.

H   When you have charges—

P   Here's the point. Let me—let me tell you what's going to happen in my view. And by charges, I don't mean indictments. But when they finally make their deal with Magruder (unintelligible) out of the D.C. jail—they're going to take him into open court. This is their deal, now because Sirica question (unintelligible) John last night. They are going to make this statement. I would assume then the charges would be made, at least as far as Magruder is concerned.

H   And they said Magruder makes charges against me? Interesting!

P   Bob, I don't know whether he does or not. Let's be damned sure (unintelligible). He's certainly going to say that Dean was involved and that Mitchell was involved.

E   And he'll say Strachan was involved.

P   He'll say Strachan was involved.

E   And, "Who's Strachan?" Well, Strachan was Mr. Haldeman's employee. But, my prediction is that if the Judge says, "Well, did Mr. Haldeman tell you to do anything or this or that," he'll say, "No sir, he was never involved in this."

H   He told me that is what he would say.

E   And he told me that is what he would say.

H   He told John that is what he would say in front of his lawyers. That's what he had said, and he flatly says that is what is the truth.

P   Yeah.

H   And it is what's the truth.

P   Alright. So your view, John, Bob, is that—you know that you got to look at—at being eaten away and then having to come in and say look, "I'm so impaired, I—"

H   No, I don't expect to be eaten away. I think when I get hit, I mean publicly. Let's say Magruder does name me. Let's say Magruder does implicate me publicly."

P   Or Dean. Say Dean names you.

H   Someone that's known publicly. As soon as Dean is known publicly—my view would be than I should then—I should request you to give me a leave of absence so that I can deal with this matter until it is cleared up.

P   You agree with that John?

E   It'll depend a little bit, I should think on degree. If it is a Jack Anderson column,—

P   (unintelligible) another point I make (unintelligible) relation that I have now is this case. Suppose that the Assistant Attorney General comes in, Magruder and Dean have made charges. His argument is, "You have an option sir, and you as President should act. And I'm telling you now that those charges are in the possession of the government." That's what I'm—

H O.K., but what's (unintelligible) you do that. I happen to know what his motive is and I'll sure as hell use it (unintelligible).

E O.K. You say, "Mr. Assistant Attorney General, I want to explain my policy to you so that you'll know what our relationship is. Our policy is that I will immediately suspend—on leave—anybody against whom formal charges are filed by indictable information.

P By information you mean—

E In other words, formal charges are filed. "As soon as that happens those men will go on leave. This is a town that is so full of wild charges that if I operated on any other basis, even of those who were brought to me by 20 Bishops and an Attorney General, I couldn't be suspending people around here or the place would look like a piece of Swiss cheese. But let me suggest you do this. You go ahead and diligently pursue the Haldeman and Ehrlichman case because I need to know."

P Right.

E And, if you come to me and say that you filed charges and I'll have really no discretion in the matter.

P If you come to me and say that you are planning to indict criminal charges, then I'll—at that time—move instantly, before we do it publicly.

E Or Dean, or anybody else. But I can't treat them any different than anybody else. And you have brought me basically, uncorroborated charges. You've said so yourself that you aren't going to be able to deal with Dean.

P I feel comfortable with that.

E But, if you lay out the general ground rules first—

P What, what basically, John, what the hell is the Garment, Rose I guess Moore (unintelligible).

E They're writing a *New York Times* editorial which is that this is a terrible cancer at the heart of the Presidency and that there must be drastic surgery. And that in a case like this you lean over backwards and fire and so forth. And, I'm sure it will be an editorial in many, many newspapers, that Dean has raised serious charges and so on so forth. And you'll hear a lot of that. Maybe the thing to do is for Ziegler—if he gets a question about suspension or firing—to say, "This is the President's general policy—without regard to individuals—any individual whose bound by the Grand Jury—"

P Why don't I say that today?

E That's fine.

P Fine. All right. I think I got the message. If you will write up a brief, brief, brief statement. You know—I can use—or do you have one you can get back to me? I have to do it at 3:00. How much time do I have?

E You've got about 45 minutes.

P I've got plenty of time.

H Ziegler should delay the 3:00. They've only scheduled a posting. He can make it 4:00. Briefing at 4:10.

P Yeah, that's right.

H You ought to tell him now, though, that you're going to do it though.

P I better do that.

H Better get Ron in quickly and review this. Just tell them to send Ron in.

E Sure.

H Would you get Ziegler?

H Any question about my theory now?

E I wonder if we should talk to him about how to operate the next couple days? (unintelligible) suspicion before grant him immunity. I thought so too. (unintelligible) be on the wires, I would think.

H Even if they have, could withdraw (unintelligible) get him before he acts.

E I don't know.

E Now, with us out of the play here for a couple weeks ah, you're going to need a different mode of operation, I would think on the domestic side—

P Yeah, Cole.

E And, Ken is fully abreast of everything.

P All right.

E And I think you ought to just call him direct when you have something.

P I will. I'll use him just like I'd use you. He'll have to wear two hats for awhile.

H My office can run itself. To cover your bases, you can deal with Steve. On schedule basis you'd be better off to deal with Parker. You haven't started doing it so you probably don't want to.

P Things we do. I'd like to get acquainted with him anyway.

H Weekly review and things you would talk to me

about, Parker knows the reasons behind everything.

P   Let us not overlook one greater—let us suppose no charges are filed, and basically—charges are filed. (Unintelligible) thing. Charges might be that Haldeman had knowledge, and that he participated—cover-up—I'm trying, Bob, to put my worse—

H   Sure.

P   Do you agree Bob, they might make that a charge—the heat would really go on.

H   Sure.

P   In John's case they make the deep six charge (unintelligible). I'd (unintelligible) with you on that.

E   It's up to you.

P   No, I mean that's a difference in degree.

H   I think each of those is something that we have to deal with at the time.

P   That's right.

H   In the context of the time, because I don't think you can anticipate now what the context will be. You don't know what the newspaper stories will be. For instance, right now—and that's another argument against taking any action regarding me—is that I'm not in the thing at all in the public mind, and it would be startling as hell.

P   Yeah. The reason for not going the Garment road—he wants, John, he wants Mitchell separated. He said, "Mitchell's got to come out (unintelligible). See my point? Don't suppose that's occurred to you? I think what we do, I think I will make a brief statement today, and I was wondering how late I can make it. Don't believe I can make it at 3:00. What do you think?

Z   You got to make it at 4:00 or 4:15.

P   Fine, but I'll have to go to work on it.

Z   We'll have to call them in.

P   Let me ask you this, fellas, you want me on the television?

E   Yes sir, that would be my preference.

P   I'll just walk out.

Z   I think depending on the statement, they'll get it to the lab. Don't worry, they'll get it out.

P   (Unintelligible).

Z   I'll just say you have that flexibility from 3:30 to 4:15.

P   O.K. Fine, fine.

E   Oh, Yeah. Ron I'll need that—

562

Z   This?

E   Yes. Where's page 1?

Z   It's—says page 1—

E   Good work.

P   I wonder, John, I wonder that unless you sank Dean, basically, if we're putting too much emphasis on the fact (unintelligible) in that office. Understand, I'd just thinking what it is worth to us to get him out of that damned office. I relieve him of his duties?

E   Well, the alternative is somehow or other to pass the word to everybody in the place that he's a piranha. I don't know how you do that.

P   What? What do you mean everybody in the place.

E   I mean people like the White House Police. That if they get a subpoena they shouldn't ask him what to do. The Secret Service, a guy like Dick Howard.

H   Who should they ask?

E   Damned good question.

P   Moore?

E   Make Moore Acting Counsel. He has very good judgment.

H   Very good judgment and absolutely no procedural knowledge.

E   Garment?

H   He's worse.

P   Fielding?

H   Let Fielding be the operative. Say that he can take no action without checking with Moore.

P   How's that sound, John?

E   That's good.

H   Fielding is to be the front man as Deputy Counsel, but he is to report to Dick Moore.

P   But you see, I just don't know if that kind of action is worth taking that kind of risk.

E   Well, if he's here, people will go to him for advice. I'm just sure of it.

P   Okay. I've told him he's not to give any advice, and he's not to have anything to do with this case at all. All right?

E   I don't know. Maybe I'm being unduly harsh, but—and maybe the negatives are more than the positives—it seems to be that it can be done without breaking any asses.

P   I can just say, "Well, people are coming in. They're on the WH Police now—so forth. I think it's going to look strange if he doesn't."

E It puts him in an impossible conflict-of-interest situation.

P That's right.

H That's the problem. He knows what is coming in—what questions are coming.

P Alright. The second point, with regard to Petersen, ah, that the—that's the highest—I better get him in and tell him (unintelligible).

H Yeah, and the no immunity thing.

P And just flatly say, "Now this is the way I'm going to handle the matter. I cannot let people go simply because charges are made until they are corroborated. That's my decision," and so forth. And second, "I've thought over the immunity thing and I want nobody on the WH staff given immunity. I don't want anybody shown any consideration whatever."

E This has been a law and order administration.

P Right, and third, "I'm directing everybody to cooperate (inaudible) They've been told they are not to. I've already helped him on that. I haven't helped him, I've tried. But I will not have a member of the White House Staff testifying in the Senate against others.

E Yes, sir, and I think that the fourth point that you should cover with him is that if I'm before that Grand Jury and I am asked about Dean's information within the Grand Jury, I will have to say that Dean told me that it came from Petersen.

P Yeah.

E And, there's no point in your getting way out by saying out here to the press that I'm relying on Henry Petersen as my good right hand and then have him compromised at a later time.

P That's right.

H I think you must, from here on—

P (unintelligible)

H Yeah, but also, that you don't, from now on, until this is totally done, maybe never, express confidence in anybody. (expletive removed), don't say, I know this guy is doing the thing right or anything else." That applies to me, Ehrlichman—

P Well, you know how I feel.

H Yes, but don't say it. Just—it just doesn't serve the cause properly. And I don't think you should say it. And you should not about Henry Petersen, Dean, or anybody else. Ron must not say it either. Don't let Ron con you into saying, "Well, I have full confidence in what's his name."

E I got a name today, and I don't know anything about this fellow—but let me advance his name to you. There's a lawyer here in town by the name of Herbert Miller. You may know him. He was head of the criminal division at the Justice Department. He was there thru 61 to 67, Kennedy and Johnson, but he's a Republican.

P Yeah, alright.

E Now, it may be possible to get a fellow like that to substitute.

P I don't know. This case is moving too fast. You call in a substitute and he's got to learn the damned case.

E O.K. He reviews it. He gets the complete file with the pros and the cons. He goes through it and he draws on seven years experience and he comes over to you and he says I've got to call this shot and I wonder if you have anything to add?

P (Unintelligible) counsel?

E Yes, but as your counsel, he has no control over the prosecution.

P (Unintelligible) Petersen

E That's right, and he's feeding a bunch of baloney, in my opinion.

H He also, I understand, told you that Strachan got very good treatment over there.

P No, no, no. He told me the opposite.

H Oh.

P He said that Strachan just got the hell beat out of him.

H He did. He was absolutely astonished. He came out of there and he said it was just beyond belief. They threatened his life practically, told him he better hire—

P A lawyer.

H Best possible counsel. Provide for support for his wife, and because he'd be going to jail, and that he was in serious trouble. Said he would be disbarred.

E What they are trying to do is put him in the hands of an attorney who'll deal for immunity.

H They are trying to get him to make the same play that Magruder made.

E No doubt that they salvaged Dean the same way, and they scored on him. Well, all I'm saying to you is, I don't think in terms of the kinds of stuff they are talking

565

about. That it is all that complicated for an experienced man to pick up, so I wouldn't want you to think that this guy is indispensable.

P Yeah, but should I make that decision today?

E Well, every day that goes by is going to make it that much tougher on somebody new coming in and you got a guy in here that I wouldn't trust, knowing what I know, and maybe you can.

P This guy gets relieved, and says well I told the President that he ought to fire Haldeman and Ehrlichman and he fired Dean.

E I don't think that he would say that. He's a pro. He's been around this town a long time and he knows if he said that, that you would come right back and say, "No, the reason that I fired him is that I've reason to believe that he is responsible for leaks out of the Grand Jury," and that would destroy him.

P O.K. Can you get that paper back to me?

E Yeah, I'll get it right back.

P Shall I get Dean down first?

E I would.

P Tell him that—

E Tell him you are going to make a statement and that it is not going to refer to him.

P Yep.

E Or anybody, and that you're going to deal with the people at the White House on an individual basis.

H Maybe you ought to get Petersen in first to talk immunity.

P Yeah, get Petersen in first. Call and tell Petersen to (unintelligible)

H Alright.

Telephone conversation: The President and Ehrlichman, April 17, 1973. (2:39 - 2:40 pm)

Opr Yes, sir.

P Mr. Ehrlichman, please

Opr Thank you.

P John - I don't want to interrupt your statement preparing,

E Yes, sir. That's alright.

P But I just wanted to be sure to check the points you

want with Peterson. He will be in just 10 minutes so, (1) no immunity. However, I would say that for any of the top three.

E   Uh, huh.

P   In other words, so that I can, if it sort of appears that if you want to give it to Strachan, that is ok. See? Don't you think that is a good line?

E   I think that is good. Any of the people in—The four points as I wrote them down were to inform him that you were making a statement; Your policy with regard to suspension and firing.

P   Which is charges or indictment—

E   Indictment for suspension and firing for conviction, which will be in the statement that I am drafting.

P   Wait a minute.

E   He'll tell the press that.

P   Right.

E   Then privately to him, your policy with regard to immunity for top people.

P   Yeah, and leaks from the Grand Jury.

E   I wouldn't limit it to three. I would say any top person, like Dean or up.

P   Yeah.

E   It will sell.

P   Then I will say, as far as a fellow like Strachan, that is fine. You can do what you want.

E   Yeah

P   That strengthens the position.

E   Colson, Dean, anybody of that kind, no dice.

P   He has mentioned these four to me. I will just say that.

E   And then, of course, the leaks out of the Grand Jury. And put it to him whether he doesn't think the later exposure would prejudice the whole investigation and whether he shouldn't withdraw at an appropriate time so that a replacement can be obtained.

P   Charges and—I am going to follow a policy of accepting resignations on charges or indictment. Is that it?

E   No. Suspension on indictment and a resignation on conviction.

P   Of course. That is right. Everybody would know that. Suspension on indictment and resignation on refusing to cooperate. Right?

E   Or conviction

P   Right. And what about charges? I mean remember we had that gray area.

E   Well, there again you will have to reserve the right, depending on the seriousness of the charge—

P   Yeah. I will say if there is a serious corroborated charge,—

E   Then you want him to bring it to you and you will reserve judgment on the individual case.

Meeting: The President and Petersen, Oval Office, April 17, 1973. (2:46 - 3:49 pm)

Steward   - Mr. Petersen

P   Right.

P   All right - he can come in.

Steward - Have him come in now, Sir?

P   Yeah.

P   Hi.

HP   Mr. President, how are you?

P   Sit down, sit down.

HP   Thank you, Sir.

P   (Inaudible) meeting - in the middle of the night for a change. The, ah, anything new I need to know?

HP   No, Sir, ah.

P   Don't. As a matter of fact, I don't want you really to tell me anything out of the Grand Jury unless you think I need to know it. If it corroborates something or anybody here I need to know it - otherwise I don't want to know about it.

HP   No, Sir.

P   That's good, because I find - Incidentally, if I might - I don't think I like - for example, I haven't been in touch with John Mitchell but he might call me sometime and I don't want to be a position of ever saying anything, see?

HP   Well, I understand how you feel - its a -

P   I guess it would be legal for me to know?

HP   Well yes, I think it is legal for you to know.

P   Is it? Well, but don't do it, right. The problem that concerns me some there (inaudible) - I did see Rogers last night as you know -

HP   Yes, Sir.

P   I wanted to get an independent judgment on this when I was talking (inaudible) . . .

HP   He is an admirable man.

P   Able fellow - was a fine Attorney General, and so forth. I gave it all to him with the bark off and (inaudible). And, his views are somewhat different from yours and I am sure you would respect them - perhaps mine as well - because it is a tough call.

HP   Indeed so.

P   I might say somewhat different - I don't mean in terms of where you come out eventually,

HP   I understand

P   but in terms of timing, and so forth, and so forth. First, there is a problem of - oh - which I don't want you to get in the wringer on this but, the leaks from the Grand Jury you remember I have already mentioned that to you before.

HP   Yes sir.

P   I think you have to know that Dean has talked very freely to Mitchell.

HP   I am sure that's so.

P   And Mitchell, of course, is—I can imagine, I don't know, but I think you should know that. Whether he has talked to others about that, I do not know.

HP   Well he feels a very close personal relationship with Mitchell. I am almost positive of that—

P   The point is I think you will have to assume that Dean in this period, who was basically sort of in charge of it for the White House (and the rest of us were out campaigning - traveling, so forth, so on) will probably have told people that he has information from the Grand Jury. Now you just have to evaluate that yourself. I just don't want the Department of Justice, and you particularly, after your, ah - the way you have broken your—

HP   Mr. President - I am sure that is so.

P   I don't want to get embarrassed, see?

HP   I have no concern about that.

P   After the pumping of Rogers - I am not enough of a criminal lawyer to know enough about it - but Rogers was greatly concerned about the leaks from the Grand Jury. He asked me that - he said

HP   Well, two things are occurring - one, Magruder is talking, Magruder is going around trying to make peace with each - in other words, he will come in to me and say look I am in this bind and I have to testify and there is nothing I can do but I got to tell the complete truth about the others but with respect to you I am doing the best I can.

P   Yeah.

HP   Which is the pitch he is making, Now,

P   You've talked to - ?

HP   We have talked to his lawyers about that. With respect to Dean - it doesn't surprise me that he has gone to Mitchell. He's, he's,

P   Understand what I am driving at?

HP   He's probably getting information from the Grand Jury.

P   What I am concerned about is leaks and leaks from the Grand Jury, not now but leaks during the period—the summer.

HP   Oh, Oh yes.

P   That's the point - during - June, July, August, September, and so forth that is the point that I mean, that a—

HP   I don't think that is a critical problem so far as I am concerned, Mr. President for this reason.

P   See we don't want - after all this agony - I don't want the - well - the man that I'm relying on to be any kind of a (inaudible) position.

P   Well no, you've got your life (inaudible) ahead.

HP   Mr. President, I don't to be in that position.

HP   Let me tell you - when I spoke to Dean and I for example, am not going to, I'm not worried about this, I

P   I just want to be sure that -

HP   Well, let me make three points - when I say this, and it's almost awkward to say this

P   That is why Rogers for example is recommending a special counsel -

HP   Right

P   he is very much afraid that anybody who has been handling the damm thing up to this point is going to have somebody -

HP   Well, there, ah

P   (Inaudible) feel about that?

HP   Well with respect to John Dean - it is almost awkward to say it - my conversation with Dean touched upon three things: (1) leaks - which frankly I tell you I don't take very seriously - see what I mean - that's part and parcel of the Washington business;

P   Yeah.

HP   (the second) was Dean's personal involvement - that is to say

P   What did he do.

HP   Well we didn't suspect him, but what did he do with respect to the securing of the equipment and records in Hunt's office in connection with the motion to suppress where he was a potential witness for the defense on the motion to suppress. And the third was status reports - now from those status reports, I spoke to him in terms of ultimates. Magruder was a good witness in his own behalf. Magruder - the Grand Jury didn't believe what he said about the money - but not the testimony itself - the result of the testimony. So I don't have any problem . . .

P   That has no problem of (inaudible)?

HP   No sir, and I can disclosure to an attorney for the government in the course of my work. Dean was in addition to Counsel for the President, obviously an attorney for the government - and there is not anything improper in that.

P   Right - well good, I am relieved to hear that.

HP   Now, politically if someone wants to say - as they said to Pat Gray - you shouldn't have been talking to John Dean. Well, there is no way out of that.

P   You see that is why I am raising the point.

HP   There is no way out of that.

P   That was perfectly proper for Pat Gray to talk to Dean you know - as a matter of fact, it would be improper for him not to . . .

HP   Indeed

P   . . . Dean was running the investigation of the damn thing and I certainly expected him to get all of the FBI information he could.

HP   Yes.

P   What the hell is the FBI for?

HP   That's right. You know - I don't -

P   Gray got a bad rap on that

HP   I don't think that - that's demagoguery I think - I don't take that seriously.

P   That's right - quite right. The second point is that with regard to our statement now - the one we talked about yesterday - I am working on it today - I don't know whether I can get it ready - for probably this afternoon - but I will give you a call if I do have one. I have decided - I want to tell you - roughly it is sort of like the one we worked on yesterday - but also covers the Ervin Committee too. We worked out a deal with them now where everything on executive session, no, everything on executive privilege we have in Executive Session.

HP   Right.

P   The right of executive privilege will be reserved and all witnesses will appear in public session - that's the way

571

the deal was signed. So they will take all of our people in executive sessions discuss matters - you know like they bring - the judge brings the lawyers around the bench.

HP   I understand - yes sir.

P   Does that sound like a good procedure to you?

HP   Yes sir - I've only got one reservation and we alluded to this earlier in connection with the Magruder plea, and that is - whether or not Senator Ervin will be willing to hold off public sessions that might interfere with the right of fair trial for the others.

P   Well you and I know it shouldn't but I mean my point is I've got to say our (inaudible) should work for the (inaudible) at the White House on it, but that is your job.

HP   OK. Just so there is nothing (inaudible) with it.

P   I don't want the damn Ervin Committee to go forward -

HP   All right. Okay

P   I think frankly if I were Mitchell I would be praying that the Committee did.

HP   Yeah. It gives him delay if nothing else.

P   Correct. Delay! If the Committee gets up there and they will splash a lot of this—I mean McCord and all the rest - in there he's sure to get a change of venue for one thing. Secondly, the thing that he'd be (inaudible) of these days, seems to me, venue is the television and the rest, it's ah, I think the Ervin Committee would be highly irresponsible to move forward.

HP   That's right

P   (inaudible)

HP   That's right.

P   So they should drop the Committee investigation the day the Grand Jury took it up seriously.

HP   Well your accommodation with the Committee makes my job much easier now.

P   Good - how's that? Because -

HP   Well I think he would have been very suspicious if I had gone up there and there was still the possibility of some confrontation between you and he.

P   (inaudible)

HP   No, because we still haven't gotten the assent from—

P   Sirica?

HP   Well, not only Sirica but Magruder's lawyers - we are still waiting for them to come back.

P   It takes a long time -

HP   Yes, sir.

P   Now with regard to my policy, I think you should know I thought it over a lot - where we come out in the end we shall see, but can be sure Haldeman, Ehrlichman . . . Dean naturally will have to go because he has admitted very deep complicity. Right? There will be no question about it.

HP   I don't think that . . .

P   Haldeman and Ehrlichman at this point had (inaudible) with Rogers - I not only let him read what you had given me but then I elaborated everything I knew about this thing. His judgment is this that on Ehrlichman it is a very thin (inaudible)

HP   Very thin indeed

P   never going to (inaudible) - he said particularly he said if they have any witnesses for the fact that he handed a packet to the Director of the FBI and Hunt didn't leave the country (inaudible) discussions. I don't know - I am not trying to judge it - but

HP   No, I understand - I agree that it is very thin

P   They better have a damn lot more than that or they are not going to get Ehrlichman

HP   That's right.

P   on that - they may get him on something else. And the other point was, that you made, was Dean said that he had talked - that Liddy had told him everything on June 19th. You remember?

HP   Yes, sir.

P   Do you know when he told Ehrlichman?

HP   No, sir.

P   In California after Ehrlichman had been there in March - Februrary?—in March.

HP   Dean told Ehrlichman then?

P   That's right. So, it is a curious thing as to - Gray's concern to me. I said Dean hasn't told you he didn't tell him ahead of Ehrlichman but I mean that he didn't run right over and tell him.

HP   No, No

P   The point is that Dean conducted his investigation and did not come to Ehrlichman and say "look we have to go on Mitchell" because that's what that was really about.

HP   Yeah.

P   Liddy had involved himself and subsequently said Mitchell and Magruder. That's what I understand to be the truth of the case.

HP   Well what Liddy in effect said was - what he admitted was that he was present at the Watergate - Dean
already knew from prior dealings that Liddy was involved;
you see?

P   Oh, I see - present at Watergate?

HP   That's right.

P   Oh, I thought he also - I thought you said - he told
everything - that you had copies of everything . . .

HP   Well I think that is correct. He probably filled in
the details but you recall at least from the meeting in February in Mitchell's office, Dean knew what Liddy was up
to.

P   Yeah.

HP   Because he had come back to Haldeman and said
we should

P   Yeah

HP   not be involved with that—

P   That's right - with that—(expletive deleted)

HP   That's right. That's right.

P   (laughs)

P   Which makes it more credible when you use all
salty words.

HP   Laughter.

P   OK Now - this brings us to a basic command decision with regard - with regard to what you do about
White House people. The main thing is (inaudible) and
you can look at it in terms of the fact that anybody who
this touches should go out - without - (inaudible). You can
look at it in terms of the fact that if it touches them
(inaudible) that clearly apart from whether or not anything legal stands up. Let's suppose - just take Ehrlichman
is a case in point - that this thing brought in by (inaudible) that proves to be (inaudible) don't get anything else
on Ehrlichman then the question is that nevertheless that
in itself would raise a cloud over Ehrlichman. That would
mean that he would be no longer be useful. Therefore,
your advice - on Sunday or least it was now - sack Haldeman, Ehrlichman and Dean now - all three - because in
the one case Dean should know he has admitted complicity - in the other case there is a possibility of charges
which may not be true and which may not be indictable
but which from the standpoint of the public will so involve them that it will cut off their legs. And let me say I
understand the point as well—the only thing is the question of how and when you do it - and as that I (inaudible). And so I have decided to handle each on an individ-

ual basis - and by that I mean that our policy generally will be that anyone who refused to cooperate will, of course, be sacked immediately. Anyone who is indicted at this time will be put on leave - indefinite leave - until he is tried. You don't - That is our system. Now, if you indict somebody, I will then put them on leave indefinitely which means he is out of a job - he'll have to go. What would happen in that instance I think, of course, is that most of the people that are involved here would resign immediately so that - I am just saying

HP   I understand

P   That the least of the (inaudible) is that you are going on leave - the guy says - oh hell no, I can never come back after four or five months of trial. That's what we would say at this point. It gives them a chance. Now comes the gray area - if any charge is made publicly - you see - I don't mean in the *Washington Post* of the *Los Angeles Times* but I mean publicly by Magruder in open court - any charges are made (not released by the Grand Jury) publicly which corroborate in any way against anybody on the White House staff then he will be asked to take leave also.

HP   Umm - uh

P   Then, of course, what will happen probably - I would predict - I know - they will come in and resign. I mean they will come in and say, look I can't do my job so I am going to go. But what I mean, the point is - my position is - indictment means - well, ah - failure to cooperate - you're fired; indictment means you are asked to take leave until you are cleared. Then the individual will say "I can't do my job" if he is a top individual, or if it is a secretary, for example . . .

HP   Oh, yeah, I understand.

P   (inaudible) - The big three - Dean, Haldeman and Ehrlichman - and third, in the area of charges - charges are made - what I am thinking of here is Magruder - Magruder goes into open court - As I understand what will happen is you make a statement in open court which will name Mitchell for sure

HP   Well

P   and might name Haldeman and might name Ehrlichman. Right?

HP   Well what we propose to do is file a one count conspiracy indictment that would name Magruder and unindicted co-conspirators.

P   And put their names in the indictment?

HP Yes sir.

P Unindicted . . .

HP Co-conspirators. Then when the court questions the defendant with respect to the facts that reflect his guilt, Magruder then would be expounding on the indictment and in effect stating what the evidence was.

P On the unindicted co-conspirators this is Magruder - but that would be on the Watergate side - that would be both before and after. Magruder is mainly before on this—

HP Well he is also involved in the obstruction.

P He is, Fine, then he is—

HP Because he perjured himself before the Grand Jury—

P Yep

HP . . . at the suggestion of others.

P So what you would have on Magruder you would say we hereby indict Magruder and the following unindicted co-conspirators which means that an undicted . . . (explain to me what unindicted co-conspirators means).

HP That just means that for one reason or another we don't want to charge them at the time. For example, I am indicted - you're named as an unindicted co-conspirator. You are just as guilty as I am but you are a witness - we are not going to prosecute you.

P I need to know that because . . . (inaudible)

HP But all those people that we name - we propose to name only to the extent that we feel we can corroborate. The one thing we can't afford to do is to name, for example, John Mitchell and then come up six months later without enough evidence to nail him.

P Or for that matter - Ehrlichman.

HP That's right.

P Or Haldeman or anybody else.

HP That's right.

P In other words, you are going to put in there people you know you can indict.

HP That's right. Now -

P Well then I'll (inaudible) - I can consider that a charge?

HP That's right.

P That's right - in other words, if they're in that I would then say - anybody that was an unindicted co-conspirator would then be immediately put on leave

HP It would . . .

P   Get my point?

HP   That's right.

P   That's what I'll tell them I will do. Now the other thing I want to tell you though that - and I say this strongly - I have thought about it a lot - I don't care what you do on immunity to Strachan or any other second people but you can't give immunity to any top people - not Dean - needless to say you don't want to to Haldeman or Ehrlichman. Dean is the counsel to the President - after the flap with Gray - I went over this with Rogers - he says - after your flap on the Gray thing and the rest - it would like that you're . . .

HP   Right - you know why I asked

P   I just want you to know that you that you if give immunity but I will have to talk (inaudible).

HP   OK, well, let me put it this way, I will not do that without your knowledge. If it is necessary for me to do that I will come to you first and then we can reach an agreement that yes you will have to disavow it and that was the decision of the prosecutor. I don't want to make that decision, Mr. President. I don't want to immunize John Dean; I think he is too high in the echelon but—it's a—

P   The prosecutor's got the right to make that decision?

HP   Yes, sir

P   You better, I think . . .

HP   . . . the point of it is, if it comes to a question of—

P   I think it would - look - because your close relationship with Dean - which has been very close - it would look like a straight deal - now that's just the way you've got to figure it.

HP   That's right.

P   The prosecutor has got to know - I can say as far as the President is concerned if John Dean gets (inaudible) then I don't care - but Ehrlichman, Haldeman and all the rest (inaudible) - why the hell did we give him immunization and not the poor damn Cubans? It just doesn't sound right.

HP   Right.

P   It doesn't sound right - it isn't going to sound good for you - because of your relationship - it isn't going to sound good for the President.

HP   Ah, well I hope we don't have to do that - I

would rather have a plea to a lesser offense by Dean. I think too that it's going to look awful. We are in no disagreement on that at all.

P   It would look awful, it really would, particularly . . .

HP   The thing that scares the hell out of me is this - suppose Dean is the only key to Haldeman and Ehrlichman and the refusal to immunize Dean means that Haldeman and Ehrlichman go free. That is the decision that we are going to ultimately come down to.

P   Well you will have to come into me with what you've got (inaudible) then there . . .

HP   I will

P   and let me handle Haldeman and Ehrlichman.

HP   I will sir.

P   Do you get my point?

HP   Yes, sir.

P   If it comes down to that - I may have to move on Haldeman and Ehrlichman - then for example you come to me and say look here's what—Look I am not going to do anything to Haldeman and Ehrlichman just because of what Dean says - I can't do that. Its got to be corroborated.

HP   I agree with that.

P   Do you agree with that?

HP   Yes sir - I am not going to do anything with those two unless it is corroborated either.

P   Dean is - I find, has told two or three different stories. I didn't realize it until lately. I guess when a guy is scared he doesn't—

HP   He is a man under great pressure.

P   Sure, I fell for the poor—

HP   So do I. He took a lot—he knows

P   He is a fine lawyer

HP   A thirty-four year old man with a bright future -

P   Sure, he's worked his—and (inaudible) everything - I understand it, but I cannot, for example, in good conscience and, you can't in good conscience say that you are going to send Haldeman and Ehrlichman - or anybody for that matter - or Colson - down the tube on the uncorroborated evidence of John Dean. You see - so basically what your problem is and the problem of the prosecutors is to find some corroboration for Dean.

HP   Precisely right.

P   If you come in to me with Dean plus corroboration and you tell me that - then we have a difficult decision on whether or not we want to immunize him

HP   That the importance . . .

P   . . . or whether we have these fellows just leave.

HP   That is the importance of Strachan.

P   It may be that in that instance - you see that is the other point - of course with Strachan you're (inaudible). Another way you can handle that - it occurs to me - is that - Haldeman & Ehrlichman - well let's take one, let's take Haldeman, for example, no - Ehrlichman - Ehrlichman is the best case - or Colson even, because they seem to be more tangential than Haldeman, right?

HP   Both are more tangential than Haldeman - yes, sir.

P   Right, let's take Ehrlichman - let's say that the only testimony we have is something about (inaudible) - and so forth and so on - something about that Dean is supposed to have told him about the Liddy operation or something in March. All right - so is he a co-conspirator? Let's suppose you cannot get anybody to corroborate that - All right, then the question is, however, then that is one thing. If on the other hand - you wouldn't sack Ehrlichman for that?

HP   Mr. President, I wouldn't prosecute Ehrlichman for that.

P   But you might sack him?

HP   Yes sir.

P   Now the second point is, let us suppose, . . .

HP   I mean if he were a junior partner in the Petersen-Nixon law firm out in Oskosh, I would not. But as senior advisor to the President of the United States I would. That is the difference.

P   Yeah. Now you come to the other point. Suppose you have Dean in a position of where he makes this charge against Ehrlichman - no, what I am getting at - no, no, no my point is where you come in and say look I've got this charge—wait a minute this is unsubstantiated - but let us suppose you have witnesses who give testimony - and credible witnesses who give testimony - and credible witness - the other way? Then what would you do with Ehrlichman on that? You have heard - Colson apparently for example is supposed to know about that - and who else was there when they talked about the, the, ah?

HP   Clemency?

P   What? Pat Gray oh talked

HP   About—Pat Gray?

P   Leaving the country and all that business - Colson?

HP   Liddy -

P   Was Liddy there?

HP   Liddy gets his instructions from Dean.

P   Yeah, All right, so Dean . . .

HP   Liddy passes the information on to Hunt.

P   Dean

HP   Hunt tells us in the Grand Jury that Liddy said his principals said that I should so this.

P   Yeah.

HP   Hunt doesn't know who the principals are

P   Right

HP   . . . he says at this stage of the proceeding. Even if he does know,

P   Right

HP   he knows only by hearsay

P   Right

HP   . . . and probably not going to be admissible.

P   This is where you're going to get the corroboration.

HP   I am not sure that we are. I am not sure that we are.

P   See that's where you give me the tough problem. But on the other hand it seems to me that on that basis the better way to handle it is for you to rather than immunizing Dean - you see if you immunize him for something that can't be corroborated, it's a straight deal between - you know what I mean. Well, I can see Mitchell saying - well John Dean was talking too much to Henry Petersen, and Petersen did this and Dean pulled the plug on him and he had no time to lie. You know?

HP   It's possible.

P   And it's a bad rap, but ah, I'm (inaudible).

HP   But we are not going to do that Mr. President - we are going to have . . . will have corroborative witnesses all along the line,

P   Yes, sure

HP   But I see the problem and I feel - I think we are looking at it a little bit differently -.

P   Sure.

HP   And I see the problem in two dimensions and, of course, I see it in this respect as a neophite. Obviously you and Bill Rogers are much more experienced in these affairs than I, but maybe because I am a neophite and one of the public I see it perhaps more clearly - at least from a different point of view. It seems to me

P   It's the taint

HP   that it's just the things that they have done impairs you.

P   I understand. Understand and I agree with you on

580

that. My point though now is a different one - it is the question of the immunity. That worries hell out of me.

HP   Well that -

P   The immunity worries me for the reason that it just is . . . I don't think it's good to give it. I don't think in view of the fact that we had this hell of a flap - you know that is the reason Gray wasn't confirmed - because of Dean.

HP   Well Mr. President -

P   We go in and give it . . .

HP   if I could only put your mind at ease - I have been arguing with those prosecutors for three days on this issue—

P   I think you've got to understand, I am not saying this because of Haldeman - I am not suggesting this about Strachan or a secretary or anybody else - no immunity all the way down the line, but it occurred to me that particularly in talking to Rogers said how in the hell can they give John Dean immunity after he's the guy that sunk Pat Gray.

HP   Well if I sound like a devil's advocate - I am. I have been saying the same to the prosecutors - how in the hell can I immunize John Dean?

P   That's the point. Well, I feel it strongly - I mean - just understand I am not trying to protect anybody - I want the damn facts if you can get the facts from Dean and I don't care whether -

HP   Mr. President, if I thought you were trying to protect somebody, I would have walked out

P   If he doesn't testify in open court - or anything of that sort it doesn't make any difference - I am going to make my decision on the basis of what you tell me Dean has told you and - just a little feel of the whole thing. But I've got to do it my way.

HP   I know - no problem with that.

P   I've got to get (inaudible) handle on it so what I am going to do is this - when charges are made - if your charge is made that certain co-conspirators, and so forth and so on - out! - even when they are unindicted - out, out - so that takes care of that. But that is the time to do it, and I am going to say that - oh, I am not going to use your technical terms -

HP   Well that is understandable.

P   But I am just going to indicate that there must be cooperation, that if there is any evidence to indict anybody on . . .

HP Let me ask you this, Mr. President, what would you do if we filed indictment against Magruder, hypothetically, and

P Yeah - Magruder or Dean?

HP Magruder

P Magruder - oh you have indicted him.

HP To which he is going to plead, and we named as unindicted co-conspirators everybody but Haldeman and Ehrlichman - never mind that the variation improves between them for the moment -

P That you would name Colson for example?

HP Well I don't know about Colson - Colson is again peripheral, but Mitchell, LaRue, Mardian - what-have-you . . .

P Colson was a big fish in my opinion.

HP Yeah, and a

P Would you name Dean for example?

HP Oh yes.

P Oh yes he was -

HP And we name all of those people. We leave out Haldeman and Ehrlichman. Now one of the things we had thought about -

P I get your point

HP leaving them out was to give you time and room to maneuver with respect to the two of them.

P Let me ask you - can I ask you - talking in the President's office

HP Yes sir. [Sets up appointment - had to take time out to sign some papers]

P You see we've got to run the government too (inaudible).

P You mean if Haldeman and Ehrlichman leave you will not indict them?

HP No sir, I didn't say that.

P That would be a strange (inaudible).

HP No - it was not a question of that - it was a question of whether or not they were publicly identified in that pleading at that time.

P Yeah.

HP And, well, for example, as a scenario - that comes out and you say -

P (inaudible)

HP this is a shocking relevation -

P Yeah.

HP as a consequence of that I have consulted and I have just decided to clear out everybody here who might have had—and as a consequence Mr. Ehrlichman and Mr. Haldeman are going. Thereafter, we would proceed with the evidence wherever it took us. That is what we were thinking about to be perfectly honest with you.

P   Well you really ought to include them (inaudible) if you include the others.

HP   Well

P   Oh, you don't want names in the indictment of Magruder.

HP   That's right - unless we were able to go forward. Well, I don't want to belabor the point - I have made it clear that my view that I think they have made you very vulnerable. I think they have made you wittingly or unwittingly very very vulnerable to rather severe criticism because of their actions. At least in public forums they eroded confidence in the office of the Presidency by their actions. Well you know it, I don't have to belabor it here—

P   Well, let's begin with this proposition. Let's not get in the wicket where we've got Dean in an immunity position. He'll talk. He'll talk.

HP   Well that's another thing. Have you decided to accept Dean's resignation?

P   No, I have decided I have to treat them all the same.

HP   I was going to say that would be terrible the effect is he would be out talking to the Press immediately.

P   On no, no, no - I told Dean I was going to handle them all the same (inaudible) - no that would be unfair.

HP   I agree.

P   Absolutely.

HP   I agree.

P   No, No, I talked to Dean about it - he said well he would do it if they did it too. He would like to do it if they did too, and I said well we are not going to do it on a conditional basis - I said stay on until we see what happens. No, I am not going to condemn Dean until he has a chance to present himself. No he is in exactly the same position they are in.

HP   Alright, O.K.

P   You see that's the point: see I put all three in the same bag.

HP   Very good.

P   How does that sound to you? Do you see what I mean?

HP   Yes, indeed

P   So they have the same rule and if Strachan comes in, I am not going to throw Strachan out simply because he's been down before the Grand Jury.

HP   No - I agree with that.

P   If you put his name in that indictment, I'm going to throw him out.

HP   Well you know Strachan right at this point is debating whether he wants to be a potential defendant or a witness.

P   You've got him down there now haven't you?

HP   Well, he's not down there now - his lawyer called around noon time and we told him go back and talk to your client and let us know one way or another.

P   Right. (pause) Oh you mean you're not covering the immunity thing there?

HP   No - but we have to distinguish between variations of immunity.

P   What?

HP   In all probability there is not enough evidence to implicate Strachan as a -

P   Principal

HP   principal. There may be some evidence to reflect some degree of culpability, but he is at least at this point in our judgment a fringe character. The type of person where we would not have to formally immunize him - we would say look,

P   Yeah.

HP   you are a witness rather than a defendant - tell us what you know.

P   What you mean—you are telling him you will not prosecute him?

HP   That's right but it is distinguished from formal immunity which requires -

P   Oh, I see . . .

HP   a filing in court.

P   What you say - Look we are having you here as a witness and we want you to talk.

HP   That is described as immunity by estoppel.

P   I see, I see - that's fair enough.

HP   That is really the prosecutor's bargain.

P   That is much better basically than immunity - let me say I am not, I guess my point on Dean is a matter of principle - it is a question of the fact that I am not trying to do Dean in - I would like to see him save himself but I think find a way to do it without - if you go the immunity route I think we are going to catch holy hell for it.

HP Scares hell out of me.

P Rogers says (expletive removed) he says "tell Petersen (expletive removed) if you give them immunity here - he sees (inaudible) the Gray thing and all the rest - Dean is." Whatever area we think Dean is in, in the public mind, he is a big shot. Ervin thinks he is a big shot, the whole Senate Judiciary Committee - Dean is the guy that the whole Executive Privilege thing is about. So we give him immunity? I hadn't thought about it when you first talked about it.

HP Sounds . . .

P But you must have thought about it.

HP I have - indeed. It is the toughest decision I have facing me.

P Well what the hell - he can talk without any immunity can't he? Oh I guess if he is a defendant he wouldn't talk to you.

HP That's right.

P (inaudible) of course he wouldn't (inaudible). Is that your problem?

HP You know if I get - yes - of course even if I come up with a lesser charge that damn Sirica is just liable to blast hell out of all of us to prevent him to plead even to a lesser charge. The ideal position would be the same as Magruder - you plead to one count felony indictment - take your chances.

P That is what Magruder agreed to plead to?

HP That's right.

P To one count felony indictment.

HP And that's what we are trying to work out with Dean and that's where the . . .

P (inaudible)

HP Five years - max.

P Five years - Out in two years?

HP Probably

P That's the way it works, isn't it?

HP Yes Sir.

P Dean's lawyers say (inaudible)

HP Dean's lawyers say we will try this whole damn Administration.

P Huh?

HP They say we'll try this whole Administration.

P Yeah, I know. I heard that. So that puts you in a hard spot.

HP   That's right. I don't know, I am just aghast at the whole damn thing and you must be too. Because I see no rhyme, reason -

P   Slightly

HP   anything to . . .

P   Yeah - for all this treatment - for this?

HP   And you know, I look at John Mitchell and I have admired him - and

P   Yeah - I know - good man.

HP   and I'm just shocked.

P   But what happened we know is this: These jackasses got off . . . see this Liddy is crazy and Hunt and that whole bunch conducted this (inaudible) Mitchell wasn't minding the store and Magruder is a weak fellow - and the damn thing - and then afterwards they compounded it by what happened afterwards.

HP   That's right.

P   They were caught in it and they said - Oh we can't and basically they were trying to protect Mitchell - let's face it. You know that.

HP   Well, you know LaRue broke down and cried like a baby yesterday.

P   He did? That's too bad.

HP   He was not so bad on admitting the obstruction of justice and subornation. Resigned, said he'd probably plead - said he didn't even think it worthwhile to bring a lawyer with him - ah,

P   He had (inaudible)

HP   Not fully he broke down but when it came to testifying about John Mitchell he just broke down and started to cry. It is a terrible thing . . .

P   (inaudible) as we all do, but we are going to do the right thing. Don't you worry about that. I am just trying to do the right thing in the way that is . . .

HP   Mr. President, if I didn't have confidence in you - I wouldn't be here.

P   Yeah

HP   You know—

P   Yeah. Did we do any good on the Liddy call?

HP   I don't know - Maroulis,

P   (inaudible)

HP   his lawyer, flew down

P   (inaudible)

HP   and we had Liddy brought over to a cell block of DC Court and made him available - and that was yesterday and of course I am sure Liddy is thinking it over -

but - we'll see. That man is a mental case . . . (inaudible)

HP   I guess Bill Rogers was shocked too? (Pause) God Almighty.

P   Bill - I think everybody is shocked, but we are in it. So what do you do? In this thing - in these things - you've got them, you handle them and go on to something else - that's what we are going to do.

HP   Damn, I admire your strength. I tell you.

P   Well, that's what we are here for.

HP   Well I know but I've been around government long enough . . .

P   Frankly, the Dean thing troubles the hell out of me - I would like in one sense I would like to see the poor bastard you know, out of it and in another sense I think the immunity thing scares me to death.

HP   Well it does me too. I agree.

P   How shall we leave that? You will go back and - you haven't made a decision then?

HP   Well we're still negotiating.

P   You are going to try to see if you can get it another way -

HP   That's right - that solves the problem for me - and if . . .

P   But you may not be able to and then we will have to get Dean. He is the only one, so - otherwise you go the other way.

HP   Yeah. Incidentally. I talked with Pat Gray again-

P   Yeah

HP   I went back again today

P   Do you think you can put that piece together?

HP   Yes sir - I'll tell you what happened. He said he met with Ehrlichman - in Ehrlichman's office - Dean was there and they told him they had some stuff in Hunt's office that was utterly unrelated to the Watergate Case. They gave him two manilla envelopes that were sealed. He took them. He says, they said get rid of them. Dean doesn't say that. Dean says I didn't want to get rid of them so I gave them to Gray. But in any event, Gray took them back, and I said Pat where are they, and he said I burned them. And I said -

P   He burned them?

HP   I said that's terrible.

P   Unrelated - only thing he can say was - he did it because it was political stuff I suppose?

HP   Well, you know, the cynics are not going to believe it was unrelated.

P   Oh yes of course.

HP   I said, did you read it?

P   Who handed it to him, Dean? Who knows the contents?

HP   Dean and Ehrlichman. Dean—Gray says he never looked at it - never read it.

P   Did Dean? - did we ask Dean what the contents were?

HP   I didn't ask Dean because he said it was -

P   Did anybody?

HP   Not at this point. We'll have to get to that obviously.

P   Sure. Dumb damn thing to do.

HP   I think it is incredible and I just -

P   Why didn't he just put it (inaudible)

HP   I said Pat why did you do it.

P   Pat's naive.

HP   He said - well, I suppose because I took them at their word.

(Apparently someone brought in a statement)

P   (Inaudible) Oh this is a (inaudible) Senate Select Committee. Let me read it to you if you can (inaudible) it for me a little. "For several weeks Senator Ervin and Senator Baker and their counsel have been in contact with White House representatives, Mr. Ehrlichman and Mr. Garment. They have been talking about ground rules to preserve the separation of powers without stressing facts. I believe that the Committee ground rules that have been adopted totally preserve the doctrine. They provided the . . . appearance by a witness named - in the first instance to be in executive session if appropriate. Second, the executive privilege would be expressly preserved (inaudible) proceeding would be televised (inaudible) . . . that has never been a central issue especially since the separation of powers problem is otherwise solved." (inaudible) Does that sound right to you?

HP   Yes sir.

P   Forthcoming and so forth, and so forth? All White House staff will appear and testify under oath and (inaudible) all proper questions fully as far as I am concerned. Second announcement - "When the Watergate Case (inaudible) several weeks ago, I began to look into this

588

matter as a result of printed stories in the press and private information which had come to me - private information?

HP I don't think that ought to be there.

P Basically it was the LaRue thing - not the LaRue - but the McCord thing that really set my invest . . . that is when I started to work with my . . .

HP I don't see how you can say private information that came to you

P Yeah

HP Almost becoming personally involved - at least as a result of a witness . . .

P As a result of some very serious charges that were

HP Yes, I think that has to be modified. (noise of paper being moved around—obviously the President was working on the statement)

P We could say that I - what was the term we used? - this says real progress has been made - that isn't very good—what is the term that we wanted to say about significant developments?

HP Significant developments is a term -

P Any person in the Executive Branch who is indicted by the Grand Jury my policy would be to immediately suspend him. If he is convicted he would be automatically discharged. No person in past or present positions of importance can (inaudible) the prosecution.

HP I don't think you ought to say that Mr. President. I mean, I think that is fine for you and I to share your concerns on that, but to state that publicly seems to me will have tendency to prevent people from coming in. In effect, we will be right back to where we were without the immunity statute - where the Fifth Amendment is a complete bar. Now even if we never utilize immunity the fact that it is there and can be used to strip them of the Fifth Amendment rights is a terrible important tactic to have available. That phrase in there takes that tactic away from us.

P The tactic of?

HP of immunity

P This doesn't refer to . . .

HP For example, we might want to immunize Strachan

P Well no, no -

HP Well then you get into a question of who is a person of importance—*Washington Post* may very well think that Strachan is a person of importance. Anybody who works at the White House is a person of importance as distinguished from—minor underlings so far as you are concerned.

P   Should we say major government employees? Government employees holding major positions - how is that?

HP   I would prefer that we not say it.

P   Well I am just trying to cover my tracks on the Dean thing - that is all.

HP   Yes.

P   And if he is - then that is the U.S. Attorney's job.

HP   But that is a sophisticated point isn't it?

P   Yeah. Sure, we could say that Dean was let off? Oooh

HP   Oh, it is a sophisticated point after the fact but at this point in time in conjunction with this statement it is going to take a rather astute reporter to raise it. Is immunity going to be utilized? - the question is easily defended - you know - that is a prosecutorial tactic and that will be handled by the prosecutors if and when it is necessary.

P   Right.

HP   You could say I would hope -

P   Yeah

HP   That no significant figures would be immunized

P   I express my - I want to put something - many of you know—I would hope—what could I say? I would hope any major - any official holding a major position, ah

HP   I have expressed my concern

P   My - I express my view

HP   To the Department of Justice

P   to the Department of Justice that no person, that it is my expressed view to the Dept. that no persons should be immunized.

HP   No - that is too strong.

P   Huh?

HP   That is too strong. That's a double entendre if you like -

P   Alright - what would you say then?

HP   In effect that says that you are taking away a prosecutorial tool from them.

P   I express my view to the appropriate authorities shall we say -

HP   That would weaken it

P   to the appropriate authorities that I do not favor—

HP   I have expressed my hope to the appropriate authorities that it would not be necessary to immunize any major official in order to develop a prosecutable case.

P Ok - I've got it Henry - otherwise it is nothing new - (inaudible) through the appropriate ways—that all White House especially are expected to cooperate fully - we said that - with the U. S. Dept.

HP With the prosecution

P With the prosecution

HP With the prosecution team.

P With the prosecution team. It says I have (inaudible) an occasion to attempt to pass the word to others who might be able to help to (inaudible) cooperation. I don't that means anything

HP I don't think that means anything and I think it says too much.

P Yes.

P Yeah - well what you are in effect saying to me - as I say - I want to be very clear on the Haldeman/Ehrlichman thing. That if they were left out of the non-indictable list it gives me a little running room. I want to be very clear - that understood?

HP That's right, that's right.

P It doesn't mean that they aren't eventually be indicted if you get the facts.

HP That's right

P But it does mean that they have an oppor . . . they aren't canned as a result of the fact - that is what we are really getting down to isn't it—you would have to put Dean on that list wouldn't you?

HP Yes Sir

P I guess you would have to with everything with him because basically Magruder is going to name him

HP That's right.

P Hmp

HP And, if we get down to . . .

P Magruder is not naming Haldeman and Ehrlichman though. That is the problem is it?

HP Yes but he does - but not in firsthand sense -

P Only by hearsay

HP But you see - if he makes that statement in open court -

P Yeah, I get it

HP It seems to me it makes your practical difficulties just as severe as if we had named him in the first place.

P Well I am glad to get this kind of stuff so I get a clear view of everything - what the options are—

HP And if we frankly - if we think that Sirica is

going to elicit that kind of statement we will include him in the charge to the extent that we can.

P   Yeah - sure you don't want to . . .

HP   Subject only to the fact that we can corroborate it later on.

P   Timing now. What about Magruder - you don't expect him tomorrow?

HP   Well I told them . . . Probably not today, but I guarantee you at least twelve hours notice.

P   Can you give me that much?

HP   I will guarantee you that. I will hold it up to make certain you get it.

P   Yeah. The only - Yeah. On the other hand I suppose you should say (inaudible) story - it got a hell of a big play.

HP   I didn't see it.

P   And other stories that are not so likely to (inaudible) could, could - everything is likely to blow around here. But at least you give me the - there is nothing in this that we irritate the fact that do we (inaudible) til down there in that court we know this damn (inaudible).

HP   That's right

P   So basically we are in a pretty good position to say - that except as I said I don't want the *Washington Post* to break this case.

HP   That's right. We don't either.

P   I want the Department of Justice - and, frankly, the White House - because as you can see we'll cooperate (inaudible).

P   OK - I can see what you mean. You would anticipate then that if you didn't include Haldeman and Ehrlichman in your general thing that Sirica will question the defendant - Magruder - and he then will bring in—

HP   If he brings that out—if we think that is a real possibility then we will have to decide whether or not as a matter of conscience and professional ethics we can put them in. If we can answer that yes - then we will put them in. If on the other hand, we think there is no basis for it - even if Sirica does bring out the hearsay - we will just have to take the knuckle for it.

P   Sure - which is basically what Sirica wants. Colson - I think we should know about him too.

HP   Well,

P   Not yet, huh?

HP   Well, Bittman went to Colson to urge leniency - Colson then got in touch with Ehrlichman and Dean.

Ehrlichman is alleged to have said -

P Make no commitments

HP we'll do the best we can - make no commitments. Then thereafter you know apparently money flows - or so we are told - whether there is any relevancy or relationship remains to be determined.

P What did Bittman want?

HP Well apparently the funds, but that remains to be developed - ah, Dorothy Hunt was, according to McCord, the intermediary the leniency thing (inaudible)

P Right.

HP And another intermediary was LaRue and LaRue used the alias of Baker - two aliases - one was Baker and I have forgotten the other one, for the transmittal of money. One of the things that concerns me in this area and you know again an area in which I may have made a mistake earlier in the game was with respect to Kalmbach. Now I understand he is your personal lawyer - is that a fact?

P Yes, yes - very capable guy. (inaudible) - as I understand - they called and said raise some money for the (inaudible) and so forth. I am sure he was no damn co-conspirator. (inaudible) after the campaign.

HP Here's one thing - in the earlier stages of the proceedings when they had Segretti in the Grand Jury -

P Yeah.

HP I told Silbert - now—damn it Silbert keep your eye on the mark - we are investigating Watergate - we are not investigating the whole damn realm of politics and I don't want you questioning him about the President's lawyer.

P Right

HP Well, he didn't. Well now Kalmbach comes up and you heard on the news I am sure today - he apparently is going to be called by the Senate Committee - but he also comes up in this investigation with respect to actually Kalmbach raising money - or passing on money at Mitchell's direction for the co-conspirators - So we are going -

P Sure

HP to have Kalmbach back into the Grand Jury.

P Well in that instance, I suppose there you've got to prove what he thought he was raising it for.

HP Well, even if he didn't know or he was misled - the fact that he

P (inaudible)

593

HP   did at the time we may very well end up with him being a witness.

P   Damn right - oh I know that. I would seriously - I mean. And again on that particular count - I guess you were the one, I think who said the question is motive - what they raised the money for.

HP   That's right

P   If you are trying to help them out with their defense - that is one thing - but if you are helping them out to keep them quiet that is a hell of (inaudible) - that is an obstruction job.

HP   That's right - you know if you are acting out of Christian charity -

P   Right

HP   that is fine.

P   That would be Mitchell's defense on that.

HP   O course all the inferences run the other way and that is a hell of a defense to have to put to the Jury.

P   Well I guess you have given me enough to chew on here - whether I get something out today and we'll know how - about it tonight - I'll see—I may have a little bit of time. You don't think that you are going to indict sometime today.

HP   I will be glad to give you twelve hours notice. Nothing is going to happen today I am certain - even if we get an agreement today - you know I can still hold it off a day.

P   Yeah - you might hold if off even tomorrow, huh?

HP   That's right. If we have to go see Ervin and Sirica - both of them - it may very well take a full day before we can get both things accomplished.

P   I've got to accept a big huge schedule tomorrow - energy message, and so forth, and so forth, and I don't want to tell you to hold it off except apparently it is going to take you some time anyway - I mean there is always a chance of leaks - leaks aren't going to mean much -

HP   There are so many i's to dot and t's to cross on this thing - when you talk about holding off a day or two if doesn't make that much difference.

P   Except leaks - what do you think on (inaudible)?

HP   I think it is terribly important -

P   Get out front?

HP   for you to get out front on this thing - irrespective of

P   Even with a statement like this that doesn't say much. Well cooperating with Ervin but that's

HP It says that - that is significant news. I think it is significant that it reflects that you are taking a personal interest in it - I think it is significant that you say there are significant developments which means you are personally informed and not only have endorsed what the prosecution is doing. It certainly is not significant in terms of evidentiary facts but we are never going to be in a position to do that anyway unless the public exposure in the court. You know there is another dimension, Mr. President. These fellows Magruder, Dean have talked to us - they'd be less than human if they didn't watch to see if the system was surviving the test - so there is another reason for their delay. Conceivably they say well this may be too strong for the Department of Justice or the President - or the people at the White House - they're not going to have the courage to face up to this—let's wait and see what happens and if we don't see some movement then our bargaining position will become increasingly tougher day by day by day.

P Yeah. (inaudible) - keep in my mind - (inaudible) get the damn thing over with - and I know the trials of Mitchell and all these people will take a long time - (inaudible) - Mitchell will never plead guilty, never. Fight it all the way down the line. (inaudible) What would you do if you were Mitchell?

HP I think I would probably go to Saudi Arabia to tell you the truth.

P Poison

HP When I think the former Attorney General of the United States being subject to criminal trial is just—

P For obstruction of justice - not the bugging - the obstruction of justice.

HP It is just terrible.

P OK - alright - thanks for your help. I'll see if I can work something out today and if I don't, maybe tomorrow. We'll see about it.

HP Thank you. Have a good day Mr. President.

P Yep - we'll try.

Meeting: The President, Haldeman, Ziegler and Ehrlichman, Oval Office, April 17, 1973.
(3:50 - 4:35 pm)

E   This is John Ehrlichman for Bill Timmons.

E   Ah, I'm in the President's office Bill, can you call—get the first page, first two lines of the second page (unintelligible). Pardon me? No, just tell him that's the statement. Bill, just go ahead and do it. Thanks.

P   I completed the round with Petersen and he said he completely agreed with me, that he's been arguing that with the U. S. Attorneys. He says the problem—

E   He's in total control

P   He said the problem is (unintelligible). I said, "Well you're going to corroborate it, aren't you?" "Yes, of course." But I put it bluntly. No individual—

Z   Ya, I just want to check. Are we already to go?

P   I don't know if I can really make it. How late can I go? About 4:30. O. K. Don't tell anybody yet. Thank you. I'll let you know.

P   Quickly. The new evidence, new leaks. First, I said, I said Rogers and I talked about it and Rogers thought it was totally wrong to immunize the President's counsel. Rogers did say that. However, I talked about the leaks in the Grand Jury (unintelligible) Mitchell, Dean. I said I just want you to know that you are vulnerable. He said, "Well I never gave them substance, I just gave them (unintelligible) on how they did and so forth and so forth." He says, After all, it's my responsibility." But anyway, I don't know. I didn't get far with that (unintelligible). He talked to Pat Gray and Pat Gray has now told him that he destroyed the packet. He just shakes his head.

H   Why would Gray do that?

P   Gray was told it was political, was told to destroy. I don't know Gray was told it was material, actually nothing to do with Watergate. He was told to destroy it, but Petersen says that's that. Here's the situation, basically, (unintelligible). They're going to haul him in court, have him plead guilty, put a statement out because Sirica always questions the witnesses who plead guilty. They are going to make it as broad as they can and as narrow as they can at the same time. By being as broad as they can, they are going to say that he has named certain people

596

and they are going to name a group of people that is non-indictable co-conspirators. They're going to include everybody on that list. I said, "Is Dean going to be on that list?" He said, "Yes." He said, "Frankly (unintelligible) not include Haldeman and Ehrlichman, which gives you an option." I said, Are you telling me that if Haldeman and Ehrlichman decide to take leave, that you will not then proceed with the prosecution. "No," he said, "I don't mean that." He said, "What I mean is that they are not going to appear on that list and that (unintelligible) Grand Jury and make case there (unintelligible). So there's the—

E Well, whether we take leave or not doesn't effect the list that they read off.

P Yes. Yes.

E Oh, it does? Yes, it does. They will put us on the list if we don't take leave?

P Yes, because otherwise, he says, he says Sirica is going to question Magruder and he's going to question (unintelligible) and it appears (unintelligible). If he does that, then it will appear that the Justice Department again is covering up. Two questions: One, should we go forward with an announcement today or not, or should—

E Well, from your standpoint, you must. Even so. This thing will get away from you otherwise.

P Well, the real question, I suppose, John is (unintelligible). I don't think we can—here's the whole point, in effect—if the—your names will probably be on the list. That's what he's saying unless you decide not to, decide that you're not (unintelligible).

H It isn't that (unintelligible), we have to resign. The (unintelligible) doesn't accomplish anything.

P (unintelligible)

H What does he mean from that? I don't understand?

E The guy to gain from that is Dean.

H Ya, they're putting us in the same bag with him.

E Ya.

P (unintelligible) he said Dean's lawyers say Dean is going to make a case against this Administration. They're going to try this Administration. That's what he said. So, I guess that's where we stand with Dean.

E Well, it's as broad as it is long as far as I'm concerned. If I'm to take leave—you think I should—that is or has the same effect as being—

P As resigning? (unintelligible) taking leave you couldn't come back.

E Ya, I'll never come back.

P Of course not. I understand that.

E On the other hand, if I'm indicted and take leave, and then I'm acquitted, I could come back. But to take leave and then not appear on the Magruder list, it's a confession.

P That's right. So I think their (unintelligible) approach just doesn't work.

H Well, then you look worse by that than you do the other way. You look better to have us on the list, than to have us take leave and then not be on the list.

E Cause that looks like you're covering up, that it hasn't come out.

P I think so, too.

H If we're going to be on the list, so be it!

P That's right. I think you're right.

H I think we're in a terrible—These guys are working in a most bloodthirsty way. They've lied to Strachan. They've told him they had all this stuff. They've not told him what his rights are properly. I'm sure his lawyer has gotten it straightened out, but it's really something.

E They're trying to get him.

H Trying to get him to take a cop-out and they won't make a deal. They told Strachan if he covered everything that he had, everybody he knows, they assured him they already had it anyway—

P That's a tactic.

H They said you, Strachan, have a chance of getting out because you'll become a witness and not a defendant, but they will not give him immunity.

P That is immunity, however.

H Well, unless—it keeps their options open and his closed.

P Strachan is (unintelligible).

H (expletive removed), I hope so. And the (expletive removed) you know Strachan made that mistake on the 350, called Silbert the next day and said, "I would like to correct that. I made a mistake." They said, "Fine, come up in the morning and we'll straighten it out." He went up Monday morning, and they laughed at him and said we're not going to put you before the Grand Jury. See that's when they kicked him around, yesterday morning. Then today when he went in they said, "We will not let you correct your statement on the 350, we've got you on a perjury count.

P That's not true.

H   That's what they told him.

E   It certainly is not fair.

H   Well, apparently by the law.

P   I think under the law if you go forth and volunteer something—

H   But they wouldn't let him go in, so he didn't volunteer, but he sure did it constructively as far as—

P   Well, shall we get to work? Shall I just go out and read it.

E   I think so. I'm having Timmons just read this first part to Ervin.

P   All members of the White House staff will appear (unintelligible) when requested by the Committee and will testify under oath and answer all proper—Are you getting all this or should I get a girl in?

E   Voluntarily, when requested by the Committee—O.K.

P   The next part is what I'm concerned about. "I began new inquiries," shall we say?

E   Well, I don't know.

P   "I began new inquiries into this matter as a result of serious charges which were reported publicly and privately." Should we say that?

E   Publicly, comma "which in some cases were reported publicly."

P   "Four weeks ago we," Why don't we say, shall we set a date? That sounds a hell of a lot stronger if we set a date.

E   All right.

P   "On March 21, I began new inquiries," Strike that. "I ordered an investigation, new inquiries throughout the government—"

E   How about saying, "On March 21 as a result of serious charges which were reported publicly and"—

P   "Some of which were reported publicly and some of which were reported privately to me"

E   "Some of which I subsequently"

P   "As a result of serious charges reported publicly and privately"—

E   "Some of which were reported publicly"—and then not say about the result of them. I—

P   In other words, "On March 21 we started an investigation because of the public hearings."

E   That's right.

P   "As a result of serious charges reported publicly—publicly reported—"I began intensive new inquiries into

599

this whole matter." I think we better get Petersen back in here.

E   Name him.

P   Ya. After all, this Kleindienst thing is very general (unintelligible)

E   "And Assistant Attorney General Petersen."

P   "Assistant Attorney General Petersen have met to review the facts at length in my investigation and the progress of the Department of Justice Investigation." How's that? "I can report today that there have been major new developments in the case." Right? That sound right?

E   How about just saying, "Have been major developments in the case concerning which I should not be more specific now, except to say that real progress has been made."

P   "Major developments in the case, concerning which—specific—which would be improper for me to be more specific now except to say that real progress has been made in getting to the bottom." What do you say, "in getting to the bottom of this matter?"

E   "Has been made in exposing the truth."

P   "In finding the truth."

E   All right.

P   "In this whole matter."

E   Well, we've already said matter.

P   Well.

E   "I can report today that major developments in the case, concerning which it would be improper to be more specific now, except to say that real progress has been made in finding the truth."

P   "Real progress has been made in finding the truth." And then you go on to the (unintelligible).

E   If you don't mind.

P   I don't want to put the immunity thing in. I don't think there's a hell of a lot gained by saying it publicly.

E   Except—

P   All right. "If any person in the Executive Branch is indicted by the Grand Jury, my policy will be to immediately suspend"—Shall we (unintelligible) of what we know is going to happen? Should we say "indicted"? Why don't we just leave it "indicted" and not indicate what charges are made? Don't you agree?

E   I think so. I think "indicted" ought to be the test.

P   "Indicted by the Grand Jury." My policy would be,

600

"If he is convicted," and then I would say, "If he is convicted, he would be automatically discharged." And then, the way I could put it, "I expressed to the appropriate authorities my views that no individual holding a position of major importance should be given immunity from prosecution. That means that no person can expect"—

E   Yep, this is fine.

P   I don't think I want to say "lead to believe." Do we have to say that?

E   No, I was just trying to get you off the hook, and say, you know, well, this—How about going on with the next sentence?

P   "The judicial process is moving to get all the facts." Or, "Moving—"

E   "moving ahead as it should."

P   "Moving ahead as it should. As I have said before, all government employees, especially members of the White House staff, are to fully cooperate with the Grand Jury." Or do we want to say "Grand Jury"?

E   How about "fully cooperate"—period.

P   "Fully cooperate in this investigation." "to fully cooperate with law enforcement authorities." How's that?

E   Ervin and Baker are out of pocket.

P   I don't want to use the next sentence, John.

E   All right.

P   Then I think the last sentence should be—I think if he puts that in there we're going to have a hell of a tough time. (unintelligible)

H   I think if he'll cover the truth—

P   Yep.

H   That's what he's got to do. Answer their questions truthfully.

P   Why didn't he say, "Sure I'll be a witness." Why didn't he just say that, take their offer? Maybe that's what he said. "I'll take your offer."

H   I think that's what we want him to do.

P   I think what you should do is say, "I don't have anything to hide. I'll take your offer," and just make the point.

H   Given that offer, he doesn't have to volunteer anything. All he has to do is answer their questions.

P   That's right Bob, he should just take their offer. Believe me, we don't have to have (unintelligible). He isn't trying to hide anything.

H   I'd feel fine with his doing that, cause—so he says

601

some things that are damaging. They are only slightly damaging, and we've had plenty of damaging things already.

P   That's right. Bob, just tell him to take it. All right? Tell him to take it but tell them the mere truth. You see, they think it is worse than it is. They think he is covering up and they are wrong. That's what it really gets down to.

H   They are trying to confuse him. That's what has him bothered. The poor guy. What's really worried him is that he's covered everything with Dean, every step of the way. Everything he has done, he's talked with Dean about it over the last year and he's scared to death Dean will make up something or take something that is partly right and twist it, which is what Dean is doing, and hang him on it. And I think what he's got to do is just go with what he believes is correct and hang with it.

P   Don't you think we are right (unintelligible) tell the U. S. Attorney, "Fine. You want to name Haldeman and Ehrlichman. You just (unintelligible) they put you on as unindictable co-conspirators, then they've got a case to prove. Now they aren't going to do that unless they figure they can prove the case, so that would give them the problem. I think his argument is, and I must say I don't know what to hell Petersen is up to (unintelligible) I think, on the other hand, it looks like. Let's look at that.

H   That makes his case for him. That makes his case for him.

P   Maybe you're right. I was going to suggest that we would get back, call you, and we get Rogers over here. And I think in this instance, you and Ehrlichman with Rogers can just sit down and talk about this?

H   I think so. Yes.

P   You don't have any other lawyer? Would you mind getting him over at 5:00 p.m.

H   We're meeting with our lawyer at 4:30 to 5:30, which is the only time we could get him. Would you want me to get him in at 5:30?

P   Sure, Bob, my time is your time.

H   Well, I don't want to screw up your time.

P   You're not.

H   That was the only time he could take us. He's taking time out of a deposition.

P   I understand, but hope he can learn from it in that time.

H   Well, we'll give him a quick fill and get him started

on it. That's all we can do now, but we need to get started on it.

P I guess (unintelligible) may resign.

H That would be a very foolish thing for him to do.

P Hmm?

H That would be a very foolish thing for him to do.

P He didn't say that. But, I meant, you know how strongly he feels. He's wrong. He's wrong, Bob. Look, the point is, (unintelligible) throwing you to the wolves with Dean. What does that accomplish? I don't know what it accomplishes. Except the President learns the facts and as a result of learning the facts (unintelligible). I say, "Fellas, you've been charged and I know that Dean has made some charges." Right?

H There's another way you could do it. John won't buy this if I don't. I won't do it if John won't. We've got to do it together. Either one of us has to hang together playing this game. But, maybe we request of you a leave of absence on the basis of the information you have, which we have, because we've been involved in the investigation too. Now if we're going to be on that list, we're going to have to ask for a leave of absence anyway, if he puts the list out, and has us on it.

P It's going to be out. And I don't know that you'll be on it. That's the point. We've got to see. Nevertheless, you will be called. But we've always talked about being called to the Grand Jury.

P That's right.

H And said that we would appear. You made a statement weeks ago saying that anybody in the White House would welcome the opportunity to testify before the Grand Jury. Ah. Do you automatically suspend any witness whose called before a Grand Jury? Of course not.

P Well, now, if you come on that list, the only problem here is that (unintelligible).

E Oops.

P The problem we have here, John, as I was just saying (unintelligible) Dean's lawyers, are they going to try this Administration?

E Believe me, everybody is going to try this Administration regardless of what (unintelligible). Ervin's going to try this Administration.

H We went through your statement. Why don't we go see the lawyers? Why don't we re-group at 5:30 and decide then

E   You have the first page intact?

P   Did she use the speech typewriter? I don't want to go through this.

E   Take this back and put it on the speech typewriter. She's running it off on the typewriter now.

P   Well, maybe it's too soon for Rogers. Well, I guess we just let Dean go ahead and try the Administration.

E   He's going to do his work anyway, with or without immunity. Ervin is going to get him up there if he has immunity or not and will take him over the jumps. What you've done here is to lay a ground rule for Ervin on immunity which is going to be very tough for him to live with if there are Ervin hearings. But eventually there will be Ervin hearings. I don't think there's much (unintelligible). The more—

P   There will be Ervin hearings, Bob.

E   The more battles the President wins, like the economical stabilization performance, the more urgent the Ervin hearings become. It's the only thing they have left, now. You're winning all the big ones.

H   We better leave now. It's 4:30.

E   Yep, ya.

H   If you want to see Bill at 5:00 p.m. ahead of us, we can join you at 5:30.

P   You may not be ready by then.

E   He can only stay an hour.

P   Fine. I'll see him at 5:00. And the situation that you have here is a (unintelligible). Dean (unintelligible) Administration if I'm wrong? Damn, no, it can't.

E   I'll tell you as we lay this out, and I'll be anxious to see what this lawyer has to say, Dean's testimony may not be admissible.

P   On what grounds?

E   That his communication to us was a communication to you, and vice versa. As an alter ego to the President.

P   I don't have any separate existence.

E   But you have to assert privilege, in a sense, but I don't know what kind of political problems that make (unintelligible) Solicitor General, as a disability, strictly from that standpoint (unintelligible)

P   Would you discuss with your lawyer the legal (unintelligible) and let's think about this business, about whether—Ron?

Z   Ya

P   Come on in.

Z   Len needs the ground rules before he calls, and he's

in my office. Could you fill him in?

E   All he has to do is read that to them. Period. He doesn't have any comment, he doesn't have any reflection. O.K.?

P   Who is this?

E   Len Garment. He's going to call back. He's just reading the first page since we can't get Ervin. Look, I don't want him to get into an argument with him.

Z   O.K. All right, fine. Then John, afterwards when they ask me what the ground rules are, I'll just say—

E   Up to the Committee (unintelligible)

Z   We have plenty of video tape recorders, so there's no film problem.

P   They got it yet? Bring it in.

Z   Ya. Did John raise with you the couple of questions in terms of the next day or so? And afterwards just say, "Is Dean still in charge of the investigation?" We ought to just say, "No."

P   Just say." that the President—that we discussed and that, "No," that the President is dealing with that the Assistant Attorney General, Mr. Petersen, is in charge of the investigation.

Z   Then, secondly, they will say does the President stand by the August 29 statement that no one presently employed in the White House had knowledge and so forth? There, I think, I suggested to John, that this is an operative statement—position as it stands.

P   You could say that the August 29 statement—that was the report that was made to the President by White House Counsel at that time—and the facts will determine whether that statement is correct, and now it would be interfering with the judicial process to comment further.

Z   I will just say that this is the operative statement.

P   You're not going to answer questions today are you?

Z   No, no. But I mean if I walk into the Press Room they'll be pounding on my door.

P   Of course, Ron. Go ahead. Don't (expletive removed) on Dean.

Z   No, I'm not going to.

P   He is, just say he—

Z   I'll try to avoid it altogether, but I just want to get guidance. Then I could give the wires some background on how aggressively and how much time you've spent on this the past three weeks and so forth. Should I do a little of that?

Statement: The President,
April 17, 1973. (4:42 - 4:45 pm)

THE PRESIDENT: Be seated, please:

Ladies and gentlemen:

I have two announcements to make. Because of their technical nature, I shall read both of the announcements to the members of the press corps.

The first announcement relates to the appearance of White House people before the Senate Select Committee, better known as the Ervin Committee.

For several weeks, Senator Ervin and Senator Baker and their counsel have been in contact with White House representatives John Ehrlichman and Leonard Garment. They have been talking about ground rules which would preserve the separation of powers without suppressing the facts.

I believe now an agreement has been reached which is satisfactory to both sides. The committee ground rules as adopted, totally preserve the doctrine of separation of powers. They provide that the appearance by a witness may, in the first instance, be in Executive session, if appropriate.

Second, Executive privilege is expressly reserved and may be asserted during the course of the questioning as to any question.

Now, much has been made of the issue as to whether the proceedings could be televised. To me, this has never been a central issue, especially if the separation of powers problem is otherwise solved, as I now think it is.

All members of the White House staff will appear voluntarily when requested by the committee. They will testify under oath and they will answer fully all proper questions.

I should point out that this arrangement is one that covers this hearing only in which wrongdoing has been charged. This kind of arrangement, of course, would not apply to other hearings. Each of them will be considered on its merits.

My second announcement concerns the Watergate case directly.

On March 21st, as a result of serious charges which

606

came to my attention, some of which were publicly reported, I began intensive new inquiries into this whole matter.

Last Sunday afternoon, the Attorney General, Assistant Attorney General Petersen and I met at length in the EOB to review the facts which had come to me in my investigation and also to review the progress of the Department of Justice investigation.

I can report today that there have been major developments in the case concerning which it would be improper to be more specific now, except to say that real progress has been made in finding the truth.

If any person in the Executive Branch or in the government is indicted by the Grand Jury, my policy will be to immediately suspend him. If he is convicted, he will, of course, be automatically discharged.

I have expressed to the appropriate authorities my view that no individual holding, in the past or at present, a position of major importance in the Administration should be given immunity from prosecution.

The judicial process is moving ahead as it should; and I shall aid it in all appropriate ways and have so informed the appropriate authorities.

As I have said before and I have said throughout this entire matter, all government employees and especially White House staff employees are expected fully to cooperate in this matter. I condemn any attempts to cover up in this case, no matter who is involved.

Thank you.

END

(At 4:45 P.M. EST)

Meeting: The President, Rogers, Haldeman and Ehrlichman, EOB Office, April 17, 1973.
(5:20 - 7:14 pm)

P   Come in.
R   Mr. President
P   Well.
R   Well, did you make the announcement?
P   Yeah.
R   Sounds good, I hope.
P   See if I—
R   See I heard it when you did it.

P   Won't hurt anything. I think it was the right move.

R   Yeah - right.

P   After our talk yesterday, I referred to—I was aiming at the Ervin Committee—managed to get that one over (unintelligible) terms we discussed. Figures though—I mean—Len Garment is pretty good. Talked to Petersen again today—he was down here at the White House. And (unintelligible) charged with "got to resign." Just figures you can't keep them. Walked out in the sun and frankly put them ahead of Mitchell. But I just don't think—you have any different views today?

R   No, I don't.

P   You think this is the right step to go?

R   I do.

P   It can occur—it's going to be—it's going to be bloody.

R   I think that.

P   Believe me.

R   That the top people in government deserve the same consideration as anybody else.

P   Damn right.

R   The idea that a top person in government is, you know—it isn't the question beyond reproach, you know. A person could be beyond reproach. Take me—I should have been fired many times because I've been so heavily criticized in the press, many of those were things I didn't do. You remember.

R   Well, as a matter of fact, it's a little bit the same attitude that Lucius Clay had about you and the fund.

P   Right.

R   That there's Mr. Eisenhower and you should get off. Well, that wasn't really what he said.

P   I think the people will probably—they will have a view that—the *New York Times* will have a view in an editorial tomorrow that the President should fire the whole White House staff.

R   Oh well, that isn't—

P   Anybody who did it. But I think the people—I don't know. Correct me if I am wrong. I think they like a man who stands up to them—not to condemn people before they're proven. I don't know.

R   Well, I think that—what did Petersen say on Ehrlichman? Does he have any other evidence except what's in that piece of paper because if he doesn't there wasn't anything in there.

P   Nope—nope. Well, it's hardly anything. Except that

Pat Gray now recollects he did get the damn piece of paper and he destroyed it, because he was told it was political material, had nothing to do with Watergate. We'll take him on on this—this has destroyed him. There's no place in the FBI to (unintelligible) it—it's an unbelievable story.

R   Well, now Ehrlichman didn't tell him to destroy it?

P   Hell no. Gray went back—Dean did give it to him. It was in Ehrlichman's office. And, incidentally, I put it hard to Petersen. I'll tell you about that point. I even used your name. I said, "I talked to Bill Rogers about it yesterday and I had a very (unintelligible)." I said, "He looked over this and he said, 'You don't have much of a case on Ehrlichman.' " That problem—and he said—

R   That piece of paper didn't have anything on Ehrlichman.

P   They'll pound on that. They're trying like hell to just frighten people to death. They're going to send 'em to jail and so forth. Strachan—they're trying to break him. I don't understand. Hell, he can either be a witness or a defendant. So—well, the other thing—and I told Haldeman, I said, "Tell him to be a witness."

R   What's happened to Dean?

P   They made a deal with him. And that's why I put in that statement, I hope—that's the point. I said, "Look, I talked to Rogers." I said, "We think we have a grave problem in giving immunity to the President's Counsel." He said, "But, suppose that it's Dean's testimony that we need to get Haldeman and Ehrlichman. Then should we give him immunity—shouldn't we give him immunity?" I said, "No—not unless you have corroboration."

R   Well, well, what you do, Mr. President, on things like that is you say to a fellow, "Well, you've got to—you violated the law. You've got to be indicted. We'll consider the help you've given us when it comes to the question of sentence." In other words, you—

P   Yeah.

R   Hold out the prospect to him.

P   But, how could you give John Dean, the President's Counsel, total immunity when he's involved? He admits involvement throughout.

R   Of course, if you gave him immunity—

P   But, I—

R   You—you get.

P   I said no. I said, by no means, I'd get the rack.

R   They'd say that you worked it out so Dean—

P   Well, they're going to. Then the other way—the way Dean's appeal is the U.S. Attorney's people. Well, Petersen said he agreed with that. He was trying to convince the U.S. Attorneys of that, but they are hot on trying to give him immunity and they're going to. And they want to (unintelligible) Haldeman and Ehrlichman. Frankly, that's it. And then they said—and then it's a cop out (unintelligible). Why do you think they should go? On what basis? Here's what we have in mind. I'll tell you what this statement was on. They're going to have Magruder in open court eventually. Haven't made the deal with him yet either, but they will. (Unintelligible) questions (unintelligible) they're going to put out this statement in which they will name other what they call non-indicted co-conspirators. I keep hearing about the names of people that he must charge. That's all (unintelligible). He said Sirica, otherwise, will ask him questions and he's going to testify publicly in open court about other people. I think that is a hell of a prejudicial thing to do—the rights of an individual—but I don't know how—have you ever heard of that? And I said—and then they said, "Haldeman and Ehrlichman will not be on that list if they take a leave—if you fire them." I said, "Are you telling me if I fire them, you won't prosecute them?" "Oh, no, no, but I mean won't be on that list." "But you—have you said if they're on that list they'll have to take 'em?" And then they said—I said, "Well, what are you saying?" He said, "Well, we just felt we were giving you an option, that you could move ahead of the herd basically by just letting them go." But on the other hand, Bill, I think—I think that whether they're on the list—if I let 'em go they're on the list anyway. It appears that I just—I heard they were going to be on the list and I fired them and they were on it. Then it looks as if we're not prosecuting. That's my problem. We're not prosecuting my two top people and I let them go. I don't think that makes sense at all or do you agree? Am I missing something here?

R   You don't seem to.

P   Well, tell me that. Well, wouldn't it look bad? Bad?

R   Oh, sure. From your standpoint. Yeah.

P   If I let Haldeman and Ehrlichman go and they didn't have them on the list, they will call them before the Grand Jury and then indict them if they get information.

R   Well you see, Mr. President, the only reason a judge questions a defendant when there's a plea of guilty—

P   Yeah.

R   Is to make sure that he's pleading voluntarily and that he knows the nature of his pleading.

P   Yeah. But right. Right. But Sirica has exceeded that hasn't he, Bill? That's the point.

R   Well.

P   He's asking now who else was involved. See that's what he's going to ask. "Was he involved?"

R   It seems to me that if he's doing that—

P   I think he'll act like he did over McCord.

R   Well, if he does that, that's a perversion of the Grand Jury process. The whole idea of the Grand Jury process is to protect people—

P   Yeah.

R   Until they are indicted. And once they are indicted, then they are presumed to be innocent until we go to trial. One of the reasons you have a Grand Jury proceeding is so you don't have innocent names and then (unintelligible) to the public.

P   Well, I'll tell you. Let me put it this way. (Unintelligible) Haldeman, and Ehrlichman, on a thing like this —Ehrlichman—frankly, I think he's going to beat it. I don't think it's going to help him, if by letting him go, I know that he's gone to the prosecution. I told him—

R   You shouldn't—you shouldn't be faced with those problems.

P   I know I don't have any (unintelligible). Don't you agree with me that that was—you know I am concerned about my people. I know that Haldeman and Ehrlichman are not guilty of a damn thing. You know what I mean. It's only tangential on that, Bill—tangential. Sure they knew we were raising money for these damn defendants, but they were (unintelligible) in the campaign. I mean, I mean (unintelligible) Dean at the meeting, wasn't he?

R   Yeah.

P   Ehrlichman was handling the whole domestic thing and Haldeman was working with me at the time. They didn't work in the campaign. It was all over with Mitchell. Mitchell was—in this whole thing—and frankly, Dean was handling it for the White House. (unintelligible). Our people were aware that he was. We were aware about that.

R   How did you leave it with Petersen? I don't know whether—I think from now on you better let him go into the brawl. I don't know.

P   I have. I left it with Petersen. He's going to report

to me and I said, "If you get any corroborating testimony, I'd like to know." I think that's better.

R Sure.

P And if I get some corroborative testimony, I said, "I'd like to be warned and I can call in my people and say, 'Look, I found this out and I've got information and you—Therefore, you ought to consider whether you shouldn't resign.'" That's all I told him. Well, I'm not going to talk to him any more about that. After all, I'm the President of the country—and I'm going to get on with it and meet Italians and Germans and all these others. You know, really—

R Oh, you do that. I think you, I think that—

P I've been living with this for (unintelligible) that's all I've been doing for half the time now. And having all these (unintelligible) that I had trust in. What trust. I trust Ehrlichman. I had him working. I must say he completed the job. He got to the bottom of the thing. Had a meeting with Mitchell and questioned (unintelligible). This was before Magruder went to the (unintelligible). And he said, "There is a possible, possible situation of the act of—What do you call it?

R (Unintelligible).

P If the individuals knew that the purpose was to keep people from talking in court. In court, not openly. Apparently, it's—You might keep 'em from it—but he said, "Anyway, that's the problem." So, I don't know. I still don't know if it is a problem. I don't—see, I'm thinking of Haldeman and his kids, Ehrlichman and Dean and his. You know what I mean. I'm thinking of the possibility of their mocking a great career. Their service has been efficient—marvelously (unintelligible). It's been all over (unintelligible). I'll tell you, if they aren't convicted, Bill, they'll come out. You know what I mean. (Unintelligible) charge, and everybody's going to understand. This'll be in better perspective in a year, I think.

R I think so. I think once that the—well, the first blush will be—

P Terrible

R It'll be terrible.

P Yes, sir.

R No doubt about that.

P Oh, yes!

R And it will—it has so many little ramifications that you—

P Yeah.

R   To this story.

P   Right - right.

R   But when it's all over—finished—

P   The Watergate mess.

R   When it's finished—

P   I'll be here, all along, Bill. The Jury indicts, moves. We're going to get on with this country. A lot of people in the country, we may find, they feel the President is doing the best he can in the damn thing. If I had wanted to cover-up—they probably think the President can cover-up. If I wanted to, I sure haven't done it very well, have I?

R   See, you only got what your—what the press will do to your own people. Press will persecute people.

P   They prosecuted Mitchell.

R   Did Dean at any time give you any indication of what he's going to do?

P   Make a deal. Both—make a deal with Dean. Make a deal. I would think that Dean would just say, "Look son, if you're indicted, I'm coming (unintelligible). Gee, fellows, what the hell is (unintelligible)" and any of the others. But he's going to try this whole Administration I would expect. And my view on that is let him try the whole Administration. Ron Ziegler has an interesting point. He said, "Dean had in February, had said, 'I, for nine months conducted this investigation.' Now he comes in and charges inaction." Dammit, why didn't he come in earlier, and tell me these things, Bill? Why didn't he do it? If he knew, I would think that—

R   It's one of those things that I just—(unintelligible) Mitchell

P   Oh.

R   Well, these things happened.

P   And once it did happen, not cutting it off right then—stepping forward and saying, "I (unintelligible) this. These kids shouldn't have done this and that's my (unintelligible) best judgment." Well, I think I know they just thought that might hurt the election.

R   Same thing is true in Vesco. That case he's involved in.

P   Belongs to the courts. I'd rather have it there than in the Committee.

R   Oh, sure.

P   Wouldn't you? At least the court doesn't try—

R   Well, that's the way it's supposed to be. That's the system. The system is—

P It sure shows the system works, though, doesn't it? And I get amused. I had (unintelligible) in all Sunday, had 'em in Monday, I had him in here today. I fired out my statement, and I said—

R What'd he say about your statement?

P Petersen? Oh, he thought it was fine. I got to thank him for it.

R Is he going to (unintelligible) accuse other people in open court?

P That's just like Sirica (unintelligible).

R Well, I can see, I can see—Sirica was, he was suspicious there was a cover-up.

P That's right.

R He was trying to, he was trying to put pressure on the ones who knew so he could—

P Not only to confess about themselves, but about other ones. That point, of course, they'd say that Magruder has acknowledged, Magruder has confessed—but what about others? What about (unintelligible)?

R What I mean is here you've got a willing witness. Before he was doing it to reluctant defendants. Here you got a willing, as I understand it, a willing one.

P Who will testify.

R Who will testify, has been working with the prosecutor and who's going to, will be called before the Grand Jury. Why the hell he's—that (unintelligible) open court. That's the—that's what the Grand Jury's for. Makes a nice little backdrop for your Italian dinner.

P Oh, it'll be alright. They'll have a fine dinner and wine. They just heard the story. "Thank God, the President's finally said something about Watergate." That, I think, is going to be the partial reaction.

R I do too.

P I don't know. I'm not taking any—

R No. I don't either.

P Comfort out of it, because for a period of time it's going to be painful. When Mitchell gets indicted, and when possibly Haldeman and Ehrlichman get—

R (Unintelligible).

P They're talking to them now. I've asked them both to come over here for a minute when they get (unintelligible). I feel frankly that we should. And a question that he makes now which is still open, you see, he still left it open. They, they'll leave if evidence (unintelligible) brought to my attention.

R Yeah.

P (unintelligible) Approach that I have my sources. Now, if he doesn't have enough to sink 'em, but he makes these, he's doing enough to sink them—where are you getting (unintelligible) on the other story? Whether or not Haldeman and Ehrlichman ought to wait until their names are publicly brought into this. Magruder shouldn't. He said he'd give me twelve hours' notice on that, but I—I think that probably it's going to (unintelligible).

R I think John and Bob ought to resign, but talk to their lawyer first (unintelligible) but I don't think—

P Your immediate reaction though is—

R My reaction is I don't understand.

P What should I do?

R What the hell they're going to. What Magruder's going to do. I don't know. It seems to me if Dean has mentioned them that way that they ought to then take a leave of absence.

P Yeah.

R I don't see how—

P But you would wait until their names were mentioned? That's the whole point.

R Yeah. I don't see on what basis you need to do it. Now in the case of—

P Well, on this basis now, let's say that the President had knowledge from the U.S. Attorney that charges had been made against them. Let me emphasize, I nailed him hard. I said, "now let's—" I said, "Rogers and I read this whole thing over. But it's uncorroborated." He says, "I agree."

P But he wants me to sack 'em.

R He can't corroborate it?

P And I have a feeling for a guy that's supposed to uphold the rights of innocent before (unintelligible) are guilty or not. Well, let me say this. I've got to live with myself. I don't want to do it in that (unintelligible). That isn't fair. On the other hand, I'm trying to think of their standpoint. If they're going to get—if they could get some advantage, either—any advantage by not thereby being named in this statement and then, of course, not even being indicted. Maybe that's something. But they're going—

R (unintelligible) specifically almost have to point out—

P They, they, on the other hand, they're going to be called. They'll be indicted and (unintelligible) Although, I guess appearing as non-indicted co-conspirators—what the hell do you say to that? I mean (unintelligible).

R   When you have a case that's serious and when you have people who are on the periphery and you want to name them in order to have them available as witness, you name them as a co-conspirator without indicting them. Well, the problem first—

P   These guys are available.

R   the problem first—that's just as bad as being indicted, especially when you know somebody was (unintelligible) lying. So you're named, but you can't clear your name.

P   That's right.

R   But in case you're indicted, then you have the opportunity to clear the record. Little trial, then acquittal, then you—this is as if it didn't happen. If you're named as a co-conspirator and forced to resign, then you're convicted without a trial. In that case I'm no really—you got to protect them because I don't—I think probably in the final analysis they—I'm afraid Bob is probably in—

P   Going to be indicted?

R   trouble. But—

P   I'm not sure he'll be indicted.

R   I'm not sure he'll be indicted but—

P   Well, staying too close to the money. He never can explain that. In terms of legal involvement though but he could never explain to the people and you (unintelligible) some of that damn money back there for 'em. Testified by Mitchell, by, by Dean. Was it a (unintelligible) of the defense?

R   Why don't we do this? (unintelligible)—or, they're just talking to lawyers. You don't have a chance to assimilate it. But don't let them (unintelligible).

P   Well

R   And you're going to have twelve hours.

P   Yeah - twelve. I would like for you to put your mind to the problem, if you would, because I really think we've got to start helping 'em. Help advise them. They're in the eye of the hurricane.

R   All right. It gives us a little time to see how your, how your statement plays.

P   Always had a (unintelligible) had (unintelligible) I really did think—

R   Oh.

P   But that he probably didn't know about—know what I mean? My feeling was that Mitchell—basically always thought Magruder knew the damn thing. Mitchell just wasn't tending the shop. That's what I understand.

R   I'm surprised about Dean. I thought—I thought. Well from the beginning, I thought Magruder lied and I thought Mitchell probably—he may well have given the go ahead and said, "Oh yeah, to hell with this," and the damn thing was then approved.

P   Yeah. "Don't tell me about it."

R   "Go ahead. Don't tell me. Go ahead and do it." Well I'm surprised about Dean because I didn't think—

P   Now Dean claims that he didn't have anything to do with having them go ahead. Understand that. After that Dean came in in terms of the obstruction of justice. There's where he's vulnerable. That's all. He's not vulnerable on the first part in my opinion. I think he—

R   From the same position if he's gotten two people he's trying to bargain with—Dean and Magruder—and he—did he say he got written statement from both of them?

P   I don't know—I think what they've done is just sat down and debriefed. That's what they call it. It's all (unintelligible) with an agreement certainly, though. Where Dean is concerned, nothing they can do to shake him. On that one he stands firm.

R   I would think that the one fellow that had to know about this and should just take a leave of absence is Dean.

P   (unintelligible) what about this—who the hell wants to (unintelligible)? It looks like this might (unintelligible) of course, set him off.

R   We don't.

P   Worse than he is.

R   Well I think your point is true enough. He appears beyond the thing, although he—

P   He was the one.

R   Pretty hard. Pretty hard to say, "The lawyers—"

P   Well he was—he was not. Not in this matter, I can assure you. He handled the whole thing. He was depending upon—regarding the fact—when I started my investigation on the 21st of March. I saw Dean at least (unintelligible) times. At Camp David, he was to write the (expletive deleted) up so we could put out a statement. He said, "I really can't write a statement that you can put out." So I must say, I've done everything I can get to the bottom, Bill, as you can see. I said, "John, you got to let it all hang out—now find out—you got to tell me what

617

the hell the score is so we'll know how to deal with this. We're not going to be nibbled to death by a thousand hurts." That's exactly what we've done. So we've got just (unintelligible) The time when McCord, which I—I don't know what he's talking about. There are—at least, he's made a lot of allegations that he can't prove. But there's enough there that would put anybody on notice that without a doubt there's something wrong.

R   Yeah.

P   That's why I had to move and I have—at least I produced—good. I thought the statement should reveal that I have been working on the (expletive deleted) since the twenty-first of March.

R   (unintelligible) why don't we—why don't we try it again tomorrow night and then—

P   Right.

R   why don't you get—still in the—in the—in a real sense, it's up to the—it's up to John and Bob.

P   Yeah.

R   It's damn difficult for anybody else who doesn't know what the hell he's talking about. For example, I don't really know—you know—what the facts are.

P   Yeah.

R   I.—

P   I'm not sure that I know.

R   You don't either. So it's very difficult for others. Your judgment tends to be superficial. Although a sophisticated fellow John, after all, is a lawyer so he claims that he's (unintelligible). Thoughtful kind of a fellow, and if he isn't shaken now, this is a fellow that's not just a rambling idiot.

P   Yeah—he's taking (unintelligible). Had everybody over this morning. "Going to fight, discredit Dean—discredit the prosecutor." You know—"going to fight." That'll be one hell of a big fight but (unintelligible) the Administration (unintelligible)

R   (unintelligible)

P   Dean's (unintelligible)

R   You don't expect the head of the FBI to pick up and burn the damn stuff. You can always put it in your safe and say it is unrelated to the investigation. But, burn it? Makes you look like a common crook.

P   We're working as hard as we can. The guy we're thinking of Bill (unintelligible) frankly (unintelligible) a Democrat, Irish, Catholic, bachelor, forty-two years of age. He's finishing the Ellsberg case and received plaudits for being just as fair as he can. Thank God there's a jurist of that kind. And based on (unintelligible) sense of (unintelligible.) And I feel I think he'd get a hundred percent because he has the best investigative experience. A great man for the job.

R (unintelligible)

P He will get a hundred votes in the Senate. I think (unintelligible) Why did you burn it? Wouldn't you say, "There's no place in the FBI. We have nothing to do with politics. This is political material. Turned it over to us, showed it to us because they wanted to be sure they weren't suppressing anything and it did not involve the Watergate. (unintelligible) thought the best thing to do was the FBI."

H Do you want us or not?

P Oh sure, come on in.

R I was just saying to the President maybe we ought to wait until overnight. The two of you buzzed or just not feeling well—

E We talked to your Mr. Wilson.

P Was he lying down? Wilson? An old-timer?

H Nothing like—contrary to your feeling that we wouldn't want to work with him, I think we'll find him very good and tough.

E He's very knowledgeable.

H Sharp as hell. Technically, he's too old, but mentally he's very bright.

P Just let me say, I'm so glad that you have him, somebody, to talk to. I definitely—

R My only reservation would be—(unintelligible).

H Well, that's a problem. If we go to trial, he's got a heart problem and all that so you can't—

P You don't need a trial lawyer—

H We need brains right now.

P What you need is brains, judgment.

H He's got that.

E Well, he knows the cast of characters. He knows Petersen. He knows Glanzer. He knows all those people and he despises them.

R All the people we don't like.

H Maybe he started out that way before we said anything.

R Well, I'm glad because I was worried about his condition.

619

P   Bill brought—incidentally, I asked him about it again, how he liked the Garment approach. And he said, "No problem." We should go with him. I told him this is the only question you see, I don't have anybody to talk to. I never talk to Petersen any more. That's done, except—except for all the information I want. You know what I mean.

E   Wilson said to us, "Beware of Petersen. He talks." He said, he cited a case that he had that Petersen was involved in—

H   And he said that one problem in dealing with him was that every point he makes is accompanied by a story, and that latter is so.

P   He probably foxed him. Well, then maybe all I'll do with Petersen—he said that he'd give me 12 hours notice with regard to the Magruder thing and I think I want that.

H   Yeah.

P   Bill doesn't know how the hell that procedure works—

E   Let me tell you what that procedure is. Wilson explained that to us too. He said that where a man goes in on an information and pleads guilty in this District, it is customary for the judge to interrogate if he wishes to. And also for there to be filed a statement of the case - ah - in the nature of information. Now the information which they will file instead of indictment names the co-conspirators in the conspiracy charge who are not indicted.

E   That does not mean that you won't be indicted later. It means for the purpose of that information which is then filed, you are not indicted. And so this is a list of people who in a description of a conspiracy pattern are co-conspirators. His analysis of the pros and cons of this are that for the prosecutor to come forward and say, "If you will suspend these birds, I will name them in the list of co-conspirators," gets the prosecutor off a difficult political hook because when the judge asks, "Were there any other co-conspirators and so on?" He says, "Well, they have already been suspended—ah, and may be indicted." We reserve the right to indict them but we are going to have them before the Grand Jury.

R   So, are they going to help a bit?

E   Well, it doesn't help us. It helps the prosecutor with his problem. On the other hand, he says, there is a certain negative in it. From a political standpoint for the Administration in that the question will arise, "Well, why weren't their names on there if they're co-conspirators?"

P   Right.

E   Somebody's covered up.

R   Yes.

H   That's worse than putting them on the list.

E   Yeah, and so, he said—

R   I don't know, John. And let me go back for just a moment on this procedure. The information is filed by the prosecutor himself, without a Grand Jury action?

H   Yeah.

R   If the prosecutor names, for all practical purposes, the fact—

P   In the public mind—

R   Particularly that you are going to leave public service—

E   That's what Wilson said.

H   That's what Wilson said.

P   If they are indicted.

R   Well. You've been indicted.

P   That's right. Let's face it.

R   The indictment, Bob, is a charge—

P   It doesn't convict anybody.

R   What the Constitution provides is that before charged, a group of citizens to view the evidence—

E   In secret—

R   In secret, to see if there is sufficient evidence to make a public charge against them. That's the protection that everybody has. If there is an exception and I guess there is in this case, the lesser crime would result. But in this case the gravity is such that it is all baloney. That's all right if somebody is accused of stealing an automobile from the sidewalk or something. You know, people in government positions are entitled to the protection of the Grand Jury because if they want to make a public charge against an individual then present it to the Grand Jury. That's what you have. But here you have a perversion of the system.

E   Sure.

R   Being compelled to leave the government. "Hell, as far as the public is concerned, you are already indicted.

E   Really, the job—they have this capacity by using that process. They could ruin you and never give you a day in court.

R   Of course.

E   They could list you as a co-conspirator, don't call you to the Grand Jury, don't take an indictment against you—

H   Force the President to suspend you and—

E   You are cooked forever. You are a conspirator in the Watergate case.

R   As far as the public is concerned, you are indicted even if they don't call it that.

E   That's right.

R   That's what it is nowadays. The President has been forced to have you leave.

E   It's non-actionable. It's privileged. You can't sue for slander.

H   We do have a public record in that regard in that we have a public position that commands substantial attention.

R   See, Bob, the protection of the Grand Jury gives a citizen is that first the charge is heard in public.

H   That's right. To turn this around.

R   Then the charge—then everybody shuts up. The evidence is not disclosed. Nobody says a word and the Judge cautions everybody to take the oath not to repeat the evidence and then you go to trial. And everything is then controlled by the rules of evidence. The the Jury makes a decision based on that evidence. That's the system. Now if you do it the other way, you don't get the trial. You both would be indicted and convicted by the public beforehand.

E   That's a tough political call—that we were framed up there. In this conversation, we don't need to decide here beyond mentioning it, but it's something that will have to be decided. Our relationship to Dean—probably was client to attorney. Because we were already noted and present in all these transactions. What I said to Dean and what Dean said to me is private conversation with no third party present. It could be a question of privilege. The question is, if requested by the prosecutor, to waive the privilege. It is that Dean conversation where he says he came and told me that Liddy had confessed.

P   But he did it in California, didn't he?

E   Well, the only reason to tell me was not for me as me but because I was one of two conduits that he had to the Boss. He didn't have, I mean, the organizational set-up was that way.

H   The President's log is very interesting. I don't know if you've gotten through all of this, but from the time of the Watergate break-in until the end of August when he signed your votes in the office, you never saw John Dean.

P   That's of course—

H   During July and August the President had no communication with Dean at all.

E   Now, he gave a lot of legal advice about this case. A lot of traffic and all that, but there's also developed a poor relationship and sooner or later the President is going to have to decide whether he wants to consider privilege—if Dean becomes—

P   My privilege? Lawyer-client privilege?

E   Yes. In Dean's communications to me and my communications to him. And the same with Bob. I think. That's a tough problem. You probably won't want to reserve it.

P   I'll take a look. In fact I don't mean this politically. What do you think about that?

R   It is really ticklish.

E   Probably the first time it's come up in this generation. Mr. Wilson would like to do a lot of erudite thinking about that for a while.

P   Great old man.

E   He was at the White House once before.

P   I remember. It's almost a year now.

E   Dixon-Yates thing.

H   He was offered the Budget thing. He refused.

E   Canal is open.

H   He stayed at the White House for several months.

R   My only thought on (unintelligible) maybe he is looking out to not hurt himself at all.

P   Like what?

R   Well, what it really means is - it is hard to understand he was Counsel to you as well as to the President.

E   I appreciate what you are saying and that is important and I understand.

R   How did he contact the President?

H   Dean? He dealt with one of us.

E   In our capacity to make decisions. He was really an advisor in that situation. Not a (unintelligible) and sometimes he followed and sometimes he didn't.

P   That's common. Everyone wants to carve his place.

H   Yeah.

R   Problem is, what do other people say about him?

E   He's a jerk. Sure, that's right.

P   And I deferred to him in this damned investigation. Remember you said, "I think you ought to talk to John Dean." Remember. And I called him in there. And,—, I listened ad infinitum and carted him off to Camp David.

H   (unintelligible) I deferred to him on most occasions.

R   Well, why don't we think it over?

P   Well, let's start with one thing. I don't see anything to be gained by the procedure of Haldeman and Ehrlichman. You see, here's the problem. Kleindienst, Bill, on Sunday - they both came in and said, "Because of Haldeman and Ehrlichman—just the fact that both of these clowns had implicated them and they ought to resign. They haven't served you well, Mr. President." and all that sort of thing.

R   I think that's—

P   They said, "Make them resign, resign, resign." I said, "Well, Damn it, I can't do it on un-corroborated testimony." The point is—I think—a moment of truth for them when they come in—and say they've got corroborative testimony. Do I have to examine the damned testimony? I say, "Look, fellows, I think under these circumstances, you had better voluntarily—" say—See—what I mean? That's what, my concern—Bill has made the point that a person in public office should have no more and no less rights than a person out of public office. That's my theory. Right, Bill?

H   Well, there is a good counter argument which is that a person in public office has a higher obligation than a person not in public office. This is one of their points.

R   I think though, that is for the individual to decide. That in effect has to be done. It hasn't been done.

E   I think that if we turned up in this crazy information—junk—even though we are not charged with a crime, in the ultimate sense—I could write you a letter and say that due to these charges, that obviously I don't want to impair your situation and I am going to take a leave.

P   You could say I have asked you to put me on leave until the charges are cleared up.

E   Sure, and I think that is the direction from which it ought to come.

P   I personally think that is really the course of action we should take and let them put it out if they want to that way. And if they do and if you are named you can immediately say, "I am confident that these charges will not stand up and that I, that I, and so forth"—and, "My usefulness, of course, will be seriously impaired and I therefore request a leave until the matter is cleared up." I think that's, I think we can all agree on that without an indictment. I might put a P.S. on there and say, "I am shocked with the procedure followed and when I am reinstated I am going to see to it that the Justice Department changes its procedure."

R If the prosecutor came to the President and advanced sufficient evidence for you to ask them to resign, and he looks at that evidence and says, "I agree." That's your decision. But in this kind of a case, normally, that kind of a judgment wouldn't mean indictment—that's all we have (unintelligible) but under these circumstances (unintelligible) in effect, Dean would be doing a greater disservice to you than a bonafide Grand Jury indictment.

P That's right, he would.

R He's working for and already decided before the Attorney General could come on the case.

P I think that, I think that before you have your day in Court. That really means something to me.

R Well, if you were to consult aside from the Attorney General, that's a different matter. I don't—the thing I think—based on what Petersen gave to the President, which I looked at, I don't think there's sufficient there. There may be something I don't know about.

E Well, I put those to Wilson and he said, "Well, I'll have to—take it with my bed crumbs tonight." You know, his reaction was . . .

P What are we going to do to—go ahead . . .

R The *Star* Newspaper said that you had meetings in June or something.

P Say it again. That's what Dean's saying.

E And even then, after that.

P That cannot be proper, Bill.

R But even supposing you had said that. Suppose you said that. Then there was, then it isn't what you say, it's what you did.

P Yeah.

R So, what did they do? They turned all. Everything in the safe over to the FBI. They turned over the materials dealing with the Watergate to the agents that were investigating it, they turned over other material not related to Watergate and was not under investigation to the head of the FBI. Now how in hell can you say, "That is obstruction of justice to turn over all the evidence to the FBI?"

P   Except that, when Pat Gray burned it, it makes it look like it—

E   His wild geese—"Deep Six."

R   Pat Gray says, Pat Gray was told to do that. He said—

P   He was not told to do that.

E   On the other business, which is very suspicious, and that is the business of "should he leave the country," I've checked with everybody in that meeting and they don't remember anything like that. It turns out Dean called Liddy and told him to have Hunt leave the country. Colson recalls Dean mentioning this to him, not in my office, and Colson saying to Dean, "You stupid bastard. What a terrible mistake." Then it was countermanded so—

H   And he didn't leave the country.

E   And he didn't leave the country, so I suspect that Dean may have acted unilaterally on that.

P   Here again—

H   Colson brought him up short.

P   Here he is trying to pass this up to Ehrlichman, too.

E   Well, he has to have an explanation for why he did it.

P   And how is that going to come out from the others if they said, "He was told to leave the country"? Or has Hunt already said it?

E   Well, yeah. There is no question that he got orders from Liddy who said that, "my principals say—" And he said, "Who are your principals?" and he said, "John Dean."

P   John Dean said, "Oh no, it's Ehrlichman"?

E   Yeah. Get into one of these "he said," "I said" sort of thing it's going to be miserable. But the probabilities against the surrounding circumstances at least as of now look good. Now I have no illusions about this process, when you give it the test of credibility. Everybody gets used up. There is nothing left so you just have to expect that that's the end of the ball game.

P   Well, it is for this time, but now and then you have one fight and win the battle. The three, the three-fifty thing is the toughest thing, Bob, about this whole thing. Mainly, to me there's no question about it, just basically that they had knowledge that it was going to those defendants and so forth. They wanted it for that purpose. And the question is what you thought it was. And then again they'll say that they don't believe you. It'll get down to that.

R   Dash, etc.

P   There again, though, course they have a route to this. LaRue. He broke down and cried, I guess.

E   That's a-right. Are you going to have spaghetti tonight?

R   Spaghetti and singing Toscanini.

P   Well, Bill. You go ahead. I'll—let them go home. it's possible we may ask your advice tomorrow with all—

R   I have reason to feel good that you got John Wilson.

H   We sure appreciate your help.

R   Yeah.

E   He was enormously gratified to hear that you had recommended him.

H   We told him you had suggested him and it was the only name you could suggest and he said that, "Bill, and I have been on the same side and on opposite sides. He wouldn't speak to me on one matter."

E   It was on the Swiss deal—

H   Something he wouldn't speak to me—never (unintelligible) worked over here three days a week and never saw President Eisenhower. Never got an autographed picture and so we said, "Maybe in this case that could be arranged."

P   Provided he had nothing to do with Watergate!

E   He's very clean by the looks of it.

P   Well, so are you. Damn it!

R   OK. Good bye, Mr. President.

P   I'm glad he feels good about having him come over here.

H   Yeah. Well, I don't know about that. I don't know anything about lawyers. I never had one before so. For exactly reasons Bill thought we wouldn't like it—he's an old man and we won't like working—I do like him.

P   How old is he? Seventy?

H   Seventy-two. Well, he's well-preserved. He has some difficulties. But I'll tell you the guy has got—his mind isn't slow at all. He is right with us and then some. He's got an abundance of stories

P   Sure.

H   Well, I fell pretty good about him.

P Well, it's good to have him. Very good. It's a fight.

H I need—a—he is so devoted to other things. He's just devoted to the cause.

H He said, "It's a great honor to meet you men."

P What is his reaction to the whole damned thing? Comic tragedy? Tragedy of Errors?

H He didn't characterize it. He didn't, ah—

P Hello. Have you been busy? Yes. How did it go? I've heard that. Yeah. Yeah. Yeah, for later. That's right. Either way. That's right. Sure. Well, get a question about whether I talked to Mitchell. Huh? Yeah, Mitchell. But there was a time set. From this period on. From the 21st on, did you talk to Mitchell? Very good. (unintelligible) Very good. How are you? Good luck. (unintelligible) Well. I just feel that, I just went through that, now they may have told you that the basic heart of the matter—

E Well, I tell you. I think you've put him in a box on that. They are going to have to have some damn good reason for that Sirica thing.

P Dean's credibility is totally destroyed you know.

H Dean (inaudible)

P Sure, Dean was in charge of the investigation. Did they ask him that? Yes. I put it up to Ron and I made this point to Ron. "You know Dean somehow has sold out the White House, the Administration, etc."

H That's a good statement. It is a good idea. It puts you exactly in the position that you should be in now.

P We'll get kicked by the press on it.

H For giving in on Ervin, etc.

P Giving in on Ervin. Oh Ervin's great—Hell, that doesn't bother me a bit. I was always ready to give in on Ervin and I said, "This is very satisfactory now. We have now accomplished our purpose. This is a good deal. I said, "It not only applies to this case but it can apply to other things." I ad libbed that when I said it. I worked it in.

H It was a very good answer.

P No, I shouldn't pick on the press but, "why did the President act so late on this case? Why didn't he act earlier on this matter? He had the charges floating around." The answer is that they are charges that were just floating. I mean, I think really, that's true, newspaper charges and so forth.

E They were all relying on Dean, frankly.

H Well speed was not of the essence in this case. It

wasn't a matter of whereby moving quickly we would stop something. It was done. It was a matter now of doing it properly. Not quickly.

P   That's right, Bob. That's the point of the whole Garment thing. There is this tendency John, to talk, and basically I thought he was a (unintelligible) but he was totally non-plussed by that.

H   He said, "Where's the Attorney General?" He's taken himself out of it. Wilson said, "Where's the Deputy Attorney General?" He's not involved in it. Where's the Chief District Attorney? Where's Titus? Who should be on top of this? Why did Silbert call me instead of Titus? Silbert—he's an old boy from the Justice Department and they band together." He said, "Did John Dean ever work for the Justice Department?" He also said, "I bet you those lawyers that Dean has—and Magruder has—both were old Justice Department types." He says that Glanzer is a very bad operator. He knows him well. He doesn't know Silbert but he knows Glanzer very well. Says he's a bad guy. (Unintelligible.)

P   Well, don't you both agree though, John and Bob?

H   He did it. But I've heard he was the *L.A. Times* leak this morning.

P   I knew about the leak. It was going to come yesterday.

H   No, I don't think it was intended as that. And I don't—not because it triggered us, but because it set the stage.

H   It let out ahead of time that the White House was going to move on something. And then you did.

P   Well, did that sotry say the White House was going to move? Oh, oh, oh. Heads are going to roll. That probably came directly from Dean. I think Dean did that.

H   "White House likely to admit some Watergate responsibility—will have a dramatic admission of whether one or more high level officials bear responsibility." It doesn't say White House officials. Your action now saying something substantial will develop, and then when the Mitchell bomb breaks, that's all going to fit together rather, rather—

P   Yeah. Yeah (unintelligible). about that—Tell us about that ransacking and (unintelligible). It's been about two years ago. It's about not letting (unintelligible).

H   He said it was 22,000. Was the difference in money material? Can a case be made out of that? Did he keep the money or was there something about that?

P   He called the same day, too, didn't he?

H   No, he called - the next day. He called within twenty-four hours. That was the next day. Testified on Thursday and called on Friday.

E   They are using every lever they can lay their hands on—these guys that say that.

H   I saw on ABC news tonight, which also fits into all this. It was in the last three weeks in the White House, Haldeman has been coming down very hard on everybody: "If you have anything to say to say it now. This was the message that was given to Mitchell Saturday at the White House. Haldeman evinced no protection and no apologies. Anyone and everything will be disclosed." It should have been Ehrlichman instead of Haldeman, or get out White House for cracking down hard on the Watergate. It's not bad. It's a damned good position to be in. And when Ziegler talked to him he said, "I can't give you anything official on that but off the record you are not going off base."

P   Was Bill Gill on that one?

H   Not tonight. Gill called and asked for confirmation and said he was going with the story and he wanted Ziegler's comment. Ziegler said, "I can't give you any comment."

P   The story probably isn't even out.

H   Well, that's what I said to Ron, "Hold the statement until tomorrow," and looked up my story (unintelligible) was on. No. It will be on. It's on. There's another item.

P   The right day too. We had to get it out. (Unintelligible.)

H   That's right. That's right. The *Post* won't put it in tomorrow. If the *Post* had something to go with tomorrow, I would say they wouldn't go. They'll hold up now and watch for something. They are playing the long game.

P   I get your point, John. On the (unintelligible), I think we, I think we have sped the process up. This kind of stuff, this kind of stuff here would have had stories for three of four months.

H   That's right.

P   That Ervin. Right. We get into the Grand Jury and then they get an indictment.

H   Well, there's no question that it's the best way compared to the Ervin process. It is essential to go this way.

P That's right. If it weren't for the fact (unintelligible) possibility of (unintelligible). I (unintelligible) my theory to take this thing to the Grand Jury.

E Yep.

H We have to face the possibility of indictments and those would have to come anyway. They wouldn't have let you get away with it.

P Well, I think what would happen for instance with Ervin's problem. They would be saying, "We refer this to the Grand Jury."

H They would have murdered us. Something would be out every minute. Demanding that you fire everybody. Demanding that you do this and that.

E Well, as a matter of fact, you might have turned the set up some day and watched your White House Counsel crap—for the glorious television. It would be at least surprising.

H That's right.

P Oh, it's done up there?

H Sure, he pulls it up there.

P Let's face it, up to this thing, Dean handled a lot of stuff well.

H That's right. Yes.

E I would hate to have you appear in the position of not, (unintelligible) sort of conditionally holding the job open much beyond the time that Dean is—

P I'll say this. I think that one thing for sure John is—I think that I've got to play, I want to play, I know the Dean thing very well. We have played it fairly well. I think what we ought to do—make our deal or not with Dean within a week. I don't see how Dean can possibly miss being involved in whatever they put out on Magruder. He can't miss being—and the way this guy talks, I think all of you, all of you, everybody may get it.

E He may get it. He's had (unintelligible) go around and talk with the U.S. Attorney types. I think we may have Wilson go over on the Hill (unintelligible) and say, "OK, you are about to ruin these guys. I just want you to know that they are going to have to go out and protect themselves." You are going to be in a knotty problem. (Unintelligible) I mean. He has quite a close relationship with Titus. He's not going to get much of a total on this. This statement, and he's going to make it, anything he can to press for, not immunity, but functional immunity, so-called where he doesn't need to make a side deal with the

631

boys and they can grant immunity. And that would be my hunch.

P   Alright, we shall go over—Come in.

H   Hello, Mr. President.

P   Same old thing, huh?

E   I would force him to go to Sirica.—

P   Put that in the library.

E   Showing the Judge what kind of a witness this is. Come on, get the Hill off the hook of the Executive Branch by having the Judge grant the immunity.

P   The Judge can attack that statement.

E   You are putting yourself with the angels on that.

P   I am just saying that immunity is not granted to any major—

E   I think that will be read as relating to Mitchell and three or four of that ilk as well.

P   Oh, sure.

H   They may decide not to do this.

P   That's the point.

H   Dean will be (unintelligible) or it could be done quickly.

P   But I have told the big five, I told the Assistant Attorney General, specifically, that nobody should be granted immunity in any case. Rogers agrees with this and—(unintelligible).

H   The other point that our attorney makes, which is significant: "That's right, the Judge can grant immunity, but that in the Executive, only the Attorney General can grant it." That holds somewhere else too.

P   Dean is the only one who can sink Haldeman or Ehrlichman.

H   How am I going to explain that, after putting out a statement?

E   What do you say, "Dean is some little clerk?" He's my Counsel.

P   That's right, he's involved in the Gray thing. They are not going to throw the whole thing in there. I am thinking whether to see Dean again unless it's useful—I don't think you can control him, he's fanatic. If you feel it would be useful, let me know.

E   I will tell you what is lurking in the back of my mind is that, based on the chain of circumstances, Dean may be provoked to make a public statement which is slanderous and hostile.

P   Another thing. I would like the libel suits. I think

both of you, and Bob particularly, you ought to get yourself a libel lawyer, Bob, and check the or have Wilson check and use the most vicious libel lawyer there is. I'd sue every (expletive deleted) (unintelligible). There have been stories over this period of time. That will make—that also helps with public opinion. Sue right down the line. It doesn't make any difference now about the taking depositions and the rest, does it? The important thing is the story's big and I think you ought to go out and sue people for libel.

H   Do you mean Senator Weicker?

P   He's covered.

E   Oh, he's not, not when he was on Issues and Answers.

H   (unintelligible) or using newspaper interviews.

E   That's right.

H   It was not on the Floor, he's too buzzy, stupid.

P   The point is the thing with Weicker (unintelligible) is whether he said—how did he say that? Was it libelous?

H   I think so. I better ask a lawyer.

P   Was he that specific?

H   He was damned specific.

P   That Haldeman knew?

H   Yes. "That Haldeman directed and Haldeman was in personal command of all personnel." I repeat, "all personnel at the Re-election Committee."

P   Good, sue him.

E   I think you should.

H   He said that I was in personal command of Liddy and Hunt.

P   I would sue.

H   And McCord (unintelligible) I have never met or heard of him.

P   John, this libel thing. You may as well get at the libel thing and have yourself a little fun.

E   Might make expenses.

H   Operating procedure-wise we've got to, or my recommendation would be that we should maintain a facade of normal operations as long as you have taken this position. I don't think we want to look like something is radically changed.

P   Nope.

H   Then I think we should come into the office at the normal time in the morning—and a

P   Right. And have your staff meeting, plus you will be at the meeting tomorrow with the energy conference and you should be at the Quadriad meeting. You are right.

H   Go and go as we go along.

P   Unless and until something happens. Now the only exception here is Dean.

H   Dean should not, but nobody would know whether he does his normal job or not. But see that nobody gives a damn, he is not visible.

P   Well, the thing that—

H   And he has been out of here for a month anyway.

E   Any objection to going to Florida this weekend, if you go?

P   Would you like to go down?

E   Yes

H   I don't expect to get much sunshine but—

E   It might help.

H   I think we should unless our lawyer keeps us here and he could.

P   Yeah.

H   We normally would and I think we should.

P   Oh, I think you should Bob. Right, now understand that if they crack this—

H   Oh well, then that would be a problem.

E   One concession that I would ask and that is that people on leave be considered for use of Camp David occasionally.

P   Let me say, what I had in mind. I want you to go forward and if this thing comes out which I can't believe, I want you to go forward at all costs to beat the damned rap. They'll have one hell of a time proving it. Yours is a little tougher I think Bob, and it shouldn't be—the 300. That's why I hope you could raise with the Judge and your attorney—that at least gave you the law on that point.

H   Yes, sir. On that point, yeah. We haven't gotten into (unintelligible) of the law at all on obstruction of justice.

E   He's briefing that tonight for us.

H   He says it's damn tough, loose.

E   He cites Glanzer as the leading authority on it. He uses it like a bludgeon.

P   Only if it's a (unintelligible)

E   Oh, he hasn't given us that yet.

H   He didn't give us the opinion. He just said, "I'll tell you on the top that it's very tough. It's Luke's law and cases go all ways."

P   I hope he has an opinion sometime on the case involving Dean to the effect (unintelligible) establishing—

H   Why the hell we didn't see then—

P   Remember I was a little suspicious of Chuck. I was not, after all, I said, "Damn it, what's he talking to these people for?" And remember the way I put it is, "He was saying, 'gee, I have talked to these guys and they're mind-picking.' "

H   Well, they're not in error.

P   And I said, "I think they are taken." Remember? I said that.

H   Yeah, sure did.

P   Well, I don't—I think he was being taken by the Senator.

E   Well, I think he figured rape was inevitable so he was going to enjoy it.

P   Bob, remember, I said, "I think they are taking Dean."

H   Sure do.

E   Well, as I said before. We beat the rap but we're damaged goods.

P   Right, you can't go back in the government, but I will tell you one thing, you are not damaged goods as far as I am concerned. It's one hell of a thing. The point is that let's wait and see what happens before we see where we are.

H   Sure.

P   We ought to expect the worst but I think that what I would like both of you to consider 50 of your time also for editing etc., and so on, with the Foundation. The Foundation is going to be a hell of a big thing, it's bound to be. These first four years are terribly important and so forth. I mean after all, you understand, that looking down the road, looking down the road, as far as—you say your Dad was good at looking down the road?

H   Yep.

P   If you are indicted and tried and found innocent, it washes away.

H   Well—

P   Agree? For government service, I mean.

E   Or for the practice of law.

P   I don't think so. Really?

E   Well, I think so. I think so. Jeanne if furious about it.

H   That isn't true John.

E   It depends on the circumstances. There is nothing I

635

can be discouraged about at this point. But I think we've just about had it. I think the odds are against it.

H You can always handle traffic cases—

E Well I am not too pleased with the traffic cases.

P The hell with the traffic cases. Well, anyway—

H Well there's all kinds of things we could do.

P Well I have a Foundation. I just think it is fair, I don't know whether I can find anybody to do it. I don't know whether you would even do it. Incidentally, it is terribly important that poor Kalmbach get through this thing.

H I think he is alright.

P How could he learn? Did you talk to him there? Did Dean call him about the money?

H Yes, Sir.

P Does he say what said?

E Dean told me that he told him what it was for. I don't believe him. Herb said that he just followed instructions, that he just went ahead and did it and sent the money back and—

P They said they need it for?

E I don't even know if they told him what for. It was an emergency and they needed this money and I don't know whether he can get away with that or if it's more specific than that.

P You can corroborate then Herb on that one.

E I can if Dean is the accuser. I can.

P If Dean is the accuser, you can say that he told you on such and such a date that he did not tell Herb Kalmbach what the money was for.

E That he has told me—that he has told me—

P That's right - that's right.

H If we have to get out of here, I think the Foundation funding - is one thing - but there is a lot of intrigue too—I hope to get funding for the ability to clear my name and spend the rest of my life destroying what some people like Dean and Magruder have done to the President.

Telephone conversation: The President and Petersen, April 18, 1973. (2:50 - 2:56 pm)

Opr   Yes, please.

P   Would you get me Assistant Attorney General Petersen, please?

P   Hello.

HP   Hello, Mr. President.

P   Well what's—anything I need to know today?

HP   No sir. There is no significant developments

P   Right. Uh, huh. Alright.

HP   Strachan is coming in. Fred Vinson, former Assistant Attorney General under Johnson, is representing him.

P   Representing who?

HP   Strachan, I think it is, who is going to come in.

P   Strachan? Oh, yeah, yeah. Gordon Strachan.

HP   But there have been no developments. We are still negotiating. We have a problem with the Grand Jury. The only copy of the Grand Jury transcript has been locked up in the prosecutor's office. We have the FBI checking out the reporter on the ground that they have leaked it. The Judge called us in about it this morning.

P   Uh, huh. Sirica did.

HP   Yeah.

P   About what? About part of it leaking?

HP   He was concerned about leaking and, of course, Anderson has been printing some of it. We have changed reporters. We haven't even been bringing it over here for security reasons.

P   Yeah. I would hope to keep the Grand Jury from leaking. But—

HP   Well, you know I don't want to go too far on it either, because I don't want to get into a diversionary battle with Anderson.

P   Hell, no. I wouldn't pay that much attention to it. I agree, I agree. What I meant is just do the best to control it.

HP   We are indeed.

P   Because we know that its just wrong. Now we are handling it over here, I trust, aren't we? I just told Ziegler

637

he won't comment on anything because it might effect the rights of either the prosecution or the rights of innocent people or the rights of defendants.

HP   We are not taking any calls from them over here.

P   So that is all we are saying.

HP   You can't talk to them at all.

P   Fine.

HP   I was kind of pleased with the reaction your statement got.

P   I think it was probably the right thing to say.

HP   Yeah.

P   What have you got—you haven't made—you haven't finished the thing with Magruder yet, then, huh?

HP   No, we haven't finished the thing with Magruder. Ah,—

P   Dean the same, huh?

HP   Dean's, well, we have just backed off of him for a while. His lawyers want time to think.

P   I have deliberately, Henry—I left Dean in a position where I said look he was going to be treated like everybody else because it wasn't fair, I mean for him to be at all, you know—what I mean, like when we talked about resignation, etc., since he was making some charges. Well, it isn't that. Since he has at least had some private discussions, but they haven't yet been in the Grand Jury forum, so I have to respect those.

HP   I think that is right.

P   So that was your suggestion, at least, that we should not do anything on Dean at this point.

HP   I think that is right. I think you ought to just let him sit.

P   All I have is just information—

HP   That's right.

P   basically from you and from him, but it is information the gravity of which I just can't judge until I see whether it is corroborated.

HP   You have to treat that as private, in any event.

P   Private, don't I? Yeah. And for that reason if I were to move to do it—so I think we are in the right position and, then, fine. Ok - Then I won't expect any more from you today. I won't bother you.

HP   No. I am a little concerned about Senator Ervin's Committee. They have just, under the agreement Kleindienst worked out with Senator Ervin, have called the Bureau and asked to see the interview statements of Magruder, Porter, Sloan and LaRue.

P   Oh, my (expletive removed).

HP   Ah, and I feel like I am sitting on a powder keg there, but I don't feel like I can dare go to Senator Ervin until I get a definite commitment from Magruder.

P   Yeah, yeah. On Magruder, what's waiting besides the Committee with him? Oh, the deal with the DC jail and—

HP   Well that is right and whether or not the Judge is going to clap him in right away, and whether or not the Committee is going to put pressure on him.

P   In other words, you think—you haven't yet tried to talk to Ervin?

HP   No, Sir, and I don't want to until I can tie him down.

P   Til you've got him tied? I get it.

HP   Well, I've got to be able to say that I am coming out with something public in terms of a charge.

P   I see. Right, right.

HP   You know, have a valid basis for asking him to slow it up.

P   Ok. Well, in any event, I am glad you thought the statement went well. I worked on it to be sure that it didn't compromise anybody one way or the other and as you noticed too I put the immunity thing. It leaves the ball in your court, but—

HP   I noticed.

P   But on the other hand, I had to express the view because basically people are going to ask me, what about Mitchell, what about, you know, a lot of people and you know I just can't be in this position.

HP   I agree wholeheartedly.

P   Lower people are different. But you know, upper people, you know, they might think I am protecting (unintelligible)

HP   I agree.

P   Ok.

HP   Alright, Mr. President.

P   Fine.

Meeting: The President, Wilson and Strickler,
EOB Office, April 19, 1973.
(8:26 - 9:32 pm)

P   This is my EOB Office where I do a lot of—

W   Yes, We were—you know those initials that we were—

P   This is where I do most of my speech writing—

S   We saw your Oval room tonight.

P   What's that?

S   I said, "We saw your Oval Office tonight."

P   Oh, you were over there? You hadn't seen it before?

S   No.

W   No. I've never been in it.

P   My gosh.

W   You know we are local boys here and—

P   You are going to get to see the things that tourists see—

W   Yes. One of our dear friends is a dear friend of yours and that is the Marriotts.

P   Oh, aren't they great people?

W   Aren't they? We have represented them for years—until young Bill got so he wanted large out-of-town law firms.

P   Foolish.

W   But Bill and Ollie and I have been—I have been friends with them forty years; they are the sweetest people in the world.

P   Well, they are really fine Americans, and you know.—And gee whiz, they don't drink themselves but they make a lot out of selling it.

(Laughter)

S   There was a time when they didn't do that, as you well know.

P   Oh, I know and it's interesting they were telling me that they had a custom now in some of their houses where they—where they reserve a couple of floors for people who don't smoke.

W   Yes.

P So people who come in—incidentally, do you guys smoke?

S I gave it up.

W I never started.

S —five or six years ago. I feel that—

P You didn't start? Cigarettes or—

S I was a cigarette smoker—about three packs a day. When I gave them up, I missed them. I was a hopeless addict.

W I never smoked in my life.

P Like some coffee? Uh? Coffee or Sanka?

W A little Sanka—would be nice.

S Coffee.

P Coffee or Sanka? I have Sanka, I guess, Manolo?

M Yes Sir.

P Get a little sleep tonight.

W I don't guess you get very much. (Laughter)

P Yet all of our other problems we've got—we've got the one you've got.

W Yes. We admire you so much; that we both are dyed-in-the-wool Republicans. I was just telling Bob Haldeman that I joined the party years ago. I said, "No sign of beating Calvin Coolidge with a Liberal!"

(Laughter)

P Well, tell me where it stands and—

W Yes.

P And, if you will, both from the standpoint of the people you are representing and from the standpoint of the Presidency, which, of course, we got to (unintelligible) and I—

W I can tell you (unintelligible)

P Oh, sure, one of those things where people with the best of intentions—I mean everybody. John Mitchell I love.

W Of course.

P He did things here, you know, that were (unintelligible) on a less, here we have people who got involved—tangentially. Really an—

W We have had three days—three different daily sessions with Bob and John.

P Right.

W And two today. And two were—

P (unintelligible)

641

W   by our visit to the District Attorney's office.

P   Right.

W   This afternoon. Uh—We want to first, go over the Bob situation. He's written a memo of things which boils down the sensitive area—

P   You're talking about Haldeman now.

W   —boils down to Bob—boils down to the matter of $350,000.

P   Three fifty - right. I am aware of that.

W   And what knowledge he has—

P   And I have questioned him very thoroughly on all things myself.

W   —Uh—I'm sure you have and he said that Dean had come to him and told him of the need of this money.

P   For what purpose?

W   To help alleviate families and legal counsel of the Watergate people.

P   All right.

W   And that was one occasion. Later on, when the money was transferred over to the Committee, he just wanted to be rid of it. And he had no intention as to where it might go. And—uh—that's that. Now we said to him that we don't doubt that—about the truthfulness and what parties in these two effects (unintelligible) We said, "Circumstantially, if it be wrong to have done this, a jury might think that he did it with (unintelligible).

P   If what? If what? That it would look—

W   It'd look like it to an impartial jury.

P   When you put it to a jury it looks like—it's just very questionable?

W   Yes. Yes.

S   Depending upon how the testimony comes out of the various people, it could become an issue.

P   Right.

W   Now that we—he said, "But wait a minute. What is this sin? What is wrong with this?" Well, by a far stretch, this might be something of accessory after the fact to a conspiracy at the Watergate. This, Mr. President.—

P   Accessory? For what? For the purpose of?

W   Of sort of aiding the consequences. I gave an example of Dr. Mudd.—

P   Yeah.

W   —in the John Wilkes Boothe case.

P   Just got that pardon.

W   Yes. I pointed out that he didn't commit the crime

but he did sort of aid in the thing afterwards.

P   Right.

W   Uh.

P   Now, I suppose—it was evident? I suppose there, too, the motive as to whether he gave it to Dean with the knowledge and with the intent of keeping the defendants quiet. That—

W   That would be the argument. Uh—

P   The argument of the prosecution?

W   Yes.

S   Exactly. Now, we don't know what Dean will say on this.

P   Well, I guess you don't because he is involved himself.

S   Yes, this is right.

W   But—

P   (unintelligible) you've got to.

S   We assume the worst. In our thinking, we assume the worst.

P   Exactly. Absolutely.

W   Now, we are old prosecutors, Mr. President.

P   Good.

W   And we think that this is not a case, according to our standards. This is not an indictable case against Bob. On the other hand, bear in mind that we have got a group of zealots—uh, particularly in Seymour Glanzer who is a fire-eating prosecutor, and uh—these zealots always shoot for the top.

P   Sure.

W   And they are not always conscientious enough to, uh—

P   To see what's wrong about it.

W   Whether it's a convicting case of whether it's—

P   In other words, they may indict even though they don't think they can (unintelligible)

W   That's it exactly. I couldn't—we couldn't exclude the possibility that the prosecutors might take this up. On the other hand, we—we—we don't think it amounts to a criminal case in a practical sense.

P   In other words, if it goes to a court—you—whoever tries it—you think you might be able to defend him?

S   On the evidence that we how have, yes.

W   Yes. That's our feeling.

P   Now, that's (unintelligible).

W   I want you to know we are guessing at this, Mr. President.

P   The letter to LaRue—was it to LaRue?

S/W   Yes. Yes.

P   The letter to LaRue—was in one sense a—(unintelligible) admitted that he was raising money for the defendants—have you got that?

S   Yes. We have that.

P   You must have it all, you see.

W   Yes. We have that. When I say that we don't think this is really a good case, this is just our best judgment.

P   Sure. I understand.

W   We could be as wrong as the devil about this thing and, yet, coming to certain conclusions—that's the reason we are presenting it to you in this way. Now this is Bob's situation—Bob and John brought us their problems three days ago. I want you to know that I never knew these guys.

S   But they are wonderful fellows.

P   They are. They're great, fine Americans. And they tell the truth, too.

W   Yes—

P   I can tell you one thing about your clients. They'll tell you the truth. They don't lie.

W   Yes. Yes. Now, now—we took up John's situation about the Deep Six.

P   Yes. This is Ehrlichman.

W   Yes.

P   Okay.

W   And—he tell's us that he (unintelligible) Hunt's safe and that there was a pistol there; there was some electronic—

P   Right.

W   Equipment. Bob didn't think it was bugging. But it was more recording than bugging. But this is unimportant.

S   And a batch of papers.

P   Right.

W   Sensitive or semi-sensitive in nature.

P   Sensitive in what respect—political or other?

W   I don't think it was as much political as it was—didn't he have something to do with national security?

P   Yes.

S   I think it was a mixture of both.

W   Was it—guess it might have been.

P   Yeah.

W   Anyway. Uh—what I was going to say today.

P   Go ahead.

W   The same day, or almost—Yes, I do.

S   So the FBI was brought in and it seems that.

P   They got the pistol.

S   They got the pistol. They got the bugging equipment. And they got a large quantity of papers.

P   Which they gave to Dean—I mean to Gray.

W   Well, presumably not this particular sensitive area.

P   Oh.

W   Gray, as the head of the Department, may have seen it. But this is not the particular instance where we see Gray. Uh, Dean held back some papers.

P   Oh. They gave some of the papers to the FBI?

W   Most of them. Now Frank, correct me if this—

P   Thank goodness, they did that.

W   Oh yes. It was promptly done, wasn't it?

S   Yeah, it was.

P   They saw the papers and they secured the area and they gave them to the FBI.

W   Yes.

P   And other papers though they didn't give to the FBI?

W   Now, do you recall whether John said that Dean informed him he was holding these back.

S   Yes, not contemporaneously but later on.

W   Yes.

S   Dean had—

W   Not at the moment.

S   Not at the moment.

W   Now let me go on. Dean had a little envelope which was unopened as far as John was concerned. He was unaware of its contents. And Gray was sent for. I think Dean suggested that Gray be sent for. Or maybe that was John.

S   I'm not sure whether it was Dean or John—I think it was John, though.

W   We have taxed our system in the last seventy-two hours.

P   I know, I know.

S   (unintelligible) did not make (unintelligible)

W   At any rate, this next meeting which was almost the next day—it wasn't more than twenty-four hours after the FBI had entered and as John described—Gray sat over there and John sat—he sat here—and Dean handed Gray this package of papers which as I say for John's purposes was sealed. He never saw the contents. Gray took it—the meeting did not last over four minutes. And left. Now Gray approached John.

S   Ehrlichman

W   And said, I want you to not mention the fact that I received those papers.

P   Gray said that? To Ehrlichman?

W   Yes. And John said, "Well, I can't do that." He said, "This was a—you were (unintelligible) in this somewhere. I didn't know where it was—I never asked you what was in it." And Gray said, "Well, I'm embarrassed because I destroyed it." Now this is Gray's fault.

P   Terrible damned thing to do.

W   Oh terrible.

S   Wasn't there a solicitation from Gray on the basis that he had testified to the contrary?

W   I think he had.

S   And the.—and then.

P   I don't think he—as I recall—he didn't testify. He told the U. S. Assistant—U. S.—Petersen.

S   He's got it wrong.

P   Yeah. It's in the record.

S   John left a rather equivocal response to the request. He called him back, upon reflecting, and said, "Look, I want you to know that I have got the question of papers."

P   John Ehrlichman?

S   John Ehrlichman, yes.

P   Then Gray got to Petersen and said, "look, I did get it. And I destroyed it."

S   Yes, that's right.

P   That's the story.

S   Incidentally, you mentioned Petersen—

P   And I guess the only basis Gray could say that it was political stuff and I didn't want to appear—pretty bad.

W   Yes. Yes. With respect to Petersen, I must give you an aside. I don't trust him. Myself.

P   You don't?

W   We both have had one experience with him. He divulged things we thought was confidential in a very serious matter to a potentially co-defendant's lawyer who was an ex-Department of Justice lawyer when we played golf over the weekend, uh—and told him the whole of our business and I got it back from a lawyer in Philadelphia who heard it from the golf partner the next day. And I'm always aware that Petersen is dealing with ex-employees of the Department of Justice.

P I'll remember that.

W Well, I wish you would.

P Well, I've got to talk to him now.

W I know you do, but I don't go around maligning everyone.

P I know—I understand. I need to know.

W He's on my list of people I don't trust.

P I understand.

W Now, the second phase of John Ehrlichman was the idea of raising funds.

P Which he was approached on.

W Yes, and this was not to come out of the three-fifty. This was—

P He didn't know about the three-fifty.

W Oh, I think he knew about it—the—he must have according to the—

P Well, what I meant is, it wasn't his field.

W That's right. But he did get (unintelligible)

P Raising money and Dean says, "Can I talk to Kalmbach?" And he said, "Yes." And—

W And Kalmbach went out and did raise the money. Now these matters involving John alarm us even less, if I can make a comparison, than Bob's do. Because I don't quite—

P Do you mean from a criminal side?

W Yes, that's it. See—

P He said they come to him and they say, Look here. I'm going to raise some money. And Kalmbach here suggests okay." You mean that doesn't make him guilty of something?

W Well, let's go back to the accessory after the fact idea. This gets even removed further than the release of the money from the (unintelligible).

P Yeah.

W of the White House fund to be used for that purpose. Now this compares—this contrast is not to be taken as making any great division between Haldeman and John. Well, frankly, our judgment is that neither one can be successfully prosecuted.

P Because of what you see here?

W Yes.

P Well, now wait a minute. Let me ask you this, though. When you talked—give me a little rundown of your talk with the U. S. Attorney.

W I certainly have.

P   Have you?

W   Yes, now we have—neither of us—I -

P   And also give me your judgment on this thing that Petersen told me about this—rather, I—I—

W   Non-indicted—they're better -

P   It seems to me the moment they come out of that, they killed themselves. They are dead.

W   Let me, yes.

P   I have never heard of that procedure before. But I may be naive about the law.

W   Let me answer that one, first, because that is more brief. In conspiracy indictments, very frequently they will name express defendants—conspirators—and they will name co-conspirators by name as well as other people to the Grand Jury unknown. But will not indict them. Now that's the (unintelligible) it's characterized as a non-dicting. It isn't—the word is not unindictable—non-in-dicting.

P   Which means that they were indicted in public—

W   Well, it's—they certainly are. And usually from that group they find witnesses who will testify against the defendants. Now that's what that phrase is. It's common-place in the law of conspiracy. And, uh, I've seen it—I've been privy to it as a prosecutor myself.

P   Yes.

W   I'm sure Frank has too. Some of that (unintelligible) it's a black market. It might be compared to the treatment over (unintelligible) that people think that I'm guilty.

P   Well, for Bob and John—if they put them on that list—it kills them.

W   Oh.

P   I mean—it may not. It may not kill them legally, but it kills them from the standpoint of the public.

W   Now, as to our visit with these gentlemen this afternoon. We contacted—we sought to contact Glanzer first, whom we both know very well, and he was—uh—said to be unavailable and we asked Silbert, whom I had met on one occasion. Frank didn't know him at all.

P   Yeah. Yeah.

W   And so we were—we made an engagement for 4:30 and they said—this was with—do two things—and that they were going to go before the Grand Jury and that they were going to be very busy and they couldn't give us more than an hour. We came in—I'm telling you this so you'll be (unintelligible) We were taken into the room at (unintelligible) I began the presentation by saying that we were there representing Haldeman and Ehrlichman. And I had the strange feeling—and I think Frank will—now, you weren't there for the first few minutes—

S   I was not there the first ten minutes.

W   I think he indicated surprise to me—I think it was a mixture.

P   Glanzer?

W   Yes. He was alone with me until a subordinate named Campbell came in. And then eventually Silbert. But his surprise to me, I felt was that in a certain sense he was surprised that Haldeman and Ehrlichman had engaged me. This gave me a little encouragement as to whether he thought that they should engage (unintelligible). I will tell you why in a couple of minutes. Uh, secondly, I—he suspected that we were down there possibly representing John Mitchell. And I said, "Well, that isn't so." Anymore—and he said. "well, these people— these perspective people have been switching counsels," and he said, "I wasn't sure Mitchell was going to keep his counsel." And I said, "Who was his counsel? and he said (unintelligible). Now, somebody said this. But anyway, uh—I said, "Now Seymour, you know I have heard you tell me before and I said I will (unintelligible) if my clients are being kicked around at the Courthouse." I asked him many questions. Get as many answers as you can. I don't come away with many answers. But I'll get mine. I said, "I asked you pertinent questions and I am not offended if you say you can't." Now, this is the way we talked. And we thought he was a little tight today because he was in the presence of his superior. We have found him more loose—and maybe on other occasions we'll be able to get him alone. And I said, "What have you got planned for these two? You going to have them before the Grand Jury?" He said, "We'll have an office interview which will not be recorded. We'll take no notes and you can be present while you take no notes. We want to know what they will say before we take them before the Grand Jury—if we go."

P   Petersen had told me they were going going to be called before the Grand Jury.

W   Well, this is—this is quite possible. We've got some more to tell you.

P   I'm (unintelligible) about this thing.

W   Silbert arrived about this time and I repeated everything that had transpired. (unintelligible) And he qualified Glanzer by saying, "Well, I think we are going to have to talk to the Department of Justice about the interview." This wasn't the interview versus the Grand Jury, I don't think. This was interview at all. Did you get that impression? So, we—then he said to me—said to us Silbert did—"We see from the papers that Ehrlichman has been conducting investigations." Can you admit this? (unintelligible) have been witnesses. I said, "We would like to have his notes on this." And I said "We had them." He says, "It's all in the paper."

P This is true.

W. Ehrlichman says (unintelligible) I don't know and I'm not getting any answer from him (unintelligible) "Now I'm going to ask, you what have you (unintelligible) from the other? He said, "Nobody's giving us any cooperation." And then Silbert said, "You know," he said, "this will (unintelligible) against the (unintelligible) problem. (unintelligible) And he said, "Well, if you come up with one of them (unintelligible) proceeding (unintelligible) and then Glanzer came to his rescue and said, "What could be—what is morally wrong with this whole thing—(unintelligible)" Then we got into—they volunteered this quite interesting problem. They volunteered that these leaks from the Grand Jury were irritating the hell out of them. And I said—

P Do you think (unintelligible) put it out (unintelligible)?

W Well, I do too—but they think a court reporter. I said—

P Bull (Laughter) A court reporter!

W He says Anderson's getting it right from the court reporter.

S Fire him.

W Well, I said, "Why do you bring the court reporter back the next day for?" I said, "This is a crime in itself."

P And a very bad thing.

W They—we didn't take him seriously. Now, general inquiries. "Oh," I said, "How are you proceeding? Are you proceeding with packages? Have you got a forerunner of some indictments? Have you got a package of other people? A second set of indictments? "He can't answer that. So I said, "Well, we understand—we'd be happy—we know you can't stay any longer. Can we leave here with the assurance that you will communicate with us?"

(unintelligible)—an agreement with us that whatever you're going to do in the way of getting a Grand Jury—we got it pretty well committed there that (unintelligible) permitted. The interview would come first.

P   Yeah.

W   And he, and we left there with a commitment from them. I think that's—a commitment for what it's worth. (unintelligible) We didn't—we didn't trap people like this. This is a (unintelligible) thing. Anyway, we left there with sort of a commitment that this would happen. Now this wasn't much, but at least we have kind of (unintelligible) and then I added a question. I said, "Are you going to get around to this before Senator Ervin begins his proceedings?" He said, rather deliberately, rather hesitating, Silbert said, "yes, they would get around before then." Now, I had in mind the fifteenth of May, which is (unintelligible).

P   Yeah.

W   But that's the only point—any point there was. This was a relaxed meeting except that Silbert is not a (unintelligible) fellow. He is a serious man and a business-like man. But that's because, it seems to me, I met him one day (unintelligible) Chambers.

P   (unintelligible)

W   He didn't even remember me that day. He said, "(unintelligible) who you are." Glanzer, (unintelligible) with his boasting—and with some of his weaknesses. Isn't that right?

S   Oh yes, oh yes. Glanzer (unintelligible).

P   Yeah. He is obviously rough—

W   Oh, he is a rough, rough fellow. He exaggerates and at times he doesn't tell you the truth. And at other times he tells you half the truth. But we couldn't go about it any other way today. And with Silbert practically sitting in his lap. We couldn't handle it any other way, but when the chips are down—

S   He is obviously clear (unintelligible) point.

P   Do you think he'll go back and (unintelligible)?

W   Oh, I think he will (unintelligible) But Hunt was before the Grand Jury this afternoon.

P   Yeah.

W   And his lawyer was in two rooms from where we were meeting.

P   What happened? Of course, nobody knows what happened.

W No—and then they—apparently nobody got the press in, to give them an opportunity to see him—he possibly went out a back door. I ran into a photographer down there and I said, "Did you get a picture of him?" And he said, "NO—we—they shipped him out the back way."

P Hmmmm.

W So, that's where that stood. Now, Mr. President, Frank and I—uh—have these conclusions if I may get the conclusions.

P Right.

W Now, do you have any questions before this?

P No. I'd like your conclusions and then I'll ask some questions. You've thought it over. You know what my questions are.

W We think—we think that you and these two men—

P Let me say my good friend Len Garment and some others think that—uh—that Dean out there is a loose cannon—

S Yes.

P Threatening, and all that sort of thing. And I think obviously what is happening—and I think that Glanzer and Silbert are giving, trying to give, Dean an incentive to lie in order to get Haldeman and Ehrlichman. Dean is scared and Dean is capable of doing that. Do you agree with that?

S I think so.

P And Mitchell told him so. But, of course, that wouldn't get him out of it. There's no way he'd (unintelligible) criminal, (unintelligible). Now, that's one point.

W Let me say this.

P Yeah.

W (unintelligible) see if this (unintelligible) I don't know whether Frank wants to talk to you about it. When I was at that meeting today, I had a feeling—and here again it's only my (unintelligible) have a feeling that these two men—Ehrlichman and Haldeman are really not (unintelligible)

P But Petersen certainly indicated, when he came to see me here last Sunday—he said Haldeman and Ehrlichman should resign, and so forth (unintelligible) it is non-corroborated testimony, you know. General Eisenhower where Adams was thrown out for this sort of little thing—the poor guy—he sort of got—

W And he served him well.

P   For seven years and that damned vicuna coat. Unfortunate thing.

S   Yes.

P   But my point is we have very great pressures, you know—quite candid about this—and say that Haldeman and Ehrlichman destroyed in the public mind and they'll say breach of a public trust." (unintelligible) two questions that I really think—one, I don't want to do anything—the heat's going to be on anyway. I don't want to do anything that would jeopardize their case. I want these men to be (unintelligible). I know there is. I really.

W   Quite so. We (unintelligible)

P   The second point, however, I have (unintelligible) And they know that. And if—if—uh—you conclude that the best thing to do is for Haldeman to step forward and say, "you're not guilty of a doggone thing." They have released the Grand Jury notes. I've been attacked by the press; I've been (unintelligible) all this (unintelligible) outside of this office including (unintelligible). In it, one (unintelligible) regard to the (unintelligible) as to whether it affects their (unintelligible) too in regard to the President. You've thought of both of those points?

W   We have. Yes. We have.

P   All right. What is your present conclusion?

W   Well, these are related items and in the area of Presidential judgment, we are (unintelligible). You know you've had such an awful experience. Excuse me, if I state it frankly. I think that either a suspension which I understood has been proposed by Petersen on the basis that—

P   They've been attacked.

W   Yes.

P   They've been named.

W   But there would be a suspension or either their resignation is no assurance that they would not be indicted.

P   I asked Petersen that today. He said it would—

W   There's no assurance.

P   That's right.

W   Yes.

P   Frankly, I said, "Now look here. If they resign does that mean that—" I put it straight to him.

W   Well, then my guess is—

P   If I thought their resignation would avoid an indictment, I would have them resign.

W   Yes, Yes Sir.

P All right.

W Now, I trespass on your area of judgment when I say—I think that if they resign or are suspended that this is a reflection on the Presidency.

P Well, if they don't resign or are suspended and then are indicted, that's all (unintelligible).

W Well, yes. But if—you have already announced you would suspend them then.

P That's true.

W And—

P Anybody who was indicted will be suspended—anybody who is indicted will resign.

W Is there, except for their own (unintelligible) is there any difference between—if they stay? By the way, you know this. I don't have to tell you. They are willing to leave.

P Oh, I know—they're—(unintelligible) my (unintelligible) Absolute (unintelligible)

W And yet on the other hand they are willing to stand up to this thing.

P Oh, yes. Yes.

W If it doesn't hurt you.

P Yes.

W And that's the reason I look at these two things in a kind—of a best—

P Right. Right. Right.

W Because of—in an urgent way, I think if they resign or are suspended then—that it reflects on you. I think if they are indicted and you suspend them or they resign upon indictment, I imagine that they wouldn't even expect you to—

P No - they know (unintelligible) Or if they are even included in this list of co-conspirators . . .

W Yes. I just don't think—

P Already said, of course . . .

W That—there's any difference. I really don't.

P What do you think, Frank?

S This is my feeling. I feel that resignation now by these two gentlemen will be a tremendous reflection on the Presidency. There are—the effect to it—because the public statement says that this is only in Senator Ervin and other sources, because there is no evidence to tie them into a criminal situation. Now if they stepped out at this point there is going to be a public feeling that this is an admission of guilt and this is going to flow over from them right to the (unintelligible) and I have a very strong feeling that this is not one—and I don't want to say you shouldn't run from it. It's not running from it—but it's facing up to it. That's the way I feel about it.

P Now, on the other hand—then just take—you would say that you would lean in the direction of taking the risk which there would be—that they may be named as so-called co-conspirators? And, if they are, then we just have to move in.

W That's it. As I see this, Mr. President, and I hope this time schedule works out—it is possible that if these gentlemen submit to this informal interview—and we haven't decided that question yet—but I think we are leaning toward doing it and I think they are leaning toward having it, too. And maybe we will be present at the interview. And I told them, I said, "We don't sit silent in these interviews. We're not just spectators. We cover for our client. And if the question is unfair, I enter into the act."

P Absolutely.

W Oh, yes. This is not a thing where we are throwing the sheep to the wolves. And so, they, I think they—we didn't make a decision, but I think they—I think they are inclined to think that way. Did you get that?

P I wonder if you could give that interview soon? Is there any way? If you could get that timing some way—or other.

W I think that—

P Or maybe you don't want it soon.

W This was a little (unintelligible) that I had with him. Silbert turned to me and said, "(unintelligible)." He said, "the man who is being talked about seeks the interview, or seeks to go before the Grand Jury. This, I—this, I never would seek. You are in there alone with no counsel and the prosecutor has been in there for months and he controls the Grand Jury and this is the score—of the rule. And I said—now the other point is whether we would ask for the interview or that he would call us for it. I said, "Listen, Silbert, (unintelligible) not taking it in the order in which the thing is supposed to. You suggested, first, that you want them for the interview. Why don't you play your cards? Why don't you call upon us first? I would prefer it that way."

P In other words, wait 'til they're ready?

W Yes. Yes, I would. Uh, now I—

P   I told Petersen they'd côme anytime he wanted them. That's the way I felt it.

W   Well, this is—we did not resist it. (unintelligible) any idea (unintelligible) to the interview for. It wasn't that at all. It wasn't that we said, "If they didn't come— nothing like that." But I have said—Frank, if you don't agree with this, please tell the President.

S   No—whenever I don't disagree with John—I agree.

W   He's

S   But I am not hesitant to disagree.

P   I understand.

W   Oh yes - he is. He's just awful at times.

P   Good.

W   And he's always willing to be critical when he thinks I'm going astray.

P   Let me ask—in other words, your advice at the present time is stand with these men, because basically if you flush them now, it's going to probably hurt—let me put it this way—it will hurt their case. Wouldn't it?

W   Yes. That's right.

P   Unless we can look at their case first and then everybody. It will hurt their case, don't you think?

W   I—it will—in the public eye.

P   And you think that—but—and my point is—so take the risk of going down and letting them be indicted and then if they—

W   Well, so you take a risk, hopefully, of the interview.

P   Oh, the interview. Certainly.

W   Yes.

P   Then what?

W   Well, let's find out—let's find out—

S   Then you take another look at it—

W   What question they ask and what they appear to have and what they are after—and then reappraise this situation. This—this thing, Mr. President, in my judgment has to be played in steps.

P   Don't go too fast?

W   Well, no.

P   You don't know how much they have and what they can prove?

W   That's it, exactly.

P   Then, you got to remember Dean, as I have said, is a loose cannon.

W   I know he is.

P The damndest charges you've ever heard. Some of them are unbelievable.

W Yes.

P This fellow that was sitting in here and who in the Office of the President—a very bright young guy and these guys would talk to him and so forth—but he now wants to drag them down with him.

W Yes. Oh, he's bad.

P They must have told him what I—they—I think—have told Dean that, "If he'll—if he can get Haldeman and Ehrlichman—he gets immunity." Now, on that point, do you want Petersen to give him immunity, or not?

W Uh—

P Dean.

W Well.

P Should he?

W Uh. Let me—as I understood, they were hung up on that right now.

P They are.

W Now.

P See, that's why—I put out a statement that no major figure should be given immunity.

W Let me tell you—

P Basically, because I think it would look bad if—(unintelligible) from our standpoint. What do you think about it?

W Let me tell you about the two kinds of immunity, may I get to this?

P Sure—anything.

W The prosecutor has the power, of course, to say I'm going to (unintelligible) that man, usually use him as a witness and he may have other reasons (unintelligible). So, he'd get case immunity. But it gets to the prosecutor now to use him as a witness and he'd involve in the cross-examination of (unintelligible). You admit he's named you, involving your total service. You are going scot-free while you hope that this will contaminate him before the Jury.

P I see.

W So that's case immunity. Now, the immunity statute that has been on the Federal statutes for years—up to 1968—was a confusing statute. It was to be co-terminus with the Fifth Amendment. That is to say, that no testimony was to be used against you. But the (unintelligible) in the courts has variously confused. It was because

657

of that fact and so nobody would ever believe that it was co-determinus with the Fifth Amendment. So in '68, perhaps it was, thereabouts, Congress passed a statute which we call "Use Amendment"—Use means use of the testimony. This does not exonerate him from indictment. This merely says that what you tell us cannot be used against you, except for perjury.

P   I see.

W   And that we can turn around and indict you the next day if we can indict you on independent evidence, having no source. So we call it case immunity in the instance where the prosecutor turns a fellow loose, and that's it. And use immunity. Now I don't know whether Dean is dickering for—by the way, this use immunity is a very elaborate procedure. This Attorney General must ask the District Judge for it and the District Judge gives it to him. As far as I know, I guess this is an open court proceeding. We considered one but it never seemed to work.

S   I mean, we got them sufficiently confused enough at one time on this very question, but—

W   But we got it resolved in the meantime. But this is a—this is a fairly new statute—but if this means—in the use immunity case—that the man can incriminate—get himself immunity. Now this is devastating where there is a witness on the stand too.

P   Yes.

W   This is a weak link in the prosecutor if he has to use a witness who got immunity by trading off his friends. And for that reason I don't know what he is trading with you—trading with trading loose on this whole mess.

P   Yeah.

W   Or whether he's trading him loose on himself.

P   I don't think Dean's lawyers—Schaffer is his name. Do you know him?

S   Who is he

P   I think Dean's lawyers are just trying to get him off.

W   Yes. On this one case.

P   Off the whole damned thing.

S   What we have found in other cases with Glanzer is that they don't want to go to the elaborate statutory procedure and just want to have an oral understanding, "If you cooperate with us, we'll give you our word we won't prosecute you."

P   That's what they told Dean.

S   That's generally their procedure when there are conspirators.

W This is Petersen's style. He practically gave us this in another case but he double-crossed us gently and we just don't believe him. You see, let me tell why we—why we are a little cocky. And maybe this—this is a bad basis for judgment. But a very prominent national industrialist was charged with—threatened with perjury before a Grand Jury. In order to get him to testify against a dubious lawyer and it was said that Mitchell wanted to get and uh—the man had been threatened by—on the perjury thing before the Grand Jury. If a man gets indicted he's not entitled to (unintelligible). We studied law for two years on that case until finally we got alarmed and we brought our client and we said, "Mr. So and So. We've got to take a chance. The time is running out on you, the time is running out on the District Attorney, but if you just want to stand the way you've stood it for two years and—you can't do that for two years—it's your risk. You can only judge us as you would be judged."

P By the fact.

W He says, "To hell with it. I will stand up to it. He hasn't got a perjury case. He didn't say anything."

S What this was—they were applying the screws to get this industrialist to testify against the lawyer more than they wanted the one against the industrialist. They didn't have the evidence against the industrialist but they would just sit down in that office and swear they had enough to return an indictment. This—this, I think—this is what they are doing. I am confident that they are going to tell each one of these witnesses that are scattered around—potential witnesses against Mr. Ehrlichman and Mr. Haldeman—they are putting the screws on them—they are scaring them. And they are using psychology. Now this overflows—it overflows on John, it may and the (unintelligible). You have to recognize this—have to recognize what we've got here. Go from that to the merits of the case—this is what I am trying to do, and when I look at it from the merits of the case, I don't think they have a criminal case against these gentlemen at this point.

P Even on conspiracy? You see, the thing is, I understand that conspiracy is very broad—

S One overt act and they can bring conspiracy.

P But you have to have an overt action.

W Not on the part of every defendant. Not on the part of every defendant. But the overt act could be in itself innocent if they are part of the pattern.

P I think that is really what they are going to try to nail Haldeman and Ehrlichman on. Not on the—not the Watergate thing—they can't do that. (unintelligible) had approved the budget that (unintelligible). They can never prove that whole thing. Never prove that that's what (unintelligible) never prove that.

S Sure. Sure.

P But on the other hand, they will say that on the three-fifty—"Haldeman and Ehrlichman were involved with Dean and Magruder in an effort to get the money to keep the defendants quiet." What's the answer to that? (unintelligible) McCord—you say—

W Well, of course—Dean's—if I understand John and Bob

W correctly—Dean's presentation goes no further, as far we know, than money to take care of their families.

P That's right.

W And legal counsel.

P That's right.

W Well, you might say circumstantially that helping the defendants—

P Yeah.

W And (unintelligible) it, but it isn't quite as wrong as—having to pay the money to the defendants for the purpose of shutting their mouths.

P Yeah. The other thing - there was perhaps one instance—very little—very little where it said there is the matter of (unintelligible). I am confident their motive in every instance was to help their families and with their legal counsel.

W Yeah.

P I can't see that that's wrong.

S I cannot either. No, there's no crime in this. And we—we asked them because the innuendos and inferences of pay-off to keep the defendants quiet—yes—surfaced quite a while ago.

P Well, McCord has said it. Yes, and the defendants may so now testify.

S Yes. That's right. But none of these actions have we been able to pin down occurred after these allegations arose. This to us—

P I see your point.

S Is significant. If they had—

P If they knew that these allegations had been made

and they still were (unintelligible)—

S   Yes. That's right. If they were chargeable with newspaper stories of allegations of payoffs and then they sent the money over, for the families—

P   I think there were newspaper stories that the defendants were getting money and so forth, but the allegations that they were paid off to keep quiet—I think it was the first time in Court—but you better check that. But I know—I don't think anything after that. It is a point worth checking.

W   You know, Mr. President, it may appear to you and I repeat only because I, (unintelligible) if you had the interview (unintelligible) and given these two men together on the basis of what we call the vernacular of capital appeals.

P   Oh, I understand.

W   And, I really—

P   Well, there are no good choices in a case like this.

W   No.

P   Just take the least bad one.

W   That's right.

P   Your point is that, which has some merit to me, that probably it's just as bad—let's look at it—at its worst. It's just as bad to sink them now as it is to sink them if they are indicted.

W   Sure.

P   Isn't that the point?

W   Yeah.

P   If they are indicted, then I've given them every chance. And if they are indicted, we'll let them go.

W   That's right.

P   If on the other hand they are not indicted—

W   You may—

P   You have to remember, though, that they may even if they are not indicted—this is the argument that these prosecutors and Petersen will make—that if they are not indicted, they will be indicted in the public mind with all this stuff.

W   That's right.

P   Well, put your hat on now.

W   If they are named as not involved—

P   Not named at all. Not named at all. Because of the newspaper stories, and the leaks and the columns and in the attacks by the Weickers, et cetera—these men are going to be really merciless by—Dean's testimony. They are going to be indicted in the public mind. Do you think their usefulness will be destroyed by that?

S Won't there come a time when they will testify before Senator Ervin's Committee and have a chance to make their public presentation?

P Yes. Well, no. I think they will be testifying in court before that.

S In court before then.

P I don't see how—I personally don't see how the Ervin Committee can possibly be allowed to go forward at a time when these court suits develop.

S Yeah. They will probably say that (unintelligible) too.

W Going back to the Petersen—

P Yeah.

W And here again you must take my observations with the fact that I am prejudiced against him.

P Yes. Tell me about—

W Dean's getting off the hook, possibly,

P For having revealed too much to Dean?

W No. From indicting your top men.

P He didn't want to indict them.

W Well, yes. And I—in other words—

P Well, he doesn't seem to be concerned about indicting Mitchell. He is concerned—he is petrified. And Mitchell will be indicted.

W That's what I am told. I have never been in quite this far as they are with this situation, but I know—

P You mean they are going to be reluctant to indict the two top men.

W That's—that's what I would say except you know—I would put it this way—Petersen will handle—this problem. I guess—a holdover from the Democratic Administration.

P That's right. He is.

W Well, I doubt (unintelligible)

P What's your judgment?

S I was following Petersen. I don't know his (unintelligible)

W I said, "His background—his background as a Democrat—"

S Oh, Assistant Petersen?

W I thought as the prosecutor he would love to—unless he was just crazy or ruthless to want to indict the top of the ladder.

S   Without the strongest case and I think—

P   He didn't want to indict unless he can convict.

S   Yes. But this is not one. I don't think he would throw in your two top assistants—into an indictment as defendants, without clear evidence against them.

P   How about this co-conspirators—not-indicting? Think they would do that?

S   Not without clear evidence. I equate either one as being one and the same.

P   I do, too. Because they know if they are named as that then I would have to suspend them. They have to fight that. It's a hell of a procedure—that co-conspiracy.

W   Yes. But it's been going on since time immemorial.

P   Unindicted co-conspirators?

W   Yes. And using that phrase the man who hands down unindicted guys would say—and others to the Grand Jury unknown—so they have a sweeping cover that way in getting them confused. I just think—

P   Well, at this point, I think the thing to do is to stand firm.

W   That's what I wanted to say.

P   Stand firm.

W   Let's play this almost—

P   Don't panic.

W   That's a very good phrase. And let's play this slowly and as things develop and take another—

P   These are good men. I just hope we can save them. It's a miserable thing to have them go through.

W   But you do know, I am sure, we have said to you that while we have their interests—well, I'll say, not primarily, but largely—in our heart, they are—because they are our friends.

P   Sure.

W   We are equally interested in this possibility.

P   I understand.

W   We think it spills over other people.

P   If anything's done now—let's just sit it out awhile—take the smears for awhile.

S   One thing I was wondering and I hesitate to bring it up because it is more of my problem. The statement from Huston—interviews in depth with your top assistant that you have gone into the facts with them—that you've put your confidence in them—believe what they say.

P   If I said that to them?

S   Yes.

P Want me to say that?

S Yes.

P Want me to say that?

S Well, I'm wondering, I'm curious - and you put this critic and foe that you have had this in-depth contact with him on this basis—that you believe them - you place your faith and credit in them—and from what they have told you—they have not done anything wrong.

W If you come to the conclusion to do this, Mr. President, and while I like Frank's presentation of that—I'm concerned about the credit.

S I haven't given it any thought.

W But I think you could add—I'm not trying to get any bouquets for this and their counsels then (unintelligible). I don't know that you want to say that, but support for you because that—

P Their counsels advise me that.

W No, not advised (unintelligible)—

P That they have not—

W That they have not - I mean I don't—

P I think the timing on that—let's have that in a reserve - I think that's a good point.

W I wouldn't mix the (unintelligible)—

P Let's let Easter go by—hope the weekend survives.

W Now Magruder isn't coming back 'til Monday, have you been informed of that?

P No.

W They heard that this afternoon while—

P Hunt was there today.

W Yes.

S But, somebody is coming in tomorrow—it was flashed by very rapidly in an exchange. I don't know who it was.

W The thing is if they can work and we're going to be—obviously, we'll see these men tomorrow again.

P We appreciate your work.

W And, any time over the weekend that they—

P You going to go back and talk to Glanzer again some time?

W Yes, aren't we, Frank?

S Oh yes, there's always been that we have a formal conference—then maybe another one. Then you can drop in the office and see them informally and see—you go down on another matter and Seymour is very cooperative.

W You couldn't do that initially—this had to be a

scheduled conference. He had a man there—he didn't know us and besides he was jumping in first (unintelligible).

S The problem—that we should be trying to get information at Seymour Glanzer's level and you're in conversation with the Assistant Attorney General, but yet it seems worthwhile and productive.

P I'm not sure that Glanzer is telling the truth.

W Well, on occasion I've never been (unintelligible) to that—He did some good opinions.

S You know why I remember that case. He was an Assistant Attorney General then but—

W Yes, he was one of the (unintelligible)—

S He was doing all the work. Well, we're at your disposal.

P Well, as I say, you've got honest men; I know they're telling the truth.

W I'm extremely impressed with them.

P Well, they're touched by this because anybody who was in the campaign is touched by everything about it. And frankly, Mitchell's an honest man. He just wasn't tending the shop—he had problems with his wife—these jackass kids and other fools around did this thing and John should have stepped up to it—that's what happened in my opinion. And I think I -

W Sure, I know.

S Well, we're available to them and if you would like to see us again any time you want to and we can tell you always be delighted.

P Well, I appreciate that.

W It's nice to talk to you even under these circumstances.

P Well, we hope that by Golly—that we'll talk under better—

S Last time I saw you it was crowded—out at the Wardman Park—the Shoreham—I could have lifted my feet off the floor and watched you—you and your famliy on the podium.

P What was that?

S That was election night.

P Election night—you were there? Oh boy. That was a great night? Well, that was what it was all about.

S Yes, it sure was.

P Well, we'll survive this. You know—people say this destroys the Administration and the rest - but what was this? What was Watergate? A little bugging! I mean a terrible thing—it shouldn't have been done—shouldn't have been covered up. And people shouldn't have and the rest, but we've got to beat it. Right.

W Everybody does—the Democrats have been doing—going on for 20 years. (Laughter)

S Mr. President, on behalf of my daughter Nancy—she asked me to do it.

P How old is she?

S She's sixteen.

P Next time you come in—I'll give her a little something—You've got—they have good men to (unintelligible).

Meeting: The President and Petersen, Oval Office, April 27, 1973. (5:37 - 5:43 pm)

P Come in.

HP How are you today?

P How was your hard day?

HP I'm sure no harder than yours, sir.

P Sit down, sit down. I was down in Mississippi today. We have gotten a report that, ah, that really we've got to head them off at the pass. Because it's so damned —so damn dangerous to the Presidency, in a sense. There's a reporter by the name of Hersch of the *New York Times* you probably know.

HP He's the fellow that did the Vietnam stories.

P Right. Who told Bittman, who told O'Brien, apparently that they have information—Hersch has information I don't know. You can't ever tell who is saying "this is from Hersh" or "this is from Bittman." Information indicating that Dean has made statements to the prosecuting team implicating the President. And whether—and whether—the *Post* has heard similar rumors. Now, Henry, this I've got to know. Now, understand—I have told you everything I know about this thing.

HP I don't have any problem with that, Mr. President, and I'll get in touch with them immediately, but—

P Who?

HP With Titus, Silbert and Glanzer and Campbell? Who are—

P Do you mind calling them right now?

HP   No, sir.

P   OK. Say, "Now, look. All of your conversations with Dean and Bittman, do they implicate the President?" Because we can't—I've got—if the U.S. Attorney's office and, ah

HP   Mr. President, (unintelligible) I had them over there—we had a kind of crisis of confidence night before last. I left to come over here and I left my two principal assistants to discourse with Silbert and the other three. And in effect it concerned me—whether or not they were at ease with my reporting to you, and I pointed out to them that I had very specific instructions, discussed that with them before on that subject, and—well

P   Yes.

HP   As a consequence—I kind of laid in to Titus yesterday and it cleared the air a little bit, but there is a very suspicious atmosphere. They are concerned and scared. Ah—and I will check on this but I have absolutely no information at this point that—

P   Never heard anything like that—

HP   No, sir. Absolutely not.

P   My gosh—As I said—

HP   Mr. President, I tell you, I do not consider it, you know, I've said to Titus, "We have to draw the line. We have no mandate to investigate the President. We investigate Watergate." And I don't know where that line draws, but we have to draw that all the time.

P   Good. Because if Dean is implicating the Presidency—we are going to damned well find out about it. That's—that's—because let me tell you the only conversations we ever had with him, was that famous March 21st conversation I told you about, where he told me about Bittman coming to him. No, the Bittman request for $120,000 for Hunt. And I then finally began to get at them. I explored with him thoroughly, "Now what the hell is this for?" He said "It's because he's blackmailing Ehrlichman." Remember I said that's what it's about. And Hunt is going to recall the seamy side of it. And I asked him, "Well how would you get it? How would you get it to them?" so forth. But my purpose was to find out what the hell had been going on before. And believe me, nothing was approved. I mean as far as I'm concerned—as far as I'm concerned turned it off totally.

HP   Yeah. My understanding of law is—my understanding of our responsibilities, is that if it came to that I

667

would have to come to you and say, "We can't do that." The only people who have jurisdiction to do that is the House of Representatives, as far as I'm concerned.

P   That's right. But I want you to know, you tell me, because as far as I'm concerned—

HP   I'll call them. Do you want me to call from here or outside?

P   Use the Cabinet Room and you will be able to talk freely. And who will you call, who will you talk to there?

HP   I'll call Silbert. If he's not there, I'll get Titus.

P   You'll say that "This is the story some *New York Times* reporter has and Woodward of the *Post*, but Hersh is reporting that Dean had made a statement to the prosecutors." Now understand that this is not a Grand Jury thing. Now damnit, I want to know what it is.

HP   I'll call right away.

P   And I need to know.

HP   Yes, sir.

Meeting: The President, Petersen and Ziegler, Oval Office, April 27, 1973. (6:04 - 6:48 pm)

P   Come in. As, like all things, some substance, some falsity.

HP   Ah, last Monday Charlie Shaffer was in the office, and a continuation of the negotiations. Charlie Shaffer is the lawyer. Charlie is a very bright, able bombastic fellow. And he was carrying on as if we're making a summation in a case. And he said—that—ah he was threatening, "We will bring the President in—not this case but in other things" What "other things" are we don't know what in the hell they are talking about.

P   Don't worry.

HP   "In other areas," more specifically is the word he used. That they regarded—and didn't consider of importance they regarded as the elaboration of his earlier threat. You know, "We'll try this Administration—Nixon—what have you, what have you." There's a new conversation by them with Dean since the Sunday we first met (unintelligible) Whatever is said is through Shaffer the lawyer.

P   What else do you have besides that?

HP Well, let's see. They did say that at a later date in the proceedings that Dean went to the President, and I assume that's the February or March or whatever that date was. But that's in the course of your trying to find out. Ah, today they were after the Cubans and the receipt of the money which they confirmed. Dorothy Hunt on being the intermediary that passed it through. They are going to have Butterfield in in a few minutes.

P What I am getting at, Henry, about this threat that—

HP There's no more on that other than I've just told you.

P Why in the hell can't we stop though—the paper that Hersh—to think that to bring the President with a thing like that. (expletive removed), you know. Understand. Let me say this. If it were in with the Grand Jury I want to know that too.

HP All right. Well—

P (expletive removed). You've got to believe me. I am after the truth, even if it hurts me. But believe me, it won't.

HP I understand that, you see. But, you know—

P Just like it won't hurt you. We are doing our job. And somebody was in here the other day and they were saying, well, Dean is going to blackmail you because of something you're supposed to have told me. And I said, (expletive removed) I said, you have a right to tell me what was going on.

HP The only thing I think is that it's either Dean or Shaffer or this McCandless. Now, Shaffer says that it's McCandless that's leaking this stuff to the press.

P Who is McCandless?

HP McCandless is another lawyer that Dean has retained.

P He's leaking to the press that they are going to try the President, huh?

(unintelligible)

HP Other areas, but what those areas are, we don't know. Now, Silbert said, "Stop." So, he didn't let them go on. He said, "why get into that?" Ah—

P It's not this case. Go ahead. (unintelligible)

HP Well, I told those fellows, look. I told those fellows this. I know you can't believe these reporters all the time. He's had one or preferably two weeks—

P I'm glad we have that then. When I heard that, I

thought that Dean must be out of his damned mind or something. The man is not, ah—I don't know. Going to have Butterfield in? Good.

HP   Well, that's in connection with the $350,000. Now, we are going to have Jack Caulfield in to the Grand Jury.

P   That's on, because he worked on—

HP   He set up the intermediaries that were being used as couriers to transfer money either to or from LaRue.

P   Oh, he did? Caulfield, eh. What would be the liability of a man like that? Would he be a conspirator?

HP   If it's done with knowledge—if it's done with knowledge—

P   Yeah, with knowledge. But also, there is a certain—it has to be willful or—there are two statutes—

HP   When you talk about conspiracy, you are impugning knowledge, and you impugn the knowledge of the facts unless there's specific evidence of the—

P   (unintelligible) I just don't want to see guys get hurt that didn't know what the hell they were doing.

HP   And we don't want to either.

P   (unintelligible)

HP   But we are looking for witnesses, to be perfectly honest.

P   Sure.

HP   Strachan, they are still negotiating with him on having flunked the lie detector test.

P   Maybe the best thing to do is to plead guilty to the prosecutor—plead guilty?

HP   Well, you know, ah—

P   What?

HP   Basically, I mean, what we are telling Strachan is that he has got to make the choice whether he wants to be a witness or a defendant. "You can just hang tough, and you can be technically be a witness."

(Ziegler enters)

P   That story, according to Henry Petersen—he just called the U. S. Attorney's office. It is totally false story. Needs to be totally knocked down.

Z   Yes, sir.

P   Read me exactly what you can recall the U. S. Attorney—

HP   Called U. S. Attorney and said that in the past an

attorney representing John Dean was in his office and indicated that if we insisted on Dean, that they would be tying in the President, not in the Watergate, but in other areas.

P   That's not Watergate, but in other areas.

HP   Whatever that means.

P   Well, that's fine. Just let them tie us in.

HP   Now, to put that in context, they had previously said that if we insisted on trying Dean and not Ehrlichman and Haldeman that they would be "trying this Administration," the President and what have you.

P   So basically that's the game they are playing.

Z   I can understand how—you indicated that their attorney, the other day, said they would resist in tying in—did you say? I not the Watergate, but—

HP   They would be tying in the President. I mean it was an emotional statement.

P   Emotion at tying in the President, not in Watergate but in other things. Right.

HP   Not in the Watergate, but other things. Whatever they would be—

P   When was this?

HP   Monday. Monday of this week.

P   Monday of this week.

HP   Monday of this week.

P   Well, I think this—I think this thing we just hit back on.

HP   Well, that's the only thing. And I don't know that. And they had no idea.

P   But Dean give them

HP   What?

P   But Dean gave them

HP   Oh, yes, but, but—

P   That basically ties in the White House.

HP   That was one of the reasons that was so important to disclose that because they could have hung that over our heads, you see and—

P   You remember my call from Camp David. I said, "Don't go into the national security stuff." I didn't mean—

HP   Oh, I understand.

P   'cause I remember I think we discussed that silly damned thing. I had heard about it, just heard about. You told me that. That's it, you told me.

P   What (expletive removed) did they break into a

psychiatrist's office for? I couldn't believe it.

Z   I think what all of this is—

P   What do you think it is?

Z   I think it's the attorney

P   I think he is bargaining for Dean.

Z   I had occasion to talk to Dean a few minutes ago, but a call—

P   You did?

Z   He is a very good friend of mine.

P   Well, tell us what you—now understand we have to watch how we handle him now, because we've got

Z   It was a very good conversation. He said, "Ron, I am issuing no statements." Incidentally, he said, "I got a telephone call."

P   A telephone call from the President. You know, that shows you what a person he is. I called—you know—some nice things we do—I called six people, members of my staff. I called Ron, Henry Kissinger, Ehrlichman, and Rose, my secretary and John Dean. I just go down a list of people, and just say, I want to wish you a Happy Easter" That's all I did. And it's all over the press!

HP   Well, you know, we got a report. Again, I got it through Charlie Shaffer that he was pleased and elated and reassured. And you know, as a human being—

P   I don't want to hurt John Dean. Believe me—I'd like to help him.

Z   He went out of his way to make the point to me, just in this two-minute conversation, he said "I didn't make that telephone call, Ron" I don't know who may have done it cause he knows—

P   Oh, you did not discuss this crazy Hersch story.

Z   No

P   Now the problem about this Hersch story, is that if the *Times* comes out and run this—

Z   Oh, no. As a matter of fact I talked to Clifton Daniels this afternoon, and he didn't raise it.

P   The Woodward story. Woodward also has the same story. Woodward of the *Post*.

Z   Woodward said that reliable sources said that someone had implicated the President in their testimony, or referred to him.

P   In the Dean story?

Z   No, that was Hersch.

P   What did Woodward say?

Z   Woodward said they had two stories; one was the

fact that it was reaching a new plateau, and he was not ready to read the story because he was still working on it, and Woodward was taking the position that he was confused and needed to talk to someone to get a perception

HP   They are trying people.

Z   What they are trying to do is to get a fix on what's happened over here.

P   OK. Take a hard line. Gergen to Woodward. Anything on that they better watch their damned cotton picking faces. Because boy, if there's one thing in this case as Henry will tell you, since March 21st when I had that conversation with Dean, I have broken my ass to try to get the facts of this case. Right? Tried to get that damn Liddy to talk. We tried to get—finally got Gray to refresh his memory. (unintelligible) We finally got—incidentally, we put Ruck in that thing rather than—I don't think based on what you had told me earlier, we should put Feld—because there's too much (unintelligible) over there and Ruckelshaus is a perfectly trustworthy man. He'll stay 30 days—

HP   I know him and I think well of him.

P   and for that matter, we'll have another man ready. Does that sound alright to you? I told Ruck, incidentally, that he was to cooperate with the investigation and I said, "Ruck you are to do anything that the prosecutor says to do, Henry Petersen, or the prosecutors, leave no stone unturned and I don't give a damn who it hurts. Now believe me, that's what he's been told. So you got a man there who will—

HP   I know him and I think well of him, Mr. President.

P   Well, he's Mr. Clean, you know so you understand

HP   Yes, indeed. He's quite able, he is indeed.

P   So there you are. You've got to knock that—Crack down. If there's one thing you have got to do, you have got to maintain the Presidency out of this. I have got things to do for this country and I'm not going to have—now this is personal. I sometimes feel like I'd like to resign. Let Agnew be President for a while. He'd love it.

HP   I don't even know why you want the job?

P   You are talking about this story—that Agnew is getting ready to resign? That's the *Post* also?

Z   Well, that's the *Post* and *Times*.

P   *Post*? Well, what did Agnew say?)

Z   "That's ridiculous." Marsh Thompson's going to

turn it off. Well, Look. Let me have Gergen call him back, and say, "He raised two points with me. Let me tell you what is going on here. What's going on here, Bob, is the President is going to get to the bottom of this.

P   That's right.

Z   And then have Gergen say, I have checked this at a very high level and you'd better, absolutely not even go into any emotional concerns of running a story like this. You had better just wipe it out of your mind. Because there is nothing to it.

P   That's right.

Z   If you say you want to be responsible and fair, "Well, you had better not go with a source that you have to speculate on.

P   Right. The same with the *Times*.

Z   The *New York Times* man, I'm sure—

P   Well, Hersch is so damn unreliable.

Z   (Unintelligible)

P   I'd call Daniels. Hersch told Bittman who told O'Brien that Dean had testified that there was a new—that the President was involved, right?

Z   Not testified, but told the prosecutor or something.

P   Told the prosecutor that the President was involved, right?

P   Let me ask Henry a question. You have Titus and those saying Dean, neither Dean or his lawyers, have said anything of that sort except this one thing.

HP   They said, "tying in the President" not in the Watergate but in other areas and the prosecutor said, "Stop! We don't want to get in this. We don't want to discuss this."

P   (unintelligible)

HP   What I think is its bombast, its negotiation—it's ah—

P   Again make it clear that Henry's made his check.

Z   Just to put this into prospective. This is not, as I sense it, about to break in the papers. This is just rumor type.

P   Well, kill it. Kill it hard.

Z   Ok, sir. (Ziegler leaves)

P   Let me say this, let me ask you about (unintelligible). First, on Dean—I would not want to get into a position—You have told me now, "You can do what you want with Dean." You have given up. You mean, in other words, fire him, hire him, leave him, treat him like the others, wait until the Grand Jury acts, or something. You see, I have three courses: I can wait until the Grand Jury acts, I can take leaves of absence, or I can take resignations, I have three different courses on all three men. I can do different things with each one of them. Right?

HP   Yes, sir.

P   These are the options, but what I will do remains to be seen. Now in Dea's case, I do not want the impression left that—I have gone over with you before, that by saying "Don't grant immunity to a major person." that in so doing I am trying to block Dean giving evidence against Haldeman or Ehrlichman.

HP   I understand that.

P   I have applied that to others, and I don't want to—no. Do I make myself clear?

HP   Yes, let me make myself clear.

P   Yes.

HP   I regard immunity authority under the statues of the United States, to be my responsibility, of which I cannot divest myself.

R   Right.

HP   And—ah—we take options, but I would have to treat this as advisory only.

P   Right. Well understand, I only expressed an opinion.

HP   I understand.

P   And understand you have got to determine who is the major culprit too.

HP   Yes, sir.

P   If you think Dean is an agent—Let me say. If Dean, I—I think Haldeman and Ehrlichman in the case of themselves with Dean. But my point is, you have got to—ah—I don't know what you prosecutors think, but if your prosecutors believe that they have got to give Dean immunity, in whole or in part, in order to get the damned case, do it. I'm not—I'm not telling you what to do but—you understand? Your decision. Now have you talked to the prosecutor about this situation?

HP   They vascillated. In the first instance they, I think, felt quite strongly that Dean should be immunized, and I was resisting. And the last time we discussed it, why they had made other—

P   Why? Maybe because of what I said? See? I don't want—I don't want them—

HP   No. I don't so, because, one, they are in a position to simply make the recommendation and let me shoulder the heavy burden.

P Why do you think that they had turned around?

HP Well, I think they see the question of credibility. They have come to the recognition that if they are going to put him on the stand and he's going to have any credibility at all, he'll have most credibility if he goes in and pleads and testifies as a co-defendant against Ehrlichman and Haldeman as opposed to someone who has been given immunity and is testifying against them.

P Even an old man like Wilson will tear hell out of him.

HP Well, John Wilson may be old, but he's one hell of a lawyer.

P Oh, I can see—

HP A top-notch man—

P I met him last night, I said privately and I won't again, but I was impressed with him. He is a delightful man. And I could see, I can see—I would want to be on the stand with him interrogating.

HP He's a fair—

P He must be pretty good,

HP Yes, sir, he is. And did you meet Frank Strickler?

P Yeah.

HP They are both delightful people.

P Yeah. Strickler, he just looks like sort of a big country bumpkin, but there is a sharp mind in there.

HP Very able fellow. And they are decent people to deal with—as adversaries. They are decent. They are honorable lawyers, they are a pleasure to deal with.

P All right. We have got the immunity problem resolved. Do it. Dean if you need to, but boy I am telling you—there ain't going to be any blackmail.

HP Mr. President, I—

P Don't let Dick Kleindienst say it. Dean ain't "Hunt is going to blackmail you." Hunt's not going to blackmail any of us. "It is his word, basically, against yours." It's his word against mine. Now for—who is going to believe John Dean? We relied on the damned so— Dean, Dean was the one who told us throughout the summer that nobody in the White House was involved when he, himself apparently, was involved, particularly on the critical angle of subornation of perjury. That's the one that—I will never, never understand John.

HP I, I can almost quote him. He said, "Henry, God

damn it, I need this information. That man has designated me to get all these facts." And he calls me in there and chews my ass off.

P Do you know something?

HP And this was before the trial—

P Dick Kleindienst, incidentally, Dick Kleindienst told me this last night when I talked to him. He said, "You know, Mr. President—" And I said, "Do you know the first time I ever saw Dean alone was on February 27, 1972, except for 5 minutes when I signed my will on August the 14th." Dick probably repeated, because I think you were in the room. He said, "Are you kidding?" I said, "No, why? Did you hear otherwise?" He said, "Well, Dean was around here quoting the President all the time." Did he indicate that I was telling him to do this?

HP He told me that he was been designated by you to accumulate all these facts and he was reporting to you personally. And that you'd be clearing his ass out if he didn't have it and I went back to him again, I said, "John, are you sure this information is not going laterally?" I said, "Not that I distrust you, but you, where is it going? Do you know?" He said, "Henry, it is only going upward," which I took to mean—Ehrlichman, Haldeman and you.

P Ehrlichman. It went to Ehrlichman, I am sure. And then into Haldeman. And to Ziegler, because Ziegler used Dean. But that was because he had to (unintelligible).

HP Well, I didn't have any problem with that. I got in—

P Dean. You will get Dean in there. Suppose he starts trying to impeach the President, the word of the President of the United States and says, "Well, I have information to the effect that I once discussed with the President the question of how the possibility, of the problem," of this damn Bittman stuff I spoke to you about last time. Henry, it won't stand up for five minutes before nothing was done, and fortunately I had Haldeman at that conversation and he was there and I said, "Look, I tried to give you this, this, this, this, this and this." And I said, "When you finally get it out, it won't work. Because, I said, "First, you can't get clemency to Hunt."

HP I agree.

P I mean, I was trying to get it out. To try to see what that—Dean had been doing! I said, "First you can't give him clemency." Somebody has thrown out something to the effect that Dean reported that Hunt had an idea that he was going to get clemency around Christmas. I said, "Are you kidding? You can't get clemency for Hunt. You couldn't even think about it until, you know, '75 or something like that." Which you could, then because of the fact, that you could get to the—ah—But nevertheless, I said you couldn't give clemency. I said, "The second point to remember is 'How are you going to get the money for them?' If you could do it, I mean you are talking about a million dollars." I asked him—well, I gave him several ways. I said, "You couldn't put it through a Cuban Committee could you?" I asked him, because to me he was sounding so damned ridiculous. I said, "Well under the circumstances." I said, "There isn't a damn thing we can do." I said, "It looks to me like the problem is sue John Mitchell." Mitchell came down the next day and we talked about executive privilege. Nothing else. Now, that's the total story. And—so Dean—I just want you to be sure that if Dean ever raises the thing, you've got the whole thing. You've got that whole thing. Now kick him straight—.

HP That's—I mean—that's what we had to do. I just don't see how we can minimize that man. That's all there is to it.

P But I suppose he talks to his friends. Is he talking to Bittman? No, Dean was talking to O'Brien, wasn't he? Dean wasn't talking to Bittman.

HP Not to my knowledge. Wasn't that story that Bittman? That Bittman talked to O'Brien—Bittman, Bittman to O'Brien—

P No. Bittman to O'Brien said, "Look, we need the money."

HP That's right.

P Or was it Bittman to Dean? I don't know. What kind of a guy is O'Brien?

HP I've only met O'Brien one time and then only recently at a recent Bar dinner. I don't know him. Bittman, I know well. I just thank God I broke off social relations with him from the time he represented Hunt. We had a golf date, and I just broke it and I haven't seen him since then.

P What about Bittman?

HP What he's concerned about is the allegation that he, in behalf of Hunt, was attempting to blackmail the White House for substantial sums of money in return for

Hunt's silence. That's the allegation. And that's what McCord said—ah

P   McCord said that Bittman—

HP   McCord said that Dorothy Hunt told him all this sort of thing.

P   And so how do you get to them? Do you have to call Bittman? What do you do?

HP   Well, we may get into the fee. Fees are not privileged.

P   I see.

HP   Now—

P   You say, "Where did he get your fee?"

HP   That's right.

P   And how would you go about that one?

HP   We'll have to subpoena the fee records out of the law firm.

P   And then if he got the fees, you say, "Did blackmail the White House for this?"

HP   Well, ah.

P   How did he pay the fee?

HP   No, no. I think that—one, we try and find out whether or not the amount of fees reflected on the books of the law firm were consistent with the amount of money that was—oh—to have gone to the law firm. In other words, what we think happened is that a considerable amount within the law firm was paid out in fees and the balance went on to Dorothy Hunt for distribution to the Cubans and what have you.

P   For support.

HP   The strange thing about this one, Mr. President, is that they could have done it openly.

P   Why, of course!

HP   If they had just come out in the *Washington Post* could say, "Well these people were—"

P   They helped the Scotsboro people, they helped the Berrigans, you remember the Alger Hiss defense fund?

HP   And we're going to help these—They were doing this—Once you do it in a clandestine fashion, it takes on elements—

P   Elements of a cover-up.

HP   That's right and obstruction of justice.

P   That's what it is, a question of the way it was done.

HP   Sir.

P   Curious thing. I get your point there, I see that in other words, the—so let's look at Bittman. Bittman says he is trying to blackmail the White House. Alright you called Bittman. Bittman says that—he says that O'Brien—Where did you get the money? And so forth—

HP Now Bittman maintains that it's a lie.

P He'd be better off to say it's a lie.

HP Yeah. He simply says that this is a statement by McCord that is lacking veracity.

HP And is attributed to (unintelligible) and Dorothy Hunt.

P Of course, you've got Dean now corroborating—

HP Well, we have Dean alluding to it, but not in circumstances that we can use it. It depends upon whether or not—

P But Dean must say—this is also hearsay on that point. I had forgotten this is hearsay. Because he says that he had heard that Bittman needed money, I mean, Bittman had said had had to have a hundred—

HP The link here is O'Brien.

P Huh?

HP The link here is O'Brien.

P I—oh, I see.

HP The lawyer.

P I see, That Dean had heard from O'Brien. Bittman or O'Brien?

HP No. I say the link we can break into this is O'Brien. Cause O'Brien's lawyer. He very scared and—

P Yeah. So O'Brien, Let's see what he says. I am just trying to see where it sorts out. O'Brien—can you get him in? What's he done? Has he spoken up?

HP Well, I don't know that I can really predict—ah—ah—but conceivably if he said—ah—

P Bittman.

HP "As part of the scheme to ensure silence of those that were convicted, we made an arrangement whereby money would flow through Bittman in the form of legal fees for distribution to those people."—Then you've got it.

P In the form of legal fees, I see. And then you've got Bittman and then you've got O'Brien and then you got the people that did it. If they—ah—At least those that knew. Like Kalmbach, might not have known.

HP That remains to be seen. And La Rue,

P LaRue? LaRue did know. He had to. And Mitchell. You've got Mitchell there, you've got LaRue. Who else is missing? La Rue, is he the one that used the code name of Rivers?

HP   I don't know whether—

P   I have heard that name Rivers.

HP   I heard Baker. Now there's two, but these may be couriers that Caulfield recruited, I am not sure.

P   And in all that Caulfield is involved, probably only coincidentally. You can't—they say some of these down there. But O'Brien in other words. O'Brien is scared. And O'Brien says that Bittman—I am just trying to see how they ever got—The only way you could ever get—Let me say, there is no way they could get that to the President without going through Haldeman and Ehrlichman. But I am referring to this man here. There's no way they could get it to here except through the fact that on March 21st Dean, as I had reported to you, did report to me that Bittman had told O'Brien that they needed the money. They needed the money. It was discussed and we, I said, "It can't be done. We can't do it." He went on to see Ehrlichman, and Ehrlichman said, "No dice." Nothing could be done. Now that is the fact. As far as we're concerned. That isn't much of a thing for Dean to have.

HP   Yeah.

P   But you could have Bittman I suppose Dean. He could have talked to him—but then you have hearsay. But Dean is not credible. He is not credible. He really can't. He can't go out and say, "Look I've talked to the President and he told me this and that and the other thing." First, it's not true.

HP   That's the reason I say, in order to make Dean a credible witness; one, it seems to me that he has to plead and two, he has to be corroborated in an essential degree, not everything he says. But in sense an essential number of factors by other witnesses. And he may be corroborating in one respect by LaRue and in another respect by O'Brien, and in still a third respect by someone else, and in a fourth respect by Magruder. You know, and that's the way it goes and the case is being built. So, maybe we can bring O'Brien out

P   Well, there's only this one charge I give to you, among many others, and that is: If any of this— —I mean, I can't allow it. Believe me that even prosecutors shouldn't even have informed you of this one. Or me—I—

HP They have described it as bombast, and rhetoric, and—you know, posing—

P You examine them tomorrow. And you tell them, they are my men. I'm for them too. I want them to do the job. I want this to come out solid and right here. And they will start right in to get the big fish. Let's come to the Dean thing again. I can give you some more time if you want to negotiate with him. I mean, when I say I—more time—

HP He needs more pressure. It's become counterproductive of the President.

P What?

HP It's become counterproductive. I think he was pressed up against the wall, he's seen the early-morning crisis pass and now he's had resurgence. You know, he sees Ehrlichman here. He sees Haldeman here. He sees John Dean still here. Nothing happens. His confidence is coming back rather than ebbing. And

P What do you think? Without your advice—Is the proper course of action to have Dean to either—There are two courses of action I can take. I can take a leave of absence until they clear. You know what I mean. Which of course is a very—Bill Rogers thinks is the fairest. And in the and and then they resign, of course. Or I can ask—just resign. Now the problem with resignation, which hits at—There isn't any question about what I will do when you get through with your damned Grand Jury. I just don't—I don't want to—you know what I mean? I don't want him in effect—by something that I do—to totally prejudice even Dean. You understand what I mean?

HP I understand that aspect of it.

P As President I shouldn't give a damn about that, but as President—I'll speak to the country on this. And I will soon. But my point is with a leave of absence, with a leave of absence for all three.

HP With a leave of absence, you have the best of both worlds. You have given them the benefit of the doubt and you haven't cut the Gordian knot. You haven't asked for their resignations.

P I have asked for a leave of absence. And I say, "Now I will determine at the conclusion not just of the Grand Jury, but at the conclusion of this entire investigation, that means the Ervin Committee is in there too." If, for example, you don't happen to indict one of these three, or one or two or three. I am not going to take that as clear evidence—it is not enough to serve the President simply to get by—

HP   I understand—

P   And I have told them all of that. They have got to be—

HP   I don't see that we're in any disagreement there. The problem is one of timing, as I see it. I think, in my humble judgement, that the question of timing is working first to your detriment, with respect to your image, before the press and public.

P   Do you mean now would be a good time—

HP   And secondly, I think it is working toward the detriment of the investigation because it is giving all of these people an attitude of hope that I think is unwarranted and I think that if he—

P   Let me ask you this. How about moving Haldeman and Ehrlichman and see what that does to Dean. I am just thinking about that—Let me put it this way. I am not in communication with Dean at all. For obvious reasons. But Haldeman and Ehrlichman, I hold my damn brain sessions. I know that they are telling me the truth. Dean, I can't believe him. Because I don't know what he is up to, you see? And, this leave of absence talk, let me say—Please let us keep it within ourselves. I can't leak this out. It will kill them. It will kill the whole thing. I am particularly—can't let it out to Dean. I don't like to put the three of them in the same bag. Although they may all be there.

HP   Mr. President, why do you not like to put them in the same bag? You don't like to put them in the same bag because Haldeman and Ehrlichman are loyal to the last minute, and you—

P   No, no it isn't that. It isn't that.

HP   I am not questioning your motive.

P   I am referring primarily to the fact that I have a different relation with the others. At this point I can't get Dean in and say, "Look fella, you take a leave of absence and if you come through clean I will take you back." You know, something like that.

HP   Well, I, in all candor, I think a leave of absence—absence—is just a preliminary step to ultimate departure.

P   I see.

HP   I don't see how either way any of them could come back. But it certainly at least in terms of bias and prejudice it indicates to the public at large that you haven't completely abandoned them. You haven't completely and unalterably decided their fate. On the other hand, I am separating myself from them and saying now, by golly, you—What you say is you are guilty until you are proven innocent. That's what the leave of absence is. You see. The other way I am saying, "Resignation—you're guilty." That's the difference, isn't it? The leave of absence in effect is saying, "Look, fellas, I give you leave of absence. So I hold you, basically, not that you're guilty," but—I'm not holding you guilty, I'm not finding you guilty, but I'm saying is that you've got to prove that you are innocent before you can come back.

HP   No.

P   Now in recognition I am saying—

HP   No—you're saying that you have to prove you're worthy to work in the Office of the President.

P   Oh, I see. I understand.

HP   But I think that, I think that's a much more ritualistic way of saying—

P   Well, that's what I told them. That's what I told them. You know what I mean by guilt and innocence, I mean worthiness.

HP   That's right.

P   You have to prove you're worthy.

HP   But you see that's what I see has to get out to the public. But Mr. President, my wife is not a politically sophisticated woman.

P   That's right—

HP   She knows I'm upset about this and you know, I'm working hard and she sees it. But she asked me at breakfast—She, now I don't want you to hold this against her if you ever meet her, because she's a charming lady—

P   Of course.

HP   She said, "Doesn't all this upset you?" And I said, "Of course it does."

P   "Why the hell doesn't the President do something?"

HP   She said, "Do you think the President knows?"

And I looked at her and said, "If I thought the President knew, I would have to resign." But, you know, now there is my own family, Mr. President—

P Sure. Sure.

HP Now whatever confidence she has in you, her confidence in me ought to be unquestioned. Well, when that type of question comes through in my home—

P We've got to get it out.

HP We've got a problem.

P Well you know I have wrestled with it. I've been trying to—

HP Mr. President, I pray for you, sir.

P I have been trying to get the thing. Like even poor Gray—there was nothing we could do. Ah—wrestling with Dean's covers. But ah—

HP I wouldn't try to distinguish between the three of them.

P I understand. I understand. Well, I won't try to distinguish, but maybe they will be handled differently due to the fact that I am not communicating with Dean.

HP Mr. President, it is always easier to advise than it is to assume the responsibility.

P I will do it my way. And it will be done. I am working on it. I won't even tell you how—how—

HP I understand—

P But what are you going to do? What will happen now? The FBI will now interview Dean on that report in California?

HP Yes, sir. They will interview Ehrlichman and they will, ah, attempt to identify the psychiatrist. They will interview the psychiatrist named as Ellsberg's psychiatrist to determine whether or not they were burglarized or know they were burglarized. They will attempt to determine if there's any police report of a burglary. We will check with the Defense Department since they have been involved in this thing. We will re-check the FBI. We've already checked them once.

P What did they find?

HP Well, nothing. We've checked our own people—

P Now, the FBI did not do anything.

HP I understand. But . . . we're talking about the evidence of information that may have been stemmed from that source.

P Yeah. Well they got into the trial.

HP Whether any of that has gotten into the file in

any way. And when we do that and we do that, we have to file a report to the Court and we will and ah we'll see what develops.

P Alright. Thank you.

Statement: The President, April 30, 1973. (9:01 - 9:25)

9:01 P.M. EDT

I want to talk to you tonight from my heart on a subject of deep concern to every American.

In recent months, members of my Administration and officials of the Committee for the Re-election of the President—including some of my closest friends and most trusted aides—have been charged with involvement in what has come to be known as the Watergate affair. These include charges of illegal activity during and preceding the 1972 Presidential election and charges that responsible officials participated in efforts to cover up that illegal activity.

The inevitable result of these charges has been to raise serious questions about the integrity of the White House itself. Tonight I wish to address those questions.

Last June 17, while I was in Florida trying to get a few days' rest after my visit to Moscow, I first learned from news reports of the Watergate break-in. I was appalled at this senseless, illegal action, and I was shocked to learn that employees of the Re-election Committee were apparently among those guilty. I immediately ordered an investigation by appropriate government authorities. On September 15, as you will recall, indictments were brought against seven defendants in the case.

As the investigations went forward, I repeatedly asked those conducting the investigation whether there was any reason to believe that members of my Administration were in any way involved. I received repeated assurances that there were not. Because of these continuing reassurances—because I believed the reports I was getting, because I had faith in the persons from whom I was getting them—I discounted the stories in the press that appeared to implicate members of my Administration or other officials of the campaign committee.

Until March of this year, I remained convinced that the denials were true and that the charges of involvement by members of the White House staff were false. The comments I made during this period, and the comments made by my Press Secretary on my behalf, were based on the information provided to us at the time we made those comments. However, new information then came to me which persuaded me that there was a real possibility that some of these charges were true, and suggesting further that there had been an effort to conceal the facts both from the public, from you, and from me.

As a result, on March 21, I personally assumed the responsibility for coordinating intensive new inquiries into the matter, and I personally ordered those conducting the investigations to get all the facts and to report them directly to me, right here in this office.

I again ordered that all persons in the Government or at the Re-election Committee should cooperate fully with the FBI, the prosecutors and the Grand Jury. I also ordered that anyone who refused to cooperate in telling the truth would be asked to resign from government service. And, with ground rules adopted that would preserve the basic constitutional separation of powers between the Congress and the Presidency, I directed that members of the White House staff should appear and testify voluntarily under oath before the Senate Committee investigating Watergate.

I was determined that we should get to the bottom of the matter, and that the truth should be fully brought out—no matter who was involved.

At the same time, I was determined not to take precipitate action, and to avoid, if at all possible, any action that would appear to reflect on innocent people. I wanted to be fair. But I knew that in the final analysis, the integrity of this office—public faith in the integrity of this office— would have to take priority over all personal considerations.

Today, in one of the most difficult decisions of my Presidency, I accepted the resignations of two of my closest associates in the White House—Bob Haldeman, John Ehrlichman—two of the finest public servants it has been my privilege to know.

I want to stress that in accepting these resignations, I mean to leave no implication whatever of personal wrongdoing on their part, and I leave no implication tonight of implication on the part of others who have been charged in this matter. But in matters as sensitive as guarding the integrity of our democratic process, it is essential not only that rigorous legal and ethical standards be observed, but also that the public, you, have the total confidence that they are both being observed and enforced by those in authority and particularly by the President of the United States. They agreed with me that this move was necessary in order to restore that confidence.

Because Attorney General Kleindienst—though a distinguished public servant, my personal friend for 20 years, with no personal involvement whatever in this matter—has been a close personal and professional associate of some of those who are involved in this case, he and I both felt that it was also necessary to name a new Attorney General.

The Counsel to the President, John Dean, has also resigned.

As the new Attorney General, I have today named Elliot Richardson, a man of unimpeachable integrity and rigorously high principle. I have directed him to do everything necessary to ensure that the Department of Justice has the confidence and trust of every law abiding person in this country.

I have given him absolute authority to make all decisions bearing upon the prosecution of the Watergate case and related matters. I have instructed him that if he should consider it appropriate, he has the authority to name a special supervising prosecutor for matters arising out of the case.

Whatever may appear to have been the case before— whatever improper activities may yet be discovered in connection with this whole sordid affair—I want the American people, I want you to know beyond the shadow of a doubt that that during my terms as President, justice will be pursued fairly, fully, and impartially, no matter who is involved. This office is a sacred trust and I am determined to be worthy of that trust.

Looking back at the history of this case, two questions arise:

How could it have happened?

Who is to blame?

Political commentators have correctly observed that during my 27 years in politics, I have always previously insisted on running my own campaigns for office.

But 1972 presented a very different situation. In both domestic and foreign policy, 1972 was a year of crucially important decisions, of intense negotiations, of vital new directions, particularly in working toward the goal which has been my overriding concern throughout my political career—the goal of bringing peace to America and peace to the world.

That is why I decided, as the 1972 campaign approached, that the Presidency should come first and politics second. To the maximum extent possible, therefore, I sought to delegate campaign operations, and to remove the day-to-day campaign decisions from the President's office and from the White House. I also, as you recall, severely limited the number of my own campaign appearances.

Who, then, is to blame for what happened in this case?

For specific criminal actions by specific individuals, those who committed those actions, must, of course, bear the liability and pay the penalty.

For the fact that alleged improper actions took place within the White House or within my campaign organization, the easiest course would be for me to blame those to whom I delegated the responsibility to run the campaign. But that would be a cowardly thing to do.

I will not place the blame on subordinates—on people whose zeal exceeded their judgment, and who may have done wrong in a cause they deeply believed to be right.

In any organization, the man at the top must bear the responsibility. That responsibility, therefore, belongs here, in this office. I accept that. And I pledge to you tonight, from this office, that I will do everything in my power to ensure that the guilty are brought to justice, and that such abuses are purged from our political processes in the years to come, long after I have left this office.

Some people, quite properly appalled at the abuses that occurred, will say that Watergate demonstrates the bankruptcy of the American political system. I believe precisely the opposite is true. Watergate represented a series of illegal acts and bad judgments by a number of individuals. It was the system that has brought the facts to light and that will bring those guilty to justice—a system that in this case has included a determined Grand Jury, honest prosecutors, a courageous Judge, John Sirica, and a vigorous free press.

It is essential now that we place our faith in that system—and especially in the judicial system. It is essential that we let the judicial process go forward, respecting those safeguards that are established to protect the innocent as well as to convict the guilty. It is essential that in reacting to the excesses of others, we not fall into excesses ourselves.

It is also essential that we not be so distracted by events such as this that we neglect the vital work before us, before this Nation, before America, at a time of critical importance to America and the world.

Since March, when I first learned that the Watergate affair might in fact be far more serious than I had been led to believe, it has claimed far too much of my own time and attention.

Whatever may now transpire in the case—whatever the actions of the Grand Jury, whatever the outcome of any eventual trials—I must now turn my full attention once again to the larger duties of this office. I owe it to this great office that I hold, and I owe it to you—to our country.

I know that as Attorney General, Elliot Richardson will be both fair and fearless in pursuing this case wherever it leads. I am confident that with him in charge, justice will be done.

There is vital work to be done toward our goal of lasting structure of peace in the world—work that cannot wait. Work that I must do.

Tomorrow, for example, Chancellor Brandt of West Germany will visit the White House for talks that are a vital element of "The Year of Europe" as 1973 has been called. We are already preparing for the next Soviet-American summit meeting, later this year.

This is also a year in which we are seeking to negotiate a mutual and balanced reduction of armed forces in Europe, which will reduce our defense budget and allow us to have funds for other purposes at home so desperately needed. It is the year when the United States and Soviet negotiators will seek to work out the second and even more important round of our talks on limiting nuclear arms, and of reducing the danger of a nuclear war that would destroy civilization as we know it. It is a year in which we confront the difficult tasks of maintaining peace in Southeast Asia and in the potentially explosive Middle East.

There is also vital work to be done right here in America—to ensure prosperity, and that means a good job for everyone who wants to work, to control inflation, that I know worries every housewife, everyone who tries to balance a family budget in America, to set in motion new and better ways of ensuring progress toward a better life for all American.

When I think of this office—of what it means—I think of all the things that I want to accomplish for this nation—of all the things I want to accomplish for you.

On Christmas Eve, during my terrible personal ordeal of the renewed bombing of North Vietnam, which after 12 years of war, finally helped to bring America peace with honor, I sat down just before midnight. I wrote out some of my goals for my second term as President.

Let me read them to you.

"To make it possible for our children, and for our children's children, to live in a world of peace.

"To make this country be more than ever a land of opportunity—of equal opportunity, full opportunity for every American.

"To provide jobs for all who can work, and generous help for all who cannot.

"To establish a climate of decency, and civility, in which each person respects the feelings and the dignity and the God-given rights of his neighbor.

"To make this a land in which each person can dare to dream, can live his dreams—not in fear, but in hope— proud of his community, proud of his country, proud of what America has meant to himself and to the world."

These are great goals. I believe we can, we must work for them. We can achieve them. But we cannot achieve these goals unless we dedicate ourselves to another goal.

We must maintain the integrity of the White House, and that integrity must be real, not transparent. There can be no whitewash at the White House.

We must reform our political process—ridding it not only of the violations of the law, but also of the ugly mob violence, and other inexcusable campaign tactics that have been too often practiced and too readily accepted in the past—including those that may have been a response by one side to the excesses or expected excesses of the other side. Two wrongs do not make a right.

I have been in public life for more than a quarter of a century. Like any other calling, politics has good people, and bad people. And let me tell you, the great majority in politics, in the Congress, in the Federal Government, in the State Government, are good people. I know that it can be very easy, under the intensive pressures of a campaign, for even well-intentioned people to fall into shady tactics—to rationalize this on the grounds that what is at stake is of such importance to the Nation that the end justifies the means. And both of our great parties have been guilty of such tactics in the past.

In recent years, however, the campaign excesses that have occurred on all sides have provided a sobering demonstration of how far this false doctrine can take us. The lesson is clear: America, in its political campaigns, must not again fall into the trap of letting the end, however great that end is, justify the means.

I urge the leaders of both political parties, I urge citizens, all of you, everywhere, to join in working toward a new set of standards, new rules and procedures—to ensure that future elections will be as nearly free of such abuses as they possibly can be made. This is my goal. I ask you to join in making it America's goal.

When I was inaugurated for a second term this past January 20, I gave each member of my Cabinet and each member of my senior White House staff a special four-year calendar with each day marked to show the number of days remaining to the administration. In the inscription on each calendar, I wrote these words: "The Presidential term which begins today consists of 1,461 days—no more, no less. Each can be a day of strengthening and renewal for America; each can add depth and dimension to the American experience. I we strive together, if we make the most of the challenge and the opportunity that these days offer us, they can stand out as great days for America, and great moments in the history of the world."

I looked at my own calendar this morning up at Camp David as I was working on this speech. It showed exactly 1,361 days remaining in my term. I want these to be the best days in America's history, because I love America. I deeply believe that America is the hope of the world, and I know that in the quality and wisdom of the leadership America gives lies the only hope for millions of people all over the world, that they can live their lives in peace and freedom. We must be worthy of that hope, in every sense of the word. Tonight, I ask for your prayers to help me in everything that I do throughout the days of my Presidency to be worthy of their hopes and of yours.

God bless America and God bless each and every one of you.

9:25 P.M. EDT